The Oxford Handbook of Accurate Personality Judgment

The Oxford Handbook of Accurate Personality Judgment

Edited by

Tera D. Letzring

Jana S. Spain

OXFORD
UNIVERSITY PRESS

OXFORD
UNIVERSITY PRESS

Oxford University Press is a department of the University of Oxford.
It furthers the University's objective of excellence in research, scholarship,
and education by publishing worldwide. Oxford is a registered trade mark of
Oxford University Press in the UK and certain other countries.

Published in the United States of America by Oxford University Press
198 Madison Avenue, New York, NY 10016, United States of America.

Library of Congress Control Number: 2020950665
[Insert Cataloging Data]

ISBN 978–0–19–091252–9

1 3 5 7 9 8 6 4 2

Printed by Sheridan Books, Inc., United States of America.

DEDICATION

This book is dedicated to David Funder in recognition of his impact on the study of the accuracy of personality trait judgment. We are grateful to David for his passion for accuracy research and his willingness and ability to share that passion with others.

SHORT CONTENTS

Tera D. Letzring is a Professor of Psychology and the Director of the Experimental Psychology PhD program at Idaho State University. She earned a PhD in Psychology from the University of California, Riverside, in 2005, and a BA in Psychology from the University of Puget Sound in 1999. Dr. Letzring's research focuses on the interpersonal accuracy of judgments of personality, and in particular on the factors that moderate accuracy.

Jana S. Spain is a Professor of Psychology at High Point University. She earned her MA in 1991 and PhD in 1994 from the University of California, Riverside, and a BA in Psychology from San Diego State University in 1988. Dr. Spain's research focuses on the link between personality and daily life experience and the accuracy of personality judgments.

CONTENTS

CONTRIBUTORS

Mitja D. Back
University of Münster

Andrew Beer
University of South Carolina Upstate

Jeremy C. Biesanz
University of British Columbia

Melinda Blackman
California State University, Fullerton

Danielle Blanch-Hartigan
Bentley University

Kathryn L. Bollich-Ziegler
Seattle University

Simon M. Breil
University of Münster

Claire Campbell
Ulster University

Erika N. Carlson
University of Toronto Mississauga

Douglas E. Colman
University of Wisconsin, La Crosse

Norhan Elsaadawy
University of Toronto Mississauga

David C. Funder
University of California, Riverside

Krista Hill Cummings
Babson College

Nate Honeycutt
Rutgers University

Lauren J. Human
McGill University

Lee Jussim
Rutgers University

Sheherezade L. Krzyzaniak
Idaho State University

Tera D. Letzring
Idaho State University

Shanhong Luo
University of North Carolina at Wilmington

Thomas E. Malloy
Rhode Island College

Marie-Catherine Mignault
McGill University

Steffen Nestler
University of Münster

Joshua R. Oltmanns
University of Kentucky

Thomas F. Oltmanns
Washington University in St. Louis

Sarah Osterholz
Johannes Gutenberg University Mainz

Katherine H. Rogers
The University of Tennessee Chattanooga

Jana S. Spain
High Point University

Sean T. Stevens
New York University Stern School of
Business and Heterodox Academy

Helen J. Wall
Edge Hill University

David Watson
University of Notre Dame

History, Theory, and Measurement

CHAPTER 1

The Accuracy of Personality Trait Judgments

An Introduction

Jana S. Spain

Abstract

How accurately can we judge the personality traits of ourselves and others? What are the factors that influence our ability to make correct judgments? How can we use this information to improve our social interactions and relationships? In this introduction to the *Oxford Handbook of Accurate Personality Judgment*, the reader is introduced to the study of personality trait accuracy. Foundations of this research are reviewed and an overview of the volume is provided. Chapters explore current judgment models and review empirical work on moderators of accuracy, including characteristics of judges, targets, traits, and information. They explain the challenges encountered when judging different types of targets and examine how different kinds of information contribute to the judgment process. The applications and implications of this work for relationships, workplace interactions, and evaluations of psychological health and functioning are discussed. Ways to improve accuracy and future directions for research on trait accuracy are offered.

Key Words: personality, judgment, accuracy, trait, accuracy, ability, target, information, workplace

Each day, we make dozens of judgments about the personality characteristics of those around us. Is that barista really as unfriendly and unsociable as she seems this morning? Joe is a funny, romantic, and caring person, but will he be a committed and faithful husband? Ms. Brown's recommenders say she is very organized, productive, and conscientious, but she was aloof and unfriendly during our interview. Will she get along with her coworkers? Does that client's frown indicate that he hates our presentation or is he just a generally critical and skeptical person who is hard to impress? These judgments range from being fairly inconsequential to extremely significant and we routinely rely on them to guide our own behavior in interpersonal interactions and relationships. In this handbook, we review theory and research on the accuracy of personality trait judgments in order to answer the following questions: How accurate are personality judgments? When are judgments of ourselves and other people

more likely to be right and when are they more likely to be wrong? And, how can we use this information to improve our everyday real-life decisions?

The Importance of Accurate Personality Judgment

Understanding the factors that are related to the accuracy of personality judgments is important for both laypersons and professionals. As laypersons, we make personality judgments every day, and those judgments form the basis of much of our interpersonal interactions and relationships. Is that stranger friendly and approachable or potentially dangerous? Is your friend trustworthy enough to risk lending him a large amount of money? Is your significant other committed and faithful? We tend to assume that personality judgments will help us make accurate predictions about others' behavior, but we often do not know when and under what conditions we are most likely to be correct. Mistakes in judgment can be quite costly, and therefore understanding when you are most likely to be accurate would be of tremendous benefit.

For professionals, understanding the accuracy of personality judgments is also important. For personality psychologists, personality judgments are a preferred method of assessing personality characteristics. The field relies on self- and informant judgments of personality. In fact, such judgments are often used to evaluate the validity of other assessment methods. Understanding how individuals come to draw inferences about traits from their interactions with and observations of others can also potentially inform us about the very nature of personality and how it is manifest in daily life. For clinicians and counselors, accurately judging both the normative and non-normative dimensions of a client's personality is an essential part of the diagnostic process. For professionals in industrial-organizational psychology, human resources, or management, personality judgments are an essential part of the employee selection and placement process. References and letters of recommendation from former employers are frequently used in hiring decisions and such recommendations often include judgments about key personality characteristics. Personality self-descriptions and judgments made during interviews are often key pieces of information collected during the selection process and, once an individual is hired, supervisors' judgments are often a key part of the performance evaluation process.

Despite the fact that we make and use personality trait judgments every day, most of us seldom carefully evaluate their level or degree of accuracy. Often, we simply assume that what individuals say about themselves and what others say about them is true, while at other times we simply dismiss these judgments as either unsubstantiated self-beliefs, as attempts to impression-manage, or, when they are provided by others, as socially constructed reputations based primarily on hearsay or rumor. The field of psychology has similarly had a mixed approach to evaluating trait judgments, historically alternating between assuming that they are uniquely insightful descriptions of general tendencies or viewing them as beliefs that are, at best, fundamentally flawed and perhaps hopelessly biased. In the last several decades, however, a rich research tradition has developed that has studied the accuracy of personality judgments more systematically and empirically.

Foundations of Accuracy Research

Contemporary theory and research on the accuracy of personality judgments has its foundations in the study of person perception. In fact, the theoretical perspectives and research traditions that have guided the study of how we come to understand other people generally form the foundation for the modern models used to study the accuracy of personality judgments.

Many early approaches to understanding person perception followed the traditions and methods established by researchers who studied the visual perception of objects (Ambady & Skowronski, 2008; Kenny, 1994). They often assumed that the processes involved in object perception and person perception were either the same or very similar. There were logical reasons to make that assumption. For example, objects and people are assumed to be real and to have stable properties. Both evoke cognitive, behavioral, and emotional responses from us. And, we follow some of the same steps when perceiving persons that we follow when perceiving objects. Namely, we differentiate the object or the person from their surroundings, identify their key features, group or categorize them following certain grouping rules, and make generalizations about groups based on individual cases and vice versa.

But, despite these similarities, there are important differences between the perception of objects and the perceptions of people. First, persons are dynamic; they do things and their features are constantly changing from moment to moment, developmentally over time, across situations and roles, and from one interaction partner to another. They are causal agents who have motives, goals, and intentions and who actively attempt to control our perceptions of them via impression management strategies. The process of understanding persons is also inherently interpersonal and typically reciprocal with each partner influencing and making judgments about the other.

Historically, research in person perception was, like perception research in other areas, guided by three main theoretical perspectives: structuralist, constructivist, or ecological. These perspectives differed significantly in their approach to person perception and in their views of the accuracy of our judgments (see Zebrowitz, 1990, for a summary). For the structuralists, perceptions of any stimulus, including persons, derived from basic sensations. The process of person perception, they maintained, was data-driven or target-driven. Information came into our sensory systems from any object or person being perceived and was sent directly to the brain for processing and interpretation. This approach assumed that because perception was largely driven by the actual physical features of the stimulus, in this case the target person, all perceivers did was simply "add up" the various pieces of information to form a judgment. Thus, from this perspective, judgments should be fairly accurate as long as sensory systems are operating correctly. Because they assumed that sensation drove perceptions and judgments, there was little need to evaluate the accuracy of judgments.

The constructivist perspective, on the other hand, saw person perceptions as largely theory-driven or constructed by the mind of the perceiver. They argued that we can never completely know the nature of another person with absolute certainty. All we have to rely on are human ideas or constructions of the world, which may or may not reflect reality. Person perceptions, from this perspective, primarily reflect the constructive processes of the perceiver's mind rather than the actual physical properties of the target of their perception. These processes, they contended, were frequently prone to information processing and motivational biases that led to considerable error.

This approach is exemplified by social psychological research on errors and biases in person perception (Jones, 1990; Kahneman, Slovic, & Tversky, 1982). While some of these theorists and researchers question the very existence of personality traits, others suggest that our ability to accurately discern the characteristics of others is quite limited and maintain that the entire enterprise is extremely challenging (Ross & Nisbett, 1991). They have frequently maintained that perceptions or judgments of people might have little or no connection to the actual properties of the person being perceived. In fact, they largely suspect that they do not. Accuracy, they argue, is likely difficult to achieve and almost impossible to ascertain. These judgments might not have any grounding in reality but might simply reflect the cognitive construction processes of the perceiver. From this perspective, the closest one can come to determining the accuracy of a personality judgment is by measuring *consensus*, or the level of agreement between different judges of the same common target. The best we can do is determine whether a particular perception of an individual was collectively held by a group of others. If others agree that you were friendly, dependable, or aggressive, it largely does not matter whether or not you actually

possess those traits. Those consensual beliefs, or your social reputation, likely influence how you are treated and how you ultimately fare in life. These ideas are frequently evident in the use of consensus as a criterion for accuracy in many studies and approaches that attempt to specify the various factors that lead to dyadic agreement. Understanding the factors that contribute to consensual understandings of traits remains a goal of several modern models including Kenny's social relations model (Kenny, 1994; Kenny & Albright, 1987) and new approaches to social relations modeling presented by Malloy in chapter 3 of this handbook.

For ecologically inclined person-perception theorists, on the other hand, reality (here in the form of actual personality traits) exists but a perceiver's ability to detect it is limited by the availability of valid information about the trait and the ability of human sensory and perceptual capabilities to detect it. For ecological person-perception theorists, perceptions of a stimulus (i.e., a target's personality) are grounded in the structure of external stimuli but the structure of those stimuli are detected (not constructed or created) by perceivers themselves. Perceptions, therefore, are limited by the perceptual processes of the perceiver so a perceiver's perspective, attention, biases, skills, expectancies, and the like will have profound influences on the connection between the *perception of a stimulus* (in this case a personality judgment) and the *actual properties of the stimulus itself* (the individual's actual personality). The accuracy of a personality judgment according to this perspective would be reflected in the correspondence between a perceiver's judgment and the actual personality characteristics of the stimulus person. Determining the actual characteristics of that target person, therefore, is of profound importance but often challenging to do empirically. This ecological approach serves as the theoretical foundation for many of the models that are used today to describe the process of personality judgment including the lens and dual lens models (Brunswik, 1956; see chapter 4 by Osterholz, Briel, Nestler, & Back) and Funder's realistic accuracy model (Funder, 1995).

Most of the empirical studies reviewed in this handbook, like the models they test, fit within this broader ecological perspective. Perhaps not surprising given their origins, many contemporary approaches to the study of accuracy frequently challenge the view that our judgments of others should not be trusted. That is not to say that most researchers, or our chapter authors, try to claim that such judgments are always perfectly accurate but rather they attempt to specify when and under what conditions personality judgments can be trusted—as well as when they cannot. Additionally, throughout this handbook, the various authors attempt to provide practical information about how we can improve our knowledge of ourselves and others.

Overview of the Handbook

The primary goal of this handbook is to synthesize contemporary theory and research on the accuracy of personality judgments. To that end, we asked researchers who were currently involved in the enterprise of studying personality judgments to review the recent findings regarding when we are most likely to make trait inferences that are accurate and when we are least likely to do so. We sought to present, in a single volume, the various models, methodologies, empirical findings and applications of research on the accuracy of personality judgments, providing a snapshot of the current state of our knowledge, an identification of the limits of our knowledge, and a glimpse of the direction future work might take to advance our understanding.

The first section presents the major theoretical models that guide research in this area and describe various methodological approaches to evaluating accuracy. Many of these models are based on the lens model first proposed by Egon Brunswik (1956). In chapter 2, for example, Letzring and Funder describe the development of the realistic accuracy model, one of the first contemporary models to describe the process of accurate personality judgment. They explain how characteristics of targets, judges, traits, and information can moderate accuracy and how they may interact with one another. In chapter 4, Osterholz and her colleagues explain how lens models can be used to study the personality-expression and impression-formation processes that lead judgments to be more or less accurate. They then extend the lens model approach to the examination of both the controlled and automatic processes involved in personality judgments, providing new avenues for future research.

In chapter 3, Malloy describes another very influential approach to studying accuracy, social relations modeling, which emphasizes the interpersonal nature of the personality judgment process. He explains the historical, philosophical, and epistemological foundations of this componential approach and demonstrates how the various components of accuracy scores can be used to identify how the actor, partner, and relationship contribute to accu-

racy. He also presents two new models to guide the next generation of research in this area. The new models emphasize the need to consider accuracy and meta-accuracy in tandem and explain how biased assumptions like assumed similarity and assumed reciprocity could affect interpersonal accuracy. In chapter 5, Biesanz shows how his social accuracy model (Biesanz, 2010), a model that integrates Cronbach's componential approach with Kenny's social relations model, can be used to address the kinds of questions typically addressed by Funder's realistic accuracy model. He illustrates the advantages this approach offers over traditional correlational approaches, providing statistical and technical guidance for researchers interested in using the model to address questions of accuracy.

The second section of the handbook reviews the research findings relevant to the various moderators of accuracy: judge, target, trait, and information. In these chapters, authors address the following questions: Are some individuals particularly good at judging personality? Are some individuals simply easier to read and easier to understand? Which traits can be judged most and/or least accurately? What kind of information yields the most accurate judgments?

For example, in chapter 6, Colman examines judge moderators of accuracy. He describes the field's search for that elusive *good judge* of personality, explains the challenges that have been encountered in this long search, and describes the progress we have made in identifying the cognitive, motivational, and behavioral factors that contribute to one's judgment ability. Mignault and Human (chapter 7), on the other hand, focus on target moderators of accuracy, describing work that attempts to identify who is particularly easy to judge. They explain how target characteristics affect the various stages of the realistic accuracy model and how a target's characteristics might increase both a judge's attention and his or her motivation to be accurate.

In addition to considering how characteristics of judges and targets might moderate accuracy, recent work has advanced our understanding of the role dimensions of traits and the quantity and quality of information play in accuracy. We have long known, for example, that some traits are easier to judge than others. But what makes them so easy to judge? In chapter 8, Krzyzaniak and Letzring describe the attributes of traits, including visibility, ratability, and evaluativeness, that impact how accurately those traits are judged. In the final chapter in this section (chapter 9) Beer explains the role information plays in accurate trait judgment, considering both the amount or quantity of information and the quality of information. He reviews previous work on *the acquaintanceship effect*, or the tendency for accuracy to increase the longer you have known someone, discussing limitations and boundaries on this effect. The quality of information, however, is also very important, and Beer examines how the relevance of the information to the particular trait being judged matters.

Although much of the research that examines the accuracy of personality judgments focuses on our judgments of other people, it is also important to understand the limits of our own self-knowledge of our defining characteristics as well as our knowledge of how we are viewed. In the third section, the various chapters focus on the accuracy of self-knowledge and comparisons of the relative accuracy of self and others' judgments. In chapter 10, Bollich-Ziegler explains the differences between judgments made about the self and judgments made about others. Using Vazire's self–other knowledge asymmetry model, she reviews work that suggests that differences in information, susceptibility to biases, and motivational factors account for such differences and emphasizes the need to adopt multiple perspectives in order to accurately understand an individual. In the next chapter (chapter 11), Spain examines how well we know ourselves and addresses whether or not we are truly the "best experts" when it comes to judging our own characteristics. The chapter presents evidence from studies of self–other agreement, behavioral prediction, and the prediction of consequential life outcomes to demonstrate how well we really know our own traits. Knowing our own traits is one type of self-knowledge. Another kind of self-knowledge involves knowing how we are viewed by others. Do we know our social reputations? In chapter 12, Carlson and Elsaadawy describe the processes involved in meta-perception or our beliefs regarding how we are viewed by other people. They then review the findings regarding the accuracy of these meta-perceptions and examine the functionality of this kind of knowledge.

The next section examines the various types of information that may be used in making personality judgments, including nonverbal cues, contextual and environmental information, normative personality profiles, and group stereotypes. Briel and his colleagues (chapter 13) summarize research on how nonverbal behavioral cues such as facial expressions, gestures, posture, and vocal information contribute to accurate judgments. Which of these cues are useful indicators of personality? Are some cues more useful for judging particular traits? The authors also explain how other individual characteristics and situational factors alter the expression of nonverbal cues and, ultimately, impact the accuracy of personality judgments. Situational factors are also examined in chapter 14 by Wall and Campbell. In this chapter, the authors examine the role physical and virtual contexts play in the judgment process and how they affect accuracy. They provide an overview of studies that examine the availability of personality-relevant cues in personal spaces, social media, and the like and explain how context might affect trait accuracy.

In the other two chapters in this section, the authors consider how knowledge of the average person or beliefs based on perceived group membership affect the accuracy of our personality judgments. In chapter 15, Rogers examines how the understanding and use of typical (or normative) personality profiles can affect judgments and emphasizes the importance of accounting for this factor when assessing accuracy. She describes how researchers can measure and account for normativity when studying accuracy and provides readers with concrete steps they can follow should they wish to incorporate this approach in their studies. Jussim and his colleagues (chapter 16), on the other hand, examine the role of stereotypes in the judgment process. They point out that stereotypes are often assumed to be inaccurate but provide a cogent explanation of why that assumption may not always be warranted. They argue that stereotypes vary on a continuum of accuracy, with some being surprisingly accurate while others are inaccurate, and explain how conclusions regarding the accuracy of stereotypes might be dependent upon the criterion being employed. They then review the empirical evidence regarding the accuracy of stereotypes about gender, age, race, national character, and personality.

The fifth section provides examples of some of the various domains to which accuracy research can be applied to improve social decision-making, including interpersonal relationships, clinical practice, the workplace, and accuracy training. First, Luo and Watson (chapter 17) consider personality judgments made in the context of romantic relationships examining both sources of accuracy and of bias. Their review of the relationship literature indicates that personality characteristics, trait properties, and relationship factors can all moderate how accurately we perceive our romantic partners and our levels of accuracy and bias can have important implications for relationship functioning.

Although much of the research reviewed in this handbook focuses on the judgment of normal range personality traits like extraversion and conscientiousness, there is increasing interest in understanding how accurately individuals can judge more maladaptive, extreme, or even disordered aspects of personality. In chapter 18, Oltmanns and Oltmanns identify the factors that contribute to self–other agreement on personality disorders and maladaptive characteristics. They present the results of a new meta-analysis of dozens of studies of self–other agreement on personality disorder and compare those findings to the findings of studies on five factor model traits. They also consider the implications of these findings for clinical work.

Personality judgments are often used in other important contexts as well. Blackman (chapter 19) discusses the use of personality judgments in the workplace, focusing primarily on their use during personnel screening and selection. She describes some of the challenges involved in making accurate judgments in this context and provides considerable guidance, based on empirical studies, of how to improve interview and hiring processes to make more effective selection decisions. Improvement of the judgment process is also the focus of the chapter by Blanch-Hartigan and Hill Cummings (chapter 20). They compare the various training approaches that could be used to increase accuracy and explain how characteristics of judges, targets, and traits could impact the effectiveness of such training. They outline a variety of creative approaches and suggest future directions for interventions designed to improve the accuracy of trait judgments.

And finally, Letzring (chapter 21) identifies what we as editors see as the overarching themes that are evident in theory and research on the accuracy of personality judgments including the major theoretical approaches and the key findings. She highlights the important consequences of accurate (and inaccurate) judgments and suggests promising directions for future research on this topic. Today we have a clearer understanding that our judgments of personality, while imperfect, do have considerable validity. It is our hope that information presented in this handbook will help readers acquire a better understanding of when and under what conditions they are more accurate and provide practical suggestions for how we improve our knowledge of our own and others personality characteristics.

References

Ambady, N., & Skowronski, J. J. (Eds.). (2008). *First impressions.* New York, NY: Guilford.

Biesanz, J. C. (2010). The social accuracy model of interpersonal perception: Assessing individual differences in perceptive and expressive accuracy. *Multivariate Behavioral Research, 45,* 853–885. https://www.doi.org/10.1080/00273171.2010.519262

Brunswik, E. (1956). *Perception and the representative design of psychological experiments.* Berkeley: University of California Press.

Funder, D. C. (1995). On the accuracy of personality judgment: A realistic approach. *Psychological Review, 102*(4), 652–670. https://www.doi.org/10.1037/0033-295X.102.4.652

Jones, E. E. (1990). *Interpersonal perception.* New York: W. H. Freeman and Company.

Kahneman, D., Slovic, P., & Tversky, A. (Eds.). (1982). *Judgment under uncertainty: Heuristics and biases.* Cambridge: Cambridge University Press.

Kenny, D. A. (1994). *Interpersonal perception: A social relations analysis.* New York, NY: Guilford.

Kenny, D. A., & Albright, L. (1987). Accuracy in interpersonal perception: A social relations analysis. *Psychological Bulletin, 102,* 390–402. https://www.doi.org/10.1037/0033-2909.102.3.390

Ross, L. & Nisbett, R. E. (1991). *The person and the situation: Perspectives of social psychology.* Temple University Press.

Zebrowtiz, L. A. (1990). *Social perception.* Pacific Grove, CA: Brooks/Cole.

The Realistic Accuracy Model

Tera D. Letzring *and* David C. Funder

Abstract

This chapter describes the realistic accuracy model (RAM), starting with a history of its development. It then describes the four moderators of accuracy in personality judgment—good judge, good target, good trait, and good information—and how these moderators interact with each other. Next, it describes the four stages in the process of making accurate judgments, which are relevance, availability, detection, and utilization. Implications of the model for improving judgment accuracy and applications to judgments of states are then discussed. The chapter concludes with suggested directions for future research, including judgments of other levels of personality besides traits, interactions between moderators, the development of judgmental ability, and the consequences of judgmental accuracy.

Key Words: judgment accuracy, judgmental ability, self-other agreement, realistic accuracy, relevance, availability, detection, utilization, moderator

Do personality traits exist and, more specifically, do people behave consistently enough across situations and over time to make trait descriptions meaningful and useful? Is it possible to make accurate judgments of the personality traits of others? What factors moderate how accurately people can make judgments of others' traits? What is the process that needs to happen for accurate trait judgments to be possible?

The search for answers to these questions led to the formulation of the realistic accuracy model, or RAM. David Funder (the second author of this chapter) first formally presented this model in writing in 1995 in a paper published in *Psychological Review*, although it was foreshadowed for several years in other research and thinking. The goal of this chapter is to describe this model, including its history and its descriptions of four moderators of accuracy and the four-step process of making accurate judgments. Then, we discuss the implications of the model for improving judgment accuracy and applications to judgments of states, and point out

some promising and important future research questions that remain unanswered.

History of the Realistic Accuracy Model

A first step in the development of the RAM was taken when Funder (1980) examined relations between ratings people made of themselves and ratings other people made of them, which is referred to as *self-other agreement*. This research was grounded in attribution theory, self-concept theory, and personality theory, and addressed the question of "whether we appear to others as we appear to ourselves" (Funder, 1980, p. 473). More specifically, the research evaluated how people rated themselves and others on personality characteristics related to inner states and external behaviors. The theoretical perspective on which this work was based led to three predictions. First, how people see themselves would be similar to how others see them. Second, people would be more likely to use the situation to explain their own behavior because the situation is more salient to them from their internal perspective, whereas people would be more likely to use personality traits to explain the behavior of others because the personality of others is more salient from the external observer's perspective. And third, which trait was being judged would influence explanations of behavior such that traits related to inner states would be rated by the self as more characteristic, while traits related to external behaviors would be rated by others as more characteristic. These predictions were tested using self-reports of personality and other-reports from roommates or friends, and support was found for all three predictions. Importantly for personality theory, the article concluded that personality traits "*do* exist, at the very least as *perceptions* people have of themselves and share with the people around them" (p. 487, emphasis in original), and that perceptions of traits are based on patterns of behavior that are observed over time. This paper set the stage for continued research on agreement between self-ratings and other ratings of personality.

The need for a model of accurate personality judgment quickly became apparent (Funder, 1987). Accuracy research differed in important ways from other types of person perception research that were popular in the mid- to late-twentieth century, and a model would help guide theorizing and research on accuracy and distinguish it from similar areas. At the time, the most influential research was based on a cognitive approach and focused on describing the process of judgment in terms of how people combine information to make judgments about hypothetical targets. This came to be known as the *social-cognitive approach*. Much has been learned from research in this area, but this approach did not consider the accuracy of these judgments, as there was not a real person about whom judges could be accurate.

Not all researchers were satisfied with the social-cognitive approach. Its focus on the process of how judgments of others are made (Asch, 1946; Jones, 1985; Kelley, 1967) bypassed issues concerning the content and accuracy of such judgments in the real world (Funder, 1990). Furthermore, this approach overwhelmingly emphasized errors in judgment (Funder, 1987). Such errors were defined as any deviations from the judgment that would be expected if judges were to follow a normative model of "perfect" judgment, such as the laws of probability or logic (Nisbett & Ross, 1980; Tversky & Kahneman, 1983). Perhaps not too surprisingly, people do not always precisely follow such models and laws, and therefore often make judgments that differ from the prescribed outcomes (Nisbett & Ross, 1980; Shaklee, 1991). Within the social-cognitive

approach, any such differences, regardless of their magnitude, are labeled as errors. However, such errors tell us little about the accuracy of judgments that are made in the real world about real people, because formal normative models do not always correctly prescribe what the "correct" judgment should be in the real world[1] (Ebbesen & Konecni, 1980; Funder, 1987, 1993, 1999; Ross, Nisbett, & Funder, 2007; Trope, 1986, 1989; Trope & Lieberman, 1993). However, this conventional view of error was so pervasive that many person perception and social judgment researchers came to doubt that it was possible for people to make judgments of others that attained even moderate levels of accuracy (Evans, 1984; Ross et al., 2007).

The fundamental limitation of the social-cognitive approach is that accurate judgment requires more than simply not making errors. This limitation arises because research focusing on error begins, ironically, by assuming that judgment should be perfect, and then proceeds to catalog imperfections. However, it fails to answer the question of how judgments of any sort arise in the first place, because it fails to ask that question. To address the source of judgments—accurate and inaccurate both—requires an ecological approach that describes how judgments arise out of information that is available to the judge under realistic circumstances, and assesses the accuracy of these judgments in terms of correspondence with real-world criteria. Such correspondence is called *realistic accuracy*.

The study of realistic accuracy fits within an ecological approach that gives primary importance to the natural environment[2] in which people behave and interact with others. According to the ecological approach, accurate perceptions are defined in terms of their adaptive functions, such as helping to navigate one's social world and coordinate social interactions, and only make sense when we consider them in the context in which they were made and the purposes for which they are used (Neisser, 1988; Zebrowitz, 1990). In terms of the accuracy of trait judgments, an ecological approach assumes that traits actually exist, cues come from those traits, and people can, at least sometimes, detect those cues and use them to make accurate judgments (Funder & Sneed, 1993). Research within the tradition of the ecological approach has found substantial levels of agreement between judgments of traits and the traits themselves, and that judgments are more accurate when judges use valid cues more than invalid cues (Borkenau & Liebler, 1992, 1995; Funder & Sneed, 1993; see chapter 13 by Breil et al. in this

TERA D. LETZRING AND DAVID C. FUNDER

handbook). These findings led to the conclusion that people do have some wisdom when it comes to trait judgments (Funder & Sneed, 1993). Research within this approach has also led to ideas about how to train people to be more accurate, which could be done by helping them focus on and use valid cues while ignoring invalid cues (Borkenau & Liebler, 1992; Funder & Sneed, 1993; chapter 4 by Hirschmüller, Breil, Nestler, & Back in this handbook).

The RAM was formulated as a corrective complement to error research, by focusing on how judgments could be accurate rather than inaccurate (Funder, 1987). The development of RAM was also motivated by Gordon Allport's (1937) list of the most important problems that were related to judgments of personality, which included "(1) the nature and reliability of first impressions, (2) the chief factors involved in judging, (3) the value of interviews, (4) the question whether ability to judge people is general or specific, [and] (5) the qualifications of a good judge" (p. 499).

The desire in developing the RAM was to account for factors, or moderators, that are related to accuracy, and to describe the process that people use to make accurate inferences about personality (Funder, 1999; Funder & Sneed, 1993). The early stages of empirical research identified four moderators of accuracy, or factors that influence the level of accuracy, and later theoretical development proposed a four-stage process of accurate judgment that sought to account for these moderators (Funder, 1995, 2012). The RAM was also built on Brunswik's (1955) lens

model of perceptual constancy, which describes how cues are related to an object and used to make judgments of that object (see chapter 4 by Hirschmüller et al. in this handbook). In the lens model there are two processes, identified as cue validity and cue utilization. Cues are valid when they are related to the object being judged, and they are utilized when they are used to make judgments about the object. Accuracy will be higher when all valid cues are utilized, and lower when invalid cues are utilized or when valid cues are not utilized. In the case of the RAM, the object being perceived was a personality trait of a real person.

The RAM further broke the lens model processes down into a four-stage process for making accurate judgments of personality traits (see Figure 2.1).

Moderators of Accuracy

The first and perhaps most obvious advantage of focusing on moderators of accuracy, rather than simply on errors, is that the operation of moderator variables can explain both correct *and* incorrect judgments. The four moderators identified by Funder include categories of factors that are related to differing levels of accuracy. Some of the moderators were identified in earlier work (Allport, 1937; Funder, 1987, p. 87; 1990, p. 208; Funder & Dobroth, 1987) before all four were summarized in a review chapter (Funder, 1993). The four moderators are the good judge, good target, good trait, and good information. Each moderator is identified as "good" to emphasize a positive focus on accuracy

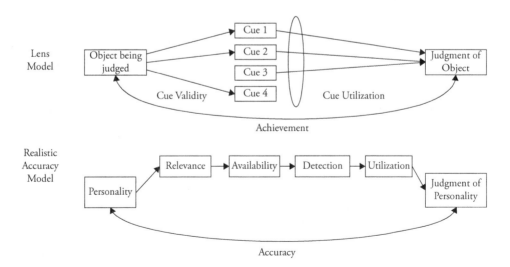

Figure 2.1. Overlap between the lens model and the realistic accuracy model. The oval represents the lens that the cues pass through in the process of cue utilization. Cues 1 and 2 are both valid and utilized, Cue 3 is not valid but is utilized, and Cue 4 is valid but not utilized. Cue validity corresponds with the relevance stage, the RAM adds the stipulation that the cues must be available, and cue utilization is broken down into the stages of detection and utilization.

(and thus suggest possible ways to improve accuracy; Funder, 1993, 1999), but as just noted, each moderator also implicitly identifies a low level of each variable as a possible source of lower accuracy.

The *good judge* moderator reflects the idea that people differ in how accurately they tend to judge others and this is due to something about the judges themselves. In general, good judges have high levels of intelligence and cognitive ability, knowledge about how behaviors and personality are related, agreeableness and social skills, perspective taking and empathy, and good psychological adjustment (Christiansen, Wolcott-Burnam, Janovics, Burns, & Quirk, 2005; Colman, Letzring, & Biesanz, 2017; Human & Biesanz, 2011; Human, Biesanz, Finseth, Pierce, & Le, 2014; Kolar, 1995; Letzring, 2008; see chapter 6 by Colman in this handbook). The *good target* moderator reflects that people differ in how accurately they are judged by others, and therefore there is something about the targets themselves that tends to make it easier for them to be judged with relatively high levels of accuracy. In general, good targets have high levels of psychological adjustment, behavioral consistency, social skills, extraversion, and expressiveness (Ambady, Hallahan, & Rosenthal, 1995; Colvin, 1993; Human, Mignault, Biesanz, & Rogers, 201; see chapter 7 by Mignault & Human in this handbook). The *good trait* reflects that personality characteristics differ in how accurately they tend to be judged, and therefore there is something about the traits that allows them to be judged with relatively high levels of accuracy across judges, targets, and situations. In general, good traits are easily observable in most situations (Funder & Dobroth, 1987; John & Robins, 1993; Paunonen & Kam, 2014; see chapter 8 by Krzyzaniak & Letzring in this handbook). Finally, *good information* reflects that information differs in how useful it is for making accurate judgments, and therefore there is something about the information that makes it easier for judges to make more accurate judgments. This moderator has two aspects. *Information quantity* reflects that having more information tends to result in more accurate judgments than having less information, which is referred to as the *acquaintanceship effect* (Biesanz, West, & Millevoi, 2007; Blackman & Funder, 1998; Colvin & Funder, 1991; Funder & Colvin, 1988; Letzring, Wells, & Funder, 2006). The other aspect, *information quality*, reflects that some types of information are more useful for making more accurate judgments than other types of information. Highly useful information includes information about general and specific behaviors, and

thoughts and feelings (Andersen, 1984; Letzring & Human, 2014; see chapter 9 by Beer in this handbook). In this handbook, an entire chapter is devoted to describing and exploring each of these moderators, so more will not be said here about individual moderators. As a whole, research has supported the usefulness of these moderators for understanding how accurate judgments are made and how various factors are related to levels of accuracy.

Interactions Between Moderators

In addition to these moderators, theoretical work on the RAM (Funder, 1995) also proposed that each moderator could interact with every other moderator and used the following terms to describe these interactions: *relationship* (interaction between judge and target), *expertise* (judge and trait), *sensitivity* (judge and information), *palpability* (target and trait), *divulgence* (target and information), and *diagnosticity* (trait and information). These terms have not come into common use to the same degree as the four basic moderators, and have not been tested as systematically, although some of the interactions have been examined empirically.

One moderator-interaction that has received a fair amount of research attention is the relationship moderator, or how something about the interaction between the judge and target could affect accuracy. The relationship moderator operates when something about the unique alignment between a target and a judge results in that judge being more accurate about the target than are any other judges and more accurate than they are when they are judging anyone else. For example, the quality of relationship between a husband and a wife could result in the husband judging his wife more accurately than anyone else judges her. His augmented ability to make an accurate judgment would not extend to other targets—just to his wife. Chapter 17 by Luo and Watson in this handbook addresses accuracy within romantic relationships and includes excellent examples of how this moderator-interaction has been examined. A meta-analysis by Connelly and Ones (2010) went a step further and examined how accuracy for specific traits differed across types of relationships, and therefore examined a three-way interaction between judge, target, and trait. Accuracy for judgments of extraversion differed little across relationships, but accuracy for judgments of emotional stability, openness, and agreeableness varied quite a bit across relationships. In particular, accuracy for these traits tended to be higher in more intimate relationships (i.e., family and friends) than less intimate relationships (i.e., work colleagues, incidental acquaintances, and strangers).

A few studies have examined expertise, which is the interaction between the judge and trait moderators, and have therefore considered how characteristics of judges are related to how accurately they judge certain traits. One study examined how several positive characteristics of judges, including intrapersonal characteristics such as satisfaction with life and positive emotions, and interpersonal characteristics such as social network size and social intimacy, were related to accuracy of ratings of five broad traits that are commonly assessed in trait accuracy research[3] (Letzring, 2015). Two types of accuracy were examined: normative accuracy, which is the level of similarity between judgments of targets and what the average person is like, and distinctive accuracy, which is the level of similarity between judgments of targets and how each target differs from the average person. Consistent with the expertise moderator-interaction, several positive characteristics of judges were positively related to normative accuracy for certain traits. For example, judges with larger social networks and higher levels of agreeableness and openness were more likely to judge targets on openness to experience in a way that was similar to the average person; and judges with higher levels of interpersonal control and support, satisfaction with life, and positive emotions were more likely to judge targets on conscientiousness in a way that was similar to the average person. However, these positive judge-characteristics were unrelated to distinctive accuracy. Another study of expertise found that judges with high social curiosity about "how other people behave, think, and feel" (Hartung & Renner, 2011, p. 796) made more accurate judgments of extraversion and openness following a 10-minute interaction with a stranger, than did judges with low social curiosity. An explanation for this finding was that judges with high social curiosity tended to detect and correctly use more cues to extraversion and openness in comparison to judges with low social curiosity. Finally, a question that is sometimes raised is whether being high on a trait makes a person an expert at judging that trait in others. However, research to date has not found that judges who are higher on a certain trait typically make more accurate judgments of that same trait in others (Hartung & Renner, 2011; Letzring, 2015).

Another moderator-interaction that has been empirically tested is diagnosticity, which is the interaction between the information and traits moderators, and can be examined when research on information quantity and quality considers accuracy for individual traits. There is evidence that some kinds of information are more useful for judging certain traits. For example, neuroticism is frequently found to be judged with low levels of accuracy, but judges were able to make relatively accurate judgments of neuroticism after observing targets in a socially stressful situation (i.e., being video-recorded while introducing one's self to strangers; Hirschmüller, Egloff, Schmukle, Nestler, & Back, 2015). Judgments of neuroticism were also more accurate when judges had more information about specific behaviors of the targets, current events in targets' lives, and when targets talked about their own personalities (Letzring & Human, 2014). Judgments of conscientiousness were more accurate when judges were given information about facts that differentiated targets from most other people than when they were given information about values that were important to targets (Beer & Brooks, 2011). Letzring and Human (2014) examined how quantities of several types of information were related to accuracy for specific traits, which yielded several interesting findings. For example, the amounts of information about targets' relationships, past events, and targets' own personalities were positively related to accuracy of judgments of agreeableness; while the amounts of information about targets' thoughts and feelings, specific and general behaviors, and current and past events were positively related to accuracy of judgments of openness (Letzring & Human, 2014). Analyses have also examined which cues are especially diagnostic for certain traits[4] and have yielded many interesting findings. For example, in photographs, a healthy appearance was diagnostic for extraversion, emotional stability, likability, and self-esteem; and smiling was diagnostic for extraversion, agreeableness, likability, self-esteem, and religiosity (Naumann, Vazire, Rentfrow, & Gosling, 2009). Additionally, a fashionable and refined appearance, energetic and expressive facial expressions, posture, and body movements, and an energetic and cheerful voice were diagnostic for extraversion (Hirschmüller, Egloff, Nestler, & Back, 2013). For more information about diagnosticity, see chapter 8 by Krzyzaniak and Letzring, chapter 9 by Beer, and chapter 14 by Wall and Campbell in this handbook.

There has been at least one study on palpability, which is the interaction between target and trait moderators such that some traits might be judged more accurately for some targets. Traits that were more central to a target's self-concept were judged with higher levels of self-other agreement by close friends, but this finding only held when targets also thought the trait had little influence on how much others liked them (Koestner, Bernieri, & Zuckerman, 1994).

Overall, research has shown that in addition to the importance of the good judge, target, trait, and information moderators, how these moderators interact with each other can influence levels of accuracy. It is possible that inconsistent findings in research that focuses on individual moderators may be due to a failure to address how the moderators interact with each other. For example, there have been some inconsistencies in studies of characteristics of the good judge (Allik, de Vries, & Realo, 2016; Christiansen et al., 2005; Letzring, 2008), and this may be due to asking judges to rate different traits, basing judgments on different types and amounts of information, and using targets that differ in important ways from each other. Examining how accuracy relates to these interactions has the potential to shed much light on the complex process of making accurate judgments.

The Process of Making Accurate Judgments

The other main contribution that resulted from the formulation of the RAM was the description of the process that needs to take place in order for accurate judgments to be possible. Notice that theorizing about the RAM does not assume that the process always happens, or even that it often (or perhaps ever) happens; these are separate empirical issues. However, the theory does assert that the process is *necessary* for accurate personality judgment—without this four-step process, accurate judgment would simply be impossible. These four stages are relevance, availability, detection, and utilization (Funder, 1995, 1999, 2012; see Figure 2.1).

Relevance

The first stage, *relevance*, indicates that there must be behavioral cues relevant to the trait or characteristic being judged. For example, let's say you are trying to assess a person's level of creativity. First, that person has to do something related to her level of creativity, such as having a thought or idea or creating something. Success at this stage is primarily influenced by the target, because targets have to do things that are relevant to and consistent with their traits. Targets tend to be judged more accurately when they are more extraverted, self-confident, emotionally stable, psychologically adjusted, and behaviorally expressive; and less

deceitful, self-defensive, and likely to keep others at a distance (Colvin, 1993; Human & Biesanz, 2013; see also chapter 7 by Mignault & Human in this handbook). This set of characteristics of good targets supports the importance of the first stage of the RAM, because targets with these characteristics are likely to behave in ways that are consistent with their personalities, which would increase relevance.

Availability

The second stage, *availability*, indicates that the cues have to be available in the external environment. If the cues are thoughts or ideas, then the target could talk or write about these in order to make the cues available. If the cues are the product of creating something, then the product has to be available to others. Success at the second stage is affected by an interaction between the target and judge, because relevant behaviors only became available in contexts that the two people share. In different contexts, such as family, work, or school, different behaviors are available for observation and therefore helpful for making accurate judgments of different traits. The accuracy that a judge attains will depend crucially on the degree to which behaviors relevant to the trait being judged are available in the contexts that the judge and target share. In addition, judges can also influence how many cues targets make available, possibly by being more agreeable, communal or interpersonally oriented, sympathetic, and warm; displaying interest in the targets; and being less domineering, avoidant, narcissistic, anxious, and condescending (Christiansen et al., 2005; Letzring, 2008; Vogt & Colvin, 2003; see chapter 6 by Colman in this handbook).

In the era of social media, "shared" contexts may also include Facebook, Twitter, Instagram, and other electronically mediated interactions. Potentially useful information about personality is available in these contexts and includes cues such as the words people use, number of friends, content of pictures and status updates or posts, and use of emoticons (Gosling et al., 2011; Hall, Pennington, & Lueders, 2014; Park et al., 2015; Qiu, Lin, Ramsay, & Yang, 2012; Wall, Kaye, & Malone, 2016). Furthermore, there is evidence that people can make accurate judgments of some personality traits based on viewing social media (Hall et al., 2014; Qiu et al., 2012; Wall et al., 2016; see also chapter 14 by Wall & Campbell in this handbook). Given the increasing use of online social media and the diversity of ways to use social media, accuracy of judging personality traits based on viewing social media and

TERA D. LETZRING AND DAVID C. FUNDER

interacting in an online environment is a promising topic for future research.

People sometimes confuse the relevance and availability stages, but they are distinct and both important. There can be many cues that are relevant to a trait, but they have to also be available to contribute to accuracy. Likewise, there can be many cues that are available, but the cues have to be relevant to the trait being judged to contribute to accuracy.

Detection

The third stage is *detection*, or noticing the relevant and available personality cues. The success of this stage is primarily influenced by the judge. Returning to the example of judging creativity, for this stage to be successful, the judge has to detect the cues to creativity. This means that the judge has to pay attention to the target. If the target is talking about her idea, then the judge has to be listening to what the target is saying; if the target wrote about her idea, then the judge has to read and understand what was written; if the target created something, then the judge has to look at and examine this product. A judge who is inattentive, distracted, uninterested, or even sensory impaired, will be less likely to detect the information necessary for accurate judgment.

This stage is typically thought of as being under the control of the judge, as it is up to the judge to pay attention to the target and detect the cues that are available. Evidence that supports the importance of the detection stage includes positive correlations between accuracy and engaging in more eye contact, seeming more interested in the targets, and reporting higher levels of perspective-taking and empathy (Colman et al., 2017; Letzring, 2008). Additionally, there may be attributes or behaviors of targets that encourage judges to pay better attention to the targets and therefore detect more cues. For example, target judgability is positively related to social status, physical attractiveness, and attempting to make a good impression (Human & Biesanz, 2013; Human, Biesanz, Parisotto, & Dunn, 2012; Lorenzo, Biesanz, & Human, 2010). Additionally, there is evidence that judges attend more to high social status and physically attractive targets who present themselves favorably (Human et al., 2012; Langlois et al., 2000; Ratcliff, Hugenberg, Shriver, & Bernstein, 2011), but not all of this research looks at whether these attributes of targets are also related to how accurately they are judged. Therefore, it would be informative to examine whether targets who are perceived as being more interesting, possibly due to have higher status or being physically attractive, are also judged more accurately, as this may reflect better attention and detection by judges.

Utilization

Finally, the judge has to correctly *utilize* the cues to make an accurate judgment. Utilization includes several more specific abilities, including being able to determine which cues are relevant to the trait being judged, giving appropriate weights to various cues, combining the cues with each other, and accounting for other characteristics, such as those of the situation, that may influence behavior. Returning to our example of judging creativity, the judge has to determine which cues are relevant to creativity, properly weight these cues and combine them with each other, and consider how the situation may influence creativity in order to make an accurate judgment.

Research supports the importance of the utilization stage in that characteristics of judges that would be likely to influence the success of this stages are related to accuracy. These characteristics include general mental ability, knowing how personality is related to behavior,[5] and making complex explanations for behavior[6] (Christiansen et al., 2005; Krzyzaniak, 2018).

Necessity of Each Stage and Multiplicativeness of the Stages

Within the RAM, these stages are all described as necessary, which means that if any stage is unsuccessful, an accurate judgment is not possible (Funder, 1995). If the target does not do anything relevant to creativity, then the process cannot even be started. If cues are not made available, then there is nothing for the judge to detect. If the judge does not detect the available cues, then there is nothing to be used to make a judgment. And if the judge does not correctly use the detected cue, or uses the wrong cues, then the judgment will not be accurate.

The stages are also multiplicative, meaning that the level of accuracy of the judgment could theoretically be determined by multiplying the levels of success for each stage. However, success is not measured in a way that is objective and quantitative enough to actually assign a number to each stage, so levels of accuracy are not really determined in this way. Rather, this is a conceptual idea and demonstrates that accuracy is influenced by the level of success at each stage. Another implication of the multiplicative nature of the stages is that 100% accuracy is unlikely, because this is only possible with 100% success at each stage of the model. However, much research supports the conclusion that judges can often make fairly accurate judgments of the personality traits of others (Brown & Bernieri, 2017; Colman et al., 2017; Connelly & Ones, 2010), and therefore the level of success for each of the stages must usually be quite high.

The processes of the RAM are often described in terms of making a judgment for a particular trait based on a particular cue, such as making a judgment of creativity based on hearing a target describe one idea she has had. However, this is a simplification designed to identify the core process of accurate judgment. In real-life settings, people are more likely to make judgments of many traits at the same time and to base these judgments on many cues they have detected, often from more than one interaction with the target. Furthermore, when people interact in groups, they may be detecting cues and making judgments of several targets simultaneously. It is easy to see how the process could get highly complex very quickly, as judges have to deal with multiple cues and decide which cues are relevant to which traits, and remember which cues came from each target. Furthermore, the situation in which the interactions take place can also change the meaning of the cues. For example, a target laughing at a party could mean something different and be utilized quite differently than a target laughing while playing a violent video game. When all of this is considered, it is quite impressive that people are able to make reasonably accurate judgments of others.

Implications for Improving Accuracy of Judgments

The moderators and stages of the RAM provide insight into ways that the accuracy of judgments could be improved. Accuracy will be highest when judgments are made by good judges who have access to a large quantity of high-quality information about good targets and are judging good traits. But what if someone is not naturally a good judge, or wants to make an accurate judgment of target or trait that is typically difficult to judge, or only has access to limited information? What should be done to increase the accuracy of those kinds of judgments? People who are not naturally good judges could learn more about how traits are related to behavior, be careful to pay attention to the targets of judgment so they can detect more cues, try to be agreeable and socially skilled so targets will feel comfortable revealing relevant information about themselves, and learn to think about what targets are thinking and feeling. When making judgments

of difficult targets, judges could gather additional information by spending more time with the targets in a variety of situations, or asking targets relevant questions in an attempt to compensate for targets with low expressiveness or consistency. When making judgments of traits that are typically more difficult to judge, judges could create situations or ask questions that are likely to elicit cues that are relevant to those traits. When only limited information is available, increasing the relevance of the information, again by creating situations or asking questions, could be especially useful.

Different situations elicit cues relevant to different traits, and therefore affect the accuracy of judgments made on the basis of observations of people in those situations (Funder, 2016; Rauthmann, Sherman, & Funder, 2015). Interacting with a person in an unstructured situation where behavior is relatively free to vary yields more informative behavioral information and more accurate personality judgments than interacting in a structured situation where behavior is more constrained (Blackman, 2002; Letzring et al., 2006). For example, in order to get to know someone in a first-date situation, it may be preferable to do something like going on a hike rather than to a movie because behavior is much more likely to be informative about personality in the less-constrained hiking situation. Moreover, certain traits may become visible under particular circumstances—recall the research, cited earlier in this chapter, that neuroticism becomes more evident when a person is under stress (Hirschmüller et al., 2015). Thus, one route to more accurate judgment is simply the selection of the situations within which one interacts with or observes a person.

Some researchers have designed programs to train people to make more accurate judgments of others, and there is evidence that some of these programs are effective (see chapter 21 by Blanch-Hartigan & Hill Cummings in this handbook). In particular, programs that include practice and feedback, or instruction, practice, and feedback, tend to be more effective than programs that have only instruction, only practice, or only instruction and practice (Blanch-Hartigan, Andrzejewski, & Hill, 2012). Additionally, programs that train people individually or in small groups tend to be more effective than programs that use large groups (Blanch-Hartigan et al., 2012).

Application to Judgments of States

The RAM was designed to describe the process of making accurate judgments about personality traits, but it can also be applied to state-level constructs, or what is happening in the moment. States that are commonly judged in research include emotions, thoughts, truthfulness versus deception, and physical pain (Bond & DePaulo, 2006; Hall, Andrzejewski, & Yopchick, 2009; Ickes, 2016; Ruben, van Osch, & Blanch-Hartigan, 2015). Judgments of these domains are likely to follow the same process as trait judgments, because in order to accurately judge what someone is feeling, thinking, or experiencing, judges would need to detect and utilize relevant and available cues. Research of accuracy of state judgments based on the RAM framework would test the generalizability of the RAM and provide another theoretical foundation for research in state domains.

If judgments of states follow the same process as judgments of traits, then the first stage would be the existence of cues relevant to the state of interest, and the second stage would be making these cues available to judges. These cues are often nonverbal and include facial expressions, body posture, and qualities of the voice such as rate of speech; although targets could also express emotions, thoughts, or inner experiences verbally (Buck, 1976; DePaulo, Stone, & Lassiter, 1985; Elfenbein & Eisenkraft, 2010; Elfenbein et al., 2010). Then, these cues would be detected and utilized by the judge to make a judgment of the state of interest.

The state and trait accuracy model (STAM) was proposed as a way to integrate the processes of making accurate judgments about states (with a focus on emotional states to begin with) and personality traits (Hall, Gunnery, Letzring, Carney, & Colvin, 2017; Letzring & Funder, 2018). Essentially, the process described in the RAM was proposed to happen twice: first for the judgment of emotions, and then for the judgment of traits. Judgments of emotions would be used as cues when making the trait judgments. The two main predictions derived from STAM are that (1) accuracy of judgments of emotions and personality traits are positively correlated when the emotions that targets experience are related to their personalities, and (2) accurate judgments of emotional states cause more accurate judgments of personality traits when judges do not have preexisting information about targets. An initial test of this model revealed that accuracy of judgments of distressed emotions, including fear and negative affect, was positively related to accuracy of judgments of neuroticism, and accuracy of judgments of positive affect was positively related to accuracy of judgments of extraversion (Hall et al., 2017). Furthermore,

the distinctive accuracy of judgments of emotional states was positively related to the distinctive accuracy of judgments of personality traits, and this was most pronounced for judgments of positive and negative affect and extraversion, and for positive affect and conscientiousness (Letzring, Biesanz, Hall, McDonald, & Krzyzaniak, 2018). Furthermore, the causal direction predicted by STAM was supported in a study that revealed that judges who were given false information about targets' emotional states made less accurate judgments of personality traits than judges who were given no information or true information about emotions (Letzring, Biesanz, Hall, Krzyzaniak, & McDonald, 2019). The STAM is an example of how to combine what is known about making accurate judgments in two domains, and research testing this kind of model can lead to advances in both research areas and to a deeper understanding of how accurate judgments can be achieved in multiple domains.

An important difference for judgments of traits versus states is that traits are assumed to be relatively consistent across situations and over time, whereas states are constantly changing. To make trait judgments, judges could rely heavily on previously detected cues and incorporate this information with new cues. On the other hand, for judgments of states, previous cues may be less useful than cues that happen in the same moment as when judgments are made. However, knowledge about previous states may help judges detect cues that are relevant to current states and to utilize these cues correctly, which would increase state accuracy. For example, knowing that someone felt proud of a previous accomplishment could help judges look for signs of pride and accurately interpret the response to a current accomplishment, or knowing that a target was often able to deceive others in the past may be useful for determining whether a person is currently being deceptive. This is especially likely to be true when targets are being observed in situations that are similar to those observed in the past, as they may be likely to have similar thoughts, emotions, and experiences when they encounter those situations again.

Future Directions

There are many unanswered questions related to the RAM. A few especially promising future direction are described next.

Other Levels of Personality

The RAM was originally conceptualized as a way to understand the process of making accurate judgments of broad personality traits that are relatively consistent across situations and over time, but it is possible to apply the model to judgments of other levels of personality such as personal concerns and identity (McAdams, 1995). Personal concerns differ importantly from traits because they take the context or situation into account; therefore personal concerns are expected to differ across time, situations, and roles that people have (such as friend or mother). Personal concerns are often related to motivation, development, or strategies for achieving one's goals. Examining the accuracy of judgments of personal concerns would be more complex than examining the accuracy of trait judgments because the situation in which the judgments are made would need to be accounted for, possibly by asking judges to describe targets in specific situations or roles and comparing the ratings to assessments of personal concerns in those same situations or roles.

An even more complex level of personality is identity, or one's definition of the self in terms of one's "overall unity and purpose" (McAdams, 1995, p. 381) that is usually captured in the answer to the question, "Who am I?" Having a clear identity is associated with having unity, purpose, and meaning in life (McAdams, 1995). Examining accuracy for judgments of identity would be quite complex, given that identity continually evolves over the lifespan and is typically assessed through the use of narrative descriptions of people's life stories (Adler et al., 2017; McAdams, 1995, 2012). The narrative descriptions are coded to identify elements that include themes, images, integrative meaning such as how one's view of the self or world has changed in response to the environment, and structural elements such as coherence and complexity. Judges would have to rate targets' identities, and then the level of correspondence between the target's identity and the judge's ratings would have to be determined. One way this could be accomplished would be to have judges rate targets on the elements that have been coded from the narratives, and then compare these judgments to the codings. Assessing accuracy of judgments of identity and personal concerns would allow researchers to examine the extent to which accuracy is possible at these deeper levels of personality and how the moderators of accuracy function within these levels.

When assessing accuracy of levels of personality other than broad-level and decontextualized personality traits, researchers will need to think about and examine how the situation in which targets are observed and judgments are made influences accu-

racy. It is likely that accuracy for different types of personal concerns will vary across situations and roles that people have. For example, achievement motivation may be easier to judge in academic or work settings than in social settings. The situation may be less influential for judgments of identity, as this should be consistent across situations. The key for revealing identity would be to have targets discuss their life story and how they see themselves, which is more likely to happen in some situations than others (e.g., within intimate relationships rather than casual or professional relationships).

Interactions Between Moderators of Accuracy

A second future direction that is likely to yield useful results is a more systematic evaluation of how interactions between moderators influence accuracy. Some work has already been done in this area, as described previously in the section "Moderators of Accuracy," but not all interactions have been carefully tested. Examining interactions may resolve some of the inconsistencies that have been found in previous work and deepen our understanding of the factors that influence and are related to accuracy.

Development of Judgmental Ability

An aspect of judgment accuracy that has received little if any research attention is how the ability develops over time. It is likely that it is not possible to judge others accurately until a theory of mind has developed, which involves developing an understanding of other people as mental beings and acquiring the ability to attribute mental stages such as desires, beliefs, and knowledge to the self and others. Theory of mind typically develops by around 4 or 5 years of age (Astington & Edward, 2010; Wellman, 2017). Such an ability is likely needed to understand that other people differ from one's self and to make accurate judgments of others. One study examined the development of theory of mind and the ability to identify emotions based on vignettes, and found evidence that theory of mind develops before children are able to accurately identify emotions in others, but also that children with more fully developed theories of mind were able to more accurately identify emotions (Brown, Thibodeau, Pierucci, & Gilpin, 2015). A longitudinal study that examines theory of mind and accuracy of trait judgments across the lifespan, from preschool children to adults, would begin to shed light on the development of judgmental ability. A longitudinal study that tracked the development of these and other related abilities and perceptions would be even more informative. These kinds of studies could also examine how moderators function at different ages and developmental stages of judges and targets.

Consequences of Judgmental Accuracy

Finally, more research that examines the consequences of judgmental accuracy is needed. This could be particularly important for relationships, as knowing when and under what conditions accuracy is associated with good versus bad relationship outcomes could point to ways to increase overall relationship quality and satisfaction, as well as relationship maintenance. For example, do more accurate judgments of potential or actual relationship partners enhance the probability of having or maintaining a good relationship with that person? The answer, as always, is probably "it depends." Additional research would help us determine what factors and conditions lead to increases or decreases in accuracy, and how accuracy is related to outcomes such as relationship quality and maintenance. In some situations, seeing only the best in a person could lead to enhanced relationships; whereas in other situations it may be more beneficial to see relationship partners as they truly are and to be aware of what makes them different from other people. Research on empathic accuracy, or knowing what someone is thinking and feeling, has shown that empathic accuracy has complex relationships with relationship satisfaction, feelings of relationship closeness, and rates of relationship dissolution (Sened et al., 2017; Simpson, Ickes, & Grich, 1999; Simpson, Oriña, & Ickes, 2003). It would be useful to examine how accuracy of judgments of personality traits relates to or predicts these types of relationship variables. Additionally, being oblivious to incompatible traits or character flaws could lead to unsatisfactory or even disastrous outcomes such as partner violence (i.e., Clements, Holtzworth-Munroe, Schweinle, & Ickes, 2007). Some cross-sectional research has found that normative accuracy based on viewing videos of targets is related to relationship variables such as perceptions of interpersonal support and social intimacy (Letzring, 2015), but longitudinal studies that examine how accuracy predicts these kinds of outcomes at later points in time would provide important insight about the consequences of accuracy for interpersonal relationships.

Other relationships that may be affected by accuracy of personality judgments could be within contexts such as relationships at work between colleagues or between managers and subordinates, relationships within educational settings such as between teachers and students, and relationships within athletics such as between coaches and athletes. Accurate judgments in these contexts could lead to more satisfying working, learning, and playing conditions, and to higher levels of success for companies, students, and teams. A good deal remains to be learned about the consequences of accuracy.

Conclusion

The RAM is based on the assumption that personality traits exist and that people behave relatively consistently across situations and over time. The ability of people to make accurate judgments of others provides evidence for these assumptions. Substantial research shows that people can make accurate judgments of the personality traits of others, although levels of accuracy differ across judges, targets, traits, and quantity and quality of information. Continuing to increase our understanding of the process, moderators, and consequences of accuracy will allow researchers to design even more effective training programs to increase levels of accuracy for judging others and for increasing the accuracy with which one's self is judged. Increased accuracy is likely to lead to better decisions in multiple realms of life and to many favorable outcomes.

Acknowledgments

Work on the state and trait accuracy model presented in this chapter was supported by the National Science Foundation Award No. 1551822 to Drs. Tera D. Letzring, Judith A. Hall, and Jeremy C. Biesanz.

References

Adler, J. M., Dunlop, W. L., Fivush, R., Lilgendahl, J. P., Lodi-Smith, J., McAdams, D. P.,...Syed, M. (2017). Research methods for studying narrative identity: A primer. *Social Psychological and Personality Science, 8,* 519–527. doi:10.1177/1948550617698202

Allik, J., de Vries, R. E., & Realo, A. (2016). Why are moderators of self-other agreement difficult to establish? *Journal of Research in Personality, 63,* 72–83. http://dx.doi.org/10.1016/j.jrp.2016.05.013

Allport, G. W. (1937). *Personality: A psychological interpretation.* New York, NY: Holt.

Ambady, N., Hallahan, M., & Rosenthal, R. (1995). On judging and being judged accurately in zero-acquaintance situations. *Journal of Personality and Social Psychology, 69,* 518–529.

Andersen, S. M. (1984). Self-knowledge and social inference: II. The diagnosticity of cognitive/affective and behavioral data. *Journal of Personality and Social Psychology, 46,* 294–307.

Asch, S. E. (1946). Forming impressions of personality. *Journal of Abnormal and Social Psychology, 9*, 258–290.

Astington, J. W., & Edward, M. J. (2010). The development of theory of mind in early childhood. In R. E. Tremblay, M. Boivin, R. de V. Peters (Eds.), & P. D. Zelazo (topic ed.), *Encyclopedia on early childhood development* [online]. http://www.child-encyclopedia.com/social-cognition/according-experts/development-theory-mind-early-childhood

Beer, A., & Brooks, C. (2011). Information quality in personality judgment: The value of personal disclosure. *Journal of Research in Personality, 45*, 175–185. doi:10.1016/j.jrp.2011.01.001

Biesanz, J. C., West, S. G., & Millevoi, A. (2007). What do you learn about someone over time? The relationship between length of acquaintance and consensus and self-other agreement in judgments of personality. *Journal of Personality and Social Psychology, 92*, 119–135. doi:10.1037/0022-3514.92.1.119

Blackman, M. C. (2002). Personality judgment and the utility of the unstructured employment interview. *Basic and Applied Social Psychology, 24*, 241–250. http://dx.doi.org/10.1207/153248302760179156

Blackman, M. C., & Funder, D. C. (1998). The effect of information on consensus and accuracy in personality judgment. *Journal of Experimental Social Psychology, 34*, 164–181.

Blanch-Hartigan, D., Andrzejewski, S. A., & Hill, K. M. (2012). The effectiveness of training to improve person perception accuracy: A meta-analysis. *Basic and Applied Social Psychology, 34*, 483–498. doi:10.1080/01973533.2012.728122

Bond, C. F., Jr., & DePaulo, B. M. (2006). Accuracy of deception judgments. *Personality and Social Psychology Review, 10*, 214–234.

Borkenau, P., & Liebler, A. (1992). Trait inferences: Sources of validity at zero acquaintance. *Journal of Personality and Social Psychology, 62*, 645–657. https://psycnet.apa.org/doi/10.1037/0022-3514.62.4.645

Borkenau, P., & Liebler, A. (1995). Observable attributes as manifestations and cues of personality and intelligence. *Journal of Personality, 63*, 1–25. https://doi.org/10.1111/j.1467-6494.1995.tb00799.x

Brown, J. A., & Bernieri, F. (2017). Trait perception accuracy and acquaintance within groups: Tracking accuracy development. *Personality and Social Psychology Bulletin, 43*, 716–728. https://doi.org/10.1177/0146167217695557

Brown, M. M., Thibodeau, R. B., Pierucci, J. M., & Gilpin, A. T. (2015). Supporting the development of empathy: The role of theory of mind and fantasy orientation. *Social Development, 26*, 951–964. doi:10.1111/sode.12232

Brunswik, E. (1955). Representative design and probabilistic theory in a functional psychology. *Psychological Review, 62*, 193–217.

Buck, R. (1976). A test of nonverbal receiving ability: Preliminary studies. *Human Communication Research, 2*, 162–171. doi:10.1111/j.1468-2958.1976.tb00708.x

Christiansen, N. D., Wolcott-Burnam, S., Janovics, J. E., Burns, G. N., & Quirk, S. W. (2005). The good judge revisited: Individual differences in the accuracy of personality judgments. *Human Performance, 18*, 123–149.

Clements, K., Holtzworth-Munroe, A., Schweinle, W., & Ickes, W. (2007). Empathic accuracy of intimate partners in violent versus nonviolent relationships. *Personal Relationships, 14*, 369–388.

Colman, D. E., Letzring, T. D., & Biesanz, J. C. (2017). Seeing and feeling your way to accurate personality judgments: The moderating role of perceiver empathic tendencies. *Social Psychological and Personality Science, 8*, 806–815. doi:10.1177/1948550617691097

Colvin, C. R. (1993). "Judgable" people: Personality, behavior, and competing explanations. *Journal of Personality and Social Psychology, 64*, 861–873.

Colvin, C. R., & Funder, D. C. (1991). Predicting personality and behavior: A boundary on the acquaintanceship effect. *Journal of Personality and Social Psychology, 60*, 884–894. doi:10.1037/0022-3514.60.6.884

Connelly, B. S., & Ones, D. S. (2010). An other perspective on personality: Meta-analytic integration of observers' accuracy and predictive validity. *Psychological Bulletin, 136*, 1092–1122. doi:10.1037/a0021212

DePaulo, B. M., Stone, J. I., & Lassiter, G. D. (1985). Telling ingratiating lies: Effects of target sex and target attractiveness on verbal and nonverbal deceptive success. *Journal of Personality and Social Psychology, 48*, 1191–1203.

Ebbesen, E. B., & Konecni, V. J. (1980). On the external validity of decision-making research: What do we know about decisions in the real world? In T. S. Wallsten (Ed.), *Cognitive processes in choice and decision behavior* (pp. 21–45). Hillsdale, NJ: Erlbaum.

Elfenbein, H. A., & Eisenkraft, N. (2010). The relationship between displaying and perceiving nonverbal cues of affect: A meta-analysis to solve an old mystery. *Journal of Personality and Social Psychology, 96*, 301–318. doi:10.1037/a0017766

Elfenbein, H. A., Foo, M. D., Mandal, M., Biswal, R., Eisenkraft, N., Lim, A., & Sharma, S. (2010). Individual differences in the accuracy of expressing and perceiving nonverbal cues: New data on an old question. *Journal of Research in Personality, 44*, 199–206. doi:10.1016/j.jrp.2010.01.001

Evans, J. St. B. (1984). In defense of the citation bias in the judgment literature [Comment]. *American Psychologist, 39*, 217–236.

Funder, D. C. (1980). On seeing ourselves as others see us: Self-other agreement and discrepancy in personality ratings. *Journal of Personality, 48*, 473–493.

Funder, D. C. (1987). Errors and mistakes: Evaluating the accuracy of social judgment. *Psychological Bulletin, 101*, 75–90.

Funder, D. C. (1990). Process versus content in the study of judgmental accuracy. *Psychological Inquiry, 1*, 207–209.

Funder, D. C. (1993). Judgments of personality and personality itself. In K. H. Craik, R. Hogan, & R. N. Wolfe (Eds.), *Fifty Years of Personality Psychology* (pp. 207–214). New York, NY: Plenum Press.

Funder, D. C. (1995). On the accuracy of personality judgment: A realistic approach. *Psychological Review, 102*, 652–670.

Funder, D. C. (1999). *Personality judgment: A realistic approach to person perception.* San Diego, CA: Academic Press.

Funder, D. C. (2012). Accurate personality judgment. *Current Directions in Psychological Science, 21*, 177–182. doi:10.1177/0963721411244530

Funder, D. C. (2016). Taking situations seriously: The situation construal model and the Riverside Situational Q-sort. *Current Directions in Psychological Science, 25*, 203–208. https://doi.org/10.1177/0963721416635552

Funder, D. C., & Colvin, C. R. (1988). Friends and strangers: Acquaintanceship, agreement, and the accuracy of personality judgment. *Journal of Personality and Social Psychology, 55*, 149–158.

Funder, D. C., & Dobroth, K. M. (1987). Differences between traits: Properties associated with interjudge agreement. *Journal of Personality and Social Psychology, 52*, 409–418.

Funder, D. C, & Sneed, C. (1993). Behavioral manifestations of personality: An ecological approach to judgmental accuracy. *Journal of Personality and Social Psychology, 64,* 479–490.

Goldberg, L. (1990). An alternative "description of personality": The big-five factor structure. *Journal of Personality and Social Psychology, 59,* 1216–1229. doi:10.1037/0022-3514.59.6.1216

Gosling, S. D., Augustine, A. A., Vazire, S., Holtzman, N., & Gaddis, S. (2011). Manifestations of personality in online social networks: Self-reported Facebook-related behaviors and observable profile information. *Cyberpsychology, Behavior, and Social Networks, 14,* 483–488. doi:10.1089/cyber.2010.0087

Hall, J. A., Andrzejewski, S. A., & Yopchick, J. E. (2009). Psychosocial correlates of interpersonal sensitivity: A meta-analysis. *Journal of Nonverbal Behavior, 33,* 149–180. doi:10.1007/s10919-009-0070-5

Hall, J. A., Gunnery, S. D., Letzring, T. D., Carney, D. R., & Colvin, C. R. (2017). Accuracy of judging affect and accuracy of judging personality: How and when are they related? *Journal of Personality, 85,* 583–592. doi:10.1111/jopy.12262

Hall, J. A., Pennington, N., & Lueders, A. (2014). Impression management and formation on Facebook: A lens model approach. *New Media and Society, 16,* 958–982. doi:10.1177/1461444813495166

Hammond, K., R. (1996). *Human judgment and social policy: Irreducible uncertainty, inevitable error, unavoidable injustice.* New York, NY: Oxford University Press.

Hartung, F., & Renner, B. (2011). Social curiosity and interpersonal perception: A judge x trait interaction. *Personality and Social Psychology Bulletin, 37,* 796–814. doi:10.1177/0146167211400618

Hirschmüller, S., Egloff, B., Nestler, S., & Back, M. D. (2013). The dual lens model: A comprehensive framework for understanding self-other agreement of personality judgments at zero acquaintance. *Journal of Personality and Social Psychology, 104,* 335–353. doi:10.1037/a0030383

Hirschmüller, S., Egloff, B., Schmukle, S. C., Nestler, S., & Back, M. D. (2015). Accurate judgments of neuroticism at zero acquaintance: A question of relevance. *Journal of Personality, 83,* 221–228. doi:10.1111/jopy.12097

Human, L. J., & Biesanz, J. C. (2011). Through the looking glass clearly: Accuracy and assumed similarity in well-adjusted individuals' first impressions. *Journal of Personality and Social Psychology, 100,* 349–364. doi:10.1037/a0021850

Human, L. J., & Biesanz, J. C. (2013). Targeting the good target: An integrative review of the characteristics and consequences of being accurately perceived. *Personality and Social Psychology Review, 17,* 248–272. doi:10.1177/1088868313495593

Human, L. J., Biesanz, J. C., Finseth, S. M., Pierce, B., & Le, M. (2014). To thine own self be true: Psychological adjustment promotes judgeability via personality-behavior congruence. *Journal of Personality and Social Psychology, 106,* 286–303. doi:10.1037/a0034860

Human, L. J., Biesanz, J. C., Parisotto, K. L., & Dunn, E. W. (2012). Your best self helps reveal your true self: Trying to make a good impression leads to more accurate personality impressions. *Social Psychological and Personality Science, 3,* 23–30. doi:10.1177/1948550611407689

Human, L. J., Mignault, M. C., Biesanz, J. C., & Rogers, K. H. (2019). Why are well-adjusted people seen more accurately? The role of personality-behavior congruence in naturalistic social settings. *Journal of Personality and Social Psychology, 117,* 465–482. https://psycnet.apa.org/doi/10.1037/pspp0000193

Ickes, W. (2016). Empathic accuracy: Judging thoughts and feelings. In J. A. Hall, M. Schmid Mast, & S. G. West (Eds.), *The social psychology of perceiving others accurately* (pp. 52–70). Cambridge, UK: Cambridge University Press.

John, O. P., Naumann, L. P., & Soto, C. J. (2008). Paradigm shift to the integrative Big Five trait taxonomy: History, measurement, and conceptual issues. In O. P. John, R. W. Robins, & L. A. Pervin (Eds.), *Handbook of personality: Theory and research* (3rd ed, pp. 114–158). New York, NY: The Guilford Press.

John, O. P., & Robins, R. W. (1993). Determinants of interjudge agreement on personality traits: The Big Five domains, observability, evaluativeness, and the unique perspective of the self. *Journal of Personality, 61,* 521–551.

Jones, E. E. (1985). Major developments in social psychology during the past five decades. In G. Lindzey & E. Aronson (Eds.), *The handbook of social psychology* (3rd ed., Vol. l., pp. 47–107). New York, NY: Random House.

Kelley, H. H. (1967). Attribution theory in social psychology. In D. Levine (Ed.), *Nebraska Symposium on Motivation* (Vol. 15, pp. 192–240). Lincoln: University of Nebraska Press.

Koestner, R., Bernieri, R., & Zuckerman, M. (1994). Self-peer agreement as a function of two kinds of trait relevance: Personal and social. *Social Behavior and Personality, 22,* 17–30.

Kolar, D. W. (1995). *Individual differences in the ability to accurately judge the personality characteristics of others* (Unpublished doctoral dissertation), University of California, Riverside, Riverside, CA.

Krzyzaniak, S. L. (2018). *Personality judgment accuracy and the role of physical fitness, cognitive functioning, and psychological well-being* (Unpublished master's thesis), Idaho State University, Pocatello, Idaho.

Langlois, J. H., Kalakanis, L., Rubenstein, A. J., Larson, A., Hallam, M., & Smoot, M. (2000). Maxims or myths of beauty? A meta-analytic and theoretical review. *Psychological Bulletin, 126,* 390–423. doi:10.1037//0033-2909.126.3.390

Letzring, T. D. (2008). The good judge of personality: Characteristics, behaviors, and observer accuracy. *Journal of Research in Personality, 42*(4), 914–932. doi:10.1016/j.jrp.2007.12.003

Letzring, T. D. (2015). Observer judgmental accuracy of personality: Benefits related to being a good (normative) judge. *Journal of Research in Personality, 54,* 51–60. doi:10.1016/j.jrp.2014.05.001

Letzring, T. D., Biesanz, J. C., Hall, J.A., Krzyzaniak, S., & McDonald, J. S. (2019, February). *Testing the State and Trait Accuracy Model II: Effect of Information Validity on Accuracy of Trait and State Judgments.* Poster presented at the annual meeting of the Society for Personality and Social Psychology, Portland, OR.

Letzring, T. D., Biesanz, J. C., Hall, J.A., McDonald, J. S., & Krzyzaniak, S. (2018, March). *Testing the State and Trait Accuracy Model I: Relationships between Accuracy of Judging Affective States and Accuracy of Judging Personality Traits.* Poster presented at the annual meeting of the Society for Personality and Social Psychology, Atlanta, GA. osf.io/2j6ey

Letzring, T. D., & Funder, D. C. (2018). Interpersonal accuracy in trait judgments. In V. Zeigler-Hill & T. K. Shackelford (eds.), *The SAGE Handbook of Personality and Individual Difference (Volume 3: Applications of Personality and Individual Differences).* Thousand Oaks, CA: Sage Publications. http://dx.doi.org/10.4135/9781526451163

Letzring, T. D., & Human, L. J. (2014). An examination of information quality as a moderator of accurate personality judgment. *Journal of Personality, 82*, 440–451. doi:10.1111/jopy.12075

Letzring, T. D., Wells, S. M., & Funder, D. C. (2006). Information quantity and quality affect the realistic accuracy of personality judgment. *Journal of Personality and Social Psychology, 91*, 111–123. doi:10.1037/0022-3514.91.1.111

Lorenzo, G. L., Biesanz, J. C., & Human, L. J. (2010). What is beautiful is good and more accurately understood: Physical attractiveness and accuracy in first impressions of personality. *Psychological Science, 21*, 1777–1782. doi:10.1177/0956797610388048

McAdams, D. (2012). Exploring psychological themes through life-narrative accounts. In J. A. Holstein & J. F. Gubrium (Eds.), *Varieties of Narrative Analysis* (pp. 15–32). Thousand Oaks, CA: Sage Publications.

McAdams, D. P. (1995). What do we know when we know a person? *Journal of Personality, 63*, 365–396.

McCrae, R. R., & Costa, P. T. Jr. (1999). A five-factor theory of personality. In L. A. Pervin & O. P. John (Eds.), *Handbook of personality: Theory and research, 2nd ed.* (pp. 139–153). New York, NY: The Guilford Press.

Naumann, L. P., Vazire, S., Rentfrow, P. J., & Gosling, S. D. (2009). Personality judgments based on physical appearance. *Personality and Social Psychology Bulletin, 35*, 1661–1671. doi:10.1177/0146167209346309

Neisser, U. (1988). The ecological approach to perception and memory. *New Trends in Empirical and Clinical Psychiatry, 4*, 153–166.

Nisbett, R., & Ross, L. (1980). *Human inference: Strategies and shortcomings of social judgment*. New York, NY: Prentice Hall.

Park, G., Schwartz, H. A., Eichstaedt, J. C., Kern, M. L., Kosinski, M., Stillwell, D. J., ... Seligman, M. E. P. (2015). Automatic personality assessment through social media language. *Journal of Personality and Social Psychology, 108*, 934–952. doi:10.1037/pspp0000020

Paunonen, S. V., & Kam, C. (2014). The accuracy of roommate ratings of behaviors versus beliefs. *Journal of Research in Personality, 52*, 55–67. doi:10.1016/j.jrp.2014.07.006

Qiu, L., Lin, H., Ramsay, J., & Yang, F. (2012). You are what you tweet: Personality expression and perception on Twitter. *Journal of Research in Personality, 46*, 710–718. http://dx.doi.org/10.1016/j.jrp.2012.08.008

Ratcliff, N. J., Hugenberg, K., Shriver, E. R., & Bernstein, M. J. (2011). The allure of status: High-status targets are privileged in face processing and memory. *Personality and Social Psychology Bulletin, 37*, 1003–1015. doi:10.1177/0146167211407210

Rauthmann, J. F., Sherman, R. A., & Funder, D. C. (2015). Principles of situation research: Towards a better understanding of psychological situations (target article). *European Journal of Personality, 29*, 363–381. https://doi.org/10.1002/per.1994

Ross, L., Nisbett, R. E., & Funder, D. C. (2007). Issue 3: Are our social perceptions often inaccurate? In J. A. Nier (Ed.), *Taking sides: Clashing views in social psychology* (pp. 52–73). New York, NY: McGraw-Hill.

Ruben, M. A., van Osch, M., & Blanch-Hartigan, D. (2015). Healthcare providers' accuracy in assessing patients' pain: A systematic review. *Patient Education and Counseling, 98*, 1197–1206. doi:10.1016/j.pec.2015.07.009

Sened, H., Lavidor, M., Lazarus, G., Bar-Kalifa, E., Rafaeli, E., & Ickes, W. (2017). Empathic accuracy and relationship satisfaction: A meta-analytic review. *Journal of Family Psychology, 31*, 742–752. http://dx.doi.org/10.1037/fam0000320

Shaklee, H. (1991). An inviting invitation [Review of *An invitation to cognitive science: Vol. 3. Thinking*]. *Contemporary Psychology, 36*, 940–941.

Simpson, J. A., Ickes, W., & Grich, J. (1999). When accuracy hurts: Reactions of anxious-ambivalent dating partners to a relationship-threatening situation. *Journal of Personality and Social Psychology, 76*, 754–769.

Simpson, J. A., Oriña, M. M., & Ickes, W. (2003). When accuracy hurts, and when it helps: A test of the empathic accuracy model in marital interactions. *Journal of Personality and Social Psychology, 85*, 881–893. doi:10.1037/0022-3514.85.5.881

Trope, Y. (1986). Identification and inferential processes in dispositional attribution. *Psychological Review, 93*, 239–257.

Trope, Y. (1989). Levels of inference in dispositional judgment. *Social Cognition, 7*, 296–314.

Trope, Y., & Lieberman, A. (1993). The use of trait conceptions to identify other people's behavior and to draw inferences about their personalities. *Personality and Social Psychology Bulletin, 19*, 553–562.

Tversky, A., & Kahneman, D. (1983). Extensional versus intuitive reasoning: The conjunction fallacy in probability judgment. *Psychological Review, 90*, 293–315.

Vogt, D. S., & Colvin, C. R. (2003). Interpersonal orientation and the accuracy of personality judgments. *Journal of Personality and Social Psychology, 71*, 267–295.

Wall, H. J., Kaye, L. K., & Malone, S. A. (2016). An exploration of psychological factors on emoticon usage and implications for judgement accuracy. *Computers in Human Behavior, 62*, 70–78. https://doi.org/10.1016/j.chb.2016.03.040

Wellman, H. M. (2017). The development of theory of mind: Historical reflections. *Child Development Perspectives, 11*, 207–214. doi:10.1111/cdep.12236

Zebrowitz, L. A. (1990). *Mapping social psychology series: Social perception*. Belmont, CA: Thomson Brooks/Cole.

Notes

1. This is because the laws of probability or logic are assessed by "coherence" criteria, whereas the accuracy of a judgment in relation to a real-life criterion is assessed by "correspondence" criteria (Hammond, 1996).
2. In contrast to judgments about hypothetical stimuli or people.
3. These are the Big Five traits of extraversion, agreeableness, conscientiousness, neuroticism, and openness to experience from the five factor model of personality (Goldberg, 1990; John, Naumann, & Soto, 2008; McCrae & Costa, 1999).
4. These analyses are referred to as lens model analyses because they are based on Brunswik's lens model and have the goal of determining which cues are valid and utilized. See chapter 4 by Hirschmüller, Breil, Nestler, and Back in this handbook for a complete description of the lens model.
5. Which is known as dispositional intelligence.
6. Which is known as attributional complexity.

Social Relations Modeling of Interpersonal Accuracy

Thomas E. Malloy

Abstract

Interpersonal perception is a dyadic phenomenon with multiple perspectives; dyad members reciprocally perceive one another (perceptions), while also assessing how the other perceives them (meta-perceptions). Because accuracy is inherently dyadic, social relations modeling is appropriate for partitioning interpersonal perceptions into theoretically meaningful components called *perceiver, target,* and *relationship.* Estimation of accuracy should use only the relevant components when assessing if perceptions conform to a validity criterion. Moreover, interpersonal perception exists within a broader nomological network of perceptual phenomena. People assume that others' traits are similar to their own traits (assumed similarity), and that others judge them as they judge others (assumed reciprocity). Each has implications for accuracy. Theoretical models are developed that specify the effect of perceivers' assumptions about others (i.e., top-down processes), and the effect of others' behaviors (i.e., bottom-up processes) on perceivers' judgments of targets' traits, and their impact on accuracy.

Key Words: social relations model, accuracy, meta-accuracy, accuracy process model, ARRMA

The accuracy of interpersonal perception is a core problem psychologists have addressed since the early twentieth century (Cleeton & Knight, 1924; Hartshorne, May, & Shuttleworth, 1930). In this endeavor there is a basic epistemological challenge highlighted by Donald T. Campbell, who was concerned with the limits of human knowing.[1] He quipped, "Cousin to the amoeba, how can we know for certain" (Mark, 1998)? Campbell was a realist who believed in an extant external world that is not mere construction, yet like our evolutionary cousins the amoeba, humans are embedded in the world we attempt to know. As the biological limits of the amoeba preclude epistemological certainty, so too the biological limits of humans makes all knowing indirect and presumptive. Despite epistemological limits and a predilection for biased social judgments (Tversky & Kahneman, 1973, 1974), human knowing had to be sufficiently accurate (i.e., accurate enough) given the evolutionary, scientific, cultural,

economic, architectural, and artistic success of Homo sapiens. Accurate judgments of the physical world occur because people have a direct sensory experience of that which they are attuned; for example, light energy contains information about a verdant forest, the length of a timber, a galaxy, or a predator (Gibson, 1966). Accurately knowing a person's traits is another matter. While some features are readily apparent (e.g., height, weight, age), trait judgments are inferences about characteristics that have never been observed. Personality traits are hypothetical unobservable constructs, and must be inferred using observable cues (e.g., behavior) presumed to be caused by the latent trait (Brunswik, 1956; Funder, 1995). Traits of most interest are typically manifest in the dyadic context (Funder & Fast, 2010; Guillaume et al., 2016; Kluger & Malloy, 2019; Malloy & Kenny, 1986). Interpersonal accuracy entails detecting cues during dyadic interaction and making valid judgments of the other (Funder, 2012), while at the same time validly predicting the other's likely response to one-self (i.e., meta-perception; Leary, 1957; see chapter 12 by Carlson & Elsaadawy in this handbook). Reciprocal interpersonal judgments in dyads operate for the coordination of human interaction (McArthur & Baron, 1983), and theories of interpersonal behavior offer guidance regarding the functional roles of dyadic perceptions and meta-perceptions in everyday life.

Goals of This Chapter

This chapter presents the social relations model (SRM) as a method for research on interpersonal accuracy. Theoretical analysis shows that interpersonal perception and meta-perception co-occur for dyad members, and should be considered simultaneously. Theoretical models proposed here are premised on the assumption that the accuracy of interpersonal judgments exists within a broader nomological network of other perceptual phenomena. For example, people assume that others' traits are similar to their own traits (assumed similarity), and that others judge them as they judge others (assumed reciprocity). Both can impact accuracy. These models specify the effect of perceivers' assumptions about others (i.e., top-down processes), and the effect of others' behaviors (i.e., bottom-up processes) on perceivers' judgments of targets' traits.

The theoretical models specified in this chapter respond to the *first* and *second Cronbach critiques* of interpersonal perception (Malloy, 2018b). In the first, Cronbach (1955) showed that interpersonal perception is componential with implications for estimating accuracy. In personal communication, Professor Cronbach (1996) raised a basic question regarding the process of interpersonal perception: "What is the object perceived in social perception?" I have referred to this as the second critique (Malloy, 2018b). Borsboom, Mellenbergh, and van Heerden (2003) addressed the general form of the second critique when considering the causal effect latent constructs have on measured variables. Individuals' latent traits are invisible and presumably displayed by actions, verbalizations, and non-verbal behavior. Because this is possibly Cronbach's last public discussion of interpersonal perception (he died on October 1, 2001), I quote him directly:

> "There is a serious lack of thought, so far as I know, given to the question "What is the object 'perceived' in social perception?' Some who see constructs as representing 'reality' might say that the target 'has'

the Big Five traits, and use sampled, coded actions as a basis for inference. Some who think in more dynamic terms might infer motives or idiographic structures in the mind of the target, and derive the response (e.g., ratings) from what is expected from that structure. Then the structure is the object. Some postmoderns would say there is no true 'message' to be perceived: 'What the person is' can be *only* a construal and different construers would bring different cultural histories to bear and so report different messages.
>
> Toulmin says that one part of the Cartesian program was, self-consciously, cryptanalysis, decoding the messages God had built into his construction.[2] Accuracy in person perception has often been seen as cryptanalysis, but it is not at all clear what the distal signal is. To construe is human; to construct, divine."
>
> (personal communication, June 30, and August 31, 1996)

The SRM and the process models developed here respond to Cronbach's two critiques in three ways. One, the SRM partitions generalized (i.e., perceiver and target effects) and dyadic (i.e., relationship) components of interpersonal trait perceptions. This is a response to Cronbach's first critique. Second, relevant SRM effects are variables in a model called ARRMA, which integrates *A*ssumed *R*eciprocity and actual *R*eciprocity while considering their joint effects on *M*eta-perception *A*ccuracy. Third, perceivers' top-down interpersonal assumptions are integrated with bottom-up effects of targets' behaviors in the accuracy process model (APM); their joint effects on accuracy and meta-accuracy are specified at the individual and dyadic levels. Both ARRMA and the APM integrate the bottom-up (i.e., behavior) and top-down (within the perceiver) processes that impact accuracy and meta-accuracy. A discussion of theories of interpersonal behavior that informs this modeling follows.

Interpersonal Theories of Dyadic Behavior

Theories of interpersonal behavior (Leary 1957; Schutz, 1966; Sullivan, 1939, 1949; Swann, 1984) specify bidirectional, functional processes in face-to-face interaction. Sullivan (1949) claimed that dyad members must understand their own behavior and that of the other to achieve "consensual validation" or the "degree of approximate agreement with a significant other person or persons which permit…the drawing of generally useful inferences about the action and thought of the other" (p. 177). Leary (1957) also viewed the dynamic interaction between two people as the appropriate focus for the study of behavior, and stated, "The interpersonal theory…requires that for each variable or variable system by which we measure the subject's behavior…we must include an equivalent set for measuring the behavior of each specified 'other' with whom the subject interacts" (p. 39). Similarly, Schutz's (1966) theory of interpersonal behavior proposes: "An interpersonal situation is one involving two or more persons, in which these individuals take account of each other for some purpose or decision" (p. 14). Swann (1984) theorized that in dyads people negotiate their identities, and use that information to accurately know "How will this target behave with *me*?" (p. 472). Overall, theories of dyadic behavior propose that human interaction necessitates a simultaneous, ongoing evaluation of the self, the other, and the other's response to the self to achieve core social motives (Fiske, 2014).

The importance of the dyad was recognized by Tagiuri (1958), who stated, "The two-person group is without doubt the most crucial social situation, perhaps even the most crucial of all human situations" (p. 329). The necessity of studying reciprocal perceptions (A's judgment of B, and B's judgment of A) and meta-perceptions (A's prediction of B's judgment of A, and B's prediction of A's judgment of B) in dyads follows from interpersonal theories. Cognitive theory applied in the dyadic context reveals mechanisms that operate when making these assessments. Specifically, an *availability-balance model* proposes cognitive processes of dyad members who perceive and meta-perceive the other (Malloy, 2018a, 2018b). When judging another, one's self-perceived traits, affect, and behavioral intentions are available cognitively, and serve an anchoring function when assessing the other (Tversky & Kahneman, 1973, 1974). This is why people assume that others are as attracted to them, as they are attracted to those others (Malloy, 2018a), and that others reciprocate their interpersonal similarity judgments (Malloy, 2019). Sometimes, trait judgments are informed by population base rates and conform to rational statistical models. Knowing that extreme violence is relatively rare is a basis for accurately assessing aggression or inferring the behavior of another in the absence of other information. But when ostensibly diagnostic information is available (e.g., a group stereotype), base rate information is ignored and judgments are biased by salient, category defining features. This is why available cognitive representations of one's own traits are so important when assessing the traits of another, and when anticipating the other's judgment of oneself. Coupled with available information about oneself is the motivation to perceive balance in social relationships (Heider, 1958), especially when consequential for the self. This availability-balance principle provides conceptual guidance when considering perceived and meta-perceived trait judgments (Malloy, 2018a, 2018b). Its implications for accuracy and inaccuracy are considered in theoretical models at the end of this chapter.

Milestones in Accuracy Research

Important milestones have characterized accuracy research up to the present, and it is useful to consider them as theory development continues. The *componential approach to accuracy* was the first substantial theoretical breakthrough (Cronbach, 1955, 1958; Gage & Cronbach, 1955) and has endured in the SRM (Kenny & Albright, 1987; Kenny, West, Malloy, & Albright, 2006). Cronbach was the first to recognize that interpersonal perception scores have a componential structure, and that estimation of accuracy requires the use of only the relevant components. This first Cronbach critique ushered in complex statistical modeling that was impractical before access to high-speed computing. Consequently, accuracy research was in a state of abeyance, and would not be reignited until the publication of Kenny and Albright's seminal paper (1987) on how to estimate accuracy using the SRM. A specialized application (*Soremo*; Kenny & Xuan, 2004) made componential analysis practical. The Kenny-Albright approach is componential, but fundamentally different from Cronbach's. Cronbach's idiographic approach was concerned with individual differences in accuracy, whereas Kenny and Albright were focused on nomothetic accuracy; the level that can be attained when people judge the traits of others. Their different orientations were discussed by Cronbach in 1996: "There is a basic difference between Kenny and me.…In my social perception work I saw perceiver and target as asymmetric; perceiver was typically 'responsible for' target in some sense: teacher, therapist, assessor, leader…these were the motivating problems when I began." Cronbach also acknowledged that the SRM advanced theory and research on interpersonal perception and accuracy beyond what he had done and stated, "I see Kenny as offering something I did not" (personal communication, August 31). The SRM approach to accuracy is nomothetic, interpersonal, componential, bidirectional, and multilevel.

Theoretical tension between nomothetic and idiographic approaches to accuracy continues to the present, and there is more support for the former than the latter. Compelling evidence is available that interpersonal trait perception is accurate beyond chance (e.g., Albright, Forest, & Reiseter, 2001), whereas the evidence for individual differences in accuracy has been mostly elusive (Kenny, 2020). Consider honesty, a trait of interest since the early 20th century (Hartshorne et al., 1930). Although meta-analysis documents the ability to accurately judge honesty (54% accuracy that is greater than 50% chance accuracy; Bond & DePaulo, 2006), a meta-analysis of individual differences in honesty detection concluded that they are "minute" and that "judges range no more widely than would be expected by chance" in terms of their accuracy (Bond & DePaulo, 2008, p. 477). In a critique of idiographic accuracy, Zaki and Ochsner (2011) argue that "no matter how organized accuracy researchers might have made their search for good judges, those judges—at least in the way researchers conceived of them—may have been more myth than reality" (p. 161). While this conclusion is disputed (see Schmid Mast & Hall, 2018), individual differences in interpersonal accuracy are not supported convincingly when estimated using componential methods.

Consideration of the *criterion problem* is another milestone in accuracy research (Kenny & Albright, 1987; Kruglanski, 1989), and this chapter offers a new perspective on this issue. The use of self-assessment as a validity criterion is rejected, as is interpersonal agreement or consensus. As will be seen, the criterion problem remains a fundamental philosophical, epistemological, and empirical concern in research on the accuracy of trait judgments.

Another milestone was the specification of the realistic accuracy model (RAM; Funder, 1995; see chapter 2 by Letzring & Funder in this handbook) that is an alternative to bias models of human judgment. The RAM assumes that observable cues are caused by latent traits and must be available, detected, and utilized to achieve accuracy. The RAM has emerged as an important heuristic device embraced by researchers because of its explicit discussion of the process of achieving accuracy. Yet, the RAM does not consider perceptual phenomena that operate in tandem with available cue detection and utilization, and models developed in this chapter fill this gap.

Two theoretical models of interpersonal accuracy and meta-accuracy presented here acknowledge the tension between bias and accuracy models of human trait judgment. One, called ARRMA (Assumed Reciprocity, Reciprocity and Meta-perception Accuracy) emphasizes the human penchant for bias in trait perception and meta-perception. The integration of this tendency with the pragmatic need for accuracy is inherent in the specification of the accuracy process model (APM). Both models are discussed later; but to understand them, it is first necessary to consider the SRM componential approach to accuracy.

Social Relations Components of Interpersonal Trait Judgments

A principle in Leary's (1957) theory of interpersonal behavior is that attention must be directed to "multilevel" causal effects, and has implications for designing research on, and estimation of, interpersonal accuracy. Studying accuracy at multiple levels requires a multiple interaction research design (e.g., round robin; Malloy, 2018b) so that trait perceptions (Malloy & Albright, 1990) and meta-perceptions (Laing, Phillipson, & Lee, 1966) can be studied at the individual and dyadic levels. In a round robin design each member judges a trait of all the other members; these are individual-level responses of one to many. Imagine that A consistently perceives others as extroverted, whereas B consistently perceives those same people as introverted. When A and B judge targets' traits consistently, but differ from each other, *perceiver effects* are operative. This is a top-down, eye-of-the-beholder effect on trait judgments. Now imagine that one person (i.e., a target) is consensually judged as extroverted by perceivers, and that another is judged as introverted by them. In this case, perceivers' judgments of targets' converge. The consensual responses of many to one are termed *target effects* in the SRM. Thus, A's perception of B is a function of how A generally perceives others (A's perceiver effect) and how B is typically perceived by others (B's target effect). Respectively, they are effects of the one to many, and the many to the one. The perceiver and target effects of the SRM are at the individual level of analysis. In Cronbachian fashion, only the appropriate individual level components should be used when conceptualizing and estimating accuracy and meta-accuracy at this level.

The psychological meaning of the perceiver and target components of interpersonal perceptions and meta-perceptions are different. Meta-perceptions are predictions of how others judge one's traits; perceiver effects quantify individual differences in these predictions. Target effects quantify agreement in perceivers' predictions that a target will judge them similarly on a trait. Usually, this agreement in meta-perceptions is very low because different people are unlikely to agree that person A judges their traits similarly.

In accord with Leary's call for a "multilevel" approach, the SRM also conceptualizes a dyadic determinant of trait perception called the *relationship effect*. Not only is A's judgment of B's trait determined by A's perceiver effect and B's target effect but also this specific combination of A and B can uniquely determine trait perception and meta-perception. The relationship effect is dyadic, meaning that it is concerned with specific dyads that produce uniquely high or low levels of trait judgments and meta-perceptions.

The componential approach to trait perceptions and meta-perceptions at the individual and dyadic levels is formalized by the SRM. If for example, A judges B a 7 on a 9-point scale of extroversion, this whole score (i.e., 7) contains the perceiver, target, and relationship components that must be partitioned for conceptual and empirical clarity. If not partitioned, these components are confounded. Kluger and Malloy (2019)show how this confounding leads to conceptual errors and invalid inferences regarding dyadic behavior.

Theoretically, the componential structure of person i's perception (p) of person j on trait X is specified in equation 1.

$$X_{ijp} = \mu_p + \alpha_{ip} + \beta_{jp} + \gamma_{ijp} + \varepsilon_{ijp} \qquad (1)$$

Equation 1 states that in a group of interactants (e.g., a round robin of coworkers), i's judgment of j's trait is equal to the average level of judgments on trait X among the coworkers (μ_p), plus the consistency of i's judgments of the members on X (i's perceiver effect α_{ip}), plus j's effect on the members' trait judgments (j's target effect β_{jp}), plus i's unique judgment of j on X (relationship effect γ_{ijp}), after controlling for α_{ip} and β_{jp}. There is also random error in i's perception of j (ε_{ijp}). Person j's perception of i on X is represented by equation 2, where the subscripts change appropriately. That is:

$$X_{jip} = \mu_p + \alpha_{jp} + \beta_{ip} + \gamma_{jip} + \varepsilon_{jip} \qquad (2)$$

Equations 1 and 2 are theoretical specifications of the SRM components of dyadic trait judgments. The perceiver effect (α) reflects individual differences when judging others' traits and the target effect (β) is the level of a trait judgment elicited by different targets. Statistically, individual is the unit of analysis for perceiver and target effects. The relationship effect (γ) is dyadic and quantifies the unique component of a perception when a specific perceiver judges a specific target's trait, after controlling their respective perceiver and target effects. Statistically, the dyad is the unit of analysis.

Variance Components in Dyadic Trait Judgments

Variance component analysis (Searle, Casella, & McCulloch, 1992) estimates interpersonal perceptual phenomena with random effect variances of the components of equations 1 and 2. Random effect estimation permits generalization to the population from which the dyad members were drawn, whereas fixed effect estimation permits generalization only to those included in the study. The variances of perceiver, target, and relationship effects estimate three perceptual phenomena: assimilation, consensus, and uniqueness, respectively. *Assimilation* occurs when perceivers make similar trait judgments of multiple targets but differ from one another, *consensus* is agreement in judgments, and *uniqueness* is a uniquely high or low judgment of a specific partner's trait. Random variance components are in the metric of the measure, and are standardized by computing the proportion of total variance and range from 0 to 1.00. A technical discussion of the SRM is available elsewhere (Malloy, 2018b).

The Criterion in Accuracy Research

To establish the accuracy of trait judgments, a validity criterion is required, and remains one of the thorniest philosophical and empirical issues in this endeavor (Kenny, 1994, 2020; Kruglanski, 1989). The fundamental problem in trait accuracy research is the absence of an objective, unmediated criterion for truth. Logical positivism once considered science the means for providing an explanation of the true state of nature (i.e., a Cartesian endeavor); yet general relativity theory (Einstein, 1951) and the Heisenberg (1930) uncertainty principle cast doubt on an immutable objective world that can be known with absolute truth. A thought experiment devised by Einstein illuminated the relativism of accurate perception of objects in motion. In that experiment, Einstein instructs us to imagine a train that travels down a rail line at a constant rate of speed. Identical two-dimensional coordinates (X and Y) are affixed to both the train and the railway embankment. A person's hand holding a pebble is placed out a window of the moving train, and is released without applying energy to it. To further simplify, no friction with air molecules is assumed. What is the trajectory of the pebble as the earth's gravitational effect impacts its movement? Einstein showed that the trajectory of the pebble varies as a function of the system of coordinates serving as the validity criterion; the coordinates on the train suggests a straight line, whereas that on the embankment suggests a parabolic function. Einstein's thought experiment showed that the concept of the "true path" is meaningless, and that there are simultaneous trajectories each defined by observations relative to a specific set of coordinates (i.e., validity criteria). This relativism has implications for the accuracy of trait judgments. Imagine that four people interact in all dyadic combinations and their behaviors and trait judgments are recorded. Across the six dyadic interactions, responses to others and by others are expected to vary around the average response of the four people. Each specific dyadic arrangement introduces unique behaviors and perceptions. Unlike the two identical X and Y coordinates in the thought experiment, each member of the round robin has a unique experience when interacting with each other member. This is why social knowing is fundamentally different from object knowing: every person has psychological coordinates that are brought to bear on each social interaction that yields nontrivial, unique social knowing. Moreover, people do not behave identically in different dyads. This is why interpersonal knowing and associated relationship outcomes at the dyadic level have become increasingly important (Kluger & Malloy, 2019; Malloy, Kluger, & Martin, 2018).

Kruglanski (1989) evaluated philosophical and logical approaches to accuracy as well as the criterion problem. He defined three types of accuracy: correspondence of a judgment and a criterion (Kenny & Albright, 1987), interpersonal consensus (Funder, 1987; Hastie & Rasinski, 1988), and pragmatic utility (McArthur & Baron, 1983; Swann, 1984). Yet, a careful reading of Kruglanski shows that treating consensus and pragmatic (i.e., functional) utility as accuracy is unwarranted because both are subsumed logically by the correspondence of a judgment and a criterion. Consensus is a necessary, though insufficient, condition for accuracy; although mariners who judged the earth as flat (consensus), successfully navigated from port to port and never fell off the edge (utility), their assessment of the earth was wrong. Kruglanski shows that even when pragmatic utility follows from a judgment, its accuracy rests ultimately on the congruence of the judgment and a criterion. My perspective is

that accuracy is only established when a judgment conforms to a criterion (c.f., Kenny, 2020; Kenny & Albright, 1987). A criterion for assessing the accuracy of judgment may be: (1) directly observable and available to the perceiver; (2) unobservable and mediated by perceptions of experts or other measurement operations (e.g., standardized test); or (3) absent entirely. The nature of the criterion has implications for establishing the accuracy of social knowing, and each is considered.

Research on the psychophysics of trait perception is an example of experimentally manipulated criterion information that is directly available to the perceiver (Malloy, 2018b). In that research, perceivers received five self-descriptive statements purportedly made by two individuals. These statements provided perceivers with information about their extroversion, or another trait known to be independent of this factor (e.g., *achievement*, *cognitive structure*, *endurance*, *impulsivity*, *order*, and *understanding* constructs of the Personality Research Form—PRF). These other traits were selected because they correlate near zero with the *Affiliation* construct of the PRF (r's = 0.01, 0.03, 0.05, 0.04, 0.08, and 0.04, respectively; Jackson, 1974). Judges received information about target A that was always five self-descriptive extroversion statements taken from the PRF (e.g., I welcome the opportunity to mix socially with people.). A was paired with target B, C, D, E, F, or G in different experimental conditions. An example of a statement that provided information independent of extroversion is: I prefer to work on a problem until it is solved. In each of the six between-subjects conditions, the differences in extroversion information for A and the other targets was 0, 1, 2, 3, 4, or 5 units of stimulus information provided by self-statements. Social relations modeling was conducted within each of the six conditions, and target variances in extroversion judgments were computed. Target variance quantifies perceivers' consensual differentiation of the two targets' traits. Target variances were then plotted as a function of the units of difference and produced a *difference detection function*. Difference detection functions from between-subjects and within-subjects studies showed that as the units of difference in extroversion information for targets increases, target variance also increases (Malloy, 2018b). In these studies, consensual trait judgments (indicated by SRM target variances) were, in fact, estimates of consensual accuracy of extroversion judgments. Because the criterion information was known explicitly, experimentally manipulated, and directly available to perceivers in the sentences provided, consensus, in this case, is evidence for accuracy. This situation is akin to asking two people to look at the sky on a clear day at noon and judge its color; both will say blue because the air molecules scatter blue wavelengths more than other visible wavelengths. The information is in the light, and humans attuned to detect it arrive at the same veridical perception (Gibson, 1966).

A study of children's peer judgments in classrooms illustrates an accuracy criterion that is an objective test score (Malloy et al., 1996); the score is treated as a basis for establishing truth. Within classrooms in grades 1 through 6, round robins were formed randomly and children participated individually in a laboratory. Each child was guided through a protocol in which traits (e.g., popularity, cognitive ability), affect (e.g., happy), and classroom behavior (e.g., well behaved) were rated. Teachers rated their students on the same dimensions. Presented here are estimates of the accuracy of cognitive ability judgments. Measures of mathematics and reading ability from standard educational testing were the validity criteria. Correlations of children's target effect estimates (with error removed) in ability judgments and the validity criterion (that contained measurement error) were: r's = 0.72, 0.56, 0.62, 0.60, 0.69, and 0.60, respectively, in grades 1 through 6. Teachers' ability ratings were undecomposed, because each child was rated by only one teacher; correlations of these ratings and the validity criterion were: r's = 0.71, 0.67, 0.56, 0.53, 0.63, and 0.63, respectively, in grades 1 through 6. All accuracy correlations were reliably different from zero; children and teachers were highly accurate when judging children's cognitive ability. In contrast to the previous study of extroversion judgments, in this study consensus (i.e., SRM partner variance) is not indicative of accuracy; only agreement. Unlike directly observable extroversion statements, in this case the validity criterion is latent and indicated by a measured test score. Accuracy required that the consensual judgments of targets (SRM partner effect estimates) conform to the objective criterion.[3] In this approach to accuracy estimation, when $r = 0$ there is no accuracy and when $r = 1.00$ there is perfect accuracy.

In the third case there is no validity criterion, and all that is possible is estimation of consensus. This approach is illustrated in a study of interpersonal trait judgments among family member, friends, and co-workers that used the key-person design (Malloy, Albright, Kenny, Agatstein, &

Winquist, 1997). In that study, key-persons were recruited and each nominated three family members, three friends, and three coworkers. Within groups members were highly acquainted, but across groups were unacquainted and produced the *non-overlapping key person design*. The key-person was the only common member of the three groups. Members of each group made judgments of one another on indicators of the Big Five personality factors, but because no criterion was available, all that could be studied was consensus. In all groups, all target variance components were reliably different from zero and showed that targets' traits were consensually differentiated by perceivers. The mean standardized target variance across five factors in the family friend and coworker groups were 0.30, 0.32, and 0.34, respectively. This showed that about one-third of the variance in trait judgments was consensual. I suspect these consensual judgments were probably accurate, but in the absence of a validity criterion, this is unknowable. Meta-accuracy was estimable because perceivers' actual judgments of targets were criteria for the validation of targets' predictions of how perceivers judged their traits. In the family, friend, and coworker groups, the mean meta-accuracy correlations were r's = 0.51, 0.44, and 0.39, respectively. In the core groups of life, people knew accurately how others judged their traits.

Social relations modeling of interpersonal accuracy views the correspondence of the judgment and a behavioral criterion as the gold standard (Kenny, 2020), and acknowledges that each has the componential structure specified in equations 1 and 2. The concept of absolute truth is avoided; rather, in most cases the judgment and the criterion are unobserved latent variables. The association of latent variables quantifies if the judgment conforms to the validity criterion and establishes accuracy. Treating consensus as accuracy is rejected (Kenny, 1994, 2020) because consensus is a necessary, yet insufficient condition, for interpersonal accuracy (Kruglanski, 1989).

Self-assessment is rejected as an acceptable validity criterion, because self-assessments are too prone to bias to serve this function. Mothers, for example, judge their relationships with family members as more positive than their relationships with each other (Cook, 2015). Mothers also report that other family members feel more positive toward her than they do toward one another. In addition, self-perception is not a single unitary structure (Malloy, 2018b). For example, Kwan and colleagues (2004) conceptualized self-perception as a componential structure determined by a general self-perceived component, an effect of the other on self-perception, and a unique self-perception when interacting with a specific person. A single, measured self-perception confounds these components and vitiates its use as a validity criterion. The validity criterion should generally not be one's self-assessment in dyadic relationships because of the potential for bias but, if used, should only be the theoretically relevant component of the self (Kwan et al., 2004; Malloy, 2018b).

The Componential Approach to Interpersonal Accuracy

Equations 1 and 2 specify the theoretical components of interpersonal trait perceptions, and there must be a criterion to validate group, individual, and dyadic components. To illustrate, imagine a round robin ($n = 4$) and in all dyads extroverted behavior is measured by the number of questions asked and speaking time. These variables would indicate a latent extroversion construct that serves as a behavioral criterion. After each interaction, dyad members rate the other on extroversion and outgoing; these variables would indicate a latent perception of extroversion construct.

The perceived and behavioral extroversion constructs can be partitioned in accord with equations 1 and 2 because each has a round robin structure. After the componential structures of the judgments and behavioral criteria are partitioned, estimation of accuracy can proceed. Different types of accuracy can be estimated using specific components of SRM judgment and criterion scores and are summarized in Table 3.1.

Base Rate or Elevation Accuracy

Can people judge a behavioral criterion (i.e., a base rate) accurately at the level of a group? This is a form of accuracy when *many respond to many*; on average, do the perceptions of others' behaviors conform to their actual behaviors? There is evidence this can be done (Albright et al., 2001), but equally compelling

evidence that people will often be biased when making these judgments (Tversky & Kahneman, 1973). If a group of psychologists is told that a population consists of 70 social psychologists and 30 personality psychologists and that one person is selected randomly from that population; they will use the base rates of 0.7 and 0.3 to make an accurate inference that the one selected is probably a social psychologist. But, if given the same base rate information and told that the psychologist selected is inclined to see traits as the cause of behavior, this seemingly diagnostic information (from the perspective of statistical models of human reasoning such as Tversky & Kahneman, 1974) will lead to probability estimates greater than 0.3 that the one selected is a personality psychologist. From this perspective, the base rate has not changed, but the inference is biased because the diagnostic information is used. From the normative perspective, inaccuracy results when people believe salient information is diagnostic of a groups' characteristic, and use it to make a judgment while ignoring the actual base rate. Alternatively, from a Bayesian perspective an estimate greater than 0.3 is potentially accurate because prior probabilities, based on the fact that personality psychologists tend to see traits as the cause of behavior, is a rational judgment strategy for achieving accuracy (Tenenbaum, Griffiths, & Kemp, 2006). This debate is beyond the scope of this chapter (see Marcus & Davis, 2013, for this).

Perceiver Accuracy

When perceiver *i*'s judgments of how others generally behave with i (α_i) conform to how others actually behave with i (β_i), perceiver accuracy is revealed. Perceiver inaccuracy is expected for two reasons. The SRM perceiver effect in judgments emerges when perceivers: (1) fail to differentiate targets, and (2) differ among themselves. Inaccuracy will result when targets do not behave consistently (and differently from each other) with different perceivers. This is typically a source of inaccuracy in *one's responses to many*. One perceiver may believe that

Table 3.1. SRM Componential Interpersonal Accuracy

Component of Perception	Component of Behavior	Level of Analysis	Accuracy/Focus
μ	μ	Group	Base rate accuracy/Many to Many
α_i	β_i	Individual	Perceiver accuracy/One to Many
β_i	α_i	Individual	Generalized accuracy/Many to One
γ_{ij}	γ_{ji}	Dyad	Dyadic accuracy/One-to-One

Note. Persons *i* and *j* are dyad members. Based on Kenny & Albright (1987) and Kenny (1994, 2020).

partners were consistently extroverted, and another believes that those same partners were consistently introverted. When asked how family members, friends, and coworkers judge their personality traits, people inferred that members of those groups make very similar judgments of them. We (Malloy et al., 1997) found that the consistency of these inferences were quite stable across groups with correlations of $r = 0.73$ (coworkers and family), $r = 0.73$ (coworkers and friends), and $r = 0.74$ (family and friends). However, this predicted consistency of trait judgments was illusory; in these groups the agreement in trait judgments across the Big Five factors were $r = 0.14$, $r = 0.34$, and $r = 0.25$, respectively. For trait judgments in different contexts, people perceive much more consistency in others' responses to them than is warranted. These patterns can be explained by the availability-balance model; one's self-assessed traits are available cognitively and people use that information to judge others, and to infer others' judgments of them. The motivation to maintain balanced interpersonal relations in different spheres of life is why people predict that others judge their traits similarly (Heider, 1958; Malloy, 2018a, 2018b) even though they do not.

Generalized Accuracy

This is the classic form of accuracy and is concerned with the question: Do people accurately judge the traits of other people? The focus is on the accuracy of the perceptions of *many when assessing the one*. Do perceivers' consensual judgments of a target's traits, captured by the SRM partner effect (βi) in perception, conform to actor effects (αi) in the behavioral criterion? For generalized accuracy there must be consensus, but that consensus must be related to an acceptable validity criterion.

Dyadic Accuracy

Can people make accurate judgments of a specific others' traits? This is *one-to-one accuracy*, and is similar to Swann's (1984) concept of circumscribed accuracy. If A perceives B as uniquely extroverted and C as uniquely introverted, do judgments of these specific partners conform to their unique behavior with A? Dyadic accuracy is often neglected because multiple interaction designs and social relations analysis with multiple indicators of constructs are required. Much more attention to dyadic accuracy is warranted because many interpersonal behaviors are inherently dyadic phenomena(e.g., questioning [Kluger & Malloy, 2019]; listening [Malloy, Kluger,

& Martin, 2018]; attraction [Malloy, 2018a]), and this is where the search for accuracy is likely to be most fruitful. In the absence of componential analysis, dyadic accuracy is invisible.

The Componential Approach to Interpersonal
Meta-Accuracy
THE BIVARIATE APPROACH

Interpersonal theory proposes that dyad members assess their own behavior, and attempt to predict the behavior of the other to coordinate action (Leary, 1957; Schutz, 1966; Sullivan, 1939, 1949). This theoretical analysis necessitates a simultaneous consideration of perceptual and meta-perceptual accuracy. Meta-perceptions (m) are predictions of others' trait judgments of, or affective and behavioral responses to, oneself. Like perceptions, meta-perceptions have the same SRM componential structure although the psychological meaning of the components differs. For example, when i predicts (m) j's trait judgment of i, yielding Y_{ijm}, this score can be partitioned into SRM perceiver, target, and relationship components discussed previously for trait perceptions. Equation 3 shows this structure for i's prediction (m) of j's trait judgment (X) of i.

$$X_{ijm} = \mu_m + \alpha_{im} + \beta_{jm} + \gamma_{ijm} + \varepsilon_{ijm} \qquad (3)$$

When j predicts i's response to j, this score X_{jim} can likewise be partitioned in accord with equation 4.

$$X_{jim} = \mu_m + \alpha_{jm} + \beta_{im} + \gamma_{jim} + \varepsilon_{jim} \qquad (4)$$

Equations 3 and 4 are theoretical SRM specifications of the componential structure of dyadic meta-perceptions. Meta-perception accuracy is estimated by the covariance of specific components of perceptions (equations 1 and 2) and meta-perceptions (equations 3 and 4) at the individual and dyadic levels. Interpersonal trait perception is the focus. Table 3.2 presents SRM components in interpersonal perceptions (or behavior) and meta-perceptions, the level of analysis of estimates, and the specific form of meta-accuracy.

Base Rate Meta-Accuracy

Are individuals' average predictions of others average judgments of their traits accurate? Considering interpersonal trait perception, base rate accuracy is estimated by the covariance of the grand mean in perceptions, which is the validity criterion, and the grand mean in meta-perceptions. Group is the unit of analysis.

Table 3.2. SRM Componential Meta-Accuracy

Component Perception (p) or Behavior (b)[a]	Component of Meta-Perception (m)	Level	Meta-Accuracy/Focus
μ_p	μ_m	Group	Base rate meta-accuracy/Many to Many
α_{ib}	α_{im}	Individual	Generalized behavioral meta-accuracy/One to Many
β_{ip}	α_{im}	Individual	Generalized perceptual meta-accuracy/Many to One (β_{ip}) and One to Many(α_{im})
γ_{ijb}	γ_{ijm}	Dyad	Dyadic behavioral meta-accuracy/One-to-One
γ_{jip}	γ_{ijm}	Dyad	Dyadic perceptual meta-accuracy/One-to-One

Note. [a] Validity criterion for meta-accuracy correlations.

Generalized Behavioral Meta-Accuracy

When predicting others' judgments of one's traits, do these judgments conform to behavior presumed to be caused by the trait? Imagine that person i interacts with multiple partners who judge i's extroversion, and that i's behavior presumed to be caused by i's latent extroversion is recorded. Person i also predicts those partners' judgments of i's extroversion. Generalized behavioral meta-accuracy is indicated when i's predictions of others' trait judgments (α_{im}) correlate with i's consistent behavior (α_{ib}) presumed to be caused by the trait being judged. There has been insufficient attention to behavioral meta-accuracy, which is a promising direction for future research (see Albright et al., 2001, for an exception).

Generalized Perceptual Meta-Accuracy

Can people accurately predict others' judgments of their traits? Meta-analytic results suggest the answer to this question is yes for trait judgments; Kenny (1994) reported a median generalized meta-accuracy correlation of $r = 0.58$. This form of meta-accuracy is indicated when people can predict (α_{im}) accurately others' consensual judgments of their traits (β_{ip}).

Dyadic Behavioral Meta-Accuracy

When people predict how a specific other judges them on a trait, does that prediction correlate with a unique behavior presumed to be cause by that trait? For example, imagine a dyad composed of i and j, and assume that i is aware that her behavior with j was agreeable and behavior indicative of this trait (e.g., smiles, eye contact) was measured. When predicting j's judgment of i's agreeableness, if i bases that judgment on how she actually behaved, dyadic behavioral meta-accuracy is indicated. One would also presume that j's judgment is consistent with how i actually behaved. This form of accuracy can be viewed as self-insight into one's own behavior, and its effect on a specific other's trait judgment.

Dyadic Perceptual Meta-Accuracy

Do people know accurately how specific others judge their traits? In this case, a specific other's relationships effect in a trait judgment is the validity criterion. Estimates of dyadic meta-accuracy for trait judgments are weak; a meta-analytic estimate of $r = 0.13$ was reported by Kenny (1994). For interpersonal attraction among well acquainted family members, friends, and coworkers, median estimates of dyadic meta-accuracy were r's = 0.19, 0.08, and 0.24, respectively (Malloy, 2018a). While somewhat counterintuitive, people do not accurately know how specific others judge their traits or feel about them.

Interpersonal theory proposes that people monitor their own and others' behavior to coordinate adaptive responses in a situation. In essence, one must consider the actual behavior of self and other, as well as assumptions about responses that will likely be made by the other. Recent theoretical analysis shows that generalized and dyadic meta-knowledge are intertwined conceptually and statistically with the actual reciprocity of dyadic responses. When interpersonal assumptions and actual behavior are commensurate, accuracy results; but when the two are not commensurate, inaccuracy results. Multivariate models linking assumed and actual interpersonal behavior at the individual and dyadic levels have been proposed, and offer insight into the origins of meta-inaccuracy. When predictions of how others will behave are inaccurate, assessments of how they actually behave may also be flawed. That is, meta-inaccuracy has implications for perceptual accuracy, and understanding the mechanisms that produce meta-inaccuracy will also shed light on how they limit accuracy. To this we turn.

ARRMA: A Model of the Determinants of Meta-Accuracy
Individual Level ARRMA

Theoretical analysis (Malloy, 2018a, 2018b, 2020) proposes that meta-perception accuracy should not be studied in isolation of two conceptually and statistically intertwined phenomena at the individual and dyadic levels. This theoretical model, called ARRMA, captures the dynamic interplay of three interpersonal phenomena that occur in dyadic interaction: *Assumed Reciprocity, Reciprocity,* and *Meta-perception Accuracy.* Assumed reciprocity is A's belief that B will respond (e.g., a trait judgment) to A as A responds to B. Reciprocity is the extent to which A's response to B and B's response to A are similar, different, or independent. Meta-perception accuracy is the veridicality of A's assumptions about how B will respond to A, and the criterion is how B actually responds to A. Until now, these phenomena have been conceptualized and studied independently although, as ARRMA shows, they are theoretically and empirically dependent. The formal statistical derivations of ARRMA at the individual (Malloy, 2018a; 2018b) and dyadic levels (Malloy, 2020) are presented elsewhere. Here, the focus is conceptual.

The estimation of ARRMA parameters is a two-step process. First, a social relations analysis is conducted to isolate SRM effect estimates at the individual (i.e., perceiver and target) and dyadic (i.e., relationship) levels for trait judgments (as in equations 1 and 2) and meta-perceptions (as in equations 3 and 4). Then, the appropriate effect estimates become variables in second-stage individual and dyadic ARRMA models. Consider the path model of ARRMA at the individual level of analysis presented in Figure 3.1 for interpersonal trait judgments.

ARRMA in Figure 3.1 includes three variables that are SRM components (i.e., effect estimates): perceiver effects in trait judgments (α_{ip}), target effects in trait judgments (β_{ip}), and perceiver effects in meta-perceptions of trait judgments (α_{im}). These SRM components are terms from equations 1 through 4, and reveal why the initial social relations analysis is the necessary first step in ARRMA parameter estimation. The impact of perceiver effects in judgments on perceiver effects in meta-perceptions estimates assumed reciprocity (AR in Figure 3.1); that is, do judgments of others' traits impact predictions of others' judgments of one's own traits? Evidence shows that assumed reciprocity is quite robust (Malloy, 2018a; Tagiuri, 1958), and Kenny (1994) concluded that "Assumed reciprocity correlations are some of the largest correlations in interpersonal perception" (p. 103). ARRMA shows that ignoring assumed reciprocity when studying meta-perception accuracy can lead to conceptual and statistical bias. Reciprocity is also intertwined with meta-perception accuracy. At the limit, when reciprocity (R in Figure 3.1) is perfect (A's judgment of B's trait is the same as B's judgment of A on that trait), and assumed reciprocity is perfect (A assumes that B will judge A on a trait as A judges B on the trait), then meta-perception will be perfectly accurate (MA in Figure 3.1). Empirically, reciprocity at the individual level has been notoriously elusive (Kenny, 1994; Newcomb, 1979) with most estimates near zero. Kenny (1994) concluded, "There appears to be no evidence of individual-level reciprocity of attraction" (p. 114). However, ARRMA provided reliable evidence for the reciprocity of attraction at the individual level among highly acquainted family members, friends, and coworkers (Malloy, 2018a). Meta-perception accuracy at the individual level is substantial; Kenny (1994)

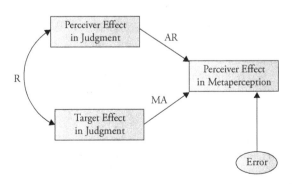

Figure 3.1. ARRMA at the individual level of analysis: AR is assumed reciprocity, R is reciprocity, and MA is meta-perception accuracy.

provides a median meta-analytic estimate of r = 0.58 for trait judgments. Using ARRMA, I found (Malloy, 2018a) that meta-perception accuracy for interpersonal attraction was the weakest of the three phenomena in the model. Although componential analysis was used in this research, differences between Kenny's (1994) and my estimates (Malloy, 2018a) probably originate in: measurement operations, level of acquaintance, and bivariate versus multivariate (i.e., ARRMA) modeling of meta-perception accuracy. I discuss these differences in detail elsewhere (Malloy, 2018a; 2018b).

In a recent study that used the nonoverlapping key person design, family members, friends, and co-workers judged the similarity of other group members to themselves (Malloy, 2019). Five indicators of a perceived and meta-perceived similarity construct based on the factor analytic work of McCroskey, McCroskey, and Richmond (2006) were used. The following variables were all indicators of a latent interpersonal similarity construct: "This person and I are from a similar social class," "This person thinks like me," "This person treats people like I do," "This person is similar to me," and "This person behaves like me." Perceptions and meta-perceptions were measured using a 7-point scale (1 [completely disagree]–7 [completely agree]). Following the initial social relations analysis, relevant SRM effect estimates for the five indicators were averaged. Path modeling was then used to estimate ARRMA parameters at the individual level.

Assumed reciprocity of similarity judgments were reliably different from zero in all groups with a median unstandardized estimate of b = 0.88 (standard error, SE = 0.06) across them. If another is judged as similar to or different from oneself, people assume that these judgments are reciprocated. The actual reciprocity of similarity judgments were reliably different from zero in all groups, though weaker than assumed reciprocity with a median unstandardized estimate of b = .47 (SE = 0.09). Individuals' similarity judgments tended to match reliably. Meta-perception accuracy was the weakest of the three phenomena, and only one estimate in families (b = 0.21, SE = 0.07) was reliably different from zero; the median estimate was b = 0.10 (SE = 0.08). People did not know accurately how similar to themselves others judged them to be. These results show that when assumed reciprocity is robust and reciprocity is less than perfect, meta-inaccuracy is the consequence, and shows why studying meta-accuracy while ignoring these related phenomena is

theoretically unwarranted. Later, the implications of the processes that produce meta-inaccuracy for the accuracy of trait judgments are discussed; but now, it is necessary to consider the dyadic ARRMA model when members are distinguishable and indistinguishable.

Dyadic ARRMA with Distinguishable and Indistinguishable Dyad Members

The ARRMA model for trait judgments is also estimable at the dyadic level; although different approaches are dictated when dyad members are distinguishable or indistinguishable. All people are distinguishable because of genetics and/or social experience; however, in this context, distinguishability is concerned with differences on a variable that can impact trait judgments. For example, leadership judgments by African American males and females were impacted by the gender of the perceiver and the target (Peters, Kinsey, & Malloy, 2004). The distinguishability of dyad members has important implications for ARRMA modeling.

DISTINGUISHABLE DYAD MEMBERS

When interpersonal trait judgments and meta-perceptions are collected from distinguishable dyad members, the parameters of dyadic ARRMA can be estimated. The full ARRMA model with distinguishable dyads is displayed in Figure 3.2 as a path diagram.[4] To estimate the parameters of dyadic ARRMA with distinguishable members, SRM relationship effects are the variables in the model. The SRM relationship effect estimates (i.e., GIJ and GJI in Figure 3.2, γ_{ij} and γ_{ji} in equations 1 through 4) for interpersonal judgments and meta-perceptions are computed for each member of each dyad, and are output to a data file.[5]

The dyadic ARRMA model in Figure 3.2 is just-identified, meaning that all parameters of the model can be estimated, but with no residual degrees of freedom. Consequently, measures of fit cannot be computed for the full model because the chi square for a just-identified model is undefined. In the dyadic ARRMA model with distinguishable members (Figure 3.2), there are two estimates of assumed reciprocity (AR and AR'), one estimate of reciprocity (parameter R), and two estimates of meta-perception accuracy (MA and MA'). Because dyad members are distinguishable (e.g., male or female), it is possible to estimate assumed reciprocity, reciprocity, and meta-perception accuracy for trait judgments when responding to members of the

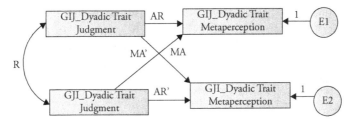

Figure 3.2. Dyadic ARRMA with distinguishable dyad members: GIJ and GJI are SRM relationship effect estimates. AR and AR' are assumed reciprocities, R is reciprocity, MA and MA' are meta-perception accuracies.

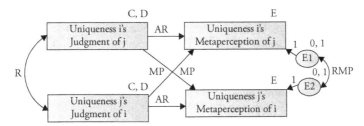

Figure 3.3. Dyadic ARRMA for Indistinguishable Dyads with Olsen and Kenny (2006) constraints. The same letters, combinations of letters, or numbers indicate an equality constraint.

other category. When parameters are expected to be equivalent for different categories, equality constraints can be imposed, and in this case the chi square is defined. This chi square tests if a constraint impairs, or fails to impair, model fit. In addition to assessing meta-perception accuracy, the proportion of variance in meta-perceptions explained by the exogenous (i.e., presumed causal) ARRMA variables is also of interest.

INDISTINGUISHABLE DYAD MEMBERS

When dyad members are indistinguishable, estimation of the dyadic ARRMA phenomena requires imposing constraints on model parameters, and adjustments of measures of model fit and degrees of freedom (Olsen & Kenny, 2006; see Figure 3.3). These constraints and adjustments are required because the designation of dyad members as *i* or *j* is arbitrary rather than based on a differentiating variable (e.g., male or female). Consequently, implicit statistical constraints on the model are imposed that, in effect, force the analysis to the dyadic level. Constraint to the dyad level is necessary even though *i*'s and *j*'s unique interpersonal responses to one another are variables in the model. Details on the implementation of the Olsen-Kenny (Olsen & Kenny, 2006) constraints on ARRMA are in the appendix.

If the unconstrained ARRMA model is estimated without the Olsen-Kenny constraints, there are two estimates of assumed reciprocity and meta-perception accuracy, whereas with them these parameters are constrained to equality. Note that the values of the parameter estimates constrained to equality using the Olsen-Kenny method are equal to the average of the parameter estimates in the unconstrained model within rounding error.

The Implications of ARRMA

Theories of interpersonal behavior converge in their emphasis on the simultaneity of interpersonal perception and meta-perception in dyadic interaction (Leary, 1957; Schutz, 1966; Sullivan, 1939, 1949). An important implication of ARRMA is the stipulation that meta-perception accuracy for trait judgments should not be studied independently of the two phenomena with which it is inextricably bound: assumed reciprocity and actual reciprocity. A logical extension is that the ARRMA phenomena also have implications for the accuracy of trait judgments. ARRMA raises two basic questions: (1) do people accurately know how others will judge their traits based on social experience with them, or (2) do people achieve meta-accuracy for trait judgments by simply assuming reciprocity when there is concomitant reciprocity? The former is bottom-up or data driven meta-accuracy, whereas the latter is top-down assumptive meta-accuracy. Bottom-up behavioral information and top-down processes of

ARRMA are further integrated in the Accuracy Process Model (APM). The APM extends beyond ARRMA to explain how bottom-up and top-down processes each impact both accuracy and meta-accuracy of trait judgments at the individual and dyadic levels.

The Accuracy Process Model

Existing theoretical models offer explanations of the process of forming trait perceptions (e.g., Kenny, 2004; Kenny, Albright, Malloy, & Kashy, 1994) and achieving accuracy (Funder, 1995; Kenny, 1991, 1994). Here, a theoretical APM is specified to explain how interpersonal accuracy and meta-accuracy can be achieved at the individual and dyadic levels. At each level, the APM integrates the impact of behavior (i.e., bottom-up data), self-perception, assumed similarity, and assumed reciprocity (i.e., top-down perceptual phenomena) that impact accuracy and meta-accuracy of trait judgments. In the context of ARRMA, the availability-balance model (Malloy, 2018a; 2018b) explained how information about oneself is readily available, and intertwined with the motivation to maintain balanced interpersonal cognitions when assessing others' traits. Consequently, assumed similarity and assumed reciprocity, which are themselves offspring of self-perception, are among the most impactful top-down social cognitive processes impacting perceivers and the accuracy and meta-accuracy of trait judgments.

Individual Level APM

The APM at the individual level integrates top-down assumptive process, like those of ARRMA, with the effects of behavior on trait judgments and meta-perceptions. To illustrate, consider individual i who judges the traits of multiple partners in a round robin. The initial step is a social relations analysis and the production of SRM effect estimates at the individual level. These include: i's self-perception,[6] i's perceiver effect in trait judgments, i's perceiver effect in meta-perceptions of trait judgments, i's actor effect in trait-relevant behavior (i.e., i's behavioral consistency in multiple dyads), and i's target effect on partners' trait judgments of i. These variables are at the individual level of analysis, and their hypothesized relationships are specified in Figure 3.4.

When self-perception affects one's perceiver effect in trait judgments, assumed similarity occurs, and across four studies, Kenny (1994) reported assumed similarity correlations ranging from $r = 0.27$ (Extroversion) to $r = 0.65$ (Agreeableness), with a median of $r = 0.37$. People nontrivially perceive others' traits as they perceive their own traits. When perceiver effects in trait judgments impact perceiver effects in trait meta-perceptions, assumed reciprocity occurs. People assume that others judge their traits as they judge the traits of others. Assumed similarity and assumed reciprocity are the top-down mechanisms of the APM. Now considered are the bottom-up mechanisms originating in the actual behavior of social interaction partners.

Interpersonal accuracy requires that trait judgments of partners are determined by their actual behavior. Meta-perception accuracy requires that a prediction of a partner's judgment of one's traits conforms to that partner's actual judgment. Actual trait-relevant behavior can be the driver of interpersonal accuracy and meta-accuracy, but can be compromised when similarity and reciprocity are assumed but do not occur. An ingenious accuracy study illuminates the impact of experimentally manipulated actor behavior on the accuracy of trait perception, and on actors' meta-accuracy regarding their partners' judgments of them (Albright, Forest, & Reiseter, 2001). In that study, actors' dyadic

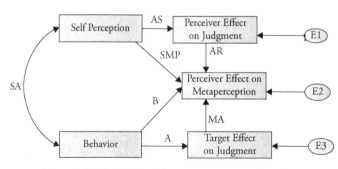

Figure 3.4. Accuracy process model—individual level: SA is self-accuracy, AS is assumed similarity, AR is assumed reciprocity, B is the effect of behavior on meta-perception, SMP is the effect of self on meta-perception, A is accuracy, and MA is meta-accuracy.

behavior (i.e., optimism or pessimism) was scripted and manipulated experimentally, thus making it orthogonal with their true standing on this construct; that is, how they behaved was independent of how optimistic/pessimistic they actually were. Results showed that partners' judgments of actors' traits (i.e., motivated, optimistic, nonjudgmental, hopeful, confident, and positive) conformed strongly to scripted verbal and nonverbal behavior coded from videotapes. The median accuracy correlation between the SRM target effect in trait judgments and the behavioral criterion was $r = 0.93$ (range $r = 0.86$ to $r = 0.96$). This documented that scripted actors' behaviors had a very strong effect on judgments of behavior-relevant traits. Additionally, this study showed that scripted actors' meta-perceptions of partners' trait judgments were also determined substantially by actual, experimentally controlled dyadic behavior. The median correlation of coded verbal and nonverbal behavior and meta-perceptions was $r = 0.92$, with a range from $r = 0.76$ to $r = 0.95$. Behavior determined meta-perceptions that were also accurate; the median correlation between actors' predictions of partners' trait judgments and their actual trait judgments (i.e., meta-perception accuracy) was $r = 0.95$ with a range from $r = 0.70$ to $r = 0.96$. These substantial accuracy and meta-accuracy correlations show that behavior is a driver of both; too often actual behavior is ignored in interpersonal perception and accuracy research (see Borkenau et al., 2004 for an exception).

Now consider other results from Albright et al. (2001) that inform the APM. Self-assessments by partners who judged the behavior of the experimentally scripted actors, correlated substantially with their trait judgments of those actors; the median correlation was $r = 0.93$. This showed that assumed similarity was substantial. In contrast, the median estimate of assumed similarity among the experimentally scripted actors was much weaker with $r = 0.31$. Assumed reciprocity was not directly estimated

in this study; however, correlations between self-assessments and partners' meta-perceptions of how the actors' judged them were estimated, and are treated as a proxy for this variable. This is defensible because self-perceptions are known to correlate reliably with perceiver effects in trait judgments; Kenny (1994, p. 184) reports an average correlation of $r = 0.42$ across the Big Five factors. Among partners, the median correlation was $r = 0.71$, whereas the equivalent estimate for the experimentally scripted actors was $r = 0.27$. The median correlations for the trait perceptions of actors, whose behavior was controlled experimentally, and their unscripted interaction partners in the Albright et al. (2001) study are summarized in Table 3.3.

Before considering the estimates of APM phenomena, realize that when actors' behaviors were controlled experimentally and scripted there were still highly stable individual differences among them; standardized SRM actor variance in overt optimistic/pessimistic behavior was 0.94. As predicted by the APM, behavior should have a strong effect on perceptions of the target, and indeed this was the case. Median standardized SRM partner variance (i.e., consensus) in judgments of actors' traits was 0.83, and showed that actors' behaviors (i.e., a bottom-up effect) had a very strong impact on their partners' judgments of their traits. As Table 3.3 shows, the top-down processes of assumed similarity ($r = 0.31$) and assumed reciprocity ($r = 0.27$) of trait judgments were weaker among actors, because their perceptions were "selfless" according to the authors, and their meta-accuracy was substantial ($r = 0.92$). Actors knew that their scripted behavior impacted their partners' judgments of their traits. Their partners, whose judgments were not "selfless," displayed strong assumed similarity ($r = 0.93$) and assumed reciprocity ($r = 0.71$). Meta-accuracy was not estimated for the partners. Partners' trait judgments of actors showed that even though assumed similarity and assumed reciprocity were substantial,

Table 3.3. Estimates of Parameters of the Accuracy Process Model for Experimentally Scripted Actors and Their Partners

Phenomenon	Optimistic/Pessimistic Actors	Unscripted Partners
Assumed Similarity	.31	.93
Assumed Reciprocity	.27	.71
Target Accuracy	—	.93
Meta-perception Accuracy	.92	—

Note. — indicates not estimated. Based on Albright et al. (2001).

accurate judgments of actors' behaviors was robust ($r = 0.93$). These results show that interpersonal accuracy can be achieved even when assumed similarity and assumed reciprocity are operative, when observable, bottom-up behavior directly relevant to the trait judgment task is available. In the absence of explicit behavioral information, when assumed similarity and assumed reciprocity are strong, target accuracy should be weak. There has been an insufficient focus on overt behavior in accuracy research, and the study by Albright et al. (2001) documents its substantial effect on interpersonal trait judgments. In the absence of explicit bottom-up information, top-down interpersonal assumptions such as those specified in the APM, should breed inaccuracy.

Dyadic Level APM

The APM is also specified at the dyadic level with distinguishable and indistinguishable members. Recall that when members of a dyad are differentiated on a variable that can impact trait judgments, they are distinguishable; when their differentiation is arbitrary, they are indistinguishable. Each dyad type is considered.

DISTINGUISHABLE DYAD MEMBERS

Imagine that males and females interact in dyads; in each dyad there is male i and female j. Assume that the concern is with accuracy when females judge males' traits and meta-accuracy when males predict females' judgments of their traits. In an initial social relations analysis, the following dyadic variables (i.e., relationship effects) are produced: male i's relationship effect in self-perception when interacting with female j,[7] i's relationship effect when judging j's trait, i's relationship effects in a meta-perception

of j's judgment of i's trait, i's relationship effect in behavior with j, and j's relationship effect when judging i's trait. These variables are represented in the dyadic APM in Figure 3.5.

The dyadic APM with distinguishable dyads permits estimation of the following parameters: the accuracy of dyadic self-perception (DSA), dyadic assumed similarity (DAS), dyadic assumed reciprocity (DAR), dyadic accuracy (DA), the effect of dyadic behavior on dyadic meta-perception (DBMP), and dyadic meta-accuracy (DMA). The dyadic APM pits the assumptive processes of assumed similarity and assumed reciprocity against behavioral effects on meta-perception and judgments of one's traits by specific partners. When one's behavior with specific partners is the driver of dyadic self-perception, dyadic meta-perception, and that partner's judgment of one's trait; dyadic self-accuracy, dyadic meta-accuracy, and dyadic accuracy should be evident. When dyadic self-perception is not determined by one's actual behavior but by assumptions about self and others resulting in dyadic assumed similarity and assumed reciprocity, dyadic meta-accuracy and dyadic accuracy of trait judgments should be attenuated.

INDISTINGUISHABLE DYAD MEMBERS

The dyadic APM with indistinguishable dyad members forces one to confront the same issue discussed previously with dyadic ARRMA; that is, the arbitrary designation of one member as i and the other as j. The implicit constraints discussed in the Appendix that must be imposed when dyad members are indistinguishable and structural or path modeling is used (Olsen & Kenny, 2006) are again relevant with APM.[8] However, because the dyadic APM is much more complex structurally than dyadic

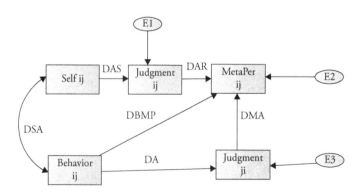

Figure 3.5. Accuracy process model, dyadic level with distinguishable dyads: DSA is dyadic self-accuracy, DAS is dyadic assumed similarity, DAR is dyadic assumed reciprocity, DMA is dyadic meta-accuracy, and DA is dyadic accuracy. DBMP is the effect of dyadic behavior on dyadic meta-perception (MetaPer). Dyads are composed of members i and j.

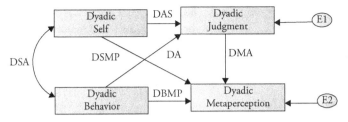

Figure 3.6. Accuracy process model, dyadic level with indistinguishable dyads: DSA is dyadic self-accuracy, DAS is average dyadic assumed similarity, DMA dyadic meta-accuracy, DBMP is the effect of dyadic behavior on dyadic meta-perception, DSMP is the effect of dyadic self on dyadic meta-perception, and DA is dyadic accuracy.

ARRMA, a simplified approach to accomplishing the Olsen-Kenny constraints is offered. The first step is to conduct a social relations analysis and organize the relationship effect estimates as a dyadic structure. This means that for each member of the dyad, the relevant relationship effect estimates are on the same row of the data set. Then, simply average the members' relationship effect estimates; this is equivalent to imposing the Olsen-Kenny equality constraints presented in the Appendix. The average relationship effect estimates are then used to estimate the dyadic APM with indistinguishable members (Figure 3.6), and the phenomena estimated are at the level of two-person arrangements. The following parameters are estimable: dyadic self-accuracy (DSA), dyadic assumed similarity (DAS), the effect of dyadic behavior on dyadic metaperception (DBMP), and dyadic accuracy (DA). If dyadic meta-perceptions are determined by dyadic behavior, then meta-accuracy can be inferred. Note that implementing the Olsen-Kenny constraints precludes estimation of dyadic reciprocity.

Implications of APM Models
The APM models integrate top-down and bottom-up processes that impact accuracy and meta-accuracy. The top-down processes originate in the availability of self-perception and a strain toward balance (assumed similarity, assumed reciprocity) that compromises accuracy and meta-accuracy. The bottom-up process is actual behavior that fosters these accuracies. As demonstrated in the research by Albright et al. (2001), when an actor's behavior is available to a perceiver and to the self, very strong accuracy and meta-accuracy can be achieved. Insufficient attention to the effect of behavior on the accuracy of trait judgments has had two effects: self-perceptions have been used as an accuracy criterion, and consensus has been treated as evidence for accuracy. Alternatively, the individual and dyadic APMs integrate perceivers' interpersonal

assumptions with the effects of targets' actual behaviors in single models at each level. At present, the APM models are theoretical specifications awaiting empirical assessment.

Conclusion
Levels of Analysis
A social relation modeling of accuracy is interpersonal, bidirectional, componential, multilevel, and nomothetic. Future research should heed prescriptions of interpersonal theory that accuracy and meta-accuracy should be considered simultaneously at multiple levels of social organization (cf. Leary, 1957). Levels of analysis are also emphasized in Mischel's theory of the cognitive-affective processing system. When elaborating this theory, Mischel (1999) presented different situations that a person might experience: "criticism from teacher," "criticism from mother," "rejection from girlfriend," and "scolding from father." These person–situation descriptions contain two components: a specific social partner, and specific negatively valenced interpersonal responses. If, for example, the recipient accurately judged the basis of the teacher's criticism, one cannot know whether this accuracy would be achieved when criticized by any person (i.e., a generalized effect), when criticized by any high-status person (a category effect), or when criticized by the specific teacher (i.e., a dyadic effect). Would accuracy or meta-accuracy be achieved when the partner is someone with whom one has a close relationship (e.g., parent or girlfriend) compared to someone known formally (e.g., teacher)? Estimation of interpersonal accuracy and meta-accuracy should vary in different contexts because, as theorized by Wright and Mischel (1987), there is "local predictability" of dyadic social behavior, as well as "contextualized behavior patterns" when interacting with specific people in different contexts (Shoda, Mischel, & Wright, 1993). These principles are consistent with Swann's (1984) concept of circumscribed accuracy (and

meta-accuracy). Moreover, these accuracies are likely to be at different levels (i.e., individual or dyadic). Social relations modeling offers sophisticated methods for studying accuracy and meta-accuracy at these levels.

Multivariate Accuracy Models

The ARRMA and APM models offer guidance for next-generation approaches to accuracy informed by theories of interpersonal behavior that emphasize the necessity of studying accuracy and meta-accuracy in tandem. Partitioning the phenomena as separate is artificial and fails to capture perceptual processes that unfold naturally and simultaneously in interacting dyads. While ARRMA highlights processes that promote inaccuracy of meta-perception, the APM integrates these top-down effects with bottom-up processes that promote accuracy. Next-generation accuracy research should direct more attention to the effect of behavior on accuracy; the utility of this focus is demonstrated in the research of Albright et al. (2001) and Borkenau et al., (2004). With a behavioral criterion, many vexing aspects of the criterion problem become irrelevant.

Behavioral Consistency and Accuracy

Behavioral consistency is a necessary, though insufficient, condition for interpersonal accuracy. Imagine a target whose behavior varies randomly from situation to situation; judgments of the target's behavior-relevant traits should correlate at 0 across those situations. But when behavior is stable across situations, accuracy of trait judgment entails detecting consistent trait-relevant behavior and basing inferences on it, while ignoring unstable or situation specific behavior. Consequently, the consistency of targets' behaviors sets a limit on the accuracy that can be achieved. Borkenau and colleagues (2004) report a mean consistency coefficient for trait judgments across situations of $r = 0.43$. Yet, even when consistency of judgments across situations is much less than perfect (i.e., $r = 1.00$), substantial accuracy can be achieved. This can be demonstrated using the *binomial effect size display* (BESD; Rosenthal & Rubin, 1982). For example, what level of accuracy can be achieved when the overall Borkenau et al. (2004) consistency coefficient is rounded down to $r = 0.40$? The BESD permits taking a correlation (in this case a cross-situational consistency coefficient) and computing the likelihood of success (i.e., accuracy) and failure (i.e., inaccuracy). With behavioral consistency of $r =$ 0.40, interpersonal trait judgments will be accurate 70% of the time and inaccurate 30% of the time (Rosenthal & Rosnow, 2008, p. 320).[9] In research where target behavior was highly consistent because it was scripted by the experimenters (Albright et al, 2001), available over time in the educational context (Malloy et al., 1996), or based on observation of targets' behaviors in multiple contexts (Borkenau et al., 2004), substantial accuracy was achieved. When actors' optimistic behavior was experimentally scripted, judgments on traits relevant to optimism by interaction partners were highly accurate; judgments of actors' behaviors correlated with relevant behavior coded from videotapes at $r = 0.93$ (Albright et al., 2001). Among classroom peers in grades 1 through 6 (Malloy et al., 1996), interpersonal judgments of academic ability correlated with standardized ability measures at a median value of $r = 0.61$ across grade levels. The median correlation of teachers' judgments of children's academic ability was $r = 0.63$ across the six grade levels. Judgments of intelligence based on observation of the targets' behaviors in 15 different contexts correlated with two standardized intelligence tests at $r = 0.41$ and $r = 0.53$ (Borkenau et al., 2004). Even when behavioral consistency is low (e.g., $r = 0.10$), 55% accuracy can be expected, and when consistency doubles (i.e., $r = 0.20$) accuracy of 60% is expected. Note that if behavioral consistency is absent entirely (i.e., $r = 0.00$), chance accuracy (50%) is the expectation. So although behavioral consistency is a necessary condition for accuracy, even when behavior is quite inconsistent interpersonal accuracy can be achieved.

Taking Seriously the First and Second Cronbach Critiques

Interpersonal accuracy and meta-accuracy have been, and remain, challenging phenomena. As revealed in the first Cronbach (1955; 1958) critique of interpersonal perception, what is intuitively a simple phenomenon, has posed exceedingly complex conceptual and empirical challenges. As seen in this chapter, the SRM approach to interpersonal accuracy and meta-accuracy is capable of managing the conceptual complexity, and provides precise estimates of generalized and dyadic components. The SRM, ARRMA, and APM models respond to Cronbach's first and second critiques of interpersonal perception. The ARRMA and APM models show that the concept of accuracy should not be conceptualized independently of other perceptual phenomena that attenuate it and overt behavior that should strengthen it. The APM models respond to the question: "What is the object perceived in social perception?"

Acknowledgments

Work on this chapter was supported by RI-INBRE Grant # 8P20GM103430-12 from the National Institute of General Medical Sciences (NIGMS), a component of the National Institutes of Health (NIH), and a US–Israel Binational Science Foundation (BSF) Grant # 2018055. Its contents are solely the responsibility of the author, and do not represent the official views of NIGMS, NIH, or the BSF. David A. Kenny, Avraham N. Kluger, Tera D. Letzring, Melvin M. Mark, and Jana S. Spain provided valuable comments or suggestions for this chapter. Address communication to Thomas E. Malloy at tmalloy@ric.edu.

Notes

1. Epistemology is a branch of philosophy concerned with knowledge acquisition and justification.
2. Stephen Toulmin was a 20th-century philosopher known for his analysis of arguments (e.g., scientific claims), the data on which they rest, and the logical implications that underlay claims derived from data. Rene Descartes was a 17th-century philosopher. The Cartesian program treated the mathematics of physics (i.e., mechanistic science) as foundational for all other science with the goal of understanding God's creation. Cronbach's critiques were concerned with the mathematics of accuracy estimation (the first), and with the bottom-up (i.e., behavior) and top-down (i.e., processes within the perceiver) Cartesian mechanisms that operate during interpersonal perception that promote accuracy and inaccuracy. The theoretical and statistical models presented in this chapter seek to address both facets of his critiques.
3. One could argue that only agreement is manifest when students' perceptions conform to a test score. This philosophical debate is beyond the scope of this chapter.
4. A minimal form of dyadic ARRMA is also estimable when meta-perceptions are available from only one member of the dyad, along with reciprocal interpersonal judgments. This model is discussed elsewhere (Malloy, 2020).
5. When using Soremo software (Kenny & Xuan, 2004) for the initial social relations analysis, these uniqueness effect estimates are output in roundrobin format, and must be restructured into an individual level format, and then restructured again into a dyad format. With dyad format, interpersonal judgments and meta-perceptions for each member of each dyad are on a single row in the data set. A guide to accomplish this reformatting using SPSS is available at www.thomasemalloy.org, or by contacting the author.
6. This could be a single measure of self-perception. If self-perception is measured in every dyadic interaction, this would be the actor effect in self-perception.
7. Note that self-perception would be measured in each dyadic interaction.
8. Alternatively, multilevel modeling can be used when dyad members are indistinguishable. Kluger et al. (2019) provide an example of this approach.
9. I thank Dave Kenny for his guidance regarding behavioral consistency and accuracy using the BESD.

Appendix

Implementing Olsen-Kenny (2006) Constraints on ARRMA

The estimation of dyadic ARRMA parameters with indistinguishable members can be accomplished with different data arrangements; this is, dyad input discussed previously or the double entry, pairwise method (Malloy & Albright, 2001) may be used. The specific data structure has implications for ARRMA parameter estimation, and the double entry method of data organization offers distinct advantages. To illustrate, for dyad 1 (first subscript), member 1 (second subscript), variables X_{11}, X'_{12}, Y_{11}, and Y'_{12} are entered on the first row of the data set. The data for member 2 of dyad 1 is entered on the second line and double entered; that is, X'_{12}, X_{11}, Y'_{12} and Y_{11}. Each member's data is entered twice; once on one line for that dyad, and then on that dyad's second line, but the order of the variables is reversed. For example, the double entry structure for 3 dyads and 4 variables is:

Variables			
Dyad	X	X'	Y	Y'
1	X_{11}	X'_{12}	Y_{11}	Y'_{12}
1	X'_{12}	X_{11}	Y'_{12}	Y_{11}
2	X_{21}	X'_{22}	Y_{21}	Y'_{22}
2	X'_{22}	X_{21}	Y'_{22}	Y_{21}
3	X_{31}	X'_{32}	Y_{31}	Y'_{32}
3	X'_{32}	X_{31}	Y'_{32}	Y_{31}

Note that X and Y are scores for one member of the dyad, and X' and Y' are scores for the other member of the dyad.

When dyad members are indistinguishable, the Olsen and Kenny (2006) constraints on the ARRMA model must be imposed (Malloy, 2020). The dyadic ARRMA model with the Olsen-Kenny constraints, represented by letters and numbers, are presented in Figure 3.3. Letters (or letter combinations) and numbers that are the same indicate that parameters are constrained to equality.

The constraints that follow are specifications of those imposed in Figure 3.3. Relationship effects are symbolized by γ, dyad members are designated i and j. For example, $\gamma_{i,mp,j}$ is uniqueness in i's meta-perception of j's response to i, and $\gamma_{j,mp,i}$ is uniqueness in j's meta-perception of i's response to j, M is an intercept for an outcome meta-perception, and d is disturbance in an exogenous variable. Specifically, the Olsen-Kenny constraints on the dyadic ARRMA model with indistinguishable members are:

$$\gamma_{ij} = \gamma_{ji} \ (\text{equal predictor means} : C)$$

$$S^2_{\gamma ij} = S^2_{\gamma ji} \ (\text{equal predictor variances: D})$$

$$M_{\gamma i,mp,j} = M_{\gamma j,mp,i} \ (\text{equal outcome intercepts: E})$$

$$E1 = E2 \ (\text{equal disturbance means: 0.00})$$

$$S^2_{E1} = S^2_{E2} \ (\text{equal disturbance variances: 1.00})$$

$$1 = 1 \ (\text{equal disturbance effects(E1 and E2)}$$
$$\text{on the outcomes } (M_{\gamma i,mp,j} \text{ and } M_{\gamma j,mp,i}))$$

The Olsen and Kenny (2006) constraints on ARRMA with indistinguishable members are the same as those imposed on the actor–partner interdependence model when dyad members are not distinguished (APIM; Kenny, 1996). Although ARRMA and APIM are structurally equivalent, the meanings of their parameters are not, and a discussion of these details is available elsewhere (Malloy, 2020).

The dyadic ARRMA model begins with dyad members' relationship effect estimates in trait judgments and metaperceptions computed in an initial social relations analysis. The Olsen-Kenny constraints yield what is referred to as the I-SAT (indistinguishable, saturated) model that is a function of which dyad member is designated as i or j, and I-SAT is used to adjust the degrees of freedom when testing the fit of the ARRMA model with the chi-square. With the double entry, pairwise data structure, the χ^2 produced for dyadic ARRMA while ignoring the implicit constraints on the model, is equal to the I-SAT χ^2 (see Olsen & Kenny, 2006, p. 134). This is one advantage of the double entry method. When dyad entry (i.e., not double entry) is used, the chi-square and degrees of freedom for the I-SAT would be subtracted from the chi-square and degrees of freedom for the unconstrained ARRMA model. Olsen and Kenny (2006) provide detailed guidance on how this is to be done.

References

Albright, L., Forest, C., & Reiseter, K. (2001). Acting, behaving, and the selfless basis of metaperception. *Journal of Personality and Social Psychology, 81,* 910–921. doi:10.1037/0022-3514.81.5.910

Bond, C. J., & DePaulo, B. M. (2006). Accuracy of deception judgments. *Personality and Social Psychology Review, 10,* 214–234. doi:10.1207/s15327957pspr1003_2

Bond, C. J., & DePaulo, B. M. (2008). Individual differences in judging deception: Accuracy and bias. *Psychological Bulletin, 134,* 477–492. doi:10.1037/0033-2909.134.4.477

Borkenau, P., Mauer, N., Riemann, R., Spinath, F. M., & Angleitner, A. (2004). Thin slices of behavior as cues of personality and intelligence. *Journal of Personality and Social Psychology, 86*(4), 599–614. https://doi-org.ric.idm.oclc.org/10.1037/0022-3514.86.4.599

Borsboom, D., Mellenbergh, G. J., & van Heerden, J. (2003). The theoretical status of latent variables. *Psychological Review, 110,* 203–219. doi:10.1037/0033-295X.110.2.203771 0146167295214001

Brunswik, E. (1956). *Perception and the representative design of psychological experiments* (2nd ed.). Berkeley: University of California Press.

Cleeton, G. U., & Knight, F. B. (1924). Validity of character judgments based on external criteria. *Journal of Applied Psychology, 8,* 215–231. doi:10.1037/h0072525

Cook, W. L. (2015). Mother's family psychology: A social relations model analysis of maternal perceptions of the family system. *Testing, Psychometrics, Methodology in Applied Psychology, 22,* 1–18. doi: 10.4473/TPM22.2.

Cronbach, L. (1955). Processes affecting scores on "understanding of others" and "assumed similarity." *Psychological Bulletin, 52,* 177–193. doi:10.1037/h0044919

Cronbach, L. J. (1958). Proposals leading to analytic treatment of social perception scores: Social preference and its perception.

In R. Tagiuri & L. Petrullo (Eds.), *Person perception and interpersonal behavior* (pp. 353–379). Stanford, CA, Stanford University Press.

Cronbach, L. J. (1996) (Personal Communication, June 30 and August 31, 1996).

Einstein, A. (1951). *Relativity: The special and the general theory.* New York, NY: Bonanza Books.

Fiske, S. T. (2014). *Social beings: A core motives approach to social psychology.* Hoboken, NJ: Wiley.

Funder, D. C. (1987). Errors and mistakes: Evaluating the accuracy of social judgment. *Psychological Bulletin, 101,* 75–90. https://doi-org.ric.idm.oclc.org/10.1037/0033-2909.101.1.75

Funder, D. C. (1995). On the accuracy of personality judgment: A realistic approach. *Psychological Review, 102,* 652–670. doi:10.1037/0033-295X.102.4.652

Funder, D. C. (2012). Accurate personality judgment. *Current Directions in Psychological Science, 21,* 177–182. doi:10.1177/0963721412445309

Funder, D. C., & Fast, L. A. (2010). Personality in social psychology. In S. T. Fiske, D. T. Gilbert, & G. Lindzey (Eds.), *Handbook of social psychology* (5th ed., Vol. 1, pp. 668–697). Hoboken, NJ: John Wiley.

Gage, N. L., & Cronbach, L. J. (1955). Conceptual and methodological problems in interpersonal perception. *Psychological Review, 62,* 411–422. doi:10.1037/h0047205

Gibson, J. (1966). *The senses considered as perceptual systems.* Oxford, UK: Houghton Mifflin.

Guillaume, E., Baranski, E., Todd, E., Bastian, B., Bronin, I., Ivanova, C., … Funder, D. C. (2016). The world at 7:00: Comparing the experience of situations across 20 countries. *Journal of Personality, 84,* 493–509. doi:10.1111/jopy.1217

Hartshorne, H., May, M. A., & Shuttleworth, F. K. (1930). Integration and honesty in relation to sundry abilities. In *Studies in the nature of character, Vol. 3: Studies in the organization of character.* (pp. 335–347). New York, NY: MacMillan Co. https://doi-org.ric.idm.oclc.org/10.1037/13357-023

Hastie, R., & Rasinski, K. A. (1988). The concept of accuracy in social judgment. In D. Bar-Tal & A. W. Kruglanski (Eds.), *The social psychology of knowledge* (pp. 193–208). New York, NY; Paris, France: Cambridge University Press.

Heider, F. (1958). *The psychology of interpersonal relations.* Hoboken, NJ: Wiley & Sons. doi:10.1037/10628-000

Heisenberg, W. (1930). *The physical principles of the quantum theory.* Chicago, IL: University of Chicago Press.

Jackson, D. N. (1974). *Personality research form manual.* Goshen, NY: Research Psychologists Press.

Kenny, D. A. (1991). A general model of consensus and accuracy in interpersonal perception. *Psychological Review, 98,* 155–163. doi:10.1037/0033-295X.98.2.155

Kenny, D. A. (1994). *Interpersonal perception: A social relations analysis.* New York, NY: Guilford Press.

Kenny, D. A. (1996). Models of non-independence in dyadic research. *Journal of Social and Personal Relationships, 13,* 279–294. doi:10.1177/026540759613200

Kenny, D. A. (2004). PERSON: A general model of interpersonal perception. *Personality and Social Psychology Review, 8,* 265–280. doi:10.1207/s15327957pspr0803_3

Kenny, D. A. (2020). *Interpersonal perception: The foundation of social relationships.* New York: NY, Guilford Press.

Kenny, D. A., & Albright, L. (1987). Accuracy in interpersonal perception: A social relations analysis. *Psychological Bulletin, 102,* 390–402. doi:10.1037/0033-2909.102.3.390

Kenny, D. A., Albright, L., Malloy, T. E., & Kashy, D. A. (1994). Consensus in interpersonal perception: Acquaintance and the big five. *Psychological Bulletin, 116,* 245–258. doi:10.1037/0033-2909.116.2.24

Kenny, D. A., West, T. V., Malloy, T. E., & Albright, L. (2006). Componential analysis of interpersonal perception data. *Personality and Social Psychology Review, 10,* 282–294. doi:10.1207/s15327957pspr1004_1

Kenny, D. A., & Xuan, Z. (2004). *WinSoremo.* http://davidakenny.net/srm/soremo.htm.

Kluger, A. N., & Malloy, T. E. (2019). Question asking as a dyadic behavior. *Journal of Personality and Social Psychology, 117,* 1127–1138. https://doi-org.ric.idm.oclc.org/10.1037/pspi0000156

Kluger, A. N., Malloy, T. E., Itzchakov, G., Castro, D. R., Lipetz, L., Sela, Y.,…New, M. (2019). *Dyadic listening in teams: Implications for intimacy, and helping organizational citizenship behavior.* Unpublished manuscript, The Hebrew University of Jerusalem.

Kruglanski, A. W. (1989). The psychology of being "right": The problem of accuracy in social perception and cognition. *Psychological Bulletin, 106,* 395–409. doi:10.1037/0033-2909.106.3.395

Kwan, V. Y., John, O. P., Kenny, D. A., Bond, M. H., & Robins, R. W. (2004). Reconceptualizing individual differences in self-enhancement bias: An interpersonal approach. *Psychological Review, 111,* 94–110. doi:10.1037/0033-295X.111.1.94

Laing, R. D., Phillipson, H., & Lee, A. R. (1966). *Interpersonal perception: A theory and a method of research.* Oxford, UK: Springer.

Leary, T. (1957). *Interpersonal diagnosis of personality.* NY, NY: Ronald Press.

Malloy, T. E. (2018a). Interpersonal attraction in dyads and groups: Effects of the hearts of the beholder and the beheld. *European Journal of Social Psychology, 48,* 285–302. doi:10.1002/ejsp.2324

Malloy, T. E. (2018b). *Social relations modeling of behavior in dyads and groups.* Amsterdam: The Netherlands: Elsevier.

Malloy, T. E. (2020). ARRMA: An Integrative Theoretical Model of Assumed and Actual Interpersonal Responses in Dyads Unpublished manuscript, Rhode Island College.

Malloy, T. E. (2019). Self-referenced interpersonal similarity phenomena: Theoretical specification and empirical assessment at the individual, dyadic, and group levels. *European Journal of Social Psychology, 49*(6), 1255–1271. https://onlinelibrary.wiley.com/doi/abs/10.1002/ejsp.2324

Malloy, T. E., & Albright, L. (1990). Interpersonal perception in a social context. *Journal of Personality and Social Psychology, 58,* 419–428. doi:10.1037/0022-3514.58.3.419

Malloy, T. E., & Albright, L. (2001). Multiple and single interaction dyadic research designs: Conceptual and analytic issues. *Basic and Applied Social Psychology, 23,* 1–19. https://doi-org.ric.idm.oclc.org/10.1207/153248301750123032

Malloy, T. E., Albright, L., Kenny, D. A., Agatstein, F., & Winquist, L. (1997). Interpersonal perception and metaperception in nonoverlapping social groups. *Journal of Personality and Social Psychology, 72,* 390–398. doi:10.1037/0022-3514.72.2.390

Malloy, T. E., & Kenny, D. A. (1986). The social relations model: An integrative method for personality research. *Journal of Personality, 54,* 199–225. doi:10.1111/j.1467-6494.1986.tb00393.x

Malloy, T. E., Kluger, A. N., & Martin, J. (2018). Women listening to women at zero-acquaintance. Unpublished raw data, Rhode Island College.

Malloy, T. E., Yarlas, A., Montvilo, R. K., & Sugarman, D. B. (1996). Agreement and accuracy in children's interpersonal perception: A social relations analysis. *Journal of Personality and Social Psychology, 71,* 692–702. https://doi-org.ric.idm.oclc.org/10.1037/0022-3514.71.4.692

Marcus, G. F., & Davis, E. (2013). How robust are probabilistic models of higher-level cognition? *Psychological Science, 24,* 2351–2360. https://doi-org.ric.idm.oclc.org/10.1177/0956797613495418

Mark, M. M. (1998). The philosophy of science (and of life) of Donald T. Campbell. *American Journal of Evaluation, 19,* 399–402. doi: 10.1177/109821409801900314

McArthur, L. Z., & Baron, R. M. (1983). Toward an ecological theory of social perception. *Psychological Review, 90,* 215–238. doi:10.1037/0033-295X.90.3.215

McCroskey, L. L., McCroskey, J. C., & Richmond, V. P. (2006). Analysis and improvement of the measurement of interpersonal attraction and homophily. *Communication Quarterly, 54,* 1–31. doi:10.1080/101463370500270322

Mischel, W. (1999). *Introduction to personality.* Fort Worth, TX: Harcourt Brace.

Newcomb, T. M. (1979). Reciprocity of interpersonal attraction: A nonconfirmation of a plausible hypothesis. *Social Psychology Quarterly, 42,* 299–306. doi:10.2307/3033801

Olsen, J. A., & Kenny, D. A. (2006). Structural equation modeling with interchangeable dyads. *Psychological Methods, 11,* 127–141. doi:10.1037/1082-989X.11.2.127

Peters, S., Kinsey, P., & Malloy, T. E. (2004). Gender and leadership perceptions among African Americans. *Basic and Applied Social Psychology, 26,* 93–101. https://doi.org/10.1207/s15324834basp2601_8

Rosenthal, R., & Rosnow, R. L. (2008). *Essentials of behavioral research.* Boston: McGraw Hill.

Rosenthal, R., & Rubin, D. B. (1982). A simple, general purpose display of magnitude of experimental effect. *Journal of Educational Psychology, 74,* 166–169. https://doi-org.ric.idm.oclc.org/10.1037/0022-0663.74.2.166

Schmid Mast, M. S., & Hall, J. A. (2018). The impact of interpersonal accuracy on behavioral outcomes. *Current Directions in Psychological Science, 27,* 309–314. https://doi-org.ric.idm.oclc.org/10.1177/0963721418758437

Searle, S. R., Casella, G., & McCulloch, C. E. (1992). *Variance components.* New York, NY: Wiley Series in Probability and Mathematical Statistics.

Schutz, W. C. (1966). *FIRO: A three-dimensional theory of interpersonal behavior.* New York, NY: Holt, Rinehart & Winston.

Shoda, Y., Mischel, W., & Wright, J. C. (1993). Links between personality judgments and contextualized behavior patterns: Situation-behavior profiles of personality prototypes. *Social Cognition, 11,* 399–429. doi:10.1521/soco.1993.11.4.399

Sullivan, H. S. (1939). A note on formulating the relationship of the individual and the group. *American Journal of Sociology, 44,* 932–937. doi:10.1086/218180

Sullivan, H. S. (1949). Multidisciplined coordination of interpersonal data. In S. S. Sargent & M. W. Smith (Eds.), *Culture and personality.* New York, NY: Viking.

Swann, W. B. (1984). Quest for accuracy in person perception: A matter of pragmatics. *Psychological Review, 91,* 457–477. doi:10.1037/0033-295X.91.4.457

Tagiuri, R. (1958). Social preference and its perception. In R. Tagiuri & L. Petrullo (Eds.), *Person perception and interpersonal behavior* (pp. 313–336). Stanford, CA: Stanford University Press.

Tenenbaum, J. B., Griffiths, T. L., & Kemp, C. (2006). Theory-based Bayesian models of inductive learning and reasoning. *Trends in Cognitive Sciences, 10,* 309–318.https://doi-org.ric.idm.oclc.org/10.1016/j.tics.2006.05.009

Tversky, A., & Kahneman, D. (1973). Availability: A heuristic for judging frequency and probability. *Cognitive Psychology, 5,* 207–232. doi:10.1016/0010-0285(73)90033-9

Tversky, A., & Kahneman, D. (1974). Judgment under uncertainty: Heuristics and biases. *Science, 185,* 1124–1131. doi:10.1126/science.185.4157.1124

Wright, J. C., & Mischel, W. (1987). A conditional approach to dispositional constructs: The local predictability of social behavior. *Journal of Personality and Social Psychology, 53,* 1159–1177. doi:10.1037/0022-3514.53.6.1159

Zaki, J., & Ochsner, K. (2011). Reintegrating the study of accuracy into social cognition research. *Psychological Inquiry, 22,* 159–182. doi:10.1080/1047840X.2011.551743

Lens and Dual Lens Models

Sarah Osterholz, Simon M. Breil, Steffen Nestler, *and* Mitja D. Back

Abstract

This chapter presents variants of Brunswik's lens model aimed to understand whether, when, and why trait judgments are more or less accurate. After outlining the basic concepts of lens models, it describes exemplary studies that have applied the lens model to unravel personality expression and impression formation processes that lead to more or less accurate judgments. Next, it gives an overview of factors that can influence the accuracy of trait judgments and explains these accuracy moderators within the lens model framework. It then describes an extension of the lens model, the dual lens model, that differentiates more controlled versus more automatic aspects on all levels of the lens model (i.e., personality self-concept, cues, personality judgments). It also briefly summarizes further extensions and highlights the lens model as a flexible tool to study cue processes underlying accuracy and related interpersonal perception phenomena. Finally, the chapter concludes by outlining suggestions for future lens model applications in accuracy research.

Key Words: lens model, dual lens model, personality judgment, accuracy, personality expression, impression formation, cue processes, interpersonal perception

Personality judgments of others are ubiquitous and formed by lay persons and professionals (e.g., psychologists, teachers, human resource managers) as part of daily life. For example, we make personality inferences about others when we are looking for new friends, hiring a new employee, or deciding whether we should lend someone a large amount money. As a new friend, we may prefer someone who seems extraverted because we think we can have a lot of fun with this person. As new employees, we might only consider people whom we judge as conscientious, and we would probably only lend money to someone whom we judge as trustworthy. That is, whether accurate or mistaken, these personality judgments can have important consequences in life and influence our decisions about whom we, for example, befriend, hire for a job, or trust (Harris & Garris, 2008). Consequently, it is crucial to understand how accurate these judgments typically are

as well as the processes that underlie more or less accurate personality judgments. Here, we introduce the lens model by Brunswik (1956) and show how it can be applied to inform research on the accuracy of personality judgments.

We first provide a broad definition of accuracy and describe ways to assess the accuracy of personality judgment. Then, we introduce the assumptions of Brunswik's (1956) lens model and apply it to the issue of personality judgment accuracy. Next, we describe exemplary lens model studies that have analyzed the processes of personality expression and impression formation underlying more or less accurate personality judgments across several trait domains. Based on our expositions, we then briefly introduce various important factors that may influence the degree of accuracy of personality inferences. Subsequently, we present the dual lens model (Hirschmüller, Egloff, Nestler, & Back, 2013), which allows for a differentiated examination of accuracy and underlying processes and we portray further extensions of the lens model. We conclude this chapter by outlining suggestions for future lens model applications in accuracy research.

Capturing the Accuracy of Personality Judgments

Observers (often also called *judges*, *perceivers*, or *decoders*) can perceive and judge many aspects of other people (also called *targets* or *encoders*; see Letzring & Funder, 2018). Here, we are interested in the accuracy of trait inferences at *zero acquaintance* (i.e., when the observer does not interact with the target prior to making judgments; Kenny & West, 2008). This includes judgments regarding broad personality dimensions such as the Big Five traits (i.e., extraversion, neuroticism, agreeableness, conscientiousness, and openness to experience; Borkenau & Liebler, 1992, 1993; Naumann, Vazire, Rentfrow, & Gosling, 2009), related interpersonal circumplex traits (e.g., dominance and warmth; Gifford, 1994), and intelligence (Borkenau & Liebler, 1993; Reynolds & Gifford, 2001; Zebrowitz, Hall, Murphy, & Rhodes, 2002; Zebrowitz & Rhodes, 2004), as well as more specific personality characteristics including people's level of self-esteem (Hirschmüller, Schmukle, Krause, Back, & Egloff, 2018; Kilianski, 2008), narcissism (Vazire, Naumann, Rentfrow, & Gosling, 2008), trustworthiness (Rule, Krendl, Ivcevic, & Ambady, 2013), or sociosexuality (Gangestad, Digeronimo, Simpson, & Biek, 1992).

Accuracy can broadly be defined as the level of correspondence between observers' personality judgments and targets' "true" personality (Funder, 1999). To approximate targets' "true" personality, typically three kinds of criterion measures are applied: self-reports, acquaintance (also called informant or peer) reports, and behavioral assessments (Back & Nestler, 2016). As accuracy criteria for the trait of extraversion, for example, one could gather targets' self-ratings of extraversion, peer-reports of targets' extraversion, and behavioral indicators of targets' extraversion assessed in the laboratory and/or naturally occurring situations. When self-ratings of targets are used as personality criterion, accuracy is often called *self-other agreement*. The combination of these criterion measures can be regarded as the "gold standard," as each single criterion measure captures valid aspects of "true personality," but also entails its limitations and blind spots (Back & Vazire, 2012; Funder, 1999).

In this chapter, we focus on *trait accuracy* in terms of a trait-based (i.e., variable-centered) approach. The trait accuracy approach differs from a profile-based (i.e., person-centered) approach (for detailed descriptions of both accuracy approaches, see Back & Nestler, 2016; Hall et al., 2018; Letzring & Funder, 2018; Nestler & Back, 2017). *Profile accuracy* assesses an observer's ability to judge each target's idiosyncratic ordering of traits relative to other traits. Profile accuracy is determined by comparing an individual observer's ordering of trait judgments for a single target (e.g., concerning the traits extraversion, conscientiousness, and trustworthiness) with the corresponding profile of the target's trait criterion values. The profile-based approach allows one to determine how much an observer can evaluate whether a target is, for example, more extraverted than conscientious and whether certain observers are particularly good at judging a target's idiosyncratic personality profile (cf. Back & Nestler, 2016).

The trait accuracy approach assesses an observer's ability to judge targets' actual trait standings relative to other targets separately for each specific trait. Trait accuracy is determined by correlating an observer's judgments about targets for a specific trait with the criterion measure(s) of targets' actual values for this trait. It indicates whether observers are able to judge the rank order of targets concerning the trait, for example, whether they can infer in a target sample who is more and who is less extraverted (cf. Funder, 1999).

Trait accuracy correlations can be computed both at the level of the *aggregated observer* and the *single observer* (Nestler & Back, 2017). The *aggregated observer* approach uses an aggregate of the judgments of several observers in computing accuracy correlations yielding an overall aggregate observer accuracy. This approach does not yield accuracy scores for individual observers, and one should be aware that results depend on the number of observers in a given study, with more observers leading to higher accuracy scores because of higher reliability of those judgments (cf. Back & Nestler, 2016; Hall & Bernieri, 2001; Nestler & Back, 2017). The *single observer* approach correlates the accuracy criteria with each observer's judgments separately. Thereafter, an average single observer accuracy estimate across observers and the variability of the individual observer's trait accuracy is computed. This approach, thus, allows one to study the determinants, moderators, and consequences of individual differences in accuracy (Back & Nestler, 2016; see Nestler & Back, 2017, for a more advanced single-step approach).

The Lens Model: A Framework to Explain the Accuracy of Personality Judgment Trait Accuracy Viewed Through Brunswik's Lens

Brunswik's (1956) lens model provides a conceptual framework that can be applied to explain how lay observers make sense of personality characteristics of targets that are not directly observable (see Figure 4.1). It, thus, aims to understand associations between people's personality traits and others' judgments of those personality traits (i.e., trait accuracy correlations). Observable cues (e.g., a stylish appearance, a loud voice) are assumed to serve as a kind of "lens" through which observers can indirectly perceive the underlying personality trait of targets (e.g., extraversion). By distinguishing three classes of variables (i.e., personality criteria, cues, and personality judgments), the lens model thereby reflects a two steps process: (1) personality expression (relations between personality criteria and observable cues; i.e., *cue validities*) and (2) impression formation (relations between observable cues and personality judgments; i.e., *cue utilizations*).

Regarding the left side of the lens model, each cue can be characterized by how much it is a valid indicator of targets' personality traits in a given context (cue validity). The validity of each cue is often determined by computing its correlation with the trait criterion. For example, targets' stylish appearance and loud voice but not facial attractiveness might prove to be associated with their self-rated extraversion. However, this correlational approach does not account for the intercorrelations between cues. Therefore, alternatively, each cue's unique validity can be calculated as its regression weight when regressing the trait criterion on all available cues. Regarding the right side of the lens model, each cue can be characterized by how much it is related to observers' personality judgments (cue utilization). For example, observers' judgments of targets' extraversion might be associated with targets' stylish appearance and loud voice but not with their facial attractiveness. The utilization of each cue is often determined by each cue's correlation with the trait judgment. Alternatively to this correlational approach, each cue's unique utilization can be calculated as its regression weight when regressing the trait judgment on all available cues.

In addition to these cue-specific indicators, the lens model framework allows researchers to explain the amount of trait accuracy by determining lens model indices across all examined cues (cf. Back & Nestler, 2016; Karelaia & Hogarth, 2008). Regarding the left side of the lens model, *predictability* of a trait in a given context pertains to how

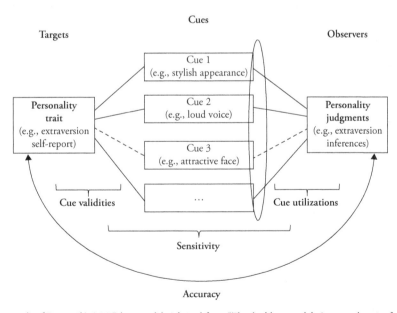

Figure 4.1. An example of Brunswik's (1956) lens model. Adapted from "The dual lens model: A comprehensive framework for understanding self-other agreement of personality judgments at zero acquaintance," by S. Hirschmüller, B. Egloff, S. Nestler, & M. D. Back, 2013, Journal of Personality and Social Psychology, 104, p. 336.

much a personality trait expresses in observable cues (e.g., the combined validity across all available cues for the trait of extraversion). It is assessed by the multiple regression coefficient when regressing the trait criterion on all observable cues. With regard to the right side of the lens model, the *response consistency* (i.e., how much observers apply cue information consistently across targets) can be determined. Response consistency is calculated as the multiple correlation when regressing the trait judgment on all available cues and indicates how much an observer applies his/her judgment model across all targets (e.g., always judges targets as extraverted if s/he has a stylish appearance and loud voice). Finally, linking both sides of the lens model, the *sensitivity* of observers (i.e., how much observers make stronger use of valid as compared to invalid cues) can be calculated. Sensitivity is given by the correlation between the predicted values of the aforementioned two kinds of regressions and it reflects the extent to which observers are sensitive to the validity of observable cues. With regard to the example, sensitivity is high when an observer uses the valid cues stylish appearance and loudness of voice rather than the invalid cue facial attractiveness to judge targets' extraversion.

Importantly, all perceptual lens model indices (cue utilizations, response consistency, and sensitivity) cannot only be determined at the level of the aggregated observer (by averaging across trait judgments of all observers before computing lens model indices), but also at the level of the individual observer (cf. Karelaia & Hogarth, 2008; Nestler & Back, 2017). It is important to note that only if the full range of valid and invalid cues is captured, one can meaningfully calculate an observer's sensitivity to the validity of observable cues (Back & Nestler, 2016). Thus, researchers should aim to fully cover all observable cues in the given judgment context, including invalid ones.

The amount of accuracy is determined by the multiplication of predictability, consistency, and sensitivity; that is, to achieve accurate judgments, all three need to be positive. For accuracy to occur, first a trait needs to be expressed in available valid cues, which would be mirrored in a high predictability. If valid cue information for the trait to be judged is not sufficiently elicited/expressed, observer judgments will be based on invalid cues and, thus, be inaccurate. A second reason why an observer's trait judgments may be inaccurate is because s/he does not utilize cues consistently across targets, which would be mirrored in a low response consistency.

Third, an observer can be inaccurate because of a lack of sensitivity for what valid and invalid cues are, which would be mirrored in a low sensitivity for this observer. In summary, a high level of trait accuracy results when the personality trait to be judged manifests in (i.e., is predicted by) observable valid cues in the given situation, when an observer uses cues consistently across judgments of different targets, and finally, when s/he is sensitive to validity differences of these cues by appropriately relying on valid cues and ignoring invalid ones (Back & Nestler, 2016; Nestler & Back, 2013).

Taken together, when analyzing accuracy data for multiple observers that all judged the same targets (e.g., based on targets' videotapes), accuracy can be calculated both for the *aggregated observer* (by averaging across observers before computing accuracy correlations) and for *single observers*. Further, lens model parameters (e.g., average accuracy of individual observers, interindividual variations in accuracies) may be estimated with a single unified approach using cross-classified structural equation models (CC-SEMs; cf. Nestler & Back, 2017; see e.g., Hirschmüller et al., 2018). The CC-SEMs can be specified to analyze a number of important research questions including, for example, whether observer characteristics can explain variations in trait accuracies and whether the strength of valid cue utilization is influenced by certain observer characteristics (cf. Nester & Back, 2017). In addition to these classic lens model analyses, one can try to fit mediational models to formally test whether the revealed valid and utilized cues indeed mediate the relation between the accuracy criterion and the personality judgments. To do so, first one typically would identify the most important valid and utilized cues (e.g., fashionable appearance, expressive gestures, cheerful voice in the case of extraversion), and then use them as process variables mediating the relation between the trait criterion (e.g., extraversion self-reports) and the personality judgments (e.g., extraversion judgments; see Hirschmüller et al., 2013).

Previous Lens Model Research on the Accuracy of Personality Judgments

How accurate are trait judgments? How are targets' personality criteria and observers' personality judgments associated with targets' observable behaviors and physical appearance? In the following, we describe two exemplary studies that have applied Brunswik's (1956) lens model framework to comprehensively analyze levels of trait accuracy as

SARAH OSTERHOLZ, SIMON M. BREIL, STEFFEN NESTLER, AND MITJA D. BACK well as cue validities and cue utilizations for zero-acquaintance personality judgments based on short video clips, audiotapes, and/or photographs of targets.

Borkenau and Liebler (1992) videotaped 100 target persons while they entered and walked through a room, sat down, looked into the camera, and read a standardized text. Targets completed Big Five self-reports and six unacquainted observers each provided Big Five personality judgments of the targets in one of four conditions (based on targets' videotapes with or without sound, the audios, or targets' photographs). In addition, personality judges in the sound film condition rated a large number of observable attributes of targets (i.e., 45 audible, static, and dynamic visible cues). This study, thus, provided accuracy (i.e., self-other agreement) values for the aggregated observer for each of the Big Five dimensions in each of the four conditions.

Based on the sound film, for example, strangers inferred extraversion most accurately and neuroticism least accurately (i.e., self-other correlations ranged from $r = .51$ for extraversion to $r = .10$ for neuroticism). These differences in zero-acquaintance accuracy could be explained with the help of lens model analyses. For extraversion, targets' self-reports were significantly associated with a number of cues (23 of the 45 attributes), and observers' extraversion judgments based on the sound film proved to be substantially influenced by valid observable attributes (20 of 23 valid cues showed significant cue utilization correlations). People with a powerful voice, stylish hair, a fashionable style of dress, and a friendly expression, for example, were judged as more extraverted, cues that were indeed associated with self-reported extraversion. However, a few valid cues for targets' extraversion were overlooked by observers (e.g., full lips, lifting feet while walking), and observers used some cues that were not valid (e.g., a pleasant voice, relaxed sitting, frequent hand movements) explaining why accuracy was far from perfect. For neuroticism, only three significant cue validity correlations emerged (e.g., wearing dark garments, stiff walking), and observer judgments in the sound film condition were largely based on invalid cues. In particular, only one of the three valid cues (i.e., stiff walking), but 18 invalid cues (e.g., hectic speaking, concerned expression) showed significant cue utilization correlations. Taken together, this study revealed accuracy differences across traits and various information channels which could be explained by analyzing the associations of people's Big Five self-reports as well as unacquainted observers' Big Five judgments with observable cues.

Borkenau and Liebler's (1992) comprehensive work has inspired subsequent research examining the processes underlying personality judgment accuracy. For example, Naumann et al. (2009) examined the accuracy of personality judgments for 10 personality traits including the Big Five, self-esteem, and religiosity based on physical appearance alone apparent in full-body photographs of targets with either a standardized or spontaneous pose. An aggregate of self- and acquaintance-reports was used as accuracy criterion, and both aggregated-observer and single-observer trait accuracies were reported. In addition, independent cue coders rated a number of static and dynamic physical appearance cues apparent in targets' spontaneously posed photographs. Results showed, for instance, that single-observer trait accuracy based on targets' photographs with a standardized pose was significantly above chance for the trait of extraversion only. Single-observer trait accuracies based on targets' photographs with a spontaneous facial expression and pose were significantly above chance for the traits extraversion, openness, self-esteem, and likability. Further, lens model analyses indicated that various traits, such as extraversion and self-esteem, are manifested through both static (e.g., healthy appearance) and expressive (e.g., smiling, energetic stance) cues captured in spontaneous photographs. A few cues appeared to be invalid (i.e., uncorrelated with the respective traits), such as targets' distinctive appearance and looking away from the camera for the traits extraversion and self-esteem. Results further showed that observers used most of the valid (besides some of the invalid) cue information to form quite accurate personality inferences (Naumann et al., 2009).

Taken together, research has shown that lay observers can form quite accurate trait judgments of strangers based on minimal information (i.e., thin slices of behavior, cf. Ambady, Bernieri, & Richeson, 2000; for meta-analytic results, see Connelly & Ones, 2010). Although most lens model studies have used self-reports as personality criteria, a number of studies assessed additional criteria beyond targets' self-report including informant reports (e.g., Hirschmüller et al., 2018; Naumann et al., 2009; Vazire et al., 2008) and/or behavioral or other more objective assessments as accuracy criteria (e.g., measured intelligence; Borkenau & Liebler, 1993; Reynolds & Gifford, 2001). Some studies provided accuracies at the level of single observers in addition to the typically reported aggregated-observer trait accuracies (e.g., Hirschmüller et al., 2018; Naumann et al., 2009). Moreover, lens model research has identified numerous specific cues explaining trait accuracies (or the lack thereof; for overviews see Hall, Horgan, & Murphy, 2019; chapter 13 by Breil, Osterholz, Nestler, & Back in this handbook). For example, intelligence has been shown to manifest mainly in auditory cues and less in visual cues, explaining higher trait accuracy levels based on targets' audio-tapes as compared to a visual condition (e.g., Reynolds & Gifford, 2001).

Generally speaking, the lens model (Brunswik, 1956) is a very flexible framework that may be used to study the accuracy and underlying processes of individuals' inferences about others' traits and characteristics in broadly any judgment context (Hammond & Stewart, 2001). For instance, the lens model has been applied to study trait accuracy and underlying behavioral processes in natural contexts outside the laboratory based on people's environmental and social media cues, such as individuals' offices and bedrooms (Gosling, Ko, Mannarelli, & Morris, 2002) or online social networking sites (e.g., Stopfer, Egloff, Nestler, & Back, 2014; see chapter 14 by Wall & Campbell in this handbook) as well as to a great number of studies analyzing trait inferences in more applied contexts including practitioners' personality judgments in clinical settings (e.g., Hammond, Hursch, & Todd, 1964) as well as in employment and academic contexts (e.g., Kuncel, Klieger, Connelly, & Ones, 2013; chapter 19 by Blackman in this handbook; for meta-analyses of lens model studies, see also Karelaia & Hogarth, 2008; Kaufmann & Athanasou, 2009; Kaufmann, Reips, & Wittmann, 2013).

Moderators of Accurate Personality Judgments: Factors Associated with Lens Model Processes

What factors influence the extent of accuracy? The lens model framework can be used to explain why certain personal and contextual factors relate to more or less accurate judgments (i.e., moderate the personality criterion-judgment relation): Because they relate to differences in relevant lens model processes. In this section, we give a very broad overview of four variables that seem to affect the likelihood of accurate trait judgments (for more extensive overviews, see Back & Nestler, 2016; Leising & Borkenau, 2011; Letzring & Funder, 2018; see chapters 6 to 9, this volume).

A variant of the lens model is the realistic accuracy model (RAM; Funder, 1995, 1999; see chapter 2 by Letzring & Funder in this handbook) which conceptually divides cue validities and cue utilizations each into two sequential stages. In the RAM, the left side of the lens model capturing personality expression is differentiated into the two stages *relevance* and *availability*, the right side of the lens model capturing impression formation is differentiated into the two stages *detection* and *utilization*. This well-elaborated conceptualization of multiple stages allows for a very detailed understanding of the accuracy process and moderators of accurate personality inferences (i.e., good trait, good target, good information, good judge; Funder, 2012). A high degree of trait accuracy is most likely, when a "good trait" and a "good target" is judged, and when the personality judgment is based on "good information," and when a "good judge" makes the personality judgment (cf. Funder, 2012). However, one challenge of the RAM to date is to empirically disentangle the relevance and availability stages as well as the detection and utilization stages involved in the accuracy process.

The less differentiated original lens model version (Brunswik, 1956) allows one to empirically capture the personality-expression and impression-formation processes underlying more or less accurate judgments by means of cue-validity and cue-utilization correlations, respectively—for the average observer and for each individual observer, for different target groups, and for different contexts. Empirical findings on these lens model processes can provide guidance on how to improve trait accuracies and provide explanations for why accuracies vary for different observers, targets, and contexts.

"Good Trait"

Across observers, targets, and contexts, some personality traits tend to be easier to accurately judge than others (cf. Connolly, Kavanagh, & Viswesvaran, 2007; Connolly & Ones, 2010; Hall, Andrzejewski, Murphy, Schmid Mast, & Feinstein, 2008). Research has identified two characteristics of traits that affect accuracy: *observability* and *evaluativeness* (Funder & Dobroth, 1987; John & Robins, 1993; Vazire, 2010; chapter 8 by Krzyzaniak & Letzring in this handbook). First, accurate personality judgment is more likely, the more a trait manifests in (i.e., is predictable by) observable valid cues. Extraversion, for example, can be considered as a "good trait," as it often shows a high amount of behavioral manifestation (e.g., Borkenau & Liebler, 1995; Funder & Sneed, 1993). In contrast, traits such as neuroticism or self-esteem tend to show fewer behavioral manifestations and to be more internal in nature (Vazire, 2010). Second, highly evaluative traits (i.e., low or high in social desirability), such as agreeableness, tend to be less accurately judged than neutral traits. This may be due to response factors that may distort targets' self-ratings (e.g., individual differences in overly positive self-judgments) and observer judgments (e.g., individual differences in overly positive other-ratings) for evaluative traits (e.g., Konstabel, Aavik, & Allik, 2006), thereby, affecting self-cue relations (cue validities) and cue-judgment relations (cue utilizations).

"Good Target"

Individual differences of targets in how easily they can be judged by others (i.e., judgability) have been shown to affect the extent of accuracy (for an overview, see Human & Biesanz, 2013), however, studies and analytical approaches analyzing target moderation of trait accuracy and underlying cue processes are still limited and should be investigated in future lens model research. Research has identified a variety of target characteristics that foster greater judgability. Specifically, a "good target" is likely to be well adjusted, to have higher social status, and to be socialized to be more expressive (e.g., Colvin, 1993; Human & Biesanz, 2013; chapter 7 by Mignault & Human in this handbook). Thereby, "good targets" most likely influence the amount and type of trait-related information that is expressed (i.e., cue validities), but it is also possible that targets indirectly facilitate greater cue utilization by affecting observer behavior and cognition (e.g., by eliciting more attention; cf. Human & Biesanz, 2013). For example, well-adjusted individuals are likely to behave more authentically and to be better nonverbal senders (e.g., Riggio & Riggio, 2002), and, hence, to emit more valid cues. Further, self-presentation of targets, often involving the aim to convey a positive but authentic impression (Schlenker & Pontari, 2000), may enhance observer attention and the accuracy of respective trait inferences (e.g., Human, Biesanz, Parisotto, & Dunn, 2012). For example, targets' self-presentational goal of appearing smart led to more accurate observer impressions of individuals' intelligence (Murphy, 2007).

"Good Information"

Research has shown that the likelihood for accurate trait judgments is affected by the quantity and quality of information that observer judgments are based on (e.g., Beer & Watson, 2010; Letzring, Wells, & Funder, 2006; chapter 9 by Beer in this handbook). First, more information about targets has been linked to an increase in accuracy for personality judgments (Blackman & Funder, 1998; Brown & Bernieri, 2017; Carney, Colvin, & Hall, 2007), most likely because longer observations or greater acquaintanceship of targets enhance the availability of valid cues. Second, better information about targets makes accurate judgments more likely. Thereby, the quality of information for a given trait (estimated by cue validities or predictability) can vary across information channels (e.g., auditory vs. visual; Borkenau & Liebler, 1992; Reynolds & Gifford, 2001) and judgment contexts. Intelligence, for example, has been shown to mainly manifest in auditory cues (e.g., speech rate, number of spoken words) compared with visual cues, allowing more accurate observer judgments based on targets' audiotapes than visual material (Reynolds & Gifford, 2001). Further, one context factor that can affect trait expression in observable behavior and as a consequence, accurate personality judgment is the relevance of the situation to the given trait (i.e., trait activation; Tett & Guterman, 2000). For example, Hirschmüller, Egloff, Schmukle, Nestler, and Back (2015) showed that the trait neuroticism expressed in more valid observable cues and could be judged more accurately by strangers in a neuroticism-relevant, socially stressful situation as compared to three less neuroticism-relevant situations.

"Good Judge"

The "good judge" is one of the most pervasive topics in accuracy research (Ambady, Hallahan, & Rosenthal, 1995; Funder & Harris, 1986; Hjelle, 1969; Taft, 1955; Vernon, 1933; Vingoe & Antonoff, 1968; chapter 6 by Colman in this handbook). Research has provided evidence that some judges of personality tend to be more accurate than others (e.g., Christiansen, Wolcott-Burnam, Janovics, Burns, & Quirk, 2005; Letzring, 2008; Rogers & Biesanz, 2019). In line with the lens model, a good judge of personality can be assumed to differ in impression-formation processes (i.e., cue utilization, response consistency, and sensitivity) from less accurate judges. Specifically, a good judge is likely to utilize more personality-related cues, to apply cue information more consistently across judgments of different targets, and to make stronger use of valid as compared to invalid cue information when forming personality impressions of others. Thereby, for a good judge's superior cue-usage to enable more accurate impressions, targets must first provide sufficiently valid cues in the given situation.

Research has examined several personal (e.g., demographics, personality, cognitive, and motivational aspects) and contextual characteristics that are likely to affect judges' impression-formation processes, and, hence, accuracy (for an overview, see De Kock, Lievens, & Born, in press). A judge's cognitive ability, general intelligence, and attentiveness, for example, have been shown to be related to judgmental ability (e.g., Brtek & Motowidlo, 2002; Christiansen et al., 2005; Lippa & Dietz, 2000). Further, personality traits reflecting a higher interpersonal orientation (e.g., agreeableness, extraversion, empathy), social skill (e.g., knowledge about cue meanings) as well as higher motivation of judges, likely increasing attunement to social stimuli, have been shown to promote accuracy (e.g., Hall, Andrzejewski, & Yopchick, 2009; Letzring, 2008; McLarney-Vesotski, Bernieri, & Rempala, 2011; Vogt & Colvin, 2003; but see Hall, Blanch, et al., 2009). Overall, however, it has been difficult to find reliable stable predictors of the good judge (De Kock et al., in press), likely because in contexts where all observers make judgments based on the same target information, individual differences in observers' judgmental ability appear to be very small (e.g., Biesanz, 2010).

The Dual Lens Model: Differentiating Automatic and Controlled Lens Model Processes

Altogether, the lens model is a flexible tool that allows one to illuminate levels of trait accuracies and underlying processes of personality expression and impression formation by distinguishing three kinds of variables, that is, targets' personality criteria, observable cues, and observers' personality judgments (Back & Nestler, 2016; Brunswik, 1956; Nestler & Back, 2013). For all three classes of variables, completely separate research areas (self-concept research, behavioral activation research, and judgment and decision-making research) exist, and interestingly, in all three research fields (although previously not connected) dualistic views differentiating more controlled versus automatic aspects have been proposed. In the following, we summarize major assumptions of these dualistic approaches and show how these may be integrated within a dual lens model framework (see Figure 4.2; Hirschmüller et al., 2013; Nestler & Back, 2013).

According to dual process approaches to personality (Asendorpf, Banse, & Mücke, 2002; Back, Schmukle, & Egloff, 2009; see Back & Nestler, 2017, for an overview), one can differentiate between explicit aspects (e.g., a person's elaborated self-view of being an extraverted person) and implicit aspects

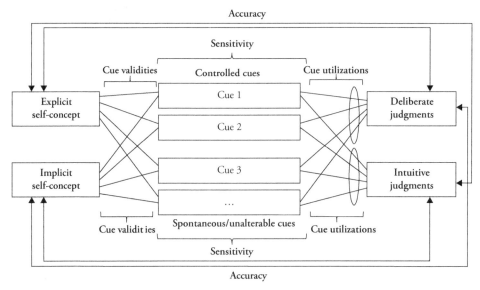

Figure 4.2. The dual lens model (Hirschmüller et al., 2013). Adapted from "The dual lens model: A comprehensive framework for understanding self-other agreement of personality judgments at zero acquaintance," by S. Hirschmüller, B. Egloff, S. Nestler, & M. D. Back, 2013, Journal of Personality and Social Psychology, 104, p. 337.

(e.g., the person's associatively stored inner self-concept of extraversion) of targets' personality. The *explicit personality self-concept* refers to individual differences in propositional representations of the self (e.g., "I am a person who likes to be around others") and is typically assessed by self-report (e.g., targets' answers in an extraversion questionnaire). The *implicit personality self-concept* refers to individual differences in rather automatic and associative mental representations of the self that are not necessarily accessible through explicit thought. They can be captured with so-called indirect tests of personality, such as an Implicit Association Test (IAT; Greenwald, McGhee, & Schwartz, 1998; e.g., targets' responses in an extraversion IAT)[1] that has been shown to predict relevant social behavior (e.g., Asendorpf et al., 2002; Back et al., 2009; Greenwald, Poehlman, Uhlmann, & Banaji, 2009). Thereby, the explicit and implicit personality self-concept tend to be only very moderately correlated (Hofmann, Gawronski, Gschwendner, Le, & Schmitt, 2005).

Furthermore, based on distinctions made in early research of facial expression (i.e., voluntary vs. involuntary; Darwin, 1872/1965) and the study of nonverbal communication and self-presentation (i.e., intentional, posed, or deceptive behavior vs. spontaneous, genuine, or natural behavior; DePaulo, 1992; Wegner & Bargh, 1998), observable personality-related cues may be differentiated with respect to the amount of their controllability. Observable cues underlying trait inferences comprise attributes of physical appearance (e.g., hairstyle, make-up, clothing, facial symmetry, height), facial expressions and body language (e.g., smiling, upright posture, fast walking), paralanguage (e.g., loudness of voice), and verbal behavior (e.g., Burgoon, Guerrero, & Manusov, 2011; Ekman, Friesen, O'Sullivan, & Scherer, 1980; Scherer, 1978). While some of these aspects appear to be intentionally generated and posed to create a certain impression, others occur more spontaneously and naturally, and certain cues may not be altered at all. That is, observable cues can range from rather *controlled* and intentionally generated aspects of people's physical appearance and expressive behavior (e.g., stylish appearance) to more *spontaneous* cues (e.g., loud voice), and virtually unalterable ones (e.g., facial symmetry). In addition, research has suggested differentiated effects of people's explicit and implicit personality aspects on those behaviors: Explicit personality aspects showed particular links to consciously controlled behavior, whereas implicit personality aspects have been particularly linked to more spontaneous behaviors (e.g., Asendorpf et al., 2002; Hagemeyer, Dufner, & Denissen, 2016; Rudolph, Schröder-Abé, Riketta, & Schütz, 2010).

Such dualities not only can be found in the ways in which the targets view themselves as well as appear and behave but also can be mirrored in observers' personality judgments. Research on social cognition and decision-making distinguishes between intuitive judgments and deliberate judgments (Evans, 2008; Kruglanski & Orehek, 2007). *Intuitive judgments* are assumed to provide a quick default solution regarding the meanings of physical appearance, behavior, and other social information and require few or no cognitive resources. *Deliberate judgments* refer to slower, higher order processes of thinking that can add to the intuitive default solution in cases in which the individual has sufficient attentional resources and the intention to override the default automatic influence (cf. Evans, 2008). Based on this dualistic research tradition, one may distinguish between two kinds of personality judgments: intuitive and deliberate personality judgments (e.g., an observer's spontaneous inference vs. reflective judgment of targets' extraversion). Although we often form personality impressions of strangers in an intuitive, quick, and effortless way, there are also situations and judgment contexts in which we deliberately reflect about the individuals we encounter by asking ourselves questions such as "What kind of person is s/he really?"

The dual lens model integrates these outlined duality perspectives allowing, among other things, to comprehensively examine the level of *accuracy* (i.e., self-other agreement) for groups of observers as well as individual observers. That is, the extent to which observers' personality judgments correspond with targets' explicit self-concept as well as targets' implicit personality self-concept can be examined. Moreover, the processes by which accuracy for the explicit and implicit personality self-concept are achieved can be investigated. This includes a fine-grained analysis of the specific cue relations of controlled and more spontaneous cues with the explicit and implicit personality self-concept as well as observers' personality judgments. Further, it can be analyzed how consistently observers utilize controlled as well as spontaneous cues for their personality judgments, and how sensitive they are regarding the validity of these cues as indicators of the explicit and implicit personality self-concept.

In addition, applying the dual lens model approach allows to examine *moderators of accuracy*:

That is, it can be analyzed whether accuracy differs as a function of the judgment mode. Whereas traditional models of rational choice assume a general superiority of deliberate decisions (for an overview, see, e.g., Hastie & Dawes, 2001), research has indicated that intuitive judgments can be very efficient (Ambady, 2010; Rule, Ambady, & Hallett, 2009) and might already capture all of the valid information available, potentially restricting the additional value of deliberate processing. Moreover, it can be explored whether certain observer characteristics (e.g., an observer's stable individual tendency to judge deliberately or intuitively; Betsch, 2008; Epstein, Pacini, DenesRaj, & Heier, 1996) affect accuracy levels for the explicit and implicit personality self-concept.

Hirschmüller et al. (2013) examined the level of zero-acquaintance accuracy and the underlying processes (i.e., cue validities and cue utilizations, response consistency, sensitivity) for explicit and implicit extraversion based on short videotapes of targets by using both a direct and an indirect measure of targets' extraversion as well as a number of more or less controlled cues (actual behaviors and appearances). Each of 41 different observers in either a deliberate or intuitive judgment condition judged extraversion of 56 targets based on short videotaped self-introductions. Observers in the deliberate judgment condition were instructed to think carefully, take as much time as needed, and judge each target's extraversion as accurately as possible. In the intuitive judgment condition, observers had to complete a concurrent task while watching targets' videotapes (a version of the n-back task; e.g., Albrechtsen, Meissner, & Susa, 2009), they had limited time to complete extraversion judgments, and they were asked to decide intuitively. In addition, observers in both conditions answered self-report measures assessing their dispositional judgment tendency. Results showed that regarding the level of accuracy, deliberate and intuitive extraversion judgments at zero acquaintance were similarly correlated with both targets' explicit and implicit self-concept of extraversion. Importantly, individual judgment analyses demonstrated a large amount of variability between observers within each judgment condition and regarding both explicit and implicit extraversion. The explicit and implicit self-concept of extraversion showed differentiated effects on actual behavior. Explicit extraversion was more strongly linked to consciously controlled aspects of physical appearance and behavior, whereas implicit extraversion primarily showed strong relations to more spontaneous and unalterable cues. For all perceptual lens model indicators, cue utilizations, but also response consistencies and sensitivities, large interindividual differences between observers within each judgment condition were revealed.

With regard to moderators, we found no superiority for observers of either the deliberate or intuitive judgment condition in inferring others' extraversion. Cue-utilization processes were relatively similar across judgment conditions. Analyses revealed that in the two judgment conditions, observers generally applied available cue information in a similarly consistent fashion across judgments of different targets and that observers proved to be sensitive to validity differences of cue domains regarding explicit and, even more, implicit extraversion. The similarity in accuracies as well as cue-usage between judgment conditions indicates that, across all observers, deliberate judgments did not add much to the intuitive use of valid cues. The large amount of interindividual differences in accuracy and judgment processes was systematically related to the observers' dispositional judgment tendency: Observers with a self-reported intuitive judgment tendency showed higher levels of accuracy for explicit extraversion across judgment conditions. Finally, higher accuracy of intuitive observers could be explained by a stronger utilization of expressive kinesics and vocal behavioral aspects in targets' self-introductions and observers' strengthened judgmental consistency.

The dual lens model may be applied to a wide range of contexts, including various traits, cues, and observers. It is not necessarily implied that the specific findings of the first empirical illustration (Hirschmüller et al., 2013) will generalize across all alternative contexts. In fact, it is an exciting empirical question whether a similar pattern of results will emerge for other traits (e.g., self-esteem) and other information channels (e.g., audio only or text-based cues) as well as lay persons' more direct everyday face-to-face social interactions and professionals' judgment situations such as clinicians', teachers', or recruiters' judgments, respectively. In all of these contexts, yet, lens model research may distinguish between explicit and implicit aspects of individuals' personality, controlled and spontaneous cues, and deliberate and intuitive personality judgments, respectively, to add to the understanding of whether, when, and why trait judgments of others are accurate.

Further Extensions of the Lens Model

In the following, we describe further extensions of the lens model that have been applied to the comprehensive investigation of accuracy and bias of personality inferences and other kinds of interpersonal judgments (see also Nestler & Back, 2013). For example, Nestler, Egloff, Küfner, and Back (2012) integrated the lens model with recent process models of hindsight bias, a well-known judgmental error (i.e., people's belief that an event is more predictable after it becomes known than it was before; see Roese & Vohs, 2012). In this integrative model, the authors propose three processes of knowledge updating (i.e., changes in cue perceptions, changes in the utilization of more valid cues, and changes in response consistency) as potential explanations for the occurrence of hindsight effects in personality judgments. By examining *hindsight effects* of personality inferences for the Big Five traits based on target pictures across two studies, the authors provided the first empirical evidence for the utility of such an integrative lens model approach. That is, participants were asked to rate each targets' level for the Big Five traits, thereafter, they received feedback of targets' actual trait levels, and they had to recall their original trait judgments of targets. The authors found hindsight effects for all of the Big Five trait dimensions and further results indicated that both the utilization of more valid cues and changes in cue perceptions—but not changes in the consistency with which cue knowledge was applied—could account for these hindsight effects in personality judgments.

Moreover, the lens model of accurate personality judgment (Brunswik, 1956) may be integrated with research traditions of related interpersonal perception phenomena to comprehensively investigate, for example, people's *impression management* (i.e., the process by which individuals control the impression others form of them; Leary & Kowalski, 1990) strategies as well as the *accuracy of meta-perceptions* (i.e., the accuracy of people's view of how others see them; Kenny, 1994; chapter 12 by Carlson & Elsaadawy in this handbook) in zero-acquaintance and other social contexts (Stopfer et al., 2014). Another integrative lens model approach is the social relations lens model (Back, Schmukle, & Egloff, 2011). This framework integrates the social relations model (SRM; Back & Kenny, 2010; Kenny, 1994; see chapter 3 by Malloy in this handbook) and the processes of personality expression and impression formation described in the lens

model (Brunswik, 1956) and can be applied to study the influence of people's personality judgments on *liking* and *popularity* and the behavioral processes underlying interpersonal attraction at first encounters, in getting-acquainted contexts, and other types of social relationships. Further, Hall and Goh (2017) recently described an integrative framework combining Brunswik's (1956) lens model with concepts of signal detection theory (Wickens, 2001) allowing for a nuanced understanding of the accuracy and inaccuracy of individuals' *stereotypes* about others.

In a nutshell, the lens model and its extensions offer flexible tools to illuminate the level and underlying processes of individuals' ability to infer others' personality traits and related interpersonal perception phenomena (Hammond & Stewart, 2001; Karelaia & Hogarth, 2008; Kaufmann & Athanasou, 2009; Kaufmann et al., 2013).

Recommendations for Future Lens Model Research

In the next paragraphs, we outline recommendations for future lens model applications along with a cautionary note on the generalizability of the reported findings illustrated in this chapter. When reviewing prior lens model research, one should keep in mind that lens model results are influenced by a number of aspects including (1) the sampling (e.g., selection and number) of targets and observers; (2) the used trait criterion measures; (3) the extent, types, and level of detail of coded cue information; (4) the applied statistical approaches; (5) the judged traits; and (6) the regarded judgment contexts. This has the consequence that findings cannot be easily generalized across individual studies.

Lens model results on the accuracy of personality judgments are dependent on a number of important aspects including the extent of *representative sampling* (cf. Brunswik, 1956). This suggests that future lens model studies should aim to assess a high number of targets and observers that are as representative as possible concerning demographics (e.g., gender, age), further characteristics (e.g., level of education) as well as trait manifestations to the populations of interest. Moreover, the applied trait criterion measure(s) typically differ across studies (e.g., self-reports only: Borkenau & Liebler, 1992; self- and acquaintance-reports: Naumann et al., 2009; direct and indirect personality measures: Hirschmüller et al., 2013), and researchers should aim for a multimethodological assessment of the examined personality trait(s). In addition, often the amount, designation, and the degree of differentiation (i.e., the coding of behavioral and appearance cues at micro-levels and/or at rather global levels) of considered cue information varies between studies (cf.chapter13 by Breil et al. in this handbook). Lens model studies should aim at a full coverage of observable (also invalid) cues and these cues should be rated by independent trained cue coders (not by the judges of personality themselves) and/or objectively measured (for recommendations concerning behavioral coding, see, e.g., Heymann, Lorber, Eddy, & West, 2014).

Further, most studies typically report lens model indices for the aggregated observer. However, as this aggregated-observer approach provides no information on the degree to which and the reasons why judges differ in their ability to form accurate personality impressions of others (cf. Back & Nestler, 2016), we suggest that future lens model studies ideally report the average and the variability of accuracy across individual observers. To analyze trait accuracy and underlying processes as well as determinants, moderators, and consequences of individual differences in accuracy, one-step statistical analyses can also be applied (cf. Nestler & Back, 2017).

Moreover, future lens model approaches to the accuracy of personality judgments should place a stronger focus on individual differences and aim to analyze the processes by which individual and context characteristics moderate the degree of accuracy of personality judgments. For example, future studies might attempt more often to analyze and compare accuracy levels and underlying cue processes across different trait-expression contexts and information channels (see e.g., Hirschmüller et al., 2015; Kaurin, Heil, Wessa, Egloff, & Hirschmüller, 2018). We suggest that future research also places more emphasis on the identification of robust cues involved in personality expression and impression formation separately for traits as well as the replication of the identified trait-related cues across target samples and situations (e.g., see Küfner, Nestler, & Back, 2013) and their eventual meta-analytic integration (cf. chapter 13 by Breil et al. in this handbook).

Prior lens model research has provided important snapshots of the extent to which, the reasons why, and the conditions under which personality judgments of others are accurate. As the lens model has been predominantly used to study trait accuracy of personality judgments, future research may

further aim to elaborate the understanding of profile accuracy and compare findings of both trait accuracy and profile accuracy within the same sets of data (e.g., Hall et al., 2018). Further, affect judgments may be integrated within the lens model to aim for a better understanding of how and when trait accuracy and accuracy in judging affect are related when forming impressions of others (see Hall, Gunnery, Letzring, Carney, & Colvin, 2017). Another exciting endeavor for future studies includes, for example, the examination of whether and why individuals can be trained to accurately judge personality (Powell & Bourdage, 2016; chapter 20 by Blanch-Hartigan & Cummings in this handbook).

In sum, lens model research on the interpersonal perception of personality traits can provide important theoretical contributions to the understanding of personality itself, personality manifestation in behavior, impression formation, as well as the processes that underlie and the factors that influence these personality judgments. We look forward to future work that applies the lens model framework to further investigate the complex nature of human trait inferences.

References

Albrechtsen, J. S., Meissner, C. A., & Susa, K. J. (2009). Can intuition improve deception detection performance? *Journal of Experimental Social Psychology*, *45*, 1052–1055. doi:10.1016/j.jesp.2009.05.017

Ambady, N. (2010). The perils of pondering: Intuition and thin slice judgments. *Psychological Inquiry*, *21*, 271–278. doi:10.1080/1047840x.2010.524882

Ambady, N., Bernieri, F. J., & Richeson, J. A. (2000). Toward a histology of social behavior: Judgmental accuracy from thin slices of the behavioral stream. In M. P. Zanna (Ed.), *Advances in experimental social psychology* (Vol. 32, pp. 201–271). New York, NY: Academic Press. doi: 10.1016/S0065-2601(00)80006-4

Ambady, N., Hallahan, M., & Rosenthal, R. (1995). On judging and being judged accurately in zero-acquaintance situations. *Journal of Personality and Social Psychology*, *69*, 518–529. doi:10.1037/0022-3514.69.3.518

Asendorpf, J. B., Banse, R., & Mücke, D. (2002). Double dissociation between implicit and explicit personality self-concept: The case of shy behavior. *Journal of Personality and Social Psychology*, *83*, 380–393. doi:10.1037//0022-3514.83.2.380

Back, M., & Nestler, S. (2017). Dual-process approaches to personality. In R. Deutsch, B. Gawronski, & W. Hofmann (Eds), *Reflective and impulsive determinants of human behavior* (pp. 137–154). New York, NY: Routledge.

Back, M. D., & Kenny, D. A. (2010). The social relations model: How to understand dyadic processes. *Social and Personality Psychology Compass, 4*, 855–870. doi:10.1111/j.1751-9004.2010.00303.x

Back, M. D., & Nestler, S. (2016). Accuracy of judging personality. In J. A. Hall, M. Schmid Mast, & T. V. West (Eds.), *The social psychology of perceiving others accurately* (pp. 98–124). Cambridge, UK: Cambridge University Press.

Back, M. D., Schmukle, S. C., & Egloff, B. (2009). Predicting actual behavior from the explicit and implicit self-concept of personality. *Journal of Personality and Social Psychology, 97*, 533–548. doi:10.1037/A0016229

Back, M. D., Schmukle, S. C., & Egloff, B. (2011). A closer look at first sight: Social relations lens model analysis of personality and interpersonal attraction at zero acquaintance. *European Journal of Personality, 25*, 225–238. doi:10.1002/per.790

Back, M. D., & Vazire, S. (2012). Knowing our personality. In S. Vazire & T. D. Wilson (Eds.), *Handbook of self-knowledge* (pp. 131–156). New York, NY: Guilford Press.

Beer, A., & Watson, D. (2010). The effects of information and exposure on self-other agreement. *Journal of Research in Personality, 44*, 38–45. doi:10.1016/j.jrp.2009.10.002

Betsch, C. (2008). Chronic preferences for intuition and deliberation in decision making: Lessons learned about intuition from an individual differences approach. In H. Plessner, C. Betsch, & T. Betsch (Eds.), *Intuition in judgment and decision making* (pp. 231–248). Mahwah, NJ: Erlbaum.

Biesanz, J. C. (2010). The social accuracy model of interpersonal perception: Assessing individual differences in perceptive and expressive accuracy. *Multivariate Behavioral Research, 45*, 853–885. doi:10.1080/00273171.2010.519262

Blackman, M. C., & Funder, D. C. (1998). The effect of information on consensus and accuracy in personality judgment. *Journal of Experimental Social Psychology, 34*, 164–181. doi:10.1006/jesp.1997.1347

Borkenau, P., & Liebler, A. (1992). Trait inferences: Sources of validity at zero acquaintance. *Journal of Personality and Social Psychology, 62*, 645–657. doi:10.1037/0022-3514.62.4.645

Borkenau, P., & Liebler, A. (1993). Convergence of stranger ratings of personality and intelligence with self-ratings, partner ratings, and measured intelligence. *Journal of Personality and Social Psychology, 65*, 546–553. doi:10.1037/0022-3514.65.3.546

Borkenau, P., & Liebler, A. (1995). Observable attributes as manifestations and cues of personality and intelligence. *Journal of Personality, 63*, 1–25. doi:10.1111/j.1467-6494.1995.tb00799.x

Brown, J. A., & Bernieri, F. (2017). Trait perception accuracy and acquaintance within groups: Tracking accuracy development. *Personality and Social Psychology Bulletin, 43*, 716–728. doi:10.1177/0146167217695557

Brtek, M. D., & Motowidlo, S. J. (2002). Effects of procedure and outcome accountability on interview validity. *Journal of Applied Psychology, 87*, 185–191. doi:10.1037//0021-9010.87.1.185.

Brunswik, E. (1956). *Perception and the representative design of psychological experiments.* Berkeley: University of California Press.

Burgoon, J. K., Guerrero, L., & Manusov, V. (2011). Nonverbal signals. In M. L. Knapp, & J. A. Daly (Eds.), *Handbook of interpersonal communication* (4th ed., pp. 239–282). Thousand Oaks, CA: Sage.

Carney, D. R., Colvin, C. R., & Hall, J. A. (2007). A thin slice perspective on the accuracy of first impressions. *Journal of Research in Personality, 41*, 1054–1072. doi:10.1016/j.jrp.2007.01.004

Christiansen, N. D., Wolcott-Burnam, S., Janovics, J. E., Burns, G. N., & Quirk, S. W. (2005). The good judge revisited: Individual differences in the accuracy of personality judgments. *Human Performance, 18*, 123–149. doi:10.1207/s15327043hup1802_2

Colvin, C. R. (1993). "Judgable people": Personality, behavior, and competing explanations. *Journal of Personality and Social Psychology, 64*, 861–873. doi:10.1037/0022-3514.64.5.861

Connolly, J. J., Kavanagh, E. J., & Viswesvaran, C. (2007). The convergent validity between self and observer ratings of personality: A meta-analytic review. *International Journal of Selection and Assessment, 15*, 110–117. doi:10.1111/j.1468-2389.2007.00371.x

Connelly, B. S., & Ones, D. S. (2010). An other perspective on personality: Meta-analytic integration of observers' accuracy and predictive validity. *Psychological Bulletin, 136*, 1092–1122. doi:10.1037/a0021212

Darwin, C. (1965). *The expression of the emotions in man and animals.* Chicago, IL: University of Chicago Press. (Original work published 1872.)

De Kock, F. S., Lievens, F., Born, M. Ph. (in press). The profile of the "Good Judge" in HRM: A systematic review and agenda for future research. *Human Resource Management Review.* doi:10.1016/j.hrmr.2018.09.003

DePaulo, B. M. (1992). Nonverbal behavior and self-presentation. *Psychological Bulletin, 111*, 203–243. doi:10.1037/0033-2909.111.2.203

Ekman, P., Friesen, W. V., O'Sullivan, M., & Scherer, K. (1980). Relative importance of face, body, and speech in judgments of personality and affect. *Journal of Personality and Social Psychology, 38*, 270–277. doi:10.1037/0022-3514.38.2.270

Epstein, S., Pacini, R., DenesRaj, V., & Heier, H. (1996). Individual differences in intuitive-experiential and analytical-rational thinking styles. *Journal of Personality and Social Psychology, 71*, 390–405. doi:10.1037//0022-3514.71.2.390

Evans, J. St. B. T. (2008). Dual-processing accounts of reasoning, judgment, and social cognition. *Annual Review of Psychology, 59*, 255–278. doi:10.1146/annurev.psych.59.103006.093629

Funder, D. C. (1995). On the accuracy of personality judgment: A realistic approach. *Psychological Review, 102*, 652–670. doi:10.1037/0033-295X.102.4.652

Funder, D. C. (1999). *Personality judgment: A realistic approach to person perception.* San Diego, CA: Academic Press.

Funder, D. C. (2012). Accurate personality judgment. *Current Directions in Psychological Science, 21*, 177–182. doi:10.1177/0963721412445309

Funder, D. C., & Dobroth, K. M. (1987). Differences between traits: Properties associated with interjudge agreement. *Journal of Personality and Social Psychology, 52*, 409–418. doi:10.1037/0022-3514.52.2.409

Funder, D. C., & Harris, M. J. (1986). On the several facets of personality assessment: The case of social acuity. *Journal of Personality, 54*, 528–550. doi:10.1111/j.1467-6494.1986.tb00411.x

Funder, D. C., & Sneed, C. D. (1993). Behavioral manifestations of personality: An ecological approach to judgmental accuracy. *Journal of Personality and Social Psychology, 64*, 479–490. doi:10.1037/0022-3514.64.3.479

Gangestad, S. W., Digeronimo, K., Simpson, J. A., & Biek, M. (1992). Differential accuracy in person perception across traits: Examination of a functional hypothesis. *Journal of Personality and Social Psychology, 62*, 688–698. doi:10.1037/0022-3514.62.4.688

Gifford, R. (1994). A lens-mapping framework for understanding the encoding and decoding of interpersonal dispositions in nonverbal behavior. *Journal of Personality and Social Psychology, 66*, 398–412. doi:10.1037/0022-3514.66.2.398

Gosling, S. D., Ko, S. J., Mannarelli, T., & Morris, M. E. (2002). A room with a cue: Personality judgments based on offices and bedrooms. *Journal of Personality and Social Psychology, 82*, 379–398. doi:10.1037/0022-3514.82.3.379

Greenwald, A. G., McGhee, D. E., & Schwartz, J. L. K. (1998). Measuring individual differences in implicit cognition: The implicit association test. *Journal of Personality and Social Psychology, 74*, 1464–1480. doi:10.1037/0022-3514.74.6.1464

Greenwald, A. G., Poehlman, T. A., Uhlmann, E. L., & Banaji, M. R. (2009). Understanding and using the Implicit Association Test: III. Meta-analysis of predictive validity. *Journal of Personality and Social Psychology, 97*, 17–41. doi:10.1037/a0015575

Hagemeyer, B., Dufner, M., and Denissen, J. J. A. (2016). Double dissociation between implicit and explicit affiliative motives: A closer look at socializing behavior in dyadic interactions. *Journal of Research in Personality, 65*, 89–93. doi:10.1016/j.jrp.2016.08.003

Hall, J. A., Andrzejewski, S. A., Murphy, N. A., Schmid Mast, M., & Feinstein, B. (2008). Accuracy of judging others' traits and states: Comparing mean levels across tests. *Journal of Research in Personality, 42*, 1476–1489. doi:10.1016/j.jrp.2008.06.013

Hall, J. A., Andrzejewski, S. A., & Yopchick, J. E. (2009). Psychosocial correlates of interpersonal sensitivity: A meta-analysis. *Journal of Nonverbal Behavior, 33*, 149–180. doi:10.1007/s10919-009-0070-5

Hall, J. A., Back, M. D., Nestler, S., Frauendorfer, D., Schmid Mast, M., & Ruben, M. A. (2018). How do different ways of measuring individual differences in zero-acquaintance personality judgment accuracy correlate with each other? *Journal of Personality, 86*, 220–232. doi:10.1111/jopy.12307

Hall, J. A., & Bernieri, F. J. (Eds.). (2001). *Interpersonal sensitivity: Theory and measurement*. Mahwah, NJ: Erlbaum.

Hall, J. A., Blanch, D. C., Horgan, T. G., Murphy, N. A., Rosip, J. C., & Schmid Mast, M. (2009). Motivation and interpersonal sensitivity: Does it matter how hard you try? *Motivation and Emotion, 33*, 291–302. doi:10.1007/s11031-009-9128-2

Hall, J. A., & Goh, J. X. (2017). Studying stereotype accuracy from an integrative social-personality perspective. *Social and Personality Psychology Compass, 11*. doi:10.1111/spc3.12357

Hall, J. A., Gunnery, S. D., Letzring, T. D., Carney, D. R., & Colvin, C. R. (2017). Accuracy of judging affect and accuracy of judging personality: How and when are they related? *Journal of Personality, 85*, 583–592. doi:10.1111/jopy.12262

Hall, J. A., Horgan, T. G., & Murphy, N. A. (2019). Nonverbal communication. *Annual Review of Psychology, 70*, 271–294. doi:10.1146/annurev-psych-010418-103145

Hammond, K. R., Hursch, C. J., & Todd, F. J. (1964). Analyzing the components of clinical inference. *Psychological Review, 71*, 438–456. doi:10.1037/h0040736

Hammond, K. R., & Stewart, T. R. (Eds.). (2001). *The essential Brunswik: Beginnings, explications, applications*. New York, NY: Oxford University Press.

Harris, M. J., & Garris, C. P. (2008). You never get a second chance to make a first impression: Behavioral consequences of first impressions. In N. Ambady & J. J. Skowronski (Eds.), *First impressions* (pp. 147–168). New York, NY: Guilford Press.

Hastie, R., & Dawes, R. M. (2001). *Rational choice in an uncertain world: The psychology of judgement and decision making*. Thousand Oaks, CA: Sage.

Heyman, R. E., Lorber, M. F., Eddy, J. M., & West, T. V. (2014). Behavioral observation and coding. In H. T. Reis, & C. M. Judd (Eds.), *Handbook of research methods in social and personality psychology* (2nd ed., pp. 345–372). New York, NY: Cambridge University Press. doi:10.1017/CBO9780511996481.018

Hirschmüller, S., Egloff, B., Nestler, S., & Back, M. D. (2013). The dual lens model: A comprehensive framework for understanding self-other agreement of personality judgments at zero acquaintance. *Journal of Personality and Social Psychology, 104*, 335–353. doi:10.1037/A0030383

Hirschmüller, S., Egloff, B., Schmukle, S. C., Nestler, S., & Back, M. D. (2015). Accurate judgments of neuroticism at zero acquaintance: A question of relevance. *Journal of Personality, 83*, 221–228. doi:10.1111/Jopy.12097

Hirschmüller, S., Schmukle, S. C., Krause, S., Back, M. D., & Egloff, B. (2018). Accuracy of self-esteem judgments at zero acquaintance. *Journal of Personality, 86*, 308–319. doi:10.1111/jopy.12316

Hjelle, L. A. (1969). Personality characteristics associated with interpersonal perception accuracy. *Journal of Counseling Psychology, 16*, 579–581. doi:10.1037/h0028439

Hofmann, W., Gawronski, B., Gschwendner, T., Le, H., & Schmitt, M. (2005). A meta-analysis on the correlation between the implicit association test and explicit self-report measures. *Personality and Social Psychology Bulletin, 31*, 1369–1385. doi:10.1177/0146167205275613

Human, L. J., & Biesanz, J. C. (2013). Targeting the good target: An integrative review of the characteristics and consequences of being accurately perceived. *Personality and Social Psychology Review, 17*, 248–272. doi:10.1177/1088868313495593

Human, L. J., Biesanz, J. C., Parisotto, K. L., & Dunn, E. W. (2012). Your best self helps reveal your true self: Trying to make a good impression leads to more accurate personality impressions. *Social Psychological and Personality Science, 3*, 23–30. doi: 10.1177/1948550611407689

John, O. P., & Robins, R. W. (1993). Determinants of interjudge agreement on personality traits: The Big Five domains, observability, evaluativeness, and the unique perspective of the self. *Journal of Personality, 61*, 521–551. doi:10.1111/j.1467-6494.1993.tb00781.x

Karelaia, N., & Hogarth, R. M. (2008). Determinants of linear judgment: A meta-analysis of lens model studies. *Psychological Bulletin, 134*, 404–426. doi:10.1037/0033-2909.134.3.404

Kaufmann, E., & Athanasou, J. A. (2009). A meta-analysis of judgment achievement as defined by the lens model equation. *Swiss Journal of Psychology, 68*, 99–112. doi:10.1024/1421-0185.68.2.99

Kaufmann, E., Reips, U. D., & Wittmann, W. W. (2013). A critical meta-analysis of lens model studies in human judgment and decision-making. *Plos One, 8*. doi:10.1371/journal.pone.0083528

Kaurin, A., Heil, L., Wessa, M., Egloff, B., & Hirschmüller, S. (2018). Selfies reflect actual personality—Just like photos or short videos in standardized lab conditions. *Journal of Research in Personality, 76*, 154–164. doi:10.1016/j.jrp.2018.08.007

Kenny, D. A. (1994). *Interpersonal perception: A social relations analysis*. New York, NY: Guilford Press.

Kenny, D. A., & West, T. V. (2008). Zero acquaintance: Definitions, statistical model, findings, and process. In N. Ambady & J. J. Skowronski (Eds.), *First impressions* (pp. 129–146). New York, NY: Guilford Press.

Kilianski, S. E. (2008). Who do you think I think I am? Accuracy in perceptions of others' self-esteem. *Journal of Research in Personality, 42*, 386–398. doi:10.1016/j.jrp.2007.07.004

Konstabel, K., Aavik, T., & Allik, J. (2006). Social desirability and consensual validity of personality traits. *European Journal of Personality, 20*, 549–566. doi:10.1002/per.593

Kruglanski, A. W., & Orehek, E. (2007). Partitioning the domain of social inference: Dual mode and systems models and their alternatives. *Annual Review of Psychology, 58*, 291–316. doi:10.1146/annurev.psych.58.110405.085629

Küfner, A. C. P., Nestler, S., & Back, M. D. (2013). The two pathways to being an (un-)popular narcissist. *Journal of Personality, 81*,184–195. doi:10.1111/j.1467-6494.2012.00795.x

Kuncel, N. R., Klieger, D. M., Connelly, B. S., & Ones, D. S. (2013). Mechanical versus clinical data combination in selection and admissions decisions: A meta-analysis. *Journal of Applied Psychology, 98*, 1060–1072. doi:10.1037/a0034156

Leary, M. R., & Kowalski, R. M. (1990). Impression management: A literature review and two-component model. *Psychological Bulletin, 107*, 34–47. doi:10.1037/0033-2909.107.1.34

Leising, D., & Borkenau, P. (2011). Person perception, dispositional inferences, and social judgment. In M. Horowitz & S. Strack (Eds.), *Handbook of interpersonal psychology: Theory, research, assessment, and therapeutic interventions* (pp. 157–170). Hoboken, NJ: John Wiley & Sons.

Letzring, T. D. (2008). The good judge of personality: Characteristics, behaviors, and observer accuracy. *Journal of Research in Personality, 42*, 914–932. doi:10.1016/j.jrp.2007.12.003

Letzring, T. D., & Funder, D. C. (2018). Interpersonal accuracy in trait judgments. In V. Zeigler-Hill & T. K. Shackelford (Eds.), *The SAGE handbook of personality and individual difference: Volume 3. Applications of personality and individual differences* (pp. 253–282). Thousand Oaks, CA: Sage Publications. doi:10.4135/9781526451248.n11

Letzring, T. D., Wells, S. A., & Funder, D. C. (2006). Information quantity and quality affect the realistic accuracy of personality judgment. *Journal of Personality and Social Psychology, 91*, 111–123. doi:10.1037/0022-3514.91.1.11

Lippa, R. A., & Dietz, J. K. (2000). The relation of gender, personality, and intelligence to judges' accuracy in judging strangers' personality from brief video segments. *Journal of Nonverbal Behavior, 24*, 25–43. doi:10.1023/A:1006610805385

McLarney-Vesotski, A., Bernieri, F., & Rempala, D. (2011). An experimental examination of the "good judge." *Journal of Research in Personality, 45*, 398–400. doi:10.1016/j.jrp.2011.04.005

Murphy, N. A. (2007). Appearing smart: The impression management of intelligence, person perception accuracy, and behavior in social interaction. *Personality and Social Psychology Bulletin, 33*, 325–339. doi:10.1177/0146167206294871

Naumann, L. P., Vazire, S., Rentfrow, P. J., & Gosling, S. D. (2009). Personality judgments based on physical appearance. *Personality and Social Psychology Bulletin, 35*, 1661–1671. doi:10.1177/0146167209346309

Nestler, S., & Back, M. D. (2013). Applications and extensions of the lens model to understand interpersonal judgments at zero acquaintance. *Current Directions in Psychological Science, 22*, 374–379. doi:10.1177/0963721413486148

Nestler, S., & Back, M. D. (2017). Using cross-classified structural equation models to examine the accuracy of personality judgments. *Psychometrika, 82*, 475–497. doi:10.1007/s11336-015-9485-6

Nestler, S., Egloff, B., Küfner, A. C. P., & Back, M. D. (2012). An integrative lens model approach to bias and accuracy in human inferences: Hindsight effects and knowledge updating in personality judgments. *Journal of Personality and Social Psychology, 103*, 689–717. doi:10.1037/a0029461

Powell, D. M., & Bourdage, J. S. (2016). The detection of personality traits in employment interviews: Can "good judges" be trained? *Personality and Individual Differences, 94*, 194–199. doi:10.1016/j.paid.2016.01.009

Reynolds, D. J., & Gifford, R. (2001). The sounds and sights of intelligence: A lens model channel analysis. *Personality and Social Psychology Bulletin, 27*, 187–200. doi:10.1177/0146167201272005

Riggio, H. R., & Riggio, R. E. (2002). Emotional expressiveness, extraversion, and neuroticism: A meta-analysis. *Journal of Nonverbal Behavior, 26*, 195–218. doi:10.1023/A:1022117500440

Roese, N. J., & Vohs, K. D. (2012). Hindsight bias. *Perspectives on Psychological Science, 7*, 411–426. doi:10.1177/1745691612454303

Rogers, K. H., & Biesanz, J. C. (2019). Reassessing the good judge of personality. *Journal of Personality and Social Psychology, 117*, 186–200. Retrieved from https://osf.io/nwkct/download. doi: 10.1037/pspp0000197

Rudolph, A., Schröder-Abé, M., Riketta, M., & Schütz, A. (2010). Easier when done than said! Implicit self-esteem predicts observed or spontaneous behavior, but not self-reported or controlled behavior. *Zeitschrift für Psychologie/Journal of Psychology, 218*, 12–19. doi:10.1027/0044-3409/a000003

Rule, N. O., Ambady, N., & Hallett, K. C. (2009). Female sexual orientation is perceived accurately, rapidly, and automatically from the face and its features. *Journal of Experimental Social Psychology, 45*, 1245–1251. doi:10.1016/j.jesp.2009.07.010

Rule, N. O., Krendl, A. C., Ivcevic, Z., & Ambady, N. (2013). Accuracy and consensus in judgments of trustworthiness from faces: Behavioral and neural correlates. *Journal of Personality and Social Psychology, 104*, 409–426. doi:10.1037/a0031050

Scherer, K. R. (1978). Personality inference from voice quality: The loud voice of extroversion. *European Journal of Social Psychology, 8*, 467–487. doi:10.1002/ejsp.2420080405

Schlenker, B. R., & Pontari, B. A. (2000). The strategic control of information: Impression management and self-presentation in daily life. In A. E. Tesser, R. B. Felson, & J. M. Suls (Eds.), *Psychological perspectives on self and identity* (pp. 199–232). Washington, DC: American Psychological Association. doi:10.1037/10357-008

Stopfer, J. M., Egloff, B., Nestler, S., & Back, M. D. (2014). Personality expression and impression formation in online social networks: An integrative approach to understanding the processes of accuracy, impression management and meta-accuracy. *European Journal of Personality, 28*, 73–94. doi:10.1002/per.1935

Taft, R. (1955). The ability to judge people. *Psychological Bulletin, 52*, 1–23. doi:10.1037/h0044999

Tett, R. P., & Guterman, H. A. (2000). Situation trait relevance, trait expression, and cross-situational consistency: Testing a principle of trait activation. *Journal of Research in Personality, 34*, 397–423. doi:10.1037/0021-9010.88.3.500

Vazire, S. (2010). Who knows what about a person? The knowledge asymmetry (SOKA) model. *Journal of Personality and Social Psychology, 98*, 281–300. doi:10.1037/a0017908

Vazire, S., Naumann, L. P., Rentfrow, P. J., & Gosling, S. D. (2008). Portrait of a narcissist: Manifestations of narcissism in physical appearance. *Journal of Research in Personality, 42*, 1439–1447. doi:10.1016/j.jrp.2008.06.007

Vernon, P. E. (1933). Some characteristics of the good judge of personality. *Journal of Social Psychology, 4*, 42–57. doi:10.1080/00224545.1933.9921556

Vingoe, F. J., & Antonoff, S. R. (1968). Personality characteristics of good judges of others. *Journal of Counseling Psychology, 15*, 91–93. doi:10.1037/h0025330

Vogt, D. S., & Colvin, C. R. (2003). Interpersonal orientation and the accuracy of personality judgments. *Journal of Personality, 71*, 267–295. doi:10.1111/1467-6494.7102005

Wegner, D. M., & Bargh, J. A. (1998). Control and automaticity in social life. In D. T. Gilbert, S. T. Fiske, & G. Lindzey (Eds.), *Handbook of social psychology* (4th ed., Vol. 1, pp. 446–496). New York, NY: McGraw-Hill.

Wickens, T. D. (2001). *Elementary signal detection theory*. New York, NY: Oxford University Press.

Zebrowitz, L. A., Hall, J. A., Murphy, N. A., & Rhodes, G. (2002). Looking smart and looking good: Facial cues to intelligence and their origins. *Personality and Social Psychology Bulletin, 28*, 238–249. doi:10.1177/0146167202282009

Zebrowitz, L. A., & Rhodes, G. (2004). Sensitivity to "bad genes" and the anomalous face overgeneralization effect: Cue validity, cue utilization, and accuracy in judging intelligence and health. *Journal of Nonverbal Behavior, 28*, 167–185. doi:10.1023/B:JONB.0000039648.30935.1b

Note

1. The personality IAT assesses the strength of people's associative semantic representation between the self and the respective trait concept (e.g., "me"–"sociable") through a series of discrimination tasks that require fast responding (cf. Back et al., 2009). For example, in the extraversion IAT, participants are instructed to categorize exemplars of self- vs. other-related words and extraversion vs. introversion words using two response keys for their categorization (e.g., left response key for self and extraversion words vs. right response key for other-related and introversion words and vice versa). Faster responses are expected when two highly associated categories (e.g., self and extraversion) share the same response key than when they are assigned to different response keys, thus indicating a higher level of the implicit self-concept of extraversion.

The Social Accuracy Model

Jeremy C. Biesanz

Abstract

The social accuracy model (SAM) is a componential model of interpersonal perception that estimates perceiver, target, dyadic, and other effects for different components or elements of accuracy. For instance, Percy may be a good judge in that she is generally accurate in her perceptions of others. As well, Taylor may be a good target in that she is generally accurately perceived by others. The SAM allows one to estimate such individual differences in components related to accuracy, bias, and generalized knowledge as well as examine moderators of such components. The present chapter provides a broad overview of the SAM, its history, and how it compares to other modeling approaches, and provides a detailed discussion of how to interpret the elements of the SAM. Finally, an appendix is provided that discusses how to create variables, analyze the model, and interpret the output from a social accuracy model analysis using R.

Key Words: person, perception, interpersonal perception, impression, personality, accuracy

Impressions matter. Our impressions of others provide the structure and coherence that allow us to understand their past behavior and then anticipate and predict their future behavior. The accuracy and positivity of impressions are critical and have real consequences for both ourselves and for others. Accurate impressions enable us to anticipate how someone will behave and appropriately adapt our responses. Inaccurate impressions can lead us to interact with others in less than optimal ways. The importance of impressions naturally raises questions. How accurate are interpersonal perceptions? To what extent are the impressions we form of others adaptive and useful? When and for whom are impressions more accurate and less biased? To what extent do we use knowledge of what people are like in general when forming impressions of others? To make these questions less abstract, consider Percy, who meets Taylor at a get-together at a friend's house. Taylor is new to town and is a manager at the company that Percy's friend works at. Percy is

considering applying to work at the same company and so Percy's impression of Taylor will influence the decision whether or not to join the company. Is Taylor organized and reliable? Smart, resourceful, intelligent, and creative? Sociable, amicable, and pleasant to work with? These are all important dimensions to consider, and the accuracy of Percy's impressions could have lasting ramifications. To what extent are Percy's impressions of Taylor's personality and characteristics valid? Are Percy's impressions positively or negatively biased?

Answering these questions requires a statistical model—and sometimes several—and there are many different approaches that one can take, as no single model of interpersonal perception can answer all of the questions that one may have (for a brief review, see Biesanz, 2018). The present chapter provides an introduction of the social accuracy model (SAM; Biesanz, 2010). SAM is a componential model of interpersonal perception that estimates perceiver, target, and dyadic effects of different components of accuracy across traits simultaneously. A componential model of accuracy breaks assessments of accuracy into different elements (components) that have specific and hopefully useful interpretations. Perceiver and target effects refer to estimates of accuracy components for each perceiver (averaged across targets) and each target (averaged across perceivers) and are analogous to main effects in ANOVA. Dyadic effects are simply the residual effect that is left over for each dyad after accounting for the perceiver and target average effects. For instance, Percy may have a large perceiver effect in that she is generally accurate in her perceptions of the personality of others and thus high in perceptive accuracy (i.e., a good judge; see chapter 6 by Colman in this handbook).[1] At the same time, Taylor may have a large target effect and is accurately perceived by others in general and thus high in expressive accuracy (i.e., a good target; see chapter 7 by Mignault & Human in this handbook). If Percy formed an especially accurate impression of Taylor, above and beyond what we would expect given their respective perceiver and target average effects, this would result in a positive dyadic accuracy score. As well, Percy may generally form favorable impressions of others whereas others tend to forwem more negative impressions of Taylor. The SAM was designed to estimate such individual differences in important components of interpersonal perception—perceiver, target, and dyadic assessments of accuracy and bias—as well as average levels of accuracy.

At a broad level, the SAM represents an integration of Cronbach's (1955) componential approach to assessing accuracy with Kenny's (Kenny, 1994; Kenny & La Voie, 1984) social relations model (SRM; see chapter 3 by Malloy in this handbook). To do this, the SAM adopts Funder's (1995) realistic accuracy model (RAM; see chapter by 2 Letzring & Funder in this handbook) for modeling accuracy in that the goal is to assess the validity of the perceiver's impressions. Initial elements of SAM can be seen in earlier work (e.g., Biesanz & West, 2000; Biesanz, West, & Graziano, 1998; Biesanz, West, & Millevoi, 2007) that adapted Cronbach's components of accuracy. Biesanz (2010) provided the first overview of the SAM as a general model that can provide answers to questions, such as those raised in Funder (1995), that cannot be addressed through other frameworks or models. Since then, the SAM has been used extensively to examine many different research questions, and the present chapter includes a brief overview of some of this work.

The goal of the present chapter is to provide an accessible overview of and introduction to the SAM. Although the SAM is a cross-classified random effects model (e.g., a two-way factorial ANOVA where the levels of each factor—perceivers and targets—are considered to be randomly sampled from larger populations) that generally requires multilevel software to estimate, a deep understanding of the model can be achieved with just a few fundamental building blocks. These necessary components are (1) an ability to interpret coefficients in one and two-predictor regression models, (2) an understanding of main effects and interactions in the two-way between-subjects ANOVA, and (3) a conceptual understanding of the sampling distribution of regression coefficients. The present chapter uses these three building blocks to explain the key elements of the SAM. If an introduction is needed, Navarro (2018) provides an excellent open-source resource to these elements using the R statistical language.

Why Not Simple Correlations?

To begin with, why are complex models like SAM needed? Can't correlations suffice to examine questions of accuracy? After all, the simple Pearson correlation has been instrumental to the field of personality psychology. Correlations are foundational to factor analysis and efforts to uncover the important dimensions of basic personality traits such as the Big Five (e.g., John & Srivastava, 1999). As well, the cumulative evidence of substantial levels of self–other agreement and consensus in personality ratings on broad traits—generally assessed using correlations—that could not be attributable to simple artefactual explanations has provided compelling evidence for both the existence of personality traits and the accuracy of interpersonal perceptions (Kenrick & Funder, 1988). The Pearson correlation has served and will continue to serve the field well. However there are severe limitations to simple correlational analyses. Correlational analyses on a single trait—such as the correlation between self and informant ratings on extraversion—do not provide the inferential leverage to examine individual differences in interpersonal perception. Such analyses provide a good estimate of the average level of self-other agreement for a single trait, but do not allow any insight into whether some perceivers are better than others, whether some individuals are more accurately perceived than others, or whether some dyads or pairs are more accurate than others. Although it is possible to examine moderators of accuracy—for instance, to examine whether judges higher in intelligence are more accurate than judges lower in intelligence—such analyses are indirect and presume both individual differences in the good judge and that intelligence is a good proxy for those individual differences. That is, we would only observe assessments of judges' intelligence moderating accuracy if (1) there are individual differences across judges in their levels of accuracy *and* (2) the judge's level of intelligence is associated with their level of accuracy. Importantly, the absence of moderation does not imply that the good judge does not exist and there are no meaningful individual differences in accuracy across judges. Indeed, much of the early work on the good judge has used this indirect moderational approach with relatively little success (e.g., see the review by Davis & Kraus, 1997), leading many to conclude that the good judge does not exist or really matter (e.g., Allik, de Vries, & Realo, 2016). However, to really address this question properly requires a model that allows one to *directly* estimate individual differences in accuracy. This is the raison d'être for the SAM. To what extent are there individual differences in the good judge, the good target, and the good pair or dyad? Once these individual or group differences are estimated it becomes easy to examine predictors of these individual differences and understand those results. If these individual differences in the good judge are essentially nil, then there is no point in examining predictors of the good judge. If there are strong individual differences associated with accuracy but proposed moderators are not associated with those individual differences, that simply means our theories and understanding of accuracy and factors associated with accuracy are incomplete and we need to look elsewhere to predict and understand those individual differences. Finally, if there are individual differences in accuracy across perceivers, targets, and/or dyads, failing to appropriately model those individual differences can lead to inflated Type I error rates and an inability to appropriately generalize results (e.g., see Judd, Westfall, & Kenny, 2012).

Accuracy and Validity

Assessing the accuracy of personality judgments may seem like a thorny and potentially impossible problem. From one perspective, assessing accuracy would require knowing someone's true personality—an impossible task, as we cannot determine or measure, for instance, how *extraverted* Taylor really is. We can certainly obtain measures of Taylor's extraversion, but assessments contain measurement error and

Taylor's true score is a latent measure in that we cannot assess it directly (Bollen, 2002). Different observers provide different answers, as consensus is not perfect. Indeed, simply asking Taylor to describe herself at different times would often yield slightly different answers, as retest reliability is also not perfect, even on broad personality traits. To avoid the philosophical trap that we can never perfectly assess personality constructs and thus assessing accuracy in interpersonal perception is a nonstarter, Funder (1995, 1999) developed the realistic accuracy model (RAM). The RAM defines a judgment or impression as accurate to the extent it maps on to realistic criteria for the target's personality, such as the target's own self-report or reports of knowledgeable informants. Moreover, the RAM outlines the necessary stages to achieve accurate impressions: specifically, *relevant* cues must be made *available* to perceivers, who must then *detect* and correctly *utilize* those cues. The RAM provides a conceptual framework that allows one to ask questions of accuracy in interpersonal perception and avoid the trap that we cannot perfectly assess Taylor's actual personality. Questions of accuracy under the RAM are really instead questions about the validity of a perceiver's impressions. Asking whether Percy's impression of Taylor is accurate, using the RAM as a theoretical framework, is really asking about the extent to which Percy's impression of Taylor is valid. The SAM adopts the RAM's philosophical perspective in that the terms "accuracy" and "validity" are used interchangeably. In the examples and models that follow I refer to validation measures—assessments of the target's personality that are used to assess the level of validity of the perceiver's impressions—and the estimates from the model provide components of accuracy in interpersonal perception.

What measures should we use to assess the validity of perceiver impressions? The ideal measure would be both highly reliable and a valid indicator of the target's personality—a good realistic measure of the target's personality. At first glance, behavioral measures are conceptually compelling to use as validity measures. However, the lessons learned from Hartshorne and May (1928) and strongly interpreted by Mischel (1968) are that direct behavioral measures correlate weakly at best with other behavioral measures. Epstein's (1983) analogy is that behavioral assessments of personality are low grade ore in that they are highly unreliable, and as a result they need to be aggregated and concentrated to yield reliable measures of personality. Wonderful empirical examples of such aggregation improving reliability and validity are provided by Moskowitz and Schwarz (1982) and Borkenau, Mauer, Riemann, Spinath, and Angleitner (2004). With considerable time, effort, and resources this aggregation of behavioral measures can be done in the laboratory and controlled well, but the funding and resources required are often not available (for an in-depth overview of assessing behavioral observations, see Nave, Feeney, & Furr, 2018). Instead we often rely on the natural aggregation of past behavior that self and knowledgeable informant assessments of behavior provide. After all, we have seen our own behavior throughout our lives and close others have observed us for long periods of time in different contexts, allowing for the concentration of the low grade ore of single behavioral measures to become highly concentrated in a manner that is much more reliable and valid (e.g., see Biesanz et al., 2007; Connelly & Ones, 2010). The starting point for any SAM should always be the assessment of the most reliable and realistically valid assessment of the target's personality that can be achieved within the constraints of the study's design. Within the contexts of specific research questions, the validation measure may be limited to a single perspective such as self-reports (e.g., see Funder & Colvin, 1997); the examples provided in the present chapter use self-, peer-, and parental reports of personality that are aggregated into a single validity composite measure that is quite reliable.

The Basic Social Accuracy Model

There are only two measures that are needed for the social accuracy model: perceiver ratings and target validity measures. These measures are needed for a set of different items or traits. Larger sets of items, such as the full 44- or 60-item Big Five Inventory (BFI; John & Srivastava, 1999; Soto & John, 2017), will provide more reliable estimates, greater statistical power (probability of correctly rejecting a false null hypothesis), and tighter confidence intervals around model estimates, and help facilitate the convergence of the model in many software programs, compared to smaller sets of items such as the Ten-Item Personality Inventory (TIPI) (Gosling, Rentfrow, & Swann, 2003). In equation (1), perceiver ratings are Y_{pti}, which indicate perceiver p's ratings of target t on item i. The target validity measure for target t on item i is V_{ti}. These are the only two assessments that are needed for a SAM analysis. However, to conduct the analysis requires separating out the validity measure into two different components—the average person's validity

measure and how different the target is from the average person. First, the average validity measure across targets is determined for each item ($Vmean_i$) by calculating the mean for each item across the t targets on V_{ti}. This provides the mean validity profile which is the profile of the average target. In small samples with relatively few targets it may be helpful to use the mean profile from a larger set of targets that are exchangeable with the targets in the analysis to have a more reliable estimate of the mean profile. The validity profile of the average target, $Vmean_i$, is then used to center the target validity measure within items by calculating $Vc_{ti} = V_{ti} - Vmean_i$. The centered validity measures for each target and the average validity profile are then used to predict the perceivers' ratings as shown in equation 1. All that is required to actually estimate equation 1 is a research design where multiple perceivers evaluate multiple targets across a large set of items. This could be a round-robin design where each perceiver meets and evaluates every target, a half-block design where a set of perceivers all evaluate a common set of targets (e.g., all of the perceivers watch and evaluate the same 10 targets in videos), or various hybrids of these designs.

$$Y_{pti} = \gamma_{0_{pt}} + \gamma_{1_{pt}} Vc_{ti} + \gamma_{2_{pt}} Vmean_i + e_{pti}$$
$$\gamma_{0_{pt}} = \gamma_{00} + u_{0_p} + u_{0_t} + u_{0_{(pt)}} \quad (1)$$

$$\gamma_{1_{pt}} = \gamma_{10} + u_{1_p} + u_{1_t} + u_{1_{(pt)}}$$
$$\gamma_{2_{pt}} = \gamma_{20} + u_{2_p} + u_{2_t} + u_{2_{(pt)}} \quad (2)$$

Equation 1 provides the full SAM, which is simply a two-predictor regression equation: validity measures, centered within item, and the average target validity profile are used to predict perceiver impressions. The unstandardized regression coefficients from this two-predictor regression equation, denoted by gamma (e.g., γ_0, γ_1, and γ_2) as is the common notational practice for multilevel models, can vary across perceivers, targets, and dyads, and are captured by the us in equation 2, as is explained and illustrated shortly.

The Basic SAM Equation: Examining a Single Dyad

To understand SAM and the interpretation of its coefficients, as well as why Vc_{ti} and $Vmean_i$ are used as the two predictors in the model instead of just V_{ti}, it is helpful to first consider in depth a single perceiver-target dyad, as illustrated in equation 3.

$$\hat{Y}_i = b_0 + b_1 Vc_i + b_2 Vmean_i \quad (3)$$

To develop a deeper understanding of the SAM, its rationale, and the interpretation of its components, consider the following example, where Percy provided her impressions of Taylor across 24 items on the Big Five. This specific dyad was chosen as the results are fairly typical and representative of the average accuracy relationships in the sample.[2] The variables of interest are Percy's impressions of Taylor (Y_i) and Taylor's validity measure (V_i), which were an average of self-, peer-, and parental-reports on the same 24 items that Percy evaluated. Figure 5.1a shows the relationship between V and Y, which appears to demonstrate a strong relationship between Taylor's personality validity measures and Percy's impressions on those same measures. At first glance this would suggest that Percy formed quite an accurate impression of Taylor. However Figure 5.1b shows the relationship between the personality profile for the average person, calculated as the average validity score for each item $\left(Vmean_i = \bar{V}_i\right)$ across targets, and Percy's impressions of Taylor. This relationship is quite strong as well and casts doubt on

using the relationship in Figure 5.1a as a measure of the accuracy of Percy's impressions. After all, if Percy's impressions are strongly related to the average person's personality, did Percy actually form an accurate impression of Taylor, or did she just use her knowledge of what the average person is like to form her impression? After all, on average people are like the average person, and the strength of this association for Taylor is shown in Figure 5.1c.

One solution to this problem is to include the average person in the model and simply partial out the average person from the relationship between Taylor's validity measures and Percy's impressions. This two-predictor regression equation, where the raw validity measure (V_i) and the average person's personality ($V\ mean_i$) are both included as predictors in the model, is illustrated in Figure 5.2.

After partialling the average personality profile from Taylor's validity scores, we observe a positive association between Taylor's validity measures and Percy's impressions (b_1=0.404) which indicates that Percy was indeed able to accurately discern Taylor's

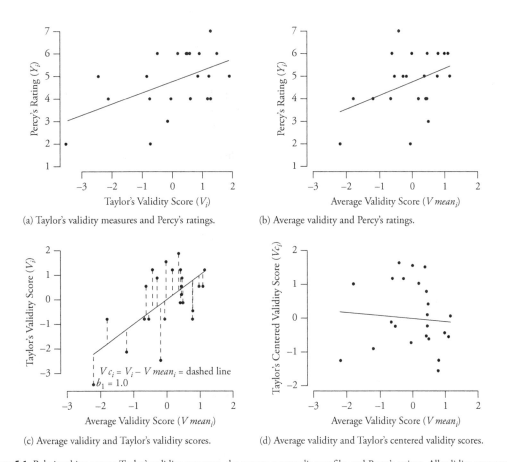

(a) Taylor's validity measures and Percy's ratings.

(b) Average validity and Percy's ratings.

(c) Average validity and Taylor's validity scores.

(d) Average validity and Taylor's centered validity scores.

Figure 5.1 Relationships among Taylor's validity measures, the average personality profile, and Percy's ratings. All validity measures are grand mean centered.

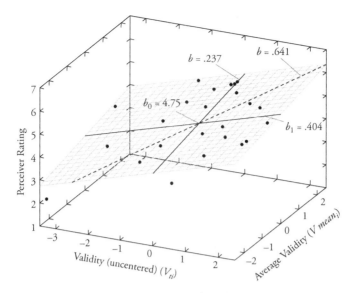

Figure 5.2 Relationship between the validity scores (not centered within items) and item means predicting perceiver ratings for a single perceiver–target dyad.

personality. However, how are we to interpret the other partial regression coefficient in this model? The coefficient ($b = 0.237$) is the relationship between the average person's personality profile and Percy's impressions of Taylor, holding Taylors's personality profile constant. As Taylor's personality profile strongly corresponds to the average person (Figure 5.1c), this coefficient tells us the relationship between the average person's personality *that is uncorrelated from Taylor's personality* is related to Percy's impressions. In other words, it partials out Taylor's personality from that of the average person and examines how this residual is related to Percy's impressions. This estimate is neither substantively useful nor informative—indeed it is quite difficult to appropriately interpret and make sense of. What would be more useful is an estimate that mirrors the relationship in Figure 5.1b—the relationship between the average person's personality profile and Percy's impressions. This relationship is present in Figure 5.2 indicated by the dashed diagonal line that has slope $b = 0.641$. The slope of this dashed line tells us the predicted change in Percy's ratings for a one-unit change in the average person's personality profile, when Taylor's personality matches the average person. In other words, instead of partialling Taylor's personality, we hold it constant at the average person (i.e., when the average person's personality *and* Taylor's personality measure both increase by 1 unit together, $b = 0.641$ is the predicted change in Percy's rating). Another way to think about this relationship is that the dashed line ($b = 0.641$) essentially attributes the overlap between Taylor's

personality and the average person to the average person instead of partialling it out.

This regression coefficient ($b = 0.641$) and its standard error are not immediately available from the model in Figure 5.2, although they can be determined through some simple but tedious algebra. Fortunately there is an easy way to determine the slope of the dashed line in Figure 5.2 directly from a statistical model with a few minor adjustments. The solution is to center Taylor's validity measure *within each item* (i.e., compute $Vc_i = V_i - Vmean_i$). This centering is illustrated in Figure 5.1c, where the difference from each of Taylor's validity measures is subtracted from the average personality profile. These new item-centered validity measures can then be used, along with the average person's personality, to predict Percy's impressions. This two-regression predictor model is illustrated in Figure 5.3 which corresponds to equation 3.[3]

There are a number of important elements to this change that are not immediately obvious.

- The slope for b_1 is exactly the same in Figures 5.2 and 5.3. This holds for all dyads, not just the present example. As well, the standard errors for b_1 do not change either so inferences are not affected by this centering.
- The slope of the diagonal dashed line in Figure 5.2 is b_2 in Figure 5.3. This is quite useful, as the model will then provide standard errors and the ability to make inferences without having to do laborious calculations.

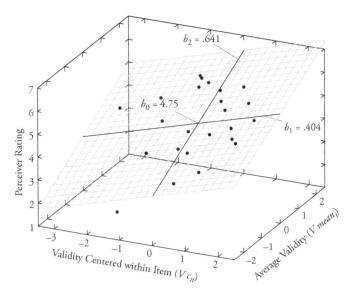

Figure 5.3 Social accuracy decomposition for a single perceiver–target dyad illustrating distinctive accuracy (b_1) and normative accuracy (b_2).

- The scatterplot in Figure 5.1c represents the predictor values for Figure 5.2; the scatterplot in Figure 5.1d represents the predictor values for Figure 5.3.
- Although the predictor values appear different, the regression models presented in Figures 5.2 and 5.3 are fully equivalent in that they make exactly the same predictions for Percy's impressions—the R^2 for each model is precisely the same.
- There is a slight relationship between the average person's personality and Taylor's centered validity scores shown in Figure 5.1d. For specific dyads there may be a positive relationship or there may be a negative relationship. This relationship is, on average across dyads, exactly 0 as the expected correlation between Vc_i and $Vmean_i$ is 0 across targets.

How do we interpret the coefficients b_1 and b_2 from the model illustrated in Figure 5.3? The coefficient b_1 provides an estimate of distinctive accuracy and b_2 an estimate of normative accuracy. *Distinctive accuracy* is the relationship between how the target is different from the average person on the validity measures across a series of items or traits and the perceiver's impressions of the target on those same traits. Distinctive accuracy is an assessment of the accuracy with which the target's unique characteristics are perceived. *Normative accuracy* is the relationship between the average target, assessed across the set the validity measures on a series of items or traits and the perceiver's impressions on

those same traits. For more detail and discussion on normative accuracy see the chapter 15 by Rogers in this handbook. Distinctive and normative accuracy are closely related to Cronbach's (1955) measures of differential and stereotype accuracy, respectively (see Biesanz et al., 2007; Furr, 2008). A more detailed discussion of the interpretation of distinctive and normative accuracy is provided shortly in the context of the full SAM.

The Full Social Accuracy Model

The full utility of SAM is not apparent when considering a single perceiver-target such as Percy's impressions of Taylor. In the present example we know that the distinctive accuracy of Percy's impression of Taylor is $b_1 = 0.404$. How do we interpret this level of accuracy? Is Percy simply perceptive and does she form more accurate impressions than others generally do? In other words, is Percy a good judge? Or is Taylor expressive and makes relevant cues about her personality available to others and thus people generally form more accurate impressions of her? Was there some synergistic effect between Percy and Taylor—for example, they bonded during their first encounter and that led to an especially accurate impression? Are several of these potential explanations responsible for the observed level of distinctive accuracy? After all, these possible explanations are not mutually exclusive. To answer these questions requires much more data than is provided by the present example, where we only have Percy's evaluation of Taylor. The inferential leverage and insight that

SAM provides can only really be achieved when many perceivers and targets are embedded within a much larger research design and each perceiver evaluates multiple targets and each target, in turn, is evaluated by multiple perceivers.

Consider first what a design that has multiple perceivers, each of whom evaluates multiple targets, provides. For each perceiver we can calculate their distinctive accuracy for each of the targets they form impressions of, exactly as in Figure 5.3. Then we can average across targets to get each perceiver's average level of distinctive accuracy across targets (e.g., $\bar{b}_{1_p}$). This is the main effect for perceiver distinctive accuracy as we are essentially conducting a two-way ANOVA with perceivers and targets as the two factors and using $b_{1_{pt}}$ as the observation for each cell in the design. The marginal means for each perceiver, $\bar{b}_{1_p}$, provide an estimate of that perceiver's average level of distinctive accuracy—how good a judge of personality they are averaged across the targets that they formed impressions of. These specific estimates of the average slopes can be useful but difficult to interpret directly. After all, these are estimates that contain measurement error. If we had each perceiver evaluate a new set of targets, or the same targets again if we could wipe their memories and have perceivers repeat the study, we would likely end up with different estimates for each perceiver simply from sampling variability and measurement error. Each perceiver, under this model, has a true level of distinctive accuracy, averaged across targets, that is denoted as u_{1_p} in equation 2. The good judge estimate for each perceiver, $\bar{b}_{1_p} = u_{1_p} + \varepsilon_{1_p}$, where ε_{1_p} represents the error that here is due primarily to sampling variability. Although we would like to determine u_{1_p} for each perceiver, we are not able to determine the "true" good judge score for each perceiver, as that is an unobserved or latent variable. However, even though we cannot estimate each perceiver's "true" good judge score, we can estimate the variance in u_{1_p} across perceivers, denoted as $\tau^2_{1_p}$. This is the random effects variance in perceiver distinctive accuracy slopes and *represents the estimate of individual differences in the good judge*. Although computing this variance can be computationally difficult in certain designs, conceptually it is quite simple. If we calculate the variance across perceivers in the estimates of $\bar{b}_{1_p}$ and then can calculate the sampling variability of $\bar{b}_{1_p}$—the weighted average of the squared standard errors for each of these average regression coefficients—$\tau^2_{1_p}$ is just the difference between these two estimates. Specifically the random effects variance estimate is the extent to which the variability in the good judge estimates ($\bar{b}_{1_p}$)

across perceivers is greater than we would expect to see from sampling variability. If we observe more variability across the good judge estimates, $\bar{b}_{1_p}$, then we would expect to see from sampling variability, this leads to higher estimates of $\tau^2_{1_p}$, the true individual differences in the good judge scores for the group of perceivers in the sample. To illustrate this concept more clearly, Figure 5.4 presents the relationship between V_c and perceiver ratings for 35 perceivers. Each perceiver has their own linear relationship ($\bar{b}_{1_p}$), which represents the observed good judge score estimate for each perceiver, and these clearly differ across perceivers. Even if each perceiver's true level of accuracy was exactly the same, we would expect these plotted lines in Figure 5.4 to vary due to sampling variability.[4] The random effects variance estimate $\tau^2_{1_p}$ represents an estimate of the *excess* variance that we observe across those slopes that cannot be accounted for by sampling variability and therefore reflects the estimate of the actual differences across perceivers in their ability to form accurate judgments.

The same process is used to understand and estimate the extent to which some individuals are more accurately perceived by others. For instance, if we had the impressions of Taylor from a larger set of perceivers beyond simply Percy, we could calculate the average accuracy of these perceivers' impressions of Taylor ($\bar{b}_{1_t}$). If these perceivers also formed impressions of others, we can then examine the average accuracy with which each of these other targets were perceived. The extent to which there is more variability in the average accuracy with which each target is perceived than we would expect to see by simple sampling variability provides the estimate of the target distinctive accuracy random effects, $\tau^2_{1_t}$. This provides an estimate of the true latent variance in the good target—individual differences in expressive accuracy that reflect the accuracy with which their personality is perceived by others.

The good judge and the good target estimates are actually main effects from a two-way between-subjects ANOVA conducted on the regression slopes, each of which is obtained originally from equation 3. When the research design incorporates multiple perceivers evaluating multiple targets we are able to estimate the average accuracy of each perceiver's impressions (the good judge), the average accuracy with which each target is perceived (the good target), and the variance across judges and targets that is not accounted for by sampling variability. These represent estimates of actual true individual differences in interpersonal perceptual accuracy.

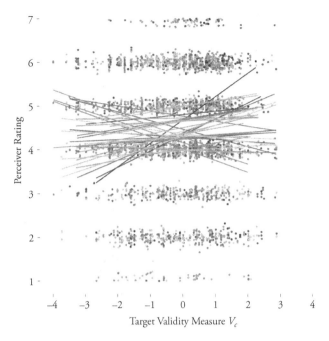

Figure 5.4 Relationship between the target validity measure and perceiver ratings for 35 perceivers. Data on perceiver ratings are slightly jittered to reduce overplotting, and individual linear relationships for each perceiver are plotted.

There is a third component that can be estimated from this model, namely the interaction between perceiver and target, also known as dyadic accuracy. Consider the accuracy of Percy's impression of Taylor. Is this level of accuracy what we would expect given Percy's good judge score as well as Taylor's good target score? Or is it different from what we would expect given those two scores? To what extent is the accuracy of Percy's impression of Taylor greater than, equal to, or less than we would expect given those two general factors? This residual, or difference, between what we observe and what we expect given the two main effects of Percy's good judge score and Taylor's good target score represents the statistical interaction effect in a two-way ANOVA. Across different dyads we can estimate whether there is more variability in the accuracy of impressions than we would expect given the residual accuracy of an impression after subtracting the main effects of the good judge and the good target. This dyadic accuracy assesses the extent to which perceivers form accurate impressions beyond what we would predict from the good judge and good target scores for that dyad.

There are additional random effects that can be also be estimated depending on the design. For instance, group-level effects examine whether the levels of distinctive and normative accuracy are higher for some round-robin groups. As well, it is possible that the average level of dyadic accuracy within pairs

(e.g., the average of distinctive accuracy of Percy's impression of Taylor with Taylor's impression of Percy) might be reliable if some encounters lead to stronger rapport between individuals which then leads both to achieve more accurate impressions.

Empirical Effects

It is helpful to examine the model with real data. Table 5.1 provides the results of the social accuracy model for a set of participants who engaged in a round-robin design where each perceiver met individually with each target for 3 minutes in an unstructured getting-acquainted interaction. Impressions were made on 24 personality items, and validity measures were a composite of self-, peer-, and parental reports.

There are fewer targets than perceivers in the analysis, as validity data were not available for all targets. This set of data is just one part of a larger study (Stewart & Biesanz, 2017) and the data and analytical code in R that produces the results in Table 5.1 are archived and available at http://osf.io/96t8f. All ratings and validity measures were assessed on 1–7 Likert-type scales and the validity measures (centered within items) and the mean validity measure were both grand mean centered. Annotated output from R is provided in the Appendix to illustrate where each of the coefficients discussed in what follows are located within the output.

Table 5.1. Social accuracy model Estimates on 24 Personality Traits and Motives from Impressions Formed During 3-Minute Interactions in a Round Robin. Data and code in R that created this Table are archived at http://osf.io/96t8f.

Parameter	Estimate (SE)
Fixed Effects	
Intercept $\hat{\gamma}_{00}$	4.55 (0.03)***
Distinctive Accuracy $\hat{\gamma}_{10}$	0.14 (0.02)***
Normative Accuracy $\hat{\gamma}_{20}$	0.92 (0.03)***
Random Effects	
Perceiver (Perceptive Accuracy)	
Intercept $\hat{\tau}_{0_p}$	0.31***
Distinctive Accuracy $\hat{\tau}_{1_p}$	0.05**
Normative Accuracy $\hat{\tau}_{2_p}$	0.38***
Target (Expressive Accuracy)	
Intercept $\hat{\tau}_{0_t}$	0.12***
Distinctive Accuracy $\hat{\tau}_{1_t}$	0.24***
Normative Accuracy $\hat{\tau}_{2_t}$	0.19***
Dyad (Interaction Accuracy)	
Intercept $\hat{\tau}_{0_{(pt)}}$	0.13***
Distinctive Accuracy $\hat{\tau}_{1_{(pt)}}$	0.13***
Normative Accuracy $\hat{\tau}_{2_{(pt)}}$	0.21***
Residual SD	1.12
Sample Sizes	
Perceivers	196
Targets	188
Dyads	1100

Note. **$p < .01$ ***$p < .001$. Random effect estimates $\hat{\tau}$ are the estimated standard deviations across the vs from equation 2. All estimates are unstandardized and reflect the 1–7 point scales used in the present study.

• **Fixed Effects.** The fixed effects represent the average relationship across perceivers and targets. These coefficients represent the weighted average two-predictor regression model coefficients across perceivers and targets (e.g., the model illustrated in Figure 5.3) in the data. Specifically, given the grand mean centering of both validity measures:

• $\hat{\gamma}_{00}$ is the predicted rating at the mean validity measure for the average personality item. This is often not of substantive import.

• $\hat{\gamma}_{10}$ is the average distinctive accuracy slope across perceivers and targets. This estimates the average relationship between how the target t is different from the average person on the validity measures across a series of traits and perceiver p's impressions of the target on those same traits. Distinctive accuracy assesses the perceiver's ability to accurately recognize the unique characteristics of the target. In other words, on average in the present sample, how accurate was

this group of perceivers in recognizing the unique traits of this group of targets?

• $\hat{\gamma}_{20}$ is the average normative accuracy slope across perceivers and targets. This estimates the average relationship between the average target on the validity measures across a series of traits and the perceiver's impressions of the target on those same dimensions. In other words, on average in the present sample, how accurate was this group of perceivers in recognizing the average target's personality?

• **Random Effects.** The random effects represent variability attributable to perceiver, targets, and dyads around the fixed effects. For instance, $\hat{\tau}_{1_t}$ represents the standard deviation in distinctive accuracy—good target scores—after adjusting for sampling variability. In the present sample there is substantial variability attributable to all three sources—perceiver, targets, and dyads—for both distinctive and normative accuracy. Tests for random effects can be made by examining the difference in model fits with a restricted model where that specific random effect is removed from the model. This results in a χ^2-test whose p-value should be halved as tests of random variances are one-tailed (see West, Ryu, Kwok, & Cham, 2011, p. 29, for more discussion of this specific issue). However, regardless of the results of null hypothesis significance tests, random effects should be included in the model to maintain appropriate Type I error rates and to allow the ability to generalize to the broader population of potential perceivers and targets. For a more detailed discussion of the importance of modeling random effects, see Judd et al. (2012).

Interpreting Distinctive Accuracy

What is distinctive accuracy, and how do we interpret it? Distinctive accuracy is computed as profile agreement across a series of items or traits, and this is made salient in Figure 5.3. However, the SAM does not just estimate a single dyad's accuracy but instead considers *all* of the data present across perceivers, targets, and domains of personality. Consequently, the fixed effect for distinctive accuracy ($\hat{\gamma}_{10}$ in Table 5.1) provides an estimate of the average trait-level accuracy across traits (i.e., the average relationship between the validity measure and perceiver ratings when analyzed separately for each item in the SAM analysis). Kenny and Winquist (2001) and Biesanz (2010) note that variable and person-centered analyses provide the same overall summary of the available data. Indeed, Allik,

Table 5.2. Percy's Impressions and Target Validation Measures Centered Within Target and Item.

Trait	Target					Trait	Target			
	Taylor	Tom	Terry	Tad			Taylor	Tom	Terry	Tad
sociable	4	6	4	5		*sociable*	−1	1	−1	1
nervous	2	4	5	4		*nervous*	−1	1	−1	1
reliable	3	4	4	2		*reliable*	1	−1	1	−1
intelligent	5	3	6	4		*intelligent*	1	−1	1	−1

      (a) Percy's impressions of four targets.   (b) Validity measures for the four targets.

Borkenau, Hřebíčková, Kuppens, and Realo (2015) provide this mathematical equivalence for correlations, which requires double standardization (both rows and columns). The use of the correlational metric for assessing accuracy obscures the relationship between profile (distinctive accuracy) and the average trait-level relationship, as computing correlations separately for each trait involves different weighting for perceivers and targets on every single trait. Averaging the correlations together across traits then can result in a slightly different estimate than the SAM's distinctive accuracy. Biesanz (2018) provides an empirical demonstration of how the average level of (unstandardized) distinctive accuracy is exactly the same across different units of analysis including trait/item, perceiver, target, and dyad.[5] All that is required to see this exact relationship is (1) center the validity scores within target and (2) weight each regression coefficient (slope) by the variance of the predictor (the variance of the validity measures for each target) to give each coefficient the same weight when computing the average. As an illustration, Table 5.2 provides a small dataset of Percy's impressions of four individuals across four personality traits.

As well, we have those four target individuals' validity measures (centered within traits as well as within targets—that is, the rows and the columns sum to 0). Note that the variance across the validity measures in Table 5.2b is the same for each target, so we do not have to weight each slope to see the equivalence. Table 5.3 provides the univariate regression slopes (unstandardized) for the validity measure predicting Percy's impressions for each trait (across the four targets) as well as for the four targets (across the four traits).

The average across those different analyses is exactly identical. In practice, even if the validity measure is not centered within target, a topic that will be discussed in more depth shortly, and simple unweighted averages are computed, the estimate of the

Table 5.3. Distinctive Accuracy Coefficients (*b*) for Trait and Profile Level Analyses for Percy's Impressions Presented in Table 5.2.

Trait-Level Analysis		Profile Analysis	
Trait	*b*	Target	*b*
sociable	0.75	Taylor	0.50
nervous	0.25	Tom	0.75
reliable	0.25	Terry	0.25
intelligent	1.00	Tad	0.75
Mean	0.5625	Mean	0.5625

average level of distinctive accuracy is often very close to that of the average trait-level relationship.

Given that distinctive accuracy is the same estimate as the average trait-level accuracy relationship, does the choice of analysis matter? Again, why not use a simpler analytical approach such as correlations? Allik (2017) argues strongly that levels of accuracy and agreement are roughly comparable across personality traits (although differences may exist at the very initial impressions). The commonality across traits is the striking factor, and assessing distinctive accuracy maximizes statistical power by aggregating all available data into the analysis. Even if perceivers are better able to distinguish between targets on a particular dimension, or if that is how they develop their judgments and ratings of others when completing assessments in research labs, profile analyses such as distinctive accuracy that average across dimensions is an appropriate analytical strategy and trait-level analyses are not required. Trait level analyses may supplement profile analyses, but care must be taken when interpreting such simple main effects, as more focused accuracy measures are based on less data, are less reliable, and have much less statistical power. Finally, trait-level analyses preclude questions of the good dyad and the good target and do not allow one to directly estimate these individual differences which appear to be robust and strongly consistent across situations and contexts.

In sum, given that distinctive accuracy is calculated as a profile measure across traits/items, how do we interpret this component of accuracy? There are two interpretations of the fixed effect for distinctive accuracy ($\hat{\gamma}_{10}$). First, distinctive accuracy is an assessment of the accuracy with which the target's unique characteristics are perceived, on average across targets. Second, distinctive accuracy is the average trait-level accuracy across the different items that were assessed in the design. Both of these interpretations are correct and are, paradoxically, exactly equivalent interpretations, which has understandably led to some confusion.

Interpreting Normative Accuracy

What is normative accuracy, and how do we interpret it? Normative accuracy is the relationship between the average person's validity measure profile and perceiver impressions. At first glance, this would seem to indicate that this component of interpersonal accuracy would reflect knowledge of the average person. Complicating this interpretation is the extraordinarily strong relationship between the average person's personality profile and social desirability. For instance, Rogers and Biesanz (2015) reports that the relationship between the average personality profile and average ratings of social desirability across the 44-item BFI (see John & Srivastava, 1999) is $r(42) = 0.86$, which has 95% CI [0.75, 0.92]. This substantial relationship is well known and quite expected, as socially desirable behaviors are more common than socially undesirable behaviors (e.g., see Edwards, 1957). Thus normative accuracy is strongly associated with the positivity of impressions and can be interpreted as a measure of positivity. However, positivity and normative knowledge can be separated out and estimated separately even when they are correlated as high as $r = 0.90$, as is described next under extensions of the SAM.

Extensions of the SAM and Additional Components

There are a number of extensions to the basic SAM analysis that one could make. The basic SAM analysis provides information on average levels of accuracy and individual, dyadic, and potential group differences (random effects) around these average levels. However, the question of interest may be on understanding and predicting these random effects. These questions of interest are addressed by including these predictors as moderators in equation 2 as shown in equation 4 for moderator M, which could be a measure of the perceiver or target's personality, a dyadic variable, or a code that captures group differences in an experimental design.

$$\begin{aligned} \gamma_{0pt} &= \gamma_{00} + \gamma_{01}M + u_{0p} + u_{0t} + u_{0_{(pt)}} \\ \gamma_{1pt} &= \gamma_{10} + \gamma_{11}M + u_{1p} + u_{1t} + u_{1_{(pt)}} \\ \gamma_{2pt} &= \gamma_{20} + \gamma_{21}M + u_{2p} + u_{2t} + u_{2_{(pt)}} \end{aligned} \quad (4)$$

For more details on interpreting interactions with continuous and categorial variables, see Aiken and West (1991) and West, Aiken, and Krull (1996). In brief, the interpretation of the coefficients for distinctive and normative accuracy depend on the scaling of the moderator variable M. Specifically, γ_{10} and γ_{20} are the model-implied estimates of distinctive and normative accuracy, respectively, when $M = 0$. The coefficients γ_{11} and γ_{21} are the relationship between the moderator variable and distinctive and normative accuracy, respectively. For instance, a positive value of γ_{11} indicates that as the moderator variable increases, so does the level of distinctive accuracy.

• **Perceiver and target effects.** A number of studies have examined characteristics of the perceiver and target that are related to distinctive and normative accuracy including Colman, Letzring, and Biesanz (2017); Letzring (2015); Human and Biesanz (2011a); and Human, Mignault, Biesanz, and Rogers (2019). When designing studies to examine perceiver and target effects, the critical sample size in the design for determining statistical power is the number of perceivers or targets. If examining the relationship between target self-esteem and distinctive accuracy, for instance, then the number of targets is the critical sample size. Increasing the number of perceivers per target or the number of items in the analysis will both help increase the reliability of the estimates of the good target, but the functional sample size is the number of targets.

• **Dyadic effects**. Measures related to the dyad can be included in the SAM and examined as potential moderators. For instance, the provided dataset includes a rating of how *likeable* the perceiver thought each target was. For dyadic measures it can be helpful to separate out perceiver and target main effects on the dyadic measure first and then use the residual component to examine dyadic relationships. In other words, what is the average *likeable* rating for each perceiver (across targets) and the average *likeable* rating for each target (across perceivers)? These are interesting moderators to examine in their own right, but to examine dyadic effects, these main effect measures need to be separated to isolate the actual dyadic measure. For instance, how much does Percy like Taylor above and beyond Percy's general tendency to like others as well as how much Taylor tends to be liked by others? For additional examples of these analyses, see Biesanz et al. (2011) for assessments of the awareness of the accuracy of one's impressions and Lorenzo, Biesanz, and Human (2010) for perceptions of the attractiveness of the target. The Appendix provides code and annotated output for these analyses.

• **Experimental studies**. Conducting SAM analyses within the context of an experimental design is straightforward (e.g., see Biesanz & Human, 2010; Human, Biesanz, Parisotto, & Dunn, 2012). All that is required is including a variable that codes group membership (e.g., a dummy or indicator code) as a moderator. For a discussion of group codes in regression analysis, see West et al. (1996).

There are additional decompositions or extensions to the SAM that one can employ. These include assumed similarity, within target centering of the validity measure, and separating social desirability from normative knowledge.

• **Assumed Similarity**. Assumed similarity is the association between how a perceiver sees themselves and how they view others. In other words, to what extent does one see oneself in others? By including the perceiver's self-reported personality profile in equation 1, it is possible to assess the impact of assumed similarity on the perceiver's impressions of others as well as directly estimate the extent to which there are individual differences in assumed similarity. Kenny and Acitelli (2001) provide an excellent overview of these questions as well as the need to partial the overlap between the self-report and the validity assessments. Examples of using SAM to address questions of assumed similarity can be found in Human and Biesanz (2011b, 2012).

• **Validity Measure**. Even after centering the validity measures for each target within items there may be differences between targets on their means on Vc_{ti} across items. As effects can vary across levels of analyses—the average relationship within a group can be different than the relationship between

groups—it may be worth examining whether such effects exist within a particular sample. This is equivalent to examining within-group centering (e.g., Enders & Tofighi, 2007) and requires centering the validity score within target. For instance, if we compute the mean for each target's set of centered (within item) validity scores, $\overline{Vc_t}$, then centering within targets (*cwt*) is computed as $Vcwt_{ti} = Vc_{ti} - \overline{Vc_t}$. Then both $Vcwt_{ti}$ and $\overline{Vc_t}$ would be included in the SAM analysis as predictors along with $Vmean_i$. Note that one can estimate the random effects for $\overline{Vc_t}$ across perceivers, but not targets, as there is no variance on this measure across targets. For SAM analyses based on a small set of items, this approach may yield results that are of interest. However, as the set of items becomes larger and is well balanced with respect to the normative means (i.e., many infrequently endorsed items along with endorsed items), then there should be relatively little useful information on the target's personality contained in the measure $\overline{Vc_t}$. This between-target's accuracy score will also be difficult to interpret and less reliable than the average distinctive accuracy coefficient $\hat{\gamma}_{10}$, as it is based on much less data as the maximum number of data points is the number of targets in the analysis.

• **Separating Normative Knowledge from Social Desirability**. As discussed earlier, the normative component in equation 1 is composed of two parts: the influence of normative knowledge and positivity on impressions. Even though the normative personality profile is extremely highly correlated with social desirability across personality trait items, it is possible to disentangle these two influences and assess their impact separately. Indeed, these two components of interpersonal accuracy are distinct and are associated with different processes (e.g., see Rogers & Biesanz, 2019; Rogers & Biesanz, 2015; Wessels, Zimmermann, Biesanz,& Leising,2020; Zimmermann, Schindler, Klaus, & Leising, 2018). To estimate normative knowledge and social desirability (positivity) simultaneously alongside distinctive accuracy, all that is required is to include the estimate of social desirability of each item within equation 1 as another predictor that can vary randomly across perceivers, targets, and dyads. However, for the same reasons that centering the validity measures within items is recommended for interpretational reasons, a similar centering process is recommended in this context as well. Specifically, one should either subtract the social desirability estimate from the normative mean profile or use the residuals from the univariate regression analysis where social desirability is used to predict the normative validity profile. This creates orthogonal measures between the (residual) normative profile and social desirability and allows for a cleaner interpretation of the results. This process creates orthogonal scores between social desirability and the (residual) normative profile and attributes the overlap between these two assessments to social desirability. The residual normative profile then represents the impact of normative knowledge on impressions, and the relationship of social desirability on impressions represents the positivity of impressions.

Modeling Notes

An excellent introduction, overview, and discussion of multilevel models can be found in West et al. (2011). What follow are several design and modeling notes that are specific to the SAM.

• **Sample sizes.** There are three primary sample sizes of interest in the SAM: items, perceivers, and targets. Larger sample sizes for all three dimensions are beneficial for different reasons. More items provide a better estimate of the accuracy relationship for a single perceiver–target dyad. Increasing the number of perceivers and targets is needed to obtain more reliable estimates of the good judge and good target, respectively. For instance, in a design where each perceiver evaluates five targets, increasing the number of targets would likely have a very beneficial impact on statistical power, as each perceiver's good judge estimate is made from the average of only five regression coefficients, which vary strongly across targets and dyads, as well as from sampling variability. Increasing the number of targets that each perceiver evaluates will have a strong impact on the reliability of each perceiver's good judge score. Similar results occur for the target—the more perceivers that evaluate each target, the greater the reliability of the good target estimates that result from the analysis. Thus, even though it is feasible to run the SAM (or an SRM analysis) based on a round robin with 4 participants, a round robin with 12 participants provides much more reliable estimates and greater statistical power than 3 round robins with 4 participants each. It is not important in the SAM to keep the round robins the same size, as multilevel modeling software easily accommodates unbalanced designs.

• **Reverse coding.** When creating composites or scales it is necessary to have all of the items coded in the same direction so that larger values reflect higher quantities of the construct of interest. There is indeed a temptation to reverse code items in the cleaned datafiles. This is a temptation that should be resisted. Reverse coding items in the SAM can create interpretational problems and does not solve any. If all of the items are coded such that higher values indicate more socially desirable levels of that item/trait, then the average value of each target's validity measure ($\overline{Vc_t}$) will reflect social desirability and social desirability/positivity will be reflected within the estimate of distinctive accuracy unless further partitioning is done to remove that component. For that reason, the ideal set of items for the SAM are fairly balanced across the spectrum of social desirability—roughly half are undesirable and half desirable—and items are *not* reverse coded. This will also increase the statistical power for analyses examining positivity and normative components.

• **Estimating the normative validity profile.** In some designs there may only be a small number of targets (e.g., 7–10). In general this is not recommended as there are substantial individual differences in the good target and a small number of targets in a design will result in unstable estimates of accuracy (i.e., large standard errors) and a limited ability to generalize. However, in such circumstances, how should one determine the average validity profile when there are only a few targets? Although one could base the normative mean on the specific set of targets examined within a study, means based on a relatively few number of observations have a large amount of uncertainty associated with those estimates. If the targets are selected from a larger set and can reasonably be considered exchangeable, using the normative means from that larger sample will provide more reliable estimates of the mean validity profile and increase the reliability of the predictors in the SAM.

Critiques of the SAM

The primary difficulty with the SAM is that it is more complicated than traditional correlational accuracy measures. Not only are the analytical techniques more difficult but also they require more intensive research designs and data collection, as multiple perceiver, targets, items, and validation measures are needed. In short, it is difficult to collect the data and requires more advanced statistical expertise. These barriers are not insurmountable, and more sophisticated statistical analyses and expertise are quickly becoming necessary to conduct research across diverse areas of psychology. For observational research, simple research designs and analytical strategies can often only address simple questions. More complex and nuanced questions require more sophisticated research designs and analyses.

An indirect critique of the SAM was recently presented by Hall et al. (2018), who provide an empirical examination of several profile analyses and compare those measures to trait-level analyses. The conclusion is "Different ways of measuring individual differences in personality judgment accuracy are not conceptually and empirically the same, but rather represent distinct abilities that rely on different judgment processes" (p. 220). The theoretical argument is that judging a profile of traits within a person (e.g., is Jane more *reliable* than she is *talkative?*) is a different process and skill than distinguishing between individuals on a single trait (e.g., is Jane more *reliable* than Jake and Jasper?). Consequently these different processes should require different summary statistics—one should pick the appropriate tool to address the research question of interest. In contrast, I argue that the distinction between trait and profile analyses is misleading. Regardless of whether or not there are different judgmental processes at play in making intra- versus interindividual judgments, for understanding accuracy of individual differences trait-level analyses and distinctive profile accuracy are exactly related (*distinctive* accuracy is the average trait-level accuracy, as shown in Table 5.3) and provide the same insight and statistical summary. In contrast, other profile measures such as normative accuracy and positivity do provide different insights as those measures are lost in trait-level correlational analyses. Hall et al.'s (2018) analyses examine distinctive accuracy along with other profile measures that do not separate out the normative component which render them hard to interpret. Although the basic theoretical premise of Hall et al. (2018) may be true, that requires different assessments of perceiver impressions, not different statistical techniques for assessing accuracy.

A more direct critique of the SAM comes from Allik et al. (2016) and Allik (2017), who argue that individual differences in accuracy components such as perceivers and targets are modest at best and the field of personality psychology should focus instead on average levels of accuracy. For this, correlational methods suffice and such data are much easier to collect and examine. In support of this argument, Allik et al. (2016) examine a very large representative sample of the population of Estonia to argue that differences in accuracy across perceivers and targets are essentially trivial. Although Allik's (2017) argument is primarily theoretical, the ultimate resolution of this question and the social accuracy model will be derived from empirical evidence on the utility of the SAM and the insights that it provides.

Conclusion

The proof of the pudding is famously in the eating. The utility of the SAM rests on the existence of substantial individual differences in components related to interpersonal accuracy. Researchers continue to provide empirical evidence that the good target is a core and strong individual difference as it correlates across contexts, domains, and situations (Human & Biesanz, 2013; Human, Mignault, et al., 2019; Human, Rogers, & Biesanz, 2018; Stewart & Biesanz, 2017). As well, building on earlier work on the good judge (e.g., Letzring, 2008), Rogers and Biesanz (2019) demonstrated across several large sample studies how there are substantial individual differences in the assessment of the good judge, but only when forming impressions of the good target. As this empirical body of evidence grows, it is becoming clearer that there are strong individual differences in the good judge, the good target, and the good pair (dyad) that need to be modeled and better understood. For these and similar questions, analytical models such as the SAM that are designed to directly assess and model those individual differences are needed.

Appendix

Annotated R code and output. The code and data are available at http://osf.io/96t8f. The SAM was estimated using R version 3.5.1 and lme4 version 1.1–19. These data are just a small part of a larger project and represent 24 items from the BFI collected from a round-robin design. All ratings were on 1–7 Likert-type scales.

Variables:

PID: Perceiver ID variable. First 3 digits correspond to the session, last 2 digits to the participant within the session. For instance, PID == 21308 is participant 08 in session 213.

TID: Target ID variable created like PID. For instance, TID == 21307 is participant 07 in session 213.

RATING: Perceiver rating (impression) of the target on ITEM i

ITEM: 24 BFI Items that correspond to Human, Biesanz, Finseth, Pierce, and Le (2014) Appendix A.

LIKEABLE: How likeable the perceiver rated the target to be. TSELFR: Target's self-report on ITEM i. TPEER: Target's peer-report on ITEM i. TPARENT: Target's parental-report on ITEM i.

Data Preparation and Variable Creation

Loading needed libraries for this code and reading in the datafile. options(scipen=99) helps to suppress scientific notation. Note that using lmer in R (as well as nlme, which is another package for multilevel models), requires a long datafile where each rating has its own row in the datafile. See Wickham (2014) for more details on and tools for creating long datafiles.

```
library(psych)
library(cwhmisc)
library(lme4)
library(optimx)
library(lmerTest)
options(scipen=99) #suppresses scientific notation
sam <- read.table(file="SAM_Chapter_Data.csv",sep=',', header=TRUE)
```

Creating unique DYAD values for each perceiver-target pairing. Note that the example used in the chapter for Percy and Taylor (Figures 5.1–5.3) corresponds to sam$DYAD == 2130821305 which is PID == 21308 and TID == 21305. Taylor's perception of Percy would correspond to sam$DYAD == 2130521308.

```
sam$DYAD <- sam$PID*100000 + sam$TID
```

The target validation measure V is the composite of self, peer, parent responses based on available data.

```
sam$V <- rowMeans(cbind(sam$TSELFR, sam$TPEER, sam$TPARENT), na.rm=TRUE)
```

Computing the average validity profile based on the present data. The remove.dup.rows() function from the cwhmisc library reduces the tid dataset so that each target has only one observation per item. Duplicate rows are removed. Without doing this reduction, targets in larger round robins appear more frequently in the sam dataset and have greater influence on the mean. This reduction ensures that each target contributes only 1 observation when calculating the means. The validity means (the average target's validity measures) for the 24 item is in the dataset vmeans. The merge() function merges the sam and vmeans datasets, matching on ITEM.

```
tid <- remove.dup.rows(as.data.frame(cbind(sam$ITEM, sam$TID, sam$V)))
```

```
colnames(tid) <- c("ITEM","TID","V")
tid <- as.data.frame(tid)
vmeans <- matrix(NA, nrow=24, ncol=2)
for (i in 1:24){
    =vmeans[i,1] <- i
    vmeans[i,2] <- mean(tid$V[tid$ITEM==i], na.rm=TRUE)
}
vmeans <- as.data.frame(vmeans)
colnames(vmeans)< c("ITEM","VMEAN")
sam <-merge(sam, vmeans, by="ITEM")
```

Centering within items and grand mean centering. Vc is the validity measure for each target, centered within items, and VMEANc is the average target's validity measure, grand mean centered. It is good practice to examine descriptives after making and transforming variables to ensure that variable means, ranges, minimums and maximums are appropriate.

```
sam$Vc <- sam$V - sam$VMEAN
sam$VMEANc <- sam$VMEAN
- mean(sam$VMEAN, na.rm=TRUE)
describe(sam, skew=FALSE)
```

BASE SOCIAL ACCURACY MODEL CODE USING LMER

Different optimizers in lmer can sometimes aid in convergence. In the present model with the dyadic random effects, the model will not converge with the default optimizer. The present example does converge with the nlminb optimizer from the optimx package. However, the model takes several minutes to estimate on older computers, so be patient. For degrees of freedom and approximate t-tests, the lmerTest package will provide a decent approach. Note that the the 1 in the formula is a placeholder for the intercept in the model as formulae in R follow Wilkinson notation (see Wilkinson & Rogers, 1973). If the 1 in the formula is not present, the intercept will still be estimated, but it is good practice to be explicit about every element that one is estimating in a model.

```
model <- lmer(RATING ~ 1 + Vc + VMEANc
+ (1 + Vc + VMEANc|PID)← coefficients vary by perceiver (PID)
+ (1 + Vc + VMEANc|TID)← coefficients vary by target (TID)
+ (1 + Vc + VMEANc|DYAD),← coefficients vary by dyad (DYAD)
data = sam,
control = lmerControl(optimizer ='optimx', optCtrl=list(method='nlminb'))) summary(model)
```

CONDENSED AND ANNOTATED OUTPUT FOR THE BASE SOCIAL ACCURACY MODEL

Linear mixed model fit by REML. t-tests use Satterthwaite's method

Formula: RATING ~ 1 + Vc + VMEANc +
(1 + Vc + VMEANc | PID) +
(1 + Vc + VMEANc | TID) +
(1 + Vc + VMEANc | DYAD)
Data:sam

Random effects:

Groups	Name	Variance	Std. Dev.	
DYAD	(Intercept)	0.017703	0.13305	$\leftarrow \hat{\tau}_{0_{(p')}}$
	Vc	0.017954	0.13399	$\leftarrow \hat{\tau}_{1_{(p')}}$
	VMEANc	0.044475	0.21089	$\leftarrow \hat{\tau}_{2_{(p')}}$
PID	(Intercept)	0.098240	0.31343	$\leftarrow \hat{\tau}_{0_{p}}$
	Vc	0.002236	0.04728	$\leftarrow \hat{\tau}_{1_{p}}$
	VMEANc	0.144775	0.38049	$\leftarrow \hat{\tau}_{2_{p}}$
TID	(Intercept)	0.015428	0.12421	$\leftarrow \hat{\tau}_{0_{t}}$
	Vc	0.059361	0.24364	$\leftarrow \hat{\tau}_{1_{t}}$
	VMEANc	0.037047	0.19248	$\leftarrow \hat{\tau}_{2_{t}}$
Residual		1.263935	1.12425	$\leftarrow \hat{\sigma}$

Note: Correlations among the random effects are not shown here but are provided in the full output.

Number of obs:26417, groups: DYAD, 1100; PID, 196; TID, 188

Fixed effects:

		Estimate	Std. Error	df	t value	Pr(>|t|)
(Intercept)	$\hat{\gamma}_{00}$	4.54836	0.02573	233.308	176.761	< 0.00001
Vc	$\hat{\gamma}_{10}$	0.13756	0.02012	183.09	6.836	< 0.00001
VMEANc	$\hat{\gamma}_{20}$	0.92137	0.03273	252.44	28.151	< 0.00001

MODERATOR ANALYSES

The following code illustrates how to prepare the data and conduct moderator analyses in the social accuracy model. Using the perceiver's assessment of how likeable the target is, three new measures are created to illustrate perceiver, target, and dyadic moderators. These new variables are (1) each perceiver's average level of liking for targets, (2) the average level that each target is liked by different perceivers, and (3) the residual level of liking that a perceiver has for a given target after accounting for the average (main) effects of perceiver and target. To determine these three measures we first must predict ratings of LIKEABLE with perceiver (PID) and target (TID) as random factors. This is done in order to extract estimates of the main effects of perceiver and target on LIKEABLE.

```
LikeModel <- lmer(LIKEABLE ~ 1 + (1 |PID) +
(1 |TID), data = sam) summary(LikeModel)
```

The model-implied grand mean of LIKEABLE is the intercept from LikeModel. fixef() provides the fixed effect coefficient estimates (e.g., $\hat{\gamma}_0$) from the model which, here, provides that grand mean as there only is one fixed effect in this model.

```
fixef(LikeModel)
```

Extracting and saving the perceiver main effect for LIKEABLE. This code extracts the random effects PID from the LikeModel model and saves it as a dataframe. Note that the values of PID are the row names when we run the as.data.frame(ranef(LikeModel)$PID) code so we explicitly need to save the rownames as a variable to use as the matching variable to correctly merge back with the sam dataset. PID.LIKE contains the measure for each perceiver on their predicted average level of liking across targets. The ranef() function extracts the empirical Bayes estimates of the random effects from a multilevel model. These are centered around the fixed effect (i.e., grand mean centered) and represent estimates that are "pre-shrunk" back to grand mean to account for regression to the mean. See Casella (1985) for a somewhat accessible introduction and Morris and Lysy (2012) for a somewhat more technical overview of these estimates.

```
PID.LIKE <-as.data.frame(ranef(LikeModel)
$PID)
    colnames(PID.LIKE)<-c("PID.LIKEABLE")
    PID.LIKE$PID <-as.numeric(rownames(PID.
LIKE))
```

Extracting and saving the target main effect for LIKEABLE. This code for the target (TID) parallels that of the perceiver to extract the target main effect estimates for LIKEABLE—how much each target is liked, on average, across perceivers.

```
TID.LIKE <- as.data.frame(ranef(LikeModel)
$TID)
    colnames(TID.LIKE)<-c("TID.LIKEABLE")
    TID.LIKE$TID <-as.numeric(rownames(TID.
LIKE))
```

Merging PID.LIKE and TID.LIKE with the sam dataset. Each row of the sam dataset will have the variables PID.LIKEABLE and TID.LIKEABLE. As this is a long dataset, these values will be the same for each dyad's 24 ratings. For instance, for PID==21308 and TID==21305, there are 24 rows in the dataset that correspond to ITEM 1 to 24. Each of these rows will have the same value of PID. LIKEABLE and TID.LIKEABLE.

```
sam <- merge(sam, PID.LIKE, by="PID")
    sam <- merge(sam, TID.LIKE, by="TID")
```

Creating the residual dyadic measure of liking. For instance, this measure for dyad 2130821305 is how much perceiver 21308 likes target 21305 after accounting for perceiver 21308's general tendency to like targets (the perceiver's score on PID. LIKEABLE) as well as target 21305's general tendency to be liked by perceivers (the target's score on TID.LIKEABLE). Recall that fixef(LikeModel) is the estimate of the grand mean of likeable—the estimated average level of likeable across perceivers and targets. The code below grand mean centers DYADIC.LIKE as we are substracting out the grand

mean. Recall that PID.LIKEABLE and TID. LIKEABLE are both grand mean centered (around fixef(LikeModel)), so DYADIC.LIKE is a residual and grand mean centered.

```
sam$DYADIC.LIKE <- sam$LIKEABLE -
fixef(LikeModel) - sam$PID.LIKEABLE -
sam$TID.LIKEABLE
```

PERCEIVER, TARGET, AND DYADIC MODERATOR MODELS

The first moderator model examines whether the main effect of perceiver liking moderates distinctive and normative accuracy. To examine this question we estimate the interaction that the moderator has with Vc and with VMEANc. Note that R will automatically create the lower-order terms (Vc, VMEANc, and PID.LIKEABLE), so we do not need to include them in the model explicitly. They will be estimated and appear in the output.

```
pid.like.model <- lmer(RATING ~ 1 + Vc*PID.
LIKEABLE + VMEANc*PID.LIKEABLE
    + (1 + Vc + VMEANc|PID)
    + (1 + Vc + VMEANc|TID)
    + (1 + Vc + VMEANc|DYAD),
        data = sam,
        control = lmerControl(optimizer
='optimx',
        optCtrl=list(method='nlminb')))
    summary(pid.like.model)
```

This second model examines whether the main effect of target liking (TID.LIKEABLE) moderates distinctive and normative accuracy.

```
tid.like.model <- lmer(RATING ~ 1 + Vc*TID.
LIKEABLE + VMEANc*TID.LIKEABLE
        + (1 + Vc + VMEANc|PID)
        + (1 + Vc + VMEANc|TID)
        + (1 + Vc + VMEANc|DYAD),
        data = sam,
        control = lmerControl(optimizer
='optimx', optCtrl=list(method='nlminb')))
    summary(tid.like.model)
```

Finally, the third model examines whether the dyadic (residual) effect of liking moderates distinctive and normative accuracy. The annotated and condensed output for this model is provided in what follows. Note that this model does result in a "failure to converge" warning message. The perceiver variance for distinctive accuracy ($\hat{\tau}_{1_p}$) is very close to 0, and random effects estimates near this boundary will often lead to warning messages, as variances cannot be negative and the model might have difficulty determining the best estimate of a parameter that is near a boundary. If the random effects for PID in the model are changed from $(1 + Vc + VMEANc|PID)$ to $(1 + VMEANc|PID)$, which constrains the estimate of $\hat{\tau}_{1_p}$ to be 0, the model converges without issue and the other parameter estimates are essentially unchanged. This provides confidence that we can safely ignore the warning message and interpret the output of the full model that follows. My experience using the SAM has been that random effects with the DYAD (e.g., $(1 + Vc + VMEANc|DYAD)$) are often difficult to estimate with fewer than 300 perceivers and targets in a round-robin design and the model becomes stable only with ~ 500 participants in a round robin. This is why I had to change the estimator from the default setting. That solution does not always work for small to moderately sized samples as in the present example. The main effects for good judge and good target (PID and TID, respectively), are generally easily estimated with smaller sample sizes.

```
dyad.like.model <- lmer(RATING ~ 1 +
Vc*DYADIC.LIKE + VMEANc*DYADIC.LIKE
    + (1 + Vc + VMEANc|PID)
    + (1 + Vc + VMEANc|TID)
    + (1 + Vc + VMEANc|DYAD),
    data = sam,
    control = lmerControl(optimizer
='optimx', optCtrl=list(method='nlminb')))
    summary(dyad.like.model)
```

CONDENSED AND ANNOTATED OUTPUT FOR THE DYADIC LIKING AS A MODERATOR IN THE SAM

Linear mixed model fit by REML. t-tests use Satterthwaite's method

Formula: RATING ~ 1 + Vc *DYADIC.LIKE + VMEANc *DYADIC.LIKE
    $(1 + Vc + VMEANc | PID) +$
    $(1 + Vc + VMEANc | TID) +$
    $(1 + Vc + VMEANc | DYAD)$
Data: sam

Random effects:

Groups	Name	Variance	Std. Dev.	
DYAD	(Intercept)	0.011971	0.10941	$\leftarrow \hat{\tau}_{0_{(pt)}}$
	Vc	0.015368	0.12397	$\leftarrow \hat{\tau}_{1_{(pt)}}$
	VMEANc	0.019884	0.14101	$\leftarrow \hat{\tau}_{2_{(pt)}}$
PID	(Intercept)	0.098985	0.31462	$\leftarrow \hat{\tau}_{0_p}$
	Vc	0.001626	0.04032	$\leftarrow \hat{\tau}_{1_p}$
	VMEANc	0.146740	0.38307	$\leftarrow \hat{\tau}_{2_p}$
TID	(Intercept)	0.016226	0.12738	$\leftarrow \hat{\tau}_{0_t}$
	Vc	0.059752	0.24444	$\leftarrow \hat{\tau}_{1_t}$
	VMEANc	0.040885	0.20220	$\leftarrow \hat{\tau}_{2_t}$
Residual		1.265642	1.12501	$\leftarrow \hat{\sigma}$

Note: Correlations among the random effects are not shown here but are provided in the full output.

Number of obs: 26417, groups: DYAD, 1100; PID, 196; TID, 188 Fixed effects:

		Estimate	Std. Error	df	t value	Pr(>|t|)
(Intercept)	$\hat{\gamma}_{00}$	4.54814	0.02578	236.02	176.444	< 0.00001
Vc	$\hat{\gamma}_{10}$	0.13751	0.02003	181.55	6.864	< 0.00001
DYADIC.LIKE	$\hat{\gamma}_{01}$	0.09407	0.01160	764.84	8.110	< 0.00001
VMEANc	$\hat{\gamma}_{20}$	0.92101	0.03282	262.33	28.060	< 0.00001
Vc:DYADIC.LIKE	$\hat{\gamma}_{11}$	−0.02729	0.01070	555.04	−2.550	0.011
DYADIC.LIKE:VMEANc	$\hat{\gamma}_{21}$	0.19781	0.01400	752.75	14.132	< 0.00001

Interpretation of the coefficients from this model, given that all predictors are grand mean centered.

- $\hat{\gamma}_{00}$ is the intercept. Recall that *all* of the variables in this analysis are grand mean centered. The intercept is the predicted mean rating across perceivers, targets, and items and often not of substantive interest.
- $\hat{\gamma}_{10}$ is the level of distinctive accuracy when dyadic liking = 0, which is the average level of liking. Thus this estimate represents the average level of distinctive accuracy in the present sample. Note how close it is to the estimate from the base SAM analysis without the moderator.
- $\hat{\gamma}_{01}$ is the relationship between dyadic liking and perceiver ratings. Higher levels of liking lead to higher ratings (averaged across the items), when Vc and VMEANc both are at 0.
- $\hat{\gamma}_{20}$ is the level of normative accuracy when dyadic liking = 0. Thus this estimate represents an estimate of the average level of normative accuracy in the present sample and, like $\hat{\gamma}_{10}$, is quite close to the estimate from the base SAM analysis without the moderator.
- $\hat{\gamma}_{11}$ is the interaction between dyadic liking and distinctive accuracy. When a perceiver likes a target more, distinctive accuracy is lowered. Note that given dyadic liking is centered within perceivers and targets, this represents the average within-perceiver and target effect.
- $\hat{\gamma}_{21}$ is the interaction between dyadic liking and normative accuracy. When a perceiver likes a target more, normative accuracy is substantially increased. Again, note that given dyadic liking is centered within perceivers and targets, this represents the average within-perceiver and target effect.

Notes

1. The terms "judge" and "perceiver" are used interchangeably in this chapter.
2. In the empirical dataset described shortly and available at http://osf.io/96t8f, this example corresponds to perceiver (PID) 21308 and target (TID) 21305.
3. The original examples of the SAM in Biesanz (2010) did not center within item but instead used partialling, as in Figure 5.2. However, subsequent research that we have conducted has always centered within items as this greatly increases the interpretability of b_2 as in Figure 5.3.
4. For fully balanced designs, the random effects variance can be calculated by hand. However, designs in interpersonal accuracy are generally not balanced and the estimation of random effects is solved iteratively. The present explanation is provided solely for broad conceptual understanding.
5. The data, materials, and code in R to reproduce that exact equivalence is archived and available at http://osf.io/5u6hw.

References

Aiken, L. S., & West, S. G. (1991). *Multiple regression: Testing and interpreting interactions*. Newbury Park, CA: Sage Publications.

Allik, J. (2017). The almost unbearable lightness of personality. *Journal of Personality, 86*, 109–123. doi:10.1111/jopy.12329

Allik, J., Borkenau, P., Hřebíčková, M., Kuppens, P., & Realo, A. (2015). How are personality trait and profile agreement related? *Frontiers in Psychology, 6*, 1–11. doi:10.3389/fpsyg.2015.00785

Allik, J., de Vries, R. E., & Realo, A. (2016). Why are moderators of self-other agreement difficult to establish? *Journal of Research in Personality, 63*, 72–83. doi:10.1016/j.jrp.2016.05.013

Biesanz, J. C. (2010). The social accuracy model of interpersonal perception: Assessing individual differences in perceptive and expressive accuracy. *Multivariate Behavioral Research, 45*, 853–885. doi:10.1080/00273171.2010.519262

Biesanz, J. C. (2018). Interpersonal perception models. In V. Zeigler-Hill & T. K. Shackelford (Eds.), *The SAGE handbook of personality and individual differences* (pp. 519–534). Thousand Oaks, CA: Sage Publications. doi:10.4135/9781526451163.n24

Biesanz, J. C., & Human, L. J. (2010). The cost of forming more accurate impressions accuracy-motivated perceivers see the personality of others more distinctively but less normatively than perceivers without an explicit goal. *Psychological Science, 21*, 589–594. doi:10.1177/0956797610364121

Biesanz, J. C., Human, L. J., Paquin, A.-C., Chan, M., Parisotto, K. L., Sarracino, J., & Gillis, R. L. (2011). Do we know when our impressions of others are valid? Evidence for realistic accuracy awareness in first impressions of personality. *Social Psychological and Personality Science, 2*, 452–459. doi:10.1177/1948550610397211

Biesanz, J. C., & West, S. G. (2000). Personality coherence: Moderating self–other profile agreement and profile consensus. *Journal of Personality and Social Psychology, 79*, 425–437. doi:10.1037/0022-3514.79.3.425

Biesanz, J. C., West, S. G., & Graziano, W. G. (1998). Moderators of self–other agreement: reconsidering temporal stability in personality. *Journal of Personality and Social Psychology, 75*, 467–477. doi:10.1037/0022-3514.75.2.467

Biesanz, J. C., West, S. G., & Millevoi, A. (2007). What do you learn about someone over time? The relationship between length of acquaintance and consensus and self-other agreement in judgments of personality. *Journal of Personality and Social Psychology, 92*, 119–135. doi:10.1037/0022-3514.92.1.119

Bollen, K. A. (2002). Latent variables in psychology and the social sciences. *Annual Review of Psychology, 53*, 605–634. doi:10.1146/annurev.psych.53.100901.135239

Borkenau, P., Mauer, N., Riemann, R., Spinath, F. M., & Angleitner, A. (2004). Thin slices of behavior as cues of personality and intelligence. *Journal of Personality and Social Psychology, 86*, 599–614. doi:10.1037/0022-3514.86.4.599

Casella, G. (1985). An introduction to empirical Bayes data analysis. *The American Statistician, 39*, 83–87. doi:10.2307/2682801

Colman, D. E., Letzring, T. D., & Biesanz, J. C. (2017). Seeing and feeling your way to accurate personality judgments: The moderating role of perceiver empathic tendencies. *Social Psychological and Personality Science, 8*, 806–815. doi:10.1177/1948550617691097

Connelly, B. S., & Ones, D. S. (2010). An other perspective on personality: Meta-analytic integration of observers' accuracy and predictive validity. *Psychological Bulletin, 136*, 1092–1122. doi:10.1037/a0021212

Cronbach, L. J. (1955). Processes affecting scores on "understanding of others" and "assumed similarity." *Psychological Bulletin, 52*, 177–193. doi:10.1037/h0044919

Davis, M. H., & Kraus, L. A. (1997). Personality and empathic accuracy. In W. J. Ickes (Ed.), *Empathic accuracy* (pp. 144–168). New York, NY: Guilford Press.

Edwards, A. L. (1957). *The social desirability variable in personality assessment and research*. New York, NY: Dryden Press.

Enders, C. K., & Tofighi, D. (2007). Centering predictor variables in cross-sectional multilevel models: A new look at an old issue. *Psychological Methods, 12*, 121–138. doi:10.1037/1082-989X.12.2.121

Epstein, S. (1983). Aggregation and beyond: some basic issues on the prediction of behavior. *Journal of Personality, 51*, 360–392. doi:10.1111/j.1467-6494.1983.tb00338.x

Funder, D. C. (1995). On the accuracy of personality judgment: A realistic approach. *Psychological Review, 102*, 652–670. doi:10.1037/0033-295X.102.4.652

Funder, D. C. (1999). *Personality judgment: A realistic approach to person perception*. San Diego, CA: Academic Press.

Funder, D. C., & Colvin, C. R. (1997). Congruence of others' and self-judgments of personality. In R. Hogan, J. Johnston, & S. Briggs (Eds.), *Handbook of personality psychology* (pp. 617–647). San Diego, CA: Academic Press.

Furr, R. M. (2008). Framework for profile similarity: Integrating similarity, normativeness, and distinctiveness. *Journal of Personality, 76*, 1267–1316. doi:10.1111/j.1467-6494.2008.00521.x

Gosling, S. D., Rentfrow, P. J., & Swann, W. B. (2003). A very brief measure of the Big-Five personality domains. *Journal of Research in Personality, 37*, 504–528. doi:10.1016/s0092-6566(03)00046-1

Hall, J. A., Back, M. D., Nestler, S., Frauendorfer, D., Mast, M. S., & Ruben, M. A. (2018). How do different ways of measuring individual differences in zero-acquaintance personality judgment accuracy correlate with each other? *Journal of Personality, 86*, 220–232. doi:10.1111/jopy.12307

Hartshorne, H., & May, M. A. (1928). *Studies in the deceit*. New York, NY: Macmillan.

Human, L. J., & Biesanz, J. C. (2011a). Target adjustment and self-other agreement: Utilizing trait observability to disentangle judgeability and self-knowledge. *Journal of Personality and Social Psychology, 101*, 202–216. doi:10.1037/a0023782

Human, L. J., & Biesanz, J. C. (2011b). Through the looking glass clearly: Accuracy and assumed similarity in well-adjusted individuals' first impressions. *Journal of Personality and Social Psychology, 100*, 349–364. doi:10.1037/a0021850

Human, L. J., & Biesanz, J. C. (2012). Accuracy and assumed similarity in first impressions of personality: differing associations at different levels of analysis. *Journal of Research in Personality, 46*, 106–110.

Human, L. J., & Biesanz, J. C. (2013). Targeting the good target an integrative review of the characteristics and consequences of being accurately perceived. *Personality and Social Psychology Review, 17*, 248–272. doi:10.1177/1088868313495593

Human, L. J., Biesanz, J. C., Finseth, S. M., Pierce, B., & Le, M. (2014). To thine own self be true: Psychological adjustment promotes judgeability via personality–behavior congruence.

Journal of Personality and Social Psychology, 106, 286–303. doi:10.1037/a0034860

Human, L. J., Biesanz, J. C., Parisotto, K. L., & Dunn, E. W. (2012). Your best self helps reveal your true self: Positive self-presentation leads to more accurate personality impressions. *Social Psychological and Personality Science, 3*, 23–30.

Human, L. J., Mignault, M.-C., Biesanz, J. C., & Rogers, K. H. (2019). Why are well-adjusted people seen more accurately? The role of personality-behavior congruence in naturalistic social settings. *Journal of Personality and Social Psychology, 117*, 465–482. doi:10.1037/pspp0000193

Human, L. J., Rogers, K. H., & Biesanz, J. C. (2018). *Is expressive accuracy a core individual difference? The cross-contextual consistency of being transparent*. Manuscript under review.

John, O. P. & Srivastava, S. (1999). The Big Five trait taxonomy: History, measurement, and theoretical perspectives. In L. A. Pervin & O. P. John (Eds.), *Handbook of personality: Theory and research* (Vol. 2, pp. 102–138). New York, NY: Guilford.

Judd, C. M., Westfall, J., & Kenny, D. A. (2012). Treating stimuli as a random factor in social psychology: A new and comprehensive solution to a pervasive but largely ignored problem. *Journal of Personality and Social Psychology, 103*, 54–69. doi:10.1037/a0028347

Kenny, D. A. (1994). *Interpersonal perception: A social relations analysis*. New York, NY: Guilford Press.

Kenny, D. A., & Acitelli, L. K. (2001). Accuracy and bias in the perception of the partner in a close relationship. *Journal of Personality and Social Psychology, 80*, 439–448. doi:10.1037/0022-3514.80.3.439

Kenny, D. A., & La Voie, L. (1984). The social relations model. *Advances in Experimental Social Psychology, Volume 18*, 141–182.

Kenny, D. A., & Winquist, L. (2001). The measurement of interpersonal sensitivity: Consideration of design, components, and unit of analysis. In J. A. Hall & F. J. Bernieri (Eds.), *Interpersonal sensitivity: Theory and measurement* (pp. 265–302). Mahwah, NJ: Erlbaum.

Kenrick, D. T., & Funder, D. C. (1988). Profiting from controversy: Lessons from the person-situation debate. *American Psychologist, 43*, 23–34. doi:10.1037/0003-066X.43.1.23

Letzring, T. D. (2008). The good judge of personality: characteristics, behaviors, and observer accuracy. *Journal of Research in Personality, 42*, 914–932. doi:10.1016/j.jrp.2007.12.003

Letzring, T. D. (2015). Observer judgmental accuracy of personality: Benefits related to being a good (normative) judge. *Journal of Research in Personality, 54*, 51–60. R Special Issue. doi:10.1016/j.jrp.2014.05.001

Lorenzo, G. L., Biesanz, J. C., & Human, L. J. (2010). What is beautiful is good and more accurately understood: Physical attractiveness and accuracy in first impressions of personality. *Psychological Science, 21*, 1777–1782. doi:10.1177/0956797610388048

Mischel, W. (1968). *Personality and assessment*. New York, NY: Wiley.

Morris, C. N., & Lysy, M. (2012). Shrinkage estimation in multilevel normal models. *Statistical Science, 27*, 115–134. doi:10.1214/11-sts363

Moskowitz, D. S., & Schwarz, J. C. (1982). Validity comparison of behavior counts and ratings by knowledgeable informants. *Journal of Personality and Social Psychology, 42*, 518–528. doi:10.1037/0022-3514.42.3.518

Navarro, D. (2018). *Learning statistics with R: A tutorial for psychology students and other beginners (version 0.6)*. University of New South Wales. Sydney, Australia. Retrieved from http:// compcogscisydney.org/learning-statistics-with-r/

Nave, C. S., Feeney, M. G., & Furr, R. M. (2018). Behavioral observation in the study of personality and individual differences. In V. Zeigler-Hill & T. K. Shackelford (Eds.), *The SAGE handbook of personality and individual differences* (pp. 317–340). Thousand Oaks, CA: Sage Publications.

Rogers, K. H., & Biesanz, J. C. (2015). Knowing versus liking: Separating normative knowledge from social desirability in first impressions of personality. *Journal of Personality and Social Psychology, 109*, 1105–1116. doi:10.1037/a0039587

Rogers, K. H., & Biesanz, J. C. (2019). Reassessing the good judge of personality. *Journal of Personality and Social Psychology, 117*, 186–200. doi:10.1037/pspp0000197

Soto, C. J., & John, O. P. [Oliver P.]. (2017). The next Big Five Inventory (BFI-2): Developing and assessing a hierarchical model with 15 facets to enhance bandwidth, fidelity, and predictive power. *Journal of Personality and Social Psychology, 113*, 117–143. doi:10.1037/pspp0000096

Stewart, J., & Biesanz, J. C. (2017, May). *Good targets in text: Individual differences in distinctive expressive accuracy through writing samples*. Poster session presented at the meeting of the American Psychological Society. Boston, MA.

Wessels, N. M., Zimmermann, J., Biesanz, J. C., & Leising, D. (2020). Differential associations of knowing and liking with accuracy and positivity bias in person perception. *Journal of Personality and Social Psychology, 118*, 149–171 doi:10.1037/pspp0000218

West, S. G., Aiken, L. S., & Krull, J. L. (1996). Experimental personality designs: Analyzing categorical by continuous variable interactions. *Journal of Personality, 64*, 1–48. doi:10.1111/j. 1467-6494.1996.tb00813.x

West, S. G., Ryu, E., Kwok, O.-M., & Cham, H. (2011). Multilevel modeling: current and future applications in personality research. *Journal of Personality, 79*, 2–50. doi:10.1111/j.1467-6494.2010.00681.x

Wickham, H. (2014). Tidy data. *Journal of Statistical Software, 59*. doi:10.18637/jss.v059.i10

Wilkinson, G. N., & Rogers, C. E. (1973). Symbolic description of factorial models for analysis of variance. *Applied Statistics, 22*, 392. doi:10.2307/2346786

Zimmermann, J., Schindler, S., Klaus, G., & Leising, D. (2018). The effect of dislike on accuracy and bias in person perception. *Social Psychological and Personality Science, 9*, 80–88. doi:10.1177/1948550617703167

PART 2

Moderators of Accuracy

Characteristics of the Judge That Are Related to Accuracy

Douglas E. Colman

Abstract

There exists a substantial body of work, dating back nearly a century, exploring individual differences in the ability to accurately judge the personality traits and characteristics of other people. While the picture of the good judge of others' personality remains somewhat abstract, there are some characteristics that consistently bear out as important, such as intelligence and emotional stability. Overall, there are five characteristics that have been investigated as correlates of this ability: (1) cognitive functioning, (2) personality, (3) motivation, (4) gender, and (5) behavior. This chapter opens with an introduction to this area of scholarship, a brief coverage of the conceptual framework, and the definitions and measurement of accuracy. A description of the research within each of the five areas is then provided. Next, some theoretical considerations for ongoing research on the good judge are illuminated. Finally, this chapter concludes with some worthy directions for future research related to the good judge of personality.

Key Words: accuracy, personality, trait, cognitive functioning, intelligence, motivation

One fundamental aspect of life is the social interactions we have with other people. As a result of these interactions we learn, fall in love, set and work toward goals, and decide to undertake countless other activities. With considerable reliance on our interpersonal experiences to navigate the complex world within which we live, there should be no doubt as to the importance of accurately coming to understand those around us. An important part of this is making judgments of others' personalities, their enduring characteristics that can be used to make predictions of future thoughts, feelings, and behaviors. Our perceptions of those around us—physically, virtually, or otherwise—affect how we think about and organize our world and influence our own actions (Schmid Mast & Hall, 2018).

The results of our encounters with others provide social feedback as to our interpersonal effectiveness and are even related to our well-being (Letzring, 2015). We use this information to adjust and refine our patterns of interaction with others. Successive trials of

engaging in this ubiquitous social process add up drastically over time, and are important not only for understanding but also for continuing to successfully navigate our social world.[1] Thus, the accumulation of these interactions—or *social-at-bats*—in which we attempt to make accurate judgments of others' personalities, can have real and compounding consequences (Funder, 2018, March).

As with most things in life—such as academic pursuits, salesmanship, and athletics—some people are better at accurately inferring the personality characteristics of other individuals. This is precisely the focus of this chapter—to provide a synthesis of the literature that has evaluated personality judgment abilities. Before we start, I first provide a description of the process by which accurate judgments come to be made and then briefly conceptualize accuracy and its measurement. Next, I take a more in-depth look at five characteristics that have been explored in the search for understanding the good judge of personality: (1) cognitive factors, (2) personality, (3) motivation, (4) gender, and (5) behavior. Finally, I wrap up by illuminating some theoretical considerations for ongoing work and intriguing directions for future research aimed toward increasing understanding of the *good judge*.

Model for the Occurrence of Judgment Accuracy

The realistic accuracy model (RAM) was developed to address the critical question of *when*, rather than *if*, judgments are accurate (Funder, 1999). This model specifies the process that *must occur* for accurate judgments of others to be made (see chapter 2 by Letzring & Funder in this handbook for a comprehensive review of the RAM). The judgment process moves through four distinct stages—relevance, availability, detection, and utilization—each of which must be successfully navigated in an ordered manner. Specifically, the RAM requires the person who is being judged to make *relevant* information about themselves *available* so such information can be *detected* and then *utilized* by the individual making the judgment. Evident from this simple description, there are two focal persons in the judgment process: the person being judged, whom I refer to as the *target*, and the person making judgments, whom I refer to as the *judge*.[2]

These four stages of the RAM are related multiplicatively; if any of the stages is not at least partially completed, accuracy becomes zero. Said differently, only when there is a substantial degree of success in all four stages—on the part of both the *target* and the *judge*—will a high level of accuracy be achieved (Funder, 1995). For this reason, much research has been directed toward moderator variables that make accuracy more or less likely by interacting with one or more stages of the RAM. Such moderator variables are placed into four discrete categories—properties of *traits*, quantity and quality of *information*, characteristics of the *target*, and characteristics of the *judge*. Most often the term *good* precedes each moderator (e.g., good trait), as the focus of research has been the correlates and/or causal mechanisms of enhanced accuracy (Funder, 1993).

Accuracy as a Measurable Construct

There have been a variety of approaches to the computation of accuracy (Funder & West, 1993). A large portion of personality judgment accuracy research has implemented a self–other agreement analytical strategy that uses either the summation of difference scores or correlation coefficients (based on different items for a single target or the same item across targets) as the metric for overall accuracy. While these appear to be straightforward measures, Cronbach (1955) demonstrated that such indices are composed of multiple perceptual components and recommended that researchers should go beyond singular indicators of accuracy such as overall accuracy correlations. The two most central components identified were stereotype accuracy and differential accuracy. Stereotype accuracy, now commonly termed normative accuracy or normativity, refers to the ability to judge the generalized or *statistically average* target, which is dependent on the judge's understanding of the "relative frequency or popularity of possible responses" on the characteristic(s) of interest (Cronbach, 1955, p. 179). Differential accuracy, now commonly referred to as distinctive accuracy, represents judges' ability to perceive targets' traits relative to the normative level, as well as the ability to order targets accurately on each attribute (Biesanz, 2017; Furr, 2008; Zebrowitz, 1990). This is what most people think of when talking about accuracy—the ability to judge others' unique levels and ordering for a given set of characteristics (e.g., personality traits).

The measurement of accuracy necessitates some objective standard or criterion to which the judgment is compared. In concise and simplistic terms, judgment accuracy is the "relation between what is perceived and what is" (Funder, 1999, p. 3). For the purpose of this chapter (and this edited handbook), the focus is on personality—enduring patterns of thoughts, feelings, and behaviors. Because of the abstract, intangible nature of personality—compared to more "objective" characteristics of people such as height, weight, and hair color—there has been much disagreement and theoretical argument surrounding what is the best measure or criterion of *what is* (Kruglanski, 1989). Most often, the criterion has been a self-assessment of the characteristic of interest. That said, people are not always the most accurate judges of their own personality (John & Robins, 1993; Vazire, 2010). Therefore, composites combining self-reports with behavioral assessments, clinical ratings, and/or ratings by close acquaintances (e.g., family, significant others, long-term friends) have been used as accuracy criteria when computing accuracy, and provide a more *realistic* understanding of an individual's personality (Funder, 1995; Kolar, Funder, & Colvin, 1996; Vazire, 2010).

A Perpetual Question: What Makes Good Judges?

Due to much theorizing, many analytical innovations, and myriad empirical investigations that have taken place over the last century, we know that people have the impressive ability to make judgments of others that are largely accurate in both description of personality and prediction of behavior (e.g., Allport, 1937; Ambady, Hallahan, & Rosenthal, 1995; Back, Schmukle, & Egloff, 2008; Barrick, Patton, & Haugland, 2000; Borkenau & Liebler, 1993; Estes, 1938; Kolar et al., 1996). Some researchers have gone so far as to propose that making accurate impressions is a rather simple task at which most people are proficient (Allik, de Vries, & Realo, 2016; Haselton & Funder, 2006). If true, however, this would *not* render moot the core perpetual question within this domain of scholarship: "What are the defining characteristics of good judges of personality?" This is because some individuals might still be better than others in this ability, and such a possibility is important to fully explore.

Indeed, there are numerous characteristics of judges that have been linked to the achievement of greater levels of accuracy (e.g., Bernstein & Davis, 1982; Biesanz, 2010; Colman, Letzring, & Biesanz, 2017; Funder, 1980, 1987, 1995; Harackiewicz & DePaulo, 1982; Letzring, 2008; Lippa & Dietz, 2000; McLarney-Vesotski, Bernieri, & Rempala, 2011), and a review of this expansive literature has centered around five core characteristics of judges: (1) cognitive functioning, (2) personality, (3) motivation, (4) gender, and (5) behavior. Even with such thematic organization, this moderator of accuracy, of the four outlined by the RAM, has seen the least consistency in results. In the following sections I unpack each of these judge characteristics, first by outlining how each should theoretically relate to personality judgment accuracy, then synthesizing the extant empirical literature, and finally in providing a brief take-away for each.

Judge's Level of Cognitive Functioning

The first cluster of variables—cognitive functioning—are cerebral in nature and involve the higher order mental processes essential for the gathering and processing of information. For the current purposes, discussion will focus on intelligence, attention, and memory. Intelligence has been widely discussed as the most consistent characteristic that differentiates good judges from those who are less skilled (Allport, 1937; Christiansen, Wolcott-Burnam,

Janovics, Burns, & Quirk, 2005; Funder, 1999; Lippa & Dietz, 2000). In particular, greater dispositional intelligence should aid in the understanding of how different personality traits are likely to manifest through behaviors exhibited by targets (Allport, 1937; Christiansen et al., 2005). Attention is another cognitive process that should be significant in aiding good judges at generating accurate judgments. To be accurate in assessments of targets, judges need to, at minimum, actively attend to relevant information made available by the targets (Cardy & Kehoe, 1984). This is because inattention will result in fewer cues being detected, which, even at high levels of correct utilization of cues on the part of the judge, would cause lower levels of accuracy to be achieved (Funder, 1995). Likely working in tandem with attention processes, memory also plays a role in achieving accuracy. Regardless of the amount of cues detected, if one does not have sufficient ability to recall and utilize information about a target, accuracy will remain elusive (Christiansen et al., 2005).

INTELLIGENCE

There are many ways that intelligence can be conceptualized—such as verbal, social, and spatial abilities—but at the apex of them all is general mental ability (GMA; Jensen, 1991). General mental ability denotes the ability to reason, use logic, and forecast behaviors and outcomes from complex and sometimes abstract information, and has been shown to predict a wide array of life outcomes (Gottfredson, 1997; Kuncel, Hezlett, & Ones, 2004). According to the RAM, GMA should be positively related to the utilization stage of the judgment process. Indeed, a meta-analysis found this intelligence–accuracy link for judgments being made on a wide range of target aspects—such as affective and nonaffective states, personality traits, roles and status, as well as prediction of actual target behaviors—with an average effect of $r = 0.23$ (Davis & Kraus, 1997).

The proposition that intelligence is positively correlated with accuracy of personality judgments is clearly tenable; empirical work spans back to the early 20th century. Adams (1927) discovered that the ability to rate others was positively correlated ($rs > 0.15$) with being both mentally bright and quick, and with a tendency for observation. While not a surprising finding, the tendency for observation to be related to judgmental ability is in line with the importance of the detection stage of the RAM. In a similar vein, Vernon (1933) found that abstract intelligence and scholastic performance were positively related to the ability to judge strangers (rs = 0.31 and 0.16, respectively). On the contrary, a study using multiple methods for assessing accuracy was unable to substantiate earlier findings, as the relation between intelligence and accuracy for targets was not significant (r = 0.04; Estes, 1938), but several methodological differences may explain this finding.[3] That said, a later investigation during this early research era found that accuracy—operationalized as a composite of (1) judging targets' self-reported personality and (2) predictions of targets' actual behavior—was positively associated with intelligence (r = 0.30; Cline, 1955).

Expanding on these early works, many studies have explored the intelligence–accuracy link for a variety of relationships and in different contexts. For instance, both GMA and verbal intelligence were significantly positively correlated with personality judgment accuracy for same-sex twin siblings, even after controlling for similarity among twin pairs (rs = 0.12 and 0.13, respectively; Harris, Vernon, & Jang, 1999). Furthermore, a series of studies measuring intelligence using the Wonderlic Personnel Test have returned mixed results. Scores were found to be related to accuracy of personality judgments made based on nonverbal cues of strangers (Lippa & Dietz, 2000) and for judging acquaintances (r = 0.24), but not when judging targets engaged in an interview (r = 0.13; Christiansen et al., 2005). However, a more recent study did not replicate the relation between judges' intelligence scores on that test and overall accuracy (r = −.01; Letzring, 2008).

In addition to GMA, the narrower construct of dispositional intelligence has also been found to be related to accuracy of personality judgments (r = 0.52; Christiansen et al., 2005). Dispositional intelligence is very similar to the construct of emotional intelligence (see Mayer, Roberts, & Barsade, 2008), but rather than a focus on emotions, emphasis is placed on thoughts and knowledge about the interrelations among behavior, traits, and situations (Christiansen et al., 2005). De Kock, Lievens, and Born (2015) have fully replicated the work of Christiansen and colleagues (2005) within the field of industrial and organizational psychology. Specifically, it was found that dispositional intelligence was significantly related to judges' level of accuracy in assessments of targets in the domain of communication and people management, and this connection was stronger for dispositional intelli-

gence than GMA (r = 0.34 vs. 0.20). Relatedly, it has been found that both emotional intelligence and dispositional intelligence were significantly related to distinctively accurate judgments of extraversion and, the notoriously difficult to judge, neuroticism (Premack, 2011). In sum, while there is mixed evidence of a link between general intelligence and accuracy, more narrow intellectual functions do appear positively associated with personality judgment accuracy.

ATTENTION

Attentiveness to the target, whether in-person, while observing audio-video recordings, or evaluating social media profiles, should play a role in the accuracy of judgments. This makes theoretical sense, as inattention would result in fewer cues being detected (Funder, 1995), which even for high levels of cue utilization would likely result in lower levels of accuracy. In support of this position, Cardy and Kehoe (1984) found that selective attention was positively and significantly related to distinctive accuracy for hypothetical instructors' classroom behavior based on vignettes.[4] Not surprisingly the differences in accuracy found between those high versus low in selective attention were greater when cognitive demands were high rather than low. In a similar vein, another investigation also demonstrated the importance of attentional demands of the situation in which the judgment process occurs (Biesanz, Neuberg, Smith, Asher, & Judice, 2001). Specifically, distracted judges—those making judgments in situations with high attentional load—were more prone to committing errors and achieving lower personality judgment accuracy. Alternatively, a more recent study investigated the role of being an active and selective, compared to a passive but attentive, perceiver of information available on the social media platform of Facebook (Waggoner, Smith, & Collins, 2009). It was found that judges choosing the quantity and type of information they viewed (i.e., paid attention to) achieved similar levels of accuracy on judgments of political affiliation, religiosity, and the Big Five personality traits as did judges who viewed the same information but without an active role in selecting which cues to see. Taken together, these three studies provide evidence for the importance of attention to judgmental ability, and that it is more about actually attending to the information (i.e., cues) than taking an active role in selection of informational cues one evaluates.

MEMORY

Another important factor is the working memory of judges. Even if detection of information is rather high, judges must possess an ability to recall the behaviors and expressions of targets, and then consider how those might be indicative of targets' stable personality attributes. In sum, memory capabilities are thought to be critical for proper utilization of cues (Christiansen et al., 2005; Fletcher, Danilovics, Fernandez, Peterson, & Reeder, 1986). While not a direct look at this connection, research has demonstrated that working memory is positively related to making accurate judgments based on rules or a set of criteria (Hoffmann, von Helversen, & Rieskamp, 2014). For instance, a rules-based judgment process to what makes a job attractive might include evaluation of criteria such as salary, workplace collegiality, technology, vacation time/sick leave, and so forth. In short, executing such rule-based strategies while forming judgments involves inhibiting irrelevant cue information and attending to cues that are important, which is precisely what is suggested by the utilization stage of the RAM. Aside from this study, research evaluating the relation between accuracy of personality judgments and judges' memory capability is virtually nonexistent. In fact, I am only aware of one such study (Krzyzaniak, 2018), which looked directly at this relation as part of a larger investigation of effects of cognitive functioning and physical fitness on personality judgment ability. The results of this study failed to demonstrate that memory, specifically recall of target behaviors, was significantly predictive of either normative (d = 0.03) or distinctive accuracy (d = 0.12). However, this single test of the relation between memory and accuracy, which was embedded in a larger study, should not inhibit further scholarly attention. Rather, given the theoretical role of memory to the judgment process and the current scarcity of research, I assert that this is an area of scholarship ripe for empirical exploration.

Judge's Own Personality

The second cluster of correlates is the personality characteristics of judges themselves, and is very likely the most extensively investigated. Studies have found links between judgmental ability and a multitude of favorable personality characteristics such as higher levels of agreeableness, psychological adjustment, social skills, greater tendencies for perspective-taking and empathy, and lower levels of neuroticism (Beer & Watson, 2008; Christiansen et al., 2005; Colman et al., 2017; Hall, Andrzejewski,

& Yopchick, 2009; Human & Biesanz, 2011; Letzring, 2008; Taft, 1955). For this chapter, three aspects of personality are considered as characteristics of good judges and thus reviewed here: (1) Big Five personality traits, (2) the empathic response, and (3) psychological adjustment.

BIG FIVE FACTORS

The five factor model is the most widely accepted taxonomy of personality traits (John, Naumann, & Soto, 2008), and encompasses the traits of openness to experience, conscientiousness, extraversion, agreeableness, and neuroticism (the opposite of emotional stability). Such characteristics of individuals have important consequences in life (Ozer & Benet-Martinez, 2006), including our ability to understand others' nonverbal behavior, emotions, honesty, and personality (Davis & Kraus, 1997; Hall, Andrzejewski, et al., 2009). Given that a large percentage of research studies require judgments of targets' personality to be made on measures of the Big Five traits, it is not surprising that such characteristics of judges themselves have been evaluated as potential correlates of accuracy. In general, however, there is not a large degree of consistency in how these traits are related to judgmental ability.

The relation between judges' openness to experience and their judgment accuracy has been marked by mixed findings. Early research found that qualities related to openness (such as interests in arts and drama) were related to a judge's accuracy (Estes, 1938; Vernon, 1933). More recent research had a similar finding with openness being positively associated (r = 0.23) with accuracy for judging targets' self-reported trait-relevant behavioral tendencies (Christiansen et al., 2005). On the other hand, a different study found this trait to be negatively associated with judges' overall accuracy (r = −.20), and with the accuracy of their judgments of targets' neuroticism in particular (r = −0.30; Lippa & Dietz, 2000). It is possible that such findings might also be dependent on gender of the judge, as Kolar (1995) found that openness was related to judgmental ability for females, but not males. In a related vein, it was also found that good male, but not necessarily female, judges tend to be extraverted and emotionally stable (Kolar, 1995). But for extraversion, too, there are mixed results. For example, Vernon (1933) found that good judges of others tend to be less sociable (i.e., less extraverted)—but this study did not disentangle the potential effect of gender.

More consistent findings, at least with regard to the direction of the relationship to judgmental ability, are found for the traits of agreeableness, conscientiousness, and neuroticism. Controlling for gender, individuals who were more agreeable and conscientious and less neurotic made more accurate judgments of personality from first-person text passages of responses to various contextual prompts (Hall, Goh, Schmid Mast, & Hagedorn, 2016). In a related vein, a review of early investigations supported the idea that emotional stability is a key feature of judgmental ability (Taft, 1955). Other research has found that judges' agreeableness was positively associated with both overall accuracy and normative accuracy in judging another's personality, but not associated with distinctive accuracy (Letzring, 2008, 2015).

EMPATHIC RESPONSE

The conscious process of attempting to envision others' points of view, termed perspective-taking, is a highly valued skill for positive interpersonal relations (Davis, 1996; Riggio, Tucker, & Coffaro, 1989); so too is empathy, the extension of this practice to include the matching of the thoughts and emotions of the other. Much research has shown positive relations between these tendencies and interpersonal sensitivity (Hall, Andrzejewski, et al., 2009), but there is relatively little work exploring such relations with personality judgment accuracy. That which does exist, and especially more recent work, seems to paint a rather consistent picture. An early study explored the relation of perspective-taking with accuracy in matching target self-descriptions using a forced-choice accuracy paradigm, for which a significant positive relation was found (Bernstein & Davis, 1982). However, this link was also mediated by length of observation, in that the combination of short observation lengths with high perspective-taking resulted in lower accuracy. Thus, it was argued that cognitively placing one's self in the shoes of the target, if undertaken too soon after meeting or observing someone, can perhaps hinder accuracy. This is because doing so has the potential to draw attention away from the target person, and instead place focus on imagining one's self in the given scenario.

The previous study aside, there have been several recent studies that have demonstrated the positive link between judgmental accuracy and the empathic responses of perspective-taking, empathy, fantasy, and personal distress. First, the ability to judge personality from passages of typed text was significantly associated with the tendency for empathic concern and marginally related to perspective-taking (Hall,

Goh, et al., 2016). In another investigation, a reliable link was found between the empathic tendencies and normative accuracy, distinctive accuracy, and assumed similarity (Colman et al., 2017). Specifically, each empathic tendency was related to distinctive accuracy, while perspective-taking, empathic concern, and fantasy, but not personal distress, were correlated with normative accuracy and judges' projection of themselves in perceptions of others (i.e., assumed similarity). Building on this latter work, another investigation was undertaken to explore the causal direction of the empathy–accuracy link (Colman, 2018).[5] While experimental evidence for directionality of the empathy–accuracy relation was not found, this study replicated the prior studies in that empathic concern, perspective-taking, and fantasy correlated with normative accuracy; however, only personal distress was significantly related to distinctive accuracy. More importantly, though, this study found that state perspective-taking and state empathy correlated positively with personality judgment accuracy.

Reviewing each of these investigations through the lens of the RAM, empathic tendencies seem to be correlated with judgmental ability through the detection and utilization stages (Colman et al., 2017). First, the processes of perspective-taking and exhibiting empathy are active endeavors, which likely increase the attentiveness of judges to targets, thereby increasing the detection of relevant cues. Second, these practices are likely to help judges better utilize cues through increased appreciation of the others' current physical context and their affective state of mind. In sum, possessing greater empathic tendencies—being able to cognitively and emotionally step into others' shoes—is both a theoretically reasonable (within the framework of RAM) and rather intuitive (lay persons often claim it promotes insight—*if you could only see from my point of view*) characteristic of good judges of personality.

PSYCHOLOGICAL ADJUSTMENT

It stands to reason that well-adjusted individuals— marked by qualities such as high life satisfaction, self-esteem, and general well-being, and less depressive symptomology—are likely to experience less social anxiety and be able to focus their efforts on the detection and utilization of informational cues, thus allowing for greater accuracy. Indeed, it has been found that greater purpose in life was positively related to overall accuracy ($r = 0.18$; Letzring, 2008). However, subsequent research has indicated that psychological adjustment is not related to distinctive accuracy of personality judgments (Human & Biesanz, 2011; Letzring, 2015). Alternatively, it might also be the case that psychological adjustment is related to greater normative accuracy, as increased outward focus during social interactions would provide a better understanding of what people are like on average. Indeed, recent work provides evidence that psychological adjustment is positively related to normative accuracy (Human & Biesanz, 2011; Krzyzaniak, 2018; Letzring, 2015). Based on the available research, the take-away message is that psychological adjustment is not the most central characteristic of good judges, but having high levels should not be inhibitory to one's judgmental ability. In fact, well-adjusted judges are likely to be more adept at creating comfortable interactions in which targets would make more relevant cues available (Letzring, 2008), a point that is further elucidated in a later section of this chapter, "Behaviors of Judges."

Motivation of the Judge

The third of the five individual characteristics of judgmental accuracy is motivation. According to the RAM, motivation should affect the detection and utilization stages of the judgment process; yet findings are mixed. On the affirmative, using a novel five-item measure of motivation to be accurate, one investigation demonstrated that a rather strong link exists between this characteristic and both normative and distinctive accuracy for judgments of video-recorded targets (ds = 0.36 and 0.64, respectively; Letzring & Colman, 2018). In several other studies using videotaped targets, however, motivation was not found to be related to accuracy. In one of the studies (Hall, Blanch, et al., 2009; Study 5) both monetary (participants were told the top percent of judges would receive compensation) and ego-relevant (participants were told skill for judging other people is related to positive attributes, such as intelligence) manipulations were tested. The monetary manipulation resulted in a nonstatistically significant decrease (d = −.36) in the accuracy of judgments of personal status and trait dominance compared to a control condition. Moreover, the ego-relevant manipulation showed no effects on accuracy (d = 0.00). Adding to this, two other studies manipulating ego relevance reported in Hall, Blanch, et al. (2009) failed to impart differences for levels of accuracy for judgments of extraversion (d = 0.01; Study 6) and judgments of trait dominance (d = 0.01; Study 7).

These video-observation studies notwithstanding, information-gathering behaviors by judges is another important avenue by which motivation can impact the level of accuracy achieved for targets with whom judges directly interact. For example, one study found that judges who were motivated to create accurate impressions were more succinct and direct in their questioning and were also less biased while gathering information from targets (Neuberg, 1989). To this end, Neuberg and his colleagues have also discovered that expectancies on the part of judges led targets to behave in line with those expectations; that is, the judge created a self-fulfilling prophecy (Judice & Neuberg, 1998; Neuberg, 1989; Neuberg & Fiske, 1987). For instance, in simulated interviews, judges with a motivation to confirm negative expectations of targets asked fewer questions and were less encouraging.[6] This behavior resulted in targets' confirmation of the negative expectations (Judice & Neuberg, 1998). Alternatively, interviewers with the goal of being accurate overcame the negative expectations by asking more questions and being more encouraging of targets. Adding a wrinkle to these empirical findings, Biesanz et al. (2001) found that attentional demands for judges moderate the effect of accuracy motivation. Specifically, distracted judges are more prone to expectancy effects in their questioning of targets as well as to making judgments that are in line with those expectancy effects.

Lastly, a few studies have investigated the effect that explicit accuracy goals have on personality judgment accuracy. In one such study, it was explained to the experimental group of participants, "it is important that you form the most accurate impressions possible for each person" (Biesanz & Human, 2010, p. 591). The group receiving this explicit goal (as compared to a no-goal group) achieved a significantly greater level of distinctive accuracy, but also had a reduced level of normative accuracy. In another study (Colman, 2015), an attempt was made to replicate and extend these findings. In particular, this investigation sought to independently increase either normative accuracy without decrement to distinctive accuracy, or increase distinctive accuracy without a decrement to normative accuracy. Ultimately, neither the direct replication nor the extension of the study was successful. However, an important take-away was that none of the explicit goals produced a reduction in judgmental accuracy. In sum, the relation between motivation and personality judgment accuracy seems to be rather complex. That said, it seems harm is unlikely to result from attempting to induce motivation for accuracy (with the exception of offering a monetary incentive).

Gender of the Judge

The fourth characteristic, which has been a recurring theme in this area of scholarship, is the gender of judges. It has been speculated that gender differences in judgmental ability might arise due to a motivation to adhere to accepted gender roles (e.g., women being more socially sensitive; Graham & Ickes, 1997; Ickes, Gesn, & Graham, 2000). To this point, research cutting across a wide range of content domains such as lie detection, personality traits, thoughts and feelings, intelligence, and dominance has relatively consistently revealed that women have a slight advantage over men when it comes to interpersonal accuracy (Hall, Gunnery, & Horgan, 2016). Compared to other characteristics that have been widely explored (e.g., nonverbal behavior, judgments of affective states), however, investigations on gender differences in personality judgment ability is limited. Additionally, a large proportion of such research comes from secondary or supplementary analyses in studies designed to answer other research questions, although some investigations seeking primarily to explore gender differences do exist.

For instance, one such study demonstrated that women provide more positive ratings of targets than men, although this effect was rather small (rs = 0.10 to 0.25; Winquist, Mohr, & Kenny, 1998). Even so, the effect was consistent across each of the Big Five traits at zero-acquaintance, short-term acquaintance, and long-term acquaintance. Expanding on this *female positivity effect*, a more recent study sought to explore the role of gender on the normative and distinctive accuracy of first impressions of personality (Chan, Rogers, Parisotto, & Biesanz, 2011). Paralleling previous research (Marcus & Lehman, 2002; Winquist et al., 1998), female judges in this sample consistently formed more positive (i.e., normatively accurate) impressions of targets.

The results have been mixed, however, among studies chiefly concerned with the ability to accurately judge the unique characteristics of others (i.e., distinctive accuracy). Much research has failed to find any gender differences at all for the Big Five traits or otherwise (e.g., Christiansen et al., 2005; De Kock et al., 2015). For example, using a gender-balanced round-robin design with 25 eight-person groups, there were no gender differences in either consensus (i.e., interjudge agreement) or self–other agreement for judgments of the Big Five personality factors (Marcus & Lehman, 2002). However, some investigations do report an accuracy advantage for females across the Big Five traits based on ratings of individuals shown in videotaped dyadic interactions (Carney, Colvin, &

Hall, 2007; Schmid Mast, Bangerter, Bulliard, & Aerni, 2011; Vogt & Colvin, 2003) and based on first-person text passages (Hall, Goh, et al., 2016).

Given the inconsistent results of studies exploring gender differences in personality judgment accuracy, a review at the trait level is warranted. To start, while Schmid Mast and colleagues (2011) found that women were better assessors of personality than men, it was also noted that the gender effect seemed to be driven primarily by differences in judgments of neuroticism. Similarly, in another study gender differences did not emerge for judgments across the traits of extraversion, neuroticism, and masculinity-femininity (Lippa & Dietz, 2000). However, when accuracy was analyzed by each individual trait, women achieved greater self–other agreement than men for judgments of neuroticism. Additionally, there is evidence that females are more accurately able to judge intelligence (Carney et al., 2007; Murphy, Hall, & Colvin, 2003) and openness to experience (Carney et al., 2007) based on video recordings of targets. Moreover, there is some evidence for gender differences, with females being more accurate for judgments of extraversion as well as positive and negative affect (Ambady et al., 1995; Carney et al., 2007).

An interesting, yet noteworthy, twist to this is the effects of judge-target similarity for gender and ethnicity on accuracy. It has been shown that female judges of female targets achieved higher accuracy than male judges of male targets (Letzring, 2010). This may be due to similarity between the judges and targets promoting understanding of likely trait-behavior associations, and therefore enabling better detection and utilization of relevant cues in making judgments (De Kock, Lievens, & Born, in press; Letzring, 2010). However, the fact that judge–target similarity was only found for women may be a reflection of females being both better judges and better targets. Overall, if a gender difference in judgmental ability exists, it would likely favor women. That said, I caution against making any large and sweeping generalizations, since differences that were found were of rather small magnitude.

Behavior of Judges

A rather new area of scholarship, and the fifth and final characteristic related to the understanding and description of good judges of personality, surrounds the behaviors that contribute to this important ability. The RAM outlines that judges are responsible for recognition and processing of cues that are made available by targets, regardless of why they are made available. Even so, it is commonplace for individuals to elicit information from others during interpersonal dealings. Thus, a possible characteristic of good judges would be skills for such cue elicitation. Indeed, it has been demonstrated that judges are able to behave in ways that increase cue availability, and those cues aid in the achievement of greater judgment accuracy (Letzring, 2008; Lievens, Schollaert, & Keen, 2015).

In one study (Letzring, 2008) it was discovered that judges' use of basic social skills (e.g., eye contact, expressing warmth) and a lack of negative behaviors (e.g., seeking reassurance or advice, undermining or obstructing the target) were positively related to accuracy. It was concluded that such behaviors on the part of judges serve to increase targets' comfort and increase their willingness to reveal information (i.e., cues) about their true selves, which can then be detected and utilized when making judgments of the targets. Indeed, exploring this proposition, Letzring (2008) specifically evaluated the impact of having good judges present during interactions with targets. The assumption was that *if* good judges are cue elicitors, *then* having more good judges within a recorded situation should increase observer accuracy. This was precisely what was found—observers of groups that contained at least one good judge had higher accuracy than observers of groups with no good judges. A subsequent series of studies (Lievens et al., 2015) investigated this cue elicitation prospect within assessment centers. It was found that role-players can be trained to elicit trait specific cues by behaving in a predetermined manner and/or asking specific questions aimed at invoking trait-relevant behavior. Indeed, these cue elicitation strategies resulted in significantly greater levels of accuracy by assessors who only observed the assessment center exercises. In sum, the currently available evidence supports the notion that good judges are more skilled at eliciting relevant informational cues from targets.

It should also be noted that this behavioral characteristic may operate in harmony with some of the factors already discussed. For instance, specific motivations activating attentional processes toward targets, such as anticipation of future interactions (Neuberg & Fiske, 1987), may also lead judges to increase cue elicitation behaviors. In a similar fashion, those who have a propensity for perspective-taking and empathy may also naturally engage in behaviors that provide comfort for interaction partners. Additionally, highly empathic individuals may inquire about current thoughts and feelings, which

might allow additional cues to be offered by targets. Furthermore, it is possible that those who are more sociable or extraverted will naturally elicit more cues as a by-product of continuing their interaction with targets, as compared to introverted individuals, who may actively seek to reduce such stimulating experiences. In a similar vein, those who are well adjusted have greater social skills and experience less social anxiety (Langston & Cantor, 1989; Riggio, Watring, & Throckmorton, 1993), which in turn allows for increased engagement with targets in a reposeful manner. Ultimately, these are questions that can, and should, be answered by future research. At this time, it can simply be concluded that cue eliciting behaviors is but one of many characteristics of good judges.

Theoretical and Methodological Considerations

Having now concluded our review of the correlates of the ability to make accurate judgments of others' personalities, let us now review a few important theoretical and methodological considerations for the continuation of research in this area. First, as explored in the preceding sections, there are inconsistencies in conclusions that have been drawn within this expansive literature. It is probable that such discrepancies are, at least in part, a reflection of the varying methodological approaches used up to this point. Providing some support for this position, when studies use tests in similar domains and/or use similar methodologies for investigating judgment accuracy, results are more consistent with one another (Schlegel, Boone, & Hall, 2017). This indicates that the contextual specificity of judgment accuracy becomes an important question to explore, and that such factors are important to consider when trying to build on the current literature through replication and extension, as well as when attempting to synthesize and/or meta-analyze the existing literature. Alternatively, the inconsistencies may also be a reflection of different researchers having examined psychometrically different constructs. For instance, the judgment measures for personality vary widely—even when similar on a conceptual level. For example, much work has used variations of the Big Five Inventory (John et al., 2008), but others have used the HEXACO (Ashton & Lee, 2009) or versions of personality trait measures from the International Personality Item Pool (Goldberg et al., 2006). It is important that subsequent work in this area of scholarship consider these possibilities.

Another issue worthy of mention is the fact that research on the good judge has almost exclusively focused on the detection and utilization stages of the RAM. Recall that these two stages are associated with the judge, while the relevance and availability stages are associated with the target (Funder, 1995). Because of this, much research has only passively considered the heterogeneity of the target pool. Intuition suggests the ability to judge others accurately should not necessarily be dependent on the target person. That is, part of being a good judge is the ability to correctly ascribe the personality characteristics of those who are least understood, as well as those who are the most understood. This implicit assumption has led some to use a diverse set of targets in terms of factors such as personality, experiences, and gender, as well as situations in which targets are observed or interactions occur.

This methodological decision, which is commonplace, is opposite of what the RAM, with the multiplicative conceptualization of the judgment process, would suggest is best. To this point, recent work by Rogers and Biesanz (2018) has demonstrated that good targets should be evaluated by judges in order to promote the observation of maximal differences in judgmental ability. Centrally, good targets are characterized by making a substantial number of relevant cues available in the external environment for judges to detect and use. Recall that according to the RAM, if cues are not relevant to the attribute being judged and/or available for detection, even great judges will be unable to make accurate judgments. Admittedly, however, the exclusive use of good targets would change the search for characteristics of the good judge in an important way. Specifically, the primary question would change from *Who is the good judge of everyone?* to asking the narrower question, *Who is a good judge of easy targets?* While this is certainly an important question to answer, it is not the original question that has driven nearly a century's worth of empirical effort. Perhaps, however, the original question is too broad and thus should be narrowed to provide a realistic opportunity to find consistent results. Even so, if researchers move forward with the exclusive use of good targets when investigating variables thought to be related to good judges, it would behoove them to consider how such findings are likely to generalize to the accurate perception of *all targets*.

Future Directions

If the past century is any indication, it is likely that this area of research will continue to develop, as interest in the good judge of personality is not likely to dwindle. As noted in the previous section, the inconsistencies in conclusions that have been drawn to this point may be, at least in part, a reflection of the varying conceptual and methodological approaches that have been used. Therefore, the development of new methodological techniques and further refinement of core theoretical underpinnings should allow for more nuanced investigations of the correlates of good judges. Incremental change is often the most prudent path to success, and I suggest that future research within this domain should take a similar approach. To this end, I now outline several worthy future directions including the development of a standardized measure, investigation of context specificity, and exploring best practices in training for and application of superior personality judgment skills.

Standardizing the Assessment of Judgmental Ability

The development and utilization of standardized measurements and methodological protocols is seen within other fields of psychological inquiry (e.g., clinical). While these, too, can be seen for some areas of interpersonal perception, such as for decoding nonverbal cues (e.g., Nowicki & Duke, 1994; Rosenthal, Hall, DiMatteo, Rogers, & Archer, 1979), a standardized measure of the ability to accurately judge personality traits does not yet exist. This state of affairs necessitates that researchers create their own stimulus materials (e.g., videos of targets) in order to assess accuracy, which is time-consuming and slows the pace of confirming previous findings and making new discoveries. Moreover, the lack of a standardized measure makes it difficult to compare findings across time, research groups, and even similar studies in the same domain of judgment (Schlegel et al., 2017), which is important to ensuring a generalizable and replicable scientific literature. As such, one important future undertaking for scholars immersed within this research field is to develop and validate a standardized assessment for personality judgment ability. Such a test (or set of tests) would certainly be useful (Murphy, 2016), especially if it would allow for cross-domain comparisons and longitudinal designs (Hall, Andrzejewski, Murphy, Schmid Mast, & Feinstein, 2008). Admittedly, this would be a large undertaking, but worthwhile nonetheless. To this point, some preliminary work has demonstrated feasibility of such a measure, and identified some basic attributes a standardized measure should incorporate (e.g., length of stimuli, # of targets; Letzring & Colman, 2018).

Assessing the Developmental Trajectory of Judgmental Ability

A second worthy area for exploration is the development of judgmental ability over the lifespan, particularly in childhood. Research has explored when and how theory of mind develops in children (Wellman, Cross, & Watson, 2001) and how it is associated with accuracy (Bernstein & Davis, 1982; Colman et al., 2017). Yet, little research has explored the early development of personality judgment ability. However, one such cross-sectional study explored accuracy of judgments by 8-, 13-, and 18-year-olds of other individuals in their age group (McLarney-Vesotski, Bernieri, & Rempala, 2006), and found that accuracy for judgments of the Big Five personality traits generally improved with age. Eight-year-olds were accurate only in judgments of extraversion; 13-year-olds achieved accuracy for the traits of extraversion, openness, and conscientiousness; and 18-year-olds were accurate in judgments of extraversion, openness, conscientiousness, and neuroticism, but were significantly inaccurate on the trait of agreeableness. This study certainly gives some important insights on judgmental ability of youth, but still more can and should be learned about the development of this skill given the importance of accuracy to everyday life. This is certainly an area where a standardized measure of personality judgment accuracy would be beneficial, as longitudinal investigations are necessary for this suggested line of inquiry.

Exploring Contextual Specificity of Judgmental Ability

There is ample research exploring the generality of judgmental ability, but findings have been mixed (e.g., Boone & Schlegel, 2016; Cline & Richards Jr, 1960; Schlegel et al., 2017). This leads to the question of whether some people are more accurate at assessing personality within certain contexts. This is not reframing the generality question of whether a good judge of personality is also a good judge for other domains (such as emotion, honesty, etc.), but rather if some contexts are better for making accurate judgments than others due to individuals' experience and knowledge of trait-behavior links. For example, might teachers be better at judging broad personality attributes when assessing others in a learning situation? Alternatively, might performance assessors have a knack for accurately rating employees based on cues available within the workplace (see De Kock et al., in press)? This is an interesting empirical question now that the psychological nature of situations are being conceptualized and quantified (Funder, 2016; Rauthmann, Sherman, & Funder, 2015), which might allow for a more nuanced understanding of the processes that might underlie situational specificity. If this is indeed a factor that contributes to variability in judgmental ability, it would likely provide insight into avenues for beneficial application of such skills.

Applied Opportunities for Good Judges of Personality

Another important direction for research within this domain is exploring the manners in which good judges are able to capitalize on their skills. One such realm where superior skills in judgmental ability should be valued is leadership (Colman, Letzring, & Lion, 2018; Schmid Mast, Jonas, Cronauer, & Darioly, 2012). This is because leaders with accurate understanding of followers are better positioned to design work for, inspire motivation within, and provide intellectual stimulation to their employees (Colman & Lion, 2018). Beyond leadership, there are other domains in which good judges are likely to provide advantages. For instance, teachers who are good judges might be able to structure content in more interesting ways for students to engage with and learn material. Additionally, it is possible that healthcare providers with high judgmental accuracy ability are especially likely to make decisions among treatment options based on which an individual is most likely to implement and adhere to. In short, researchers should keep an eye toward the value of this skill while continuing their research agenda. Coverage of other applied implications and applications of trait accuracy research is provided in Section V of this handbook.

Training and Development of Good Judges

Under the assumption that there are a multitude of areas that would benefit from increased judgmental ability (as just discussed), it would be advantageous for future empirical work to explore the training and ongoing development of this important skill (see also chapter 21 by Blanch-Hartigan & Cummings in this handbook). It has been concluded that on average across psychological domains (e.g., emotion recognition, lie detection), training aimed at increasing person perception accuracy is effective (Blanch-Hartigan, Andrzejewski, & Hill, 2012). However, virtually nonexistent are studies looking at the trainability of personality judgment accuracy. One recent study (Colman, 2018) attempted to increase personality judgment accuracy by training perspective-taking or empathy skills. However, the brief, text-based intervention was not successful and led to more questions than answers. For instance, given that in-person training with practice and feedback is the most effective strategy for other person perception accuracy domains (e.g., empathic accuracy, deception detection; Blanch-Hartigan et al., 2012), it remains unclear whether such training designs are efficacious for the domain of personality. Ultimately, this line of inquiry is ripe for investigation, and is certain to be of interest to basic and applied researchers alike.

Conclusion

As Gage (1953) noted more than 60 years ago about what characterizes good judges of personality, "the results are far from conclusive...[and the] full story is not yet in." Even with that conclusion, scholars were not convinced that meaningful moderators of this ability simply did not exist—hence, research continued then and is still thriving now. Today, looking at variability among people's level of accuracy in judging personality, there is adequate evidence that this is an individual difference (Christiansen et al., 2005; Letzring, 2008; Rogers & Biesanz, 2018), and many possible correlates have been identified, most of which were discussed in this chapter. Although smaller and more inconsistent effects are found for this moderator of accuracy than others outlined by the RAM (e.g., the target; Biesanz, 2010), individual differences in this ability deserve no less scholarly consideration or empirical attention moving forward.

Much as other scholars have indicated, there does not yet exist an extremely clear portrait of the good judge of others' personality. However, if pressed to describe the profile of a good judge, I would tentatively describe *her* as being *agreeable*, *emotionally stable*, *psychologically well adjusted*, and having *above average intelligence* with the *motivation* to make accurate impressions. When engaging in the personality judgment process, she would have a *tendency for empathy* and *actively engaging with targets* in an effort to elicit information to which *attention is given* and *recalled* as judgments are being made. Even with this tentative description of an optimal profile of the good judge, there is much work to do, and, dare I say, this is an exciting time for such research. Scholars are now in a position, especially with the increasing number of analytical tools at their disposal, to make great strides in further identifying, characterizing, and hopefully training *good judges* of others' personality.

References

Abelson, R. P. (1985). A variance explanation paradox: When a little is a lot. *Psychological Bulletin, 97*, 129–133.

Adams, H. F. (1927). The good judge of personality. *The Journal of Abnormal and Social Psychology, 22*, 172–181. doi:10.1037/h0075237

Allik, J., de Vries, R. E., & Realo, A. (2016). Why are moderators of self-other agreement difficult to establish? *Journal of Research in Personality, 63*, 72–83. doi:10.1016/j.jrp.2016.05.013

Allport, G. W. (1937). *Personality: A psychological interpretation.* New York, NY: Holt, Reinhart, & Winston.

Ambady, N., Hallahan, M., & Rosenthal, R. (1995). On judging and being judged accurately in zero-acquaintance situations. *Journal of Personality and Social Psychology, 69*, 518–529. doi10.1037/0022-3514.69.3.518

Ashton, M. C., & Lee, K. (2009). The HEXACO-60: A short measure of the major dimensions of personality. *Journal of Personality Assessment, 91*, 340–345. doi:10.1080/00223890902935878

Back, M. D., Schmukle, S. C., & Egloff, B. (2008). How extraverted is honey.bunny77@hotmail.de? Inferring personality from e-mail addresses. *Journal of Research in Personality, 42*, 1116–1122. doi:10.1016/j.jrp.2008.02.001

Barrick, M. R., Patton, G. K., & Haugland, S. N. (2000). Accuracy of interviewer judgments of job applicant personality traits. *Personnel Psychology, 53*, 925–951. doi:10.1111/J.1744-6570.2000.Tb02424.X

Beer, A., & Watson, D. (2008). Personality judgment at zero acquaintance: Agreement, assumed similarity, and implicit simplicity. *Journal of Personality Assessment, 90*, 250–260. doi:10.1080/00223890701884970

Bernstein, W. M., & Davis, M. H. (1982). Perspective-taking, self-consciousness, and accuracy of person perception. *Basic and Applied Social Psychology, 3*, 1–19.

Biesanz, J. C. (2010). The social accuracy model of interpersonal perception: Assessing individual differences in perceptive and expressive accuracy. *Multivariate Behavioral Research, 45*, 853–885. doi:10.1080/00273171.2010.519262

Biesanz, J. C. (2017). Interpersonal perception models. In V. Ziegler-Hill & T. K. Shackelford (Eds.), *The SAGE handbook of personality and individual differences.* Thousand Oaks, CA: Sage.

Biesanz, J. C., & Human, L. J. (2010). The cost of forming more accurate impressions: Accuracy-motivated perceivers see the personality of others more distinctively but less normatively than perceivers without an explicit goal. *Psychological Science, 21*, 589–594. doi:10.1177/0956797610364121

Biesanz, J. C., Neuberg, S. L., Smith, D. M., Asher, T., & Judice, T. N. (2001). When accuracy-motivated perceivers fail: Limited attentional resources and the reemerging self-fulfilling prophecy. *Personality and Social Psychology Bulletin, 27*, 621–629.

Blanch-Hartigan, D., Andrzejewski, S. A., & Hill, K. M. (2012). The effectiveness of training to improve person perception accuracy: A meta-analysis. *Basic and Applied Social Psychology, 34*, 483–498. doi:10.1080/01973533.2012.728122

Boone, R. T., & Schlegel, K. (2016). Is there a general skill in perceiving others accurately? In J. A. Hall, M. Schmid Mast, & T. V. West (Eds.), *The social psychology of perceiving others accurately* (pp. 379–403). Cambridge, UK: Cambridge University Press.

Borkenau, P., & Liebler, A. (1993). Consensus and self-other agreement for trait inferences from minimal information. *Journal of Personality, 61*, 477–496.

Cardy, R. L., & Kehoe, J. F. (1984). Rater selective attention ability and appraisal effectiveness: The effect of a cognitive style on the accuracy of differentiation among ratees. *Journal of Applied Psychology, 69*, 589–594. doi:10.1037/0021-9010.69.4.589

Carney, D. R., Colvin, C. R., & Hall, J. A. (2007). A thin slice perspective on the accuracy of first impressions. *Journal of Research in Personality, 41*, 1054–1072. doi:10.1016/j.jrp.2007.01.004

Chan, M., Rogers, K. H., Parisotto, K. L., & Biesanz, J. C. (2011). Forming first impressions: The role of gender and normative accuracy in personality perception. *Journal of Research in Personality, 45*, 117–120. doi:10.1016/j.jrp.2010.11.001

Christiansen, N. D., Wolcott-Burnam, S., Janovics, J. E., Burns, G. N., & Quirk, S. W. (2005). The good judge revisited: Individual differences in the accuracy of personality judgments. *Human Performance, 18*, 123–149. doi:10.1207/s15327043hup1802_2

Cline, V. B. (1955). Ability to judge personality assessed with a stress interview and sound-film technique. *Journal of Abnormal and Social Psychology, 50*, 183–187.

Cline, V. B., & Richards, J. M., Jr. (1960). Accuracy of interpersonal perception—A general trait? *Journal of Abnormal and Social Psychology, 60*, 1–7. doi:10.1037/h0041320

Colman, D. E. (2015). *Motivated accuracy: Investigating the effect of task goals on normative and distinctive components of accuracy of personality trait judgments* (Unpublished masters thesis). ID State University, Pocatello, ID.

Colman, D. E. (2018). *The effects of training, practice, and feedback of the empathic response on accuracy of personality trait judgment* (Unpublished doctoral dissertation). ID State University, Pocatello, ID.

Colman, D. E., Letzring, T. D., & Biesanz, J. C. (2017). Seeing and feeling your way to accurate personality judgments: The moderating role of perceiver empathic tendencies. *Social Psychological and Personality Science, 8*, 806–815. doi:10.1177/1948550617691097

Colman, D. E., Letzring, T. D., & Lion, R. W. (2018). *The perceptive leader: A preliminary look into trait judgment accuracy*. Paper presented at the Western Academy of Management, Salt Lake City, UT.

Colman, D. E., & Lion, R. W. (2018). *Contextualizing leadership upon followers' unique characteristics: An argument for explicit consideration of accurate person perception*. Manuscript in preparation.

Cronbach, L. J. (1955). Processes affecting scores on "understanding of others" and "assumed similarity." *Psychological Bulletin, 52*, 177–193.

Davis, M. H. (1996). *Empathy: A social psychological approach*. Boulder, CO: Westview Press.

Davis, M. H., & Kraus, L. A. (1997). Personality and empathic accuracy. In W. Ickes (Ed.), *Empathic accuracy* (pp. 144–168). New York, NY: The Guildford Press.

De Kock, F. S., Lievens, F., & Born, M. P. (2015). An in-depth look at dispositional reasoning and interviewer accuracy. *Human Performance, 28*, 199–221. doi:10.1080/08959285.2015.1021046

De Kock, F. S., Lievens, F., & Born, M. P. (in press). The profile of the "Good Judge" in HRM: A systematic review and agenda for future research. *Human Resource Management Review*. doi:10.1016/j.hrmr.2018.09.003

Estes, S. G. (1938). Judging personality from expressive behavior. *Journal of Abnormal and Social Psychology, 33*, 217–236.

Fletcher, G. J. O., Danilovics, P., Fernandez, G., Peterson, D., & Reeder, G. D. (1986). Attributional complexity: An individual differences measure. *Journal of Personality and Social Psychology, 51*, 875–884. doi:10.1037/0022-3514.51.4.875

Funder, D. C. (1980). On seeing ourselves as others see us: Self-other agreement and discrepancy in personality ratings. *Journal of Personality, 48*, 473–493.

Funder, D. C. (1987). Errors and mistakes: Evaluating the accuracy of social judgment. *Psychological Bulletin, 101*, 75–90.

Funder, D. C. (1993). Judgments as data for personality and developmental psychology: Error versus accuracy. In D. C. Funder, R. D. Parke, C. Tomlinson-Keasey, & K. Widaman (Eds.), *Studying lives through time: Personality and development* (pp. 121–146). Washington, DC: American Psychological Association.

Funder, D. C. (1995). On the accuracy of personality judgment: A realistic approach. *Psychological Review, 102*, 652–670.

Funder, D. C. (1999). *Personality judgment: A realistic approach to person perception*. San Diego, CA: Academic Press.

Funder, D. C. (2016). Taking situations seriously. *Current Directions in Psychological Science, 25*, 203–208. doi:10.1177/0963721416635552

Funder, D. C. (2018, March). *Implications of the depletion replication study for meta-science and behavioral research*. Paper presented at the Society for Personality and Social Psychology, Atlanta, GA.

Funder, D. C., & West, S. G. (1993). Consensus, self-other agreement, and accuracy in personality judgment: An introduction. *Journal of Personality, 61*, 457–476.

Furr, R. M. (2008). A Framework for profile similarity: Integrating similarity, normativeness, and distinctiveness. *Journal of Personality, 76*, 1267–1316. doi:10.1111/j.1467-6494.2008.00521.x

Gage, N. L. (1953). Explorations in the understanding of others. *Educational and Psychological Measurement, 13*, 14–26.

Goldberg, L. R., Johnson, J. A., Eber, H. W., Hogan, R., Ashton, M. C., Cloninger, C. R., & Gough, H. G. (2006). The international personality item pool and the future of public-domain personality measures. *Journal of Research in Personality, 40*, 84–96. doi:10.1016/j.jrp.2005.08.007

Gottfredson, L. S. (1997). Why g matters: The complexity of everyday life. *Intelligence, 24*, 79–132. doi:10.1016/S0160-2896(97)90014-3

Graham, T., & Ickes, W. (1997). When women's intuition isn't greater than men's. In W. Ickes (Ed.), *Empathic accuracy* (pp. 117–143). New York, NY: Guilford.

Hall, J. A., Andrzejewski, S. A., Murphy, N. A., Schmid Mast, M., & Feinstein, B. A. (2008). Accuracy of judging others' traits and states: Comparing mean levels across tests. *Journal of Research in Personality, 42*, 1476–1489. doi:10.1016/j.jrp.2008.06.013

Hall, J. A., Andrzejewski, S. A., & Yopchick, J. E. (2009). Psychosocial correlates of interpersonal sensitivity: A meta-analysis. *Journal of Nonverbal Behavior, 33*, 149–180. doi:10.1007/s10919-009-0070-5

Hall, J. A., Blanch, D. C., Horgan, T. G., Murphy, N. A., Rosip, J. C., & Schmid Mast, M. (2009). Motivation and interpersonal sensitivity: Does it matter how hard you try? *Motivation and Emotion, 33*, 291–302. doi:10.1007/s11031-009-9128-2

Hall, J. A., Goh, J. X., Schmid Mast, M., & Hagedorn, C. (2016). Individual differences in accurately judging personality from text. *Journal of Personality, 84,* 433–445. doi:10.1111/jopy.12170

Hall, J. A., Gunnery, S. D., & Horgan, T. G. (2016). Gender differences in interpersonal accuracy. In J. A. Hall, M. S. Mast, & T. V. West (Eds.), *The social psychology of perceiving others accurately* (pp. 309–327). Cambridge, UK: Cambridge University Press.

Harackiewicz, J. M., & DePaulo, B. M. (1982). Accuracy of person perception: A component analysis according to Cronbach. *Personality and Social Psychology Bulletin, 8*(2), 247–256.

Harris, J. A., Vernon, P. A., & Jang, K. L. (1999). Intelligence and personality characteristics associated with accuracy in rating a co-twin's personality. *Personality and Individual Differences, 26,* 85–97.

Haselton, M. G., & Funder, D. C. (2006). The evolution of accuracy and bias in social judgment. In M. Schaller, J. A. Simpson, & D. T. Kenrick (Eds.), *Evolution and social psychology* (pp. 15–38). New York, NY: Psychology Press.

Hoffmann, J. A., von Helversen, B., & Rieskamp, J. (2014). Pillars of judgment: How memory abilities affect performance in rule-based and exemplar-based judgments. *Journal of Experimental Psychology General, 143,* 2242–2261. doi:10.1037/a0037989

Human, L. J., & Biesanz, J. C. (2011). Through the looking glass clearly: Accuracy and assumed similarity in well-adjusted individuals' first impressions. *Journal of Personality and Social Psychology, 100,* 349–364. doi:10.1037/a0021850

Ickes, W., Gesn, P. R., & Graham, T. (2000). Gender differences in empathic accuracy: Differential ability or differential motivation? *Personal Relationships, 7,* 95–110. doi:10.1111/j.1475-6811.2000.tb00006.x

Jensen, A. R. (1991). General mental ability: From psychometrics to biology. *Diagnostique, 12,* 134–144.

John, O. P., Naumann, L. P., & Soto, C. J. (2008). Paradigm shift in the integrative big five trait taxonomy: History, measurement, and conceptual issues. In O. P. John, R. W. Robins, & L. A. Pervin (Eds.), *Handbook of Personality: Theory and Research* (pp. 114–158). New York, NY: Guilford Press.

John, O. P., & Robins, R. W. (1993). Determinants of interjudge agreement on personality traits: The big five domains, observability, evaluativeness, and the unique perspective of the self. *Journal of Personality, 61,* 521–551.

Judice, T. N., & Neuberg, S. L. (1998). When interviewers desire to confirm negative expectations: Self-fulfilling prophecies and inflated applicant self-perceptions. *Basic and Applied Social Psychology, 20,* 175–190.

Kolar, D. W. (1995). *Individual differences in the ability to accurately judge the personality characteristics of others* (Unpublished doctoral dissertation). University of California, Riverside, Riverside, CA.

Kolar, D. W., Funder, D. C., & Colvin, C. R. (1996). Comparing the accuracy of personality judgments by the self and knowledgeable others. *Journal of Personality, 64,* 311–337. doi:10.1111/1467-6494.ep9606164112

Kruglanski, A. W. (1989). The psychology of being "right": The problem of accuracy in social perception and cognition. *Psychological Bulletin, 106,* 395–409.

Krzyzaniak, S. L. (2018). *Personality judgment accuracy and the role of physical fitness, cognitive functioning, and psychological well-being* (Unpublished masters thesis). Idaho State University, Pocatello, ID.

Kuncel, N. R., Hezlett, S. A., & Ones, D. S. (2004). Academic performance, career potential, creativity, and job performance: Can one construct predict them all? *Journal of Personality and Social Psychology, 86,* 148–161. doi:10.1037/0022-3514.86.1.148

Langston, C. A., & Cantor, N. (1989). Social anxiety and social constraint: When making friends is hard. *Journal of Personality and Social Psychology, 56,* 649–661. doi: 10.1037/0022-3514.56.4.649

Letzring, T. D. (2008). The good judge of personality: Characteristics, behaviors, and observer accuracy. *Journal of Research in Personality, 42,* 914–932. doi:10.1016/j.jrp.2007.12.003

Letzring, T. D. (2010). The effects of judge-target gender and ethnicity similarity on the accuracy of personality judgments. *Social Psychology, 41,* 42–51. doi:10.1027/1864-9335/a000007

Letzring, T. D. (2015). Observer judgmental accuracy of personality: Benefits related to being a good (normative) judge. *Journal of Research in Personality, 54,* 51–60. doi:10.1016/j.jrp.2014.05.001

Letzring, T. D., & Colman, D. E. (2018). *The Idaho Test of Accurate Person Perception (ITAPP): Preliminary results from the creation of a standardized measure of individual differences in the accuracy of perceiving others.* Manuscript in preparation.

Lievens, F., Schollaert, E., & Keen, G. (2015). The interplay of elicitation and evaluation of trait-expressive behavior: Evidence in assessment center exercises. *Journal of Applied Psychology, 100,* 1169–1188. doi:10.1037/apl0000004

Lippa, R. A., & Dietz, J. K. (2000). The relation of gender, personality, and intelligence to judges' accuracy in judging strangers' personality from brief video segments. *Journal of Nonverbal Behavior, 24*(1), 25–43.

Marcus, D. K., & Lehman, S. J. (2002). Are there sex differences in interpersonal perception at zero acquaintance? A social relations analysis. *Journal of Research in Personality, 36,* 190–207. doi:10.1006/jrpe.2001.2346

Mayer, J. D., Roberts, R. D., & Barsade, S. G. (2008). Human abilities: Emotional intelligence. *Annual Review of Psychology, 59,* 507–536. doi:10.1146/annurev.psych.59.103006.093646

McLarney-Vesotski, A. R., Bernieri, F., & Rempala, D. (2006). Personality perception: A developmental study. *Journal of Research in Personality, 40,* 652–674. doi:10.1016/j.jrp.2005.07.001

McLarney-Vesotski, A. R., Bernieri, F. J., & Rempala, D. (2011). An experimental examination of the "good judge." *Journal of Research in Personality, 45*(4), 398–400. doi:10.1016/j.jrp.2011.04.005

Murphy, N. A. (2016). What we know and the future of interpersonal accuracy research. In J. A. Hall, M. Schmid Mast, & T. V. West (Eds.), *The social psychology of perceiving others accurately* (pp. 404–424). Cambridge, UK: Cambridge University Press.

Murphy, N. A., Hall, J. A., & Colvin, C. R. (2003). Accurate intelligence assessments in social interactions: Mediators and gender effects. *Journal of Personality, 71,* 465–493.

Neuberg, S. L. (1989). The goal of forming accurate impressions during social interactions: attenuating the impact of negative expectancies. *Journal of Personality and Social Psychology, 56,* 374.

Neuberg, S. L., & Fiske, S. T. (1987). Motivational influences on impression formation: Outcome dependency, accuracy-driven attention, and individuating processes. *Journal of Personality and Social Psychology, 53*, 431–444. doi:10.1037/0022-3514.53.3.431

Nowicki, S., Jr., & Duke, M. P. (1994). Individual differences in the nonverbal communication of affect: The diagnostic analysis of nonverbal accuracy scale. *Journal of Nonverbal Behavior, 18*(1), 9–35.

Ozer, D. J., & Benet-Martinez, V. (2006). Personality and the prediction of consequential outcomes. *Annual Review of Psychology, 57*, 401–421. doi:10.1146/annurev.psych.57.102904.190127

Premack, D. R. (2011). The role of emotional intelligence in the judgmental accuracy of neuroticism (Unpublished masters thesis). University of Guelph, Guelph, ON.

Rauthmann, J. F., Sherman, R. A., & Funder, D. C. (2015). Principles of situation research: Towards a better understanding of psychological situations. *European Journal of Personality, 29*, 363–381. doi:10.1002/per.1994

Riggio, R. E., Tucker, J., & Coffaro, D. (1989). Social skills and empathy. *Personality and Individual Differences, 10*, 93–99.

Riggio, R. E., Watring, K. P., & Throckmorton, B. (1993). Social skills, social support, and psychosocial adjustment. *Personality and Individual Differences, 15*, 275–280. doi: 10.1016/0191-8869(93)90217-Q

Rogers, K. H., & Biesanz, J. C. (2018). Reassessing the good judge of personality. *Journal of Personality and Social Psychology, 117*, 186–200. doi:10.1037/pspp0000197

Rosenthal, R., Hall, J. A., DiMatteo, R. M., Rogers, P. L., & Archer, D. (1979). *Sensitivity to nonverbal communication: The PONS test.* Baltimore, MD: Johns Hopkins University Press.

Schlegel, K., Boone, R. T., & Hall, J. A. (2017). Individual differences in interpersonal accuracy: A multi-level meta-analysis to assess whether judging other people is one skill or many. *Journal of Nonverbal Behavior, 41*, 103–137. doi:10.1007/s10919-017-0249-0

Schmid Mast, M., Bangerter, A., Bulliard, C., & Aerni, G. (2011). How accurate are recruiters' first impressions of applicants in employment interviews? *International Journal of Selection and Assessment, 19*, 198–208.

Schmid Mast, M., & Hall, J. A. (2018). The impact of interpersonal accuracy on behavioral outcomes. *Current Directions in Psychological Science, 27*, 309–314. doi:10.1177/0963721418758437

Schmid Mast, M., Jonas, K., Cronauer, C. K., & Darioly, A. (2012). On the importance of the superior's interpersonal sensitivity for good leadership. *Journal of Applied Social Psychology, 42*(5), 1043–1068. doi:10.1111/j.1559-1816.2011.00852.x

Taft, R. (1955). The ability to judge people. *Psychological Bulletin, 52*, 1–23.

Vazire, S. (2010). Who knows what about a person? The self-other knowledge asymmetry (SOKA) model. *Journal of Personality and Social Psychology, 98*, 281–300. doi:10.1037/a0017908

Vernon, P. E. (1933). Some characteristics of the good judge of personality. *The Journal of Social Psychology, 4*, 42–57.

Vogt, D. S., & Colvin, C. R. (2003). Interpersonal orientation and the accuracy of personality judgments. *Journal of Personality, 71*, 267–295.

Waggoner, A. S., Smith, E. R., & Collins, E. C. (2009). Person perception by active versus passive perceivers. *Journal of Experimental Social Psychology, 45*, 1028–1031. doi:10.1016/j.jesp.2009.04.026

Wellman, H. M., Cross, D., & Watson, J. (2001). Meta-analysis of theory-of-mind development: The truth about false belief. *Child Development, 72*, 655–684. doi:10.1111/1467-8624.00304

Winquist, L. A., Mohr, C. D., & Kenny, D. A. (1998). The female positivity effect in the perception of others. *Journal of Research in Personality, 32*, 370–388.

Zebrowitz, L. A. (1990). *Social perception.* Belmont, CA: Thomson Brooks/Cole.

Notes

1. Abelson (1985) provided a sophisticated and analytical account of this proposition. He used baseball to outline how what are perceived as small differences in batting averages can amount to very meaningful differences over the course of an entire season. Now imagine the impact of this over a lifetime, not just a season's worth, of social interactions!

2. I exclusively use the terms "judge" and "target" to provide consistency throughout this chapter. Please note, however, that across the literature many terms have been used and are considered synonymous—judges have been referred to as "perceivers, raters, assessors, and decoders, while targets have also been referred to as subjects, ratees, and encoders.

3. In this study, accuracy was measured in several atypical manners. As related to this particular result, the first was having judges select the 10 most applicable descriptors of targets from a checklist of 41 options and comparing those selections to criteria obtained in a clinical setting. The second relevant method was to have judges attempt to match a description of two behaviors with a correct personality sketch for a total of seven targets.

4. The measure used for making judgment ratings was a Behavioral Anchored Rating Scale (BARS) with five different dimensions. For each vignette used, three critical incidents were incorporated for each dimension. The accuracy criterion for each dimension rated for each hypothetical instructor was the averaged effectiveness rating by trained assessors across the three critical incidents included in each vignette.

5. This study also incorporated a manipulation of training design, but discussion of that aspect is not within the purview of this chapter. Interested readers may contact the author for a copy of the complete write-up of this study.

6. The negative expectations were based on purported low scores on three job-related dimensions: being goal-driven, sociability, and problem-solving skills.

CHAPTER 7

The Good Target of Personality Judgments

Marie-Catherine Mignault *and* Lauren J. Human

Abstract

Being a *good target, judgeable*, or high in *expressive accuracy* plays a fundamental role in the accuracy of personality judgments. In line with Funder's realistic accuracy model (RAM), targets are responsible for the quality and quantity of information—or cues—they provide to judges, and have the potential to influence how much attention and cognitive resources judges dedicate to those cues. In this chapter, target characteristics are discussed, such as psychological adjustment and social skills, which influence each stage of the RAM, thereby distinguishing good targets from targets that are more elusive or difficult to read. To conclude, possible intra- and inter-personal benefits of expressive accuracy and potential ways to enhance expressive accuracy are considered.

Key Words: good target, judgeability, expressive accuracy, personality judgment, psychological adjustment, social skill, realistic accuracy model

We are what we pretend to be, so we must be careful what we pretend to be.

(Vonnegut, 1962)

This quote by Kurt Vonnegut adeptly captures the critical role of the target—the person being judged—in the formation of accurate personality judgments. Responsible for the information they provide and for the attention they draw to themselves, targets have substantial influence over others' judgments of them (Funder, 1995; Human & Biesanz, 2013). For example, some people may downplay, hide, or overemphasize certain aspects of their personalities, whereas others may strive to be seen in line with who they are. There are large individual differences in the tendency to be a *good target* or *judgeable*, that is, the tendency to express one's personality accurately (or *expressive accuracy*; Biesanz, 2010; Human & Biesanz, 2013), which appear to be stable over time (Colvin, 1993a) and across diverse social contexts (Human, K. H. Rogers, & Biesanz, 2018). In turn, good targets may reap intra- and interpersonal benefits (e.g., Human,

Carlson, Geukes, Nestler, & Back, 2018; see Human & Biesanz, 2013). We therefore devote this chapter to understanding the good target. First, we discuss the role of the good target in contributing to the overall accuracy of personality judgments. Second, following Funder's realistic accuracy model (RAM; 1995), we consider the characteristics that distinguish targets who are easier versus more difficult to read. Then, we explore benefits of being a good target for psychological well-being and interpersonal relationships and briefly consider ways to improve expressive accuracy.

The Role of the Target in Accurate Personality Judgments

Historically, research has focused more on good judges—people who are particularly skilled at forming accurate personality impressions—than good targets. However, although some individual characteristics have been found to differentiate good from bad judges of personality (e.g., L. Christensen, 1974; Colman, Letzring, & Biesanz, 2017; Letzring, 2008;

see also chapter 6 by Douglas Colman in this handbook), finding consistent predictors has been challenging (Kenny, 1994). This may be because there tends to be less variability in the ability to form accurate impressions; indeed, most people appear to be able to form somewhat accurate judgments of others (Biesanz, 2010; Human & Biesanz, 2013; K. H. Rogers & Biesanz, 2018). In contrast, people vary much more widely in the tendency to be viewed accurately, defined as the degree of agreement between a personality judgment and a realistic accuracy criterion, such as self- and/or close-other reports (Funder, 1995). The greater individual differences in accuracy for targets as compared to judges suggest that any variability in overall personality judgment accuracy may be particularly dependent on who the target of that judgment is. Indeed, K. H. Rogers and Biesanz (2018) found that variability in the ability to accurately judge others only emerges when observing and interacting with good targets. This indicates that being a good judge may not be helpful unless one is judging people who express themselves accurately, a finding echoed in empathic accuracy research (Zaki, Bolger, & Ochsner, 2008).

Why do targets play such a critical role in accurate personality judgment? One reason is that, as information providers, targets are especially important to the initial stages of personality judgment. That is, based on the RAM proposed by Funder (1995), personality judgment accuracy is achieved through four steps: (1) targets make *relevant* personality cues (2) *available* to judges, (3) who *detect* the cues and (4) appropriately *utilize* them. Targets thus play a direct role in the first two stages, consciously or unconsciously selecting the cues they emit, thereby influencing the quality of the information they provide, and displaying those cues in a way that is available (or not) for judges to see, in turn also influencing the quantity of the information they provide. Importantly, targets can also influence the last two stages, albeit more indirectly, through attributes or behaviors that capture judges' attention and enhance their motivation to be accurate, thus potentially enhancing cue detection and utilization. Thus, according to this model, targets have the ability to influence each stage of accurate judgment formation. Although the same is true for judges, that targets have the most direct control over the first two stages is critical, given the multiplicative nature of the RAM. That is, accuracy cannot be achieved if any stage is skipped, making it essential that first and foremost relevant cues be made available, especially given how naturally judges may detect and utilize the cues they are exposed to. Indeed, people naturally attend to others' cues (New, Cosmides, & Tooby, 2007) and make personality judgments based on that information automatically, even when cognitively distracted (Gilbert, Pelham, & Krull, 1988). Therefore, by being the ones chiefly responsible for the first two stages, targets occupy at least an equally, and potentially more, important role as judges in the accuracy of personality judgments. Thus, the extent to which people, in Vonnegut's terms, pretend to be who they actually are, is critical in determining how accurately they will be judged.

Characteristics of the Good Target

Thus far we have established that targets play a key role in the accuracy of personality judgments. But what makes some people better targets than others? To shed light on this variability, we review characteristics found to predict the tendency to be seen accurately. We have divided these characteristics according to how they might influence expressive accuracy at each stage of the RAM: cue relevance, availability, detection, and utilization. At the relevance stage, we discuss how characteristics such as psychological well-being, personality coherence, self-knowledge, social skills, power, and physical attractiveness may facilitate the provision of higher-quality cues to judges. At the availability stage, we consider characteristics such as extraversion and emotion expressiveness, which may enhance the amount of information targets provide. Next, we discuss how targets may heighten judges' attention and motivation through qualities related to likability, social communication skills, power, and physical attractiveness, thereby indirectly influencing the cue detection and utilization stages.

Relevance Stage

Given the multiplicative nature of the RAM stages, the very first stage, *cue relevance*, plays a foundational role in enabling the formation of accurate judgments: if the cues targets provide do not reveal their true selves, whether they make those cues available or whether judges detect and use those cues will not affect accuracy. In this section, we discuss how psychological well-being, personality coherence, self-knowledge, social skills, power, and physical attractiveness may lead targets to provide judges with more relevant information about their personality traits.

PSYCHOLOGICAL ADJUSTMENT

Humanists have long associated psychological well-being with a "transcendence of the environment, independence of it, ability to stand against it" (Maslow, 1968, p. 180), suggesting that individuals high in well-being may be more likely to embrace their true selves, including their quirks and flaws, regardless of the environment they find themselves in. Indeed, empirical evidence suggests that individuals who are well adjusted, that is, generally high in self-esteem, satisfied with their lives, and/or low in depression, tend to be judged in line with their unique profile of personality traits—and not overly normatively or positively (Colvin, 1993b; Human & Biesanz, 2011a, Human, Biesanz, et al., 2014, Human, Carlson, et al., 2018; Human, Mignault, K. H. Rogers, & Biesanz, 2019). Specifically, well-being is associated with greater personality expressive accuracy with new acquaintances (Human, Biesanz, et al., 2014; Human et al., 2019), peers and objective observers (Colvin, 1993a, 1993b), parents and close friends (Human, K. H. Rogers, et al., 2018), and online (Human, K. H. Rogers, et al., 2018). Indeed, recent work demonstrates that well-being predicts expressive accuracy across these different contexts to quite a similar degree (Human, K. H. Rogers, et al., 2018).

Although theoretically well-being could promote expressive accuracy through each stage of the RAM, there is evidence that it is specifically linked to the cue relevance stage. That is, well-being is associated with a greater tendency to emit cues that reflect one's "true" personality traits, in other words, cues that reflect target's self and close-other reports of how they generally are (Human, Biesanz, et al., 2014; Human et al., 2019). In contrast, well-adjusted individuals have not been found to provide more information or engender more attention from judges (Human, Biesanz, et al., 2014), and judges tend to detect and utilize target behavioral cues regardless of the target's well-being levels (Human, Biesanz, et al., 2014; Human et al., 2019). Importantly, paying more attention to targets only helps accuracy to the extent that one is judging a well-adjusted target, as targets with lower-than-average well-being may not be providing sufficiently relevant cues about themselves (Human, Biesanz, et al., 2014), in line with findings that good judges only emerge when perceiving good targets (K. H. Rogers & Biesanz, 2018).

But what makes well-adjusted people more likely to provide relevant information about themselves? Different mechanisms may be at play. For instance, less-adjusted individuals, such as those with lower self-esteem, may assume others will be more rejecting than accepting of them, in turn leading them to be cautious in expressing their less-desirable qualities (Baumeister, Tice, & Hutton, 1989; Gaucher et al., 2012), or they may have emotion regulation difficulties likely to trigger more "out-of-character" reactions to certain events (Tangney, Baumeister, & Boone, 2004). These examples illustrate the long-theorized link between psychological adjustment and personality coherence, or having and expressing a consistent, stable personality profile (Block, 1961; Campbell, Assanand, & Paula, 2003; Clifton & Kuper, 2011; Diehl & Hay, 2007, 2010; Donahue, Robins, Roberts, & John, 1993; Erickson, Newman, & Pincus, 2009; McReynolds, Altrocchi, & House, 2000; Sheldon et al., 1997; Sheldon & Kasser, 1995, but see Baird, Le, & Lucas, 2006). Highlighting the role of this association in expressive accuracy, there is evidence that behaving in line with one's personality may partly mediate the link from well-being to expressive accuracy (Human, Biesanz, et al., 2014; Human et al., 2019). An alternative, though less investigated, explanation linking well-being to the emission of relevant cues may be that well-adjusted individuals know themselves better (Jahoda, 1958; C. R. Rogers, 1961; Human & Biesanz, 2011a; Vogt & Colvin, 2005) and hold self-views with a greater level of certainty (Campbell, 1990). Arguably, they may then also be more articulate in expressing their self-beliefs (Campbell, 1990), thereby providing clearer cues of who they are. Later we review the empirical evidence linking personality coherence and self-knowledge to the relevance stage of the RAM, and briefly discuss other possible predictors of cue relevance in need of more empirical attention: power and physical attractiveness.

PERSONALITY COHERENCE

As mentioned, personality coherence is defined as behaving in a predictable manner, following a lawful patterning of personality traits (Allport, 1937, 1955; Cervone & Shoda, 1999), and has long been considered a predictor of expressive accuracy. Over the years, personality coherence has been operationalized in a number of ways, such as self-reported behavior consistency, self-reported personality stability over time, and personality-behavior congruence. These various indicators of coherence and their links to expressive accuracy are reviewed in this section.

Self-reporting higher consistency in behavior across situations or roles has been shown to predict greater agreement between the self and close others about one's personality (Baird et al., 2006; Bem & Allen, 1974; Cheek, 1982; Kenrick & Stringfield, 1980; Zuckerman, Bernieri, Koestner, & Rosenthal, 1989), as well as between close other-rated personality and observer-rated behaviors (Bem & Allen, 1974). That said, other studies failed to establish the link between self-reported consistency and self-other agreement (Chaplin & Goldberg, 1984; Paunonen & Jackson, 1985). Beyond self-reported consistency, there is also evidence for an association between coherence and self-close other agreement using temporal stability in behavior as an indicator of coherence, with experience sampling measures over the course of one week (Baird et al., 2006), or repeated measures across several weeks (Biesanz, West, & Graziano, 1998; Biesanz & West, 2000; Baird et al., 2006).

There is also evidence that personality coherence is linked to expressive accuracy in first impressions (Human, Biesanz, et al., 2014; Human et al., 2019), using personality-behavior congruence as an indicator of coherence. Specifically, targets who behaved more in line with their self- and close-other rated personality traits in initial interactions in the lab, as rated by outside observers, or in daily life assessed with experience sampling reports, tended to be viewed more accurately by new acquaintances (Human, Biesanz, et al., 2014; Human et al., 2019). Importantly, in those first-impression interactions, targets were judged in line with how they behaved, regardless of how congruent the target's behaviors were with the target's personality. This highlights that coherence is more likely to facilitate cue relevance, rather than cue utilization. That is, new acquaintances do not necessarily know which targets are providing more relevant cues—they are likely to utilize whatever information is given to them, congruent or otherwise. As such, behaving congruently with one's personality is critical to fostering more accurate judgments because it ensures that relevant, rather than irrelevant, cues will be utilized.

SELF-KNOWLEDGE
Another predictor of cue relevance may be self-knowledge. Though far from being a perfect—unbiased—tool (Vazire, 2010; Vazire & Carlson, 2010, 2011), it seems individuals do have some insight into their trait tendencies, and this insight could in turn help guide the cues one chooses to emit. Here we look at two indicators of self-knowledge—self-reflectiveness and self-concept clarity—and their associations to cue relevance.

Self-Reflective Tendencies
People who tend to reflect on their thoughts, feelings, and motives are found to reap greater self-awareness and in turn provide clearer and more relevant cues of who they are. The tendency to reflect on aspects of the self is also termed "private self-consciousness," and has been compared to "public self-consciousness," the concern with others' perceptions and approval of the self (Fenigstein, Scheier, & Buss, 1975). Turner (1978) showed that individuals high in private self-consciousness, as well as those low in public self-consciousness, reported more consistency in their personality traits, endorsing to a lesser extent that their expression of a given trait "*depends on the situation.*" In a study by Scheier, Buss, and Buss (1978), individuals who endorsed high private self-consciousness (but not those who endorsed high public self-consciousness) showed greater congruence between self-ratings of aggression-related personality traits and experimentally induced aggressive behavior. Similarly, B. Underwood and Moore (1981) found that highly self-reflective individuals were more likely to behave in line with self-reported trait sociability. In turn, at least one study has found that private but not public self-consciousness is associated with greater self-peer agreement across personality traits (Cheek, 1982), suggesting this indicator of self-knowledge may indeed promote expressive accuracy. On the other hand, certain forms of self-reflective tendencies—such as rumination, typically endorsed by less-adjusted individuals—may induce emotional distress and shame (Trapnell & Campbell, 1999), potentially motivating those individuals to conceal aspects of themselves they come to be aware of, thereby reducing cue relevance and expressive accuracy. In sum, there is evidence that greater self-reflective tendencies may promote the relevance of cues provided to others; however, additional research is needed to determine how robustly self-reflection in turn fosters accuracy, as well as possible contexts in which self-knowledge may hinder accuracy.

Self-Concept Clarity and Traitedness
Another indicator of self-knowledge is self-concept clarity, the extent to which one's beliefs about the self are clear and confidently defined (Campbell, Chew, & Scratchley, 1991). It appears that those high in self-concept clarity tend to have a greater need to be judged as stable in their behavior to confirm their self-views or to promote consensus among their own and others' views of the self (Robin & John, 1997). For example, an individual higher in

self-concept clarity who views the self as conscientious may be particularly motivated to take necessary steps to behave conscientiously and provide cues of his or her conscientiousness to others. Indeed, Lewandowski and Nardone (2012) found that targets with higher self-concept clarity were better at predicting their own subsequent behavior and agreed more with judges about their personality.

Other related indicators involve "traitedness" or "self-schema," the extent to which given traits are relevant to one's self-views (Baumeister & Tice, 1988; Bem & Allen, 1974; Reise & Waller, 1993; Markus, 1977). Whereas self-concept clarity focuses on a broader understanding of how one's personality is defined overall, traitedness and self-schema look at self-concept at a narrower level, examining the identification to specific personality traits. It appears that traits that individuals particularly identify with are more accurately judged by close others (Cheek, 1982; Zuckerman et al., 1989; Zuckerman, Kuhlman, & Camac, 1988), possibly because strong self-views toward a given trait lead to displaying clearer behavioral cues of that trait (e.g., Swann & Ely, 1984). It follows that the more traits one finds pertinent to one's self-views, the more one might provide relevant cues of those traits to others, and the more one's global personality profile is likely to be accurately judged. Indeed, individuals diagnosed with borderline personality disorder—characterized in part by unclear and unstable self-views—are found to have greater context-dependent variability in affect and behavior (Hopwood et al. 2009; Sadikaj, Russell, Moskowitz, & Paris, 2010). This is likely to result in being viewed less accurately by others.

SOCIAL SKILLS

Another important predictor of cue relevance appears to be social skills, described as the ability to regulate the expression of speech and nonverbal behavior to facilitate communication with others (DePaulo Blank, Swaim, & Hairfield, 1992; Friedman, Prince, Riggio, & DiMatteo, 1980). One indicator of self-reported social skill is the "Acting" subscale of the Self-Monitoring Scale (Briggs, Cheek, & Buss, 1980), thought to tap enjoyment as well as skill in speaking to and entertaining others (Snyder, 1974). Targets high on this indicator are found to be more accurately judged both by acquaintances (Cheek, 1982), and by strangers viewing videotapes of them (Tobey & Tunnel, 1981), arguably because those targets communicate to others more specific, nuanced, and detailed information. Another indicator of social skill may be self-presentation,

that is, the ability to manage the impression one is making on others (Baumeister, 1982; Goffman, 1959; Schlenker, 1980). When people are given the instruction to self-present (i.e., to make a "good impression"), their personality profiles are judged more accurately (Human, Biesanz, Parisotto, & Dunn, 2012). Similarly, when targets are told to "try to appear intelligent," targets' intelligence levels are judged more accurately (Murphy, 2007). Back and Nestler (2016) argue that self-presenting leads targets to make specific behaviors more observable, thereby providing more relevant information to others. Additionally, self-presenting may result in eliciting judges' attention and motivation (Human et al., 2012), to be discussed in the cue detection and utilization section.

POWER

Power is generally defined as the capacity to control one's own and others' resources and outcomes (Keltner, Gruenfeld, & Anderson, 2003; Magee & Galinsky, 2008). Individuals who are high in power or dominance tend to feel less socially constrained, thereby promoting more open expression of self-related characteristics. Both trait dominance and experimentally manipulated power are shown to foster the expression of true opinions and values (Anderson & Berdahl, 2002; Berdahl & Martorana, 2006), an effect explained by self-reported feelings of dominance, suggesting the importance of status awareness in selecting the cues to emit (Anderson & Berdahl, 2002). Experimentally manipulated high dominance may also facilitate acting in line with one's values (Lönnqvist, Verkasalo, & Walkowitz, 2011), and a lower likelihood to engage in behavioral confirmation of others' expectations (D. Christensen & Rosenthal, 1982; Cooper & Hazelrigg, 1988; Copeland, 1994; Hilton & Darley, 1985; Smith, Neuberg, Judice, & Biesanz, 1997; Snyder & Haugen, 1995). Thus, people who are generally higher in power or dominance may be more expressively accurate, but it may also be possible to boost expressive accuracy via contextual increases in power.

PHYSICAL ATTRACTIVENESS

Physically attractive individuals tend to be treated more favorably in daily social interactions and regarded with more respect (Dion, Berscheid, & Walster, 1972). Being systematically viewed and treated more positively by others could lead attractive people to feel that social acceptance does not depend on their specific behaviors, potentially allowing them to behave more freely and provide more valid cues of their personalities. This may help to explain why attractive individuals are seen not just more positively but also more accurately (Lorenzo, Biesanz, & Human, 2010). In addition, evolutionary, socialization, and social expectancy theories argue that the positive judgments of attractive people, or the attractiveness stereotype or "halo effect," promotes the development of characteristics in the target that are in line with the stereotype. Indeed, meta-analyses suggest that attractive people may in fact be more socially competent (Langlois et al., 2000). This enhanced social competence of attractive individuals may reflect more opportunities and experience interacting with others and potentially practicing nonverbal skills (Adams, 1977; Sabatelli & Rubin, 1986), in turn promoting the ability to emit more relevant or clearer information about themselves (Lorenzo et al., 2010). Overall, then, physically attractive people may be viewed more accurately because greater social acceptance and social skills may enable them to provide more relevant cues to their personalities. In parallel, physical attractiveness is also linked to greater judge attention and motivation (Langlois et al., 2000; Maner et al., 2003), potentially providing another route to greater judgeability, which is discussed in the cue detection and utilization section.

RELEVANCE STAGE SUMMARY

Overall, one of the most robust predictors of being a good target is psychological well-being, most likely because it facilitates cue relevance. In particular, well-adjusted individuals appear to provide more relevant cues of themselves because they tend to behave coherently with their traits. Thus, another important, more proximal, predictor of cue relevance and therefore expressive accuracy is personality coherence, the tendency to behave (or to report generally behaving) in line with one's personality across contexts or over time. Another characteristic that appears to facilitate expressive accuracy, likely via cue relevance, is greater self-knowledge, as this characteristic may lead people to share more relevant information about who they are. Additionally, there is preliminary evidence suggesting that greater social skills may help targets provide more nuanced information about themselves, in a more effective manner, thereby enhancing cue relevance. Further, characteristics such as power and attractiveness may foster fewer social constraints and greater social skills, leading more dominant and attractive people to emit clearer information about themselves. Future

research could examine whether self-knowledge, like coherence, also partly mediates the link between well-being and cue relevance, and clarify the role of social skills, power, and physical attractiveness in specifically promoting cue relevance.

Availability Stage

In line with the RAM, making more personality cues available to others should promote accuracy. Indeed, targets' self-reported personality profiles tend to be in greater agreement with close-others' ratings than with new acquaintances' or strangers' ratings (Connelly & Ones, 2010; Connolly, Kavanagh, & Viswesvaran, 2007; Funder & Colvin, 1988), suggesting that people who have more information about a target will judge that target more accurately. In addition, greater length of acquaintanceship in longitudinal designs (Kurtz & Sherker, 2003; Paulhus & Bruce, 1992) and in cross-sectional designs (Biesanz, West, & Millevoi, 2007), as well as increasing length and number of behavioral slices (i.e., brief excerpts of social behavior; Ambady, Bernieri, & Richeson, 2000; Murphy et al., 2015) in experimental designs (Borkenau, Mauer, Riemann, Spinath, & Angleitner, 2004; Carney, Colvin, & Hall, 2007; Letzring, Wells, & Funder, 2006) also promote accuracy. Of note, improvements in accuracy quickly taper off when no new information about a given target is introduced (Carney et al., 2007; Hall, Andrzejewski, Murphy, Mast, & Feinstein, 2008), suggesting that it is indeed the number of relevant cues, rather than the sheer amount of time spent around targets, that improves judges' accuracy. However, even if amount of acquaintanceship is held constant, some individuals may provide more information about themselves than others, making them better targets. In this section we consider some characteristics of targets that may facilitate such enhanced cue availability.

EXTRAVERSION

Extraverted individuals are identified by a tendency to be talkative, social, gregarious, and active (McCrae & Costa, 1999). These qualities promote the provision of a greater quantity of cues, as extraverted targets may naturally seek to be around others more frequently, for longer periods, and disclose more information to them. Indeed, extraverts' intelligence (Paulhus & Morgan, 1997), states (Borkenau & Liebler, 1992; Buck, Miller, & Caul, 1974; R. E. Riggio, Widaman, & Friedman, 1985), and personality traits

(Colvin, 1993b; Human, K. H. Rogers, et al., 2018) tend to be more accurately judged. Further, Human, K. H. Rogers, and colleagues (2018) found that extraverts were expressively accurate across various contexts such as in first impressions, with close peers, and on social media. Future research is needed to directly link greater extraversion to greater judgeability via cue availability, however, as it is also possible that extraversion could facilitate other stages such as cue detection, given the links between extraversion and social skills (see subsequent section for discussion of social skills and cue detection).

EMOTIONAL EXPRESSIVENESS

Another characteristic likely to foster the provision of more information to both new acquaintances and close others is the tendency to be high on emotional expressiveness or to be low on emotion suppression—the tendency to inhibit the display of felt emotions (Gross, 1998). In fact, greater emotional expressiveness may partly explain the link between extraversion and greater expressive accuracy, given that extraverted individuals have been found to be lower in emotion suppression (Gross & John, 2003) and high on self-report and behavioral indicators of emotion expressiveness (H. R. Riggio & Riggio, 2002). Expressiveness can be operationalized as the extent to which targets' emotional reactions can be read from their faces when they are not deliberately attempting to communicate those emotions (e.g., when they are alone watching emotionally loaded stimuli; Buck, 1984; Halberstadt, 1991; Manstead, 1991), or the extent to which targets are judged as expressive, open, and uninhibited in nonverbal or verbal behavior (e.g., DePaulo & Kirkendol, 1989; R. E. Riggio & Friedman, 1986). We distinguish this operationalization of emotion expressiveness, which refers to a general tendency to be expressive, from one's skill or ability to control their expressiveness to convey a particular emotion. We discuss the role of skillful self-expression on expressive accuracy when we consider the role of social skills more generally in the relevance section (previously) and detection/utilization section (subsequently).

Emotion expression is theorized to provide information about behavioral intentions (Ekman, Friesen, & Ellsworth, 1972) and to indicate boundaries, interests, and preferences (Walden, 1991), thus providing idiosyncratic cues about who a person is. Indeed, personality judgment accuracy is enhanced when more private information about thoughts and feelings—as opposed to information about overt actions—is provided (Andersen, 1984; Beer &

Brooks, 2011; Beer & Watson, 2010, Letzring & Human, 2014). Self-reported emotional expressiveness has been found to enhance accuracy in first impressions for at least the more affect-related traits such as neuroticism and agreeableness (Ambady, Hallahan, & Rosenthal, 1995). Further, targets who report "masking" their inner experiences—on items such as *"the way I feel is different than other people think I feel,"* tend to be less accurately judged on their unique personality traits (Lewis, 2014). Recent findings suggest overlap in judges' self-reported ability to understand as well as feel others' emotions and make accurate judgments of targets' unique personality profiles (Colman et al., 2017). Thus, it would be interesting to investigate whether there is overlap for targets as well, that is, whether their emotional expressiveness translates to expressiveness of their traits, particularly traits most relevant to emotions, such as neuroticism and extraversion.

Given that women and feminine individuals tend to exhibit greater emotion expressivity (Hall, 1979; Zuckerman et al., 1982), we may hypothesize that their personalities might also be judged more accurately. However, this does not appear to be the case, as research to date has not found robust gender differences in the good target of personality (Chan, K. H. Rogers, Parisotto, & Biesanz, 2011). Females' tendency to provide more emotion-relevant cues may therefore not translate to the tendency to provide more personality-relevant cues. One potential rationale for this may be that, whereas females may be more socialized (or males less motivated) to learn about emotions and show them (Gross & John, 2003; M. K. Underwood, Coie, & Herbsman, 1992), males and females may be equally socialized and motivated to express their unique personalities.

AVAILABILITY STAGE SUMMARY

Characteristics found to promote cue availability include extraversion and emotional expressiveness. It would be interesting to examine additional potential predictors, such as socialization in the family environment, in promoting communication and emotional expression, thereby enhancing cue availability (Cassidy, Parke, Butkovsky, & Braungart, 1992; Halberstadt, 1983, 1986; Hodgins & Belch, 2000; see Human & Biesanz, 2013, for further discussion). Along similar lines, future research could shed light on the role of the judge (being agreeable and making the target feel comfortable; Letzring, 2008) in eliciting a greater quantity (and potentially also quality) of cues from the target.

Detection and Utilization

The judge's task involves noticing the target's cues (e.g., momentarily looking away would hinder the detection of a target's blushing), but also that he or she have sufficient cognitive resources and social skills to notice and decode target cues (Funder, 1995). Assuming that targets have made available adequate information, how can they then help judges in the last two stages, in detecting and utilizing the cues? Some target characteristics may prompt judges to pay more attention to them (e.g., Human et al., 2012), and to engage in a more thoughtful information-processing style (Biesanz & Human, 2010; Clark, Wegener, & Fabrigar, 2008; Devine, Sedikides, & Fuhrman, 1989; Erber & Fiske, 1984; Neuberg & Fiske, 1987; Ruscher & Fiske, 1990), in turn promoting more individuated and accurate personality judgments. In this section, we review how likability, social skills, power, and physical attractiveness may enhance targets' ability to influence judges' detection and utilization of cues.

LIKEABILITY

Targets who are liked by judges tend to be judged positively and in line with how judges see themselves (e.g., Aron, Aron, Tudor, & Nelson, 1991; Human & Biesanz, 2011b); but importantly, their unique personality traits also tend to be judged more accurately (Colvin, 1993b; Human & Biesanz, 2011b). Why does being liked promote expressive accuracy? Possibly, judges may be more motivated to pay attention and decode the cues of targets they like or find pleasant (Human et al., 2012). Targets judged to have likable voices have been argued to be more expressive—to some extent suggesting they make information more available, but also elicit a positive mood in judges (Larrance & Zuckerman, 1981), potentially leading judges to pay more attention to them (see Human & Biesanz, 2013, for further discussion). Importantly, experimental research manipulating liking of a target (via inducing dislike by giving judges bogus negative feedback from targets) found that dislike reduced both positivity bias and accuracy in judgments of a target's unique personality traits (Zimmermann, Schindler, Klaus, & Leising, 2018). Because this study relied on judgments of targets in video clips, and therefore judges could not influence target behavior, it provides support for the idea that judge liking (or disliking) can influence accuracy via the cue detection and/or utilization stages, Nevertheless, it is possible that judge liking could also enhance cue relevance and availability by put-

ting targets at ease, thereby enhancing the quality and quantity of information that targets provide. Of note, the influence of liking on accuracy may not be long-lasting, as recent prospective data indicates that liking does not promote accuracy over time (i.e., at the beginning vs. end of the semester; Human, Carlson, et al., 2018). Combined, these studies suggest that liking may have an immediate benefit to accuracy, likely via cue detection and/or utilization, but less so over longer time periods. Future research would benefit from examining whether liking also influences cue relevance and availability.

SOCIAL SKILLS

Targets who have greater social skills, such as communication or self-presentation skills, have been shown to elicit greater cue detection and utilization from judges. As discussed in the relevance stage section, communication skills generally refer to the ability to regulate the intensity as well as the content of self-expression based on the context (DePaulo et al., 1992). Self-presentation is defined similarly, though involving the specific objective to make a good impression on others (Schlenker, 1980). Broadly, socially skilled individuals have been described as having a "healthy dramatic flair," argued to "move, inspire, or captivate others" and keep them engaged (Friedman, Prince, Riggio, & DiMatteo, 1980, p. 348). Indeed, some people have a greater natural ability to be charismatic or socially engaging, and this ability is associated with a higher frequency of attention-getting behaviors (e.g., DePaulo et al., 1992; Friedman et al., 1980). Although social skills are associated with a greater capability to deceive (DePaulo et al., 1992), the way people use social skills on a daily basis generally involves remaining authentic (Leary, 1995; Schlenker & Pontari, 2000). Indeed, self-presentation has been associated with being viewed more, not less, accurately in first impressions.

For example, in a study on the impression management of intelligence, targets were either given no instruction or told to "*try to appear intelligent*" prior to engaging in a videotaped getting-acquainted interaction with another participant (Murphy, 2007). Results showed that participants in the impression-management condition were perceived both as more intelligent and as more in line with their actual intelligence levels (IQ test scores) by judges (their interaction partners and outside observers). Murphy argued this may be because participants in the impression-management condition were found to use more eye-contact, potentially attracting their interaction partners' attention, thereby enhancing cue detection for those judges. Similarly, experimentally manipulating general positive self-presentation by asking participants to "*put their best face forward*" prompted targets to behave in a more engaging and pleasant way, thus drawing judges' attention and leading them to form more accurate personality judgments (Human et al., 2012). These experimental manipulations lend support to the causal interpretation of the link between social skill and cue detection and use. Further, the malleability of self-presentation suggests that it may be not only an individual difference but also context-specific, partly driven by the target's expectations and motivation in a given situation. Similarly, then, expressive accuracy may also be affected by targets' motivations in specific situations.

POWER

In addition to providing more relevant cues, high target power may also facilitate cue detection and use. Specifically, judges who interact with higher-power or more dominant targets may be particularly motivated to pay attention to cues and to make sense of those cues, given the greater control higher-status individuals generally have over outcomes (Fiske, 1993). Alternatively, lower-power targets may be seen less accurately because higher-power judges experience greater cognitive load of responsibility-related information, reducing the motivation and cognitive resources they would otherwise allocate to judging their subordinates (Overbeck & Park, 2001). A host of studies show that individuals who report lower status or trait dominance (Ratcliff, Hugenberg, Shriver, & Bernstein, 2011) or who are in an experimentally induced low dominance condition (Dépret & Fiske, 1999; Erber & Fiske, 1984; Neuberg & Fiske, 1987; Ruscher & Fiske, 1990) tend to pay more attention to high-power individuals, while high-power or dominant individuals tend to pay less attention to subordinates or low-dominance individuals (Goodwin, Gubin, Fiske, & Yzerbyt, 2000; but see Overbeck & Park, 2001; Weick & Guinote, 2008; Schmid Mast, Jonas, & Hall, 2009).

There is also evidence to suggest that target power promotes greater judge cue utilization as well as attention and cue detection. For example, when rating high-status (as compared to low-status) targets, judges engage in more deliberate processing of personality-relevant information (Erber & Fiske, 1984; Neuberg & Fiske, 1987; Ruscher & Fiske, 1990). This enhanced processing suggests that

judges may devote more cognitive resources, and use superior encoding strategies, when attempting to understand high-status versus low-status individuals. In line with those findings, Galinsky, Magee, Ines, and Gruenfeld (2006) showed that judges in a high-power condition tended to be more self-focused than controls, that is, less likely to take into account others' perspectives. However, Schmid Mast and colleagues (2009) found that high-power individuals who endorsed more other-focused as opposed to self-focused tendencies were better judges of targets' feelings and thoughts than their lower-power counterparts. Thus, higher-power judges might in fact make more accurate judgments of others, but possibly only if motivated to detect target cues, which may not always be the case. Future research could examine how various types of power may differentially promote self- or other-focused tendencies, in order to disentangle the cases in which more versus less power promotes expressive accuracy.

PHYSICAL ATTRACTIVENESS

People tend to like physically attractive individuals and seek to spend more time with them (Langlois et al., 2000). Further, research shows that judges differ in their interactive style based on their interaction partner's attractiveness (Dion, 1974; Langlois, Ritter, Casey, & Sawin, 1995; Snyder, Tanke, & Berscheid, 1977; D. W. Stewart, 1984; J. E. Stewart, 1980), and are likely to pay more attention to targets they find attractive (Langlois et al., 2000; Maner et al., 2003). In addition, judges' greater motivation to engage in interactions and bond with physically attractive targets (Lemay, Clark, & Greenberg, 2010) may make them eager to know and understand them (De La Ronde & Swann, 1998). In turn, a judge's motivation to connect with (Maner, DeWall, Baumeister, & Schaller, 2007; Pickett, Gardner, & Knowles, 2004) and accurately perceive (Biesanz & Human, 2010) a given target is shown to promote accuracy of that target's unique personality profile. Thus, to the extent that people pay more attention and are more motivated to understand attractive individuals, they may view them more accurately. In line with this, Lorenzo et al. (2010) found that the link between physical attractiveness and being viewed more accurately depends not only on the target's objective attractiveness but also on the judge's subjective ratings of that target's attractiveness. That is, judges who rated a target as more physically attractive, above and beyond consensually determined attractiveness, judged that target's personality more accurately. This judge-specific effect of perceived attractiveness on accuracy suggests that enhanced judge motivation to pay attention and devote cognitive resources, and not just the attractive target's natural tendency to provide more relevant cues, contributes to accuracy for that target.

CUE DETECTION AND UTILIZATION SUMMARY

Being liked, socially skilled, high in power, or physically attractive are all pathways that enhance the attention targets receive and the cognitive resources that judges devote to deciphering them, providing indirect routes to being a good target. Nonetheless, the research reviewed in this section does not adequately disentangle detection from utilization processes. Future studies should attempt to separate detection from utilization, for example with tasks involving gaze-tracking (assessing detection) or experimentally induced cognitive load (manipulating utilization). This will begin to shed light on the extent to which these characteristics influence detection, utilization, or both simultaneously.

Benefits of Being a Good Target

As described previously, several stable individual differences appear to distinguish the good target of accuracy. Interestingly, many of these characteristics seem to be linked to positive psychological and social processes. Therefore, we posit that there may be something inherently adaptive in being a good target, in turn promoting positive consequences. This section explores the possible intrapersonal and interpersonal benefits that good targets may reap.

Intrapersonal Benefits

Though typically theorized as a predictor of expressive accuracy, evidence suggests that greater psychological adjustment could also be a consequence of being viewed more accurately. Indeed, both disclosing personal information to others (i.e., self-disclosure), indicating that one may be making relevant cues available, and receiving feedback about the self in line with one's own self-views (i.e., self-verification), indicating being perceived in line with one's unique characteristics, are shown to be intrinsically gratifying experiences. For example, disclosing high-quality personal information, that is, less observable information about one's feelings and thoughts as opposed to one's behaviors (Laurenceau, Barrett, Pietromonaco, 1998), appears to promote greater target liking of their interaction partner, possibly in part because disclosing feels good

(Jourard, 1971). In fact, both introspecting on one's own personality traits and, to a greater extent, sharing the content of that introspection with others, have been associated with greater activation of neural reward pathways (Tamir & Mitchell, 2012).

Further, expressing oneself in line with one's own self-views may lead targets to receive more self-verifying information from judges; that is, judges may be more likely to provide good targets with feedback in line with targets' self-views (Gill & Swann, 2004; see Swann, 2012, for review). In turn, receiving self-verifying information is found to be a subjectively pleasing experience (Swann, Pelham, & Krull, 1989), and people appear to respond positively when confronted with self-verifying information— positive or negative—by displaying more positive facial expressions and engaging in more creative behaviors (Ayduk et al., 2013). Further, self-verifying information has been argued to reduce anxiety (Swann, Chang-Schneider, & Angulo, 2007) and to increase one's sense of authenticity (Kernis, 2003; Leary, 2003), which is also related to greater well-being (Sheldon & Kasser, 1995).

Though not directly related to personality judgments, there is preliminary work linking being judged accurately to biological processes and better physical health. For example, adolescents whose parents accurately perceive their daily experiences, agreeing more with the adolescent regarding how positive their day was and how much stress they experienced, tend to have more effective inflammatory regulation (Human, Chan, et al., 2014), which is in turn linked to reduced systemic inflammation and risk of chronic disease (Chung et al., 2009). Relatedly, expressing emotion is related to lower blood pressure reactivity (e.g., Buck, Savin, Miller, & Caul, 1972; Dan-Glauser & Gross, 2015; but see Mendolia & Kleck, 1993), though this may potentially depend on whether emotion expression is valued within a given culture (Butler, Lee, & Gross, 2009). Similarly, obtaining self-verifying information is shown to reduce blood pressure reactivity (Ayduk et al., 2013). Conversely, suppressing emotions and thoughts is shown to increase blood pressure reactivity (Butler et al., 2003). Of note, it appears to be the intensity of the emotion, rather than the valence, that is distressing, as suppressing emotions to both positive and negative stimuli, but not to neutral stimuli, is linked to greater reactivity (Butler et al., 2009). It is argued that these physiological responses, such as poor inflammatory regulation and increased blood pressure reactivity, reflect the stressful experience of not being able to accurately express oneself and in turn be accurately judged (Human, 2017).

Interpersonal Benefits

In addition to being intrinsically beneficial for individual adjustment, expressive accuracy may also benefit social interactions and relationships. For instance, targets who are seen more accurately in first impressions tend to be better liked by judges. Indeed, longitudinal studies have demonstrated that judges better liked targets that they more accurately perceived in initial impressions over time (Human et al., 2013; Human, Carlson, et al., 2018). Furthermore, among newlyweds, accuracy is linked to greater relationship satisfaction both in the target and the judge (Luo & Snider, 2009), and being accurately perceived by one's spouse predicts a lower likelihood of divorce (Neff & Karney, 2005). Thus, liking and positive relationship experiences may foster expressive accuracy, as discussed earlier, and expressive accuracy may foster greater liking and positive relationship experiences.

What about being a good target could improve the quality of one's interpersonal interactions and relationships? Greater target self-disclosure has been associated with greater judge and target liking (see Collins & Miller, 1994, for a review), and receiving self-verifying information from one's romantic partner has been associated with greater intimacy and relationship satisfaction (Lackenbauer, Campbell, Rubin, Fletcher, & Troister, 2010; Swann, De La Ronde, & Hixon, 1994). Good targets may also feel more familiar to judges, thereby making the judge feel more comfortable and promoting smoother interactions and greater liking (Langlois & Roggman, 1990; Reber, Schwarz, & Winkielman, 2004; Reis, Maniaci, Caprariello, Eastwick, & Finkel, 2011; but see Norton, Frost, & Ariely, 2007). Good targets also likely provide a sense of predictability, making judges feel in control of their world, which is argued to promote romantic relationship satisfaction in both partners (De La Ronde & Swann, 1998; Hardin & Higgins, 1996).

The interpersonal benefits of being a good target may also extend to the workplace. For example, when choosing among high-quality job applicants in personnel selection contexts, employers are more likely to hire those who are also good targets, arguably because they confer potential employers with a sense that their flaws may be more predictable (Moore, Lee, Kim, & Cable, 2017; see Mignault & Human, 2017, for further discussion). Providing higher-quality cues may also lead to greater person-environment fit, increasing the target's chances that judges—who use target cues regardless of cue relevance (Human et al., 2019)—will make decisions aligned to the target's personal style, skills, and interests.

Given the strong links between psychological well-being and both expressive accuracy (discussed previously) and positive interpersonal outcomes (e.g., Lyubomirsky, King, & Diener, 2005), it is plausible that the links between expressive accuracy and positive interpersonal outcomes are driven by psychological well-being. Alternatively, positive interpersonal experiences may play a mediating role linking expressive accuracy to psychological well-being. Ideally, future research will examine these possibilities by comprehensively assessing both intra- and interpersonal processes and using longitudinal and experimental designs.

Negative Consequences

Despite the aforementioned benefits, could expressing oneself accurately sometimes do more harm than good? When targets are in a situation in which there is an actual or perceived risk of being rejected, accurately expressing their negative traits and experiences may bear more negative than positive consequences (Kwang & Swann, 2010). For example, in dating contexts, where there is an actual risk of rejection, targets tend to seek positive feedback as opposed to feedback in line with their self-views (Kwang & Swann, 2010), arguably because being accurately but negatively perceived by their dating partner could lead to being abandoned (e.g., Baumeister & Leary, 1995; Wiggins & Broughton, 1985). Indeed, when judges have more information about their dating partners, they tend to like them less, potentially because it may emphasize dissimilarities between the target partner and the self (Norton et al., 2007). Rejection risk may also be perceived on a more chronic basis by certain individuals such as those who have low self-esteem (Kwang & Swann, 2010). Indeed, when self-disclosing negative information, low-self-esteem targets report feeling less valued by their romantic partners (Cameron, Holmes, & Vorauer, 2009), and appear to receive less support from their online social networks (Forest & Wood, 2012). That said, judges on average tend to appreciate the genuineness of negative self-disclosures (Gromet & Pronin, 2009), and low self-esteem targets are found to feel positively when receiving negative self-verifying feedback (Ayduk et al., 2013), thus possibly mitigating the undesirable effects of disclosing negative information about the self. Thus, being a good target may backfire when there is potential for being rejected, leading to interpersonal stress. However, the benefits likely outweigh the costs, given that the wealth of prior research tends to link being viewed accurately to positive intra- and interpersonal experiences.

Summary and Discussion

The evidence reviewed in this chapter highlights the important role of the target in the accuracy of personality judgments and reveals several potential pathways to being a good target. *Psychological well-being*, one of the target characteristics that has received the most empirical attention, along with related characteristics such as *personality coherence* and *self-knowledge*, likely lead targets to provide cues that truly reflect who they are (cue relevance). Preliminary research suggests that *power* and *physical attractiveness* may also impact targets' tendency to provide relevant cues, and may enhance judges' attention and motivation (cue detection and utilization). *Extraversion* and *emotional expressiveness* may foster expressive accuracy by increasing the amount of information targets provide (cue availability), though it is also possible that such characteristics foster cue detection and use. *Social skills* are also argued to promote expressive accuracy via cue relevance, as well as cue detection and use. Lastly, *being liked* by judges may foster greater cue detection and use, as liking potentially motivates judges to pay attention and to correctly interpret the targets' cues. Thus, there are various characteristics that may foster expressive accuracy, sometimes via multiple pathways. More research directly examining each of these characteristics and which pathway or pathways they operate through is needed. Understanding the predictors and mechanisms underlying expressive accuracy is especially important given the potential benefits to one's psychological and social health.

Enhancing Expressive Accuracy

But is being a good target an attainable experience? Interestingly, some of the aforementioned characteristics appear to be quite malleable and could possibly be trained to improve expressive accuracy. For example, interventions aimed at enhancing cue relevance could potentially involve aspects of well-being (such as self-esteem and positive mood), congruence, and self-knowledge. Specifically, it appears self-esteem can be enhanced for sustained periods through indirect means such as increased social sup-port from coaches in team sports (Smoll, Smith, Barnett, & Everett, 1993) and implicitly using a computer task in which words that are relevant to one's self-concept are systematically followed by a smiling face (Baccus, Baldwin, & Packer, 2004). Additionally, given the association between daily well-being levels and personality-behavior congruence (Human et al., 2019), it would be interesting to enhance state well-being, for example using mood inductions such as the presentation of a happy film (Westermann, Spies, Stahl, & Hesse, 1996), to examine whether that enhances cue relevance and expressive accuracy. Further, it may also be possible to train self-knowledge, through introspection (Hixon & Swann, 1993; Sedikides et al., 2007) or through feedback from close others (Bollich, Johannet, & Vazire, 2011), to examine whether that enables targets to provide others with clearer cues to their personalities.

Inducing a sense of power in targets may also promote cue relevance, as well as detection and use. This can be done, for instance, by asking targets to recall an experience in which they had control over others' outcomes (Rucker & Galinsky, 2009) or by simply asking the target for advice (Schaerer, Tost, Huang, Gino, & Larrick, 2018). Further, to enhance cue detection and use, simply encouraging targets to "make a good impression" may promote attention and motivation in judges, in turn predicting greater accuracy (Human et al., 2012). Of note, in addition to training targets, expressive accuracy might also be improved indirectly, through educating judges on the optimal conditions that make targets feel at ease to divulge their true selves, for example, by providing a warm and nonjudgmental attitude (Letzring, 2008). Critically, improving target characteristics—such as well-being, self-knowledge, self-presentation, and the sense of power—as well as the judge's attitude, is not only likely to promote expressive accuracy but also likely to have personal benefits beyond accuracy (e.g., Bollich et al., 2011), as such characteristics are found to be closely related to broader intra- and interpersonal functioning.

Conclusion

In sum, Vonnegut's warning that "we must be careful what we pretend to be" is warranted, given the important role that targets play in the overall accuracy of personality judgments. Specifically, through each stage of the personality judgment process, targets can facilitate being viewed in line with their true selves, by providing a higher quality and quantity of information and delivering that information in a way that elicits greater judge attention and motivation to be accurate. In turn, being perceived in line with one's true self may often feel inherently good and foster broader psychological and social well-being.

References

Adams, G. R. (1977). Physical attractiveness, personality, and social reactions to peer pressure. *Journal of Psychology, 96*(2), 287–296. doi:10.1080/00223980.1977.9915911

Allport, G. W. (1937). *Personality: A psychological interpretation.* Oxford, England: Holt.

Allport, G. W. (1955). *Becoming: Basic considerations for a psychology of personality.* New Haven, CT: Yale University Press.

Ambady, N., Bernieri, F. J., & Richeson, J. A. (2000). Toward a histology of social behavior: Judgmental accuracy from thin slices of the behavioral stream. In M. P. Zanna (Ed.), *Advances in experimental social psychology* (Vol. 32, pp. 201–271). San Diego, CA: Academic Press. doi:10.1016/S0065-2601(00)80006-4

Ambady, N., Hallahan, M., & Rosenthal, R. (1995). On judging and being judged accurately in zero- acquaintance situations. *Journal of Personality and Social Psychology, 69*(3), 518–529. doi:10.1037/0022-3514.69.3.518

Andersen, S. M. (1984). Self-knowledge and social inference: II. The diagnosticity of cognitive/affective and behavioral data. *Journal of Personality and Social Psychology, 46*, 294–307. doi:10.1037//0022-3514.46.2.294

Anderson, C., & Berdahl, J. L. (2002). The experience of power: Examining the effects of power on approach and inhibition tendencies. *Journal of Personality and Social Psychology, 83*(6), 1362–1377. doi:10.1037/0022-3514.83.6.1362

Aron, A., Aron, E. N., Tudor, M., & Nelson, G. (1991). Close relationships as including the other in the self. *Journal of Personality and Social Psychology, 60*, 241–253. doi:10.1037/0022-3514.60.2.241

Ayduk, Ö., Gyurak, A., Akinola, M., & Mendes, W. B. (2013). Consistency over flattery: Self-verification processes revealed in implicit and behavioral responses to feedback. *Social Psychological and Personality Science, 4*(5), 538–545. doi:10.1177/1948550612471827

Baccus, J. R., Baldwin, M. W., & Packer, D. J. (2004). Increasing implicit self-esteem through classical conditioning. *Psychological Science, 15*(7), 498–502. doi:10.1111/j.0956-7976.2004.00708.x

Back, M. D., & Nestler, S. (2016). Accuracy of judging personality. In J. A. Hall, M. Schmid Mast, & T. V. West (Eds.), *The social psychology of perceiving others accurately* (pp. 98–124). Cambridge: Cambridge University Press.

Baird, B. M., Le, K., & Lucas, R. E. (2006). On the nature of intraindividual personality variability: Reliability, validity, and associations with well-being. *Journal of Personality and Social Psychology, 90*, 512–527. doi:10.1037/0022-3514.90.3.512

Baumeister, R. F. (1982). A self-presentational view of social phenomena. *Psychological Bulletin, 91*(1), 3–26. doi:10.1037/0033-2909.91.1.3

Baumeister, R. F., & Leary, M. R. (1995). The need to belong: Desire for interpersonal attachments as a fundamental human motivation. *Psychological Bulletin, 117*(3), 497–529. doi:10.1037/0033-2909.117.3.497

Baumeister, R. F., & Tice, D. M. (1988). Metatraits. *Journal of Personality, 56*(3), 571–598. doi:10.1111/j.1467-6494.1988.tb00903.x

Baumeister, R. F., Tice, D. M., & Hutton, D. G. (1989). Self-presentational motivations and personality differences in self-esteem. *Journal of Personality, 57*(3), 547–579. doi:10.1111/j.1467-6494.1989.tb02384.x

Beer, A., & Brooks, C. (2011). Information quality in personality judgment: The value of personal disclosure. *Journal of Research in Personality, 45*(2), 175–185. doi:10.1016/j.jrp.2011.01.001

Beer, A., & Watson, D. (2010). The effects of information and exposure on self-other agreement. *Journal of Research in Personality, 44*(1), 38–45. doi:10.1016/j.jrp.2009.10.002

Bem, D. J., & Allen, A. (1974). On predicting some of the people some of the time: The search for cross-situational consistencies in behavior. *Psychological Review, 81*, 506–520. doi:10.1037/h0037130

Berdahl, J. L., & Martorana, P. (2006). Effects of power on emotion and expression during a controversial group discussion. *European Journal of Social Psychology, 36*(4), 497–509. doi:10.1002/ejsp.354

Biesanz, J. C. (2010). The social accuracy model of interpersonal perception: Assessing individual differences in perceptive and expressive accuracy. *Multivariate Behavioral Research, 45*, 853–885. doi:10.1080/00273171.2010.519262

Biesanz, J. C., & Human, L. J. (2010). The cost of forming more accurate impressions: Accuracy motivated perceivers see the personality of others more distinctively but less normatively than perceivers without an explicit goal. *Psychological Science, 21*(4), 589–594. doi:10.1177/0956797610364121

Biesanz, J. C., & West, S. G. (2000). Personality coherence: Moderating self–other profile agreement and profile consensus. *Journal of Personality and Social Psychology, 79*, 425–437. doi:10.1037/0022-3514.79.3.425

Biesanz, J. C., West, S. G., & Graziano, W. G. (1998). Moderators of self-other agreement: Reconsidering temporal stability in personality. *Journal of Personality and Social Psychology, 75*, 467–477. doi:10.1037/0022-3514.75.2.467

Biesanz, J. C., West, S. G., & Millevoi, A. (2007). What do you learn about someone over time? The relationship between length of acquaintance and consensus and self-other agreement in judgments of personality. *Journal of Personality and Social Psychology, 92*, 119–135. doi:10.1037/0022-3514.92.1.119

Block, J. (1961). Ego identity, role variability, and adjustment. *Journal of Consulting Psychology, 25*(5), 392–397. doi:10.1037/h0042979

Bollich, K. L., Johannet, P. M., & Vazire, S. (2011). In search of our true selves: Feedback as a path to self-knowledge. *Frontiers in Psychology, 2*, 312. doi:10.3389/fpsyg.2011.00312

Borkenau, P., & Liebler, A. (1992). Trait inferences: Sources of validity at zero acquaintance. *Journal of Personality and Social Psychology, 62*(4), 645–657. doi:10.1037/0022-3514.62.4.645

Borkenau, P., Mauer, N., Riemann, R., Spinath, F. M., & Angleitner, A. (2004). Thin slices of behavior as cues of personality and intelligence. *Journal of Personality and Social Psychology, 86*(4), 599–614. doi:10.1037/0022-3514.86.4.599

Briggs, S. R., Cheek, J. M., & Buss, A. H. (1980). An analysis of the Self-Monitoring Scale. *Journal of Personality and Social Psychology, 38*(4), 679–686. doi:10.1037/0022-3514.38.4.679

Buck, R. (1984). *The communication of emotions.* New York: Guilford University Press.

Buck, R., Miller, R. E., & Caul, W. F. (1974). Sex, personality, and physiological variables in the communication of affect via facial expression. *Journal of Personality and Social Psychology, 30*(4), 587–596. doi:10.1037/h0037041.

Buck, R. W., Savin, V. J., Miller, R. E., & Caul, W. F. (1972). Communication of affect through facial expressions in humans. *Journal of Personality and Social Psychology, 23*(3), 362–371. doi:10.1037/h0033171

Butler, E. A., Egloff, B., Wilhelm, F. H., Smith, N. C., Erickson, E. A., & Gross, J. J. (2003). The social consequences of expressive suppression. *Emotion, 3*, 48–67. doi:10.1037/1528-3542.3.1.48

Butler, E. A., Lee, T. L., & Gross, J. J. (2009). Does expressing your emotions raise or lower your blood pressure? The answer depends on cultural context. *Journal of Cross-Cultural Psychology, 40*(3), 510–517. doi:10.1177/0022022109332845

Cameron, J. J., Holmes, J. G., & Vorauer, J. D. (2009). When self-disclosure goes awry: Negative consequences of revealing personal failures for lower self-esteem individuals. *Journal of Experimental Social Psychology, 45*(1), 217–222. doi:10.1016/j.jesp.2008.09.009

Campbell, J. D. (1990). Self-esteem and clarity of the self-concept. *Journal of Personality and Social Psychology, 59*(3), 538–549. doi:10.1037/0022-3514.59.3.538

Campbell, J. D., Assanand, S., & Paula, A. D. (2003). The structure of the self-concept and its relation to psychological adjustment. *Journal of Personality, 71*(1), 115–140. doi:10.1111/1467-6494.t01-1-00002

Campbell, J. D., Chew, B., & Scratchley, L. S. (1991). Cognitive and emotional reactions to daily events: The effects of self-esteem and self-complexity. *Journal of Personality, 59*(3), 473–505. doi:10.1111/j.1467-6494.1991.tb00257.x

Carney, D. R., Colvin, C. R., & Hall, J. A. (2007). A thin slice perspective on the accuracy of first impressions. *Journal of Research in Personality, 41*(5), 1054–1072. doi:10.1016/j.jrp.2007.01.004

Cassidy, J., Parke, R. D., Butkovsky, L., & Braungart, J. M. (1992). Family-peer connections: The roles of emotional expressiveness within the family and children's understanding of emotions. *Child Development, 63*(3), 603–618. doi:10.1111/j.1467-8624.1992.tb01649.x

Cervone, D., & Shoda, Y. (Eds.). (1999). *The coherence of personality: Social-cognitive bases of consistency, variability, and organization.* New York: Guilford Press.

Chan, M., Rogers, K. H., Parisotto, K. L., & Biesanz, J. C. (2011). Forming first impressions: The role of gender and normative accuracy in personality perception. *Journal of Research in Personality, 45*(1), 117–120. doi:10.1016/j.jrp.2010.11.001

Chaplin, W. F., & Goldberg, L. R. (1984). A failure to replicate the Bem and Allen study of individual differences in cross-situational consistency. *Journal of Personality and Social Psychology, 47*, 1074–1090. doi:10.1037/0022-3514.47.5.1074

Cheek, J. M. (1982). Aggregation, moderator variables, and the validity of personality tests: A peer rating study. *Journal of Personality and Social Psychology, 43*(6), 1254–1269. doi:10.1037/0022-3514.43.6.1254

Christensen, D., & Rosenthal, R. (1982). Gender and nonverbal decoding skill as determinants of interpersonal expectancy effects. *Journal of Personality and Social Psychology, 42*(1), 75–87. doi:10.1037/0022-3514.42.1.75

Christensen, L. (1974). The influence of trait, sex, and information on accuracy of personality assessment. *Journal of Personality Assessment, 38*(2), 130–135. doi:10.1080/00223891.1974.10119949

Chung, H. Y., Cesari, M., Anton, S., Marzetti, E., Giovannini, S., Seo, A. Y.,…Leeuwenburgh, C. (2009). Molecular inflammation: Underpinnings of aging and age-related diseases. *Ageing Research Reviews, 8*, 18–30. doi:10.1016/j.arr.2008.07.002

Clark, J. K., Wegener, D. T., & Fabrigar, L. R. (2008). Attitudinal ambivalence and message-based persuasion: Motivated processing of proattitudinal information and avoidance of counterattitudinal information. *Personality and Social Psychology Bulletin, 34*(4), 565–577. doi:10.1177/0146167207312527

Clifton, A., & Kuper, L. E. (2011). Self-reported personality variability across the social network is associated with interpersonal dysfunction. *Journal of Personality, 79*(2), 359–390. doi:201110.1111/j.1467-6494.2010.00686.x

Collins, N. L., & Miller, L. C. (1994). Self-disclosure and liking: A meta-analytic review. *Psychological Bulletin, 116*, 457–475. doi:10.1037//0033-2909.116.3.457

Colman, D. E., Letzring, T. D., & Biesanz, J. C. (2017). Seeing and feeling your way to accurate personality judgments: The moderating role of perceiver empathic tendencies. *Social Psychological and Personality Science, 8*(7), 806–815. doi:10.1177/1948550617691097

Colvin, C. R. (1993a). Childhood antecedents of young-adult judgability. *Journal of Personality, 61*(4), 611–635. doi:10.1111/j.1467-6494.1993.tb00784.x

Colvin, C. R. (1993b). "Judgable" people: Personality, behavior, and competing explanations. *Journal of Personality and Social Psychology, 64*, 861–873. doi:10.1037//0022-3514.64.5.861

Connelly, B. S., & Ones, D. S. (2010). Another perspective on personality: Meta-analytic integration of observers' accuracy and predictive validity. *Psychological Bulletin, 136*(6), 1092–1122. doi:10.1037/a0021212

Connolly, J. J., Kavanagh, E. J., & Viswesvaran, C. (2007). The convergent validity between self and observer ratings of personality: A meta-analytic review. *International Journal of Selection and Assessment, 15*(1), 110–117. doi:10.1111/j.1468-2389.2007.00371.x

Cooper, H., & Hazelrigg, P. (1988). Personality moderators of interpersonal expectancy effects: An integrative research review. *Journal of Personality and Social Psychology, 55*(6), 937–949. doi:10.1037/0022-3514.55.6.937

Copeland, J. T. (1994). Prophecies of power: Motivational implications of social power for behavioral confirmation. *Journal of Personality and Social Psychology, 67*(2), 264–277. doi:10.1037/0022-3514.67.2.264

Dan-Glauser, E. S., & Gross, J. J. (2015). The temporal dynamics of emotional acceptance: Experience, expression, and physiology. *Biological Psychology, 108*, 1–12. doi:10.1016/j.biopsycho.2015.03.005

De La Ronde, C., & Swann, W. B., Jr. (1998). Partner verification: Restoring shattered images of our intimates. *Journal of Personality and Social Psychology, 75*, 374–382. doi:10.1037//0022-3514.75.2.374

DePaulo, B. M., Blank, A. L., Swaim, G. W., & Hairfield, J. G. (1992). Expressiveness and expressive control. *Personality and Social Psychology Bulletin, 18*(3), 276–285. doi:10.1177/0146167292183003

DePaulo, B. M., & Kirkendol, S. E. (1989). The motivational impairment effect in the communication of deception. In J. C. Yuille (Ed.), *Credibility assessment* (pp. 51–70). Dordrecht, The Netherlands: Kluwer.

Dépret, E., & Fiske, S. T. (1999). Perceiving the powerful: Intriguing individuals versus threatening groups. *Journal of Experimental Social Psychology*, 35(5), 461–480. doi:10.1006/jesp.1999.1380

Devine, P. G., Sedikides, C., & Fuhrman, R. W. (1989). Goals in social information processing: The case of anticipated interaction. *Journal of Personality and Social Psychology*, 56(5), 680–690. doi:10.1037/0022-3514.56.5.680

Diehl, M., & Hay, E. L. (2007). Contextualized self-representations in adulthood. *Journal of Personality*, 75(6), 1255–1284. doi:10.1111/j.1467-6494.2007.00475.x

Diehl, M., & Hay, E. L. (2010). Risk and resilience factors in coping with daily stress in adulthood: The role of age, self-concept incoherence, and personal control. *Developmental Psychology*, 46(5), 1132–1146. doi:10.1037/a0019937

Dion, K., Berscheid, E., & Walster, E. (1972). What is beautiful is good. *Journal of Personality and Social Psychology*, 24(3), 285–290. doi:10.1037/h0033731

Dion, K. K. (1974). Children's physical attractiveness and sex as determinants of adult punitiveness. *Developmental Psychology*, 10(5), 772–778. doi:10.1037/h0037030

Donahue, E. M., Robins, R. W., Roberts, B. W., & John, O. P. (1993). The divided self: Concurrent and longitudinal effects of psychological adjustment and social roles on self-concept differentiation. *Journal of Personality and Social Psychology*, 64(5), 834–846. doi:10.1037/0022-3514.64.5.834

Ekman, P., Friesen, W. V., & Ellsworth, P. (1972). *Emotion in the human face: Guidelines for research and an integration of findings*. Oxford, UK: Pergamon Press.

Erber, R., & Fiske, S. T. (1984). Outcome dependency and attention to inconsistent information. *Journal of Personality and Social Psychology*, 47(4), 709–726. doi:10.1037/0022-3514.47.4.709

Erickson, T. M., Newman, M. G., & Pincus, A. L. (2009). Predicting unpredictability: Do measures of interpersonal rigidity/flexibility and distress predict intraindividual variability in social perceptions and behavior? *Journal of Personality and Social Psychology*, 97(5), 893–912. doi:10.1037/a0016515

Fenigstein, A., Scheier, M. F., & Buss, A. H. (1975). Public and private self-consciousness: Assessment and theory. *Journal of Consulting and Clinical Psychology*, 43(4), 522–527. doi:10.1037/h0076760

Fiske, S. T. (1993). Social cognition and social perception. *Annual Review of Psychology*, 44(1), 155–194. doi:10.1146/annurev.ps.44.020193.001103

Forest, A. L., & Wood, J. V. (2012). When social networking is not working: Individuals with low self-esteem recognize but do not reap the benefits of self-disclosure on Facebook. *Psychological Science*, 23(3), 295–302. doi:10.1177/0956797611429709

Friedman, H. S., Prince, L. M., Riggio, R. E., & DiMatteo, M. R. (1980). Understanding and assessing nonverbal expressiveness: The Affective Communication Test. *Journal of Personality and Social Psychology*, 39(2), 333–351. doi:10.1037/0022-3514.39.2.333

Funder, D. C. (1995). On the accuracy of personality judgment: A realistic approach. *Psychological Review*, 102(4), 652–670. doi:10.1037/0033-295X.102.4.652

Funder, D. C., & Colvin, C. R. (1988). Friends and strangers: Acquaintanceship, agreement, and the accuracy of personality judgment. *Journal of Personality and Social Psychology*, 55(1), 149–158. doi:10.1037/0022-3514.55.1.149

Galinsky, A. D., Magee, J. C., Ines, M. E., & Gruenfeld, D. H. (2006). Power and perspectives not taken. *Psychological Science*, 17, 1068–1074. doi:10.1111/j.1467-9280.2006.01824.x

Gaucher, D., Wood, J. V., Stinson, D. A., Forest, A. L., Holmes, J. G., & Logel, C. (2012). Perceived regard explains self-esteem differences in expressivity. *Personality and Social Psychology Bulletin*, 38(9), 1144–1156. doi:10.1177/0146167212445790

Gilbert, D. T., Pelham, B. W., & Krull, D. S. (1988). On cognitive busyness: When person judges meet persons perceived. *Journal of Personality and Social Psychology*, 54, 733–740. doi:10.1037/0022-3514.54.5.733

Gill, M. J., & Swann, W. B., Jr. (2004). On what it means to know someone: A matter of pragmatics. *Journal of Personality and Social Psychology*, 86(3), 405–418. doi:10.1037/0022-3514.86.3.405

Goffman, E. (1959). *The presentation of self in everyday life*. Garden city, NY: Doubleday.

Goodwin, S. A., Gubin, A., Fiske, S. T., & Yzerbyt, V. Y. (2000). Power can bias impression processes: Stereotyping subordinates by default and by design. *Group Processes and Intergroup Relations*, 3(3), 227–256. doi:10.1177/1368430200003003001

Gromet, D. M., & Pronin, E. (2009). What were you worried about? Actors' concerns about revealing fears and insecurities relative to observers' reactions. *Self and Identity*, 8(4), 342–364. doi:10.1080/15298860802299392

Gross, J. J. (1998). Antecedent-and response-focused emotion regulation: Divergent consequences for experience, expression, and physiology. *Journal of Personality and Social Psychology*, 74(1), 224–237. doi:10.1037/0022-3514.74.1.224

Gross, J. J., & John, O. P. (2003). Individual differences in two emotion regulation processes: implications for affect, relationships, and well-being. *Journal of Personality and Social Psychology*, 85(2), 348–362. doi:10.1037/0022-3514.85.2.348

Halberstadt, A. G. (1983). Family expressiveness styles and nonverbal communication skills. *Journal of Nonverbal Behavior*, 8(1), 14–26. doi:10.1007/BF00986327

Halberstadt, A. G. (1986). Family socialization of emotional expression and nonverbal communication styles and skills. *Journal of Personality and Social Psychology*, 51(4), 827–836. doi:10.1037/0022-3514.51.4.827

Halberstadt, A. G. (1991). Toward an ecology of expressiveness: Family socialization in particular and a model in general. In R. S. Feldman & B. Rimé (Eds.), *Studies in emotion and social interaction: Fundamentals of nonverbal behavior* (pp. 106–160). New York, NY: Cambridge University Press; Paris, France: Editions de la Maison des Sciences de l'Homme.

Hall, J. A. (1979). Gender, gender roles, and nonverbal communication skills. In R. Rosenthal (Ed.), *Skill in nonverbal communication*. Cambridge, MA: Oelgeschlager, Gunn & Hain.

Hall, J. A., Andrzejewski, S. A., Murphy, N. A., Mast, M. S., & Feinstein, B. A. (2008). Accuracy of judging others' traits and states: Comparing mean levels across tests. *Journal of Research in Personality*, 42(6), 1476–1489. doi:10.1016/j.jrp.2008.06.013

Hardin, C. D., & Higgins, E. T. (1996). Shared reality: How social verification makes the subjective objective. In R. M. Sorrentino & E. T. Higgins (Eds.), *Handbook of motivation and cognition: Vol. 3. The interpersonal context* (pp. 28–84). New York, NY: Guilford Press.

Hilton, J. L., & Darley, J. M. (1985). Constructing other persons: A limit on the effect. *Journal of Experimental Social Psychology*, 21(1), 1–18. doi:10.1016/0022-1031(85)90002-2

Hixon, J. G., & Swann, W. B., Jr., (1993). When does introspection bear fruit? Self-reflection, self-insight, and interpersonal choices. *Journal of Personality and Social Psychology, 64*(1), 35–43. doi:10.1037//0022-3514.64.1.35

Hodgins, H. S., & Belch, C. (2000). Interparental violence and nonverbal abilities. *Journal of Nonverbal Behavior, 24*(1), 3–24. doi:10.1023/A:1006602921315

Hopwood, C. J., Newman, D. A., Donnellan, M. B., Markowitz, J. C., Grilo, C. M., Sanislow, C. A.,...Gunderson, J. G. (2009). The stability of personality traits in individuals with borderline personality disorder. *Journal of Abnormal Psychology, 118*(4), 806–815. doi:10.1037/a0016954

Human, L. J. (2017). Interpersonal perception. In K. Sweeny & M. L. Robbins (Eds.), *The Wiley encyclopedia of health psychology: Volume II. The social bases of health behavior.* New York, NY: Wiley.

Human, L. J., & Biesanz, J. C. (2011a). Target adjustment and self–other agreement: Utilizing trait observability to disentangle judgeability and self-knowledge. *Journal of Personality and Social Psychology, 101*, 202–216. doi:10.1037/a0023782

Human, L. J., & Biesanz, J. C. (2011b). Through the looking glass clearly: Accuracy and assumed similarity in well-adjusted individuals' first impressions. *Journal of Personality and Social Psychology, 100*(2), 349–364. doi:349.10.1037/a0021850

Human, L. J., & Biesanz, J. C. (2013). Targeting the good target: An integrative review of the characteristics and consequences of being accurately perceived. *Personality and Social Psychology Review, 17*(3), 248–272. doi:10.1177/1088868313495593

Human, L. J., Biesanz, J. C., Finseth, S. M., Pierce, B., & Le, M. (2014). To thine own self be true: Psychological adjustment promotes judgeability via personality–behavior congruence. *Journal of Personality and Social Psychology, 106*(2), 286–303. doi:10.1037/a0034860

Human, L. J., Biesanz, J. C., Parisotto, K. L., & Dunn, E. W. (2012). Your best self helps reveal your true self: Trying to make a good impression leads to more accurate personality impressions. *Social Psychological and Personality Science, 3*, 23–30. doi:10.1177/1948550611407689

Human, L. J., Carlson, E. N., Geukes, K., Nestler, S., & Back, M. D. (2018). Do accurate personality impressions benefit early relationship development? The bidirectional associations between accuracy and liking. *Journal of Personality and Social Psychology.* Advance online publication. doi:10.1037/pspp0000214.

Human, L. J., Chan, M., DeLongis, A., Roy, L., Miller, G. E., & Chen, E. (2014). Parental accuracy regarding adolescent daily experiences: Relationships with adolescent psychological adjustment and inflammatory regulation. *Psychosomatic Medicine, 76*(8), 603–610. doi:10.1097/PSY.0000000000000105

Human, L. J., Mignault, M. C., Rogers, K. H., & Biesanz, J. C. (2019). Why are well-adjusted people seen more accurately? The role of personality-behavior congruence in naturalistic social settings. *Journal of Personality and Social Psychology.* Advance online publication. doi:10.1037/pspp0000193.

Human, L. J., Rogers, K. H., & Biesanz, J. C. (2018). *Is expressive accuracy a central individual difference? The cross-contextual consistency of being transparent.* Manuscript in preparation.

Human, L. J., Sandstrom, G. M., Biesanz, J. C., & Dunn, E. W. (2013). Accurate first impressions leave a lasting impression: The long-term effects of accuracy on relationship development. *Social Psychological and Personality Science, 4*, 395–402. doi:10.1177/1948550612463735

Jahoda, M. (1958). *Joint Commission on Mental Health and Illness Monograph Series: Vol. 1. Current concepts of positive mental health.* New York: Basic Books. doi:10.1037/11258-000

Jourard, S. M. (1971). *Self-disclosure: An experimental analysis of the transparent self.* Oxford, UK: John Wiley.

Keltner, D., Gruenfeld, D. H., & Anderson, C. (2003). Power, approach, and inhibition. *Psychological Review, 110*(2), 265–284. doi:10.1037/0033-295X.110.2.265

Kenny, D. A. (1994). *Interpersonal perception: A social relations analysis.* New York, NY: Guilford.

Kenrick, D. T., & Stringfield, D. O. (1980). Personality traits and the eye of the beholder: Crossing some traditional philosophical boundaries in the search for consistency in all of the people. *Psychological Review, 87*(1), 88–104. doi:10.1037/0033-295X.87.1.88

Kernis, M. H. (2003). Toward a conceptualization of optimal self-esteem. *Psychological Inquiry, 14*(1), 1–26. doi:10.1207/S15327965PLI1401_01

Kurtz, J. E., & Sherker, J. L. (2003). Relationship quality, trait similarity, and self-other agreement on personality ratings in college roommates. *Journal of Personality, 71*(1), 21–48. doi:10.1111/1467-6494.t01-1-00005

Kwang, T., & Swann, W. B., Jr. (2010). Do people embrace praise even when they feel unworthy? A review of critical tests of self-enhancement versus self-verification. *Personality and Social Psychology Review, 14*(3), 263–280. doi:10.1177/1088868310365876

Lackenbauer, S. D., Campbell, L., Rubin, H., Fletcher, G. J. O., & Troister, T. (2010). The unique and combined benefits of accuracy and positive bias in relationships. *Personal Relationships, 17*, 475–493. doi:10.1111/j.1475-6811.2010.01282.x

Langlois, J. H., Kalakanis, L., Rubenstein, A. J., Larson, A., Hallam, M., & Smoot, M. (2000). Maxims or myths of beauty? A meta-analytic and theoretical review. *Psychological Bulletin, 126*(3), 390–423. doi:10.1037/0033-2909.126.3.390

Langlois, J. H., Ritter, J. M., Casey, R. J., & Sawin, D. B. (1995). Infant attractiveness predicts maternal behaviors and attitudes. *Developmental Psychology, 31*(3), 464–472. doi:10.1037/0012-1649.31.3.464.

Langlois, J. H., & Roggman, L. A. (1990). Attractive faces are only average. *Psychological Science, 1*(2), 115–121. doi:10.1111/j.1467-9280.1990.tb00079.x

Larrance, D. T., & Zuckerman, M. (1981). Facial attractiveness and vocal likeability as determinants of nonverbal sending skills. *Journal of Personality, 49*(4), 349–362. doi:10.1111/j.1467-6494.1981.tb00219.x

Laurenceau, J. P., Barrett, L. F., & Pietromonaco, P. R. (1998). Intimacy as an interpersonal process: The importance of self-disclosure, partner disclosure, and perceived partner responsiveness in interpersonal exchanges. *Journal of Personality and Social Psychology, 74*(5), 1238–1251. doi:10.1037/0022-3514.74.5.1238

Leary, M. R. (1995). *Self-presentation: Impression management and interpersonal behavior.* Madison, WI: Brown & Benchmark.

Leary, M. R. (2003). Interpersonal aspects of optimal self-esteem and the authentic self. *Psychological Inquiry, 14*(1), 52–54. Retrieved from http://www.jstor.org/stable/1449041.

Lemay, E. P., Jr., Clark, M. S., & Greenberg, A. (2010). What is beautiful is good because what is beautiful is desired: Physical attractiveness stereotyping as projection of interpersonal goals. *Personality and Social Psychology Bulletin, 36*(3), 339–353. doi:10.1177/0146167209359700

Letzring, T. D. (2008). The good judge of personality: Characteristics, behaviors, and observer accuracy. *Journal of Research in Personality, 42*(4), 914–932. doi:10.1016/j.jrp.2007.12.003

Letzring, T. D., & Human, L. J. (2014). An examination of information quality as a moderator of accurate personality judgment. *Journal of Personality, 82*(5), 440–451. doi:10.1111/jopy.12075

Letzring, T. D., Wells, S. M., & Funder, D. C. (2006). Information quantity and quality affect the realistic accuracy of personality judgment. *Journal of Personality and Social Psychology, 91*(1), 111–123. doi:10.1037/0022-3514.91.1.111

Lewandowski, G. W., Jr., & Nardone, N. (2012). Self-concept clarity's role in self–other agreement and the accuracy of behavioral prediction. *Self and Identity, 11*(1), 71–89. doi:10.1080/15298868.2010.512133

Lewis, K. L. (2014). *Searching for the open book: Exploring predictors of target readability in interpersonal accuracy* (Doctoral dissertation). University of Oregon.

Lönnqvist, J. E., Verkasalo, M., & Walkowitz, G. (2011). It pays to pay: Big Five personality influences on co-operative behavior in an incentivized and hypothetical prisoner's dilemma game. *Personality and Individual Differences, 50*(2), 300–304. doi:10.1016/j.paid.2010.10.009

Lorenzo, G. L., Biesanz, J. C., & Human, L. J. (2010). What is beautiful is good and more accurately understood: Physical attractiveness and accuracy in first impressions of personality. *Psychological Science, 21*(12), 1777–1782. doi:10.1177/0956797610388048

Luo, S., & Snider, A. G. (2009). Accuracy and biases in newlyweds' perceptions of each other: Not mutually exclusive but mutually beneficial. *Psychological Science, 20*(11), 1332–1339. doi:10.1111/j.1467-9280.2009.02449.x

Lyubomirsky, S., King, L., & Diener, E. (2005). The benefits of frequent positive affect: Does happiness lead to success? *Psychological Bulletin, 131*(6), 803–855. doi:10.1037/0033-2909.131.6.803

Magee, J. C., & Galinsky, A. D. (2008). Social hierarchy: The self-reinforcing nature of power and status. *Academy of Management Annals, 2*(1), 351–398. doi:10.5465/19416520802211628

Maner, J. K., DeWall, C. N., Baumeister, R. F., & Schaller, M. (2007). Does social exclusion motivate interpersonal reconnection? Resolving the "porcupine problem." *Journal of Personality and Social Psychology, 92*(1), 42–55. doi:10.1037/0022-3514.92.1.42

Maner, J. K., Kenrick, D. T., Becker, D. V., Delton, A. W., Hofer, B., Wilbur, C. J., & Neuberg, S. L. (2003). Sexually selective cognition: Beauty captures the mind of the beholder. *Journal of Personality and Social Psychology, 85*(6), 1107–1120. doi:10.1037/0022-3514.85.6.1107

Manstead, A. S. (1991). Emotion in social life. *Cognition and Emotion, 5*(5–6), 353–362. doi:10.1080/02699939108411047

Markus, H. (1977). Self-schemata and processing information about the self. *Journal of Personality and Social Psychology, 35*(2), 63–78. doi:10.1037/0022-3514.35.2.63

Maslow, A. (1968). Some educational implications of the humanistic psychologies. *Harvard Educational Review, 38*(4), 685–696. doi:10.17763/haer.38.4.j07288786v86w660

McCrae, R. R., & Costa, P. T., Jr. (1999). A five-factor theory of personality. In L. A. Pervin & O. P. John (Eds.), *Handbook of personality theory and research* (Vol. 2, pp. 139–153). New York: Guilford Press.

McReynolds, P., Altrocchi, J., & House, C. (2000). Self-pluralism: Assessment and relations to adjustment, life changes, and age. *Journal of Personality, 68*(2), 347–381. doi:10.1111/1467-6494.00100

Mendolia, M., & Kleck, R. E. (1993). Effects of talking about a stressful event on arousal: Does what we talk about make a difference? *Journal of Personality and Social Psychology, 64*(2), 283–292. doi:10.1037/0022-3514.64.2.283

Mignault, M. C., & Human, L. J. (2017). Hiring the good target: Toward more integration of expressive accuracy into personnel selection. Open Peer Commentary. *European Journal of Personality, 31*, 471–472. doi:10.1002/per.2119

Moore, C., Lee, S. Y., Kim, K., & Cable, D. M. (2017). The advantage of being oneself: The role of applicant self-verification in organizational hiring decisions. *Journal of Applied Psychology, 102*(11), 1493–1513. doi:10.1037/apl0000223

Murphy, N. A. (2007). Appearing smart: The impression management of intelligence, person perception accuracy, and behavior in social interaction. *Personality and Social Psychology Bulletin, 33*, 325–339. doi:10.1177/0146167206294871

Murphy, N. A., Hall, J. A., Schmid Mast, M., Ruben, M. A., Frauendorfer, D., Blanch-Hartigan, D.,…Nguyen, L. (2015). Reliability and validity of nonverbal thin slices in social interactions. *Personality and Social Psychology Bulletin, 41*(2), 199–213. doi:10.1177/0146167214559902

Neff, L. A., & Karney, B. R. (2005). To know you is to love you: The implications of global adoration and specific accuracy for marital relationships. *Journal of Personality and Social Psychology, 88*, 480–497. doi:10.1037/0022-3514.88.3.480

Neuberg, S. L., & Fiske, S. T. (1987). Motivational influences on impression formation: Outcome dependency, accuracy-driven attention, and individuating processes. *Journal of Personality and Social Psychology, 53*, 431–444. doi:10.1037/0022-3514.53.3.431

New, J., Cosmides, L., & Tooby, J. (2007). Category-specific attention for animals reflects ancestral priorities, not expertise. *Proceedings of the National Academy of Sciences, 104*(42), 16598–16603. doi:10.1073/pnas.0703913104

Norton, M. I., Frost, J. H., & Ariely, D. (2007). Less is more: The lure of ambiguity, or why familiarity breeds contempt. *Journal of Personality and Social Psychology, 92*(1), 97–105. doi:10.1037/0022-3514.92.1.97

Overbeck, J. R., & Park, B. (2001). When power does not corrupt: Superior individuation processes among powerful perceivers. *Journal of Personality and Social Psychology, 81*(4), 549–565. doi:10.1037/0022-3514.81.4.549

Paulhus, D. L., & Bruce, M. N. (1992). The effect of acquaintanceship on the validity of personality impressions: A longitudinal study. *Journal of Personality and Social Psychology, 63*(5), 816–824. doi:10.1037/0022-3514.63.5.816

Paulhus, D. L., & Morgan, K. L. (1997). Perceptions of intelligence in leaderless groups: The dynamic effects of shyness and acquaintance. *Journal of Personality and Social Psychology, 72*(3), 581–591. doi:10.1037/0022-3514.72.3.581

Paunonen, S. V., & Jackson, D. N. (1985). Idiographic measurement strategies for personality and prediction: Some unredeemed promissory notes. *Psychological Review, 92*(4), 486–511. doi:10.1037/0033-295X.92.4.486

Pickett, C. L., Gardner, W. L., & Knowles, M. (2004). Getting a cue: The need to belong and enhanced sensitivity to social cues. *Personality and Social Psychology Bulletin, 30*, 1095–1107. doi:10.1177/0146167203262085

Ratcliff, N. J., Hugenberg, K., Shriver, E. R., & Bernstein, M. J. (2011). The allure of status: High-status targets are privileged in face processing and memory. *Personality and Social Psychology Bulletin, 37*(8), 1003–1015.

Reber, R., Schwarz, N., & Winkielman, P. (2004). Processing fluency and aesthetic pleasure: Is beauty in the judge's processing experience? *Personality and Social Psychology Review, 8*(4), 364–382. doi:10.1207/s15327957pspr0804_3

Reis, H. T., Maniaci, M. R., Caprariello, P. A., Eastwick, P. W., & Finkel, E. J. (2011). Familiarity does indeed promote attraction in live interaction. *Journal of Personality and Social Psychology, 101*(3), 557–570. doi:10.1037/a0022885

Reise, S. P., & Waller, N. G. (1993). Traitedness and the assessment of response pattern scalability. *Journal of Personality and Social Psychology, 65*(1), 143–151. doi:10.1037/0022-3514.65.1.143

Riggio, H. R., & Riggio, R. E. (2002). Emotional expressiveness, extraversion, and neuroticism: A meta analysis. *Journal of Nonverbal Behavior, 26*(4), 195–218. doi:10.1023/A:1022117500440

Riggio, R. E., & Friedman, H. S. (1986). Impression formation: The role of expressive behavior. *Journal of Personality and Social Psychology, 50*(2), 421–427. doi:10.1037//0022-3514.50.2.421

Riggio, R. E., Widaman, K. F., & Friedman, H. S. (1985). Actual and perceived emotional sending and personality correlates. *Journal of Nonverbal Behavior, 9*(2), 69–83. doi:10.1037/h0037041

Robins, R. W., & John, O. P. (1997). The quest for self-insight: Theory and research on accuracy and bias in self-perception. In R. Hogan, J. Johnson, and S. Briggs (Eds.), *Handbook of personality psychology* (pp. 649–679). New York, NY: Academic Press. 10.1016/B978-012134645-4/50026-3

Rogers, C. R. (1961). *A therapist's view of psychotherapy: On becoming a person.* London, UK: Constable & Company.

Rogers, K. H., & Biesanz, J. C. (2018). Reassessing the good judge of personality. *Journal of Personality and Social Psychology.* Advance online publication. doi:10.1037/pspp0000197

Rucker, D. D., & Galinsky, A. D. (2009). Conspicuous consumption versus utilitarian ideals: How different levels of power shape consumer behavior. *Journal of Experimental Social Psychology, 45*(3), 549–555. doi:10.1016/j.jesp.2009.01.005

Ruscher, J. B., & Fiske, S. T. (1990). Interpersonal competition can cause individuating processes. *Journal of Personality and Social Psychology, 58*(5), 832–843. doi:10.1037/0022-3514.58.5.832

Sabatelli, R. M., & Rubin, M. (1986). Nonverbal expressiveness and physical attractiveness as mediators of interpersonal perceptions. *Journal of Nonverbal Behavior, 10*(2), 120–133. doi:10.1007/BF01000008

Sadikaj, G., Russell, J. J., Moskowitz, D. S., & Paris, J. (2010). Affect dysregulation in individuals with borderline personality disorder: Persistence and interpersonal triggers. *Journal of Personality Assessment, 92*(6), 490–500. doi:10.1080/00223891.2010.513287

Schaerer, M., Tost, L. P., Huang, L., Gino, F., & Larrick, R. (2018). Advice giving: A subtle pathway to power. *Personality and Social Psychology Bulletin, 44*(5), 746–761. doi:10.1177/0146167217746341

Scheier, M. F., Buss, A. H., & Buss, D. M. (1978). Self-consciousness, self-report of aggressiveness, and aggression. *Journal of Research in Personality, 12*(2), 133–140. doi:10.1016/0092-6566(78)90089-2

Schlenker, B. R. (1980). *Impression management.* Monterey, CA: Brooks/Cole.

Schlenker, B. R., & Pontari, B. A. (2000). The strategic control of information: Impression management and self-presentation in daily life. In A. Tesser, R. B. Felson, & J. M. Suls (Eds.), *Psychological perspectives on self and identity* (pp. 199–232). Washington, DC: American Psychological Association. doi:10.1037/10357-008

Schmid Mast, M., Jonas, K., & Hall, J. A. (2009). Give a person power and he or she will show interpersonal sensitivity: The phenomenon and its why and when. *Journal of Personality and Social Psychology, 97*(5), 835–850. doi:10.1037/a0016234

Sedikides, C., Horton, R. S., & Gregg, A. P. (2007). The why's the limit: Curtailing self-enhancement with explanatory introspection. *Journal of Personality, 75*(4), 783–824. doi:10.1111/j.1467 6494.2007.00457.x

Sheldon, K. M., & Kasser, T. (1995). Coherence and congruence: Two aspects of personality integration. *Journal of Personality and Social Psychology, 68*(3), 531–543. doi:10.1037/0022-3514.68.3.531

Sheldon, K. M., Ryan, R. M., Rawsthorne, L. J., & Ilardi, B. (1997). Trait self and true self: Cross-role variation in the Big-Five personality traits and its relations with psychological authenticity and subjective well-being. *Journal of Personality and Social Psychology, 73*(6), 1380–1393. doi:10.1037/0022-3514.73.6.1380

Smith, D. M., Neuberg, S. L., Judice, T. N., & Biesanz, J. C. (1997). Target complicity in the confirmation and disconfirmation of erroneous perceiver expectations: Immediate and longer term implications. *Journal of Personality and Social Psychology, 73*(5), 974–991. doi:10.1037//0022-3514.73.5.974

Smoll, F. L., Smith, R. E., Barnett, N. P., & Everett, J. J. (1993). Enhancement of children's self-esteem through social support training for youth sport coaches. *Journal of Applied Psychology, 78*(4), 602–610. doi:10.1037/0021-9010.78.4.602

Snyder, M. (1974). Self-monitoring of expressive behavior. *Journal of Personality and Social Psychology, 30*(4), 526–537. doi:10.1037/h0037039

Snyder, M., & Haugen, J. A. (1995). Why does behavioral confirmation occur? A functional perspective on the role of the target. *Personality and Social Psychology Bulletin, 21*(9), 963–974. doi:10.1177/0146167295219010

Snyder, M., Tanke, E. D., & Berscheid, E. (1977). Social perception and interpersonal behavior: On the self-fulfilling nature of social stereotypes. *Journal of Personality and Social Psychology, 35*(9), 656–666. doi:10.1037/0022-3514.35.9.656

Stewart, D. W. (1984). Physiological measurement of advertising effects. *Psychology and Marketing, 1*(1), 43–48. doi:10.3200/SOCP.147.3.285-298

Stewart, J. E. (1980). Defendant's attractiveness as a factor in the outcome of criminal trials: An observational study. *Journal of Applied Social Psychology, 10*(4), 348–361. doi:10.1111/j.1559-1816.1980.tb00715.x

Swann, W. B., Jr. (2012). Self-verification theory. In P. A. Van Lange, A. W. Kruglanski, & E. T. Higgins (Eds.), *Handbook of theories of social psychology* (Vol. 2, pp. 23–42). London: SAGE. doi:10.4135/9781446249222.n27

Swann, W. B., Jr., Chang-Schneider, C. S., & Angulo, S. (2007). Self-verification in relationships as an adaptive process. In J. Wood, A. Tesser, & J. Holmes (Eds.), *The self and social relationships* (pp. 49–72). New York: Psychology Press.

Swann, W. B., Jr., De La Ronde, C., & Hixon, J. G. (1994). Authenticity and positivity strivings in marriage and courtship. *Journal of Personality and Social Psychology, 66*(5), 857–869. doi:10.1037/0022-3514.66.5.857

Swann, W. B., Jr., & Ely, R. J. (1984). A battle of wills: Self-verification versus behavioral confirmation. *Journal of Personality and Social Psychology, 46*(6), 1287–1302. doi:10.1037/0022-3514.46.6.1287

Swann, W. B., Jr., Pelham, B. W., & Krull, D. S. (1989). Agreeable fancy or disagreeable truth? Reconciling self-enhancement and self-verification. *Journal of Personality and Social Psychology, 57*(5), 782–791. doi:10.1037/0022-3514.57.5.782

Tamir, D. I., & Mitchell, J. P. (2012). Disclosing information about the self is intrinsically rewarding. *Proceedings of the National Academy of Sciences, 109*(21), 8038–8043. doi:10.1073/pnas.1202129109

Tangney, J. P., Baumeister, R. F., & Boone, A. L. (2004). High self-control predicts good adjustment, less pathology, better grades, and interpersonal success. *Journal of Personality, 72*(2), 271–322. doi:10.1111/j.0022-3506.2004.00263.x

Tobey, E. L., & Tunnel, G. (1981). Predicting our impressions on others: Effects of public self-consciousness and acting, a self-monitoring subscale. *Personality and Social Psychology Bulletin, 7*, 661–669. doi:10.1177/014616728174024

Trapnell, P. D., & Campbell, J. D. (1999). Private self-consciousness and the five-factor model of personality: Distinguishing rumination from reflection. *Journal of Personality and Social Psychology, 76*(2), 284–304. doi:10.1037/0022-3514.76.2.284

Turner, R. G. (1978). Effects of differential request procedures and self-consciousness on trait attributions. *Journal of Research in Personality, 12*(4), 431–438. doi:10.1016/0092-6566(78)90069-7

Underwood, B., & Moore, B. S. (1981). Sources of behavioral consistency. *Journal of Personality and Social Psychology, 40*(4), 780–785. doi:10.1037/0022-3514.40.4.780

Underwood, M. K., Coie, J. D., & Herbsman, C. R. (1992). Display rules for anger and aggression in school-age children. *Child Development, 63*(2), 366–380. doi:10.1111/j.1467-8624.1992.tb01633.x

Vazire, S. (2010). Who knows what about a person? The self–other knowledge asymmetry (SOKA) model. *Journal of Personality and Social Psychology, 98*(2), 281–300. doi:10.1037/a0017908

Vazire, S., & Carlson, E. N. (2010). Self-knowledge of personality: Do people know themselves? *Social and Personality Psychology Compass, 4*(8), 605–620. doi:10.1111/j.1751-9004.2010.00280.x

Vazire, S., & Carlson, E. N. (2011). Others sometimes know us better than we know ourselves. *Current Directions in Psychological Science, 20*(2), 104–108. doi:10.1177%2F0963721411402478

Vogt, D. S., & Colvin, C. R. (2005). Assessment of accurate self-knowledge. *Journal of Personality Assessment, 84*(3), 239–251. doi:10.1207/s15327752jpa8403_03

Vonnegut, K. (1962). *Mother night.* Greenwich, CT: Gold Medal.

Walden, T. A. (1991). Infant social referencing. In J. Garber & K. A. Dodge (Eds.), *Cambridge studies in social and emotional development: The development of emotion regulation and dysregulation* (pp. 69–88). New York: Cambridge University Press. doi:10.1017/CBO9780511663963.005

Weick, M., & Guinote, A. (2008). When subjective experiences matter: Power increases reliance on the ease of retrieval. *Journal of Personality and Social Psychology, 94*(6), 956–970. doi:10.1037/0022-3514.94.6.956

Westermann, R., Spies, K., Stahl, G., & Hesse, F. W. (1996). Relative effectiveness and validity of mood induction procedures: A meta-analysis. *European Journal of Social Psychology, 26*(4), 557–580. doi:10.1002/(SICI)1099-0992(199607)26:4%3C557::AID-EJSP769%3E3.0.CO;2-4

Wiggins, J. S., & Broughton, R. (1985). The interpersonal circle: A structural model for the integration of personality research. In R. Hogan & W. H. Jones (Eds.), *Perspectives in personality* (Vol. 1, pp. 1–47). Greenwich, CT: JAI Press.

Zaki, J., Bolger, N., & Ochsner, K. (2008). It takes two: The interpersonal nature of empathic accuracy. *Psychological Science, 19*(4), 399–404. doi:10.1111/j.1467-9280.2008.02099.x

Zimmermann, J., Schindler, S., Klaus, G., & Leising, D. (2018). The effect of dislike on accuracy and bias in person perception. *Social Psychological and Personality Science, 9*(1), 80–88. doi:10.1177/1948550617703167

Zuckerman, M., Bernieri, F., Koestner, R., & Rosenthal, R. (1989). To predict some of the people some of the time: In search of moderators. *Journal of Personality and Social Psychology, 57*(2), 279–293. doi:10.1037//0022-3514.57.2.279

Zuckerman, M., DeFrank, R. S., Spiegel, N. H., & Larrance, D. T. (1982). Masculinity-femininity and encoding of nonverbal cues. *Journal of Personality and Social Psychology, 42*, 548–556. doi:10.1037//0022-3514.42.3.548

Zuckerman, M., Kuhlman, D. M., & Camac, C. (1988). What lies beyond E and N? Factor analyses of scales believed to measure basic dimensions of personality. *Journal of Personality and Social Psychology, 54*(1), 96–107. doi:10.1037/0022-3514.54.1.96

Characteristics of Traits That Are Related to Accuracy of Personality Judgments

Sheherezade L. Krzyzaniak *and* Tera D. Letzring

Abstract

Personality traits are characteristics of individuals that predict patterns of thoughts, feelings, and behavior over time. Research focusing on accuracy of judgments of the traits of others has found that certain traits are more easily judged than others. Traits such as extraversion tend to be judged with high levels of accuracy, while other traits such as neuroticism and openness to experience are more difficult to judge. Several factors play a role in these findings, such as the observability and ratability of traits, favorability and evaluativeness of traits, and the types of situations and relationships in which judgments are made. In this chapter, research investigating how these factors are related to accuracy of judgments for different traits is described, potential ways to improve accuracy of less easily judged traits are proposed, and directions for future research are identified.

Key Words: personality trait, accuracy, observability, ratability, favorability, evaluativeness, situation, relationship, improving accuracy

Can I trust my friend to pay back money he borrows from me? Which of my coworkers or classmates would be best to work with on an important project? Should I agree to a second date with her? Should I accept a marriage proposal from him? When we make important decisions about others, they are based in part on what we think they are like. We should lend money to an honest and reliable person, work on important projects with competent and responsible people, and date and marry people with whom our own personalities are compatible. We make better decisions when they are based on accurate judgments of characteristics or personality traits related to the decision, but what characteristics or traits are we most likely to accurately judge? The answer to this question is the focus of this chapter. We explore what is known about relationships between accurate trait judgments and characteristics of the traits themselves, the situations in which the judgments are made, the type of relationship between the person making the judgment

and the person being judged, and whether a person is judging the self or someone else.

Definitions

Let us start with some definitions. *Personality traits* are the unique, broad characteristics that make up "an individual's characteristic patterns of thought, emotion, and behavior, together with the psychological mechanisms—hidden or not—behind those patterns" (Funder, 2016, p. 5). Traits provide descriptions of an individual's typical thoughts, feelings, and behaviors and are assumed to predict what the person does across time and situations. By investigating accuracy of personality judgment at the trait level, it is possible to understand why some characteristics are relatively easier to judge compared to others and how individual differences and varying circumstances play a role in the accuracy of judging certain traits. *Judges* are the people making the judgments, while *targets* are the people being judged. Judges rate targets, and it is possible for an individual to be both a judge and a target simultaneously. Within dyads, triads, or even larger groups of people, an individual may be a judge and target of multiple individuals.

Realistic Accuracy Model

David Funder (1995, 1999, 2012) proposed the *Realistic Accuracy Model* (RAM) to describe the process that makes accurate judgments possible and the *moderators* that are related to higher versus lower levels of accuracy (see chapter 2 by Letzring & Funder in this handbook). Within the RAM, accurate judgments are described as the result of judges *detecting* and correctly *utilizing* cues that are *relevant* to the trait being judged and *available* to the judge. The four moderators within the RAM are the *good judge*, *good target*, *good trait*, and *good information*, meaning that some judges, targets, and traits are easier to judge than others, and that accuracy is higher when many high-quality cues are available to judges (see the other chapters in Section II of this handbook for in-depth discussions of the judge, target, and information moderators).

The current chapter focuses on the good trait and summarizes the research findings that indicate that certain traits tend to be judged more accurately than others (Funder & Dobroth, 1987; Letzring & Human, 2013). Several factors have been examined that may play a role in how accurately different traits are judged, including how easy it is to observe cues that are relevant for a given trait and the perceived social desirability of displaying a trait in a given circumstance. In addition, certain traits become relevant only within certain situations, such as bravery in a dangerous situation or self-control in a demanding situation. These situation-specific traits are typically judged less accurately when the judgments are first impressions formed in unstructured or neutral situations (Hirschmüller, Egloff, Schmukle, Nestler, & Back, 2015; Hirschmüller, Schmukle, Krause, Back, & Egloff, 2018). There is also evidence that some traits are more easily judged when the person being judged is the self, while other traits are more easily judged by an observer (Vazire, 2010). This chapter explores these concepts and other factors that are related to the good trait.

Assessing Accuracy

The research discussed within this chapter covers multiple ways of assessing accuracy. The simplest way to assess accuracy is by determining how well two or more judges agree about a target's personality, which is called *consensus*. The judges could all be close acquaintances of the target, strangers, or a combination such that a judgment from a stranger could be compared to a judgment from a close other, such as a parent or spouse. However, a problem with consensus is that judges can agree with each other, but all be inaccurate in terms of what the target is really like. For example, people could agree that someone is highly conscientious based on seeing them complete one task on time, but they could all be inaccurate if the target only rarely does this. Another way to assess accuracy is by determining the relationship between judgments of a target and self-ratings from that target, which is referred to as *self-other agreement*. This method of assessing accuracy uses the self-judgment as the criterion and assumes that the self-judgments are valid. This is problematic if the targets do not know themselves well or if they are asked to report on characteristics that are difficult to see in one's self, such as modesty or highly evaluative traits (Paulhus & Vazire, 2007). To minimize the bias that is likely in any single judgment of personality, the accuracy criterion could be based on a composite of ratings from multiple perspectives, including self-ratings, ratings from people assumed to know the target well such as family members and close friends, and ratings from trained coders based on behavioral observations. When these ratings agree with each other, the composite can be used as the accuracy criterion and agreement between the composite ratings and judges' ratings is referred to as *realistic accuracy*.[1]

Accuracy can also be calculated in multiple ways, which can lead to some confusion about exactly what is being assessed. First, *trait accuracy* can be used to assess accuracy for a single trait and reflects how accurately a judge orders a set of targets on a given trait, or how accurately a set of judges orders a set of targets when each judge rates only one target.[2] High trait accuracy means that a single judge was able to correctly identify which targets were higher versus lower on a trait, or that across a set of judge-target pairs, the targets were ordered accurately. For example, a judge may correctly rate Aaron as being kinder than David and Darlene. The other approach to calculating accuracy is based on correlations between judge ratings and the accuracy criteria for a set of items for a single target, which are referred to as *profile correlations*. These correlations reflect how accurately a judge can order a set of items or traits for an individual target. For example, a strong and positive profile correlation means the judge was able to correctly determine whether a target was more kind than competent, or more dominant than

SHEHEREZADE L. KRZYZANIAK AND TERA D. LETZRING

anxious (e.g., that Aaron is more kind than he is competent, and that Darlene is more dominant than she is anxious).

Accuracy of Judging Different Traits

To illustrate the idea of judging different traits, think back to a time when you were first introduced to an important person in your life. Think back to your first interactions with this person, and the behaviors that stood out right away. There were probably certain characteristics that you could not help but notice, such as how talkative this person was, their social etiquette, and the facial expressions they made as you interacted together. You may have quickly noticed their ability to make a great first impression and how much they seemed to enjoy talking to you even though you had just met. It is also possible that you noticed quite the opposite about this person, in that they were shy and quiet and did not seem to enjoy talking to you at all. Even within these first few moments, certain characteristics about this person probably stood out to you very quickly, and there is a good chance that you were able to make at least some accurate judgments about this person within this first interaction.

Now, consider the characteristics you discovered about this person over the course of your relationship. Over time you began to learn new information about this person that was not as apparent within that first interaction. You may have discovered that this individual was very organized after visiting their tidy home for the first time. You may have also discovered that under certain situations this individual became upset very easily and that they were happiest when engaging in artistic endeavors compared with more structured tasks. The more ways you engaged with this person over time, the more you learned about the more nuanced aspects of his/her personality that did not stick out right away. Perhaps this person was organized with their physical possessions, but they could not seem to get to appointments on time. These examples demonstrate that while certain personality traits are more easily judged, even with relatively little information that can be learned during a first interaction, other personality traits are not accurately judged so readily.

Before we examine what makes a trait easy versus difficult to judge accurately, it will be useful to describe a commonly used model of personality traits that identifies five broad-level traits that are useful for describing people. This model is called the *five factor model* (FFM) (Goldberg, 1999; John et al., 2008; McCrae & Costa, 1999; Soto & John, 2017), which is

also sometimes referred to as the *Big Five*. The Big Five include the traits of extraversion, agreeableness, conscientiousness, openness to experience/intellect, and neuroticism/emotional stability. Each trait can be used to predict patterns of thoughts, feelings, and behaviors people are likely to experience or engage in across situations and relationships. The traits are conceptualized at a broad and decontextualized level, which means that they describe what people are like in general across all situations they are in and over time.

Extraversion refers to how talkative, assertive, energetic, enthusiastic, outgoing, sociable, active, and prone to positive emotion an individual is. People with low levels of extraversion can be referred to as introverted, and highly introverted people like to spend time alone, are often relaxed and rarely get irritated, and typically let others take the lead. *Agreeableness* refers to how cooperative, trusting, appreciative, forgiving, caring, generous, kind, sympathetic, and likable a person is. People high on agreeableness tend to behave in ways that are altruistic, emotionally supportive, and compliant, while people low on agreeableness can be described as antagonistic and tend to look down on others. *Conscientiousness* refers to how efficient, organized, planful, reliable, responsible, thorough, careful, competent, achievement-oriented, and self-disciplined an individual is. People high on conscientiousness behave in ways that are responsible, productive, and ethical, while people low on conscientiousness can be described as messy or careless and are somewhat likely to break the rules. *Openness to experience* refers to how curious, imaginative, insightful, open to ideas, and artistic an individual is. This trait is also referred to as Intellect in some models, which highlights the importance of basic intelligence, how people approach intellectual matters, and wisdom. People high in openness are likely to have unusual thought processes and to behave in unconventional ways, while people low in openness are conservative, traditional, and prefer routine. *Neuroticism* refers to how moody, reactive, anxious, self-pitying, tense, nervous, and prone to negative emotion an individual is. People high in neuroticism tend to worry a lot, be impulsive, have fluctuating moods, and behave in self-defeating ways. People who are low on this are emotionally stable, relaxed, and comfortable with themselves. The research discussed in this chapter largely focuses on the Big Five personality traits because this model is most commonly used in accuracy research. However, findings based on other traits, such as trait mindfulness (May &

Reinhardt, 2018), supernumerary traits[3] (Paunonen & Kam, 2014), personal values (McDonald & Letzring, 2016), and self-esteem (Hirschmüller et al., 2018) are also included.

Throughout the accuracy literature, certain traits are consistently found to be judged with high levels of accuracy, while other traits are typically judged with lower accuracy. The trait of extraversion, for example, tends to be judged with higher levels of accuracy compared to any other Big Five trait regardless of the context or situation, and even when judges have access to very limited amounts of information about targets (Beer & Watson, 2008; Borkenau & Liebler, 1992; Letzring & Human, 2013). On the other hand, traits such as neuroticism, self-esteem, and openness to experience/intellect[4] all tend to be judged with lower levels of accuracy (Borkenau & Liebler, 1992; Funder & Dobroth, 1987; John & Robins, 1993; Kilianski, 2008; Yeagley, Morling, & Nelson, 2007). Other traits, such as agreeableness and conscientiousness, are not considered to be especially easy or difficult to judge, with levels of accuracy generally varying depending on other factors (Connelly & Ones, 2010).

The following sections explore research involving several factors related to accuracy of judgments of different traits, which include observability, favorability, the role of the situation, and different types of relationships, among others. As you will learn, research has investigated a variety of factors related to how accurately traits are typically judged, but it is important to keep in mind that some research findings are mixed and that there are still many unanswered questions within this literature.

Observability and Ratability of Traits and Accuracy

Observability (also termed *visibility*) refers to how likely it is for cues relevant to a given trait to be made available by targets, especially early in the acquaintance process and in many different situations. Levels of observability are typically determined by asking a group of research participants to rate how easy versus difficult they think it is to observe or judge a certain characteristic or trait in another person (Funder & Dobroth, 1987; John & Robins, 1993). These ratings showed that people do think that traits differ in terms of how easy they are to judge in others, which is consistent with the idea that traits vary in the number of relevant cues that are easily observable in most situations and initial encounters (Funder, 1995, 2012). Consider again the illustration in which you became acquainted

with an especially important person in your life—it is very likely that certain characteristics stood out much more readily than others, and this can be explained by observability. For example, extraversion is a highly observable trait because the behavioral cues related to this trait (e.g., talkativeness, sociability, dominance, energy level) are made available in many kinds of unstructured situations and are relatively easy for any type of judge to detect, including strangers. On the other extreme, neuroticism is much less observable because the behavioral manifestations (e.g., feeling depressed and tense, worrying a lot, and not handling stress well) are less likely to be made available in unstructured situations and are often difficult for others to detect.

Observability is also positively related to self-other agreement with close acquaintances for traits beyond the Big Five, including Honesty-Humility[5] as assessed by the HEXACO-PI-R (De Vries, Lee, & Ashton, 2008; De Vries, Realo, & Allik, 2016), and moral character as rated by close acquaintances (Helzer et al., 2014). For moral character, the highest level of agreement was found for the temperance facet and the lowest agreement was for the compassion facet. However, observability was not related to self-other agreement among close peers for ratings of facets of trait mindfulness (May & Reinhardt, 2018).

One of the first studies to examine how properties of traits are related to self-other agreement was conducted by Funder and Dobroth (1987). Participants in this study rated the 100 trait descriptors of the California Adult Q-Set (CAQ), which describes various aspects of personality, for how easy they thought it would be to judge each trait in another person. It was found that traits more strongly related to extraversion were seen as easier to judge, while traits more strongly related to neuroticism were seen as somewhat more difficult to judge. Then, self-other agreement (where the other-ratings were from peers who were acquainted with the targets) and peer-to-peer agreement (or consensus) were calculated and averaged to form interjudge agreement ratings for each trait, and these ratings were then correlated with ease-of-judgment. The results of this analysis are consistent with the subjective ratings of ease of judgment, as traits that were rated as easy to judge also had higher interjudge agreement, and traits that were rated as difficult to judge had lower interjudge agreement. This relationship between ease-of-judgment and accuracy has been replicated. For example, it has been replicated in multiple studies in the United States

(Funder & Colvin, 1988; John & Robins, 1993; Watson et al., 2000), Estonia, and the Netherlands (De Vries et al., 2016). Findings have also replicated in studies involving close acquaintances of the targets (De Vries et al., 2016) and among judges who had only viewed a 5-minute interaction between two people whom they did not know (Funder & Colvin, 1988). Furthermore, a meta-analysis of 24 studies with round-robin designs[6] found support for the positive relationship between observability and self-other agreement, with the effect being stronger with small group sizes and for people who were unfamiliar with each other prior to making ratings (Kenny & West, 2010).

Additional evidence for the relationship between trait observability and accuracy comes from a study that examined ratings of traits other than the Big Five, as assessed by the Supernumerary Personality Inventory (SPI; Paunonen & Kam, 2014). Rating of items that described behaviors resulted in higher self-other agreement among roommates than did ratings of items that described attitudes and beliefs. This evidence supports the role of observability in accuracy, as behaviors are more observable than attitudes and beliefs.[7] Finally, a more recent study that examined the relationship between ease-of-judgment and self-other agreement among acquaintances using the International Personality Item Pool's (IPIP; Goldberg et al., 2006) 100-item version of the NEO[8]-Personality Inventory-Revised-domains (Costa & McCrae, 1992) and a standard measure of personal values (the Schwartz Values Survey; Schwartz, 1992) did not find relations between ease-of-judgment and self-other agreement or consensus for either traits or personal values (McDonald & Letzring, 2016), nor did an early study that used ratings on the CAQ (Funder, 1980). There is not a clear explanation for this lack of replication, as the McDonald and Letzring (2016) study used the same method to assess observability as Funder and Dobroth (1987), and also assessed self-other agreement among acquaintances in the same way. Overall, research evidence supports the positive relationship between trait observability and accuracy, and the idea that traits that are easy to see are judged more accurately.

A construct that is closely related to observability is *ratability*, which includes observability but also includes whether cues relevant to a trait are more likely to be made available in public versus private situations and how difficult it is to describe the trait itself (Letzring & Funder, 2018; Paunonen & Kam, 2014). One study found that items from the

Schedule for Nonadaptive and Adaptive Personality (SNAP; Clark, 1993), which is a measure of 12 non-adaptive and adaptive personality traits and temperaments,[9] had ratability scores that correlated positively with self-other agreement among close friends (Ready, Clark, Watson, & Westerhouse, 2000). Ratability was also found to be positively correlated with self-other agreement among roommates for ratings of the Big Five traits but is less strongly correlated for ratings on the SPI (Paunonen & Kam, 2014). There is not yet enough evidence for a positive link between ratability and accuracy to claim that this is an important factor related to self-other agreement, but the existing studies certainly point in that direction.

Favorability and Evaluativeness of Traits and Accuracy

Favorability of traits (also referred to as *social desirability* or *desirability*) reflects how favorably a person would be viewed if he or she was high or low on a particular trait. Levels of favorability are typically determined by ratings of how socially desirable it is to have a given trait or characteristic (Funder, 1980), or how favorably versus unfavorably a person would be viewed if he or she possessed a given trait or characteristic (John & Robins, 1993; McDonald & Letzring, 2016). Favorability is positively related to observability for personal values (McDonald & Letzring, 2016) and the traits described by the CAQ (Funder, 1980), but not for the Big Five traits[10] (McDonald & Letzring, 2016). This relationship is important to keep in mind, as favorability and observability may be linked and therefore it is difficult to independently evaluate the effects of these factors on accuracy.

Findings are mixed in regard to the relationship between favorability and accuracy of trait judgments. Two of the earlier studies of this aspect of traits found positive relationships of moderate strength between favorability and self-other agreement among peers who knew the targets well (Funder, 1980; Funder & Colvin, 1988). It is interesting to note that this finding only held when judges were close friends or roommates of the targets, but not when judges were strangers who observed 5-minute recorded interactions (Funder & Colvin, 1988). Other research has found a curvilinear relationship between favorability and self-other agreement among acquaintances for judgments of the Big Five traits, such that agreement was higher for neutral traits than for highly favorable and unfavorable traits (John & Robins, 1993).

In contrast to the evidence of a positive relationship between favorability and self-other agreement, other research has found no relationship. This lack of a relationship has been seen among roommates or close friends for ratings of traits other than the Big Five, including traits assessed with the SPI (Paunonen & Kam, 2014) and the SNAP (Ready et al., 2000), personal values (McDonald & Letzring, 2016), and trait mindfulness (May & Reinhardt, 2018). Additionally, some studies have even found negative relationships of moderate strength between favorability and self-other agreement for the Big Five traits (McDonald & Letzring, 2016) and moral character (Helzer et al., 2014). On the whole, there is not evidence to support a robust relationship between favorability and self-other agreement.

A similar way to conceptualize favorability of traits is with the concept of *evaluativeness*. There is a u-shaped relationship between favorability and evaluativeness in that traits with high and low favorability are high on evaluativeness, whereas traits that are neither favorable nor unfavorable are low on evaluativeness. In other words, highly evaluative traits are those that are either very favorable or very unfavorable, whereas low evaluative traits are those that are neutral in terms of favorability. Evaluativeness can be used to explain the curvilinear relationship between favorability and self-other agreement as a negative linear relationship between evaluativeness and agreement because agreement was higher for traits with low evaluativeness and lower for traits with high evaluativeness (John & Robins, 1993). Some research suggests that a highly evaluative trait is intellect and the traits of extraversion and emotional stability are some of the least evaluative (John & Robins, 1993). However, other studies have not found a direct relationship between evaluativeness and self-other agreement with close informants for ratings of the Big Five traits, the HEXACO, and the SNAP (De Vries et al., 2016; Ready et al., 2000). Additionally, the study by De Vries and colleagues found that the relationship between these variables was mediated by the amount of variance in the ratings of the targets. In other words, traits that were less evaluative had more variability in how they were rated, and traits with more variability were rated with higher levels of self-other agreement.

Overall, there is not a clear picture of how favorability and evaluativeness are related to accuracy. Perhaps this relationship depends on other variables that have not yet been examined in multiple studies, such as item variance. It may also be useful to investigate various factors related to trait accuracy in a more systematic way, such as the type of relationship between judges and targets, the types of traits that are being judged, or the method of determining levels of favorability.

Other Factors That Influence Trait Accuracy

As we have learned so far, there are several factors that can influence the accuracy of a trait judgment, including the observability, ratability, favorability, and evaluativeness of a given trait. We now look at research that investigates how other factors can influence the accuracy of judgment of specific traits. These other factors include the type of situation in which an interaction occurs, the type of relationship two people share, and whether people are judging their own personality or the personality of another. As you will see, these factors can help to explain why some traits are judged more easily and accurately than others.

The Situation

Have you ever experienced a moment when a person you thought you knew very well did something that surprised you? Perhaps it was the time you worked on a time-sensitive project with a work-colleague and you noticed how calmly she handled the pressure and stress. You may have invited this same person to a dinner party and seen a different side of her compared to her work-persona. The more different kinds of situations you saw this person in, the more subtle aspects of her personality you started to see as she behaved consistently or differently across the situations.

The stages of the RAM, as described previously, are important in consideration of research involving the *situation*, or the different contexts in which the individual engages with the world. When we are placed into a new situation with someone, it is possible to discover new things about that person because the situation might elicit cues that are not usually exhibited in other contexts. In terms of the language of the RAM, relevant cues to a given trait are more likely to be available in some situations than others. For example, behaviors related to one's level of courage or bravery are only likely to be available in dangerous or risky situations, and behaviors related to how one handles stress are more likely to be available when working on important and time-sensitive projects than in other situations. More internal personality traits that are not related to as many behavioral cues are less likely to be made available in most situations, because expressing those cues in an external way simply is not as likely. Because of this, the different situations we are in with others can influence which trait-specific behaviors are performed, which in turn can influence our ability to accurately judge different traits.

Research has investigated accuracy of trait-specific judgments with the use of different types of situations. For example, research has found that neuroticism tends to be more accurately judged when judges observe targets in more socially stressful situations in which cues about neuroticism are relevant and more likely to be externally displayed (Hirschmüller et al., 2015). In a similar fashion, unacquainted judges are able to accurately judge the self-esteem of targets in a public self-presentation situation (although accuracy is still considered to be relatively low; Hirschmüller et al., 2018). Additional research found that openness to experience was judged with higher levels of accuracy when judges examined the offices or bedrooms of targets, as opposed to engaging directly in interactions or observations (Gosling, Ko, Mannarelli, & Morris, 2002). Research that intentionally selects situations that are likely to elicit cues to certain traits, especially traits that are typically judged with lower levels of accuracy, demonstrates that it is possible for judges to accurately judge these more difficult traits as long as the situation pulls for cues relevant to the trait of interest.

Relationships

Now let us add yet another piece to this puzzle. Consider the types of relationships you have with different people in your life, such as friends, family, coworkers, and your significant other. While some traits can be accurately judged regardless of relationship type, many traits show benefit from a more personal and intimate relationship. In this way, the type of relationship you have with a person is important in terms of accuracy because judgments of less observable and more internal traits made by strangers are typically less accurate compared with judgments of casual acquaintances; which in turn are less accurate compared with judgments of close friends, spouses, and family members (Connelly & Ones, 2010; see also chapter 9 by Beer and chapter 17 by Luo & Watson in this handbook). While most personality traits require a more personal relationship to be judged with especially high levels of accuracy, extraversion is the consistent exception throughout the literature because it is judged with high accuracy even among strangers (Beer & Watson, 2008; Borkenau, Brecke, Mottig, & Paelecke, 2009; Borkenau & Liebler, 1992; Letzring

& Human, 2013; Naumann, Vazire, Rentfrow, & Gosling, 2009) and sees the least improvement in accuracy as relationships become more intimate (Connelly & Ones, 2010).

While it is certainly impressive that some traits can be accurately judged at high levels by total strangers, it is a very different story for more internal personality traits. Neuroticism and openness to experience are traits that are especially difficult for strangers to accurately judge within most first-impression situations, and research shows that accuracy for these traits, as measured by self-other agreement, sees the most improvement for friends and family compared to the other Big Five traits (Connelly & Ones, 2010). When compared to accuracy of extraversion, neuroticism is judged with much lower levels of accuracy by strangers, but with about the same level of accuracy for dating and married couples (Watson et al., 2000). Friends and cohabitating romantic couples who are not married are more accurate about agreeableness and conscientiousness compared to other relationship types (Connelly & Ones, 2010). Thus, it is certainly possible for more internal traits such as neuroticism and openness to experience to be judged with high levels of accuracy, but it is much more likely for this to occur in close relationships than among strangers.

These relationships differ in important ways that can help us understand why there are differences in levels of accuracy for some traits. One of these differences is the level of intimacy. Your interactions with strangers are most likely not at all intimate and involve adherence to social norms and small talk, and not much else. Relationships with coworkers may be more intimate than relationships with strangers, but are likely still on the low end of intimacy. In comparison, you probably have far more intimate relationships with friends, family members, and romantic relationship partners. In more intimate relationships, people are more likely to share their thoughts and feelings, including thoughts and feelings relevant to less-observable traits, and this may partly explain why people tend to make more accurate judgments of friends, family members, and romantic partners than of coworkers and strangers (Connelly & Ones, 2010).

In addition to intimacy-level, another factor that varies across relationship types is the number of situations or contexts in which you are likely to see each other. The types of contexts in which you interact with strangers or coworkers are probably very limited in scope (such as only at the grocery store or at work or work-related functions). On the other hand, you have likely seen your family, friends, and romantic partners across a much wider variety of contexts (such as at home, social events, religious events, work parties, and while on vacation). Cues to different traits are more or less likely to be revealed in different situations, so seeing people in more types of situations increases the likelihood that a judge will have access to cues that are relevant to less-observable traits, and therefore are likely to make more accurate judgments about those traits than people who have seen the targets in fewer situations. In summary, judgments of friends, family, and romantic partners are likely to be more accurate than judgments of strangers, especially for less visible traits, due to increased levels of intimacy and being with other people across many types of situations, which both increase the availability of relevant cues.

Judgments of the Self and Others

Another factor that should be discussed in terms of trait judgments, and perhaps one that you have not yet considered while reading this chapter, is whether we are making judgments of others or of ourselves. We already know people make judgments of others constantly, but people also make judgments about *their own* personality traits. Most people have a fairly good idea of who they are and are able to describe what they are like and what they think and do in different situations. Within the accuracy literature, recall that the accuracy criterion often relies on a self-report measure of personality, other-report measures of personality from individuals who are well acquainted with the target, or the combination of both (Funder, 1995). Judgments made by the self or by others tell two sides of the story that make up a person, and both are certainly worth considering. While the literature discussed within this chapter up until now has focused on how we make judgments of others, here we briefly discuss the accuracy of our *self-judgments* and which traits are judged more accurately when rating the self versus others. The idea that there may be differences in judgments made by the self and others is captured in the *self-other knowledge asymmetry model* (see chapter 10 by Bollich-Ziegler in this handbook for a more detailed description of this model).

It can be argued that self-judgments and judgments of others are accurate due to different reasons. The self has access to a plethora of information, including their own thoughts, feelings, and behaviors across every situation and interaction they have been in over time. Self-perceptions are based

on internal experiences of thoughts and feelings, and awareness and observation of one's own behavior, across the lifespan. On the other hand, perceptions of others are primarily based on a more limited outside viewpoint, fewer situations and less time, and a lack of access to internal thoughts and feelings unless they are outwardly expressed. In line with this, some research has suggested that the self is likely to more accurately judge more internal personality traits that are related to emotional experiences (such as neuroticism) because the self simply has more knowledge about these internal traits (Spain, Eaton, & Funder, 2000).

On the other hand, despite having access to more knowledge and experience than anyone else, the self is not necessarily completely accurate for judgments of all traits. The self has the tendency to provide self-descriptions that are overly positive and to *self-enhance*, which means seeing the self in a more favorable way than is warranted by more objective indicators. This *positivity bias* indicates a possible cause of inaccuracy in self-judgments (Hofstee, 1994), especially for traits that are highly evaluative. Judgments of others are not as prone to this bias, although acquaintances tend to judge targets more favorably than do strangers (John & Robins, 1993). Some research suggests that judgments from outside observers capture unique aspects of a target's personality that the perspective of the self does not provide, indicating that judgments of the self and of others provide somewhat different information about the person (Vazire, 2010). This is especially likely for traits that are related to more behavioral cues such as sociability and arrogance, which tend to be more accurately perceived by others (Vazire & Mehl, 2008).

Summary

We have described how different factors, including the situation and type of judge-target relationship can influence our ability to accurately judge different traits. In review, accuracy for more internal and less observable personality traits is highly influenced by the situation and relationship type, while more externalized personality traits are more easily and accurately judged across different situations and with shorter and less intimate relationships. In addition, more internal and less evaluative traits are more accurately judged by the self, while more externalized and evaluative traits are more accurately judged by others. Considering what we have learned so far about the accuracy of different personality traits, we now discuss some possible ways to increase the accuracy of judgments of some traits, as well as some possibilities for the future of accuracy research that focuses on the good trait moderator.

Improving Accuracy of Trait Judgments

While there are many factors related to how accurately specific traits can be judged, it is important to emphasize that under the right circumstances, it may be possible to judge all traits with high levels of accuracy. The topics discussed within this chapter highlight several ways that achieving higher levels of trait accuracy is possible. While this may seem like a daunting task given the complexities we have discussed, research on the good trait suggests how accuracy could be improved. Before we discuss how to improve accuracy for a given trait, consider the answers to the questions we have addressed within this chapter.

First, what makes a trait more observable, and is this related to accuracy? An observable trait is associated with an abundance of relevant cues that are made available in many situations. It is easier to judge these traits because it is easier for judges to gather a large enough amount of relevant information about them. Furthermore, there is strong research evidence that more observable traits tend to be judged more accurately.

Second, what are trait favorability and evaluativeness, and are these related to accuracy? A favorable trait is one that is socially desirable to score high on, and evaluative traits are ones with high or low favorability. The research is less clear on whether and how favorability and evaluativeness are related to accuracy, although highly evaluative traits do seem to be judged more accurately by others than by the self.

Third, how do other factors of a trait judgment contribute to accuracy? First, cues relevant to some traits are more likely to be available in certain situations, and therefore accuracy for certain traits varies across situations. Second, individuals in more intimate relationships, including family members, close friends, and romantic partners, tend to be more accurate about each other than coworkers and strangers, especially when judging less visible or more internal traits. Third, it is possible to be accurate when judging both others and the self, but the process of gathering information and proneness to positivity bias differs for others versus the self. As a result, judgments of the self tend to be more accurate than judgments of others for more internal and less evaluative traits.

Even traits that are less easily judged, such as neuroticism, can be accurately judged in situations

that are likely to elicit cues relevant to those traits, which indicates that it is important to interact with or observe targets in a variety of situations, and especially in situations that are likely to elicit cues for these less-observable traits. As research has shown, observing someone in a socially stressful situation can lead to higher levels of accuracy for judgments of neuroticism compared to less stressful situations (Hirschmüller et al., 2015), and accuracy of self-esteem is possible within public self-presentation situations (Hirschmüller et al., 2018). But what about other traits that are difficult to judge? Can we broadly apply what we know from previous research to identify possible situations in which cues to these traits are more likely to be available? For example, openness to experience is the other trait from the FFM that tends to be judged with lower levels of accuracy. Perhaps engaging in a task with someone that requires creativity, discussing philosophical issues, or visiting a museum or art gallery would provide cues relevant to openness and intellect. An aspect of moral character that was judged with lower accuracy was compassion (Helzer et al., 2014), so observing people interacting with or helping others who are in need in some way or asking people to talk about whether they look for and act on ways to help others, could provide cues to compassion. For example, one study examined whether people are able to make accurate judgments of how others perceive risk (Vineyard, 2016). Judgments reached the highest levels of accuracy when judges observed targets discussing their attitudes toward risk as opposed to describing either a risky activity in which they had engaged, or their personality in general. So, if you want to judge less observable and more internal traits with high accuracy, be sure to ask questions that will provide information that is relevant to those traits or observe people in situations that are likely to elicit trait-relevant information.

Research has found that people tend to make more accurate judgments of low-observability traits when they have been acquainted with targets for longer and have developed a more intimate relationship with them (Biesanz, West, & Millevoi, 2007; Connelly & Ones, 2010). Based on this finding, another possible way to improve accuracy is to have longer and more intimate relationships. To perhaps hasten this process, you could spend more time with people, ask questions, and have conversations that are likely to increase the level of intimacy in the relationship. For example, instead of talking about the weather and movies you have seen recently, talk about things that are important to you (such as your life goals and motivations, and philosophical or religious worldviews) and how you typically think and feel in several types of situations. Although keep in mind that how you do this is important, as you want other people to feel comfortable to reveal their true thoughts, feelings, motivations, and so forth (see Letzring, 2008). In addition, more intimate relationships are likely to involve interactions across a wider variety of contexts compared to those that are less intimate, and seeing people in more situations is likely to increase the number of relevant cues that are available to less-observable traits. For this reason, interacting with targets in a larger variety of situations, or asking people to describe what they think, feel, and do across several types of situations, is likely to lead to higher levels of accuracy.

In addition to these suggestions, it is also important to note that targets have access to internal knowledge about themselves that is not always behaviorally externalized (Vazire, 2010). Because of this, it can be beneficial to simply ask someone what they are thinking or feeling; ask them to describe their attitudes, beliefs, or values; ask them to list unusual facts about themselves; or directly ask them what they think are like. If they respond to these questions honestly, this will also be helpful in making more relevant cues available for less judgable traits.

Future Directions

Research investigating judgment accuracy for specific personality traits has advanced our understanding of why some traits are judged more easily than others. However, there are still several areas of research that have not yet been investigated deeply in relation to the good trait and that would be interesting avenues for future work.

It is not yet clear whether and how favorability and evaluativeness of traits are related to how accurately they are judged. Research has found positive linear relationships (Funder, 1980; Funder & Colvin, 1988), curvilinear relationships (John & Robins, 1993), no relationship (May & Reinhardt, 2018; McDonald & Letzring, 2016; Paunonen & Kam, 2014; Ready et al., 2000), and even negative relationships (Helzer et al., 2014; McDonald & Letzring, 2016) between favorability and accuracy. Furthermore, these relationships have been found to vary depending on the relationship between the judges and targets (Funder & Colvin, 1988). One study suggested that rather than there being a direct relationship between favorability and accuracy, there is an indirect link that goes through variability

in how items were rated (De Vries et al., 2016). Future research should attempt to make sense of this link to determine how favorability is related to accuracy and the other variables that moderate and mediate this relationship. This is important because many consequential decisions are based on judgments of evaluative traits, such as whom to hire for a job or whom to date and/or marry, and information about how to increase the accuracy of judgments of these traits could help people to make better decisions in these areas.

Another important area for future research is to expand work that examines the role of the situation. Research investigating the role of the situation yields consistent findings, in that certain situations are more relevant for certain traits over others (Beer & Brooks, 2011; Hirschmüller et al., 2015; Hirschmüller et al., 2018; Letzring & Human, 2013). Future research investigating the role of the situation should investigate a much wider variety of situations, as the vast majority of situations explored within accuracy research are interactions between strangers in a laboratory setting. Many situations encountered in real life occur while someone is by themselves or with people they have known for a long time, as well as in familiar settings in which everyday activities take place.

Future research should also continue to investigate the role of relationship type. It is clear that accuracy for some traits tends to improve over the course of a relationship as more intimate information is more likely to be made available across a wider variety of contexts (Biesanz et al., 2007; Connelly & Ones, 2010; Watson et al., 2000). What is less clear is which traits tend to be more or less relevant across different relationship types, and therefore more or less accurately judged across relationship types (see chapter 17 by Luo & Watson in this handbook). The type of relationship may certainly influence the type of traits that are more or less likely to be expressed over time, as a casual friendship could involve very different interactions compared to an employer-employee relationship, a parent-child relationship, a teacher-student relationship, and a marriage, just to name a few.

A third future research direction could investigate how the variability of traits is related to how accurately they are judged. Fleeson (2001) proposed the idea of thinking about personality traits in terms of how states related to the traits vary over time, and later used this idea as part of his *whole trait theory* (Fleeson & Jayawickreme, 2015). Fleeson called this variability in states a *density distribution*, and the main idea is that over time, people behave in ways that are consistent with different levels of traits. For example, when people report on how extraverted they are feeling and behaving in the moment at several points over several days, there are large amounts of variability such that sometimes they report high levels of extraversion, sometimes moderate levels, and sometimes low levels. It is possible to compute a person's average state-level for each trait, as well as the variability in the state ratings (usually in terms of standard deviations). Research supports this conceptualization of traits and has found that individuals vary quite a bit in behavior and emotions related to traits (Fleeson, 2001; Fleeson & Law, 2015). However, some traits (especially extraversion, conscientiousness, and positive affect) seemed to have more within-person variability than other traits (such as agreeableness, neuroticism, and intellect; Fleeson, 2001). It is this aspect of trait variability that fits in this chapter on the good trait. If some traits have narrow density distributions, meaning that people act and feel more consistent levels of those traits across situations and over time, then those traits may be easier to judge accurately than traits with wider density distributions. To our knowledge, no one has yet investigated how accuracy is related to density distributions of specific traits, and this could be another important approach that would increase our understanding of why some traits are judged more accurately than others.

Finally, future research should continue to investigate accuracy of a wide variety of traits and could benefit by also examining accuracy at different levels of specificity or breadth. While most research has investigated accuracy of judging personality traits, and the FFM in particular, research has also investigated accuracy of judging values (McDonald & Letzring, 2016), trait mindfulness (May & Reinhardt, 2018), and self-esteem (Hirschmüller et al., 2018). Investigating accuracy of traits other than the Big Five is important to more fully understand how accurately other relatively stable characteristics of individuals are judged and the factors related to the accuracy of those judgments. Furthermore, most research has examined accuracy of judging personality traits at a broad factor level. However, there are lower-levels of these personality factors—called facets—that describe more specific patterns of thoughts, feelings, and behaviors (Costa & McCrae, 1995; Soto & John, 2009, 2017). Research that examines accuracy of personality trait judgments at the facet level could reveal additional information about how factors are related to accuracy

of judgments, such as whether accuracy of judging facets follows similar patterns to accuracy of judging personality traits as a whole and whether certain facets are more observable and relevant depending on the circumstances of the interaction.

Conclusion

Understanding accuracy of person perception for specific traits is not a straightforward process, as you may have deduced from reading this chapter. People and contexts are both complex, and some traits are simply easier to judge than others depending on the circumstances. Several characteristics of traits play a role in why some traits are judged more easily than others, including observability, the situation, and your relationship with a target. Identifying which traits are easier versus harder to judge and developing ways to increase accuracy for less easily judged traits could help people to make more accurate judgments and ultimately to make better decisions based on these judgments. It is important for people to understand that they may have to invest quite a bit of time and thought in order to make the most accurate judgments possible of different traits.

References

Beer, A., & Brooks, C. (2011). Information quality in personality judgment: The value of personal disclosure. *Journal of Research in Personality, 45*, 175–185. doi:10.1016/j.jrp.2011.01.001

Beer, A., & Watson, D. (2008). Asymmetry in judgments of personality: Others are less differentiated than the self. *Journal of Personality, 76*, 535–560. doi:10.1111/j.1467-6494.2008.00495.x

Biesanz, J. C., West, S. G., & Millevoi, A. (2007). What do you learn about someone over time? The relationship between length of acquaintance and consensus and self-other agreement in judgments of personality. *Journal of Personality and Social Psychology, 92*, 119–135. doi:10.1037/0022-3514.92.1.119

Borkenau, P., Brecke, S., Möttig, C., & Paelecke, M. (2009). Extraversion is accurately perceived after a 50-ms exposure to a face. *Journal of Research in Personality, 43*, 703–706. doi:10.1016/j.jrp.2009.03.007

Borkenau, P., & Liebler, A. (1992). Trait inferences: Sources of validity at zero acquaintance. *Journal of Personality and Social Psychology, 62*, 645–657. doi:10.1037/0022-3514.62.4.645

Clark, L. A. (1993). *Schedule for nonadaptive and adaptive personality: Manual for administration, scoring, and interpretation*. Minneapolis: University of Minnesota Press.

Connelly, B. S., & Ones, D. S. (2010). An other perspective on personality: Meta-analytic integration of observers' accuracy and predictive validity. *Psychological Bulletin, 136*(6), 1092–1122. doi:10.1037/a0021212

Costa, P. T., & McCrae, R. R. (1992). Normal personality assessment in clinical practice: The NEO Personality Inventory. *Psychological Assessment, 4*, 5–13. doi:10.1037/1040-3590.4.1.5

Costa, P. T., & McCrae, R. R. (1995). Domains and facets: Hierarchical personality assessment using the Revised NEO Personality Inventory. *Journal of Personality Assessment, 64*, 21–50. doi:10.1207/s15327752jpa6401_2

De Vries, R. E., Lee, K., & Ashton, M. C. (2008). The Dutch HEXACO Personality Inventory: Psychometric properties, self-other agreement, and relations with psychopathy among low and high acquaintance dyads. *Journal of Personality Assessment, 90*, 142–151. doi:10.1080/00223890701845195

De Vries, R. E., Realo, A., & Allik, J. (2016). Using personality item characteristics to predict single-item internal reliability, retest reliability, and self-other agreement. *European Journal of Personality, 30*, 618–636. doi:10.1002/per.2083

Fleeson, W. (2001). Toward a structure- and process-integrated view of personality traits as density distributions of states. *Journal of Personality and Social Psychology, 80*, 1011–1027. doi:10.1037//0022-3514.80.6.1011

Fleeson, W., & Jayawickreme, E. (2015). Whole Trait Theory. *Journal of Research in Personality, 56*, 82–92. doi:10.1016/j.jrp.2014.10.009

Fleeson, W., & Law, M. K. (2015). Trait enactments as density distributions: The role of actors, situations, and observers in explaining stability and variability. *Journal of Personality and Social Psychology, 109*, 1090–1104. doi:10.1037/a0039517

Funder, D. C. (1980). On seeing ourselves as others see us: Self-other agreement and discrepancy in personality ratings. *Journal of Personality, 48*, 473–493. doi:10.1111/j.1467-6494.1980.tb02380.x

Funder, D. C. (1995). On the accuracy of personality judgment: A realistic approach. *Psychological Review, 102*, 652–670. doi:10.1037/0033-295X.102.4.652

Funder, D. C. (1999). *Personality judgment: A realistic approach to person perception.* San Diego, CA: Academic Press.

Funder, D. C. (2012). Accurate personality judgment. *Current Directions in Psychological Science, 21*, 177–182. doi:10.1177/0963721412445309

Funder, D. C. (2016). *The personality puzzle* (7th ed.). New York: W. W. Norton.

Funder, D. C., & Colvin, C. R. (1988). Friends and strangers: Acquaintanceship, agreement, and the accuracy of personality judgment. *Journal of Personality and Social Psychology, 55*, 149–158. doi:10.1037/0022-3514.55.1.149

Funder, D. C., & Dobroth, K. M. (1987). Differences between traits: Properties associated with interjudge agreement. *Journal of Personality and Social Psychology, 52*, 409–418. doi:10.1037/0022-3514.52.2.409

Goldberg, L. R. (1999). A broad-bandwidth, public-domain, personality inventory measuring the lower-level facets of several five-factor models. In I. Mervielde, I. Deary, F. De Fruyt, & F. Ostendorf (Eds.), *Personality psychology in Europe* (Vol. 7, pp. 7–28). Tilburg, The Netherlands: Tilburg University Press.

Goldberg, L. R., Johnson, J. A., Eber, H. W., Hogan, R., Ashton, M. C., Cloninger, C. R., & Gough, H. C. (2006). The International Personality Item Pool and the future of public-domain personality measures. *Journal of Research in Personality, 40*, 84–96. doi:10.1016/j.jrp.2005.08.007

Gosling, S. D., Ko, S. J., Mannarelli, T., & Morris, M. E. (2002). A room with a cue: Personality judgments based on offices and bedrooms. *Journal of Personality and Social Psychology, 82*, 379–398. doi:10.1037//0022-3514.82.3.379

Helzer, E. G., Furr, R. M., Hawkins, A., Barranti, M., Blackie, L. E. R., & Fleeson, W. (2014). Agreement on the perception of moral character. *Personality and Social Psychology Bulletin, 40*, 1698–1710. doi:10.1177/0146167214554957

Hirschmüller, S., Egloff, B., Schmukle, S. C., Nestler, S., & Back, M. D. (2015). Accurate judgments of neuroticism at zero acquaintance: A question of relevance. *Journal of Personality, 83*, 221–228. doi:10.1111/jopy.12097

Hirschmüller, S., Schmukle, S. C., Krause S., Back, M. D., & Egloff, B. (2018). Accuracy of self-esteem judgments at zero-acquaintance. *Journal of Personality, 86*, 308–319. doi:10.1111/jopy.12316

Hofstee, W. K. B. (1994). Who should own the definition of personality? *European Journal of Personality, 8*, 149–162. doi:10.1002/per.2410080302

John, O. P., Naumann, L. P., & Soto, C. J. (2008). Paradigm shift to the integrative Big Five trait taxonomy: History, measurement, and conceptual issues. In O. P. John, R. W. Robins, & L. A. Pervin (Eds.), *Handbook of personality: Theory and research* (3rd ed., pp. 114–158). New York: Guilford Press.

John, O. P., & Robins, R. W. (1993). Determinants of interjudge agreement on personality traits: The Big Five domains, observability, evaluativeness, and the unique perspective of the self. *Journal of Personality, 61*, 521–551. doi:10.1111/j.1467-6494.1993.tb00781.x

Kenny, D. A., & West, T. V. (2008). Zero acquaintance: Definitions, statistical model, findings, and process. In N. Ambady & J. J. Skowronski (Eds.), *First impressions* (pp. 129–146). New York: Guilford.

Kenny, D. A., & West, T. V. (2010). Similarity and agreement in self- and other perception: A meta-analysis. *Personality and Social Psychology Review, 14*, 196–213. doi:10.1177/1088868309353414

Kilianski, S. E., (2008). Who do you think I am? Accuracy in perceptions of others' self-esteem. *Journal of Research in Personality, 42*, 386–398. doi:10.1016/j.jrp.2007.07.004

Letzring, T. D. (2008). The good judge of personality: Characteristics, behaviors, and observer accuracy. *Journal of Research in Personality, 42*, 914–932. doi:10.1016/j.jrp.2007.12.003

Letzring, T. D., & Funder, D. C. (2018). Interpersonal accuracy in trait judgments. In V. Zeigler-Hill & T. K. Shackelford (Eds.), *The SAGE handbook of personality and individual difference: Volume 3. Applications of personality and individual differences.* Thousand Oaks, CA: Sage.

Letzring, T. D., & Human, L. J. (2013). An examination of information quality as a moderator of accurate personality judgment. *Journal of Personality, 82*, 440–451. doi:10.1111/jopy.12075

May, L. M., & Reinhardt, K. M. (2018). Self-other agreement in the assessment of mindfulness using the Five-Facet Mindfulness Questionnaire. *Mindfulness, 9*, 105–116. doi:10.1007/s12671-017-0749-3

McCrae, R. R., Costa, P. T, Jr. (1999). A five-factor theory of personality. In L. A. Pervin & O. P. John (Eds.), *Handbook of personality: Theory and research* (2nd ed.). New York: Guilford Press.

McDonald, J. S., & Letzring, T. D. (2016). Judging personal values and personality traits: Accuracy and its relation to visibility. *Journal of Research in Personality, 65*, 140–151. doi:10.1016/j.jrp.2016.10.009

Naumann, L. P., Vazire, S., Rentfrow, P. J., & Gosling, S. D. (2009). Personality judgments based on physical appearance. *Personality and Social Psychology Bulletin, 35*, 1661–1671. doi:10.1177/0146167209346309

Paulhus, D. L., & Vazire, S. (2007). The self-report method. In R. W. Robins, R. C. Fraley, & R. F. Krueger (Eds.), *Handbook of research methods in personality psychology* (pp. 224–239). New York: Guilford Press.

Paunonen, S. V., & Kam, C. (2014). The accuracy of roommate ratings of behaviors versus beliefs. *Journal of Research in Personality, 52*, 55–67. doi:10.1016/j.jrp.2014.07.006

Ready, R. E., Clark, L. A., Watson, D., & Westerhouse, K. (2000). Self- and peer-reported personality: Agreement, trait ratability, and the "self-based heuristic." *Journal of Research in Personality, 34*, 208–224. doi:10.1006/jrpe.1999.2280

Schwartz, S. H. (1992). Universals in the content and structure of values: Theoretical advances and empirical tests in 20 countries. In M. Zanna (Ed.), *Advances in experimental social psychology* (Vol. 35, pp. 1–65). New York: Academic Press.

Soto, C. J., & John, O. P. (2009). Ten facet scales for the Big Five Inventory: Convergence with NEO-PI-R facets, self-peer agreement, and discriminant validity. *Journal of Research in Personality, 43*, 84–90. doi:10.1016/j.jrp.2008.10.002

Soto, C. J., & John, O. P. (2017). The next Big Five Inventory (BFI-2): Developing and assessing a hierarchical model with 15 facets to enhance bandwidth, fidelity, and predictive power. *Journal of Personality and Social Psychology, 113*, 117–143. doi:10.1037/pspp0000096

Spain, J. S., Eaton, L. G., & Funder, D. C. (2000). Perspectives on personality: The relative accuracy of self versus others for the prediction of emotion and behavior. *Journal of Personality, 68*, 837–867. doi:10.1111/1467-6494.00118

Vazire, S. (2010). Who knows what about a person? The self-other knowledge asymmetry (SOKA) model. *Journal of Personality and Social Psychology, 98*, 281–300. doi:10.1037/a0017908

Vazire, S., & Mehl, M. R. (2008). Knowing me, knowing you: The accuracy and unique predictive validity of self-ratings and other-ratings of daily behavior. *Journal of Personality and Social Psychology, 95*, 1202–1216. doi:10.1037/a0013314

Vineyard, J. (2016). *The accuracy of judging risk in others: Investigating information quality and individual differences as moderators of accuracy of risk trait judgments* (Unpublished doctoral dissertation). Idaho State University, Pocatello, ID.

Watson, D.D., Hubbard, B., & Wiese, D. (2000). General traits of personality and affectivity as predictors of satisfaction in intimate relationships: Evidence from self and partner-ratings. *Journal of Personality, 68*, 413–449. doi:10.1111/1467-6494.00102

Yeagley, E., Morling, B., & Nelson, M. (2007). Nonverbal zero-acquaintance accuracy of self-esteem, social dominance orientation, and satisfaction with life. *Journal of Research in Personality, 41*, 1099–1106. doi:10.1016/j.jrp.2006.12.002

Notes

1. It is usually preferable to use a composite for the accuracy criteria, but this is not always feasible and self-other agreement is quite commonly used in research in this area.

2. It is possible to calculate correlations in this matter for single items within a personality measure when it is assumed that each item represents an individual trait, and this is referred to as *item-level correlations.*

3. The Supernumerary Personality Inventory assesses 10 traits that do not map on to the Big Five traits. These traits are conventionality, seductiveness, manipulativeness, thriftiness, humorousness, integrity, femininity, religiosity, risk-taking, and egotism.

4. Sometimes people think that people who are high in openness reveal a lot of relevant cues about the self, which leads them to think that openness should be more accurately judged. However, revealing information about the self is unrelated to openness.

5. HEXACO-PI-R stands for Honesty-Humility, Emotionality, eXtraversion, Agreeableness, Conscientiousness, and Openness to Experience-Personality Inventory-Revised.

6. In round-robin design, a group of people rate themselves and every other member of the group.

7. However, it is interesting to note that self-other agreement did not differ for behaviors versus attitudes and beliefs when items related to religiosity were included.

8. NEO stands for neuroticism, extraversion, and openness to experience because this scale originally assessed these three traits.

9. The SNAP includes scales for mistrust, manipulativeness, aggression, self-harm, eccentric perceptions, dependency, exhibitionism, entitlement, detachment, disinhibition, impulsivity, propriety, workaholism, positive temperament, and negative temperament.

10. Favorability for personality traits was significantly correlated with a total observability score that was a composite of several ratings but was not significantly correlated with any of the individual observability ratings.

Information as a Moderator of Accuracy in Personality Judgment

Andrew Beer

Abstract

People inherently believe that additional information is helpful in making accurate personality judgment, an assertion supported by empirical evidence. This chapter reviews the evidence beginning with the cross-sectional and longitudinal study of accuracy in naturally existing groups and continuing through to laboratory-based experiments involving the intentional manipulation of available information. In doing so, it discusses the process of becoming acquainted with others in our social world and makes suggestions for future avenues of research in this area, including but not limited to more clearly defining acquaintanceship, studying information quantity and quality jointly and separately, and better connecting personality judgment with real-world phenomena.

Key Words: accuracy, information quantity, information quality, acquaintanceship, personality judgment

In most modern cultures, it would be considered reckless to propose marriage after a few weeks of dating and brazen to ask for a promotion on one's third day on the job. However, after a considerable amount of time and exposure to the relevant parties, such requests are commonplace and expected. It is natural to want to truly know a person before tying one's lot to theirs, personally or professionally, and one could argue that in many ways, knowing a person means that we feel able to accurately judge his or her personality. Evidence of the belief that greater information tends to associate with greater accuracy in personality judgment is easily available. Employers seek letters of reference from individuals who *should* know the applicant, usually based on length and depth of exposure—often specifying the length and nature of such exposure. In social settings, we make general assumptions about our knowledge of others, and this is often based on our sense of appropriate exposure (e.g., "I only know Ted from work; you might ask his brother if he would like tickets to the opera.").

In an effort to understand the psychological underpinnings of accurate personality judgment,

Funder's realistic accuracy model (RAM; 1995, 2012; see also chapter 2 by Letzring & Funder in this handbook) envisions the path to accurate judgment as occurring through four successive processes. First, potential cues must be *relevant* to an underlying personality characteristic of interest. Second, these relevant cues must be *available* to the judge[1] in question. Third, the judge must *detect* these cues, and finally, the judge must properly connect these cues to the relevant personality characteristic, a process called *utilization*. One of the principal moderators of accuracy in the RAM is information, which works primarily through the first two processes of the RAM. That is, *good information* means that the judgment context is characterized by greater availability of relevant cues to personality. More and better information helps us make more accurate personality judgments, but what do "more" and "better" mean in these circumstances? What, exactly, happens during the course of dating or during an occupational performance evaluation period? Do we come to know others via repeated bouts of small talk, or does most useful information come from long, focused conversations about important topics?

Can we come to understand someone simply by sharing a cubicle wall for 2 years, without forming a meaningful relationship? How would this occur? In this chapter, I trace empirical investigation of these questions from their origins to our present understanding of the phenomena, spotlighting a few landmark studies and concluding with some open questions and suggested directions for future research.

Origins

Research focused on the validity of observer judgments of personality has existed for the bulk of psychological scientific history (e.g., Cleeton & Knight, 1924; Estes, 1938; Shen, 1925). Almost as soon as the field began addressing research questions with data in earnest, attention turned toward identifying conditions that might yield accurate judgments of others—and determining whether this were even truly possible. One of the earlier and most-cited empirical investigations into information's connection to accurate personality judgment, however, came rather incidentally. Norman and Goldberg (1966) were attempting to address a different issue (identifying principal personality traits) when they compared the interrelations of trait judgments derived from statistical simulations to those obtained from groups of people making judgments of others. These sets of intertrait correlations were similar, but it was their secondary tests that are relevant to the topic in question. In order to determine whether relations among trait judgments were due to actual differences in a target's personality (as opposed to the simple semantic relations of trait terms in the mind of the judge), Norman and Goldberg (1966) examined the two primary types of interjudge agreement: consensus and self-other agreement. *Consensus* involves the comparison of judgments made by two or more individuals (not including the person being judged, who is referred to as the target). *Self-other agreement* involves comparing a target's self-rated personality to judgments made by others. The simulated data were compared to data obtained from four distinct groups: (1) strangers (participants made personality ratings of each other on the first day of class), (2) ROTC members (these people had typically seen each other in class or drills over a 1–2 year period), (3) Peace Corps trainees (these individuals had spent 3 months of intensive training together), and (4) fraternity seniors (this group had generally lived together over a period of 1–3 years). In this case, simulated data yielded no consensus (which was

unsurprising, as the simulated "judges'" ratings were initially determined by a random response from which an algorithm generated related trait judgments), but groups with varying levels of acquaintanceship produced different levels of consensus. Specifically, the greatest levels of agreement were found in the fraternity and Peace Corps samples, followed by the ROTC sample and, finally, the strangers who showed the lowest levels of consensus among real (as opposed to simulated) data. The authors also presented self-other agreement data for the strangers and the Peace Corps sample, demonstrating that the Peace Corps trainees were more accurate in assessing each other's personalities (mean r across five factor model [FFM] traits = 0.41) than were the strangers (mean r = 0.25). At the time, the authors (appropriately) concluded that this was solid evidence in support of the existence of personality traits in the structure suggested, but—as they would note in the discussion—some of the additional findings of this work would spur entire areas of discovery in personality perception.

The Acquaintanceship Effect

The groups in Norman and Goldberg's (1966) study could be arranged in terms of increasing levels of subjectively determined "acquaintanceship." People who had lived together for years probably knew each other better than did people who spent a couple of hours a week together over a similar period of time, and each of these groups certainly knew more about each other than did people who had just met moments prior to evaluation. But these differences were not purely tied to mere length of exposure. For example, the manner in which Peace Corps trainees and ROTC members interacted was likely qualitatively different as well. Nevertheless, on its face the acquaintanceship effect seems rather unexciting: those with greater personal knowledge of another should better understand that individual's personality, fostering more accurate personality judgments.

Much of the early empirical work directly addressing the phenomenon was cross-sectional in nature. At the same time that Norman and Goldberg reported their results, Taft (1966)—following pioneering work by Ferguson (1949) that demonstrated greater consensus in personality judgments made by employees of managers as they were better acquainted—undertook a more intentional look at the phenomenon. In Taft's study, participants nominated most- and least-known classmates, and self-other agreement was compared across these groups.

As was the case in Norman and Goldberg's data, people were more accurate in judging the most known ($r = 0.52$) than the least known ($r = 0.42$) participants. Cloyd (1977) replicated these findings using a similar method (but different analytic strategy). In each of these studies, however, the samples were fairly small and the nomination procedures were somewhat problematic. In asking people to assess those they know, it is possible that these respondents were actually identifying people whom they thought they could best evaluate, in which case the exercise becomes somewhat redundant or at least an exercise in demonstrating a connection between perceived and actual accuracy rather than demonstrating the pure influence of level of acquaintance. A similar criticism could be made for any study in which acquaintanceship is operationalized via self-reported knowledge of the target, as was the case in both Watson and Clark's (1991) and Paunonen's (1989) work demonstrating support for the acquaintanceship effect. Even so, some studies using such methodology showed only modest support for increased accuracy with increased acquaintance (Biesanz, West, & Millevoi, 2007).

In other work, researchers sidestepped this issue by employing methods more similar to Norman and Goldberg's (1966), in which consensus or agreement was compared across existing groups who differed in nature of relationship (and thus acquaintanceship). Funder and Colvin (1988) employed a unique design in which the same target was rated by each class of acquaintanceship, diminishing some concerns common in such cross-sectional comparisons—and found that, indeed, friends (mean profile $r = 0.46$) were more accurate than strangers ($r = -.03$). Later research would replicate this effect using a similar design and variable-centered[2] analyses (Funder, Kolar, & Blackman, 1995). Getting beyond simple acquainted-unacquainted differences, Watson, Hubbard, and Wiese (2000) compared self-other agreement across groups of pairs of friendship, dating couples, and married couples. In this case, the first two groups had known each other for approximately 3 years versus an average of 17 years of marriage. As hypothesized, agreement was stronger among the married couples (mean $r = 0.43$) than among friends (mean $r = 0.33$) or dating couples (mean $r = 0.35$). Allik, De Vries, and Realo (2016) also demonstrated increased self-other agreement across groups characterized by increasing levels of familiarity or intimacy (friends, family, spouses or partners).

In the end, however, all of these data are subject to a myriad of confounds with respect to explaining differences in accuracy in terms of differences in in-

formation. In studies comparing groups, the issues are particularly stark. Beyond the quantitative (length of relationship) differences, are people who stay married for 10 years qualitatively different from dating couples? Married samples tend to be older, and it may be possible that older (or, more socially experienced) individuals are simply better judges of others. Or perhaps staying married for many years requires that one be a good judge of personality (Rogers & Biesanz, 2018; see also chapter 6 by Colman in this handbook)—or a good target (Human & Biesanz, 2013; see also chapter 7 by Mignault & Human in this handbook). Further, intact groups or dyads of any sort may be more likely to be composed of well-adjusted individuals, and psychological adjustment is a predictor of both good judges (Letzring, 2008, 2015) and good targets (Human & Biesanz, 2011). Additionally, in studies involving existing relationships it is possible that people who are acquainted have communicated with each other specifically about their personalities, thus agreement may reflect a simple result of that communication rather than truly accurate personality judgment (but see Funder, et al., 1995). These are just a few examples highlighting the difficulty in interpreting the results discussed previously. In order to alleviate some of these concerns—particularly those involving group differences—longitudinal studies are necessary.

Longitudinal Studies of Acquaintanceship

Most research on judgmental accuracy in relationships that develop over time takes a fairly standard form. As an initial example, consider a frequently cited study (Paulhus & Bruce, 1992) tracking the validity of observer judgments among previously unacquainted individuals. In short, students in a personality course met weekly in small groups seven times for approximately 20 minutes per meeting. After each meeting, participants rated the personalities of the other members of their group. In keeping with expectations, self-other agreement showed a positive trend across the seven meetings: average (across FFM traits) correlations increased from $r = 0.21$ to $r = 0.30$ from the first to the last week. Kurtz and Sherker (2003) replicated this general effect with a sample of college roommates whom they assessed at approximately 2 weeks (mean $r = 0.27$) and 15 weeks (mean $r = 0.43$) of acquaintanceship. In the most recent attempt to examine the acquaintanceship effect over time, Brown and Bernieri (2017) assessed personality at zero acquaintance, after 5 minutes of interaction, and again after 10 weeks (a total of approximately 30 hours) of contact designed by the experimenters to create opportunities to become better acquainted (e.g., playing games, traveling short distances together, debating an issue, cleaning one another's rooms). They found general gains in accuracy from zero acquaintance to 5 minutes and from 5 minutes to 10 weeks, although the gains in accuracy across the two time intervals were more similar in magnitude than one might expect: the first 5 minutes seemed to provide as much relevant information as the next 30 hours! On the other hand, Park and Ryan's (1997) similarly designed—but longer (approximately 8 months at final assessment)—study revealed no increases in consensus with increased acquaintanceship. In fact, several studies of this sort (more on this later) yielded little in terms of support for increased information being associated with increased levels of consensus in personality judgment.

So why have longitudinal studies generated such a mixed bag of findings? One issue could be that very few studies start at a true zero point in terms of acquaintanceship. That is, the individuals in these groups have generally already spent some time together prior to the initial judgment of each other. As discussed later, this may be problematic for attempts to observe increasing accuracy, due to the fact that in some cases, very limited information can lead to accurate personality judgment. A second issue could be that these groups have tended to be student populations who are either thrown together by chance into work or discussion groups or even as roommates, which may not be fully representative of the natural flow of information and acquaintanceship in that it may lack the inherent motivational component of naturally forming relationships (i.e., the interactants truly care and intend to know each other). A third issue is that there tends to be fairly little control of exactly how information is being exchanged in these studies in terms of the kind of contact that is occurring and whether people are actually being exposed to more personality-relevant information.

The (Relatively Fruitless) Search for Acquaintanceship Moderators

In both cross-sectional and longitudinal studies of acquaintanceship effects, researchers have occasionally attempted to measure the precise methods by which people become acquainted. As mentioned previously, some early studies used self-reported "extent of knowledge" measures to create their comparison groups (e.g., Watson & Clark, 1991). In these studies, there is usually a relation between knowing and accuracy, but as discussed previously, it is possible that the extent-of-knowledge measures are driven by an existing sense in the judge of self-other agreement with the target in question. Thus, others have chosen to measure acquaintanceship by more objective means. One way to do this is simply asking judges to estimate the length of their relationship with a given target. This has been operationalized in various ways, but generally has not yielded strong associations between length of acquaintance and degree of accuracy (e.g., Allik et al., 2016; Biesanz, West, & Millevoi, 2007). Indeed, there are reasons to believe that just the duration of a relationship may not, in fact, be a valid measure of acquaintanceship as it is intended in this line of research. Thus, others have attempted to more clearly measure acquaintanceship. In addition to measuring length of acquaintanceship, Watson and colleagues (2000) used a modification of the Relationship Closeness Inventory (Berscheid, Snyder, & Omoto, 1989) and an ad hoc measure in which they calculated the number of shared activities (e.g., going to movies, visiting family, exercising), in their "disappointing" (p. 555) attempts to uncover a statistical moderator of accuracy in their sample. Such unfulfilled hopes are not uncommon (e.g., McCrae, 1994; McCrae, Stone, Fagan, & Costa, 1998). In their discussion of moderators of accuracy in judgments of life satisfaction, Schneider, Schimmack, Petrican, and Walker (2010) noted other issues that may have hindered identification of acquaintance duration as a moderator of accuracy—most notably that (1) effect sizes of the relationship between accuracy and length of acquaintance are small (and thus require large sample sizes) and (2) common statistical techniques for identifying these relationships assume a linear connection between variables, which, in their estimation, is unlikely in the case of acquaintance effects (i.e., the learning curve is steeper sooner).

In short, attempts to establish acquaintanceship as a moderator of accurate personality judgment have been moderately successful when examining the phenomenon across groups but less successful when examining the phenomenon over time. Further, attempts to specifically measure the way in which groups of varying levels of assumed acquaintanceship differ, and connect those differences to differences in accuracy, have also been generally unsuccessful. The various attempts and discussions thereof seem to imply that such failures are primarily measurement-based—if only we had clear, valid measures of acquaintanceship, the connection between it and accuracy would be empirically established to a greater extent. Therein lies the problem, however: prior to the development of a valid operational definition of acquaintanceship, there must be a consensual, coherent, conceptual definition of the concept. Perhaps we do not have a great sense of what is meant by "acquaintanceship" in its various applications.

A Model of Acquaintanceship

We have discussed the issues with simply relying on direct measures of acquaintanceship (e.g., How well do you know this person?), but what is to take its place? How do the members of the Peace Corps and fraternity seniors differ? What about married couples and friends? In graduate school, I had one friend with whom I routinely played basketball, another with whom I would cook and play tennis, and another with whom I would discuss and exchange music. With whom was I most acquainted? For the first few years that I worked at my current job, a geology professor from down the hall would come by once a week to tell me a joke. Around that same time in my life, I spent the better part of a day talking with someone at a conference; I have not spoken to or seen that person since. With whom am I more acquainted? What really differentiates these relationships? What is the best way to conceptualize and measure acquaintanceship? Luckily, some researchers have attempted to address these questions empirically. Starzyk, Holden, Fabrigar, and McDonald (2006) asked samples of individuals to characterize their relationships with others of varying degree of subjectively assessed "acquaintanceship."[3] To uncover dimensions of acquaintanceship, they factor analyzed responses to a lengthy list of items ranging from queries about amount of contact ("I see this person a lot") to context-specific knowledge ("I know how this person handles stress") to simple behaviors ("I hug this person a lot"). From a list of over two hundred items, the authors identified six underlying dimensions. The first two seemed to tap quantity of information and reflect some simple conceptualizations of acquaintanceship: duration (how long one has known the person) and frequency (how often one sees the person). Duration is probably the more common measure used in the literature to date as a proxy for acquaintanceship, but it is important to distinguish it from frequency. For example, I have a friend whom I have known for over 30 years, but whom I see or speak to fairly rarely these days (long duration/low frequency), whereas I see

my colleagues at work daily but have known them for a (relatively) short period of time (high frequency/short duration). Norman and Goldberg (1966), and many others that followed, were obviously sensitive to this difference in their chosen comparison groups, but they were also implicitly mindful of other distinctions. Fraternity seniors had lived together; Peace Corps volunteers likely had similar values (and lived together in that instance). Friends share information with each other and see each other in a variety of contexts, but dating and married couples are physically intimate and may have even more access to private information. These kinds of differences—which might be considered more qualitative in nature—are captured in the four other dimensions identified in Starzyk et al.'s research: Knowledge of Goals (extent to which one feels familiar with another's goals and interests), Physical Intimacy (extent to which physical contact is affectionate and common in the relationship), Self-Disclosure (familiarity with the other person's true feelings), and Social Network Familiarity (knowledge of the other person's friends and the interactions among them). Thus, one can also characterize level of acquaintance by evaluating a given relationship across these dimensions. For example, my relationship with the jokester was of moderate duration, low-to-moderate frequency, low self-disclosure, low physical intimacy, low knowledge of goals, and low-to-moderate knowledge of social network. The total relationship score across the six dimensions predicted (at least modestly) self-other agreement in the original study, but has yet to be widely applied in research focused on accuracy in personality judgment (for various applications see Fareri, Niznikiewicz, Lee, & Delgado, 2012; Gros, Simms, & Antony, 2010; Nauta, 2012; Kahn, Hucke, Bradley, Glinski, & Malak, 2012; Sparling & Cramer, 2015). Such empirically derived measures of acquaintanceship might be of substantial utility in future work in this area.

The Last Word on Acquaintanceship (Meta-Analyses)

The studies summarized thus far were designed to evaluate differences in accuracy across naturally occurring groups of varying levels of acquaintance. Thus, each study had an aim to draw conclusions about how more information was associated with more accurate personality judgment. And despite the long-standing interest in conditions giving rise to accurate personality judgment, the studies aimed directly at answering this question could be considered relatively few. Happily, however, there is a wealth of accuracy data that can be compared in this fashion via meta-analytic review—even if it was not the authors' original intent to examine this particular question. As researchers in our field and others have begun to recognize the limitations of any single study (Maxwell, Lau, & Howard, 2015), the importance of such studies has appropriately grown.

An early meta-analytic review (Kenny, Albright, Malloy, & Kashy, 1994) indicated that increasing amounts of contact did not predict greater consensus among judges of personality in longitudinal designs (they did find evidence for increasing consensus with increasing acquaintance in cross-sectional designs). However, it must be noted that this review was (1) limited to studies using specific design parameters, such as each judge rating multiple targets and each target being rated by multiple judges (limiting the number of studies included to 32) and (2) focused solely on consensus. The latter can be considered problematic in that two or more judges can agree on the nature of a given target while being entirely inaccurate. For example, two people could share the stereotype that males are more aggressive, and thus agree that Ted is more aggressive than Suzy, even if this is not true. Thus, increased exposure may not always lead to gains in consensus, though it should generally lead to gains in accuracy (Blackman & Funder, 1998). Indeed, some models (e.g., the weighted average model [WAM]; Kenny, 1991; see also chapter 3 by Malloy in this handbook) would not predict consensus to increase under the conditions observed in that analysis. Kenny and West's (2010) meta-analysis alleviates the concern that results may differ when using different accuracy measures by examining interjudge agree-

ment (1) involving the self and (2) not involving the self. Their conclusions with respect to information's moderating role on accuracy are the same, however: increased familiarity with a target does not seem to predict greater consensus or self-other agreement. It is again worth noting that this review was limited to round-robin designs, which allowed for the application of certain componential analyses (e.g., WAM; Kenny, 1991; again, see chapter 3 of this volume), and thus was limited to 24 studies.

In their meta-analysis on the utility of informant ratings of personality in general, Connelly and Ones (2010) used a more inclusive study selection strategy. They examined consensus, self-other agreement, and some instances of behavioral prediction across over 250 studies (comprising over 44,000 participants). Additionally, the authors used Starzyk et al.'s (2006) model of acquaintanceship as a means of organizing their analyses. Figure 9.1 presents the average self-other agreement correlations[4] across traits and across groups representing varying levels of acquaintanceship. As evidenced in the figure, the authors conclude that increased acquaintanceship is associated with increased accuracy (in the form of self-other agreement). Given its greater inclusivity, this study's result may be the more appropriate synopsis of the relationship between acquaintanceship and accuracy. That said, there is much to be considered regarding the mechanism of acquaintance. In Kenny et al.'s (1994) review, it was noteworthy that longitudinal studies, in particular, showed very little evidence of greater information leading to greater consensus. Indeed, Connelly and Ones (2010) suggest that sheer information quantity (e.g., greater exposure to target behavior) is only useful to a point, after which they posit that the self-disclosure

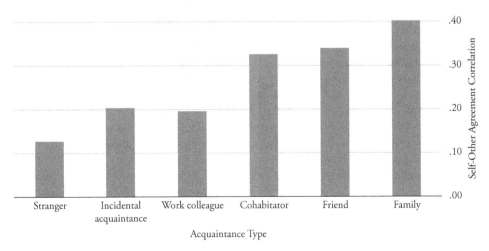

Figure 9.1. Average self-other agreement correlations (calculated from Connelly & Ones, 2010).

associated with closer relationships is what drives greater accuracy in personality judgment. In other words, the *quality* of the information explains differences in accuracy between say, a spouse and a long-term coworker. The data discussed to this point cannot directly address the mechanism of acquaintance, which is at the heart of inquiry with respect to information as a moderator of personality accuracy. In the remainder of this chapter, we turn our focus toward specific attempts to more carefully control aspects of judgment context, and the distinction between quantity and quality of information figures prominently in these discussions.

Beyond Acquaintanceship: Out of the Field and into the Laboratory

Much—though not all—of the work discussed to this point has involved examining differences in accuracy either (1) across naturally occurring groups of varying acquaintance or (2) within groups that are followed over a period of time with limited control of how information is exchanged. This lack of control makes inferences with respect to mechanism problematic. For example, in Paulhus and Bruce's (1992) discussion groups, one cannot be sure the extent to which self-disclosure occurred from week to week or what kinds of behaviors occurred in these contexts. The only sure thing is that *more* information has been exchanged. In order to better understand exactly how gains in accuracy might occur, it is necessary to exert more control over the availability of information in studies of judgment accuracy. In this section, I review some of the systematic attempts to evaluate the role of information quantity and quality in the early stages of impression formation.

Zero Acquaintance: In the Beginning, There Is Nothing (Sort Of)

Researchers have adopted the term "zero acquaintance" to describe studies in which judgments are made about individuals with whom we are unfamiliar—usually restricted to having met for the first time just prior to assessing personality. All relationships begin at a baseline of no knowledge—at least in theory. In practice, this is fairly rare, however. By the time we have met someone in person, we generally have a fair amount of potentially relevant information about them. For example, I "knew" my wife's best friend for years before having met her, so ground zero of person knowledge in this case would have to predate anything generally referred to as "acquaintance." Zero acquaintance and zero infor-

mation are not necessarily the same thing. Early research (e.g., Norman & Goldberg, 1966) would (inadvertently) highlight this point in that unacquainted individuals can nonetheless form somewhat accurate impressions of one another.

One thing that might have struck the reader in preceding sections was the magnitude of accuracy estimates for strangers across the various studies. For traits like extraversion, self-other agreement correlations in samples of strangers routinely reach $r = 0.30$ or greater. This level of agreement among strangers has also struck some researchers as a bit odd. In fact, though Norman and Goldberg (1966) did not spend time discussing this peculiarity in their data, Watson (1989) found it so unexpected that he conducted a study intended primarily to replicate these surprising zero acquaintance effects (Norman and Goldberg's strangers also generated statistically significant agreement correlations for agreeableness and openness/culture). Watson (1989) indeed replicated the effect, as have others over time (e.g., Beer & Brooks, 2011; Beer & Watson, 2008; Hirschmüller, Egloff, Nestler, & Back, 2013; Albright, Kenny, & Malloy, 1988; Kenny, Horner, Kashy, & Chu, 1992). The search for an explanation of this replicable level of accuracy is really a search for what constitutes good information—clearly, some relevant information is present almost immediately.[5] In the studies cited thus far, participants were generally able to see each other move and hear each other talk[6] (if only briefly). In some cases, there may have even been opportunity for incidental contact surrounding the experimental session. Thus, researchers began to strip all information away, adding bits at a time in order to determine how we become more accurate in judging personality.

In a landmark study in this area, Borkenau and Liebler (1992)[7] asked participants to view targets in one of four conditions. Each target had been photographed and then filmed while walking into a room, sitting down, reading a weather report, standing up, and leaving the room. One group of judges was allowed to see only the photograph of the target individual. Another group only heard the speaking portion of the film. A third group saw the film with no sound, and a fourth group saw the film with audio. One could consider this a (quasi) escalating amount of information available across observers, which should predict greater accuracy (consensus and self-other agreement) in the sound-film group than the silent film group and so forth. Indeed, there was a general trend toward greater accuracy with greater information. However, it is noteworthy that even a still photograph led to greater-than-chance levels of self-other agreement for extraversion in this sample—a finding replicated many times over (Beer, 2013, 2014; Beer & Watson, 2010; Naumann, Vazire, Rentfrow, & Gosling, 2009), even with exposure to photographs as brief as 50 milliseconds (Borkenau, Brecke, Möttig, & Paelecke, 2009).

Studies of this sort—in which information is carefully manipulated and personality accuracy measured—are actually rather uncommon in the literature. In an early systematic evaluation of differing types and levels of information on personality judgments, Weiss (1979) did not observe gains in consensus, though there was evidence of differential use of information across conditions. Further, as mentioned earlier, some models of personality accuracy (Kenny, 1991) would indeed predict that consensus may not increase with more information unless this additional information was shared across judges—judges exposed to different sets of new information about a target may not agree more with one another about that target. Other studies, however, have replicated general beneficial effects of increased quantity of information. For instance, Beer and Watson (2010) replicated the gains from still photographs to videos, demonstrating the utility of dynamic visual and audio cues (beyond static visual cues) in assessing extraversion, and another group observed increases in accuracy (for some traits) on a second live interaction of a different kind than the first (i.e., a negotiation task following an unstructured conversation with the same individual; Wall, Taylor, Campbell, Heim, & Richardson, 2018). In a more ambitious study, Borkenau, Mauer, Riemann, Spinath, and Angleitner (2004) presented videos of targets engaging in 15 different activities (e.g., building a paper tower, introducing someone to someone else, mock persuasion, singing) to different judges and found that aggregating impressions from multiple observations was associated with accuracy.[8] Although aggregating information in this fashion is not exactly equivalent to comparing evaluations made by a single individual with greater exposure to a target, it is certainly an interesting approximation of the phenomenon. Furthermore, this study shares a design complication with the others discussed in preceding paragraphs: frequently in studies of this nature—as in more naturalistic studies of acquaintanceship effects—amount of information is confounded with type of information. In Borkenau and Liebler's (1992) study, for example, one can be sure that the sound film condition contains more information than the still photo condition, but the distinction between the audio-only and still-photo condition is not solely an issue of amount.

Pure Quantity of Information

One area of study in which researchers are clearly focused on amount of information is in *thin slice* paradigms (Ambady, Bernieri, & Richeson, 2000; Ambady & Rosenthal, 1992). Typically, in this kind of work judges are exposed to small samples of verbal and/or nonverbal behavior taken from a larger behavioral observation. For example, researchers might present one or five seconds of a silent recorded lecture by a professor and use this to predict end-of-semester teaching evaluations (e.g., Ambady & Rosenthal, 1993). These thin slices have shown to be useful in predicting various social judgments including things such as sexual orientation (Ambady, Hallahan, & Conner, 1999), nature of relationships (Ambady & Gray, 1995), and intelligence (Murphy, Hall, & Colvin, 2003). This methodology has also been applied specifically to personality judgments. Though an early review indicated that gains in predictive accuracy in general are modest to nonexistent from exposures between 30 seconds and 5 minutes (Ambady & Rosenthal, 1992), more recent research indicates that small increases in exposure to the same class of information (usually a video recording of the target interacting with someone) can lead to small gains in accuracy in the domain of personality judgment. For example, Blackman and Funder (1998) observed gains in self-other agreement (but not consensus) when participants viewed 5- to 10-minute segments of target behavior versus 25- to 30-minute segments, and Carney, Colvin, and Hall (2007) noted a similar linear trend (though only for certain traits) when participants viewed clips ranging from 5 seconds to 5 minutes. Letzring, Wells, and Funder (2006) also demonstrated some increases in profile accuracy from initial acquaintance to 50 minutes of conversation (but not from 50 minutes to 3 hours). Finally, Krzyzaniak, Colman, Letzring, McDonald, and Biesanz (2018) observed a linear increase in accuracy for extraversion and a nonlinear increase for conscientiousness from 30 seconds to 5 minutes of exposure to a target. In short, there is at least some evidence for the positive impact of escalating quantity of information in both shorter- and longer-term observations of the phenomenon.

Pure Quality of Information

Increasing quantity of information while holding quality relatively steady is a simpler feat than altering the quality of information available to a judge without affecting quantity of information exchanged. Nonetheless, researchers have made a few attempts to tackle this latter issue. The first clear attempt to do so involved exposure to video recordings of target individuals discussing either (1) their thoughts and feelings with respect to range of topics (e.g., work, family, important life choices) or (2) their specific behaviors with respect to those same topics (Andersen, 1984). In keeping with lay expectations observed in another study (Andersen & Ross, 1984), the thoughts and feelings videos generated greater accuracy than did the behavioral descriptions. More recently, Letzring and Human (2014) approached information quality from a similar vantage point, pitting thoughts and feelings and discussions of behaviors against actually performed behaviors (e.g., read a poem aloud, interpret a Thematic Apperception Test card, playing games, explaining idioms)—except in this case the researchers assigned dyads to discuss these things in person as opposed to observing someone in a video. They found that distinctive accuracy (the ability to judge how people differ from the average person) was generally greater when participants discussed thoughts and feelings or discussed behaviors (specific or general) than when they actually engaged in behaviors together. Departing from thoughts and feelings versus behaviors and their descriptions, Beer and Brooks (2011) instead chose another potential parameter of information quality: varying types of self-disclosure. Building on previous work (Pronin, Fleming, & Steffel, 2008) which established that lay judges believe that learning about personal values (e.g., god, family, justice) is more informative than learning distinguishing facts (e.g., can play the trombone, owns a flying squirrel, is afraid of vending machines), participants in small groups were asked to disclose either three core personal values or three distinguishing facts about themselves. Although there was no general advantage (collapsing across trait dimensions) for one type of information over another, those in the facts condition more accurately judged conscientiousness and those in the values condition more accurately judged neuroticism. These trait × judgment-context interactions are not uncommon. Wall, Taylor, Dixon, Conchie, and Ellis (2013) evaluated accuracy while escalating "richness" of context (Internet chat, telephone, face-to-face conversation) and found greater accuracy for neuroticism and extraversion as richness increased, but the reverse pattern for openness and conscientiousness. These kinds of findings fuel speculation that relevance (the RAM stage through which information quality primarily

operates) needs to be considered in context. For example, one consistent finding in the zero-acquaintance literature is general inaccuracy in assessing neuroticism. However, this may be explained by the fact that the contexts in which we have examined accuracy at zero acquaintance afford opportunities for behavioral expressions of extraversion but not neuroticism. Indeed, neuroticism was evaluated more accurately in circumstances where the evaluative nature of the social context was particularly salient, which enhances the availability of relevant cues for this trait (Hirschmüller, Egloff, Schmukle, Nestler, & Back, 2015, see also chapter 8 by Krzyzaniak & Letzring in this handbook).

Joint Evaluations of Quantity and Quality

Studies described in the preceding two sections provide good opportunities to evaluate the impact of quantity and quality in isolation, but some researchers have been able to rather cleverly examine the influence of these factors simultaneously. In a particularly ambitious study, Letzring et al. (2006) constructed five judgment contexts representing increasing quality and quantity of information. Quantity escalated from a zero-acquaintance judgment situation to a 50-minute unstructured conversation to a 3-hour unstructured conversation. Quality, on the other hand, was represented at the low end by a 50-minute highly structured interaction (answering trivia questions as a group) and at the high end by a 50-minute conversation with explicit instructions to "get to know" the other participant. Results support that increases in both quantity and quality are associated with greater accuracy. However, in each case the most significant gains occurred from low to medium levels of quantity and quality. To date, this is the only published study in which such systematic evaluations of quantity and quality occur simultaneously.

Evaluation and Future Directions

The preceding review was hardly exhaustive, but rather meant as a primer and roadmap to the various avenues of research with bearing on the question: what is good information? In this final section, I highlight some of the themes and focus on some of the most important open questions in the subfield. I also make some suggestions based on these conclusions.

Effect Sizes

One trend in both controlled laboratory studies and more descriptive studies of existing groups is that the effect of information on personality accuracy could be considered rather small.[9] Agreement correlations in laboratory studies may shift from approximately 0.20 to 0.30 with additional exposure, and groups that one might imagine are substantially more acquainted (i.e., married couples) may only generate accuracy correlations (correlations typically 0.50–0.60) slightly greater than do relative strangers—at least for extraversion (correlations typically in the 0.30s). Biesanz et al. (2007) noted of Watson et al.'s (2000) work that 5 years of acquaintance was associated with an effect size increase of $r = 0.05$. Allik et al. (2016) observed even smaller gains. Why so modest? Should we be concerned?

One issue, as noted earlier, is that some information available quite early upon encountering a new person is fairly diagnostic, thus the lower bound for accuracy is fairly high. This is particularly true for extraversion. Similarly, one could also argue that the upper bound is not impressive. Should self-other agreement correlations among individuals married for 30 years not exceed $r = 0.60$? There are at least two possible explanations to consider for these conditions, both involving measurement and one involving a theoretical shift. First, it is possible that the standard methods for evaluating accuracy are not suited to observing information's effect on accuracy. There have been various debates about what constitutes an accuracy criterion. Clearly, self-judgments are not always accurate (Dunning et al., 2004), and we have already discussed some of the pitfalls of relying solely on consensus of observers as a measure of accuracy. Some researchers have opted to combine methods (e.g., Letzring et al., 2006) in an effort to mitigate the shortcomings of each. This can be effective and is generally recommended, though it does not protect against circumstances in which the component sources share a systematic error component, such as a positivity bias (Leising, Erbs, & Fritz, 2010). Another recommendation is to make more consistent efforts to connect personality judgments to tangible life outcomes and observable behaviors. Some early efforts to compare the accuracy of say, informants versus strangers in predicting laboratory (Vazire, 2010) or natural (Beer & Vazire, 2017) behaviors have yielded mixed results, and these studies were not carefully designed to address the particular issue of information as a moderator. It is possible that predicting concrete outcomes will depress effect sizes across the board but highlight the value of various kinds of information in ways that interjudge agreement does not capture. In sum, more carefully chosen accuracy criteria may yield larger effects.

A second possible explanation for the small effect sizes could be that the upper bound and lower bound accuracy estimates are truncated due to the decontextualized nature of standard measurements. A frequent complaint of people first encountering most common personality inventories is that the items are too broad to capture their personality fully. What does it mean to be calm and relaxed in a general sense? If one has a history of being calm in emergencies but finds herself frequently and easily agitated by fellow motorists, how does one respond to the item on a 5-point scale of Strongly Disagree to Strongly Agree? There have been strong calls for contextualizing personality in theory and empirical practice (Mischel, 1973; Shoda & Mischel, 199, 1996; Shoda, Mischel, & Wright, 1993), and it is possible that well-acquainted individuals might be more accurate in evaluating contextualized tendencies rather than general tendencies (e.g., Friesen & Kammrath, 2011). Perhaps accuracy could be better defined as the range of contexts in which one can predict how another person behaves, thinks, or responds emotionally.

Scarcity of Studies

Although there exists a large amount of data regarding accuracy of personality judgments, the number of studies explicitly dedicated to understanding the impact of information on judgmental accuracy is actually rather small. By this researcher's count, there have been fewer than 20 longitudinal investigations into accurate personality judgment, and these typically do not exceed approximately 3 months in length. Laboratory studies in which the quantity of information is increased and accuracy is observed are limited to the few outlined in this chapter, and in these there is a notable absence of within-subject designs (e.g., repeated assessments of the same target by the same judge in response to increasing information). Finally, the formal study of information quality as a moderator is in its infancy—in fact, this review *is* exhaustive in that particular case.

Why has progress been so slow on these issues? There are certainly practical concerns. Longitudinal studies of this sort are difficult and expensive to execute, and the laboratory protocols for repeated assessments can be tedious and taxing for participants. But another reason could be that the field is still searching for a unified theory to serve as the backdrop for these explorations. Information quality, in particular, has long suffered from a lack of theoretical grounding. For a long time, the simple distinction between strong situations (wherein the situation constrains individuals' behaviors) and weak situations (for an extended discussion, see Cooper & Withey, 2009) could be considered as one of the only theories of what constitutes high-quality information—that which is obtained in the context of a "weaker" situation (i.e., a cocktail party, as opposed to waiting in line at the post office). The studies aimed at evaluating the impact of information quality generally espoused some fairly arbitrarily chosen parameter (e.g., thoughts and feelings versus behaviors, distinguishing facts versus personal values, structured versus unstructured activities) and compared accuracy estimates. The field would benefit if researchers had some guiding principles as to how to manipulate quality in such studies.

In addition, the more descriptive studies of information quantity and quality could also benefit from using theory to guide the choice of comparison groups. Like the laboratory work, researchers seemed to simply grab at groups that may differ in amount of information exchanged (e.g., married couples versus dating couples, fraternity seniors versus Peace Corps trainees) without particular attention to why exactly these groups differ. Here I would like to make a case for Starzyk et al.'s (2006) work on clarifying acquaintanceship as a means to guide our empirical efforts. Figure 9.2 contains a visual representation of information quality versus quantity across various types of relationships as derived from Starzyk et al.'s (2006) model. From this schematic, one could determine that Watson et al.'s (2000) comparison of dating couples versus friendship dyads may be considered as indicative of differences in information quality alone, whereas the comparison between married couples and these groups involves a distinction in both quality and quantity. Of course, actually making that claim would require assessing a given relationship on indices of quantity and quality, rather than broadly comparing types of relationships. In addition, future studies could involve choosing groups that systematically differ on just one dimension at a time in an effort to evaluate Connelly and Ones's (2010) suggestion that differences in accuracy among acquainted individuals are largely related to quality of information. Aside from that, simply measuring acquaintance systematically may elucidate some of the murkiness in the field. For example, perhaps the aforementioned small effect sizes—particularly in longitudinal studies—may have to do with a fundamental failure of the manipulation. Perhaps roommates or discussion groups simply do not see increases in the quality of

their interactions in the form of greater self-disclosure, knowledge of goals, physical intimacy, or knowledge of social network. Quantity is increasing, but not quality (Figure 9.2 also illustrates this occasional orthogonality). Laboratory studies should involve specific attempts to increase some of these parameters (probably not physical intimacy) as fundamental ingredients in studies of information quality. Even studies of information quantity may benefit from some of the lessons from Starzyk et al. (2006) in that frequency of contact and duration of relationship are often confounded. Is greater accuracy achieved when one interacts with another person routinely for short periods of time (e.g., my interactions with the administrative office workers for the neighboring department) versus more rarely but for longer periods of time (e.g., my interactions with one of our book publisher representatives)? Does the nature of the quantity impact the quality of these interactions, such that longer interactions breed greater self-disclosure? In any case, there is a need for theory development in understanding information as a moderator of judgmental accuracy, whether it be greater attention to work like Starzyk et al. (2006) or development of new integrative frameworks. Doing so may help generate more meaningful studies and greater interest in the field among researchers.

Future Directions

I have already discussed some of the hopes I have for the future of this area of study, but I can make some more specific suggestions for empirical inquiry. The ideal descriptive study is one with a true zero-acquaintance point, involving representative samples of community-dwelling adults, spanning multiple years with multiple measurement occasions in real relationships that are not created for the purpose of the study. This is practically impossible. The most likely avenue to research of this sort would involve partnering with a dating or matchmaking website, but this would still limit the scope of understanding to the context of romantic relationships. Short of accomplishing all of these goals, researchers should strive for as many as possible in a given study. Why do each of these desired components matter? First, establishing a baseline is difficult, as some information is obtained immediately upon visual contact with an individual, and a fair amount of information can be obtained in just a few minutes of exposure. Second, many purposeful studies of acquaintanceship (particularly longitudinal studies) involve college students, whom we know do not perfectly

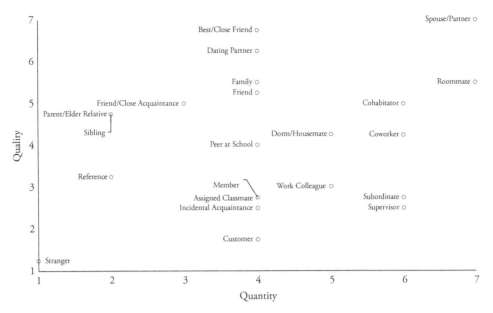

Figure 9.2. Information quantity versus quality across relationship types. To create this figure, I quantified the distinctions contained in Table 1 of Connelly and Ones (2010). They asked independent coders to evaluate each type of relationship along the six dimensions of acquaintance established in Starzyk et al. (2006) on a 7-point scale (1 = Very Low, 7 = Very High). To ease presentation, I used frequency of contact as the quantity domain and aggregated the quality-relevant indices into a single quality index.

represent the population to which we would like to generalize (Henrich, Heine, & Norenzayan, 2010). Third, the time period must be long (probably measured in years rather than weeks or months) given what is likely slow growth in accuracy over time (Biesanz et al., 2007). The measurement occasions must be fairly frequent and, perhaps as importantly, they must involve explicit measures of information quantity and quality. Finally, these must be real relationships to help ensure that personality assessments are meaningful to the interactants and the task is taken seriously. Motivation has been shown to increase accuracy (Biesanz & Human, 2010), and lack of motivation on the part of participants cannot be ruled out as a potential cause for the absence of judgmental accuracy in some research paradigms.

For laboratory work, as discussed previously, it is important that researchers have good scientific reasons for the chosen manipulations and are mindful of the implications for quantity and quality simultaneously. The field needs more systematic evaluations involving graduated exposure to information about targets. It may also behoove the field to consider reuniting to some extent with the social cognition and judgment and decision-making literature. In the 1980s, the study of accuracy and the study of error or bias in social judgment parted ways theoretically and methodologically (Funder, 1987), and in some ways, the two literatures have carried on somewhat

independently over time. But each could still inform the other, as the study of how to be right is not always entirely separate from the study of how to be wrong. Certainly, researchers in personality have bridged this gap (Luo & Snider, 2009; Rogers & Biesanz, 2014; West & Kenny, 2011; Zimmermann, Schindler, Klaus, & Leising, 2018), but there are more opportunities available. For example, the concept of dilution effects—when lower-quality information mitigates or overwhelms higher-quality information—have been established in other fields (Nisbett, Zukier, & Lemley, 1981), but not yet in the study of accurate personality judgment (but see Beer, Rogers, & Letzring, 2018).

Conclusion

In sum, there is evidence that we come to know others better over time. This evidence may not be fully consistent or statistically overwhelming, but it does exist. We have some clues as to how it happens, and a few clues as to when. We know that all information is not equally useful, but we are not entirely certain which kinds are most useful. For a field that has existed for approximately a century, we seem to still be scratching the surface to some extent. This is unfortunate for a couple of reasons. First, of the primary moderators originally enumerated by Funder (1995), some have suggested that the information moderator has the most promise for theoretical and empirical development. Allik et al. (2016) argued that the relative ease with which people can achieve judgmental accuracy in personality (contrary to Funder's [1995] claim) renders the search for evidence of good targets, good judges, and good traits generally futile, and that information (quality of information, in particular—in accordance with Connelly & Ones's [2010] assertion) is likely to yield the most useful and interesting avenues of research into moderators of accuracy. Second, the potential real-world implications of understanding information quality and quantity's impact on accuracy could represent a significant advance for personality and social psychology's standing as a practical science. Perhaps we could make better hires and have fewer divorces if we had clearer understanding of exactly how and when we can know exactly what about a person. Thus, perhaps a final suggestion I would make to researchers of these phenomena is to find more ways to clearly connect accuracy to these important real-life outcomes. Perhaps in identifying the optimal judgment conditions for producing contextualized behavioral predictions in meaningful real-world circumstances (e.g., demonstrating that certain structured interactions can allow us to determine whether someone is likely to cheat when in competition or lash out in anger when challenged), we can attract greater—and deserved, in this author's opinion—attention to this important area of inquiry.

References

Albright, L., Kenny, D. A., & Malloy, T. E. (1988). Consensus in personality judgments at zero acquaintance. *Journal of Personality and Social Psychology*, 55, 387–395. doi:10.1037/0022-3514.55.3.387

Allik, J., de Vries, R. E., & Realo, A. (2016). Why are moderators of self–other agreement difficult to establish? *Journal of Research in Personality*, 63, 72–83. doi:10.1016/j.jrp.2016.05.013

Ambady, N., Bernieri, F. J., & Richeson, J. A. (2000). Toward a histology of social behavior: Judgmental accuracy from thin slices of the behavioral stream. In M. P. Zanna (Ed.), *Advances in experimental social psychology* (Vol. 32, pp. 201–271). San Diego, CA: Academic Press. doi:10.1016/S0065-2601(00)80006-4

Ambady, N., & Gray, H. M. (2002). On being sad and mistaken: Mood effects on the accuracy of thin-slice judgments. *Journal of Personality and Social Psychology*, 83, 947–961. doi:10.1037/0022-3514.83.4.947

Ambady, N., Hallahan, M., & Conner, B. (1999). Accuracy of judgments of sexual orientation from thin slices of behavior. *Journal of Personality and Social Psychology*, 77, 538–547. doi:10.1037/0022-3514.77.3.538

Ambady, N., & Rosenthal, R. (1992). Thin slices of expressive behavior as predictors of interpersonal consequences: A meta-analysis. *Psychological Bulletin*, 111, 256–274. doi:10.1037/0033-2909.111.2.256

Ambady, N., & Rosenthal, R. (1993). Half a minute: Predicting teacher evaluations from thin slices of nonverbal behavior and physical attractiveness. *Journal of Personality and Social Psychology*, 64, 431–441. doi:10.1037/0022-3514.64.3.431

Andersen, S. M. (1984). Self-knowledge and social inference: II. The diagnosticity of cognitive/affective and behavioral data. *Journal of Personality and Social Psychology*, 46, 294–307. doi:10.1037/0022-3514.46.2.294

Andersen, S. M., & Ross, L. (1984). Self-knowledge and social inference: I. The impact of cognitive/affective and behavioral data. *Journal of Personality and Social Psychology*, 46, 280–293. doi:10.1037/0022-3514.46.2.280

Back, M. D., Schmukle, S. C., & Egloff, B. (2008). How extraverted is honey.bunny77@hotmail.de? Inferring personality from e-mail addresses. *Journal of Research in Personality*, 42, 1116–1122. doi:10.1016/j.jrp.2008.02.001

Back, M. D., Stopfer, J. M., Vazire, S., Gaddis, S., Schmukle, S. C., Egloff, B., & Gosling, S. D. (2010). Facebook profiles reflect actual personality, not self-idealization. *Psychological Science*, 21, 372–374. doi:10.1177/0956797609360756

Beer, A. (2013). Group personality judgments at zero acquaintance: Communication among judges versus aggregation of independent evaluations. *Journal of Research in Personality*, 47, 385–389. doi:10.1016/j.jrp.2013.03.008

Beer, A. (2014). Comparative personality judgments: Replication and extension of robust findings in personality perception using an alternative method. *Journal of Personality Assessment*, 96, 610–618. doi:10.1080/00223891.2013.870571

Beer, A., & Brooks, C. (2011). Information quality in personality judgment: The value of personal disclosure. *Journal of Research in Personality*, 45, 175–185. doi:10.1016/j.jrp.2011.01.001

Beer, A., Rogers, K. H., & Letzring, T. D. (2018). *Effects of escalated exposure to information on accuracy of personality judgment*. Manuscript submitted for publication.

Beer, A., & Vazire, S. (2017). Evaluating the predictive validity of personality trait judgments using a naturalistic behavioral criterion: A preliminary test of the self–other knowledge asymmetry model. *Journal of Research in Personality*, 70, 107–121. doi:10.1016/j.jrp.2017.06.004

Beer, A., & Watson, D. (2008). Personality judgment at zero acquaintance: Agreement, assumed similarity, and implicit simplicity. *Journal of Personality Assessment*, 90, 250–260. doi:10.1080/00223890701884970

Beer, A., & Watson, D. (2010). The effects of information and exposure on self–other agreement. *Journal of Research in Personality*, 44, 38–45. doi:10.1016/j.jrp.2009.10.002

Berscheid, E., Snyder, M., & Omoto, A. M. (1989). The Relationship Closeness Inventory: Assessing the closeness of interpersonal relationships. *Journal of Personality and Social Psychology*, 57, 792–807. doi:10.1037/0022-3514.57.5.792

Biesanz, J. C., & Human, L. J. (2010). The cost of forming more accurate impressions: Accuracy-motivated perceivers see the personality of others more distinctively but less normatively than perceivers without an explicit goal. *Psychological Science*, 21, 589–594. doi:10.1177/0956797610364121

Biesanz, J. C., West, S. G., & Millevoi, A. (2007). What do you learn about someone over time? The relationship between length of acquaintance and consensus and self–other agreement in judgments of personality. *Journal of Personality* and Social Psychology, 92, 119–135. doi:10.1037/0022-3514.92.1.119

Blackman, M. C., & Funder, D. C. (1998). The effect of information on consensus and accuracy in personality judgment. Journal of Experimental Social Psychology, 34, 164–181. doi:10.1006/jesp.1997.1347

Borkenau, P., Brecke, S., Möttig, C., & Paelecke, M. (2009). Extraversion is accurately perceived after a 50-ms exposure to a face. Journal of Research in Personality, 43, 703–706. doi:10.1016/j.jrp.2009.03.007

Borkenau, P., & Liebler, A. (1992). Trait inferences: Sources of validity at zero acquaintance. Journal of Personality and Social Psychology, 62, 645–657. doi:10.1037/0022-3514.62.4.645

Borkenau, P., Mauer, N., Riemann, R., Spinath, F. M., & Angleitner, A. (2004). Thin slices of behavior as cues of personality and intelligence. Journal of Personality and Social Psychology, 86, 599–614. doi:10.1037/0022-3514.86.4.599

Brown, J. A., & Bernieri, F. (2017). Trait perception accuracy and acquaintance within groups: Tracking accuracy development. Personality and Social Psychology Bulletin, 43, 716–728. doi:10.1177/0146167217695557

Brunswik, E. (1956). Perception and the representative design of psychological experiments (2nd ed.). Berkeley: University of California Press.

Carney, D. R., Colvin, C. R., & Hall, J. A. (2007). A thin slice perspective on the accuracy of first impressions. Journal of Research in Personality, 41, 1054–1072. doi:10.1016/j.jrp.2007.01.004

Cleeton, G. U., & Knight, F. B. (1924). Validity of character judgments based on external criteria. Journal of Applied Psychology, 8, 215–231. doi:10.1037/h0072525

Cloyd, L. (1977). Effect of acquaintanceship on accuracy of person perception. Perceptual and Motor Skills, 44, 819–826. doi:10.2466/pms.1977.44.3.819

Connelly, B. S., & Ones, D. S. (2010). An other perspective on personality: Meta-analytic integration of observers' accuracy and predictive validity. Psychological Bulletin, 136, 1092–1122. doi:10.1037/a0021212

Cooper, W. H., & Withey, M. J. (2009). The strong situation hypothesis. Personality and Social Psychology Review, 13, 62–72. doi:10.1177/1088868308329378

Dunning, D., Heath, C., & Suls, J. M. (2004). Flawed self-assessment: Implications for health, education, and the workplace. Psychological Science in the Public Interest, 5, 69–106. doi:10.1111/j.1529-1006.2004.00018.x

Estes, S. G. (1938). Judging personality from expressive behavior. Journal of Abnormal and Social Psychology, 33, 217–236. doi:10.1037/h0058565

Fareri, D. S., Niznikiewicz, M. A., Lee, V. K., & Delgado, M. R. (2012). Social network modulation of reward-related signals. Journal of Neuroscience, 32, 9045–9052. doi:10.1523/JNEUROSCI.0610-12.2012

Ferguson, L. W. (1949). The value of acquaintance ratings in criterion research. Personnel Psychology, 2, 93–102. doi:10.1111/j.1744-6570.1949.tb01673.x

Friesen, C. A., & Kammrath, L. K. (2011). What it pays to know about a close other: The value of if-then personality knowledge in close relationships. Psychological Science, 22, 567–571. doi:10.1177/0956797611405676

Funder, D. C. (1987). Errors and mistakes: Evaluating the accuracy of social judgment. Psychological Bulletin, 101, 75–90. doi:10.1037/0033-2909.101.1.75

Funder, D. C. (1995). On the accuracy of personality judgment: A realistic approach. Psychological Review, 102, 652–670. doi:10.1037/0033-295X.102.4.652

Funder, D. C. (2012). Accurate personality judgment. Current Directions in Psychological Science, 21, 177–182. doi:10.1177/0963721412445309

Funder, D. C., & Colvin, C. R. (1988). Friends and strangers: Acquaintanceship, agreement, and the accuracy of personality judgment. Journal of Personality and Social Psychology, 55, 149–158. doi:10.1037/0022-3514.55.1.149

Funder, D. C., Kolar, D. C., & Blackman, M. C. (1995). Agreement among judges of personality: Interpersonal relations, similarity, and acquaintanceship. Journal of Personality and Social Psychology, 69, 656–672. doi:10.1037/0022-3514.69.4.656

Gillath, O., Bahns, A. J., Ge, F., & Crandall, C. S. (2012). Shoes as a source of first impressions. Journal of Research in Personality, 46, 423–430. doi:10.1016/j.jrp.2012.04.003

Gosling, S. D., Ko, S. J., Mannarelli, T., & Morris, M. E. (2002). A room with a cue: Personality judgments based on offices and bedrooms. Journal of Personality and Social Psychology, 82, 379–398. doi:10.1037/0022-3514.82.3.379

Gros, D. F., Simms, L. J., & Antony, M. M. (2010). Psychometric properties of the State-Trait Inventory for Cognitive and Somatic Anxiety (STICSA) in friendship dyads. Behavior Therapy, 41, 277–284. doi:10.1016/j.beth.2009.07.001

Henrich, J., Heine, S. J., & Norenzayan, A. (2010). The weirdest people in the world? Behavioral and Brain Sciences, 33, 61–83. doi:10.1017/S0140525X0999152X

Hirschmüller, S., Egloff, B., Nestler, S., & Back, M. D. (2013). The dual lens model: A comprehensive framework for understanding self–other agreement of personality judgments at zero acquaintance. Journal of Personality and Social Psychology, 104, 335–353. doi:10.1037/a0030383

Hirschmüller, S., Egloff, B., Schmukle, S. C., Nestler, S., & Back, M. D. (2015). Accurate judgments of neuroticism at zero acquaintance: A question of relevance. Journal of Personality, 83, 221–228. doi:10.1111/jopy.12097

Human, L. J., & Biesanz, J. C. (2011). Target adjustment and self-other agreement: Utilizing trait observability to disentangle judgeability and self-knowledge. Journal of Personality and Social Psychology, 101, 202–216. doi:10.1037/a0023782

Human, L. J., & Biesanz, J. C. (2012). Accuracy and assumed similarity in first impressions of personality: Differing associations at different levels of analysis. Journal of Research in Personality, 46, 106–110. doi:10.1016/j.jrp.2011.10.002

Human, L. J., & Biesanz, J. C. (2013). Targeting the good target: An integrative review of the characteristics and consequences of being accurately perceived. Personality and Social Psychology Review, 17, 248–272. doi:10.1177/1088868313495593

Ivcevic, Z., & Ambady, N. (2012). Personality impressions from identity claims on Facebook. Psychology of Popular Media Culture, 1, 38–45. doi:10.1037/a0027329

Kahn, J. H., Hucke, B. E., Bradley, A. M., Glinski, A. J., & Malak, B. L. (2012). The Distress Disclosure Index: A research review and multitrait–multimethod examination. Journal of Counseling Psychology, 59, 134–149. doi:10.1037/a0025716

Kenny, D. A. (1991). A general model of consensus and accuracy in interpersonal perception. Psychological Review, 98, 155–163. doi:10.1037/0033-295X.98.2.155

Kenny, D. A., Albright, L., Malloy, T. E., & Kashy, D. A. (1994). Consensus in interpersonal perception: Acquaintance and the big five. *Psychological Bulletin, 116*, 245–258. doi:10.1037/0033-2909.116.2.245

Kenny, D. A., Horner, C., Kashy, D. A., & Chu, L. (1992). Consensus at zero acquaintance: Replication, behavioral cues, and stability. *Journal of Personality and Social Psychology, 62*, 88–97. doi:10.1037/0022-3514.62.1.88

Kenny, D. A., & West, T. V. (2010). Similarity and agreement in self- and other perception: A meta-analysis. *Personality and Social Psychology Review, 14*, 196–213. doi:10.1177/1088868309353414

Krzyzaniak, S., Colman, D. C., Letzring, T. D., McDonald, J. S., & Biesanz, J. C. (2018). *The effects of information quantity on the distinctive and normative accuracy of personality trait judgments*. Manuscript submitted for publication.

Kurtz, J. E., & Sherker, J. L. (2003). Relationship quality, trait similarity, and self-other agreement on personality ratings in college roommates. *Journal of Personality, 71*, 21–48. doi:10.1111/1467-6494.t01-1-00005

Leising, D., Erbs, J., & Fritz, U. (2010). The letter of recommendation effect in informant ratings of personality. *Journal of Personality and Social Psychology, 98*, 668–682. doi:10.1037/a0018771

Letzring, T. D. (2008). The good judge of personality: Characteristics, behaviors, and observer accuracy. *Journal of Research in Personality, 42*, 914–932. doi:10.1016/j.jrp.2007.12.003

Letzring, T. D. (2015). Observer judgmental accuracy of personality: Benefits related to being a good (normative) judge. *Journal of Research in Personality, 54*, 51–60. doi:10.1016/j.jrp.2014.05.001

Letzring, T. D., & Human, L. J. (2014). An examination of information quality as a moderator of accurate personality judgment. *Journal of Personality, 82*, 440–451. doi:10.1111/jopy.12075

Letzring, T. D., Wells, S. M., & Funder, D. C. (2006). Information quantity and quality affect the realistic accuracy of personality judgment. *Journal of Personality and Social Psychology, 91*, 111–123. doi:10.1037/0022-3514.91.1.111

Luo, S., & Snider, A. G. (2009). Accuracy and biases in newlyweds' perceptions of each other: Not mutually exclusive but mutually beneficial. *Psychological Science, 20*, 1332–1339. doi:10.1111/j.1467-9280.2009.02449.x

Maxwell, S. E., Lau, M. Y., & Howard, G. S. (2015). Is psychology suffering from a replication crisis? What does "failure to replicate" really mean? *American Psychologist, 70*, 487–498. doi:10.1037/a0039400

McCrae, R. R. (1994). The counterpoint of personality assessment: Self-reports and observer ratings. *Assessment, 1*, 159–172. doi:10.1177/1073191194001002006

McCrae, R. R., Stone, S. V., Fagan, P. J., & Costa, P. J. (1998). Identifying causes of disagreement between self-reports and spouse ratings of personality. *Journal of Personality, 66*, 285–313. doi:10.1111/1467-6494.00013

Meyer, G. J., Finn, S. E., Eyde, L. D., Kay, G. G., Moreland, K. L., Dies, R. R.,... Reed, G. M. (2001). Psychological testing and psychological assessment: A review of evidence and issues. *American Psychologist, 56*, 128–165. doi:10.1037/0003-066X.56.2.128

Mischel, W. (1973). Toward a cognitive social learning reconceptualization of personality. *Psychological Review, 80*, 252–283. doi:10.1037/h0035002

Murphy, N. A., Hall, J. A., & Colvin, C. R. (2003). Accurate intelligence assessments in social interactions: Mediators and gender effects. *Journal of Personality, 71*, 465–493. doi:10.1111/1467-6494.7103008

Naumann, L. P., Vazire, S., Rentfrow, P. J., & Gosling, S. D. (2009). Personality judgments based on physical appearance. *Personality and Social Psychology Bulletin, 35*, 1661–1671. doi:10.1177/0146167209346309

Nauta, M. M. (2012). Are RIASEC interests traits? Evidence based on self–other agreement. *Journal of Career Assessment, 20*, 426–439. doi:10.1177/1069072712448895

Nisbett, R. E., Zukier, H., & Lemley, R. E. (1981). The dilution effect: Nondiagnostic information weakens the implications of diagnostic information. *Cognitive Psychology, 13*, 248–277. doi:10.1016/0010-0285(81)90010-4

Norman, W. T., & Goldberg, L. R. (1966). Raters, ratees, and randomness in personality structure. *Journal of Personality and Social Psychology, 4*, 681–691. doi:10.1037/h0024002

Park, B., Kraus, S., & Ryan, C. S. (1997). Longitudinal changes in consensus as a function of acquaintance and agreement in liking. *Journal of Personality and Social Psychology, 72*, 604–616. doi:10.1037/0022-3514.72.3.604

Paulhus, D. L., & Bruce, M. N. (1992). The effect of acquaintanceship on the validity of personality impressions: A longitudinal study. *Journal of Personality and Social Psychology, 63*, 816–824. doi:10.1037/0022-3514.63.5.816

Paunonen, S. V. (1989). Consensus in personality judgments: Moderating effects of target-rater acquaintanceship and behavior observability. *Journal of Personality and Social Psychology, 56*, 823–833. doi:10.1037/0022-3514.56.5.823

Pronin, E., Fleming, J. J., & Steffel, M. (2008). Value revelations: Disclosure is in the eye of the beholder. *Journal of Personality and Social Psychology, 95*, 795–809. doi:10.1037/a0012710

Rentfrow, P. J., & Gosling, S. D. (2003). The do re mi's of everyday life: The structure and personality correlates of music preferences. *Journal of Personality and Social Psychology, 84*, 1236–1256. doi:10.1037/0022-3514.84.6.1236

Rogers, K. H., & Biesanz, J. C. (2014). The accuracy and bias of interpersonal perceptions in intergroup interactions. *Social Psychological and Personality Science, 5*, 918–926. doi:10.1177/1948550614537307

Rogers, K. H., & Biesanz, J. C. (2018). Reassessing the good judge of personality. *Journal of Personality and Social Psychology*. Advance online publication. doi:10.1037/pspp0000197

Schneider, L., Schimmack, U., Petrican, R., & Walker, S. (2010). Acquaintanceship length as a moderator of self-informant agreement in life-satisfaction ratings. *Journal of Research in Personality, 44*, 146–150. doi:10.1016/j.jrp.2009.11.004

Shen, E. (1925). The influence of friendship upon personal ratings. *Journal of Applied Psychology, 9*, 66–68. doi:10.1037/h0075606

Shoda, Y., & Mischel, W. (1996). Toward a unified, intra-individual dynamic conception of personality. *Journal of Research in Personality, 30*, 414–428. doi:10.1006/jrpe.1996.0029

Shoda, Y., Mischel, W., & Wright, J. C. (1993). Links between personality judgments and contextualized behavior patterns: Situation-behavior profiles of personality prototypes. *Social Cognition, 11*, 399–429. doi:10.1521/soco.1993.11.4.399

Sorokowska, A., Sorokowski, P., & Szmajke, A. (2012). Does personality smell? Accuracy of personality assessments based on body odour. *European Journal of Personality, 26*, 496–503. doi:10.1002/per.848

Sparling, S., & Cramer, K. (2015). Choosing the danger we think we know: Men and women's faulty perceptions of sexually transmitted infection risk with familiar and unfamiliar new partners. *Canadian Journal of Human Sexuality, 24*, 237–242. doi:10.3138/cjhs.243-A2

Starzyk, K. B., Holden, R. R., Fabrigar, L. R., & MacDonald, T. K. (2006). The personal acquaintance measure: A tool for appraising one's acquaintance with any person. *Journal of Personality and Social Psychology, 90*, 833–847. doi:10.1037/0022-3514.90.5.833

Taft, R. (1966). Accuracy of empathic judgments of acquaintances and strangers. *Journal of Personality and Social Psychology, 3*, 600–604. doi:10.1037/h0023288

Tskhay, K. O., & Rule, N. O. (2014). Perceptions of personality in text-based media and OSN: A meta-analysis. *Journal of Research in Personality, 49*, 25–30. doi:10.1016/j.jrp.2013.12.004

Vazire, S. (2010). Who knows what about a person? The self–other knowledge asymmetry (SOKA) model. *Journal of Personality and Social Psychology, 98*, 281–300. doi:10.1037/a0017908

Vazire, S., & Gosling, S. D. (2004). e-Perceptions: Personality impressions based on personal websites. *Journal of Personality and Social Psychology, 87*, 123–132. doi:10.1037/0022-3514.87.1.123

Wall, H. J., Taylor, P. J., Campbell, C., Heim, D., & Richardson, B. (2018). Looking at the same interaction and seeing something different: The role of informational contexts, judgment perspective, and behavioral coding on judgment accuracy. *Journal of Individual Differences, 39*, 123–141. doi:10.1027/1614-0001/a000257

Wall, H. J., Taylor, P. J., Dixon, J., Conchie, S. M., & Ellis, D. A. (2013). Rich contexts do not always enrich the accuracy of personality judgments. *Journal of Experimental Social Psychology, 49*, 1190–1195. doi:10.1016/j.jesp.2013.05.010

Watson, D. (1989). Strangers' ratings of the five robust personality factors: Evidence of a surprising convergence with self-report. *Journal of Personality and Social Psychology, 57*, 120–128. doi:10.1037/0022-3514.57.1.120

Watson, D., & Clark, L. A. (1991). Self- versus peer ratings of specific emotional traits: Evidence of convergent and discriminant validity. *Journal of Personality and Social Psychology, 60*, 927–940. doi:10.1037/0022-3514.60.6.927

Watson, D., Hubbard, B., & Wiese, D. (2000). Self–other agreement in personality and affectivity: The role of acquaintanceship, trait visibility, and assumed similarity. *Journal of Personality and Social Psychology, 78*, 546–558. doi:10.1037/0022-3514.78.3.546

Weiss, D. S. (1979). The effects of systematic variations in information on judges' descriptions of personality. *Journal of Personality and Social Psychology, 37*, 2121–2136. doi:10.1037/0022-3514.37.11.2121

West, T. V., & Kenny, D. A. (2011). The truth and bias model of judgment. *Psychological Review, 118*, 357–378. doi:10.1037/a0022936

Zimmermann, J., Schindler, S., Klaus, G., & Leising, D. (2018). The effect of dislike on accuracy and bias in person perception. *Social Psychological and Personality Science, 9*, 80–88. doi:10.1177/1948550617703167

Notes

1. It is acceptable to refer to an individual making a personality judgment as a "judge" or a "perceiver." For the sake of uniformity, in this chapter I use the term "judge" to refer to these individuals.

2. Person-centered analyses involve comparing patterns of values across items (or traits) within a dyad, resulting in what are commonly referred to as profile correlations. Thus, when using a person-centered analytic strategy, one may calculate an accuracy score that can be applied to a given case or person but that is not as easily summarized within a trait category. Variable-centered analyses compare patterns of values across an entire sample for a given item (or trait). Thus, one calculates the accuracy in a given sample for extraversion, for example. Biesanz and colleagues (2007) suggest in their discussion that perhaps different analytic strategies may yield different results with respect to the acquaintanceship effect, and while they are generally correct that different analytic strategies and foci yield different results—particularly when using person-centered analyses (e.g., Human & Biesanz, 2012) and distinguishing between normative and distinctive accuracy (e.g., Biesanz & Human, 2010)—the work reviewed here points to similar general conclusions regarding the effects of information quantity and quality on judgmental accuracy when using either person- or variable-centered analytic strategies.

3. In this case, there were three levels: low (brief duration or homogeneous interactions), moderate (moderate duration and/or varied interactions), high (long duration and varied types of interaction).

4. These are averaged across traits. To do this, I simply used Fisher's z-transformation on the average raw correlations presented in Table 5 of the original paper. The authors focus their conclusions on a different estimate, corrected for unreliability in both judgments, but I chose to use the raw correlations in keeping with other estimates provided in the text.

5. This may even occur in the form of simple markers of group membership (e.g., gender). For more on stereotype accuracy, see chapter 16 by Jussim in this handbook.

6. A person's physiognomy or actions are not the only possible cues to personality; there is an extensive literature covering other types of zero acquaintance research—particularly that which involves no contact with or direct observation of the individual. Given the ubiquity of social media in our time, there have been several studies demonstrating that people's websites (Vazire & Gosling, 2004), social networking profiles and activity (Back et al., 2010; Ivcevic & Ambady, 2012; Tskhay, & Rule, 2014), and even e-mail addresses (Back, Schmukle, & Egloff, 2008) provide valid cues to people's personalities. Additionally, personal artifacts can also be useful in understanding others. A look at one's office or bedroom can generate some accurate trait judgments (Gosling, Ko, Mannarelli, & Morris, 2002), as can listening to someone's playlist or music collection (Rentfrow & Gosling, 2003). There is even work examining the connection between personal odor and personality (Sorokowska, Sorokowski, & Szmajke, 2012) and even what can be gleaned from looking at someone's shoes (Gillath, Bahns, & Crandall, 2012). Thankfully, these two streams of research have not met. For reviews of what can be learned from personal artifacts and spaces and online presence, see chapter 14 by Wall and Campbell in this handbook. To learn more about what can be gleaned from nonverbal behavior in

low-acquaintance settings, please see chapter 13 by Breil, Osterholz, Nestler, and Back in this handbook. Finally, Connelly and Ones's (2010) meta-analysis also contains a substantial and interesting component addressing accuracy of zero-acquaintance judgments made from different types of information.

7. Aside from undertaking one of the first studies to systematically control the amount of information exchanged—essentially by removing actual interaction among participants—Borkenau and Liebler (1992) were also among the first to employ Brunswik's (1956) lens model as a means to understanding the mechanism of judgmental accuracy in personality perception. For a description of this model and myriad findings related to it with respect to accuracy in personality judgment, see chapter 4 by Osterholz, Breil, Nestler, and Back this handbook.

8. This aggregation is beneficial only to a certain point—it seems that any more than six instances yielded little gain in accuracy of aggregated perceptions.

9. The practical impact of an effect can be separated from its statistical effect size, and the desired size of an effect should be considered in context. In this section, I argue as if effects of the size described throughout this chapter are small, though researchers in this field could (convincingly) argue that they are not. See Meyer et al. (2001) for a discussion of such issues.

PART 3

Judging the Self

Self–Other Knowledge Asymmetry (SOKA) Model

Kathryn L. Bollich-Ziegler

Abstract

Despite the strong intuition that people know themselves well, much research in self-perception demonstrates the biases present when evaluating one's own personality traits. What specifically are these blind spots in self-perceptions? Are self-perceptions always disconnected from reality? And under what circumstances might other people actually be more accurate about the self? The self–other knowledge asymmetry (SOKA) model suggests that because individuals and others differ in their susceptibility to biases or motivations and in the information they have access to, self- and other-knowledge will vary by trait. The present chapter outlines when and why other-perceptions are sometimes more accurate than self-perceptions, as well as when self-reports can be most trusted. Also discussed are next steps in the study of self- and other-knowledge, including practical, methodological, and interdisciplinary considerations and extensions. In sum, this chapter illustrates the importance of taking multiple perspectives in order to accurately understand a person.

Key Words: self-perception, self-knowledge, other-knowledge, personality, accuracy

Are you an intelligent person? Extraverted and enthusiastic? Anxious and easily upset? If you were to ask your friends and family members, would they agree with you? Despite the strong intuition that people know themselves well, much research in self-perception demonstrates that people have blind spots when evaluating their own personality traits and suggests that judgments made by close others are sometimes more accurate than people's judgments of themselves. But what specifically are these blind spots in self-perceptions, and are self-perceptions always disconnected from reality? Under what circumstances might other people actually be more accurate about us?

Before these questions are addressed, examine the traits in the following list. Take a moment to consider how you see yourself on each of these traits, and rate how much you agree with each statement using the following 5-point scale.

Strongly Disagree	Disagree	Neither Agree Nor Disagree	Agree	Strongly Agree
1	2	3	4	5

I see myself as someone who...

1. ...has high self-esteem.
2. ...is anxious, easily upset.
3. ...is extraverted, enthusiastic.
4. ...is reserved, quiet.
5. ...is assertive.
6. ...is open to new experiences, complex.
7. ...is conventional, uncreative.
8. ...is intelligent.

Now, consider how accurate your ratings are. The majority of people believe they are quite accurate about themselves across a number of qualities

(Bollich, Rogers, & Vazire, 2015; Pronin, Kruger, Savtisky, & Ross, 2001; Schoeneman, 1981; Schoeneman, Tabor, & Nash, 1984; Sedikides & Skowronski, 1995; Vazire & Mehl, 2008). After all, if you cannot see yourself as you really are, who can? Not only do people assume the superiority of their self-views but also self-reports are heavily relied on in psychology to provide a picture of what someone's personality is like (e.g., how talkative, funny, hard-working, smart, or kind someone is; Baumeister, Vohs, & Funder, 2007; Gosling, Vazire, Srivastava, & John, 2004; Vazire, 2006).

Despite confidence in and reliance on self-reports, there are legitimate reasons to question their alleged accuracy. The present chapter outlines when self-reports can be most trusted, as well as when and why close others are sometimes more accurate than the self. Also discussed are next steps in the study of self- and other-knowledge, including practical, methodological, and interdisciplinary considerations and extensions. In sum, this chapter illustrates the importance of taking multiple perspectives in order to accurately understand a person.

How Is Accuracy Determined?

Before discussing research on who is more accurate and when, it is important to clarify what is meant by accuracy. When determining the accuracy of self-perceptions, self-reports are generally judged against an external criterion measure—a measurement that researchers have decided captures the true level of the trait being examined (Funder, 2012). For example, a researcher interested in self-knowledge of intelligence might use an IQ test as an accuracy criterion measure that is then compared against self-reports of intelligence. Or, someone studying self-knowledge of humor might compare self-reports of humor against trained judges' impressions of a comedy routine. Sometimes the criterion measure comprises the reports of close others like friends, family members, or romantic partners. More desirable, though, are behavioral measures that can be objectively coded or rated by another party. Perceptions are considered more accurate the more similar they are to a selected accuracy criterion.

It is also important to clarify how accuracy is generally calculated. Within the field of personality psychology, accuracy is most often determined at the sample level via rank-order correlations instead of in an absolute sense. In rank-order correlations, the ordering of people's self-perceptions from low to

high on a given trait is compared with people's ordering on an accuracy criterion measure that is also ordered from low to high. Someone whose self-views are accurate can correctly judge their trait level in the context of other people. For example, if Kramer has high self-accuracy as determined by rank-order correlations, Kramer knows he is funnier than Elaine and George, and much more hilarious than Newman, but not quite as funny as Jerry.

Rank-order accuracy is different from accuracy in an absolute sense, in which a person's score on a self-report measure is the same as their score on an accuracy criterion measure. For example, if Kramer has high self-accuracy in an absolute sense, his self-reports of humor will be the same as trained judges' impressions of his comedy routine. It is worth noting that these two types of accuracy are independent of one another. Rank-order accuracy still allows for inaccuracy in an absolute sense—for example, all five people can know how funny they are in comparison with one another, but they can all view themselves as funnier than an audience of trained judges might rate them.

Self-Perceptions Are Especially Susceptible to Biases and Motivations

Study after study has shown that self-perceptions are far from perfect. Individuals are especially prone to seeing themselves too positively or in self-enhancing ways (Sedikides, Gaertner, & Toguchi, 2003; Sedikides & Gregg, 2008). On average, people are positively biased about themselves (Epley & Dunning, 2006; Gosling, John, Craik, & Robins, 1998), for instance, seeing themselves as better than the average person. People tend to see themselves as better drivers, better teachers, more charitable, more intelligent, more responsible, more competent, and fairer than their peers and colleagues, and this occurs across ages (Alicke, 1985; Brown, 2012; Epley & Dunning, 2000; Liebrand, Messick, & Wolters, 1986; Messick, Bloom, Boldizar, & Samuelson, 1985; Sedikides, 1993; Svenson, 1981; Van Lange & Sedikides, 1998; Zell & Alicke, 2011).

People do not only self-enhance their personality traits and abilities. When processing self-relevant information, people are known to engage in a number of biased motivational processes, such as self-enhancement, self-protection, and self-verification (Alicke & Sedikides, 2009; Sedikides, 2012; Sedikides & Strube, 1995; 1997). For example, via self-protection, people avoid negative information about themselves (Alicke & Sedikides, 2009; Sedikides, 2012). Alternatively, people with a self-verification motivation seek information that is consistent with their self-views and disregard information that is inconsistent with their self-views, whether those self-perceptions are positive (e.g., "I am very funny") or negative (e.g., "I am not very funny"; Swann, 2012; Swann & Read, 1981). These motivations and others make it unlikely that individuals will be receptive to all information about themselves (e.g., information received via self-observation or feedback from others) that could allow for accurate self-views.

Unsurprisingly, the biases that people have about themselves are likely to affect the rank-order accuracy of their self-perceptions (John & Robins, 1993; Vazire, 2010). These individual differences in biases and inaccuracies can covary with traits like narcissistic tendencies (Tracy, Cheng, Martens, & Robins, 2011), but they also vary across specific domains (Paulhus & Buckels, 2012; Sedikides, Gaertner, & Toguchi, 2003), making them difficult to predict. Individuals are also very quick to engage in self-motivations like self-enhancement, especially when under cognitive load or when distracted (Beer & Hughes, 2010; Paulhus & Levitt, 1987). These tendencies can prevent people from forming accurate self-perceptions in the first place if self-relevant information is processed through a biased lens. For example, a poor test score might be dismissed and not be used to update self-perceptions of academic ability or conscientiousness.

Although self-perceptions are not always highly accurate, it is important to note that they do not completely miss the s. For one, although some people see themselves too positively or too negatively, a sizable number of people see themselves accurately (Bollich et al., 2015; John & Robins, 1994; Kwan, John, Kenny, Bond, & Robins, 2004; Schriber & Robins, 2012). In addition, correlational estimates of self-knowledge indicate that on average people's self-views are not completely untethered from reality (Vazire & Carlson, 2010; 2011). In one meta-analysis assessing the accuracy of self-reports against behaviors mostly reflecting Big Five personality traits, the relationship was moderate, with a correlation of approximately $r = 0.25$ (Vazire & Carlson, 2010). Similarly, a recent synthesis of 22 meta-analyses showed that self-perceptions of abilities such as intelligence and academic ability correspond similarly well with actual performances, with an average correlation of $r = 0.29$ (Zell & Krizan, 2014). These results are promising—as a whole, participants could somewhat accurately report their personality traits in relation to others. However, these accuracy correlations are far from perfect and raise concerns about exclusively relying on self-perceptions when assessing personality.

Close Others' Perceptions Are Also Biased, But Less So

Close others are also often biased when perceiving each other. Parents tend to think their children are better than average (Cohen & Fowers, 2004; Wenger & Fowers, 2008), and individuals in romantic relationships, especially healthy ones, usually see their partners in an overly positive light (Murray & Holmes, 1997; Solomon & Vazire, 2014; see also chapter 17 by Luo & Watson in this handbook). Indeed, close others of any kind who like each other are prone to holding overly positive views of each other, particularly for highly desirable or undesirable traits (Leising, Erbs, & Fritz, 2010).

Although close others do often see each other through rose-colored glasses (Murray, Holmes, Dolderman, & Griffin, 2000; Neff & Karney, 2005; Solomon & Vazire, 2014), there is also evidence that their perceptions are tethered to reality. For example, people know when their loved ones' reputations are different from how they see them (Solomon & Vazire, 2014), and they can be globally biased about their partners (e.g., "I feel that my spouse has a number of good qualities") but be more accurate about their specific behaviors and traits (e.g., social skills, tidiness; Neff & Karney, 2005). In a meta-analysis of self-reports and informant reports, close others were in fact more accurate than the self on desirable behaviors such as academic achievement and job performance (Connelly & Ones, 2010).

In contrast to the biases and motivations present in self-perceptions, biases in close other perceptions are also generally more predictable. Specifically, close other perceptions are more likely to be uniformly overly positive (e.g., Leising et al., 2010). Because of this general tendency, these biases are less likely to affect the rank-order accuracy of other-perceptions. That is, close others are able to achieve accurate impressions of one another (e.g., Leslie knowing that Ben is smarter than Andy), but because close others like each other, they may simply elevate those ratings (e.g., Leslie thinking Ben is "very smart" rather than just "smart"). Taken together, it is reasonable to think that even if close others are positively biased in their perceptions of each other, other-perceptions will likely be accurate in general, and more accurate than self-perceptions.

The Self and Close Others Have Access to Different Types of Information

The accuracy of self- and other-perceptions is also influenced by the availability of information on which to base judgments. When evaluating a target, what information can the self draw on, and conversely, what information can close others use? There are two primary sources of information when it comes to knowing a person's personality. One is the internal world of the target. This consists of a target's thoughts, feelings, desires, and motivations. How positively someone sees himself, how anxious or insecure he is, how motivated she is to achieve a goal, or how much someone desires time with a loved one or a promotion at work are all internally based aspects of their personality. Unless he or she chooses to relay this information to the outside world or manifests it in particular behaviors, this information is internally experienced and the self has privileged access to it, even above close others such as best friends and romantic partners.

The second broad source of information is the outward display of a target's personality. These manifestations of personality, such as physical behavior and appearance, occur outside the self, and are thus more readily accessible to outsiders than is the internal world. Certain information may be even more available to outsiders than the self, even those who are new acquaintances, given differences in visual perspective. For example, no matter how much effort is placed on imagining one's physical image, there is no disputing the fact that there are certain features of the body that are impossible to view firsthand in real time.

Not only do the self and others vary in the information they have access to, they also put different weight on that information. For instance, the actor-observer effect illustrates differences in what information is emphasized when perceiving the self versus others (Jones & Nisbett, 1987). To an actor, situational influences are more salient than the self. In contrast, to an observer, the target being observed is the most salient feature of the visual field. This leads to differences in the attributions made about a person's behavior, wherein the self explains behaviors more often as stemming from situational stimuli and other people explain the target's behavior as resulting from the target and her own agency (Jones & Nisbett, 1987; Storms, 1973; cf., Malle, 2006; Taylor & Koivumaki, 1976). Much research shows that one of the main obstacles to fruitful self-reflection is the excessive weight people place on their internal thoughts and feelings, at the expense of observing

their own behavior (Pronin, 2008; Pronin & Kugler, 2007). Furthermore, behaviors simply are not as salient to individuals as are their thoughts and feelings (Malle & Knobe, 1997). This difference in emphasis, in combination with the discrepancies in access to information, suggest valuable distinctions in accuracy between the self and her close others about her personality.

Who Knows What About a Person? The Self–Other Knowledge Asymmetry Model

Taking into account these motivational biases and gaps in access to information, the self–other knowledge asymmetry (SOKA) model was developed to illustrate where and why these bright spots and blind spots in self- and other-knowledge exist (Vazire, 2010). The SOKA model's focus is on when different perspectives are accurate or explain unique variance for a given trait—in other words, the focus is not so much who is accurate but who is *more* accurate about the self. The model posits that accuracy levels vary depending on the presence of motivational bias (low or high) and observability of the trait (low or high). In general, the greater the motivational bias, the more likely other people will be more accurate than the self, and the lower the observability, the more likely the self will be more accurate than others. The impact of trait observability on accuracy can be further explained by differentiating types of other people: People closer to the individual will have better access to qualities lower in observability than will new acquaintances. A test of differences in self- and other-knowledge thus must include traits that vary on how visible they are to other people and on how evaluative they are (i.e., highly desirable or undesirable), which in turn influences motivational biases.

With this in mind, the following predictions were tested in an initial evaluation of the SOKA model (Vazire, 2010):

1. *For traits low on observability and low on evaluativeness (e.g., self-esteem)*, outsiders should have difficulty accessing this information and the self should not be vulnerable to motivational biases. As such, the self should be more accurate than close others and new acquaintances, but close others should be more accurate than new acquaintances given the closer nature of their relationship with the self.

2. *For traits high on observability and low on evaluativeness (e.g., talkativeness)*, all

perspectives should have access to this information with little concern for motivational biases, suggesting that the self, close others, and new acquaintances should all be equally accurate.

3. *For traits low on observability and high on evaluativeness (e.g., creativity)*, the self should be at an advantage over close others and new acquaintances because of the poor observability, but the self also should be especially vulnerable to motivational biases because of the evaluativeness. Thus, on balance, close others should have better insight into these traits than the self and new acquaintances.

4. *For traits high on observability and high on evaluativeness (e.g., prosociality)*, all perspectives should have access to this information because of the high observability. However, given the high evaluativeness, the self should be motivated to distort their perceptions, meaning that close others and new acquaintances should be more accurate than the self. It is important to note that these predictions were not explicitly made or tested in the initial test of the SOKA model (Vazire, 2010).

In the original test of the model (Vazire, 2010), the accuracy of self, close other, and new acquaintance judgments of the self was examined for the first three types of traits listed previously. Groups of five friends rated themselves and each other, as did groups of five new acquaintances who had interacted with one another for approximately 10 minutes. Self-reports, close other reports, and new acquaintance reports of traits were then compared against corresponding criterion-based measures for those traits, as detailed here:

1. *To represent traits low on observability and low on evaluativeness*, self-esteem and anxiety were selected. The corresponding accuracy criteria were behaviors observed during a modified Trier stress test (Kirschbaum, Pirke, & Hellhammer, 1993), wherein participants were asked to complete a performance task intended to provoke nerves or anxiety (e.g., give a speech, serially subtract numbers). In Vazire's (2010) study, participants talked about what they liked and did not like about their bodies in the presence of a video camera and an interpersonally cold

experimenter. Trained research assistants then rated the audio-visual recording on qualities like "Says negative things about self (e.g., is self-critical; expresses feelings of inadequacy)" and coded behaviors like number of nervous mouth movements.

2. *To represent traits high on observability and low on evaluativeness*, talkativeness, dominance, and leadership were selected. The corresponding accuracy criteria were behaviors coded from a leaderless group discussion among new acquaintances who were asked to determine the allocation of funds to fictional candidates. Specifically, research assistants coded information like the amount of time each participant spent talking and instances of interrupting group members, and they also rank ordered group members' leadership ability.

3. *To represent traits low on observability and high on evaluativeness*, creativity and intelligence were selected. The corresponding accuracy criterion for intelligence was an IQ test (Wonderlic, 1983) and for creativity was the BRICK test (Friedman & Förster, 2002), which examines the creativity of novel uses a participant can name for a brick, with more creative uses (as rated by coders) scoring higher on this behavioral measure of creativity.

Results mostly supported the expectations of the proposed model, though conclusions differed when close other reports were tested individually and in aggregate. It is important to note that in general, informant reports are at an advantage when predicting behaviors or other outcomes because multiple reports can be averaged together to create a more reliable measure of personality (Vazire, 2006; 2010). Thus, it is worthwhile to test single reports of informants as well as aggregated reports of informants in order to examine what is driving any apparent advantage in informant reports. The following summarizes the results of the tested model:

1. The self was most accurate about less observable, less evaluative traits (i.e., self-esteem, anxiety). This was more pronounced for anxiety than self-esteem and when self-reports were compared against a single randomly selected friend report (rather than all four friend reports aggregated). Contrary to expectations, friends were not more accurate than new acquaintances when

judging self-esteem and anxiety, indicating that level of acquaintance did not impact knowledge of these traits.

2. As predicted, all types of judges (the self, friends, and new acquaintances) were equally accurate for more observable, less evaluative traits (i.e., talkativeness, dominance, leadership).

3. For less observable, more evaluative traits (i.e., creativity, intelligence), friends were generally more accurate than the self and new acquaintances, as predicted by the SOKA model. However, this advantage only held true when friend reports were aggregated—a single peer report performed only marginally better than did self-reports when predicting intelligence.

Overall, the SOKA model was mostly supported in its initial test. Two clear departures were that close others did not have an advantage over new acquaintances for traits low on observability and evaluativeness (e.g., self-esteem), and close others were only better than the self at predicting less observable, more evaluative traits (e.g., creativity) when their reports were aggregated.

Replications and Extensions of the SOKA Model

Outside Vazire's (2010) test, the SOKA model's hypotheses have been examined with alternative traits and behavioral accuracy criteria. These studies have given further insight into the abilities of the self and others to accurately perceive personality, as well methodological considerations in the study of self- and other-knowledge.

Everyday, Naturalistically Observed Behaviors

A recent study used the Electronically Activated Recorder (EAR) to track participants in more externally valid, naturalistic settings (Beer & Vazire, 2017). Specifically, participants were audio recorded intermittently for brief (~30 s) intervals throughout their normal day with a device worn on their belt or purse. Audio files were coded for behaviors relevant to each of the Big Five traits, which were then compared to personality ratings from the self, close others, and strangers. Strangers had no in-person contact with targets but had access to facts and values written by participants as well as a 1-minute video segment of each participant from the initial intake laboratory session that involved completing surveys and receiving the EAR device.

Across all three perspectives, ratings of extraversion corresponded to various extraversion-related behaviors (e.g., sociable behaviors like talking with friends, and general activity like energetic behavior), supporting SOKA's prediction that all perspectives can accurately predict more observable, less evaluative traits. Contrary to expectations, close others were most successful in predicting less observable, less evaluative behaviors related to neuroticism. For example, social withdrawal behaviors, like spending more time in private places and less time in public places, and mental or physical illness behaviors, like sleeping and coughing, were best predicted by close other reports. Surprisingly, no neuroticism-related behaviors were associated with self-reports, a clear departure from the SOKA model's prediction.

Results for the remaining Big Five traits (agreeableness, conscientiousness, and openness to experience) were generally unsupportive of the SOKA model, which predicted that close others would be more accurate than the self and that the self would be more accurate than strangers for these traits. For example, showing sympathy or expressing anger did not correspond to self, close other, or stranger ratings of agreeableness. Conscientious behaviors like spending more time in class and not swearing were better predicted by strangers than close others, counter to SOKA model predictions. Openness behaviors proved difficult to code from EAR files, but those behaviors that could be coded (e.g., substance use) generally provided weak support for the SOKA model's predictions. For instance, both close other and stranger reports were accurate for substance abuse, and self-reports—but not close other reports—were accurate for creativity.

Beer and Vazire's (2017) study is noteworthy due to its emphasis on naturally occurring behaviors from everyday life. How one behaves in a setting outside a contrived laboratory context is likely more representative of one's true personality. In addition, assessing multiple instances of behaviors over several hours or days provides a more reliable assessment of behavior than do the results of a one-off laboratory task. However, some of these findings also highlight how the EAR is not well suited for capturing all traits and behaviors. The EAR simply cannot capture all aspects of one's everyday experience, and it is concerning when behaviors do not correspond to any personality reports (e.g., as with agreeableness-relevant behaviors). Some behaviors occur too infrequently or are inaudible, putting the EAR at a disadvantage for accurately representing certain traits. This is an important reminder that careful consideration must be given when selecting accuracy criteria for studies on self- and other-knowledge.

Moral and Prosocial Behaviors

The SOKA model has also been extended to moral and prosocial behaviors, two particularly interpersonally consequential qualities. In line with the SOKA model, a more evaluative, more observable trait like fairness, which exemplifies prosociality, should be more accurately perceived by close others than the self, owing to its desirable nature (Thielmann, Zimmermann, Leising, & Hilbig, 2017). Honesty, on the other hand, is an evaluative trait exemplifying morality and is very low on observability, so whereas its evaluative nature puts close others at an advantage over self-reports, its particularly low observability makes it challenging for even very close others to have access to relevant information.

To test self- and other-knowledge of fairness, participants completed a dictator game that tracked how much money they shared with an unknown other participant, and this behavior was compared with self-reports and close other reports of honesty-humility (Thielmann et al., 2017). Despite the trait's evaluative nature and the concern for motivational biases, self-perceptions of fairness tracked reality. Both self-reports and close other reports of honesty-humility were moderately accurate, with some evidence that close others explained more unique variance. It is worth noting that the original test of the SOKA model (Vazire, 2010) did not include a more evaluative, more observable trait like fairness, and thus this study helps fill an empirical gap, albeit without acquaintance reports.

To test the accuracy of self and close other ratings of honesty, participants completed a quiz in which they were able to lie about their results in order to win money (Thielmann et al., 2017). Despite the original test of the SOKA model showing that close others are more accurate than the self for highly evaluative, less observable traits like creativity (Vazire, 2010), this stricter test using a trait with even *lower* observability found that close others were not at an advantage and did not achieve a statistically significant level of accuracy. Also counter to the expectation that evaluative traits would be

judged inaccurately by the self, the self was actually accurate at predicting dishonest behavior. These findings may illustrate the limits for close others when predicting very unobservable traits, or that perhaps the motivational biases impacting moral and prosocial traits operate differently than those that influence agentic traits like intelligence.

Emotional Experience

Vazire's original test of the SOKA model focused on a somewhat negative emotion that was coded from behaviors visible during a lab task. Does the self remain the best judge when emotions are positive and when different accuracy criteria are used? Other studies suggest that support for this claim of the SOKA model (that the self would be more accurate than other people) may depend greatly on the accuracy criteria used—whether that be experience sampling methods, coded lab behaviors, momentary self-reports, or physiological responses. For example, Spain and colleagues found that when emotions from experience sampling methods collected outside the laboratory were used as accuracy criteria, results were mostly in line with SOKA model predictions: For both positive and negative emotions, self-reports performed better than did close other reports (Spain, Eaton, & Funder, 2000). However, when the accuracy criteria were instead emotion-relevant behaviors coded from laboratory social interactions (e.g., shows physical signs of tension/anxiety), self-reports did perform better for positive emotion behaviors than did close other reports, but neither perspective was accurate for negative emotions. Thus, self-reports were not always at an advantage—or even accurate—when predicting emotions, depending on the accuracy criteria used.

As another example, Lieberman and colleagues also studied positive and negative emotions but used different accuracy criteria: momentary self-reports and physiological responses (Lieberman et al., 2016). Participants completed a threat task and a reward task during which momentary emotions (i.e., nervousness/anxiety and excitement, respectively) were self-reported and physiological measures were assessed (i.e., startle responses and EEG asymmetry, respectively). When accuracy criteria were momentary ratings of positive and negative affect, self-reports of affect were more accurate than were close other reports, in line with SOKA model predictions. However, when the accuracy criteria were instead physiological responses to these lab tasks, self-reports did not predict these responses and close others' reports surprisingly did. Similar to Spain et al.'s (2000) findings, there were again limits to self-reports when predicting emotions. These two studies together suggest that self-reports may be at a disadvantage when accuracy criteria are either too internal (i.e., physiological) or too external (i.e., behavioral lab codings).

In synthesizing these studies on self- and other-knowledge of naturalistically observed behaviors, moral and prosocial behavior, and emotion, it becomes clear that although extensions of the SOKA model have been promising, much work still remains. For one, it has been less common to see a study that includes both close others and new acquaintances alongside self-reports, so the full SOKA model has rarely been tested. Also needed are highly powered studies using more diverse participants, traits, types of informants, and types of accuracy criteria to clarify inconsistencies among studies presented here. For example, accuracy criteria across these studies included momentary self-reports (Lieberman et al., 2016), experience sampling methods (Spain et al., 2000), coded laboratory behaviors (Thielmann et al., 2017; Vazire, 2010), naturalistically observed behaviors (Beer & Vazire, 2017), physiological responses (Lieberman et al., 2016), and standardized tests (Vazire, 2010). Variation in accuracy criteria increases the generalizability of the findings, but may also explain inconsistencies in results.

Using the SOKA Model to Increase Accuracy of Perceptions

Given the distinctive insights that the self and close others provide about one's personality, each perspective can shine light on blind spots in personality perception. In various settings, research indicates that having accurate self-views is beneficial (e.g., Dunning, Heath, & Suls, 2004; cf., Dufner, Gebauer, Sedikides, & Denissen, 2019; Humberg et al., 2019). Knowing how much one enacts various everyday behaviors (e.g., talking, commuting, arguing, etc.) is associated with better relationship quality (Tenney, Vazire, & Mehl, 2013), as is knowing one's reputation (Carlson, 2016), and inaccurate self-views can have costly repercussions in health, education, and workplace settings (Dunning, Heath, & Suls, 2004). As such, finding ways to increase self-knowledge is warranted.

Because of the special insight and perspective to which close others have access, it is possible they can play an important role in improving self-knowledge (Bollich, Johannet, & Vazire, 2011; Srivastava, 2012).

As illustrated by the SOKA model, close others' judgments of less observable, more evaluative traits like creativity and intelligence can be more accurate than self-perceptions (Vazire, 2010), and close other perceptions can provide valuable insight into job performance and academic achievement (Connelly & Hülsheger, 2012; Connelly & Ones, 2010). Given this other-knowledge, it is possible that the biases and gaps in self-knowledge as discussed earlier may be brought to light through regular, honest conversation with close others, such as romantic partners, friends, roommates, bosses, coworkers, and therapists (Gallrein, Bollich-Ziegler, & Leising, 2019). This could take the form of people regularly asking for feedback from close others, and also close others providing direct feedback unprompted. To the extent, then, that close others' perceptions can be incorporated into one's self-views, there is potential for self-knowledge to increase.

Not only is there potential for self-knowledge to improve, but the privileged knowledge to which the self has access may also be used to improve the accuracy of others' perceptions. Qualities that are more internal such as thoughts, feelings, and desires are generally better assessed by the self than other people, especially new acquaintances (Vazire, 2010). Although others may have some insight into these qualities (Hirschmüller, Schmukle, Krause, Back, & Egloff, 2018; Spain et al., 2000), people should be cautious when evaluating another's internal world without involving that person in the conversation. For example, to understand a friend or family member's levels of happiness or depression, it is important they are asked directly for their self-views.

Conclusion

Recall the personality ratings you completed at the beginning of this chapter. Considering what you now know about the SOKA model and its related literature, can your ratings be trusted? The research outlined here suggests the answer is not straightforward, and that to really know someone is a social affair. The internal world, such as emotions, thoughts, and desires, is generally best known by the self, whereas external personality features can often be accurately assessed by the self or someone as distant as a new acquaintance. However, this is further complicated when these qualities are desirable or undesirable—in these cases, close others may know more. All in all, the SOKA model provides a framework for considering who knows what about a person that takes into account the advantages of different perspectives and variations in traits.

References

Alicke, M. D. (1985). Global self-evaluation as determined by the desirability and controllability of trait adjectives. *Journal of Personality and Social Psychology, 49*(6), 1621–1630. https://doi.org/10.1037/0022-3514.49.6.1621

Alicke, M. D., & Sedikides, C. (2009). Self-enhancement and self-protection: What they are and what they do. *European Review of Social Psychology, 20*(1), 1–48. https://doi.org/10.1080/10463280802613866

Baumeister, R. F., Vohs, K. D., & Funder, D. C. (2007). Psychology as the science of self-reports and finger movements: Whatever happened to actual behavior? *Perspectives on Psychological Science, 2*(4), 396–403. https://doi.org/10.1111/j.1745–6916.2007.00051.x

Beer, J. S., & Hughes, B. L. (2010). Neural systems of social comparison and the "above-average" effect. *Neuroimage, 49*(3), 2671–2679. https://doi.org/10.1016/j.neuroimage.2009.10.075

Beer, A., & Vazire, S. (2017). Evaluating the predictive validity of personality trait judgments using a naturalistic behavioral criterion: A preliminary test of the self–other knowledge asymmetry model. *Journal of Research in Personality, 70,* 107–121. https://doi.org/10.1016/j.jrp.2017.06.004

Bollich, K. L., Johannet, P. M., & Vazire, S. (2011). In search of our true selves: Feedback as a path to self-knowledge. *Frontiers in Psychology, 2,* 312. https://doi.org/10.3389/fpsyg.2011.00312

Bollich, K. L., Rogers, K. H., & Vazire, S. (2015). Knowing more than we can tell: People are aware of their biased self-perceptions. *Personality and Social Psychology Bulletin, 41*(7), 918–929. https://doi.org/10.1177/0146167215583993

Brown, J. D. (2012). Understanding the better than average effect: Motives (still) matter. *Personality and Social Psychology Bulletin, 38*(2), 209–219. https://doi.org/10.1177/0146167211432763

Carlson, E. N. (2016). Meta-accuracy and relationship quality: Weighing the costs and benefits of knowing what people really think about you. *Journal of Personality and Social Psychology, 111*(2), 250–264. https://doi.org/10.1037/pspp0000107

Cohen, J. D., & Fowers, B. J. (2004). Blood, sweat, and tears: Biological ties and self-investment as sources of positive illusions about children and stepchildren. *Journal of Divorce & Remarriage, 42*(1–2), 39–59. https://doi.org/10.1300/J087v42n01_02

Connelly, B. S., & Hülsheger, U. R. (2012). A narrower scope or a clearer lens for personality? Examining sources of observers' advantages over self-reports for predicting performance. *Journal of Personality, 80*(3), 603–631. https://doi.org/10.1111/j.1467–6494.2011.00744.x

Connelly, B. S., & Ones, D. S. (2010). An other perspective on personality: Meta-analytic integration of observers' accuracy and predictive validity. *Psychological Bulletin, 136*(6), 1092–1122. https://doi.org/10.1037/a0021212

Dufner, M., Gebauer, J. E., Sedikides, C., & Denissen, J. J. (2019). Self-enhancement and psychological adjustment: A meta-analytic review. *Personality and Social Psychology Review, 23*(1), 48–72. https://doi.org/10.1177/1088868318756467

Dunning, D., Heath, C., & Suls, J. M. (2004). Flawed self-assessment: Implications for health, education, and the workplace. *Psychological Science in the Public Interest, 5*(3), 69–106. https://doi.org/10.1111/j.1529–1006.2004.00018.x

Epley, N., & Dunning, D. (2000). Feeling "holier than thou": Are self-serving assessments produced by errors in self- or social prediction? *Journal of Personality and Social Psychology, 79*(6), 861–875. https://doi.org/10.1037//0022-3514.79.6.861

Epley, N., & Dunning, D. (2006). The mixed blessings of self-knowledge in behavioral prediction: Enhanced discrimination but exacerbated bias. *Personality and Social Psychology Bulletin, 32*(5), 641–655. https://doi.org/10.1177/0146167205284007

Friedman, R. S., & Förster, J. (2002). The influence of approach and avoidance motor actions on creative cognition. *Journal of Experimental Social Psychology, 38,* 41–55. https://doi.org/10.1006/jesp.2001.1488

Funder, D. C. (2012). Accurate personality judgment. *Current Directions in Psychological Science, 21*(3), 177–182. https://doi.org/10.1177/0963721412445309

Gallrein, A. M. B., Bollich-Ziegler, K. L., & Leising, D. (2019). Interpersonal feedback in everyday life: Empirical studies in Germany and the United States. *European Journal of Social Psychology, 49*(1), 1–18. https://doi.org/10.1002/ejsp.2381

Gosling, S. D., John, O. P., Craik, K. H., & Robins, R. W. (1998). Do people know how they behave? Self-reported act frequencies compared with on-line codings by observers. *Journal of Personality and Social Psychology, 74*(5), 1337–1349. https://doi.org/10.1037/0022-3514.74.5.1337

Gosling, S. D., Vazire, S., Srivastava, S., & John, O. P. (2004). Should we trust web-based studies? A comparative analysis of six preconceptions about Internet questionnaires. *American Psychologist, 59*(2), 93. https://doi.org/10.1037/0003-066X.59.2.93

Hirschmüller, S., Schmukle, S. C., Krause, S., Back, M. D., & Egloff, B. (2018). Accuracy of self-esteem judgments at zero acquaintance. *Journal of Personality, 86*(2), 308–319. https://doi.org/10.1111/jopy.12316

Humberg, S., Dufner, M., Schönbrodt, F. D., Geukes, K., Hutteman, R., Küfner, A. C.,… Back, M. D. (2019). Is accurate, positive, or inflated self-perception most advantageous for psychological adjustment? A competitive test of key hypotheses. *Journal of Personality and Social Psychology, 116*(5), 835–859. https://doi.org/10.1037/pspp0000204

John, O. P., & Robins, R. W. (1993). Determinants of interjudge agreement on personality traits: The Big Five domains, observability, evaluativeness, and the unique perspective of the self. *Journal of Personality, 61*(4), 521–551. https://doi.org/10.1111/j.1467–6494.1993.tb00781.x

John, O. P., & Robins, R. W. (1994). Accuracy and bias in self-perception: individual differences in self-enhancement and the role of narcissism. *Journal of Personality and Social Psychology, 66*(1), 206–219. https://doi.org/10.1037/0022-3514.66.1.206

Jones, E. E., & Nisbett, R. E. (1987). The actor and the observer: Divergent perceptions of the causes of behavior. In E. E. Jones, D. E. Kanouse, H. H. Kelley, R. E. Nisbett, S. Valins, B. Weiner,… B. Weiner (Eds.), *Attribution: Perceiving the causes of behavior* (pp. 79–94). Hillsdale, NJ: Erlbaum.

Kirschbaum, C., Pirke, K. M., & Hellhammer, D. H. (1993). The "Trier Social Stress Test": A tool for investigating psychobiological stress responses in a laboratory setting. *Neuropsychobiology, 28,* 76–81. https://doi.org/10.1159/000119004

Kwan, V. S., John, O. P., Kenny, D. A., Bond, M. H., & Robins, R. W. (2004). Reconceptualizing individual differences in self-enhancement bias: An interpersonal approach. *Psychological Review, 111*(1), 94–110. https://doi.org/10.1037/0033-295X.111.1.94

Leising, D., Erbs, J., & Fritz, U. (2010). The letter of recommendation effect in informant ratings of personality. *Journal of Personality and Social Psychology, 98*(4), 668–682. https://doi.org/10.1037/a0018771

Lieberman, L., Liu, H., Huggins, A. A., Katz, A. C., Zvolensky, M. J., & Shankman, S. A. (2016). Comparing the validity of informant and self-reports of personality using laboratory indices of emotional responding as criterion variables. *Psychophysiology, 53*(9), 1386–1397. https://doi.org/10.1111/psyp.12680

Liebrand, W. B., Messick, D. M., & Wolters, F. J. (1986). Why we are fairer than others: A cross-cultural replication and extension. *Journal of Experimental Social Psychology, 22*(6), 590–604. https://doi.org/10.1016/0022-1031(86)90052-1

Malle, B. F. (2006). The actor-observer asymmetry in attribution: A (surprising) meta-analysis. *Psychological Bulletin, 132*(6), 895–919. https://doi.org/10.1037/0033-2909.132.6.895

Malle, B. F., & Knobe, J. (1997). Which behaviors do people explain? A basic actor-observer asymmetry. *Journal of Personality and Social Psychology, 72*(2), 288. https://doi.org/10.1037/0022-3514.72.2.288

Messick, D. M., Bloom, S., Boldizar, J. P., & Samuelson, C. D. (1985). Why we are fairer than others. *Journal of Experimental Social Psychology, 21*(5), 480–500. https://doi.org/10.1016/0022-1031(85)90031-9

Murray, S. L., & Holmes, J. G. (1997). A leap of faith? Positive illusions in romantic relationships. *Personality and Social Psychology Bulletin, 23*(6), 586–604. https://doi.org/10.1177/0146167297236003

Murray, S. L., Holmes, J. G., Dolderman, D., & Griffin, D. W. (2000). What the motivated mind sees: Comparing friends' perspectives to married partners' views of each other. *Journal of Experimental Social Psychology, 36*(6), 600–620. https://doi.org/10.1006/jesp.1999.1417

Neff, L. A., & Karney, B. R. (2005). To know you is to love you: The implications of global adoration and specific accuracy for marital relationships. *Journal of Personality and Social Psychology, 88*(3), 480–497. https://doi.org/10.1037/0022-3514.88.3.480

Paulhus, D. L., & Buckels, E. (2012). Classic self-deception revisited. In S. Vazire & T. D. Wilson (Eds.), *Handbook of self-knowledge* (pp. 363–378). New York, NY: Guilford.

Paulhus, D. L., & Levitt, K. (1987). Desirable responding triggered by affect: Automatic egotism? *Journal of Personality and Social Psychology, 52*(2), 245–259. https://doi.org/10.1037/0022-3514.52.2.245

Pronin, E. (2008). How we see ourselves and how we see others. *Science, 320*(5880), 1177–1180. https://doi.org/10.1126/science.1154199

Pronin, E., Kruger, J., Savtisky, K., & Ross, L. (2001). You don't know me, but I know you: The illusion of asymmetric insight. *Journal of Personality and Social Psychology, 81*(4), 639–656. https://doi.org/10.1037/0022-3514.81.4.639

Pronin, E., & Kugler, M. B. (2007). Valuing thoughts, ignoring behavior: The introspection illusion as a source of the bias blind spot. *Journal of Experimental Social Psychology, 43*(4), 565–578. https://doi.org/10.1016/j.jesp.2006.05.011

Schoeneman, T. J. (1981). Reports of the sources of self-knowledge. *Journal of Personality, 49*(3), 284–294. https://doi.org/10.1111/j.1467-6494.1981.tb00937.x

Schoeneman, T. J., Tabor, L. E., & Nash, D. L. (1984). Children's reports of the sources of self-knowledge. *Journal of Personality,* 52(2), 124–137. https://doi.org/10.1111/j.1467-6494.1984.tb00348.x

Schriber, R. A., & Robins, R. W. (2012). Self-knowledge: An individual-differences perspective. In S. Vazire & T. D. Wilson (Eds.), *Handbook of self-knowledge* (pp. 105–127). New York, NY: Guilford.

Sedikides, C. (1993). Assessment, enhancement, and verification determinants of the self-evaluation process. *Journal of Personality and Social Psychology, 65*(2), 317–338. https://doi.org/10.1037/0022-3514.65.2.317

Sedikides, C. (2012). Self-protection. In M. R. Leary & J. P. Tangney (Eds.), *Handbook of self and identity* (pp. 327–353). New York, NY: Guilford.

Sedikides, C., Gaertner, L., & Toguchi, Y. (2003). Pancultural self-enhancement. *Journal of Personality and Social Psychology, 84*(1), 60–79. https://doi.org/10.1037/0022-3514.84.1.60

Sedikides, C., & Gregg, A. P. (2008). Self-enhancement: Food for thought. *Perspectives on Psychological Science, 3*(2), 102–116. https://doi.org/10.1111/j.1745-6916.2008.00068.x

Sedikides, C., & Skowronski, J. J. (1995). On the sources of self-knowledge: The perceived primacy of self-reflection. *Journal of Social and Clinical Psychology, 14*(3), 244–270. https://doi.org/10.1521/jscp.1995.14.3.244

Sedikides, C., & Strube, M. J. (1995). The multiply motivated self. *Personality and Social Psychology Bulletin, 21*(12), 1330–1335. https://doi.org/10.1177/01461672952112010

Sedikides, C., & Strube, M. J. (1997). Self-evaluation: To thine own self be good, to thine own self be sure, to thine own self be true, and to thine own self be better. In *Advances in experimental social psychology* (Vol. 29, pp. 209–269). Academic Press. https://doi.org/10.1016/S0065-2601(08)60018-0

Solomon, B. C., & Vazire, S. (2014). You are so beautiful... to me: Seeing beyond biases and achieving accuracy in romantic relationships. *Journal of Personality and Social Psychology, 107*(3), 516–528. https://doi.org/10.1037/a0036899

Spain, J. S., Eaton, L. G., & Funder, D. C. (2000). Perspectives on personality: The relative accuracy of self versus others for the prediction of emotion and behavior. *Journal of Personality, 68*(5), 837–867. https://doi.org/10.1111/1467-6494.00118

Srivastava, S. (2012). Other people as a source of self-knowledge. In S. Vazire & T. D. Wilson (Eds.), *Handbook of self-knowledge* (pp. 90–104). New York, NY: Guilford.

Storms, M. D. (1973). Videotape and the attribution process: Reversing actors' and observers' points of view. *Journal of Personality and Social Psychology, 27*(2), 165–175. https://doi.org/10.1037/h0034782

Svenson, O. (1981). Are we all less risky and more skillful than our fellow drivers? *Acta Psychologica, 47*(2), 143–148. https://doi.org/10.1016/0001-6918(81)90005-6

Swann, W. J. (2012). Self-verification theory. In P. M. Van Lange, A. W. Kruglanski, E. T. Higgins, P. M. Van Lange, A. W. Kruglanski, & E. T. Higgins (Eds.), *Handbook of theories of social psychology* (Vol. 2, pp. 23–42). Thousand Oaks, CA: Sage.

Swann, W. B., & Read, S. J. (1981). Self-verification processes: How we sustain our self-conceptions. *Journal of Experimental Social Psychology, 17*(4), 351–372. https://doi.org/10.1016/0022-1031(81)90043-3

Taylor, S. E., & Koivumaki, J. H. (1976). The perception of self and others: Acquaintanceship, affect, and actor-observer differences. *Journal of Personality and Social Psychology, 33*(4), 403–408. https://doi.org/10.1037/0022-3514.33.4.403

Tenney, E. R., Vazire, S., & Mehl, M. R. (2013). This examined life: The upside of self-knowledge for interpersonal relationships. *PloS ONE, 8*(7), e69605. https://doi.org/10.1371/journal.pone.0069605

Thielmann, I., Zimmermann, J., Leising, D., & Hilbig, B. E. (2017). Seeing is knowing: On the predictive accuracy of self- and informant reports for prosocial and moral behaviours. *European Journal of Personality, 31*(4), 404–418. https://doi.org/10.1002/per.2112

Tracy, J. L., Cheng, J. T., Martens, J. P., & Robins, R. W. (2011). The emotional dynamics of narcissism: Inflated by pride, deflated by shame. In W. K. Campbell & J. D. Miller (Eds.), *The handbook of narcissism and narcissistic personality disorder: Theoretical approaches, empirical findings, and treatments* (p. 330–343). John Wiley & Sons Inc.

Van Lange, P. A., & Sedikides, C. (1998). Being more honest but not necessarily more intelligent than others: Generality and explanations for the Muhammad Ali effect. *European Journal of Social Psychology, 28*(4), 675–680. https://doi.org/10.1002/(SICI)1099-0992(199807/08)28:4%3C675::AID-EJSP883%3E3.0.CO;2-5

Vazire, S. (2006). Informant reports: A cheap, fast, and easy method for personality assessment. *Journal of Research in Personality, 40*(5), 472–481. https://doi.org/10.1016/j.jrp.2005.03.003

Vazire, S. (2010). Who knows what about a person? The self–other knowledge asymmetry (SOKA) model. *Journal of Personality and Social Psychology, 98*(2), 281–300. https://doi.org/10.1037/a0017908

Vazire, S., & Carlson, E. N. (2010). Self-knowledge of personality: Do people know themselves? *Social and Personality Psychology Compass, 4*(8), 605–620. https://doi.org/10.1111/j.1751-9004.2010.00280.x

Vazire, S., & Carlson, E. N. (2011). Others sometimes know us better than we know ourselves. *Current Directions in Psychological Science, 20*(2), 104–108. https://doi.org/10.1177/0963721411402478

Vazire, S., & Mehl, M. R. (2008). Knowing me, knowing you: The accuracy and unique predictive validity of self-ratings and other-ratings of daily behavior. *Journal of Personality and Social Psychology, 95*(5), 1202–1216. https://doi.org/10.1037/a0013314

Wenger, A., & Fowers, B. J. (2008). Positive illusions in parenting: Every child is above average. *Journal of Applied Social Psychology, 38*(3), 611–634. https://doi.org/10.1111/j.1559-1816.2007.00319.x

Wonderlic, E. F. (1983). *Wonderlic Personnel Test manual.* Northfield, IL: Wonderlic & Associates.

Zell, E., & Alicke, M. D. (2011). Age and the better-than-average effect. *Journal of Applied Social Psychology, 41*(5), 1175–1188. https://doi.org/10.1111/j.1559-1816.2011.00752.x

Zell, E., & Krizan, Z. (2014). Do people have insight into their abilities? A metasynthesis. *Perspectives on Psychological Science, 9*(2), 111–125. https://doi.org/10.1177/1745691613518075

The Accuracy of Self-Judgments of Personality

Jana S. Spain

Abstract

How accurate are self-judgments of personality traits? When it comes to judging our own enduring personality characteristics, are we hopelessly blind, deluded, and biased, or are we generally accurate? In order to answer these questions, this chapter reviews the empirical evidence regarding the accuracy of trait self-judgments. Although self-judgments are not always perfectly accurate, the majority of studies suggest that self-judgments of personality have considerable validity. Self-judgments of both narrow, specific traits and the broad personality factors of the Big Five agree with judgments provided by knowledgeable others and predict personality-relevant states, experiences, behaviors, and consequential life outcomes. Suggestions for improving the accuracy of our self-judgments and directions for future research on the accuracy of trait self-judgments are discussed.

Key Words: self-judgment, self-perception, self-knowledge, self-rating, self-report, accuracy, personality, judgment, trait, self

Developing a clear understanding of who you are as an individual, separate from others, is seen as an important developmental task in many cultures. An inscription at Delphi exhorted the ancient Greeks to "Know thyself," reflecting the long-held belief that individuals throughout the world should have a clear sense of their own identity including their own abilities, interests, values, and personality traits. But the ancient Greeks did not have to seek the wisdom of the Delphic oracle to be encouraged to develop an accurate understanding of their own characteristics. Greek philosophers often opined that accurate self-knowledge was the foundation of all understanding and frequently encouraged their followers to actively attempt to develop such insight.

Those early Greeks were not alone in their assumption that humans should know themselves very well. Many early Western psychologists, for example, theorized that having insight about your own characteristics was an important marker of mental health and well-being. For Allport (1937), Rogers (1950, 1951), and others, a mature,

well-adjusted and well-functioning adult should have insight about their enduring characteristics, their strengths and limitations, and even how they are viewed by others (see Wicklund & Eckert, 1992, for a review). In fact, it was often assumed that an individual could not understand others until he or she first understood themselves. Those who lacked self-insight were predicted to have many difficulties in navigating their social worlds. Self-insight was seen as crucial for understanding and relating to others. To judge others accurately, you needed to first judge yourself accurately.

But how accurate are our self-views? Do most individuals know who they are? Can they accurately judge their own characteristics? Is it so easy to "know thyself"? Within the field of psychology, we have often assumed that individuals know themselves well. In fact, the field relies on self-descriptions of personality, ability, interests, attitudes, values, and behavior. Self-report measures are the most frequently used method for collecting information about individuals (Paulhus & Vazire, 2007).

Their use is often based on the assumption that no one knows you as well as you know yourself. After all, you likely possess more information about yourself than anyone else possesses about you. You have known yourself for your entire life and, despite the amnesia that accompanies the first few years of that life, you have many, many years of information upon which to draw. You have access to information about your inner experiences, like thoughts and feelings, as well as information about your overt behavior. You have seen yourself in many different situations, at different ages, interacting with a wide variety of different people. It is not surprising, therefore, that you are assumed to be the single best expert about your own behavior and characteristics. Although doubts about the validity of this assumption have been expressed from time to time (e.g., Dunning, Heath, & Suls, 2004) and empirical work has suggested this assumption might not always be warranted (Vazire & Mehl, 2008), trust in the validity of self-reports and our reliance on them continues.

Within the subfield of personality psychology, assumptions about the validity of self-descriptions are particularly apparent. As is evident in other chapters in this handbook, a self-judgment of personality is often the criterion against which other personality measures are evaluated. For example, if an informant's description of you as shy agrees with your own self-description, we are more likely to decide that the informant's description is accurate.

But should we? Are self-judgments always accurate? If not, when should we trust them and when should we not? When and under what conditions are they most likely to be valid? In order to answer these questions, this chapter reviews the empirical evidence regarding the accuracy of self-views, focusing on the accuracy of one kind of self-judgment: Judgment of your own personality traits.

Defining and Assessing the Accuracy of Self-Judgment: The Criterion Problem

What is accuracy in this context, and how can we assess it? Accuracy typically refers to the agreement between a judge's personality judgment and a target's actual personality (Funder, 1987, 1995). In this context, consistent with other work in this area, *self-judgment accuracy* refers to the agreement between an individual's judgment of his or her own personality traits and the person's actual standing on those personality dimensions (Back & Vazire, 2012).[1] But how do we determine what the individual's actual personality is in a way that is (1) not perfectly con-

founded with the trait self-description and (2) ecologically valid? This can be quite challenging because there is not a single best way to measure personality that is both independent of self-report and representative of the individual's typical patterns of thought, emotion, and behavior. One approach that has often been pursued is referred to as a *realistic approach* (see Funder, 1995, and chapter by Letzring & Funder in this handbook). This approach to measuring personality and assessing the accuracy of personality judgments is based on the process of construct validation (Campbell & Fiske, 1959; Cronbach & Meehl, 1955). That is, if an assessment of personality (in this case a personality judgment) is accurate (valid), it should converge or agree with other different ways of measuring the same construct and predict relevant outcomes such as behavior. For example, when accuracy researchers evaluate the accuracy of *others' judgments* of a target's personality, they determine whether those judgments (1) agree with self-judgments (i.e., self–other agreement), (2) agree with the judgments of others (i.e., consensus or interjudge agreement, or (3) predict some relevant outcome such as the target individual's behavior (Funder, 1987, 1995). If a judge's judgment agrees with how the target person describes themselves, agrees with how other people describe the target, and predicts what the target does, then we assume that judgment is more accurate.

Self–Other Agreement

But how do we determine the level of accuracy of a personality judgment when what we are evaluating is the accuracy of the very self-judgment we usually use as the criterion for other measures? Ideally, the criterion measure used to establish the validity of the personality judgment should be independent of the judgment measure. Self–other agreement can be used to establish convergence in this context as well. According to Allport (1937), individuals could be said to have accurate self-insight when their self-reported view of themselves agreed with others' perceptions of them. Among studies examining the accuracy of personality judgments, self–other agreement is usually used to evaluate the validity of perceptions of others, not the target's own self-perception. Studies demonstrating that targets' self-judgments are correlated with the judgments of others who are well acquainted with the targets could, however, be viewed as evidence that the self-judgment is accurate (McCrae, 1982). Ideally, the other judge should be an informant who is very knowledgeable about the target individual like a parent, sibling, spouse, or close friend. These individuals should be well informed about the target individual's personality because they have often known the person for many years and they also have had the opportunity to observe them in many different situations. Plus, because these informants observe the target person when they are just living their everyday lives, their judgments should have considerable ecological validity. In fact, the results of several studies have indicated that friends' and family members' judgments are sometimes more valid than self-judgments, predicting the target's behavior better than the target's own self-ratings (Connelly & Ones, 2010; Epley & Dunning, 2006; Gosling, John, Craik, & Robins, 1998; John & Robins, 1993; Kolar, Funder, & Colvin, 1996). Consequently, informant judgments of personality could reasonably be used as a criterion to establish the accuracy of self-descriptions of personality.

PREDICTION

If one adopts a construct validity approach, convergence or agreement between different measures is only one step in establishing accuracy. A measure should also be able to predict relevant experiences, behaviors, or outcomes. Therefore, to establish the accuracy of a self-description of personality, that self-judgment should demonstrate coherent relationships with the various ways that personality is manifest. Personality traits are relevant to and expressed in characteristic patterns of thought, emotion, and behavior, so if a personality self-judgment is accurate, it should predict how the individual thinks, feels, and behaves in everyday settings throughout life. One challenge, however, is that obtaining measures of these criteria that are independent of an individual's self-description of their own traits is sometimes difficult, if not impossible, to do. This is particularly challenging if the relevant criteria you are trying to predict are an individual's cognitive processes or emotional experiences. The fact that the self is the source for both the trait self-description and the criterion measure means that any observed correlations between them could simply reflect shared method variance or consistency in how individuals describe themselves. Nonetheless, in some contexts, correlations between trait self-reports and self-reported emotional or cognitive experiences could provide some evidence, albeit not conclusive, that the self-reports are to an extent accurate. One should always keep in mind, however, that such findings do tend to "stack the cards in favor" of providing evidence for self-judgment accuracy.

The prediction of a target's overt behavior has been described by Back and Vazire (2012) as the "gold standard" for evaluating the accuracy of self-judgments of personality. Behavioral measures, however, vary in their independence from personality self-judgments, immediacy, susceptibility to error and biases, and ecological validity. They can be collected from the individual themselves, reported by observers or acquaintances, or coded directly from observations; they can be collected at the same time as the occurrence of the behavior or after the fact; and they can be collected in carefully controlled situations like a laboratory interaction or from everyday life (Furr, 2009). Each of these approaches has strengths and weaknesses when used to obtain criterion measures to evaluate accuracy. If collected from the individual, the reports may be more prone to self-report biases or may be confounded with the personality self-judgments. If collected from other people, the behavioral measures are assumed to be independent of the target's self-views and may tend to be more objective. They may, however, be more susceptible to interpretation errors because observers may not always understand the true meaning of or motive behind a particular behavior. Behavioral measures obtained from everyday situations tend to have greater ecological validity than those obtained in the lab but require a higher investment of effort and resources to acquire. Limited access to private situations may also limit the scope of the behavioral observations. The best, therefore, of these behavioral prediction criteria are those that are collected from multiple observers, aggregated over a significant period of time, and collected from a variety of settings in the individual's daily life (Back & Vazire, 2012).

Agreement and Prediction in Everyday Interactions

In everyday interactions, we often informally attempt to use the criteria of self–other agreement and prediction to evaluate the accuracy of what someone tells us about themselves. For example, imagine that you have just started dating someone and still know very little about them. As part of the early get-acquainted ritual, you might ask them to tell you a little about themselves. How would you find out if their self-description was accurate? You might, for example, try to discover if the way they describe themselves is consistent with how their friends and family members describe them. You might also conduct some observations of your own to see if they behave in a way that fits with their self-description. If, for example, they say they are easy-going, empathetic, and generous, you might ask your mutual friends if that is really the case. You might also seek confirmation of their self-ascribed tendencies in the way they behave on your first date. If they are polite and courteous to everyone, forgive the waiter when he accidentally spills water on them, and leave a big tip at the end of the dinner, you will likely be more confident that their self-description was accurate. If, however, they are overly critical of the service, enraged about the spillage, and miserly with the tip, you might begin to doubt that they are really an empathetic and generous person who goes with the flow.

The Blind, Biased, and/or Deluded Self-Judge

If you discovered that your date's self-description was less than completely accurate, you might have begun to wonder: Can you ever trust what people say about their own personalities? You might have also begun to wonder what might have led them to be so inaccurate. Were they simply trying to manage your impression of them by describing themselves so favorably, were they deliberately lying about themselves, were they delusional, or were they simply clueless?

Many researchers would caution you against trusting any type of self-report (e.g., Dunning et al., 2004). Self-reports, they would argue, are hopelessly biased and extremely prone to error (Kenny, 1994). If you were to pick up a social psychology textbook, you would find numerous examples of biases and blind spots in our self-perceptions. For example, when we are describing ourselves, we often tend to self-enhance, exaggerating our positive characteristics while minimizing our negative characteristics (Alicke & Sedikides, 2009; Brown, 1986). This self-enhancement tendency is evident in a number of ways, including our tendency to see ourselves as better than the average person on many abilities and traits (Guenther & Alicke, 2010). Oftentimes this tendency to provide overly favorable ratings of the self is due to social desirability tendencies, or our desire to look good to other people, while at other times it may arise from the fact that we may be blissfully unaware of some of our own characteristics (Hansen & Pronin, 2012).

It appears that sometimes we may lack the appropriate objectivity or perspective necessary to judge ourselves accurately. In effect, we may have physical and/or psychological "blind spots" that could negatively impact our ability to make a valid assessment of our own traits. For example, we may not have the best visual perspective for identifying consistencies in our own behavior. This may be attributable to visual and attention processes that focus our attention outward toward other people and the environment rather than toward ourselves and consequently limit our access to relevant information (Andersen, Glassman, & Gold, 1998). Even our own personality traits may negatively impact our ability to provide accurate self-descriptions. For example, in a now classic study by John and Robins (1994), individual differences in narcissism moderated the accuracy of self-predictions of behavior. Narcissists' tendency to self-enhance resulted in predictions of their own behavior and performance that were exaggerated. Thus, we may either knowingly or unknowingly deceive ourselves about our own traits.

These biases and blind spots, however, may affect the accuracy of our trait judgments in fairly specific ways and may not result in all personality descriptions being inaccurate. In a set of studies, Paulhus and John (1998) identified two biases that compromise the validity of some trait self-judgments: an egoistic bias and a moralistic bias. An egoistic bias, which they labeled Alpha, was associated with a tendency to exaggerate one's prominence, status, and intelligence. This largely affects self-judgments of agentic traits related to extraversion, openness, and intelligence. A moralistic bias, which they labeled Gamma, was associated with a tendency to exaggerate characteristics associated with being a "nice person" or even a "saint" and to minimize or deny possession of socially undesirable or deviant attributes. This bias generally affects self-judgments of agreeableness and the self-control or restraint dimensions of conscientiousness.

These differences in perspective as well as the biases and blind spots that have been identified likely explain some of the discrepancies between self-judgments and the judgments provided by others. Recently, Vazire (2010) has developed a theoretical model to explain self–other asymmetries in knowledge about personality. The self–other knowledge asymmetry model (SOKA) describes how information and motivational differences may explain why self-judgments differ from those of other people. The model integrates decades of findings on self–other differences in the judgment of personality and explains how information differences affect the relevance and availability of cues, while motivational differences affect cue detection and utilization (for a review of the SOKA model, see chapter by Bollich-Ziegler in this handbook). According to the SOKA model, self-judgments are likely to be less accurate when judging highly socially evaluative traits, but more accurate (as compared to others' judgments) for traits that are low in both observability and social evaluativeness. For other traits that are not all that evaluative, self-judgments should be fairly accurate.

The results of a recent meta-analysis by Kim, DiDomenico, and Connelly (2019), however, suggest that trait evaluativeness and observability may not necessarily negatively impact all forms of accuracy. For this meta-analysis, the researchers compared mean self-reports of personality to mean informant reports to evaluate the elevation accuracy[2] of self-reports. Identifying mean differences in the ratings from these sources (self and informants) would indicate that systematic errors or biases may inflate or deflate ratings from at least one of the sources. First, they did not find a general tendency for self-reports to show either self-enhancement or self-effacement. Moreover, neither trait evaluativeness nor trait visibility appeared to noticeably affect elevation accuracy. We should not, therefore, always expect individuals to be generally blind, biased, or deluded about their own characteristics.

The Accurate Self-Judge

In fact, there is considerable evidence that individuals are quite knowledgeable about their own personality traits. In the last several decades, many researchers have used self–other agreement and prediction of personality-relevant experiences, states, behavior, and life outcomes to attempt to determine the accuracy of self-judgments of personality. In the following sections, their empirical findings are summarized and examples of representative studies are presented.

Evidence from Studies of Self–Other Agreement

Many studies have found impressive levels of self–other agreement for broad personality factors like the Big Five (see McCrae & Costa, 1987, or Vazire & Carlson, 2010, for summaries).

In one of the most ambitious meta-analytic attempts to date, Connelly and Ones (2010) examined the agreement between Big Five–relevant personality self-ratings and ratings provided by family, friends, cohabitators, work colleagues, incidental acquaintances, and strangers. They concluded that there was substantial evidence for self–other agreement. Although personality ratings provided by strangers,

incidental acquaintances, and work colleagues sometimes agreed with self-ratings, particularly high levels of agreement were evident between self-judgments and judgments provided by family, friends, and cohabitators. Generally, the closer the relationship, the higher self–other agreement tended to be.

It is clear that those who know you well often agree with how you view yourself. For example, using data from the Riverside Accuracy Project, Spain (1995) found self–other agreement for the Big Five factors to be substantial. In this study, approximately 200 college students provided self-judgments of their own personality and were described by two college friends, two hometown friends, and their parents using the NEO-PI (Costa & McCrae, 1985). For the female participants, agreement between self-judgments and descriptions provided by the college acquaintances across the five factors ranged from 0.23 to 0.66 (mean r = 0.49); for male participants, self-college acquaintance agreement ranged from 0.37 to 0.62 (mean r = 0.51). Self–other agreement results for parents and hometown friends were similar with average agreement correlations across the five factors ranging from 0.32 to 0.48.

Self–other agreement is evident for more specific traits as well. In a study of 211 traditional- and non-traditional-age college students, Spain and her colleagues found high levels of agreement between self-judgments and the judgments of friends, parents, romantic partners, and coworkers for both specific traits and broad personality factors (Benson, Spry, & Spain, 2004; Spain, 2007). For example, self–other agreement correlations for the Big Five ranged from 0.23–0.54 for friends to 0.21–0.49 for parents, 0.32–0.50 for romantic partners, and 0.07–0.46 for coworkers. Profile agreement correlations across the 100 specific traits included in the California Q-set (Block, 1961) averaged 0.52 for self–mother agreement and 0.49 for self–romantic partner agreement. These results are fairly typical. In three meta-analyses across 21 studies that included judgments of Big Five factors, the 100 trait items from the California Q-set, and features of personality disorders, Vazire and Carlson (2010) found that the average self–other agreement was 0.40.

Evidence from Studies Involving the Prediction of Daily Life Experiences and Behavior

If personality self-judgments are accurate, they should also predict personality-relevant criteria such as individuals' emotional reactions, personality states, behaviors, and life outcomes. In the next several sections, representative studies that have identified coherent and meaningful links between individuals' personality trait self-judgments and measures of daily life experiences, behaviors, and outcomes are reviewed.

Many of these studies use experience sampling methods (ESMs) to assess various aspects of a target's daily life. To collect data using ESMs, multiple assessments of a participant's everyday behavior and experiences are taken over a period of time. If participants are asked to record their own daily life activities and behaviors, participants are typically either signaled by an electronic device or given preset reporting times and, at each point, report what they are thinking, feeling, or doing at that moment or in the moments just prior to the reporting time.

For research on the accuracy of personality judgments, these daily life measures can be used as criteria for accuracy. These measures are a type of self-report and, as such, are not completely independent of personality self-ratings. Nevertheless, the collection of these reports is typically separated in time and location from the personality self-descriptions. Because these reports are provided in situ, usually at random times or times selected by the researcher rather than the participant, they are considered to be closer to "objective" measures of actual behavior and experiences than are most other self-report measures that are more prone to retrospective biases and/or selective reporting (Tennen, Suls, & Affleck, 1991).

Other behavioral measures can be collected either in the lab or from everyday naturalistic settings. For coded lab behavior, participants are typically brought into the researcher's lab, asked to complete a task or interact with others, and their behavior is recorded or observed obtrusively or unobtrusively. To collect in situ measures of behavior with a recording device, participants agree to wear a small recording device that usually cycles off and on capturing snippets of the participants' behavior as it occurs in everyday settings. The resulting behavioral streams are then coded by trained coders for the behaviors of interest.

PREDICTING EMOTIONAL EXPERIENCES IN DAILY LIFE

Some personality traits reflect individual differences in the chronic experience of some emotional states (e.g., depressed, angry, irritable) while others reflect variability in emotions from one moment to the next (e.g., moody) or the ability to regulate emotion (e.g., emotional stability). If an individual's self-judgment of a personality trait can predict the subsequent experience of relevant emotional states or responses, then we can be more confident that their personality judgment is accurate.

Using this emotional experience criterion, Spain, Eaton, and Funder (2000) demonstrated that self-judgments of the personality factors of neuroticism and extraversion were meaningfully related to the experience of daily life emotion collected using ESM. Participants in the Riverside Accuracy Project carried "beepers" for 8 days and were randomly signaled four times each day. Each time their beeper sounded, participants reported what they were doing and what they were feeling at that moment. Participants rated their current state using six positive emotion adjectives (calm, energetic, happy, interested, joyful, and pleased) and six negative emotion adjectives (nervous, scared, sad, hostile, distressed, and upset). The correlation between participants' self-judgments of extraversion and a composite of their everyday experience of positive emotions was 0.40 ($p < 0.05$) while the correlation between self-judgments of neuroticism and the negative emotion composite was 0.39 ($p < 0.05$).[3]

PREDICTING PERSONALITY STATES

Personality states can also serve as criteria for accuracy. According to whole trait theory (Fleeson & Jayawickreme, 2015), personality traits are best thought of as a density distribution of momentary personality states so, logically, there should be coherent links between trait ratings and the experience of personality states in daily life. Using experience sampling methods, Wilt, Noftle, Fleeson, and Spain (2012; Studies 1 & 2) found significant correlations between self-rated trait measures of extraversion and the everyday experience of extraversion states. For Study 1, 44 undergraduates carried Palm Pilots for 13 days and responded five times each day at preset intervals. For each response, participants rated the extent to which they had behaved in an energetic, assertive, adventurous, or talkative way in the last hour. For Study 2, 62 college students who ranged in age from 18 to 51 carried Palm Pilots for 10 days and also responded at five set times each day. At each of the set times, participants reported how quiet, energetic, or bold they had been in the previous hour. In both studies, trait self-ratings of extraversion were significantly related to enacted extraversion states in daily life ($rs = 0.38$ for Study 1 and 0.29 for Study 2). In other words, trait self-judgments were able to predict how the individuals behaved at specific time points later in their everyday lives.

PREDICTING BEHAVIOR AND DAILY ACTIVITIES

For studies evaluating the accuracy of personality judgments that rely on behavioral criteria, researchers have typically collected either live or videotaped laboratory behavior coded by trained observers, in situ ESM reports provided by the participants, or measures of everyday behaviors recorded by an electronic recording device. Studies linking self-reports of personality to some type of behavior observed in the lab or in naturalistic settings abound. Vazire and Carlson (2010), for example, summarized the results of seven such studies (five lab and two naturalistic settings) that examined self-accuracy using the criterion of prediction of behaviors and outcomes. The traits studied included the broad Big Five personality factors, specific traits from the California Q-Set, friendliness, and dominance. Correlations between self-ratings of traits and the various behaviors and outcomes (laughing, talking, attending class, socializing, watching TV, etc.) ranged from 0.14 to 0.34 with the average self-accuracy correlation being 0.25, indicating moderate levels of accuracy.

A number of studies have used the Electronically Activated Recorder (EAR; Mehl, Pennebaker, Crow, Dabbs, & Price, 2001) to collect snippets of ambient sound from participants' daily life. For example, Mehl, Gosling, and Pennebaker (2006) related EAR-derived information on daily experiences to Big Five ratings. Participants wore the EAR for 2 days during waking hours. The devices captured 30-second snippets of sound from the participants' environment. Sound recordings were then rated by coders for information about moods, language use, social interactions, activities, and locations. Self-rated personality showed theoretically relevant links to these daily experiences. For example, self-reported extraversion was negatively correlated with being alone ($r = -.27$) but positively correlated with time spent talking ($r = 0.30$). Individuals who described themselves as conscientious were more likely to be in class ($r = 0.42$).

In a similar study, Beer and Vazire (2017) collected 2 days of EAR measures and coded them for emotions, locations, talking, various activities, and other Big Five–relevant behaviors. Self-rated Big Five scores were again meaningfully related to naturalistic behavior. Self-rated extraversion, for instance, was positively correlated with talking to friends, laughing, singing, and gossiping.

Evidence from Studies Involving the Prediction of Life Outcomes

If one is to use the criterion of prediction to establish the accuracy of a personality judgment, some of the most compelling evidence for accuracy would be the judgment's ability to predict consequential, personality-relevant outcomes not just in the weeks or months immediately following when the judgment was initially made, but also far into the future. Considerable evidence demonstrates the ability of personality judgments to predict many important life outcomes at individual, interpersonal, and institutional levels including psychological and physical health status, changes in health, happiness and well-being, relationship quality, work outcomes like performance and job satisfaction, political and community engagement, and even criminal behavior (see Ozer & Benet-Martinez, 2006, and Roberts, Kuncel, Shiner, Caspi, & Goldberg, 2007, for reviews).

Longitudinal studies provide some of the most interesting findings. For example, Hill, Turiano, Mroczek, and Roberts (2012) examined concurrent and longitudinal associations between Big Five traits and social well-being at two points in midlife, measured approximately 9 years apart. Participants were midlife adults who participated in the Mid-Life Development in the United States (MIDUS) study. Initial self-ratings of extraversion, agreeableness, openness, and conscientiousness were positively correlated with initial ratings of social well-being, while self-ratings of neuroticism were negatively correlated with well-being. Self-rated changes on these traits also predicted changes in social well-being 9 years later.

Such longitudinal associations are not just limited to measures of social well-being; they are also evident in studies of physical health. Weston, Hill, and Jackson (2015) studied over 7,000 older adults who participated in the Health and Retirement Study. At the first time of measurement, participants completed personality measures and reported on current health status. A follow-up was conducted 4 years later to assess changes in health status. Self-ratings of conscientiousness, neuroticism, and openness to experience predicted risk of developing disease. Self-rated personality predicted likelihood of developing a heart condition, having a stroke, developing a lung condition, as well as other conditions. For example, conscientiousness was a generally protective factor while neuroticism was a risk factor. Those who were low on openness were more likely to have experienced the onset of high blood pressure, arthritis, heart disease, and stroke during the 4-year period.

Even self-ratings of traits associated with personality disorders (PDs) can predict later life outcomes. In a study of over 1,000 Air Force recruits, Fiedler, Oltmanns, and Turkheimer (2004) found that self-reports of PD-related traits measured using the Schedule for Non-Adaptive and Adaptive Personality (SNAP) predicted job status measured two years later. Self-rated PD-related traits predicted whether or not the recruit was still engaged on active duty or had been given an early discharge. These early discharges were usually due to poor performance, disciplinary problems, or serious interpersonal problems.

Conclusions and Future Directions

In sum, it is clear that self-judgments of personality, albeit prone to biases and sometimes flawed, have considerable validity. They agree with the judgments made by others, particularly if those others are close acquaintances or family members. Self-judgments can also predict many relevant behaviors measured both in the lab and in naturalistic settings from the person's daily life. They can also predict some of the most consequential life outcomes including well-being, health, relationship quality, and occupational success. Although these judgments are far from perfect, recent empirical work has advanced our knowledge of the perceptual and motivational mechanisms that account for their inaccuracy.

More work, however, remains to be done. It is, for example, still somewhat unclear exactly how self-judgments become accurate. Most models of the personality judgment process like Funder's RAM were developed to describe how we judge others, and recent work on those models has focused on how properties of the target, judge, trait, and information moderate accurate judgments of other people. These moderators are usually assumed to operate similarly for self-judgments, but scant attention has been paid to identifying any differences in how these moderators operate when the target is the self. Vazire's SOKA model and other work reviewed in this chapter make it clear that differences exist but determining the extent of those differences requires additional attention.

Consideration should also be given to other aspects of self-judgments and other types of self-knowledge. To date, research on self-accuracy has tended to focus primarily on the accuracy of judgments about *explicit* aspects of your own personal-ity. Some have argued that accurate knowledge of your own personality should include understanding the more implicit aspects of your self-concept (Back & Vazire, 2012) as well as knowledge about how you are viewed by others, or meta-accuracy. The dual process lens model described by Osterholz and her colleagues (see chapter by Osterholz, Breil, Nestler, & Back in this handbook) attempts to integrate implicit and explicit processes in one model, but to date most empirical work testing the model has focused on perceivers' judgments of a target rather than the target's own self-judgment. On the other hand, significant advances have been made in recent years by Carlson and others in understanding meta-perception processes and the factors that affect meta-accuracy (see chapter by Carlson & Elsaadawy in this handbook for a review). Although many questions remain about the accuracy of this particular kind of self-knowledge, such work should significantly advance our understanding of the general validity of trait self-judgments.

As mentioned previously, finding appropriate criteria to use when evaluating the accuracy of trait self-judgments has also been challenging. Self–other agreement and behavioral prediction are useful as criteria but there may be other criteria that can be employed that could help us better understand the factors that affect accuracy. For example, personality traits also influence an individual's choices regarding the situations they enter and the locations they occupy in their daily lives. Although ESM studies have sometimes collected situation and location information from individuals, it has seldom been used as a primary criterion for accuracy. One reason may be that we still have very little understanding of the important properties of situations or everyday locations that are relevant to personality. In the last decade or so, Funder and others have called for researchers to pay greater attention to identifying key characteristics of situations (e.g., Funder, 2006, 2009; Guillaume, Stauner, & Funder, 2017). Rauthmann, Sherman, and others have also developed new ways to more objectively measure and classify the situations individuals enter each day (Brown, Blake, & Sherman, 2017; Rauthmann et al., 2014; Rauthmann, Sherman, Nave, & Funder, 2015). Once we have a clearer understanding of how situations and locations are relevant to personality, we could use information about an individual's choice of or response to various situations and locations as criteria for accuracy.

Of even more importance than identifying new criteria for accuracy is understanding how we can improve our self-judgments. Can individuals improve their understanding of themselves and reduce the tendency for self-views to be biased or inaccurate? Wilson (2009) suggests that we should first try to be objective observers of our own behavior and, when possible, try to see ourselves through the eyes of others. He believes that if we read and apply the findings from psychological science to ourselves, that we should be more accurate. This sounds relatively straightforward, but it is far from easy to do. Leary and Toner (2012) offer additional approaches that they assert should reduce biases in perspective and evaluation. They suggest that to be an accurate self-judge, one should value accurate self-views, practice and promote ego skepticism (e.g., critically evaluate your own assumptions), accept one's fallibility and recognize one's ordinariness, and attempt to reduce defensiveness and unnecessary self-evaluative thinking. In other words, do not always assume you are right and try to avoid self-serving biases. And, when others' views of us are perceived to be inaccurate, we should explicitly examine the discrepancies in how we are viewed.

While these are logical suggestions, acquiring a truly accurate view of your own personality may not be so easy. Ben Franklin once said, "There are three things very hard: steel, diamonds, and to know one's self." We should not, therefore, be surprised that self-judgments of personality traits are not always perfectly accurate. We are not, however, as blind, biased, or deluded as some would have us believe. We do, face many challenges in developing an accurate view of our own enduring characteristics. Nevertheless, the enterprise is important enough to warrant our best efforts because, as Aristotle once so aptly put it, "Knowing yourself is the beginning of all wisdom."

References

Alicke, M. D., & Sedikides, C. (2009). Self-enhancement and self-protection: What they are and what they do. *European Journal of Social Psychology, 20,* 1–8. http://dx.doi.org/10.1080/10463280802613866

Allport, G. (1937). *Pattern and growth in personality.* London, UK: Holt, Rinehart, & Winston.

Andersen, S. M., Glassman, N. S., & Gold, D. A. (1998). Mental representations of the self, significant others, and nonsignificant others: Structure and processing of private and public aspects. *Journal of Personality and Social Psychology, 75*(4), 845–861. http://dx.doi.org/10.1037/0022-3514.75.4.845

Back, M. D., & Vazire, S. (2012). Knowing our personality. In S. Vazire & T. D. Wilson (Eds.), *Handbook of self knowledge* (pp. 131–156). New York, NY: he Guilford Press.

Beer, A., & Vazire, S. (2017). Evaluating the predictive validity of personality trait judgments using naturalistic behavior criterion: A preliminary test of the self-other knowledge asymmetry model. *Journal of Research in Personality, 70,* 107–121. https://dx.doi.org/10.1016/j.jrp.2017.06.004

Benson, G. J., Spry, W. L., & Spain, J. S. (2004, April). *Does mother always know best? Comparing the accuracy of personality judgments by mothers and significant others.* Poster presented at the meeting of the Eastern Psychological Association, Washington, DC.

Block, J. (1961). *The Q-sort method in personality assessment and psychiatric research.* Springfield, IL: Charles C Thomas. https://dx.doi.org/10.1037/13141-000

Brown, J. D. (1986). Evaluations of self and others: Self-enhancement biases in social judgments. *Social Cognition, 4*(4), 353–376.

Brown, N. A., Blake, A. B., & Sherman, R. A. (2017). A snapshot of the life as lived: Wearable cameras in social and personality psychological science. *Social Psychological and Personality Science, 8*(5), 592–600. https://doi.org/10.1177/1948550617703170

Campbell, D. T., & Fiske, D. W. (1959). Convergent and discriminant validation by the multitrait-multimethod matrix. *Psychological Bulletin, 56*(2), 81–105. https://dx.doi.org/10.1037/h0046016

Connelly, B. S., & Ones, D. S. (2010). An other perspective on personality: Meta-analytic integration of observers' accuracy and predictive validity. *Psychological Bulletin, 136*(6), 1092–1122. https://dx.doi.org/10.1037/a0021212.supp (Supplemental)

Costa, P. T., Jr., & McCrae, R. R. (1985). *The NEO Personality Inventory (NEO-PI-R) and NEO Five Factor Inventory (NEO-FFI) professional manual.* Odessa, FL: Psychological Assessment Resources.

Cronbach, L. J., & Meehl, P. E. (1955). Construct validity in psychological tests. *Psychological Bulletin, 52*(4), 281–302. https://dx.doi.org/10.1037/h0040957

Dunning, D., Heath, C., & Suls, J. (2004). Flawed self-assessment: Implications for health, education, and the workplace. *Psychological Science in the Public Interest, 5*(3), 69–106. http://dx.doi.org/10.1111/j.1529-1006.2004.00018.x

Epley, N., & Dunning, D. (2006). The mixed blessings of self-knowledge in behavioral prediction: Enhanced discrimination but exacerbated bias. *Personality and Social Psychology Bulletin, 32*(5), 641–655. https://dx.doi.org/10.1177/0146167205284007

Fiedler, E. R., Oltmanns, T. F., & Turkheimer, E. (2004). Traits associated with personality disorders and adjustment to military life: Predictive validity of self and peer reports. *Military Medicine, 169*(3), 207–211. https://dx.doi.org/10.7205/MILMED.169.3.207

Fleeson, W., & Jayawickreme, E. (2015). Whole trait theory. *Journal of Research in Personality, 56,* 82–92. https://doi.org/10.1016/j.jrp.2014.10.009

Funder, D. C. (1987). Errors and mistakes: Evaluating the accuracy of social judgment. *Psychological Bulletin, 101*(1), 75–90. http://dx.doi.org/10.1037/0033-2909.101.1.75

Funder, D. C. (1995). On the accuracy of personality judgment: A realistic approach. *Psychological Review, 102*(4), 652–670. http://dx.doi.org/10.1037/0033-295X.102.4.652

Funder, D. C. (2006). Towards a resolution of the personality triad: Persons, situations, and behaviors. *Journal of Research in Personality, 40*(1), 21–34. https://doi.org/10.1016/j.jrp.2005.08.003

Funder, D. C. (2009). Persons, behaviors and situations: An agenda for personality psychology in the postwar era. *Journal of Research in Personality, 43*(2), 120–126. https://doi.org/10.1016/j.jrp.2008.12.041

Furr, R. M. (2009). Personality psychology as a truly behavioural science. *European Journal of Personality, 23*(5), 369–401. https://dx.doi.org/10.1002/per.724

Gosling, S. D., John, O. P., Craik, K. H., & Robins, R. W. (1998). Do people know how they behave? Self-reported act frequencies compared with on-line codings by observers. *Journal of Personality and Social Psychology, 74*(5), 1337–1349. http://dx.doi.org/10.1037/0022-3514.74.5.1337

Guenther, C. I., & Alicke, M. D. (2010). Deconstructing the better-than-average effect. *Journal of Personality and Social Psychology, 99,* 755–770. http://dx.doi.org/10.1037/a0020959

Guillaume, E., Stauner, N., & Funder, D. C. (2017). Toward a psychology of situations across cultures. In A. T. Church (Ed.), *The Praeger handbook of personality across cultures: Trait psychology across cultures* (Vol. 1, pp. 309–333). Santa Barbara, CA: Praeger/ABC-CLIO.

Hansen, K. E., & Pronin, E. (2012). Illusions of self-knowledge. In S. Vazire & T. D. Wilson (Eds.), *Handbook of self-knowledge* (pp. 345–362). New York, NY: The Guilford Press.

Hill, P. L., Turiano, N. A., Mroczek, D. K., & Roberts, B. W. (2012). Examining concurrent and longitudinal relationships between personality traits and social well-being in adulthood. *Social Psychological and Personality Science, 3*(6), 698–705. http://dx.doi.org/10.1177/1948550611433888

John, O. P., & Robins, R. W. (1993). Determinants of interjudge agreement on personality traits: The Big Five domains, observability, evaluativeness, and the unique perspective of the self. *Journal of Personality, 61*(4) 521–551. https://dx.doi.org/10.1111/j.1467-6494.1993.tb00781.x

John, O. P., & Robins, R. W. (1994). Accuracy and bias in self-perception: Individual differences in self-enhancement and the role of narcissism. *Journal of Personality and Social Psychology, 66*(1), 206–219. http://dx.doi.org/10.1037/0022-3514.66.1.206

Kenny, D. A. (1994). *Interpersonal perception: A social relations analysis.* New York, NY: Guilford Press.

Kim, H., Di Domenico, S. I., & Connelly, B. S. (2019). Self–other agreement in personality reports: A meta-analytic comparison of self- and informant-report means. *Psychological Science, 30*(1), 129–138. https://dx.doi.org/10.1177/0956797618810000

Kolar, D. W., Funder, D. C., & Colvin, C. R. (1996). Comparing the accuracy of personality judgments by the self and knowledgeable others. *Journal of Personality, 64,* 311–337. http://dx.doi.org/10.1111/j.1467-6494.1996.tb00513.x

Leary, M. R., & Toner, K. (2012). Reducing egoistic biases in self-beliefs. In S. Vazire & T. D. Wilson (Eds.), *Handbook of self-knowledge* (pp. 413–428). New York, NY: he Guilford Press.

McCrae, R. R. (1982). Consensual validation of personality traits: Evidence from self-reports and ratings. *Journal of Personality and Social Psychology, 43,* 293–303. http://dx.doi.org/10.1037/0022-3514.43.2.293

McCrae, R. R., & Costa, P. T. (1987). Validation of the five-factor model of personality across instruments and observers. *Journal of Personality and Social Psychology, 52*(1), 81–90. https://dx.doi.org/10.1037/0022-3514.52.1.81

Mehl, M. M., Gosling, S. D., & Pennebaker, J. W. (2006). Personality in its natural habitat: Manifestations and implicit folk theories of personality in daily life. *Journal of Personality and Social Psychology, 90*(5), 862–877. https://dx.doi.org/10.1037/0022-3514.90.5.862

Mehl, M. R., Pennebaker, J. W., Crow, D. M., Dabbs, J., & Price, J. H. (2001). The Electronically Activated Recorder (EAR): A device for sampling naturalistic daily activities and conversations. *Behavior Research Methods, Instruments, and Computers, 33*(4), 517–523. https://dx.doi.org/10.3758/BF03195410

Ozer, D. J., & Benet-Martinez, V. (2006). Personality and the prediction of consequential outcomes. *Annual Review of Psychology, 57,* 401–421. https://doi.org/10.1146/annurev.psych.57.102904.190127.

Paulhus, D. L., & John, O. P. (1998). Egoistic and moralistic biases in self-perceptions: The interplay of self-deceptive styles with basic traits and motives. *Journal of Personality, 66,* 1024–1060. https://doi.org/10.1111/1467-6494.00041

Paulhus, D. L., & Vazire, S. (2007). The self-report method. In R. W. Robins, R. C. Fraley, & R. F. Krueger (Eds.), *Handbook of research methods in personality psychology* (pp. 224–239). New York, NY: Guilford Press.

Rauthmann, J. F., Gallardo-Pujol, D., Guillaume, E. M., Todd, E., Nave, C. S., Sherman, R. A.,… Funder, D. C. (2014). The Situational Eight DIAMONDS: A taxonomy of major dimensions of situation characteristics. *Journal of Personality and Social Psychology, 107*(4), 677–718. https://doi.org/10.1037/a0037250.supp (Supplemental)

Rauthmann, J. F., Sherman, R. A., Nave, C. S., & Funder, D. C. (2015). Personality-driven situation experience, contact, and construal: How people's personality traits predict characteristics of their situations in daily life. *Journal of Research in Personality, 55,* 98–111. https://doi.org/10.1016/j.jrp.2015.02.003

Roberts, B. W., Kuncel, N. R., Shiner, R., Caspi, A., & Goldberg, L. R. (2007). The power of personality: The comparative validity of personality traits, socioeconomic status, and cognitive ability for predicting important life outcomes. *Perspectives on Psychological Science, 2*(4), 313–345. https://doi.org/10.1111/j.1745-6916.2007.00047.x

Rogers, C. R. (1950). The significance of the self-regarding attitudes and perceptions. In M. L. Reymart (Ed.), *Feeling and emotions: The Mooseheart Symposium* (pp. 374–382). New York, NY: McGraw Hill.

Rogers, C. R. (1951). *Client-centered therapy: Its current practice, implications, and theory (The Houghton Mifflin psychological series).* Boston, MA: Houghton Mifflin.

Spain, J. S. (1995, September). *Personality and daily life experiences: Evaluating the accuracy of personality judgments. Dissertation Abstracts International: Section B: The Sciences and Engineering.* ProQuest Information & Learning.

Spain, J. S. (2007, October). The role of the perceiver-target relationship in accurate person perception: Evidence from an experience sampling study. In J. Spain (Chair), *Interpersonal perception and the eye of the beholder: Understanding the role of personality, gender, and relationship variables in perceiver judgments.* Symposium conducted at the meeting of the Society for Southeastern Social Psychologists, Durham, NC.

Spain, J. S., Eaton, L. G., & Funder, D. C. (2000). Perspectives on personality: The relative accuracy of self versus others for the prediction of emotion and behavior. *Journal of Personality, 68*(5), 837–867. https://doi.org/10.1111/1467-6494.00118

Tennen, H., Suls, J., & Affleck, G. (1991). Personality and daily experience: The promise and the challenge. *Journal of*

Personality, *59*(3), 313–337. https://dx.doi.org/10.1111/j.1467–6494.1991.tb02387.x

Vazire, S. (2010). Who knows what about a person? The self-other knowledge asymmetry (SOKA) model. *Journal of Personality and Social Psychology, 98*(2), 281–300. http://dx.doi.org/10.1037/a0017908

Vazire, S., & Carlson, E. N. (2010). Self-knowledge of personality: Do people know themselves? *Social and Personality Psychology Compass, 4,* 605–620. https://dx.doi.org/10.111/j.1751.2010.00280.x

Vazire, S., & Mehl, M. R. (2008). Knowing me, knowing you: The accuracy and unique predictive validity of self-ratings and other-ratings of daily behavior. *Journal of Personality and Social Psychology, 95*(5), 1202–1216. http://dx.doi.org/10.1037/a0013314

Weston, S. J., Hill, P. L., & Jackson, J. J. (2015). Personality traits predict the onset of disease. *Social Psychological and Personality Science, 6*(3), 309-317. https://dx.doi.org/10.1177/1948550614553248.

Wicklund, R., & Eckert, M. (1992). *The self-knower: A hero under control* (The Plenum Series in Social/Clinical Psychology). New York, NY: Plenum Press.

Wilson, T. D. (2009). Know thyself. *Perspectives on Psychological Science, 4*(4), 384–389. http://dx.doi.org/10.1111/j.1745–6924.2009.01143.x

Wilt, J., Noftle, E. E., Fleeson, W., & Spain, J. S. (2012). The dynamic role of personality states in mediating the relationship between extraversion and positive affect. *Journal of Personality, 80*(5), 1205–1236. https://dx.doi.org/10.1111/j.1467–6494.2011.00756.x

Notes

1. This definition focuses on an individual's explicit knowledge of his or her own personality traits. Other approaches consider the relations between explicit and implicit aspects of self-knowledge and the accuracy of metaperceptions of personality traits. These aspects of personality self-knowledge are considered in Back and Vazire (2012) and in chapter by Bollich-Ziegler and chapter by Carlson and Elsaadawy in this handbook.

2. Elevation accuracy is the match between perceivers' average rating on a criterion and the average rating provided by a group of targets. It refers to how accurately people can judge a criterion or base rate at the group level. Kenny (1994) provides a review of different forms of accuracy, or see chapter by Malloy in this handbook.

3. One could argue that these findings simply demonstrate consistencies in the ways that individuals describe themselves. Describing how you are feeling at the moment that you are feeling the emotion at 32 randomly selected times in your daily life, however, is rather different from rating a trait on a personality scale describing what you are generally like. It is also almost impossible to obtain a measure of emotional experience that is more objective and independent of self-evaluation. Even physiological measures of emotion often necessitate the individual specifying what the measured arousal means.

Figuring Out How Others See Us

The Formation of Accurate Meta-Perceptions

Erika N. Carlson *and* Norhan Elsaadawy

Abstract

We have a natural desire to know what other people think of us and, thus, we form beliefs regarding other people's impressions of us, called *meta-perceptions*. The extent to which these beliefs are accurate is called *meta-accuracy*, and is related to whether people like us, as well as the quality of our relationships with others. As a result, meta-accuracy has become a topic of interest in the literature on personality judgment. This chapter reviews how researchers study and index meta-accuracy and the results of the existing work on meta-accuracy. Further, it proposes studying meta-accuracy by using the Realistic Accuracy Model (RAM) as a framework. To demonstrate the utility of this approach, we use the RAM to outline the cues used in the formation of meta-perceptions, the potential moderators of meta-accuracy, and future avenues of research.

Key Words: meta-perception, meta-accuracy, realistic accuracy model, impression, personality judgment

Judging others' personalities comes easily and naturally to us. We form judgments about what others are like almost instantly (Willis & Todorov, 2006) and use these judgments to navigate our day-to-day interactions with people and to make important decisions, such as whom to befriend or whom to trust. For instance, we are much more likely to trust our reliable friend than our impulsive friend to show up on time, give good advice, or keep a promise. In turn, we realize that others form personality judgments about us as well, and we wonder about these judgments, arguably because we realize others' judgments of us can have a profound effect on us. Our beliefs about how others perceive us are called *meta-perceptions* (Kenny & DePaulo, 1993). Most of us are aware of our meta-perceptions in situations such as job interviews (e.g., we wonder if our potential employer thinks we are competent) and romantic dates (e.g., we try to guess if our date thinks we are attractive), or we have a general sense of how we think our friends or acquaintances see us (e.g., we think our friends see us as trustworthy). The degree to which our meta-perceptions are accurate, or the

degree to which we know the impressions we make on others, is called *meta-accuracy* (Kenny & DePaulo, 1993). The current chapter reviews how meta-perceptions and meta-accuracy are studied, how meta-perceptions are formed, and the factors that influence meta-accuracy.

How Are Meta-Perceptions and Meta-Accuracy Studied?

For the most part, much of the empirical work on meta-perceptions and meta-accuracy focuses on people's beliefs about how they are seen on personality traits (e.g., sociability, kindness) and attraction variables (e.g., liking, physical attractiveness). Regardless of the characteristics they are interested in, the way researchers measure meta-perceptions and meta-accuracy often depends on whether they are interested in studying first impressions or the perceptions of people who are already well acquainted. For example, researchers interested in meta-perceptions of first impressions might bring two participants (i.e., a dyad) into the lab to meet for the first time and have a short conversation.

After participants have gotten acquainted in this first impression paradigm, the researchers would ask the participants to provide judgments of each other (e.g., "how talkative is person x?") and meta-perceptions of those judgments (e.g., "how talkative does person x think you are?") for several traits (e.g., the Big Five[1]; Carlson, 2016a). Another, more common, first-impression paradigm is to bring a small group of unacquainted participants into the lab to meet as a group or in one-on-one conversations with each group member. For example, participants might take part in a competitive task (e.g., DePaulo et al., 1987), a cooperative task (e.g., Malloy & Janowski, 1992), or a "getting to know you" activity (e.g., Reno & Kenny, 1992) as a group, or they might take part in similar activities in pairs such that every person interacts with every other person in the group. After the group or dyadic interactions, participants provide round-robin ratings, whereby each person rates each group member using a Likert scale on several traits (e.g., "I think person x is extraverted; 1 = *disagree*, 7 = *agree*) and provides meta-perceptions for each person (e.g., "I think person x saw me as extraverted; 1 = *disagree*, 7 = *agree*; Reno & Kenny, 1992). For example, if there is a participant named Judy in the group, then Judy would rate the personality traits of everyone in her group, she would guess how everyone rated her, and all of her group members would do the same. This round-robin method makes it is possible to index both *differential (dyadic) meta-accuracy*, or the degree to which people know the unique impression they make on specific people (e.g., does Judy know that Paul thought she was more extraverted than Pam thought she was?), and *generalized meta-accuracy*, or the degree to which people know their overall reputation (e.g., does Judy know that the group on average rated her as fairly extraverted?; Kenny, 1994). The round-robin method is most commonly used among new acquaintances (i.e., first impressions) rather than close acquaintances, because it is easy to obtain ratings among groups when they are present in the lab, and most people's close acquaintances do not all know each other (i.e., it would be difficult for all of Judy's friends to rate each other because some of her friends do not know each other), although there are a few studies that have looked at round-robin ratings among well-acquainted groups such as family, friends, and coworkers (Cook & Douglas, 1998; Malloy & Albright, 1990). Instead, a common and logistically more feasible design for studying meta-perceptions among close others is to ask participants to guess how a few close others perceive them and then obtain actual personality impressions from those close others, usually in the form of questionnaires sent to the close others via email (e.g., Carlson & Furr, 2009). That is, Judy would provide meta-perceptions of each of her close friends, while Judy's close friends would only provide judgments about Judy and not each other. When people provide meta-perceptions for and are rated by multiple close others, it is also possible to assess whether people (i.e., Judy) know who sees them as higher or lower on a trait (i.e., differential meta-accuracy), and whether they know their reputation (i.e., generalized meta-accuracy; Carlson & Furr, 2009). Finally, some research examines meta-perceptions and meta-accuracy when people do not meet face-to-face. For example, participants might be asked to provide a screenshot of their social media profile as well as meta-perceptions for how people who see the profile might view them, and a separate set of raters would later provide personality ratings based on these stimuli (Stopfer, Egloff, Nestler, & Back, 2014). In sum, researchers assess meta-perceptions and meta-accuracy in a variety of ways in order to study a wide range of contexts and people with varying levels of acquaintanceship.

In addition to assessing meta-accuracy in different contexts, researchers also index meta-accuracy in different ways in order to address specific research goals. One common goal is to determine how accurate people tend to be about a specific trait (e.g., kindness), an approach that is especially useful when researchers want to know which traits people tend to be more accurate about. To address this goal, researchers index meta-accuracy as a correlation between people's meta-perceptions and others' judgments of those individuals on a given trait (e.g., Carlson & Furr, 2009). This approach, which is called the *trait-based approach*, reveals whether the people who tend to think they are seen as, for example, more kind, are actually seen as more kind. Overall, several studies have demonstrated that people know both their reputation (i.e., generalized meta-accuracy) and who sees them as higher or lower on a trait (i.e., dyadic or differential meta-accuracy) on a range of traits including the Big Five traits (e.g., extraversion), socially desirable traits (e.g., intelligence), and personality pathology (e.g., borderline personality disorder) among new acquaintances (DePaulo et al., 1987; Levesque, 1997; Malloy & Janowski, 1992) and close others (e.g., friends, family, romantic partners; Carlson & Furr, 2009; Carlson & Oltmanns, 2015, 2018; Malloy & Albright, 1990; Oltmanns et al., 2005).

Another common goal is to answer questions about who is accurate (e.g., do narcissists know their reputation?), which involves indexing accuracy for each participant individually. One common way to measure meta-accuracy for each participant is to index whether people know how they are perceived across a broad range of traits using what is called the *profile-based approach* (e.g., Carlson & Furr, 2013). For example, using the profile-based approach, Judy would provide meta-perceptions for several items on a Big Five measure, Tom would rate Judy on those same items, and Judy's meta-accuracy would be captured by the correlation between her meta-perception and Tom's impression of her. Thus, the profile approach indexes meta-accuracy as the degree to which meta-perceivers understand how a specific person perceives their characteristic pattern of traits (e.g., Judy realizes that Tom sees her as more kind than outgoing but more outgoing than nervous). Results from the profile approach reveal that people seem to know how others perceive their characteristic pattern of traits in a range of social contexts (e.g., in a first impression, with a friend), although there is variability in these effects such that not everyone is accurate (Carlson, 2016a; Carlson, Furr, & Vazire, 2010). Further, this approach has revealed that people who tend to have higher meta-accuracy are also seen as being more socially skilled (Carlson, 2016a).

Notably, the analytic methods used to index meta-accuracy do not necessarily influence how meta-perceptions are collected. For example, researchers who use the first-impression paradigm in which people meet someone in the lab for the first time are able to index how accurate people are in general for each of the Big Five traits (e.g., Carlson et al., 2011) as well as how accurate each person is (e.g., Carlson et al., 2010). In sum, in any given context, researchers can index meta-accuracy for each trait or for each individual.

How Do People Achieve Meta-Accuracy?

A growing body of work suggests that forming accurate meta-perceptions might be highly consequential. People who are more accurate about the impressions they make tend to be liked more by new acquaintances, friends, and romantic partners compared to people who lack this awareness, and accuracy early on can foster greater liking over time (Carlson, 2016b). The positive influence of meta-accuracy holds true even for people with higher levels of personality pathology, which arguably reflects negative or undesirable traits (Carlson &

Oltmanns, 2018). As such, forming accurate meta-perceptions is a valuable skill for people to possess and develop. What do people need to do to achieve meta-accuracy, and how can people improve the accuracy of their meta-perceptions? To better understand the nature of meta-accuracy, we propose studying meta-accuracy through the lens of the realistic accuracy model (RAM; Funder, 1995), which is a model traditionally used to describe how people form accurate personality judgments of other people (e.g., how Tom forms accurate personality judgments of Judy). In the following sections, we use the RAM as a framework to outline the cues used in the formation of meta-perceptions, the pathways and obstacles to accuracy, and the potential moderators of meta-accuracy. Finally, we use the RAM framework to make predictions regarding meta-accuracy and to outline future avenues of research in the self-knowledge literature.

The Realistic Accuracy Model: How Do People Form Accurate Personality Judgments?

Traditionally, the RAM has been used to explain how people form accurate personality judgments of others. According to the RAM, when forming a judgment about Judy's personality, Tom's accuracy involves four stages: relevance, availability, detection, and utilization of various cues (for a detailed description of RAM, see chapter 2 by Letzring & Funder in this handbook). These stages are outlined in Figure 12.1a. First, cues about Judy's personality must be relevant to the personality trait being judged by Tom. For example, Judy's generous behavior (e.g., sharing) is relevant to the trait kindness, but her sociable behavior (e.g., talking) is not relevant to kindness. Second, these relevant cues must be available to Tom, the judge of personality. In other words, Tom needs to have the opportunity to see or hear Judy do or say something kind. For example, if Judy is generous when Tom is not around, then the behavior is not available to Tom. Availability might be low if Judy and Tom just met because Tom has yet to encounter Judy in a context where generous behavior might emerge. Alternatively, the availability of a cue might be low because the behavior is infrequent. For example, Judy might be extremely brave, but because there is never a chance for her to run into a burning building to save someone (i.e., a cue relevant to bravery), Tom might never know that Judy is brave because the cue is not available to him. Thus, stages one and two are often influenced by the context because

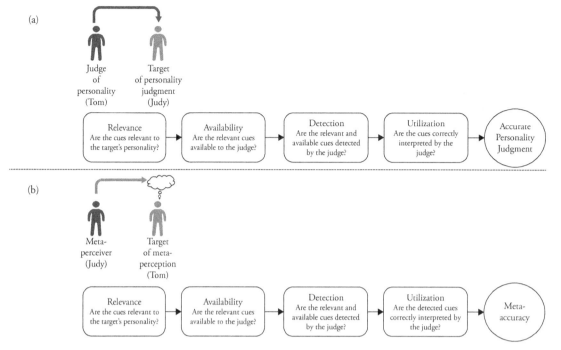

Figure 12.1. a) The stages of the realistic accuracy model (RAM; Funder, 1995) through which a judge of personality (Tom) forms an accurate personality judgment of the target of the personality judgment (Judy). b) The stages of the RAM through which a judge of meta-perception, or meta-perceiver (Judy), forms an accurate meta-perception of the target of the meta-perception (Tom).

some situations bring out cues more than others. However, in the third stage, Tom, the judge of personality, must detect (i.e., see or hear) these relevant and available cues of kindness, and in the fourth stage he must correctly utilize, or interpret, the detected cues as evidence of Judy's kind personality. Thus, in the latter two stages (i.e., detection, utilization), accuracy is more in the hands of the judge of personality. As an example, judges of personality who are motivated to be accurate about targets tend to pay more attention and thus notice more cues (Biesanz & Human, 2010), so Tom will likely be more accurate if he detects more cues related to Judy's kindness. Further, in the final stage, Tom will be more accurate if he interprets Judy's generous behavior as a signal of kindness but will be less accurate if he interprets this behavior as a signal of another trait such as extraversion. Importantly, in order for a judge of personality (e.g., Tom) to achieve accuracy, all four stages must occur successfully (Funder, 2012). While each of the stages brings Tom closer to being accurate about Judy's personality, errors at any step have a negative, additive effect on his accuracy. Sometimes this will be because Tom (the judge of personality) fails to detect or properly utilize cues. Other times, it will be because some cues are simply not relevant to a trait (e.g., how

much someone talks is not a cue relevant to kindness) or because some cues are not available in certain contexts.

We propose that the process of forming accurate meta-perceptions, which are simply a type of judgment, is similar to the process of forming accurate personality judgments and as such, the RAM might also explain when and why people have knowledge of how others experience them (see Figure 12.1b). In the same way that in the context of a personality judgment the person forming the personality judgment is the judge of personality and the person about whom the personality judgment is formed is the target, in the context of a meta-perception, the person forming the meta-perception is the *judge of meta-perception* or the *meta-perceiver*, whereas the person about whom the meta-perception is formed is the target (see Figure 12.1). For meta-perceivers to know what a target really thinks of them, they must detect and appropriately utilize relevant and available cues. For example, for Judy (the meta-perceiver) to know if Tom (the target of meta-perception) thinks she is kind, four steps are necessary: (1) relevance: there are cues that are relevant to Tom's judgment of Judy's kindness (e.g., Tom says he thinks Judy is kind), (2) availability: the relevant cues for Tom's judgment of Judy's kindness are available to Judy (e.g., Tom tells Judy that he thinks she is kind instead of telling someone else), (3) detection: Judy detects the relevant and available cues for Tom's judgment of her kindness (e.g., Judy hears Tom when he tells her he thinks she is kind), and (4) utilization: Judy correctly utilizes and interprets the cues Tom provided about his judgment of her kindness (e.g., Judy infers that Tom is saying she is kind because he thinks she is kind instead of assuming that it is because he thinks she is attractive). Similar to forming personality judgments of others, each of these steps brings Judy closer to achieving accuracy, and errors at any step reduce accuracy. That is, at times, poor meta-accuracy will be due to Judy failing to detect or properly utilize some cues. Other times, some cues will simply not be relevant or available to Judy, which means she will not be able detect or utilize cues in accurate ways. Thus, each step is critical for achieving meta-accuracy.

What Are the Cues That Can Lead to Meta-Accuracy?

In our example, we suggested that perhaps Tom simply tells Judy what he thinks of her, but in reality, there are many cues that can be used in the formation of a meta-perception. Some of these cues are simply sources of information that people rely on when forming meta-perceptions, but we refer to them as cues because they contain information that can vary in the degree to which they are relevant, available, detected, and utilized. Further, some cues we discuss are relevant to the self, while some cues are relevant to knowledge about others, which underscores the idea that forming accurate meta-perceptions involves both self-knowledge and social knowledge (Carlson & Kenny, 2012). In the following sections, we outline five cues that people use when forming meta-perceptions and discuss evidence for when these cues foster meta-accuracy.

Self-Perceptions: We Think People See Us as We See Ourselves

A large body of research suggests that the primary cue people use when forming meta-perceptions is self-perception of their personality (i.e., self-theory; Kenny & DePaulo, 1993). Put another way, when Judy thinks about Tom's impression of her kindness, she likely assumes that Tom perceives her kindness the same way she perceives her own kindness. Indeed, meta-perceptions and self-perceptions are strongly correlated for a broad range of traits and across social contexts (estimated $r = 0.87$; Kenny & DePaulo, 1993), suggesting that people tend to

think that others see them similarly to how they see themselves.

In terms of the RAM, basing a meta-perception on self-perceptions can lead to the formation of accurate meta-perceptions if people are actually seen by others as they see themselves. That is, meta-accuracy will be high if self-other agreement, or the similarity between a person's self-perceptions (Judy's self-views) and others' impressions of that person (Tom's view of Judy), is high. Arguably, such agreement occurs when a meta-perceiver's self-perceptions and their target's impressions are based on the meta-perceiver's "actual" personality via relevant, available, detected, and utilized cues. Put another way, if Judy (the meta-perceiver) and Tom (the target) use the same information about Judy and interpret that information in similar ways when forming an impression of Judy, Judy's self-views should align with Tom's view of her, which would make self-views one of the best cues for Judy to use when forming a meta-perception of Tom. Indeed, self-other agreement is higher for close others and observable traits (e.g., talkative) than new acquaintances and socially desirable traits (e.g., kind; John & Robins, 1993; Vazire & Carlson, 2010), and meta-accuracy follows the same pattern (Carlson & Kenny, 2012). Overall then, self-perceptions are likely the primary cue people utilize in the formation of meta-perceptions and are a relevant cue of others' impressions when self-other agreement is high.

Of course, self-other agreement is not perfect, and relying entirely on self-perceptions can be problematic. In general, people tend to overestimate how transparent they are to others, or the extent to which others can detect their internal states including thoughts, feelings, and intentions (Cameron & Vorauer, 2008; Gilovich, Savitsky, & Medvec, 1998; Kaplan, Santuzzi, & Ruscher, 2009; Kenny & DePaulo, 1993). In terms of the RAM, this means that people utilize self-perceptions incorrectly because they weight them too heavily (i.e., people rely too much on this information) and consequently often miss subtle ways others see them differently from how they see themselves. The other way in which self-perceptions can be a problematic cue is when self-other agreement is low, such as with new acquaintances (Connelly & Ones, 2010; Kurtz & Sherker, 2003) or when judging socially desirable traits (e.g., intelligence) or internal, unobservable traits (e.g., well-being; Oltmanns & Turkheimer, 2009; Vazire, 2010; see chapter 10 by Bollich-Ziegler in this handbook). In the context of the RAM, the use of self-perceptions when self-other agreement is low hinders the relevance stage of the RAM and leads to inaccurate meta-perceptions. In sum, assuming that others share one's self-perceptions can foster meta-accuracy to some degree, but this cue hinders accuracy when people rely too much on self-views or when self-other agreement is low.

While people rely primarily on their self-perceptions, they can and do use other cues in the formation of their meta-perceptions. For example, people realize that they make different impressions on others across social contexts, suggesting that people might be aware that they behave differently in different situations or that they are experienced differently across contexts (Carlson & Furr, 2009). Such awareness requires using information beyond a global self-view and suggests that people realize self-perceptions are not the only relevant cue and are capable of utilizing their self-perceptions along with other cues. The most powerful evidence that people use additional sources of information beyond self-views to achieve meta-accuracy comes from studies that suggest that people are able to detect how others perceive them with some degree of accuracy when controlling for their global self-perceptions, context-specific self-perceptions, and self-observations of behavior (Carlson, Vazire, & Furr, 2011; Gallrein et al., 2013, 2016; Hu, Kaplan, Wei, & Vega, 2014; Oltmanns & Turkheimer, 2009). The ability to understand how others might not share one's self-view is called *meta-insight* and has been observed for typical personality traits such as the Big Five (Carlson et al., 2011; Gallrein et al., 2013, 2016), atypical personality traits such as personality pathology (Maples-Keller, & Miller, 2018; Oltmanns et al., 2005; Yalch & Hopwood, 2016), and workplace perceptions (e.g., performance ratings; Hu et al., 2014), as well as across social contexts ranging from online social networks to close relationships (Stopfer et al., 2014). Overall, these findings suggest that people can and do successfully use cues unrelated to the self to form meta-perceptions.

Self-Observations of Behavior: We Think Our Behavior Drives the Impressions People Make of Us

While self-perceptions of personality are one type of cue people can use to achieve meta-accuracy, another possible cue is the meta-perceiver's own behavior (i.e., self-observation theory; Kenny & DePaulo, 1993). That is, when Judy considers how Tom sees her, she can look to her own behavior to infer what he might think. Self-observation of be-

havior as a cue might be especially useful because people base personality judgments on behavior (e.g., Tom bases his impression of Judy's kindness on her generous behavior) and people tend to agree about which behaviors reflect specific traits (e.g., both Tom and Judy agree that generosity demonstrates kindness; Funder & Dobroth, 1987; Funder & Sneed, 1993). Thus, if meta-perceivers (Judy) base their meta-perceptions on the same source of information used by targets (Tom), they are likely to be accurate. Indeed, there is evidence that, when it is available to them, people can use observations of their own behavior to form accurate meta-perceptions (Albright, Forest, & Reiseter, 2001; Albright & Malloy, 1999). In one study, participants were able to accurately detect how they were perceived in an interaction in which they were instructed to act overly optimistic or pessimistic (Albright et al., 2001). Acting increased the salience of participants' own behaviors, which did not reflect their self-views, suggesting that participants were able to achieve meta-accuracy by using self-observations of their behavior rather than their self-perceptions. In another study, participants interacted in a group and then formed accurate meta-perceptions of their group members after observing their own behaviors in a videotape of the group interaction (Albright & Malloy, 1999). While this is evidence that people can successfully use self-observations of their behavior as a cue, this experimental work gave meta-perceivers access to their behavior in artificial ways (e.g., videotaped interactions; Albright & Malloy, 1999) or increased the salience of their behavior experimentally (e.g., via acting; Albright et al., 2001). In contrast, there is some evidence that focusing too much on one's own behavior in more naturalistic settings (e.g., during a conversation) can backfire such that people become less accurate about their behavior (Hall, Murphy, & Mast, 2007).

In naturalistic settings, there are obstacles at each of the stages of the RAM that hinder meta-perceivers' ability to access and use self-observations of behavior as a cue. At the relevance stage, the behavioral cues the meta-perceiver uses must be the same behavioral cues that the target uses. For example, when guessing how kind Tom (the target) thinks she is, Judy (the meta-perceiver) might assume that her quiet, reserved manner indicates that she is kind because she allowed Tom to speak without interruptions, but for Tom, like for most people, quietness is not a cue for kindness (Kenny, 2004). At the availability stage, meta-perceivers have limited access to their own behavior because some behaviors are simply not visible to the self, such as facial expressions or nonverbal behavior (Barr & Kleck, 1995; Gilovich et al., 1998). Even when meta-perceivers' own relevant behaviors are available to them, there are obstacles to the successful detection and utilization of those behavioral cues. At the detection stage, people tend to focus on, and hence, remember, their internal thoughts more than their external behavior, while the people they are interacting with are more likely to recall the opposite (Chambers et al., 2008). Thus, after meeting Tom, Judy might recall her kind thoughts or feelings toward Tom but fail to recall that she said unkind things during the interaction (e.g., gossiped about a coworker), whereas Tom will primarily use what Judy said to form his impression of her. Also at the detection and utilization stages, people perceive extreme behaviors as being especially diagnostic of an individual's behavior (Skowronski & Carlston, 1987, 1989), while the extreme individual has generally habituated to their own extreme and frequent behaviors (Leising, Rehbein, & Sporberg, 2006). As such, Judy likely fails to notice the behaviors that influenced Tom's impression of her the most (e.g., Judy fails to realize that she gossips a lot and is experienced as especially unkind). Additionally, people's desire to see themselves positively (i.e., self-enhancement motivation; Gosling et al., 1998), their desire to be seen as they see themselves (i.e., self-verification motivation; Swann, 1983), and the rejection of negative self-attributes (i.e., denial; Paulhus & Reid, 1991) might also obstruct people's meta-accuracy at the detection and utilization stages of the RAM. For example, Judy thinks that she is a kind person and wants others to also think that she is a kind person, which may result in her failing to see her gossiping behavior as a sign of unkindness. Thus, while their own behaviors are an additional cue that meta-perceivers can use to form meta-perceptions, self-observation of behavior might not always be available to meta-perceivers and, when it is, it might not always lead to meta-accuracy.

Feedback and Hearsay: We Think Others Provide Cues About What They Really Think of Us

Another source of information meta-perceivers might use is feedback from the target, including direct and nonverbal feedback (Kenny & DePaulo, 1993). For example, Tom might explicitly tell Judy, or subtly imply what he thinks about Judy. According to the RAM, in order for feedback to lead to meta-accuracy, the target must provide honest, relevant feedback (e.g., Tom says that he thinks Judy is kind), the feedback must be available to the meta-perceiver (e.g., Tom directly tells Judy she is kind), the meta-perceiver must detect the feedback (e.g., Judy hears Tom when he tells her she is kind), and the meta-perceiver must correctly utilize that feedback (e.g., Judy assumes that Tom's comment means that he thinks she is kind). Some work has demonstrated that people do adjust their meta-perceptions in response to direct verbal feedback (Langer & Wurf, 1999). However, adjusting meta-perceptions in response to feedback might not always foster accuracy. For example, when individuals focus on indirect feedback such as others' reactions to them, they actually demonstrate lower meta-accuracy (Kaplan et al., 2009).

Indeed, there are several obstacles that impede the success of feedback as a cue at each stage of the RAM. For instance, at the relevance stage, people are often reluctant to provide honest feedback to others, particularly when that feedback is negative (Herbert & Vorauer, 2003). In fact, people often provide misleading or ambiguous feedback, conveying a more positive evaluation than their true impression of others (Swann, Stein-Seroussi, & McNulty, 1992). Thus, targets' unwillingness to provide meta-perceivers with honest feedback and their tendency to overstate positive reactions hinders meta-accuracy by obstructing the availability and relevance stages of the RAM, respectively. Even in the presence of relevant, available feedback, there may be attentional and motivational barriers to the successful detection and utilization of feedback by meta-perceivers, respectively. With respect to detection, social interactions are laden with attentional demands and people are often too distracted to attend to all the available cues (Gilbert & Osborne, 1989; Gilovich, Kruger, & Medvec, 2002; Lieberman & Rosenthal, 2001). Thus, subtle, nonverbal cues might be especially hard to detect (e.g., Judy might miss how Tom frowns when she gossips). However, one study suggests that people might even fail to detect or utilize direct feedback in the formation of their meta-perceptions, specifically when people share exactly what they think of each other (Shechtman & Kenny, 1994). Why would people be wrong in the face of direct feedback? Arguably, the problem lies at the utilization stage of the RAM. Self-enhancement motives, or the desire to protect one's self-esteem, and self-verification motives, or the desire to confirm one's self-views, may prevent meta-perceivers from correctly utilizing or interpreting feedback (Leary, 2007; Kwang &

Swann, 2010). For example, people often dismiss overly positive or negative feedback that is inconsistent with their self-views (Sargeant et al., 2006). People also tend to engage in feedback-seeking behaviors that either enhance or confirm their self-perceptions (Kwang & Swann, 2010). In sum, feedback is a cue people might try to use when forming meta-perceptions, but there are many obstacles to achieving meta-accuracy with feedback.

Aside from feedback from the target themselves, meta-perceivers may have insight into how a target perceives them based on how other people talk about the meta-perceiver. There is some evidence to suggest that people form impressions of others based on hearsay, or information obtained through a mutual acquaintance, and that these impressions correspond closely to the impressions held by the mutual acquaintance (Costello & Srivastava, 2017). For example, suppose Tom and Judy have never met, but they have a mutual acquaintance, Tara. Tara wants to introduce the pair at a party and tells Tom all about Judy's generous behavior beforehand. Judy knows that Tara likely shared information about her to Tom and thus, Judy assumes that when they meet, Tom will think she is a nice person because Tara seems to think that Judy is a nice person. Of course, it is also possible that Tara tells Judy exactly what she said about her to Tom. Assuming hearsay influences the impressions people form, hearsay can influence meta-accuracy at each stage of the RAM. First, how accurate the meta-perceiver's meta-perceptions are of the mutual acquaintance influences the relevance stage of the RAM such that the more aware the meta-perceiver (Judy) is of how the mutual acquaintance (Tara) perceives them (Judy), the more relevant hearsay is as a cue of the target's (Tom's) impression of the meta-perceiver (Judy). Second, if the mutual acquaintance (Tara) does not share their opinion of the meta-perceiver (Judy) with the target (Tom), then hearsay will not be an available cue to the meta-perceiver (Judy). Third, if the meta-perceiver (Judy) is unaware that the mutual acquaintance (Tara) told the target (Tom) about them (Judy), then the meta-perceiver (Judy) will have failed to detected hearsay as a cue and the meta-perceiver (Judy) will be less accurate about the target's (Tom's) impression. Fourth, the extent to which the meta-perceiver (Judy) correctly weighs the effect hearsay has on the target's (Tom's) impression of them relative to the impression they (Judy) make on the target (Tom) when they meet in person affects meta-accuracy at the utilization stage. In sum, while it may influence meta-accuracy, a meta-perceiver may not always share a mutual acquaintance with the target and, thus, hearsay is not always an available cue.

Normative Knowledge: We Think Others See Us as Being Average

One source of information that is readily available to meta-perceivers is normative knowledge, or information about what the typical person is like (Human & Biesanz, 2011; see chapter 15 by Rogers in this handbook). Normative knowledge reflects the fact that most people are, for example, more kind than cruel; thus, using this understanding of the normative person tends to boost accuracy when judging others (Biesanz, West, & Millevoi, 2007). As an example, before ever meeting Judy, if Tom were asked to rate Judy with no information about her, he would likely demonstrate above-chance accuracy about Judy because his judgments would be based somewhat on the average person. The same phenomenon would likely be observed in the context of meta-accuracy. If Judy were to guess how Tom sees her without ever meeting him, she might demonstrate above-chance meta-accuracy because she used normative knowledge to guess Tom's impression and Tom used this information too when rating her personality. Notably, normative knowledge can be indexed when meta-accuracy is measured using the profile-based approach (i.e., when meta-accuracy is the correlation between a meta-perceiver's meta-perceptions and targets' actual impressions of the meta-perceiver across several traits). Thus, in terms of the RAM, the use of normative knowledge by meta-perceivers when forming meta-perceptions influences the relevance stage because targets tend to use similar information when forming actual impressions. Indeed, recent work suggests that meta-perceivers use normative knowledge when guessing how targets view them, and this source of information tends to boost meta-accuracy (Carlson, 2016a, 2016b; Carlson et al., 2010).

Interestingly, the average person's personality is typically quite positive, suggesting that what is normative is good (Wood & Furr, 2016). Specifically, researchers have found that the normative profile, which is the average impression made by hundreds or thousands of people, is strongly correlated with a profile of the same traits rated for social desirability (Borkenau & Zaltauskas, 2009; Furr, 2008; Wood & Furr, 2016). Put another way, the pattern of traits that belong to average individuals tends to reflect a socially desirable personality. The same effect has been observed with meta-perceptions, such that

ERIKA N. CARLSON AND NORHAN ELSAADAWY

people who tend to use normative knowledge tend to assume they are seen in especially positive ways (Carlson 2016a, 2016b; Carlson & Oltmanns, 2018). For this reason, normative knowledge influences the relevance stage of the RAM in another way, such that relying on normative knowledge may enhance meta-accuracy in contexts where meta-perceivers are perceived in positive ways, and it may reduce meta-accuracy in contexts where meta-perceivers are perceived negatively. For example, assuming others see the best in us likely fosters meta-accuracy for close others (e.g., romantic partners and close friends) who actually do see us in positive ways (Leising, Erbs & Fritz, 2010). In contrast, using normative knowledge might backfire when guessing how people who dislike us see us (Zimmermann et al., 2018). Despite being highly correlated (e.g., $r = 0.87$; Carlson & Oltmanns, 2018), positivity and normative knowledge can have unique effects (Rogers & Biesanz, 2015). As such, normative knowledge likely reflects more than just a positivity bias, although most of normative knowledge appears to be positivity.

One important thing to note is that people can be accurate while also assuming that others perceive them positively (Human & Biesanz, 2011). Thus, positivity is statistically teased apart from accuracy when using the profile-based approach to index meta-accuracy. When researchers remove normative knowledge as a source of information, it is possible to test *distinctive meta-accuracy*, or whether people know how they are seen as unique from the average person (Carlson & Furr, 2013). Distinctive meta-accuracy would reveal whether Judy knows what makes her distinctive in Tom's eyes. Given that people do achieve distinctive meta-accuracy in first impressions and among close others (Carlson, 2016a, 2016b; Carlson & Furr, 2013), people can and do use valid information beyond normative knowledge to achieve meta-accuracy.

Meta-Stereotypes: We Think Others See Us as Similar to Our In-Groups

Another type of cue that people rely on is meta-stereotypes, or beliefs about the stereotypes or expectations that out-group members hold of their in-group (Malloy & Janowski, 1992; Saroglou, Yzerbyt, & Kaschten, 2011; Vorauer, Main, & O'Connell, 1998). When forming judgments of others, people place individuals in categories to reduce cognitive effort and speed up the impression-formation process using easily accessible information about that group, including stereotypes and

prejudices, to do so (Ashmore & Del Boca, 1981). Thus, meta-perceivers might use meta-stereotypes because they realize that others use stereotypes to judge them or they might use meta-stereotypes to speed up the meta-perception process. A growing body of work suggests that meta-stereotypes can and do influence meta-perceptions. For example, White Canadians expect to be perceived as arrogant and prejudiced by Aboriginal Canadians (Vorauer et al., 1998), and women expect to be perceived as low in leadership traits by men (Malloy & Janowski, 1992). When used to form meta-perceptions, these meta-stereotypes can either enhance or hinder meta-accuracy.

Specifically, meta-stereotypes influence meta-accuracy at the relevance and utilization stages of the RAM. At the relevance stage, meta-stereotypes can lead to meta-accuracy when targets rely on the same stereotypes to form impressions of the meta-perceiver. For instance, as women expect, men do perceive them as being low in leadership (Malloy & Janowski, 1992) and, as it is often assumed, people do perceive members of their out-group more negatively than they perceive their in-group (Hewstone, Rubin, & Willis, 2002). Thus, if Judy used the meta-stereotype regarding how men perceive women's leadership abilities and assumed that Tom saw her as low in leadership, it is likely that the meta-stereotype would be relevant and that she would be accurate. However, people do not always rely on stereotypes or category membership when forming impressions of others and can form individuated impressions that are driven by others' particular attributes (Neuberg & Fiske, 1987). For instance, when there are available cues that are inconsistent with the visible social category or when there is task-oriented outcome dependency (e.g., when working together toward a common goal), people are more motivated to form an accurate impression and pay greater attention to cues regarding others' attributes rather than stereotypes (Neuberg & Fiske, 1987). Thus, using a meta-stereotype or giving a meta-stereotype a lot of weight at the utilization stage when forming a meta-perception would lead Judy astray if Tom was motivated to form an accurate impression of her (Miller & Malloy, 2003).

What Factors Influence Meta-Accuracy?

As we have discussed, there are many cues that people use in the formation of meta-perceptions, including global self-perceptions, self-observations of behavior, direct and indirect feedback from others, hearsay, normative knowledge, and meta-stereotypes.

The extent to which these cues are relevant, available, detected, and utilized determines whether or not they lead to meta-accuracy. However, there are several factors that can influence the degree to which these cues foster accuracy at each stage of the RAM. According to Funder (1995), during the formation of a personality judgment (e.g., when Tom judges Judy's personality), four factors can affect the accuracy of the personality judgment: (1) the information one has (i.e., higher quality or quantity of cues), (2) the trait being judged (e.g., extraversion vs. neuroticism), (3) the target of the judgment (Judy vs. Joe), and (4) the judge (Tom vs. Tim). Each of these factors has been shown to influence the degree to which personality judgments are accurate (see Section II in this handbook). Higher quality and quantity of information improves accuracy (e.g., judges of personality who know more personal things about a target or have been acquainted with a target for longer are more accurate; Biesanz et al., 2007; Letzring, Wells, & Funder, 2006), observable traits (e.g., extraversion) are easier to judge than internal traits (e.g., neuroticism; John & Robins, 1993), some targets are easier to judge than others (e.g., people pay more attention to attractive targets; Langlois et al., 2000), and some judges of personality are more accurate than others (e.g., some judges of personality are better than others at eliciting cues from targets; Funder, 2012; Letzring, 2008; Ruben & Hall, 2016). We predict that these four types of moderators might also affect when people are meta-accurate. In what follows, we discuss each of the four moderators: information, traits, targets, and judges.

Information

Information refers to the quality and quantity of cues and it moderates the relevance and availability stages of the RAM. Judges are more accurate when there are higher quality cues (i.e., more relevant cues) or a greater quantity of cues (i.e., more available cues) about a target's impression of them. In the context of meta-accuracy, these cues include self-perceptions, self-observation of behavior, feedback, hearsay, normative knowledge, and meta-stereotypes. Situations and contextual factors likely influence the quality and quantity of cues in ways that make the target's impressions more or less relevant and available to the meta-perceiver (Fleeson, 2001, 2004).

In terms of quality, some contexts might encourage self-disclosure, which would allow meta-perceivers to convey their self-views to targets (e.g.,

Judy might tell Tom more about herself in a dating context than if they met in class) and would increase the chances that meta-perceivers' self-perceptions are a relevant cue for meta-perception. This is also observed among close others because, over time, targets (Tom) tend to eventually see meta-perceivers (Judy) as they see themselves, increasing the relevance of self-perceptions as a cue and allowing meta-perceivers (Judy) to be more meta-accurate with close others than with new acquaintances (Carlson & Kenny, 2012; Kenny & DePaulo, 1993). Likewise, some contexts might heighten observation of behavior by both the self and others (e.g., a job interview) or increase the degree to which others provide honest, direct feedback (e.g., an academic setting), which increases the relevance of behavior and feedback as a cue, respectively, and may thus promote meta-accuracy.

In terms of quantity, rather than increasing the quality, or relevance, of a given cue, simply increasing the availability of the relevant cues above might also foster meta-accuracy. For example, extended or numerous interactions between close others allow meta-perceivers to observe more of their own behavior with or feedback from a specific target, which might be why people are able to detect both which close others see them as higher or lower on Big Five traits (i.e., differential meta-accuracy; Carlson & Furr, 2009) and how they are seen independently of how they see themselves (i.e., meta-insight; Carlson et al., 2011). That is, as Judy spends more time with Tom, the availability of her own behavior and Tom's feedback increases, which provides her with more cues about what Tom thinks of her and promotes her meta-accuracy. In sum, most people will be more meta-accurate when they have more relevant cues than when they have fewer.

Traits

The second moderator is traits, which refers to the idea that some trait impressions are more available to the meta-perceiver, are easier to detect, or perhaps easier to utilize. Indeed, there is some evidence that meta-accuracy is higher for more observable traits, such as extraversion, than less visible traits, such as well-being (Carlson & Kenny, 2012), likely because observable traits are more available to both the meta-perceiver and the target. That is, it is easier for Judy to know what Tom thinks of her on traits where they can both use the same cues (e.g., both Judy and Tom can observe how talkative Judy is) versus when one person has more information than the other (e.g., Judy knows how anxious she is but

Tom cannot see her anxiety). Notably, people also know how they are seen differently from how they see themselves on observable traits (Carlson & Kenny, 2012), suggesting, for example, that even if Judy sees herself as introverted but acts extraverted with Tom, she will realize that Tom sees her as extraverted. While it is easier for meta-perceivers to be meta-accurate about observable traits, it might be more difficult for meta-perceivers to be accurate about how others see them on socially desirable traits, such as intelligence or physical attractiveness, because ego-protective biases (i.e., biases that function to protect one's self-esteem) impede the successful detection and utilization of available cues relevant to these traits (Vazire, 2010). This can happen for two reasons. First, people are motivated to think that they possess socially desirable traits, which might hinder meta-accuracy if they base their meta-perceptions on self-views. In contrast, others tend to be more accurate than the self about the self's socially desirable traits, arguably because they are not influenced by ego-protective processes (Carlson, Vazire, & Oltmanns, 2013; Vazire, 2010). Second, people might be motivated to interpret their behavior or feedback from others about socially desirable traits in positive ways because it feels good to assume that others see the best in us (Carlson, 2016b). Overall then, meta-perceivers are generally more meta-accurate about the impressions they make on observable and neutral traits than on traits that are more internal or socially desirable (Carlson & Kenny, 2012)[2].

Targets

The third moderator is the target, which refers to the idea that some targets are easier or more difficult to read than others. For example, when forming judgments of others (e.g., when Tom judges Judy's personality), there is evidence that some targets are more expressive, transparent, and easy to read (e.g., Judy might be easy to read while Jill is not; Human & Biesanz, 2013). Targets whose personalities are easily judged are high in expressive accuracy (Human & Biesanz, 2011), which is an individual difference that is stable across time (Colvin, 1993) and social contexts (Human, Rogers, & Biesanz, under review, 2017). Extraverts, women, physically attractive individuals, and well-adjusted individuals tend to be especially adept at displaying nonverbal cues and are thus high in expressive accuracy (Human & Biesanz, 2013). We predict that a similar pattern might hold for meta-accuracy such that when Judy thinks about the impression she makes

across targets, one target (Tom) might be very easy to read but another target (Tim) might be especially hard to read. We predict that one likely target moderator of meta-accuracy is expressivity; specifically, individuals who are more expressive make more relevant cues available to meta-perceivers. For example, extraverts and high-status individuals are more open and forthcoming with their emotions and opinions (Anderson & Berdahl, 2002; Riggio & Riggio, 2002), which may make their impressions of others more known and thus increase the availability of relevant cues to meta-perceivers. If Tom is a good target, he is likely to provide higher quality cues (i.e., he tells Judy what he thinks of her) and more cues in general. In addition to making more relevant cues available to meta-perceivers, good targets may also moderate the detection of cues. For instance, people pay more attention to physically attractive (Langlois et al., 2000) and high-status (Dalmaso et al., 2011; Ratcliff et al., 2011) individuals, which can facilitate successful cue detection and lead to meta-accuracy (Lorenzo, Biesanz, & Human, 2010). That is, Judy might pay more attention and notice cues from Tom if he is attractive, but might miss the same quality or quantity of cues given off by Tim if he is not attractive. Overall then, targets likely influence the quality and quantity of cues available to meta-perceivers, and as such, also influence the relevance, availability, and detection stages of the RAM.

Judges

Lastly, the fourth moderator is the judge, which refers to the idea that some judges of meta-perception, or meta-perceivers, are more accurate than others (e.g., Judy might be more meta-accurate than Jill). A meta-perceiver may influence the relevance, availability, detection, or utilization stages of the RAM. In terms of relevance, the good meta-perceiver might be someone who is seen by others as they see themselves (i.e., high self-other agreement; Carlson & Kenny, 2012). For example, if Judy is a good meta-perceiver, she might simply behave in ways that are consistent with her self-views, which would lead Tom, Tim, and other targets to perceive her as she perceives herself. In line with this idea, authentic individuals and individuals with coherent personalities provide more relevant cues about themselves (Human & Biesanz, 2013), which boosts self-other agreement. As such, authentic meta-perceivers and meta-perceivers with coherent personalities should have higher meta-accuracy because they increase the relevance of their self-perceptions as a cue. In contrast, people with poor self-knowledge, or people who hold inaccurate self-views, are likely bad meta-perceivers. Indeed, people with more personality disorder symptoms, which are disorders defined by poor self-knowledge and low self-other agreement, generally have less insight into the impressions they make on even their close others (Carlson & Oltmanns, 2015; Carlson, Wright, & Imam, 2017). Poor self-knowledge gives rise to low self-other agreement and, as a result, self-perceptions would no longer be a relevant cue of the target's impression of the meta-perceiver.

Good meta-perceivers might also be more aware of their behavior. Individuals who are high self-monitors are especially adept at managing the impressions that others have of them (Turnley & Bolino, 2001), suggesting that high self-monitors are well aware of their behaviors and the impressions they make on others. Further, there is evidence that the relationship between someone's self-reported personality traits and others' impressions of them is attenuated by high self-monitoring (Barrick, Parks, & Mount, 2005). This implies that behavior is a more relevant cue than self-perceptions in the context of high self-monitoring. As such, high self-monitors might be good meta-perceivers because they are aware of their behavior and because self-observations of their behavior are an especially relevant cue to others' impressions of them.

Alternatively, good meta-perceivers might elicit more honest feedback from targets, increasing the relevance and availability of feedback as a cue. Indeed, good judges of others' personalities are better at eliciting cues (Letzring, 2008). For example, a good judge of personality is socially skilled and agreeable, making them able to draw people's true selves out such that everyone who interacts with the target in the presence of a good judge of personality is more accurate (Letzring, 2008). In the context of meta-accuracy, a good meta-perceiver might foster a target's authenticity by reacting in less defensive ways to feedback, which in turn may lead the target to convey their true opinions of the meta-perceiver (Carlson, 2013). Further, there is evidence that people who are more meta-accurate also tend to be seen by others as more interpersonally adjusted (i.e., socially skilled; Carlson, 2016a), a finding that might be explained by the fact that good meta-perceivers tend to react to feedback in appropriate ways.

Another way a good meta-perceiver might achieve meta-accuracy is by observing more cues (i.e., better detection) or interpreting cues in less

ego-protective ways (i.e., better utilization; Funder, 1995) than other meta-perceivers. For example, individuals with high working memory capacity are more adept at decoding cues about others' impressions (Lieberman & Rosenthal, 2001), while intelligent individuals are more proficient at interpreting cues (Christiansen et al., 2005), suggesting that meta-perceivers with higher cognitive abilities might be good meta-perceivers. Theoretically, individuals high in mindfulness might also be good meta-perceivers, as increased awareness of and nonjudgmental openness to their social environment may lead to more successful detection and utilization of social cues (Carlson, 2013). In contrast, certain mood disorders can distort detection and utilization such that some meta-perceivers may notice too many negative cues or process cues in overly negative ways. For example, individuals with social anxiety (Christensen, Stein, & Means-Christensen, 2003), Post Traumatic Stress Disorder (PTSD; Christensen, Cohan, & Stein, 2004), and depression (Moritz & Roberts, 2018) tend to assume others see then in more negative ways than they really do, arguably because they fail to detect positive cues or give too much weight to negative self-views.

Thus, there are certain individual differences that meta-perceivers possess that may influence the relevance, availability, detection, and utilization of cues. Since meta-perceivers can potentially moderate meta-accuracy at any of the stages of the RAM, there are many ways that some meta-perceivers might be better than others at knowing the impressions they make.

Interactions Between the Moderators of Meta-Accuracy

The four potential moderators of meta-accuracy suggest that meta-accuracy may be the product of the judge, the target, or contextual factors such as the quantity and quality of cues available or the type of trait being judged, although it is likely that each affects meta-accuracy to different degrees. Further, the RAM posits that, in addition to the four main moderators of meta-accuracy, there might be interactions between any two of the four moderators (Funder, 1995). Next, we focus on possible interactions that involve the judge in the context of meta-accuracy (i.e., the meta-perceiver). That is, while it is possible that some meta-perceivers are more meta-accurate than others in general, we consider the possibility that there are also some meta-perceivers that are more accurate with certain

ERIKA N. CARLSON AND NORHAN ELSAADAWY

levels of information (judge × information), for certain traits (judge × trait), or with certain targets (judge × target).

Judge × Information

The judge by information interaction suggests that some meta-perceivers may be especially accurate with certain levels of information compared to others. For example, narcissists are perceived more in line with their positive self-perceptions by new acquaintances they meet in social situations compared to close others, which may be why narcissists exhibit higher meta-accuracy for some traits in a first impression context versus a close-other context (Carlson, Vazire, & Oltmanns, 2011; Paulhus, 1998). In other words, narcissists might be good meta-perceivers when they have spent less time with others and the quantity of information is low. In contrast, shy or withdrawn individuals might be perceived more in line with how they perceive themselves by close others than by new acquaintances, making it easier for them to be meta-accurate in a close-other context in which the quantity and quality of information is high compared to a first-impression context in which the quantity and quality of information is low. Overall then, some meta-perceivers may be particularly meta-accurate when informational quality and quantity is higher or lower.

Judge × Trait

Another potential interaction between moderators is the judge by trait interaction, which suggests that some meta-perceivers may be especially accurate when judging some traits compared to others. This may be the result of people's experience with or interest in specific traits. For example, narcissists are particularly concerned with possessing agentic traits (e.g., extraversion, openness) and much less concerned with being seen in communal ways (e.g., agreeable, conscientious; Campbell, Rudich, & Sedikides, 2002). As a result, narcissists may be more motivated to understand how they are seen on agentic traits, which may make them better at detecting and utilizing cues relevant to those traits (Carlson et al., 2011). Similarly, some people might identify with one trait more than others such that, for them, it is very important that others see them as they see themselves on that trait. For example, Judy might define her identity by her intellectual abilities and, as such, she might want Tom to see her as highly intellectual. Thus, Judy might be especially motivated to convey her intellectual attributes and she might be especially attuned to whether or not her efforts were successful.

Another possibility is that meta-perceivers are especially good at knowing the impressions they make on their *defining traits*, or traits that are particularly salient due to their extremity. For example, most people are less meta-accurate about evaluative traits such as agreeableness or narcissism, but perhaps narcissists are meta-accurate about their low agreeableness and arrogant reputation (Carlson et al., 2011) because their tendencies to criticize and derogate others, brag excessively, and overexaggerate their abilities are relevant cues that can be easily perceived by the people rating them as well as by the narcissist. Likewise, socially anxious individuals might be aware that others see them as anxious (Norton & Hope, 2001) because there are several behavioral cues relevant to their anxiety that are visible to everyone. Overall then, some meta-perceivers provide more relevant and available cues regarding their defining traits, which may help foster their meta-accuracy regarding those traits.

Judge × Target

The third possible moderator interaction is the judge by target interaction, which implies that some judges are more accurate at judging certain targets over others. There is evidence that some judges of personality are more accurate than others at judging people's personalities, but that this difference only arises in the presence of certain targets (Rogers & Biesanz, 2018). Similarly, it is possible that the unique relationship between a specific meta-perceiver and target is what drives meta-accuracy. This idea is supported by the fact that there are certain relationship-specific factors that influence meta-accuracy. For instance, meta-accuracy is higher when people like each other because mutual liking causes both the meta-perceiver and the target to be more open and engage in greater self-disclosure (Levesque, 1997; Ohtsubo et al., 2009), which increases the availability of relevant cues. At the same time, meta-perceivers and targets may be more motivated to make a good impression and be attentive to cues when interacting with partners who like them (Ohtsubo et al., 2009), facilitating meta-accuracy at the detection stage of the RAM. Indeed, people motivated to make a good impression tend to be seen as they see themselves (Human & Biesanz, 2011), which in turn may make it easier for them to form accurate meta-perceptions.

There are of course factors in a meta-perceiver–target relationship that may hinder meta-accuracy, such as a discrepancy in social status (Miller & Malloy, 2003; Santuzzi, 2007). While people tend to pay more attention to high-status individuals (Dalmaso et al., 2011; Ratcliff et al., 2011), high-status individuals pay less attention to lower-status individuals (Goodwin, Gubin, Fiske, & Yzerbyt, 2000), increasing the likelihood that, as meta-perceivers, high-status individuals will miss relevant and available cues. Further, people in different positions of power tend to differentially weigh the importance of certain cues or behaviors (e.g., supervisors place less importance than colleagues on the social behaviors of an employee that support the work environment), which may explain why employees exhibit low meta-accuracy regarding their supervisors' ratings of their work performance (Hu et al., 2014). Together, these findings indicate that there are several characteristics of a meta-perceiver–target relationship that might moderate meta-accuracy.

In sum, there is reason to believe that rather than meta-perceivers influencing meta-accuracy in the same way across different contexts, traits, or targets, meta-perceivers may differentially influence meta-accuracy depending on the characteristics of the other moderators. Thus, interactions between the moderators suggest that rather than being driven completely by cues, traits, judges (i.e., meta-perceivers), or targets, meta-accuracy may only be possible under limited conditions.

Future Directions

The association between meta-accuracy and interpersonal outcomes, such as liking and relationship quality (Carlson, 2016b; Carlson & Oltmanns, 2018), suggests that meta-accuracy helps us successfully navigate our interactions with others and is thus an important phenomenon to study. Fortunately, as we have summarized in this chapter, there are several studies that demonstrate that people are generally aware of the impressions they make on a range of traits and across situations (e.g., Carlson & Furr, 2009, 2013; Malloy & Janowski, 1992). Further, studies have shown that people can achieve meta-accuracy regarding their overall reputation or the unique impression they make on another person (e.g., Carlson & Furr, 2009; Levesque, 1997). To form meta-perceptions, there are at least six cues that people can use: self-perceptions, self-observation of behavior, feedback from others, hearsay, normative knowledge, and meta-stereotypes. However, these cues do not always lead to meta-accuracy; there are factors that influence

whether these cues promote meta-accuracy at each stage of the RAM. Specifically, the amount and quality of information available, the trait being judged, the target, and the judge can all potentially influence the relevance, availability, detection, and utilization of cues. In sum, meta-accuracy is both a form of self-knowledge and social knowledge (Carlson & Kenny, 2012), as it relies on the successful detection and utilization of available cues relevant to both the self (e.g., self-views, self-observations of behavior) and others (e.g., feedback, normative knowledge).

Studying meta-accuracy through the lens of the RAM helps shed light on the questions that remain unanswered in the meta-accuracy literature. For example, there is evidence that some meta-perceivers are more or less meta-accurate than others when judging close others or when judging certain traits (Carlson & Furr, 2009); however, it is unclear whether the meta-perceivers who are accurate in one context or about one trait are also accurate in other contexts or about other traits. Based on the RAM, there are at least two possible predictions. On one hand, as suggested by the judge moderator, it is possible that the meta-perceivers who are accurate in one context, with one trait, or with one target, are accurate across all contexts, traits, and targets. This would suggest that there are good meta-perceivers and that meta-accuracy is a skill, or individual difference, that meta-perceivers carry with them. On the other hand, as suggested by the interactions between moderators, it is possible that there are meta-perceivers who are accurate in only one context, with only one type of trait, or with certain targets. This would suggest that meta-accuracy is not a skill that meta-perceivers carry with them, but rather a situation-specific ability that arises within a specific context (e.g., in social situations versus professional situations), for a specific trait (e.g., kind versus reliable), or with a specific target (e.g., for Tom but not Tim or Tammy). However, to our knowledge, no studies have explicitly tested whether meta-accuracy is a skill that meta-perceivers demonstrate consistently across contexts, traits, and targets.

Future work should directly examine whether the individuals who are accurate in one context, for one trait, or with one target are accurate in other contexts, for other traits, and with other targets. Such work would have important implications for both the empirical study and the practical application of meta-accuracy. If future work suggests that there are indeed meta-perceivers who are meta-accurate across contexts, traits, and targets, then perhaps meta-accuracy is primarily in the control of the meta-perceiver and there is a set of attributes that help a meta-perceiver achieve meta-accuracy. Identifying this set of attributes would lay the groundwork for clinicians who want to help clients improve their self-knowledge by narrowing down the attributes or skills clinicians should target. In contrast, if future work suggests that meta-accuracy is a context-specific ability, then perhaps the skills or attributes that help foster accuracy in one context are not necessarily useful in other contexts. This would mean that researchers and clinicians should focus on identifying and targeting the context-specific factors that enhance accuracy. In sum, testing whether meta-accuracy is a consistent skill or a context-specific ability is both theoretically and practically useful. Thus, it is our hope that future work will strive to explicitly test the nature and consistency of meta-accuracy.

Another important avenue for future research is the process underlying meta-accuracy. As we have outlined in this chapter, there are multiple cues that are used in the formation of meta-perceptions and factors that moderate whether or not these cues lead to meta-accuracy at each stage of the RAM. However, there have been no studies to test whether meta-perceivers who achieve meta-accuracy do so because they rely on certain cues or are particularly adept at a certain stage of the RAM. For example, meta-perceivers who achieve meta-accuracy do so because they are particularly good at observing their own behaviors or others reactions to them. Or, perhaps these meta-perceivers are particularly good at eliciting plenty of honest verbal and nonverbal feedback from others. To better understand the underlying process that gives rise to meta-accuracy, future research should attempt to experimentally break down the process into the stages of the RAM and compare meta-perceivers who achieve meta-accuracy to meta-perceivers who fail to do so at each stage. Moreover, future work should compare meta-perceivers who achieve meta-accuracy to meta-perceivers who fail to do so in contexts where only one type of cue is available. Such work would provide insight into how good meta-perceivers achieve meta-accuracy and which cues they use. Overall, this work would shed light on how people in general can improve their meta-accuracy. Given that meta-accuracy is associated with positive social outcomes, learning how to improve meta-accuracy would likely be in people's best interests.

References

Albright, L., Forest, C., & Reiseter, K. (2001). Acting, behaving, and the selfless basis of metaperception. *Journal of Personality and Social Psychology*, *81*, 910–921. doi:10.1037/0022-3514.81.5.910

Albright, L., & Malloy, T. E. (1999). Self-observation of social behavior and metaperception. *Journal of Personality and Social Psychology*, *77*, 726–734. doi:10.1037/0022-3514.77.4.726

Anderson, C., & Berdahl, J. L. (2002). The experience of power: Examining the effects of power on approach and inhibition tendencies. *Journal of Personality and Social Psychology*, *83*, 1362–1377. doi:10.1037//0022-3514.83.6.1362

Ashmore, R. D., & Del Boca, E. K. (1981). Conceptual approaches to stereotypes and stereotyping. In D. L. Hamilton (Ed.), *Cognitive processes in stereotyping and intergroup behavior* (pp. 1–35). Hillsdale, NJ: Erlbaum.

Barr, C. L., & Kleck, R. E. (1995). Self-other perception of the intensity of facial expressions of emotion: Do we know what we show? *Journal of Personality and Social Psychology*, *68*, 608–618. doi:10.1037/0022-3514.68.4.608

Barrick, M. R., Parks, L., & Mount, M. K. (2005). Self-monitoring as a moderator of the relationship between personality traits and performance. *Personnel Psychology*, *58*, 745–767. doi:10.1111/j.1744-6570.2005.00716.x

Biesanz, J. C., & Human, L. J. (2010). The cost of forming more accurate impressions: Accuracy-motivated perceivers see the personality of others more distinctively but less normatively than perceivers without an explicit goal. *Psychological Science*, *21*, 589–594. doi:10.1177/0956797610364121

Biesanz, J. C., West, S. G., & Millevoi, A. (2007). What do you learn about someone over time? The relationship between length of acquaintance and consensus and self-other agreement in judgments of personality. *Journal of Personality and Social Psychology*, *92*, 119–135. doi:10.1037/0022-3514.92.1.119

Borkenau, P., & Zaltauskas, K. (2009). Effects of self-enhancement on agreement on personality profiles. *European Journal of Personality*, *23*, 107–123. doi:10.1002/per.707

Cameron, J. J., & Vorauer, J. D. (2008). Feeling transparent: On metaperceptions and miscommunications. *Social and Personality Psychology Compass*, *2*, 1093–1108. doi:10.1111/j.1751-9004.2008.00096.x

Campbell, W. K., Rudich, E. A., & Sedikides, C. (2002). Narcissism, self-esteem, and the positivity of self-views: Two portraits of self-love. *Personality and Social Psychology Bulletin*, *28*, 358–368. doi:10.1177/0146167202286007

Carlson, E. N. (2013). Overcoming the barriers to self-knowledge: Mindfulness as a path to seeing yourself as you really are. *Perspectives on Psychological Science*, *8*, 173–186. doi:10.1177/1745691612462584

Carlson, E. N. (2016a). Do psychologically adjusted individuals know what other people really think about them? The link between psychological adjustment and meta-accuracy. *Social Psychological and Personality Science*, *7*, 717–725. doi:10.1177/1948550616646424

Carlson, E. N. (2016b). Meta-accuracy and relationship quality?: Weighing the costs and benefits of knowing what people really think about you, *Journal of Personality and Social Psychology*, *111*, 250–264.

Carlson, E. N., & Furr, R. M. (2009). Evidence of differential meta-accuracy: People understand the different impressions they make. *Psychological Science*, *20*, 1033–1039. doi:10.1111/j.1467-9280.2009.02409.x

Carlson, E. N., & Furr, R. M. (2013). Resolution of meta-accuracy: Should people trust their beliefs about how others see them? *Social Psychological and Personality Science, 4,* 419–426. doi:10.1177/1948550612461653

Carlson, E. N., Furr, R. M., & Vazire S. (2010). Do we know the first impressions we make? Evidence for idiographic meta-accuracy and calibration of first impressions. *Social Psychological and Personality Science, 1,* 94–98. doi:10.1177/1948550609356028

Carlson, E. N., & Kenny, D. A. (2012). Meta-accuracy: Do we know how others see us? In S. Vazire & T. D. Wilson (Eds.), *Handbook of self-knowledge* (pp. 242–257). New York: Guilford Press.

Carlson, E. N., & Oltmanns, T. F. (2015). The role of metaperception in personality disorders: Do people with personality problems know how others experience their personality? *Journal of Personality Disorders, 29,* 449–467. doi:10.1521/pedi.2015.29.4.449

Carlson, E. N., & Oltmanns, T. F. (2018). Is it adaptive for people with personality problems to know how their romantic partner perceives them? The effect of meta-accuracy on romantic relationship satisfaction. *Journal of Personality Disorders, 32,* 374–391. doi:10.1521/pedi.2018.32.3.374

Carlson, E. N., Vazire, S., & Furr, R. M. (2011). Meta-insight: Do people really know how others see them? *Journal of Personality and Social Psychology, 101,* 831–846. doi:10.1037/a0024297

Carlson, E. N., Vazire, S., & Oltmanns, T. F. (2011). You probably think this paper's about you: Narcissists' perceptions of their personality and reputation. *Journal of Personality and Social Psychology, 10,* 185–201. doi:10.1037/a0023781

Carlson, E. N., Vazire, S., & Oltmanns, T. F. (2013). Self-other knowledge asymmetries in personality pathology. *Journal of Personality, 81,* 155–170. doi:10.1111/j.1467-6494.2012.00794.x.

Carlson, E. N., Wright, A. G. C., & Imam, H. (2017). Blissfully blind or painfully aware? Exploring the beliefs people with interpersonal problems have about their reputation. *Journal of Personality, 85,* 757–768. doi:10.1111/jopy.12284

Chambers, J. R., Epley, N., Savitsky, K., & Windschitl, P. D. (2008). Knowing too much: Using private knowledge to predict how one is viewed by others. *Psychological Science, 19,* 542–548. doi:10.1111/j.1467-9280.2008.02121.x

Christensen, P. N., Cohan, S. L., & Stein, M. B. (2004). The relationship between interpersonal perception and post-traumatic stress disorder-related functional impairment: A social relations model analysis. *Cognitive Behaviour Therapy, 33,* 151–160. doi:10.1080/16506070410026417

Christensen, P. N., Stein, M. B., & Means-Christensen, A. (2003). Social anxiety and interpersonal perception: A social relations model analysis. *Behaviour Research and Therapy, 41,* 1355–1371. doi:10.1016/S0005-7967(03)00064-0

Christiansen, N. D., Wolcott-Burnam, S., Janovics, J. E., Burns, G. N., & Quirk, S. W. (2005). The good judge revisited: Individual differences in the accuracy of personality judgments. *Human Performance, 18,* 123–149.

Colvin, C. R. (1993). Childhood antecedents of young-adult judgability. *Journal of Personality, 61,* 611–635.

Connelly, B. S., & Ones, D. S. (2010). Another perspective on personality: Meta-analytic integration of observers' accuracy and predictive validity. *Psychological Bulletin, 136,* 1092–1122. doi:10.1037/a0021212

Cook, W. L., & Douglas, E. M. (1998). The looking-glass self in family context: A social relations analysis. *Journal of Family Psychology, 12,* 299–309. doi:10.1037/0893-3200.12.3.299

Costello, C. K., & Srivastava, S. (2017). *Perceiving through the Grapevine: Consensus and accuracy of hearsay reputations.* Poster presented at the 18th annual meeting of the Society for Personality and Social Psychology, San Antonio, TX.

Dalmaso, M., Pavan, G., Castelli, L., & Galfano, G. (2011). Social status gates social attention in humans. *Biology Letters, 8,* 450–452. doi:10.1098/rsbl.2011.0881

DePaulo, B. M., Kenny, D. A., Hoover, C. W, Webb, W., & Oliver, P. V. (1987). Accuracy of person perception: Do people know what kinds of impressions they convey? *Journal of Personality and Social Psychology, 52,* 303–315. doi:10.1037//0022-3514.52.2.303

Eisenkraft, N., Elfenbein, H. A., & Kopelman, S. (2017). We know who likes us, but not who competes against us: Dyadic meta-accuracy among work colleagues. *Psychological Science, 28,* 233–241. doi:10.1177/0956797616679440

Fleeson, W. (2001). Toward a structure- and process-integrated view of personality: Traits as density distributions of states. *Journal of Personality and Social Psychology, 80,* 1011–1027. doi:10.1037//0022-3514.80.6.1011

Fleeson W. (2004). Moving personality beyond the person-situation debate. *Current Directions in Psychological Science, 13,* 83–87.

Funder, D. C. (1995). On the accuracy of personality judgement: A realistic approach. *Psychological Review, 102,* 652–670.

Funder, D. C. (2012). Accurate personality judgment. *Current Directions in Psychological Science, 21,* 177–182. doi:10.1177/0963721412445309

Funder, D. C., & Dobroth, K. M. (1987). Differences between traits: Properties associated with interjudge agreement. *Journal of Personality and Social Psychology, 52,* 409–418. doi:10.1037/0022-3514.52.2.409

Funder, D. C., & Sneed, C. D. (1993). Behavioral manifestations of personality: An ecological approach to judgmental accuracy. *Journal of Personality and Social Psychology, 64,* 479–490. doi:10.1037/0022-3514.64.3.479

Furr, R. M. (2008). A framework for profile similarity: Integrating similarity, normativeness, and distinctiveness. *Journal of Personality, 76,* 1267–1316. doi:10.1111/j.1467-6494.2008.00521.x

Gallrein, A. M. B., Carlson, E. N., Holstein, M., & Leising, D. (2013). You spy with your little eye: People are "blind" to some of the ways in which they are consensually seen by others. *Journal of Research in Personality, 47,* 464–471. doi:10.1016/j.jrp.2013.04.001

Gallrein, A. M. B., Weßels, N. M., Carlson, E. N., & Leising, D. (2016). I still cannot see it—A replication of blind spots in self-perception. *Journal of Research in Personality, 60,* 1–7. doi:10.1016/j.jrp.2015.10.002

Gilbert, D. T., & Osborne, R. E. (1989). Thinking backward: Some curable and incurable consequences of cognitive busyness. *Journal of Personality and Social Psychology, 57,* 940–949. doi:10.1037/0022-3514.57.6.940

Gilovich, T., Savitsky, K., & Medvec, V. H. (1998). The illusion of transparency: Biased assessment of others' ability to read our emotional states. *Journal of Personality and Social Psychology, 75,* 332–346.

Gilovich, T., Kruger, J., & Medvec, V. H. (2002). The spotlight effect revisited: Overestimating the manifest variability of our actions and appearance. *Journal of Experimental Social Psychology, 38*, 93–99. doi:10.1006/jesp.2001.1490

Goodwin, S. A., Gubin, A., Fiske, S. T., & Yzerbyt, V. Y. (2000). Power can bias impression processes: Stereotyping subordinates by default and by design. *Group Processes and Intergroup Relations, 3*, 227–256. doi:10.1177/1368430200003003001

Gosling, S. D., John, O. P., Craik, K. H., & Robins, R.W. (1998). Do people know how they behave? Self-reported act frequencies compared with on-line coding by observers. *Journal of Personality and Social Psychology, 74*, 1337–1349.

Hall, J. A., Murphy, N. A., & Mast, M. S. (2007). Nonverbal self-accuracy in interpersonal interaction. *Personality and Social Psychology Bulletin, 33*, 1675–1685. doi:10.1177/0146167207307492

Herbert, B. G., & Vorauer, J. D. (2003). Seeing through the screen: Is evaluative feedback communicated more effectively in face-to-face or computer-mediated exchanges? *Computers in Human Behavior, 19*, 25–38.

Hewstone, M., Rubin, M., & Willis, H. (2002). Intergroup bias. *Annual Review of Psychology, 53*, 575–604. doi:10.1146/annurev.psych.53.100901.135109

Hu, X., Kaplan, S., Wei, F., & Vega, R. P. (2014). Employees' metaperceptions of supervisor ratings on job performance. *The Psychologist-Manager Journal, 17*, 30–48. doi:10.1037/mgr0000010

Human, L. J., & Biesanz, J. C. (2011). Through the looking glass clearly: Accuracy and assumed similarity in well-adjusted individuals' first impressions. *Journal of Personality and Social Psychology, 100*, 349–364. doi:10.1037/a0021850

Human, L. J., & Biesanz, J. C. (2013). Targeting the good target: An integrative review of the characteristics and consequences of being accurately perceived. *Personality and Social Psychology Review, 17*, 248–272. doi:10.1177/1088868313495593.

Human, L. J., Rogers, K. H., & Biesanz, J. C. (under review, 2017). *Is expressive accuracy a core individual difference? The cross-contextual consistency of being transparent.*

John, O. P., & Robins, R. W. (1993). Determinants of inter-judge agreement on personality traits: The Big Five domains, observability, evaluativeness, and the unique perspective of the self. *Journal of Personality, 61*, 521–551.

John, O. P., & Srivastava, S. (1999). The Big Five taxonomy: History, measurement, and theoretical perspectives. In L. A. Pervin & O. P. John (Eds), *Handbook of personality: Theory and research* (pp. 102–138). New York: Guilford.

Kaplan, S. A., Santuzzi, A., & Ruscher, J. (2009). Elaborative metaperceptions in outcome-dependent situations: The diluted relationship between default self-perceptions and meta-perceptions. *Social Cognition, 27*, 601–614.

Kenny, D. A. (1994). *Interpersonal perception: A social relations analysis.* New York: Guilford.

Kenny, D. A. (2004). PERSON: A general model for understanding interpersonal perception, *Personality and Social Psychology Review, 8*, 265–280. doi:10.1207/s15327957pspr0803_3

Kenny, D. A., & DePaulo, B. M. (1993). Do people know how others view them? An empirical and theoretical account. *Psychological Bulletin, 114*, 145–161. doi:10.1037/0033-2909.114.1.145

Kurtz, J. E., & Sherker, J. L. (2003). Relationship quality, trait similarity, and self–other agreement on personality ratings in college roommates. *Journal of Personality, 71*, 21–48. doi:10.1111/1467-6494.t01-1-00005

Kwang, T., & Swann, W. B. (2010). Do people embrace praise even when they feel unworthy? a review of critical tests of self-enhancement versus self-verification. *Personality and Social Psychology Review, 14*, 263–280. doi:10.1177/1088868310365876

Langer, S. L., & Wurf, E. (1999). The effects of channel-consistent and channel-inconsistent interpersonal feedback on the formation of metaperceptions. *Journal of Nonverbal Behavior, 23*, 43–65.

Langlois, J. H., Kalakanis, L., Rubenstein, A. J., Larson, A., Hallam, M., & Smoot, M. (2000). Maxims or myths of beauty? A meta-analytic and theoretical review. *Psychological Bulletin, 126*, 390–423. doi:10.1037//0033-2909.126.3.390

Leary, M. R. (2007). Motivational and emotional aspects of the self. *Annual Review of Psychology, 58*, 317–344. doi:10.1146/annurev.psych.58.110405.085658

Leising, D., Erbs, J., & Fritz, U. (2010). The letter of recommendation effect in informant ratings of personality. *Journal of Personality and Social Psychology, 98*, 668–682. doi:10.1037/a0018771

Leising, D., Rehbein, D., & Sporberg, D. (2006). Does a fish see the water in which it swims? A study of the ability to correctly judge one's own interpersonal behavior. *Journal of Social and Clinical Psychology, 25*, 963–974. doi:10.1521/jscp.2006.25.9.963

Letzring, T. D. (2008). The good judge of personality: Characteristics, behaviors, and observer accuracy. *Journal of Research in Personality, 42*, 914–932. doi:10.1016/j.jrp.2007.12.003.

Letzring, T. D., Wells, S. M., & Funder, D. C. (2006). Information quantity and quality affect the realistic accuracy of personality judgment. *Journal of Personality and Social Psychology, 91*, 111–123. doi:10.1037/0022-3514.91.1.111

Levesque, M. J. (1997). Meta-accuracy among acquainted individuals: A social relations analysis of interpersonal perception and metaperception. *Journal of Personality and Social Psychology, 72*, 66–74. doi:10.1037/0022-3514.72.1.66

Lieberman, M. D., & Rosenthal, R. (2001). Why introverts can't always tell who likes them: Multitasking and nonverbal decoding. *Journal of Personality and Social Psychology, 80*, 294–310. doi:10.1037/0022-3514.80.2.294

Lorenzo, G. L., Biesanz, J. C., & Human, L. J. (2010). What is beautiful is good and more accurately understood: Physical attractiveness and accuracy in first impressions of personality. *Psychological Science, 21*, 1777–1782. doi:10.1177/0956797610388048

Malloy, T. E., & Albright, L. (1990). Interpersonal perception in a social context. *Journal of Personality and Social Psychology, 58*, 419–428. doi:10.1037//0022-3514.58.3.419

Malloy, T. E., & Janowski, C. L. (1992). Perceptions and metaperceptions of leadership: Components, accuracy, and dispositional correlates. *Personality and Social Psychology Bulletin, 18*, 700–708. doi:10.1177/0146167292186006

Maples-Keller, J. L., & Miller, J. D. (2018). Insight and the dark triad: Comparing self- and meta-perceptions in relation to psychopathy, narcissism, and Machiavellianism. *Personality Disorders: Theory, Research, and Treatment, 9*, 30–39. doi:10.1037/per0000207

Miller, S., & Malloy, T. E. (2003). Interpersonal behavior, perception, and affect in status-discrepant dyads: Social interaction of gay and heterosexual men. *Psychology of Men and Masculinity, 4,* 121–135. doi:10.1037/1524-9220.4.2.121

Moritz, D., & Roberts, J. E. (2018). Self-other agreement and metaperception accuracy across the Big Five: Examining the roles of depression and self-esteem. *Journal of Personality, 86*(2), 296–307. doi:10.1111/jopy.12313

Neuberg, S. L., & Fiske, S. T. (1987). Motivational influences on impression formation: Outcome dependency, accuracy-driven attention, and individuating processes. *Journal of Personality and Social Psychology, 53,* 431–444. doi:10.1037/0022-3514.53.3.431

Norton, P. J., & Hope, D. A. (2001). Kernels of truth or distorted perceptions: Self and observer ratings of social anxiety and performance. *Behavior Therapy, 32,* 765–786.

Ohtsubo, Y., Takezawa, M., & Fukuno, M. (2009). Mutual liking and meta-perception accuracy. *European Journal of Social Psychology, 39,* 707–718. doi:10.1002/ejsp.568

Oltmanns, T. F., Gleason, M. E. J., Klonsky, E. D., & Turkheimer, E. (2005). Meta-perception for pathological personality traits: Do we know when others think that we are difficult? *Consciousness and Cognition, 14,* 739–751. doi:10.1016/j.concog.2005.07.001

Oltmanns, T. F., & Turkheimer, E. (2009). Person perception and personality pathology. *Current Directions in Psychological Science, 18,* 32–36. doi:10.1016/j.jacc.2007.01.076

Paulhus, D. L. (1998). Interpersonal and intrapsychic adaptiveness of trait self-enhancement: A mixed blessing? *Journal of Personality and Social Psychology, 74,* 1197–1208. doi:10.1037/0022-3514.74.5.1197

Paulhus, D. L., & Reid, D. B. (1991). Enhancement and denial in socially desirable responding. *Journal of Personality and Social Psychology, 60,* 307–317. doi:10.1037/0022-3514.60.2.307

Ratcliff, N. J., Hugenberg, K., Shriver, E. R., & Bernstein, M. J. (2011). The allure of status: High-status targets are privileged in face processing and memory. *Personality and Social Psychology Bulletin, 37,* 1003–1015. doi:10.1177/0146167211407210

Reno, R., & Kenny, D. A. (1992). Effects of self-consciousness on self-disclosure among unacquainted individuals: An application of the social relations model. *Journal of Personality, 60,* 79–94. doi:10.1111/j.1467-6494.1992.tb00266.x

Riggio, H. R., & Riggio, R. E. (2002). Emotional expressiveness, extraversion, and neuroticism: A meta-analysis. *Journal of Nonverbal Behavior, 26,* 195–218. doi:10.1023/A:1022117500440

Rogers, K. H., & βiesanz, J. C. (2015). Knowing versus liking: Separating normative knowledge from social desirability in first impressions of personality. *Journal of Personality and Social Psychology, 109,* 1105–1116. doi:10.1037/a0039587

Rogers, K. H., & Biesanz, J. C. (2018). Reassessing the good judge of personality. *Journal of Personality and Social Psychology.* Advance online publication. doi:10.1037/pspp0000197

Ruben, M. A., & Hall, J. A. (2016). A lens model approach to the communication of pain. *Health Communication, 31,* 934–945. doi:10.1080/10410236.2015.1020261

Santuzzi, A. M. (2007). Perceptions and metaperceptions of negative evaluation: Group composition and meta-accuracy in a social relations model. *Group Processes and Intergroup Relations, 10,* 383–398. doi:10.1177/1368430207078700

Sargeant, J., Mann, K., Sinclair, D., van der Vleuten, C., & Metsemakers, J. (2006). Understanding the influence of emotions and reflection upon multi-source feedback acceptance and use. *Advances in Health Science Education, 13,* 275–288. doi:10.1007/s104569-006-9039-x

Saroglou, V., Yzerbyt, V., & Kaschten, C. (2011). Meta-stereotypes of groups with opposite religious views: Believers and non-believers. *Journal of Community and Applied Social Psychology, 21,* 484–498. doi:10.1002/casp.1123

Shechtman, Z., & Kenny, D. A. (1994). Metaperception accuracy: An Israeli study. *Basic and Applied Social Psychology, 15,* 451–465

Skowronski, J. J., & Carlston, D. E. (1987). Social judgment and social memory: The role of cue diagnosticity in negativity, positivity, and extremity biases. *Journal of Personality and Social Psychology, 52,* 689–699. doi:10.1037/0022-3514.52.4.689

Skowronski, J. J., & Carlston, D. E. (1989). Negativity and extremity biases in impression formation: A review of explanation. *Psychological Review, 105,* 131–142. doi:10.1037/0033-2909.105.1.131

Stopfer, J. M., Egloff, B., Nestler, S., & Back, M. D. (2014). Personality expression and impression formation in online social networks: An integrative approach to understanding the processes of accuracy, impression management, and meta-accuracy. *European Journal of Personality, 28,* 73–94. doi:10.1002/per.1935

Swann, W. B. (1983). Self-verification: Bringing social reality into harmony with the self. In J. Suls. and A. G. Greenwald (eds), *Psychological Perspectives on the Self, 2,* 33–66, Hillsdale, NJ: Erlbaum.

Swann, W. B., Stein-Seroussi, A., & McNulty, S. E. (1992). Outcasts in a white-lie society: The enigmatic worlds of people with negative self-conceptions. *Journal of Personality and Social Psychology, 62,* 618–624. doi:10.1037/0022-3514.62.4.618

Turnley, W. H., & Bolino, M. C. (2001). Achieving desired images while avoiding undesired images: Exploring the role of self-monitoring in impression management. *Journal of Applied Psychology, 86,* 351–360. doi:10.1037/0021-9010.86.2.351

Vazire, S. (2010). Who knows what about a person? The self-other knowledge asymmetry (SOKA) model. *Journal of Personality and Social Psychology, 98,* 281–300. doi:10.1037/a0017908

Vazire, S., & Carlson, E.N. (2010). Self-knowledge of personality: Do people know themselves? *Social and Personality Psychology Compass, 4,* 605–620. doi:10.1111/j.1751-9004.2010.00280.x

Vorauer, J. D., Main, K. J., & O'Connell, G. B. (1998). How do individuals expect to be viewed by members of lower status groups? Content and implications of meta-stereotypes. *Journal of Personality and Social Psychology, 75,* 917–937. doi:10.1037/0022-3514.75.4.917

Willis, J., & Todorov, A. (2006). First impressions: Making up your mind after a 100-ms exposure to a face. *Psychological Science, 17,* 592–598. doi:10.1111/j.1467-9280.2006.01750.x

Wood, D., & Furr, R. M. (2016). The correlates of similarity estimates are often misleadingly positive: The nature and scope of the problem, and some solutions. *Personality and Social Psychology Review, 20,* 79–99. doi:10.1177/1088868315581119

Yalch, M. M., & Hopwood, C. J. (2016). Target-, informant-, and meta-perceptual ratings of maladaptive traits.

Psychological Assessment, 29, 1142–1156. doi:10.1037/pas0000417

Zimmermann, J., Schindler, S., Klaus, G., & Leising, D. (2018). The effect of dislike on accuracy and bias in person perception. *Social Psychological and Personality Science, 9*, 80–88. doi:10.1177/1948550617703167

Notes

1. The Big Five is a basic framework for understanding individual differences in personality. This framework divides personality into five factors: extraversion, agreeableness, conscientiousness, emotional stability, and openness to experience (John & Srivastava, 1999). Each of these broad factors captures a group of distinct, specific personality traits. For example, some of the traits captured by extraversion are sociability, assertiveness, positive emotions, and warmth.

2. Our focus has been on traits, but people are better at detecting who likes them than they are at detecting who sees them as higher or lower on traits (Carlson & Kenny, 2012; Kenny & DePaulo, 1993). Put another way, it is easier for meta-perceivers to detect attraction than traits. Further, while people in workplace contexts are able to detect who likes them, they are not able to detect who competes against them (Eisenkraft, Elfenbein, & Kopelman, 2017). Thus, while we have focused on traits, there are many other types of attributes that might influence if and when meta-perceivers are accurate.

PART 4

Use of Nonverbal Cues and Other Information in Trait Judgments

Contributions of Nonverbal Cues to the Accurate Judgment of Personality Traits

Simon M. Breil, Sarah Osterholz, Steffen Nestler, *and* Mitja D. Back

Abstract

This chapter summarizes research on nonverbal expressions of behavior (nonverbal cues) and how they contribute to the accuracy of personality judgments. First, it presents a conceptual overview of relevant nonverbal cues in the domains of facial expressions, body language, paralanguage, and appearance as well as approaches to assess these cues on different levels of aggregation. It then summarizes research on the validity of nonverbal cues (what kind of nonverbal cues are good indicators of personality?) and the utilization of nonverbal cues (what kind of nonverbal cues lead to personality impressions?), resulting in a catalog of those cues that drive judgment accuracy for different traits. Finally, it discusses personal and situational characteristics that moderate the expression and utilization of nonverbal cues and give an outlook for future research.

Key Words: judgment accuracy, personality judgment, nonverbal behavior, behavioral cue, lens model analyses

Whenever we interact with others, we make judgments about their personalities (e.g., this person is trustworthy, this person is friendly). These judgments are typically formed within seconds (e.g., Willis & Todorov, 2006), tend to be quite stable across time (e.g., Kenny, Horner, Kashy, & Chu, 1992), and are often surprisingly accurate (e.g., Ambady & Skowronski, 2008; Funder, 2012). Most of the time, initial judgments are even formed before any (relevant) verbal information is exchanged. They are thus exclusively based on nonverbal cues (i.e., the way people look, move, or gesture) and they can have far-reaching consequences (e.g., Ambady, Bernieri, & Richeson, 2000; Harris & Garris, 2008). For example, in an employment interview, the applicant's upright posture, firm handshake, and appearance might lead to a positive evaluation (e.g., the applicant seems trustworthy and competent) and eventually to a job offer. In a get-to-know context, the broad smile of an interaction partner and the colorful clothing could lead to the

conclusion that this person is friendly, thus resulting in a friendship or a romantic relationship.

In this chapter, we present an overview of nonverbal cues and how they are related to the accuracy of personality judgments. That is, we first summarize relevant nonverbal cue domains (i.e., facial expressions, body language, paralanguage, appearance) and discuss why they might be important for the judgment of personality and how they can be assessed. Afterward, using the lens model as a conceptual framework, we summarize their role in explaining the degree of accuracy in personality trait judgments. We then present research on the validity (what kind of nonverbal cues are good indicators of "true" personality?) and utilization (what kind of nonverbal cues are good indicators of personality impressions?) of nonverbal cues. Based on this, we discuss potential moderators that might influence the relation between nonverbal cues and trait accuracy (i.e., good trait, good information, good judge, good target) and outline implications for future research.

Conceptualization of Nonverbal Cues

There has been a long history of studying nonverbal (behavioral) cues, going as far back as Darwin (1897), who examined the expression of emotions through facial cues and gestures. Numerous studies in this spirit focused on nonverbal cues and their relation to judgments of emotions and personality (e.g., Ekman & Friesen, 1969; Scherer, Scherer, Hall, & Rosenthal, 1977; Taft, 1955; for overviews of nonverbal communication and behavioral research, see Burgoon, Guerrero, & Floyd, 2010; Hall, Horgan, & Murphy, 2018; Harrigan, Rosenthal, & Scherer, 2005; Manusov, 2004). Nonverbal cues are typically divided into three domains of dynamic cues (i.e., cues that can easily be changed): face (i.e., facial expressions), body (i.e., body language; sometimes further divided into gestures and postures), and tone (i.e., paralanguage; Blanck, Rosenthal, Snodgrass, DePaulo, & Zuckerman, 1981; Elfenbein & Eisenkraft, 2010; Hall & Andrzejewski, 2008; Hall, Schmidt Mast, & West, 2016; Nowicki & Duke, 1994). In addition to these dynamic cues, there also exists a long research tradition of investigating static appearance-based cues (e.g., body shape, choice of clothing, head size; DeGroot & Gooty, 2009; Gifford, Ng, & Wilkinson, 1985; Naumann, Vazire, Rentfrow, & Gosling, 2009; Scherer et al., 1977), which also play an important role in nonverbal expression. Cues based on environmental aspects such as rooms (Gosling, Ko, Mannarelli, & Morris, 2002), music (Rentfrow & Gosling, 2006), or verbal descriptions (e.g., Borkenau, Mosch, Tandler, & Wolf, 2016; Küfner, Back, Nestler, & Egloff, 2010), as well as social media cues (e.g., Back, Schmukle, & Egloff, 2008; Back, Stopfer, et al., 2010) are discussed in chapter14 by Wall and Campbell in this handbook. Thus, for this chapter, we focus on facial expressions, body language, paralanguage, and appearance as four generally distinct domains of nonverbal behavior (please refer to Table 13.1 for an overview with examples).

Facial Expressions

Facial expressions refer to any kind of movements with the facial muscles. This most prominently includes expressions via the mouth and lips (e.g., smiling, yawning, showing teeth) as well as expressions via the eyes and eyebrows (e.g., eye contact, glazing, squinting, winking, scowling). Research on such facial expressions has predominantly focused on the recognition of emotions (e.g., Ekman & Friesen, 1969, 1971; Ekman, Sorenson, & Friesen, 1969; Izard, 1971), which are displayed through an interplay of different facial muscle movements. For example, the emotion of anger can be characterized by pulled-down eyebrows, pulled-up eyelids, and tightened lips (for an overview, see Ekman & Rosenberg, 1997). While the kind of emotion signals are often assumed to be universal across cultures (Ekman, 1994, 2016; Izard, 1994), there is large variability between individuals of how strongly emotions are expressed (e.g., Hildebrandt, Olderbak, & Wilhelm, 2015).

Individual differences in facial expressions, whether they are used for the recognition of emotions or not, can be used as cues for the judgment of underlying personality traits. One possible explanation lies in the relation between facial cues, affect, and traits. The state and trait accuracy model (STAM; Hall, Gunnery, Letzring, Carney, & Colvin, 2017), for example, posits that people first judge affective states (e.g., a person with pulled-down eyebrows might be perceived as angry, a person with a wide smile might be perceived as happy). These affective state impressions might then be used to form trait judgments (e.g., an angry person could be seen as disagreeable, a happy person could be seen as extraverted). This is based on the idea that momentary characteristics are often regarded as enduring attributes (i.e., the process of temporal extension; Knutson, 1996; Secord, 1958; Zebrowitz & Montepare, 2008). This link between facial expressions, emotions, and personality judgments has been shown in a variety of studies (for an overview, see: Zebrowitz & Montepare, 2008) and serves as a starting point for the understanding of accurate trait judgments based on facial expressions.

Body Language

Body language involves any kind of arrangement or gestures performed with the body and its limbs (i.e., every movement or arrangement of a person except the facial muscles). This includes gestures performed with the arms and hands (e.g., folded arms, waving, itching, peace sign), movement with the legs (e.g., running, walking) or head (e.g., head shake, head pointed toward the ground), as well as arrangements concerning the whole body (e.g., upright posture, energetic stance, crouched position). Some of these movements and gestures have concrete meanings within specific cultural groups (often called emblems, e.g., in many cultures a head shake stands for "no" and a thumbs up stands for "I agree," cf. Hall et al., 2018). Research on body-related cues has often focused on the display, recognition, and

SIMON M. BREIL, SARAH OSTERHOLZ, STEFFEN NESTLER, AND MITJA D. BACK

Table 13.1. Overview of Nonverbal Cue Domains

Domain	Definition	Examples
Facial expressions	Movements executed with the facial muscles	Smiling Eye contact Frowning Winking
Body language	Arrangement and gestures executed with the body and its limbs	Trunk reclines Energetic stance Body movement Head shake
Paralanguage	Nonverbal elements and features of speech	Pitch Speech rate Amplitude Voice breaks
Appearance	Static visual cues	Body shape Height Stylish clothes Makeup

relationship with dominance, power, and status (e.g., Carney, Hall, & LeBeau, 2005; Hall, Coats, & LeBeau, 2005; Henley, 1977). For example, upright postures, upright head tilts, and wide gestures are generally seen as signs of dominance.

Again, differences in the expression of such behaviors can be used as cues for the judgment of underlying traits. In addition to previously mentioned explanations (i.e., temporal extension, STAM) of how differences in expression can be related to (more or less accurate) personality judgments, body language cues especially can function via the accurate perception of underlying goals and motives. An individual who shows cues such as a huddled posture or head pointed toward the ground might, for example, be seen as someone with a (conflict) avoidance motive that wants to maintain a stable relationship with possible interaction partners. This person might then be (correctly) identified as being submissive or introverted (cf. Hall et al., 2005 for multiple explanations of how social pressures, goals, motives, emotions, and contextual variables impact nonverbal cues in the context of dominance).

Paralanguage

Paralanguage (i.e., paraverbal cues) describes nonverbal elements and general features of speech such as speech rate (number of words within a specific timeframe), voice breaks (number of pauses), fundamental frequency (mean voice pitch), pitch variability (variation of the voice pitch), amplitude

(mean loudness/intensity of the voice), or amplitude variability (variation in the loudness of the voice). These vocal cues often parallel the spoken word, but can also provide additional (e.g., emotional state) or contradictory (e.g., sarcasm, deception) information (Hall et al., 2018). There is a large amount of research focusing on the perception of different paralanguage cues which shows that people generally rely heavily on voice and speech features when forming impressions about others (e.g., DeGroot & Gooty, 2009; Kramer, 1963). One example is the relationship between cognitive ability and paralanguage: Perceptions made via acoustic cues (within a standardized content, e.g., reading the weather forecast) have been shown to relate to differences in individuals' cognitive ability measured via standardized intelligence tests (Borkenau & Liebler, 1993, 1995; Borkenau, Mauer, Riemann, Spinath, & Angleitner, 2004).

This can most likely be explained by the fact that ability measured in cognitive tests (e.g., rapid information processing, good working memory) is also important for the comprehension and fluent repetition of words and sentences (i.e., reading, see for example: Borkenau & Liebler, 1995). These possible differences in speech rate, pauses, and emphasis might then be used by observers as cues for competence. Of course, paralinguistic cues can also carry information about emotions and affective states (e.g., speaking slowly and quietly might be a sign for a sad mood, cf. Bänziger, Hosoya, & Scherer, 2015) and reveal individual motives of how one wants to appear to others that are based on stereotypes (e.g., Anna believes herself to be dominant, thus she general speaks in a loud voice when talking to others).

Appearance

Nonverbal cues relating to appearance include any static visual cues. These are physical characteristics that are usually less alterable such as height, weight, body shape, length of nose, width of chin, shape of ears, eye color, or hair color as well as more alterable features like choice of clothing, grooming, hairstyle, or makeup. All appearance-based cues have in common, however, that they are generally static within one situation and, in contrast to facial expressions and body language, cannot be easily changed within the specific judgment context. Theories and research about the relationship between static visual cues and personality dates back to *physiognomical* ideas of ancient Greek philosophers more than 2000 years ago (cf. Hassin &

Trope, 2000; Zebrowitz, 1997), who believed that there are "mystic" links between a person's character and outer appearance. While these simplified ideas have been heavily criticized, newer research has focused on more specific relationships between appearance characteristics and personality, and there are hints that appearance can provide us with at least rudimentary guidelines when judging personality (i.e., a kernel of truth; e.g., Berry, 1990; Naumann et al., 2009; Zebrowitz, 2017; Zebrowitz & Montepare, 2008).

Associations between personality and appearance can be traced back to a variety of mechanisms involving environmental and biological factors. For example, appearance and personality might be related due to common biological causes (e.g., testosterone influences facial hair growth as well as a more aggressive personality) as well as common environmental causes (e.g., the choice for a specific grooming style is specific for individuals that share the same values). Furthermore, physical differences could serve as some form of self-fulfilling prophecy (e.g., tall individuals are expected to behave more dominantly, they thus act accordingly) or they could reveal differences in past behaviors (e.g., individuals that laugh a lot might develop laugh lines and are thus judged to be happy or extraverts; see Zebrowitz & Collins, 1997 for an overview of these four explanations).

Assessment of Nonverbal Cues

To empirically investigate the contribution of nonverbal cues to trait accuracy one needs three different data sources: This includes some measure of "real" personality provided by the targets (typically assessed via self-reported personality questionnaires and sometimes supplemented by informant-reported personality), judgments on the same personality traits by unacquainted perceivers (typically based on short interactions, videos, or photos), and a listing and quantification of nonverbal cues available to perceivers. At best, these cues should be sampled with respect to their natural range and covariation and rated by independent observers.

Generally, the assessment of such cues can happen at different levels of abstraction, which include the macro level (global ratings specific to one behavioral domain; e.g., shows dominant behavior), meso level (circumscribed behavioral expressions; e.g., self-confident facial expressions), and micro level (specific behavioral acts; e.g., leaning forward). The specific cues that are to be rated are typically based on coding schemes developed for the assess-

ment of (nonverbal) cues (for overviews, see Bakemann, 2000; Brauner, Boos, & Kolbe, 2018; Heyman, Lorber, Eddy, & West, 2014; Manusov, 2004). These schemes vary in their number of cues and comprehensiveness. The Münster Behavior Coding System (Grünberg, Mattern, Geukes, Küfner, & Back, 2018), for example, differentiates between the mentioned macro, meso, and micro levels and classifies cues within the broader sections of dominance, warmth, expressiveness, arrogance, aggressiveness, nervousness, and intellectual competence, resulting in over 280 possible cues. When used for specific research questions the number of assessed cues is often considerably lower. An example are the classic studies by Borkenau and Liebler (1992a, 1992b, 1995) in which observers rated about 50 behavioral and appearance-based cues.

Cues further differ in how they can be assessed: there are cues that can be objectively determined (e.g., target wears glasses, height of target, body proportions), cues that can be counted (e.g., number of aggressive gestures, number of smiles), and cues that are rated on Likert-type scales (e.g., extent of leaning forward, extent of eye contact). Due to the sheer number of cues investigated, live rating is not an option in most cases. Thus, usually multiple observers need to watch videos or evaluate photos of targets to assess all desired nonverbal cues.

Role of Nonverbal Cues for Accuracy

How are nonverbal cues related to trait accuracy when judging personality traits? Based on the assumptions of the lens model (Brunswik, 1952, 1956 see chapter 4 by Osterholz, Breil, Nestler, & Back in this handbook for a detailed explanation; see Figure 13.1 for an example), perceivers use available cues in the environment to form judgments of personality traits that are not directly observable. This framework enables an analytic and differentiated analysis of involved processes.

For example, perceivers might observe the cheerfulness, the amount of body movement, and the lack of tension of a target and use this information to infer his/her (possibly high) extraversion. The extent to which an observer uses a specific cue for judgments is called cue utilization (see right side in Figure 13.1). For each cue, it describes the relationship between individual differences in target cue values and individual differences in how targets are judged. Cue utilizations are influenced by (intuitive) knowledge and individual experiences, as well as the utilization of stereotypes (e.g., Jussim, Cain,

Crawford, Harber, & Cohen, 2009) and exemplar information (e.g., Smith & Zárate, 1992).

Cue validity on the other side, describes, for each cue, the relationship between individual differences in targets (nonverbal) cue values and individual differences in targets actual personality trait values (typically assessed via self-report and/or informant-report questionnaires; see left side in Figure 13.1). Individuals who wear glasses, for example, might be (on average) less extraverted, while individuals who smile a lot (i.e., have a cheerful expression) might be more extraverted. Multiple (not mutually exclusive) explanations on why differences in the expression of nonverbal cues could be related to differences in actual personality traits have been discussed earlier and are displayed in Table 13.2. Nonverbal cues especially might be very well suited for the judgment of personality as they are more difficult to suppress relative to verbal behavior and are thus more revealing of internal states (DePaulo, 1992).

In summary, accuracy through nonverbal cues can be achieved when there are valid cues available in the environment, that are observable, and used in line with their degree of validity. If there are no valid cues in the environment for a given trait, this means that this trait is impossible to judge accurately within this specific context. If there are valid cues, but they are not used accordingly by perceivers, this would indicate that perceivers have missing knowledge. The utilization of cues in the absence of validity could suggest some sort of bias or false stereotype.

Empirical Results for Validity and Utilization of Nonverbal Cues Study Selection and Procedure

In this part, we summarize empirical results regarding the validity and utilization of nonverbal cues for personality traits. We decided to include results of studies investigating the relationship between nonverbal cues on the one side and personality and/or personality judgments on the other side. We hereby only included studies with (1) real targets (age ≥ 16), with (2) a natural range and covariation of cues (i.e., no experimental manipulation), with (3) nonevaluative traits (e.g., no liking or popularity), and with (4) cues that classify to one of the four categories (i.e., facial expression, body language, paralanguage, appearance; e.g., no environmental cues, no highly aggregated cues).

We identified relevant studies through multiple criteria: In a first step we scanned known studies (and cross-references within these studies) that focused on the lens model, on cue-based judgments, and on behavioral prediction. In total, 32 studies met our criteria. In a second step, we used EBSCO, including the databases PsycARTICLES, PsycINFO, PSYINDEX, PsycBOOKS, and MEDLINE, for an online literature search. The search was restricted to peer-reviewed journals. Keywords were *lens model [AND] nonverbal* (all fields, 17 results), *nonverbal cues [AND] personality* (key words only, 30 results), *personality judgment* (key words only, 271 results), *personality perception [AND] cues* (all fields, 57 results), and *big five [AND] nonverbal* (all fields, 58 results). Here we found 10 additional studies. In a last step, we scanned the first dozen pages of Google Scholar using the same criteria and identified 22 additional articles. In total, 64 articles were included (see osf.io/9p64g, Table S1 for an overview of included studies with relevant characteristics). Please note that some articles included multiple studies, while other studies were covered by multiple articles, resulting in 65 independent studies. Of these 65 studies, 33 studies included both cue validities and cue utilizations. Fifteen studies included only validities, while 17 studies exclusively focused on utilizations.

On the OSF (Open Science Framework) page of this chapter (osf.io/9p64g), we have uploaded the full table with all studies and all individual correlations. Please note, however, that this list does not aim to be fully comprehensive and should be regarded as a preliminary documentation of the existing work. On the same page, we have included a sheet in which additional relevant studies we might have missed can be added, and we invite all readers to contribute to a more exhaustive documentation on personality (judgments) and nonverbal cues.

For the presentation of results in this chapter, we have focused on the relationship (correlation) between the Big Five (supplemented by intelligence) and 39 cues (6 to 14 per domain), which were selected based on their number of occurrences across studies. We hereby summarized traits and cues to broader categories (e.g., dominance and shyness were allocated to extraversion; warmth and arrogance were allocated to agreeableness; smiles and happy expression were allocated to cheerful facial expression; stylish hair and fashionable dress were allocated to stylishness). This allocation process was done by the authors of this study and based on theoretical (e.g., childlike, feminine, and soft faces are all related to babyfaceness)

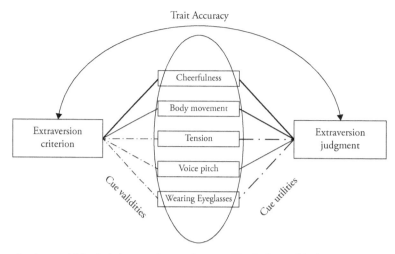

Figure 13.1. Exemplary lens model for the judgment of personality traits. The thickness of the lines indicates the strength of the relation. Solid lines indicate positive associations, dotted lines indicate negative associations.

and practical (e.g., to have multiple studies for every trait/cue combination) considerations (also see Hirschmüller, Schmukle, Krause, Back, & Egloff, 2018, for a similar allocation of cues). For an overview concerning the current allocation of traits and cues, please refer to the online supplement (osf.io/9p64g, Table S2).[1]

As some studies did not provide zero-order correlations, we used the provided partial correlations for those studies (e.g., correlations controlled for sex and age). When there were multiple correlations for a specific trait and cue combination within a sample (e.g., multiple traits within a sample allocated to extraversion, multiple cues within a study allocated to stylishness, separate results for men and women, self- and informant-reported traits), we aggregated these correlations within studies. In a next step, we meta-analyzed the resulting correlations across studies, using the R package meta (Schwarzer, 2019; R version 3.4.3, see osf.io/9p64g for data and code). Reported estimations are based on a random effects model with inverse variance weighting and DerSimonian-Laird estimation for the between-study variance. Please refer to Tables 13.3 to 13.8 for results.

Overview Results

In the following, we summarize the results separately for each trait domain. We hereby focus on cue validities and cue utilizations that were at least small in effect size ($r \geq 0.10$; Cohen, 1992). Cues that were used by observers to judge a specific trait and were at the same time related to actual trait values (in the same direction, with results from at least two

studies), were identified as potential influences that drive trait accuracies.

Neuroticism

Noncheerful expressions; a tense and nervous body language; an unexpressive, nonfluent, unpleasant, and silent voice; low amount of speaking; unattractiveness and a non-neat appearance; low height; and being less muscular were all indicators of being neurotic and led observers to the same impression. Other cues (e.g., dominant facial expression, self-assured body language, ease of understanding, powerful voice, not wearing eyeglasses) were associated with being judged less neurotic but were not related to individuals' actual neuroticism. Wearing darker clothes and having darker hair were among the few cues that were related to actual levels of neuroticism but were not used by observers when judging this trait (see Table 13.3).

Extraversion

Out of all the investigated traits, extraversion included the greatest number of valid cues that were also used by observers. These cues include cheerful facial expression, dominant facial expression, general facial expressiveness, forward leans, gestures, self-assured posture, relaxed posture, expressive/varying voice, fluent speaking, pleasantness of voice, confidence of voice, loudness of voice, speech rate, amount of talking, attractiveness, neatness, stylishness, lack of eyeglasses, volume of mouth, hair length, and the lack of dark clothes. The cues eye contact, body movement, and head movements (among others) were used by observers to judge

Table 13.2. Explanations on Why Nonverbal Cues Are Related to "Real" Personality

Reason	Explanation	Potential Examples
Temporal extension of emotion and affect	Individuals who are high in specific traits are more likely to show specific emotions and affective states. These emotions and affective states are expressed through nonverbal cues.	Extraverts are more likely to be happy, thus they smile more often. People high in neuroticism are more likely to be afraid, thus their body is shaking more often.
Motives/Goals	Individuals who are high in specific traits are more likely to have specific motives and goals when interacting with others. These motives, goals, and interests are expressed through nonverbal cues.	Introverts are more likely to have a conflict avoidance motive, thus they show submissive (gestures, facial expressions) behavior. Individuals high in openness are more likely to have goals related to the creative expression of oneself and are thus more likely to wear extravagant clothes.
Common biological cause	Individuals who are high in specific traits are more likely to show specific nonverbal cues based on genetic and biological links.	Aggressive persons are more likely to have strong beard growth (due to testosterone, which influences facial hair growth and aggressiveness). Intelligent individuals are more likely to be generally good looking (e.g., possible due to "good genes").
Common environmental cause	Individuals who are high in specific traits are more likely to show specific nonverbal cues based on correlated learning.	Individuals low in openness have generally learned conservative values and, thus, wear more formal (conservative) clothes. Individuals high in conscientiousness have learned to think first, then act, and thus have a slower speech rate.
Self-fulfilling prophecy	Individuals who are high in specific traits are more likely to show specific nonverbal cues based on self-fulfilling prophecy, which causes them to behave in a manner consistent with expectations.	Taller individuals are more likely to be dominant because they act on the expectation to be dominant. Attractive individuals are more likely to be extraverted because they get more attention and act accordingly.
Past behavior	Individuals who are high in specific traits are more likely to show specific nonverbal cues based on past behavior that led to the development of these cues.	Individuals low in conscientiousness are more likely to be overweight because they behaved less conscientiously in the past. Individuals high in extraversion are more likely to have laugh lines because they behaved extraverted in the past.

Note. For more information on these different explanations please refer to Hall et al. (2005), Hall et al. (2017), Zebrowitz & Collins (1997), Zebrowitz & Montepare (2008). Please note that the provided examples just serve as a representation of different mechanisms and not all links have been empirically investigated. Furthermore, the mechanisms are not mutually exclusive (e.g., a common environmental cause might influence motives and goals).

extraversion but were not related to actual extraversion (see Table 13.4).

Openness

For openness, only self-assured/open posture, pleasantness of voice, volume of mouth, and hair length were valid and utilized cues. There were multiple cues (e.g., cheerful facial expression, fluent speaking, attractiveness, neatness, stylishness) that were

used when judging openness, however, they were not related to actual openness. Less talking was related to actual openness, but observers did not use this cue (see Table 13.5).

Agreeableness

A cheerful facial expression, small stride length, fluent speaking, attractiveness, and neatness of appearance were the only cues that were related to

Table 13.3 Cue Validity and Cue Utilization Meta-Analyses: Neuroticism.

Cue Validity			Neuroticism	Cue Utilization		
k (n) 95% CI r			Cues	r 95% CI k (n)		
			Facial expression			
9(862)	[-.18, -.03]	-.11	**Cheerful facial expression**	-.24	[-.46, .02]	9(878)
4(414)	[-.16, .04]	-.06	Dominant facial expression	-.58	[-.74, -.36]	2(200)
1(62)		-.15	General expressiveness	n/a	n/a	n/a
3(299)	[-.16, .11]	-.03	Unconcerned (vs. serious)	.10	[-.42, .56]	3(299)
7(524)	[-.19, .07]	-.07	Eye contact	-.14	[-.24, -.04]	4(388)
2(116)	[-.55, .85]	.31	Eyebrow movements	-.01	[-.19, .18]	2(116)
			Body language			
5(498)	[-.20, .08]	-.06	Body movement	.09	[-.18, .35]	6(466)
3(365)	[-.24, .12]	-.06	Forward lean/proximity	n/a	n/a	n/a
5(420)	[-.12, .07]	-.03	Gestures	-.12	[-.25, .02]	2(200)
3(189)	[-.27, .08]	-.10	Head movements	.13	[-.21, .44]	2(140)
4(336)	[-.16, .14]	-.01	Self-assured/open vs. slouching	-.40	[-.64, -.09]	3(224)
3(313)	[-.06, .17]	.06	Closed arms	.13	[-.01, .27]	3(313)
3(208)	[-.14, .13]	-.01	Self-touch	.17	[-.29, .57]	2(164)
4(325)	[.02, .23]	.13	**Tension/nervousness (vs. relaxed)**	.29	[.00, .53]	4(325)
2(200)	[-.09, .19]	.05	Stride length	-.13	[-.28, .02]	2(200)
			Paralanguage			
2(200)	[-.09, .19]	.05	Ease of understanding	-.33	[-.51, -.14]	2(200)
2(123)	[-.43, -.02]	-.24	**Expressive/varying voice**	-.47	[-.70, -.14]	3(180)
7(698)	[-.20, -.01]	-.10	**Fluent speaking (vs. nervous)**	-.32	[-.40, -.24]	5(510)
3(299)	[-.23, .00]	-.12	**Pleasantness of voice**	-.50	[-.60, -.39]	4(323)
3(299)	[-.19, .04]	-.07	Powerful/confident voice (vs. soft)	-.28	[-.41, -.13]	4(323)
2(248)	[-.29, .02]	-.14	**Loudness**	-.17	[-.45, .13]	3(180)
(3, 299)	[-.25, .23]	-.01	Pitch	.08	[-.07, .22]	6(822)
1(54)		.20	Speech rate	-.20	[-.46, .10]	2(499)

Table 13.3   Cue Validity and Cue Utilization Meta-Analyses: Neuroticism   (Continued)

k (n)	95% CI	r		r	95% CI	k (n)
			Paralanguage			
5(446)	[-.32, .07]	-.13	**Speech vs. nonspeech**	-.11	[-.19, -.03]	3(623)
n/a	n/a	n/a	Interruptions	n/a	n/a	n/a
			Appearance			
9(865)	[-.22, -.06]	-.14	**Attractiveness**	-.33	[-.45, -.19]	10(843)
6(476)	[-.12, .10]	-.01	Babyfaceness vs. maturity	-.01	[-.26, .24]	4(276)
3(189)	[-.11, .18]	.04	Distinctiveness	.00	[-.14, .15]	3(189)
9(764)	[-.17, -.02]	-.10	**Neatness**	-.15	[-.24, -.05]	10(757)
8(752)	[-.11, .03]	-.04	Stylishness	-.15	[-.28, -.02]	8(690)
3(212)	[-.24, .24]	.00	Formality	-.08	[-.21, .06]	3(212)
3(149)	[-.22, .30]	.04	Eyeglasses	.24	[.01, .45]	2(76)
3(176)	[-.10, .20]	.06	Volume of Mouth/full lips	-.05	[-.39, .31]	3(176)
2(200)	[-.09, .19]	.05	Hair length (long)	.11	[-.03, .24]	2(200)
3(176)	[.10, .38]	.25	Dark hair color	.01	[-.14, .16]	3(176)
2(199)	[-.24, .04]	-.10	**Height**	-.18	[-.32, -.05]	2(199)
3(273)	[-.24, .00]	-.12	**Muscular**	-.33	[-.49, -.14]	2(200)
3(299)	[-.05, .18]	.07	Weight	-.04	[-.29, .21]	3(299)
2(200)	[.05, .32]	.19	Dark clothes	.08	[-.07, .21]	2(200)

Note. k = number of included samples, *n* = overall sample size. The effect size and confidence interval (CI) estimations are based on a random effects model (empty CI cells included only one study). Cues in bold showed at least small (*r* ≥ 0.10) effects for both utilization and validity (same direction; across at least two studies).

Table 13.4   Cue Validity and Cue Utilization Meta-Analyses: Extraversion

Cue Validity			Extraversion	Cue Utilization		
k (n) 95% CI r			Cues	r 95% CI k (n)		
			Facial expression			
17(1789)	[.09, .21]	.15	**Cheerful facial expression**	.54	[.32, .70]	17(1565)
6(669)	[-.08, .27]	.10	**Dominant facial expression**	.52	[.38, .64]	3(382)
3(311)	[.03, .25]	.14	**General expressiveness**	.40	[.11, .63]	4(371)
3(382)	[-.35, .26]	-.05	Unconcerned (vs. serious)	-.29	[-.75, .37]	3(382)
12(1222)	[-.02, .09]	.03	Eye contact	.21	[.11, .31]	11(1202)

(Continued)

Table 13.4 Cue Validity and Cue Utilization Meta-Analyses: Extraversion   (Continued)

			Facial expression			
4(394)	[-.17, .10]	-.04	Eyebrow movements	.07	[-.24, .37]	4(394)

			Body language			
8(733)	[-.02, .20]	.09	Body movement	.33	[.16, .48]	10(837)
7(893)	[.04, .24]	.14	**Forward lean/proximity**	.10	[.03, .18]	5(670)
12(1226)	[.11, .24]	.18	**Gestures**	.35	[.22, .46]	11(1048)
8(808)	[-.14, .13]	.00	Head movements	.26	[.17, .35]	8(802)
5(520)	[-.01, .31]	.15	**Self-assured/open vs. slouching**	.25	[-.30, .67]	4(395)
6(623)	[-.18, .05]	-.06	Closed arms	-.12	[-.23, -.01]	6(623)
7(697)	[-.03, .12]	.04	Self-touch	.07	[-.08, .22]	7(711)
7(713)	[-.24, -.08]	-.16	**Tension/nervousness (vs. relaxed)**	-.42	[-.58, -.23]	8(773)
3(382)	[-.07, .13]	.03	Stride length	.05	[-.05, .15]	4(425)

			Paralanguage			
4(449)	[-.04, .22]	.09	Ease of understanding	.30	[.11, .47]	4(449)
7(849)	[.08, .33]	.21	**Expressive/varying voice**	.36	[.20, .50]	7(514)
5(564)	[-.03, .22]	.10	**Fluent speaking (vs. nervous)**	.22	[.14, .31]	5(472)
4(455)	[.08, .26]	.17	**Pleasantness of voice**	.30	[.16, .42]	4(406)
6(894)	[.13, .30]	.22	**Powerful/confident voice (vs. soft)**	.36	[.25, .46]	5(473)
3(387)	[-.03, .43]	.21	**Loudness**	.35	[.09, .57]	6(581)
5(821)	[-.15, .08]	-.04	Pitch	.05	[-.08, .17]	7(972)
3(493)	[-.25, .52]	.16	**Speech rate**	.21	[-.10, .49]	4(609)
9(932)	[.15, .32]	.23	**Speech vs. nonspeech**	.31	[.15, .45]	7(1191)
2(197)	[-.01, .27]	.13	Interruptions	.05	[-.09, .19]	2(197)

			Appearance			
13(1603)	[.14, .27]	.20	**Attractiveness**	.47	[.37, .56]	15(1362)
8(731)	[-.04, .21]	.08	Babyfaceness vs. maturity	.06	[-.07, .19]	6(627)
3(189)	[-.29, .05]	-.12	Distinctiveness	-.09	[-.23, .06]	3(189)
11(1064)	[.15, .27]	.21	**Neatness**	.25	[.18, .32]	11(1009)
10(964)	[.14, .31]	.22	**Stylishness**	.32	[.21, .41]	9(829)

Table 13.4 Cue Validity and Cue Utilization Meta-Analyses: Extraversion   (Continued)

			Appearance			
4(367)	[-.09, .11]	.01	Formality	-.08	[-.22, .05]	4(463)
3(149)	[-.32, .07]	-.13	**Eyeglasses**	-.35	[-.54, -.13]	2(76)
4(358)	[.01, .22]	.12	**Volume of Mouth/full lips**	.16	[.05, .27]	4(358)
2(282)	[-.14, .33]	.10	**Hair length (long)**	.10	[-.02, .22]	2(282)
4(358)	[-.18, .06]	-.06	Dark hair color	-.09	[-.19, .01]	4(358)
3(382)	[-.19, .19]	.00	Height	.02	[-.08, .12]	3(382)
4(455)	[-.06, .12]	.03	Muscular	.19	[.02, .35]	3(382)
4(455)	[-.01, .18]	.08	Weight	.07	[-.03, .17]	3(382)
4(455)	[-.28, .04]	-.12	**Dark clothes**	-.11	[-.27, .06]	3(382)

Note. k = number of included samples, n = overall sample size. The effect size and confidence interval (CI) estimations are based on a random effects model (empty CI cells included only one study). Cues in bold showed at least small ($r \geq 0.10$) effects for both utilization and validity (same direction; across at least two studies).

Table 13.5 Cue Validity and Cue Utilization Meta-Analyses: Openness

Cue Validity			Openness	Cue Utilization		
k (n) 95% CI r			Cues	r 95% CI k (n)		
			Facial expression			
6(711)	[-.06, .09]	.02	Cheerful facial expression	.38	[.29, .46]	9(1026)
5(596)	[-.04, .12]	.04	Dominant facial expression	.36	[.27, .45]	3(382)
1(182)		-.01	General expressiveness	.22		1(182)
3(382)	[-.09, .11]	.01	Unconcerned (vs. serious)	-.28	[-.57, .08]	3(382)
5(645)	[-.20, .06]	-.07	Eye contact	.13	[.00, .26]	6(832)
2(116)	[-.26, .10]	-.08	Eyebrow movements	.09	[-.05, .22]	3(326)
			Body language			
4(394)	[-.13, .07]	-.03	Body movement	.02	[-.08, .11]	5(434)
1(182)		.02	Forward lean/proximity	.15	[.05, .24]	2(392)
3(394)	[-.07, .13]	.03	Gestures	.08	[-.01, .17]	3(492)
3(382)	[-.12, .09]	-.01	Head movements	.07	[-.06, .19]	5(632)
3(237)	[-.03, .23]	.10	**Self-assured/open vs. slouching**	.25	[-.07, .52]	3(335)
4(495)	[-.13, .06]	-.03	Closed arms	-.10	[-.18, -.01]	4(495)
2(282)	[-.16, .21]	.02	Self-touch	.02	[-.10, .13]	2(282)

(Continued)

			Body language			
5(507)	[-.13, .05]	-.04	Tension/nervousness (vs. relaxed)	-.16	[-.26, .05]	5(507)
3(382)	[-.13, .13]	.00	Stride length	-.01	[-.27, .24]	3(382)

			Paralanguage			
3(382)	[-.09, .14]	.02	Ease of understanding	.31	[.11, .49]	3(382)
n/a	n/a	n/a	Expressive/varying voice	n/a	n/a	n/a
4(520)	[-.13, .08]	-.02	Fluent speaking (vs. nervous)	.21	[.12, .29]	4(533)
3(382)	[.00, .20]	.10	**Pleasantness of voice**	.44	[.28, .58]	3(382)
3(382)	[-.24, .10]	-.07	Powerful/confident voice (vs. soft)	.10	[-.03, .23]	3(382)
1(182)		-.18	Loudness	-.23		1(182)
3(382)	[-.18, .07]	-.06	Pitch	.08	[-.10, .25]	4(824)
n/a	n/a	n/a	Speech rate	.05		1(442)
3(432)	[-.32, -.02]	-.17	Speech vs. non-speech	.06	[-.01, .14]	3(775)
1(182)		-.04	Interruptions	-.16		1(182)

			Appearance			
8(788)	[-.14, .09]	-.03	Attractiveness	.56	[.21, .78]	9(828)
6(571)	[-.02, .14]	.06	Babyfaceness vs. maturity	.17	[.01, .31]	5(458)
3(189)	[-.30, .25]	-.03	Distinctiveness	.05	[-.34, .42]	3(189)
8(687)	[-.22, .09]	-.07	Neatness	.32	[.12, .49]	10(840)
7(675)	[-.13, .14]	.00	Stylishness	.18	[.06, .29]	7(675)
4(394)	[-.32, .08]	-.12	Formality	.08	[-.20, .35]	4(394)
2(76)	[-.18, .28]	.05	Eyeglasses	.00	[-.23, .23]	2(76)
4(358)	[.00, .33]	.17	**Volume of Mouth/full lips**	.21	[.01, .39]	4(358)
2(282)	[-.02, .22]	.10	**Hair length (long)**	.16	[.05, .28]	2(282)
5(458)	[-.05, .14]	.04	Dark hair color	.09	[-.01, .18]	5(458)
3(382)	[-.09, .11]	.01	Height	.12	[.02, .22]	3(382)
3(382)	[-.15, .05]	-.05	Muscular	.02	[-.29, .32]	3(382)
3(382)	[-.18, .02]	-.09	Weight	-.22	[-.38, -.04]	3(382)
3(382)	[-.01, .19]	.09	Dark clothes	.05	[-.05, .15]	3(382)

Note. k = number of included samples, n = overall sample size. The effect size and confidence interval (CI) estimations are based on a random effects model (empty CI cells included only one study). Cues in bold showed at least small ($r \geq 0.10$) effects for both utilization and validity (same direction; across at least two studies).

actual agreeableness and used by observers to judge this trait. Many cues that observers associated with agreeableness (e.g., eye contact, relaxed body language, pleasantness of voice, babyfaceness) were not valid indicators. Furthermore, there were a few valid cues (high pitch, nondominant facial expression) that were not identified by observers (see Table 13.6).

Conscientiousness

Cues that drove accuracy for conscientiousness judgments exclusively belonged to the domains of body language and appearance. These were self-assured/open posture, lack of self-touch, attractiveness, lack of distinctiveness in appearance, neatness, formality, and having shorter hair. Many more cues (e.g., fluent speaking, pleasantness of voice, wearing eyeglasses) were used when judging conscientiousness, but were not actually related with individuals' conscientiousness (see Table 13.7).

Intelligence

Here, cue validities refer to the relationship between cues and intelligence measured via cognitive ability tests (with the exception of one study that only included self-reports). For intelligence, paralinguistic cues played the biggest role in explaining accuracy. Especially, easiness of understanding, pleasantness of voice, speech rate, and amount of speech were used by observers and at the same time related to actual (measured) intelligence. Cues that were used but not valid were (for example): eye contact, amount of gestures, powerful voice, and attractiveness[2] (see Table 13.8).

Summary and Comparison

Results of the included studies suggest that, for all traits, there are at least a few nonverbal cues that allow for accurate glimpses into one's personality. For most traits (i.e., extraversion, openness, conscientiousness, intelligence) this is in line with research showing above chance judgment accuracies, even by strangers (for overviews see: Connelly & Ones, 2010; Connelly, Kavanagh, & Viswesvaran, 2007; Hall, Andrzejewski, Murphy, Mast, & Feinstein, 2008; Kenny, Albright, Malloy, & Kashy, 1994; Kenny et al., 1992). However, even for traits that are typically viewed as not easily observable (i.e., agreeableness, neuroticism) we find multiple valid cues.

Nearly all the valid cues were also used by observers when judging the specific traits, showing that perceivers generally have the ability to correctly identify relevant cues. However, observers often overestimated the actual size of relationships, and this potentially resulted in lower accuracies. Furthermore, there were many cues for which the included studies did not provide evidence for validity, but that were nevertheless used for judgments. These cues, thus, might represent some sort of common bias/inaccurate stereotype when judging the respective traits.

The five most utilized cues across all traits were attractiveness, dominant facial expression, cheerful facial expression, pleasantness of voice, and ease of understanding ($r = 0.33–0.45$). The five most valid cues were speech versus nonspeech, loudness, expressive/varying voice, wearing dark clothes, and speech rate ($r = 0.14–0.18$). Generally, the portion of cues that drove accuracy was highest for the paralanguage domain, highlighting the importance of voice and speech characteristics when judging personality.

In Table S3 in the online supplement, we additionally provide vector correlations[3] for cue validities and cue utilizations across traits. Results show high intercorrelations for cue utilizations. This especially applies to extraversion, neuroticism (recoded as emotional stability), and intelligence (mean intercorrelations for the three traits = 0.68), as well as to openness and agreeableness ($r = 0.72$). This means that for judgments on these traits, available cues were used in a similar way (i.e., in the sense that the most and least utilized cues for one trait were also the most and least used cues for the other traits). The strong relationships between trait judgments might be related to general favorability of these traits and specific cues (e.g., attractive individuals, with a cheerful expression and self-assured postures were generally judged as being high in extraversion, emotional stability, and intelligence). Low correlations were found for the cue utilization regarding extraversion and conscientiousness ($r = 0.14$).

For cue validities, we found a more mixed pattern: There were high intercorrelations between the cue validities for extraversion, emotional stability, and conscientiousness (mean intercorrelations for the three traits $r = 0.51$). For example, the neatness of appearance was significantly correlated with self/informant ratings on all three traits, while voice pitch played a negligible role. Noticeably smaller or even negative (e.g., openness and conscientiousness: $r = -.27$) correlations between cue validities were found for other trait combinations. This suggests that the relationship between nonverbal cues and actual personality across traits is more diverse than the perceived associations.

Table 13.6 Cue Validity and Cue Utilization Meta-Analyses: Agreeableness

Cue Validity			Agreeableness	Cue Utilization		
k (n) 95% CI r			Cues	r 95% CI k (n)		
			Facial expression			
13(1225)	[.02, .19]	.10	**Cheerful facial expression**	.53	[.39, .64]	17(1561)
4(385)	[-.27, -.06]	-.17	Dominant facial expression	.22	[.07, .37]	2(200)
1(62)		.09	General expressiveness	n/a	n/a	n/a
2(200)	[-.19, .09]	-.05	Unconcerned (vs. serious)	-.26	[-.39, -.12]	2(200)
7(577)	[-.08, .08]	.00	Eye contact	.24	[.10, .36]	8(814)
3(136)	[-.08, .26]	.09	Eyebrow movements	-.04	[-.14, .07]	4(346)
			Body language			
4(272)	[-.23, .07]	-.08	Body movement	-.13	[-.32, .06]	7(394)
n/a	n/a	n/a	Forward lean/proximity	-.05	[-.31, .22]	3(330)
4(334)	[-.27, .17]	-.05	Gestures	-.03	[-.28, .22]	4(430)
5(323)	[-.16, .28]	.06	Head movements	.18	[.00, .35]	7(552)
4(310)	[-.20, .33]	.07	Self-assured/open vs. slouching	.14	[-.34, .56]	4(395)
3(273)	[-.05, .19]	.07	Closed arms	-.14	[-.35, .09]	3(273)
2(162)	[-.22, .19]	-.02	Self-touch	-.10	[-.37, .19]	2(160)
4(325)	[-.26, .23]	-.02	Tension/nervousness (vs. relaxed)	-.30	[-.50, -.06]	4(325)
2(200)	[-.41, -.01]	-.22	**Stride length**	-.18	[-.31, -.04]	2(200)
			Paralanguage			
1(100)		.28	Ease of understanding	.35		1(100)
n/a	n/a	n/a	Expressive/varying voice	.01	[-.45, .46]	2(81)
3(262)	[-.07, .35]	.15	**Fluent speaking (vs. nervous)**	.10	[-.27, .44]	2(200)
2(200)	[-.05, .23]	.09	Pleasantness of voice	.43	[.32, .54]	3(224)
2(200)	[-.22, .18]	-.02	Powerful/confident voice (vs. soft)	.02	[-.11, .16]	3(224)
n/a	n/a	n/a	Loudness	.18	[-.12, .45]	2(81)
2(200)	[.04, .31]	.18	Pitch	.05	[-.19, .29]	4(699)
1(54)		.11	Speech rate	-.02	[-.28, .26]	2(499)
1(112)		-.11	Speech vs. nonspeech	-.10	[-.35, .16]	2(499)
1(138)		-.22	Interruptions	-.30		1(151)

Table 13.6 Cue Validity and Cue Utilization Meta-Analyses: Agreeableness (Continued)

			Appearance			
10(983)	[.02, .18]	.10	**Attractiveness**	.32	[.19, .44]	11(897)
6(476)	[-.08, .16]	.04	Babyfaceness vs. maturity	.33	[.17, .46]	6(467)
3(189)	[-.23, .06]	-.09	Distinctiveness	.02	[-.12, .17]	3(189)
10(882)	[.03, .24]	.13	**Neatness**	.18	[.05, .30]	9(658)
8(726)	[-.11, .11]	.00	Stylishness	-.01	[-.11, .09]	6(493)
3(212)	[-.02, .25]	.12	Formality	-.01	[-.15, .13]	3(212)
4(249)	[-.15, .10]	-.02	Eyeglasses	.00	[-.15, .15]	3(176)
3(176)	[-.04, .26]	.11	Volume of Mouth/full lips	.05	[-.13, .22]	3(176)
1(100)		.16	Hair length (long)	.11		1(100)
3(176)	[-.12, .19]	.03	Dark hair color	-.02	[-.17, .13]	3(176)
2(200)	[-.35, -.01]	-.18	Height	-.04	[-.25, .17]	2(200)
2(173)	[-.27, .03]	-.12	Muscular	-.20		1(100)
2(200)	[-.18, .10]	-.04	Weight	.08	[-.06, .22]	2(200)
2(173)	[-.23, .65]	.27	Dark clothes	-.19		1(100)

Note. k = number of included samples, n = overall sample size. The effect size and confidence interval (CI) estimations are based on a random effects model (empty CI cells included only one study). Cues in bold showed at least small ($r \geq 0.10$) effects for both utilization and validity (same direction; across at least two studies).

Table 13.7 Cue Validity and Cue Utilization Meta-Analyses: Conscientiousness

Cue Validity			Conscientiousness	Cue Utilization		
k (n) 95% CI r			Cues	r 95% CI k (n)		
			Facial expression			
5(529)	[-.04, .22]	.09	Cheerful facial expression	.28	[.10, .44]	7(630)
4(414)	[-.14, .05]	-.05	Dominant facial expression	.13	[-.05, .31]	2(200)
n/a	n/a	n/a	General expressiveness	n/a	n/a	n/a
2(200)	[-.10, .18]	.04	Unconcerned (vs. serious)	-.04	[-.24, .17]	2(200)
3(363)	[-.05, .17]	.06	Eye contact	.20	[.04, .34]	4(400)
2(116)	[-.70, .47]	-.17	Eyebrow movements	.15	[-.04, .32]	2(116)
			Body language			
3(212)	[-.27, .32]	.03	Body movement	-.18	[-.36, .00]	5(316)
n/a	n/a	n/a	Forward lean/proximity	.14		1(60)

(Continued)

k (n)	95% CI	r	Body language	r	95% CI	k (n)
3(300)	[-.14, .20]	.03	Gestures	-.01	[-.22, .20]	3(260)
2(200)	[-.30, .29]	-.01	Head movements	-.23	[-.39, -.05]	3(240)
3(237)	[.04, .29]	.16	**Self-assured/open vs. slouching**	.31	[.14, .46]	2(125)
2(213)	[-.28, -.01]	-.15	Closed arms	-.03	[-.16, .11]	2(213)
2(200)	[-.34, -.07]	-.21	**Self-touch**	-.22	[-.35, -.09]	2(200)
4(325)	[-.19, .20]	.01	Tension/nervousness (vs. relaxed)	.21	[-.11, .50]	4(325)
1(100)		-.16	Stride length	-.39		1(100)

k (n)	95% CI	r	Appearance	r	95% CI	k (n)
7(606)	[-.01, .23]	.11	**Attractiveness**	.21	[.06, .35]	10(875)
5(389)	[-.10, .21]	.06	Babyfaceness vs. maturity	.06	[-.29, .40]	5(445)
3(189)	[-.33, -.05]	-.19	**Distinctiveness**	-.12	[-.26, .03]	3(189)
7(505)	[.15, .31]	.23	**Neatness**	.50	[.37, .61]	10(827)
6(493)	[-.01, .17]	.08	Stylishness	.07	[-.11, .25]	6(493)
3(212)	[-.09, .37]	.15	**Formality**	.54	[.32, .71]	5(445)
3(176)	[-.19, .24]	.03	Eyeglasses	.25	[.10, .38]	3(176)
3(176)	[-.13, .21]	.04	Volume of Mouth/full lips	.04	[-.19, .26]	3(176)
2(200)	[-.30, -.03]	-.17	**Hair length (long)**	-.14	[-.27, .00]	2(200)
3(176)	[-.12, .18]	.03	Dark hair color	.12	[-.10, .32]	3(176)
2(200)	[-.28, -.01]	-.15	Height	-.06	[-.29, .17]	2(200)
1(100)		.00	Muscular	-.17		1(100)
2(200)	[-.33, .33]	.00	Weight	.06	[-.08, .20]	2(200)
1(100)		-.13	Dark clothes	-.21		1(100)

Note. k = number of included samples, n = overall sample size. The effect size and confidence interval (CI) estimations are based on a random effects model (empty CI cells included only one study). Cues in bold showed at least small (r ≥ 0.10) effects for both utilization and validity (same direction; across at least two studies).

Table 13.8   Cue Validity and Cue Utilization Meta-Analyses: Intelligence

Cue Validity			Intelligence	Cue Utilization		
k (n) 95% CI r			Cues	r 95% CI k (n)		
			Facial expression			
4(267)	[-.22, .02]	-.10	Cheerful facial expression	.16	[.04, .27]	4(281)
1(100)		.34	Dominant facial expression	.35		1(100)

Table 13.8 Cue Validity and Cue Utilization Meta-Analyses: Intelligence   (Continued)

			Facial expression			
n/a	n/a	n/a	General expressiveness	.12	[-.10, .33]	2(122)
2(142)	[-.24, .09]	-.08	Unconcerned (vs. serious)	-.13	[-.61, .41]	2(142)
4(267)	[-.07, .22]	.08	Eye contact	.32	[.19, .43]	3(221)
n/a	n/a	n/a	Eyebrow movements	n/a	n/a	n/a

			Body language			
2(142)	[-.18, .15]	-.01	Body movement	.03	[-.11, .17]	3(202)
3(258)	[-.01, .24]	.12	Forward lean/proximity	.16		1(42)
4(267)	[-.09, .15]	.03	Gestures	.28	[.11, .43]	4(283)
2(88)	[-.22, .21]	-.01	Head movements	.16		1(42)
2(121)	[-.18, .25]	.04	Self-assured/open vs. slouching	.28	[-.09, .58]	2(121)
2(142)	[-.16, .18]	.01	Closed arms	-.12	[-.32, .10]	2(142)
2(88)	[-.10, .32]	.12	Self-touch	.06	[-.14, .25]	2(104)
3(221)	[-.39, .20]	-.10	**Tension/nervousness (vs. relaxed)**	-.15	[-.28, -.02]	3(221)
1(100)		.17	Stride length	.20		1(100)

			Paralanguage			
4(251)	[.01, .44]	.24	**Ease of understanding**	.30	[.12, .46]	4(251)
1(42)		-.02	Expressive/varying voice	.23	[.03, .41]	2(102)
3(221)	[-.28, .44]	.09	Fluent speaking (vs. nervous)	.25	[.07, .42]	6(373)
3(221)	[-.08, .32]	.12	**Pleasantness of voice**	.22	[.06, .37]	3(221)
3(165)	[-.26, .05]	-.11	Powerful/confident voice (vs. soft)	.18	[.00, .34]	2(135)
n/a	n/a	n/a	Loudness	.45		1(30)
2(142)	[-.36, -.04]	-.21	Pitch	.00	[-.25, .25]	2(142)
2(109)	[-.08, .49]	.22	**Speech rate**	.31	[.12, .47]	2(109)
4(197)	[-.01, .39]	.20	**Speech vs. nonspeech**	.30	[.13, .45]	3(151)
n/a	n/a	n/a	Interruptions	n/a	n/a	n/a

			Appearance			
3(632)	[-.26, .24]	-.01	Attractiveness	.53	[.44, .60]	2(602)
1(100)		.02	Babyfaceness vs. maturity	-.10		1(100)

(Continued)

			Appearance			
1(502)		.00	Distinctiveness	-.25		1(502)
1(100)		-.06	Neatness	.34		1(100)
1(100)		-.11	Stylishness	.13		1(100)
1(100)		-.09	Formality	.17		1(100)
n/a	n/a	n/a	Eyeglasses	n/a	n/a	n/a
n/a	n/a	n/a	Volume of Mouth/full lips	n/a	n/a	n/a
1(100)		-.05	Hair length (long)	-.01		1(100)
n/a	n/a	n/a	Dark hair color	n/a	n/a	n/a
1(100)		.03	Height	.16		1(100)
1(100)		-.07	Muscular	.20		1(100)
1(100)		-.05	Weight	-.36	[-.50, -.20]	2(130)
1(100)		.11	Dark clothes	.07		1(100)

Note. k = number of included samples, n = overall sample size. The effect size and confidence interval (CI) estimations are based on a random effects model (empty CI cells included only one study). Cues in bold showed at least small ($r \geq 0.10$) effects for both utilization and validity (same direction; across at least two studies).

Potential Moderators

The mentioned relationship between nonverbal cues and personality (judgments) can be influenced by a variety of personal, situational, and trait-specific factors that affect the strength of cue utilities/validities. Funder (1999, 2012, also see chapter 2 by Letzring & Funder in this handbook) distinguishes between four classes of moderators: differences between traits (good trait), differences regarding the available information (good information), differences between perceivers (good judge), and differences between targets (good target).

A good trait on the individual cue level refers to traits that have, relative to other traits, a high number of valid cues that are also utilized by observers. Comparing the traits, one can notice that extraversion stands out by being associated with the highest number of valid and utilized nonverbal cues. This is in line with previous research identifying extraversion as a trait that is easily observable across many different contexts (see Back & Nestler, 2016, and overviews mentioned earlier). Agreeableness however, is one of the traits hardest to judge accurately. Our results show that the lack of accuracy when judging agreeableness is not generally due to missing knowledge or judgment biases but also due to the limited number of valid cues available (e.g., for agreeableness only 10 percent of investigated cues showed validities of at least $r = 0.20$. Extraversion in contrast had a percentage of 18).

The quantity and quality of information (i.e., good information) can also influence cue validities and cue utilities. One could imagine, for example, that over time (of interacting with someone) cue validities for dynamic cues increase due to more reliable variance in cue expression between different targets (e.g., reliable differences in the amount of head movements, which could be related to extraversion, might only emerge after a few minutes of interaction). Furthermore, the type of situation and their trait relevance might serve as moderators for cue validities (e.g., a tense body language might be a highly valid cue for judging neuroticism when the situation activates this specific trait but not in a neutral situation). While levels of accuracy have shown to increase over time (e.g., Borkenau et al., 2004; Letzring, Wells, & Funder, 2006) and to differ between settings varying in trait relevance (Hirschmüller, Egloff, Schmukle, Nestler, & Back, 2015; Letzring et al., 2006), influences on single cue validities have not been investigated yet.

Considering the right side of the lens model (i.e., cue utilities), good information can also refer to the type of judgment channel (e.g., video with or without sound, audio only) observers are exposed to. For example, multiple studies included in this chapter (e.g., Borkenau & Liebler, 1992a, 1992b, 1995; Murphy, Hall, & Colvin, 2003; Reynolds & Gifford, 2001) compare cue utilizations for different kinds of judgments channels. Results by Borkenau and Liebler (1995) suggest that if valid cues are not observable (e.g., there are no paralinguistic cues), the utilization of observable nonvalid cues (e.g., specific body language cues) increases, which would result in lower accuracy.

Regarding the expression of nonverbal cues, good targets would refer to a group of individuals that provides more nonverbal cues and/or more variance in nonverbal cues, resulting in potentially stronger cue validities. Generally, research has identified the traits of extraversion and emotional stability as features of good targets (i.e., targets that act more and express their emotions, cf. Colvin, 1993; Human & Biesanz, 2011; Human, Biesanz, Finseth, Pierce, & Le, 2014), but, to the best of our knowledge, specific changes in cue validities or utilities have not been investigated. There have, however, been many studies separating results by targets' sex (e.g., Aronovitch, 1976; Berry & Landry, 1997; Lippa, 1998; Riggio & Friedman, 1986; Shrout & Fiske, 1981; Simpson, Gangestad, & Biek, 1993). Lippa (1998), for example, found multiple nonverbal cues that were valid indicators of females' extraversion but not of males' extraversion, suggesting that it should be easier to judge females' extraversion.

Someone who is identified as a good judge should be better at identifying and using valid cues (and not using nonvalid cues) compared to other judges, thus reaching higher accuracies. Another influence could be that good judges evoke more valid cues in targets. As most judgment accuracy studies do not include interactions between observers and targets, this explanation has received little empirical attention so far (but see Letzring, 2008). While the question "Who is a good judge?" has engaged researchers for a long time, results have been ambiguous (cf. Back & Nestler, 2016; see Davis & Kraus, 1997; Hall, Andrzejewski, & Yopchick, 2009; Taft, 1955 for meta-analyses). There have been a few studies analyzing cue utilities for different groups of (potentially good) judges (e.g., Hartung & Renner, 2011; Hirschmüller, Egloff, Nestler, &

Back, 2013; Nestler & Back, 2017). For example, Hartung and Renner (2011) showed that socially highly curious judges generally used more available cues and were thus more likely to detect valid cues for visible traits (in this case extraversion and openness).

Outlook and Future Research

Here we summarize suggestions that, in our view, would benefit future research on nonverbal cues and their relation to trait accuracy. First, while meta-analytical results presented in this chapter can serve as a first overview of validities and utilities for a variety of cues, more, and more comprehensive studies are needed. Most included studies only investigated a small number of cues (< 10) and there are many trait-cue combinations for which empirical evidence is limited. It would also be beneficial to replicate the presented results across more diverse target samples and judgment contexts. Furthermore, results across studies are often difficult to integrate. For example, some studies only presented correlations controlled for sex and age, while other studies only reported significant cue relationships. Furthermore, nearly all studies focused on aggregated observer utilities (i.e., correlations computed for personality judgments aggregated across observers). Results based on this approach, in contrast to the single observer approach (separate correlations for each observer), depend on the number of observers within a study (more observers lead to higher utilities because of higher reliability of those ratings, cf. Back & Nestler, 2016; Hall & Bernieri, 2001; Nestler & Back, 2017), making it difficult to compare studies with a varying number of observers. Thus, we urge researchers to (at least in online supplementaries) present comprehensive results, which include zero-order cue validities and cue utilities (aggregated and single observer) for all assessed cue and trait combinations.

Second, as stated previously, the research on how potential moderators influence cue validities and cue utilities, especially good information, good target, and good judge, is limited. Therefore, it would be beneficial to investigate how cue validities change over time and settings (good information) and to additionally present results separated by specific target criteria (besides sex), to identify subgroups that might constitute as good targets. In a similar way, systematically comparing single-observer cue utilities across judges would shed more light on the good judge.

Third, the advance of big data and accompanying machine learning techniques provides opportunities for the investigation of nonverbal cues. Research shows that, based on digital footprints, computer algorithms are often better in judging personality than humans (Youyou, Kosinski, & Stillwell, 2015) and it would be fruitful to transfer these methods to the judgment of pictures, videos, or audio files. Thus, it could be investigated if computer algorithms can outperform human judges in these contexts and how humans versus computers differ in their cue utilizations. Machine learning approaches could also be used as an economic and more objective tool for the quantification of nonverbal cues (i.e., use machine learning approaches instead of raters to judge the degree of smiling of targets).

In summary, with this chapter, we offer a first overview of how and which nonverbal cues contribute to accuracy for different traits. Results show that, for all traits, there are at least a few nonverbal cues that allow for accurate glimpses into one's personality, and perceivers often showed the ability to identify relevant cues. We plan to expand this overview in the future and to regularly update the results in the online supplement (osf.io/9p64g). We hereby invite interested readers to contribute to a more exhaustive documentation and add additional studies. In the years to come, with collaborations like this, we will be able to offer more comprehensive insights on which cues drive trait accuracies.

Further Reading

The references provided below are studies included in the meta-analysis

Albright, L., Kenny, D. A., & Malloy, T. E. (1988). Consensus in personality judgments at zero acquaintance. Journal of Personality and Social Psychology, 55(3), 387–395. doi:10.1037/0022-3514.55.3.387

Albright, L., Malloy, T. E., Dong, Q., Kenny, D. A., Fang, X., Winquist, L., & Yu, D. (1997). Cross-cultural consensus in personality judgments. Journal of Personality and Social Psychology, 72(3), 558–569. doi:10.1037//0022-3514.72.3.558

Aronovitch, C. D. (1976). The voice of personality: Stereotyped judgments and their relation to voice quality and sex of speaker. Journal of Social Psychology, 99, 207–220.

Asendorpf, J. B., Banse, R., & Mücke, D. (2002). Double dissociation between implicit and explicit personality self-concept: The case of shy behavior. Journal of Personality and Social Psychology, 83(2), 380–393. doi:10.1037//0022-3514.83.2.380

Back, M. D., Penke, L., Schmukle, S. C., Sachse, K., Borkenau, P., & Asendorpf, J. B. (2011). Why mate choices are not as reciprocal as we assume: The role of personality, flirting and physical attractiveness. European Journal of Personality, 25(2), 120–132. doi:10.1002/per.806

Back, M. D., Schmukle, S. C., & Egloff, B. (2010). Why are narcissists so charming at first sight? Decoding the narcissism-popularity link at zero acquaintance. Journal of Personality and Social Psychology, 98(1), 132–145. doi:10.1037/a0016338

Back, M. D., Schmukle, S. C., & Egloff, B. (2011). A closer look at first sight: Social relations lens model analysis of personality and interpersonal attraction at zero acquaintance. European Journal of Personality, 25(3), 225–238. doi:10.1002/per.790

Berry, D. S., & Hansen, J. S. (2000). Personality, nonverbal behavior, and interaction quality in female dyads. Personality and Social Psychology Bulletin, 26(3), 278–292. doi:10.1177/0146167200265002

Berry, D. S., & Landry, J. C. (1997). Facial maturity and daily social interaction. Journal of Personality and Social Psychology, 72(3), 570–580. doi:10.1037/0022-3514.72.3.570

Biel, J.-I., Aran, O., & Gatica-Perez, D. (2011).You are known by how you vlog: Personality impressions and nonverbal behavior in YouTube. Paper presented at the AAAI Conference on Weblogs and Social Media, Barcelona, Spain.

Borkenau, P., Brecke, S., Möttig, C., & Paelecke, M. (2009). Extraversion is accurately perceived after a 50-ms exposure to a face. Journal of Research in Personality, 43(4), 703–706. doi:10.1016/j.jrp.2009.03.007

Borkenau, P., & Liebler, A. (1992a). The cross-modal consistency of personality: Inferring strangers' traits from visual or acoustic information. Journal of Research in Personality, 26(2), 183–204. doi:10.1016/0092-6566(92)90053-7

Borkenau, P., & Liebler, A. (1992b). Trait inferences: Sources of validity at zero acquaintance. Journal of Personality and Social Psychology, 62(4), 645–657. doi:10.1037/0022-3514.62.4.645

Brown, W. M., Palameta, B., & Moore, C. (2003). Are there nonverbal cues to commitment? An exploratory study using the zero-acquaintance video presentation paradigm. Evolutionary Psychology, 1(1), 42–69. doi:10.1177/147470490300100104

Burgoon, J. K., Birk, T., & Pfau, M. (1990). Nonverbal behaviors, persuasion, and credibility. Human Communication Research, 17(1), 140–169. doi:10.1111/j.1468-2958.1990.tb00229.x

Burnett, J. R., & Motowidlo, S. J. (1998). Relations between different sources of information in the structured selection interview. Personnel Psychology, 51(4), 963–983. doi:10.1111/j.1744-6570.1998.tb00747.x

Campbell, A., & Rushton, J. P. (1978). Bodily communication and personality. British Journal of Social and Clinical Psychology, 17(1), 31–36. doi:10.1111/j.2044-8260.1978.tb00893.x

Creed, A. T., & Funder, D. C. (1998). Social anxiety: From the inside and outside. Personality and Individual Differences, 25(1), 19–33. doi:10.1016/S0191-8869(98)00037-3

Eaton, L. G., & Funder, D. C. (2003). The creation and consequences of the social world: An interactional analysis of extraversion. European Journal of Personality, 17(5), 375–395. doi:10.1002/per.477

Ferguson, N. (1977). Simultaneous speech, interruptions and dominance. British Journal of Social and Clinical Psychology, 16(4), 295–302. doi:10.1111/j.2044-8260.1977.tb00235.x

Funder, D. C., & Sneed, C. D. (1993). Behavioral manifestations of personality: An ecological approach to judgmental accuracy. Journal of Personality and Social Psychology, 64(3), 479–490. doi:10.1037/0022-3514.64.3.479

Gifford, R. (1991). Mapping nonverbal behavior on the interpersonal circle. Journal of Personality and Social Psychology, 61(2), 279–288. doi:10.1037/0022-3514.61.2.279

Gifford, R. (1994). A lens-mapping framework for understanding the encoding and decoding of interpersonal dispositions in nonverbal behavior. Journal of Personality and Social Psychology, 66(2), 398–412. doi:10.1037//0022-3514.66.2.398

Gifford, R., & O'Connor, B. (1987). The interpersonal circumplex as a behavior map. Journal of Personality and Social Psychology, 52(5), 1019–1026. doi:10.1037/0022-3514.52.5.1019

Hartung, F.-M., & Renner, B. (2011). Social curiosity and interpersonal perception: A judge x trait interaction. Personality and Social Psychology Bulletin, 37(6), 796–814. doi:10.1177/0146167211400618

Hirschmüller, S., Egloff, B., Nestler, S., & Back, M. D. (2013). The dual lens model: A comprehensive framework for understanding self-other agreement of personality judgments at zero acquaintance. Journal of Personality and Social Psychology, 104(2), 335–353. doi:10.1037/a0030383

Hirschmüller, S., Egloff, B., Schmukle, S. C., Nestler, S., & Back, M. D. (2015). Accurate judgments of neuroticism at zero acquaintance: A question of relevance. Journal of Personality, 83(2), 221–228. doi:10.1111/jopy.12097

Hirschmüller, S., Schmukle, S. C., Krause, S., Back, M. D., & Egloff, B. (2018). Accuracy of self-esteem judgments at zero acquaintance. Journal of Personality, 86(2), 308–319. doi:10.1111/jopy.12316

Ickes, W., & Barnes, R. D. (1977). The role of sex and self-monitoring in unstructured dyadic interactions. Journal of Personality and Social Psychology, 35(5), 315–330. doi:10.1037/0022-3514.35.5.315

Kaurin, A., Heil, L., Wessa, M., Egloff, B., & Hirschmüller, S. (2018). Selfies reflect actual personality—Just like photos or short videos in standardized lab conditions. Journal of Research in Personality, 76, 154–164. doi:10.1016/j.jrp.2018.08.007

Kendon, A., & Cook, M. (1969). The consistency of gaze patterns in social interaction. British Journal of Psychology, 60(4), 481–494.

Kenny, D. A., Horner, C., Kashy, D. A., & Chu, L.-C. (1992). Consensus at zero acquaintance: Replication, behavioral cues, and stability. Journal of Personality and Social Psychology, 62(1), 88–97. doi:10.1037//0022-3514.62.1.88

Koppensteiner, M., & Grammer, K. (2010). Motion patterns in political speech and their influence on personality ratings. Journal of Research in Personality, 44(3), 374–379. doi:10.1016/j.jrp.2010.04.002

Koppensteiner, M., Stephan, P., & Jäschke, J. P. M. (2016). Moving speeches: Dominance, trustworthiness and competence in body motion. Personality and Individual Differences, 94, 101–106. doi:10.1016/j.paid.2016.01.013

Levesque, M. J., & Kenny, D. A. (1993). Accuracy of behavioral predictions at zero acquaintance: A social relations analysis. Journal of Personality and Social Psychology, 65(6), 1178–1187. doi:10.1037/0022-3514.65.6.1178

Lippa, R. (1998). The nonverbal display and judgment of extraversion, masculinity, femininity, and gender diagnosticity: A lens model analysis. Journal of Research in Personality, 32(1), 80–107. doi:10.1006/jrpe.1997.2189

Lyons, K. D., Tickle-Degnen, L., Henry, A., & Cohn, E. (2004). Impressions of personality in Parkinson's disease: Can rehabilitation practitioners see beyond the symptoms? Rehabilitation Psychology, 49(4), 328–333. doi:10.1037/0090-5550.49.4.328

Mallory, E. B., & Miller, V. R. (1958). A possible basis for the association of voice characteristics and personality traits. Speech Monographs, 25(4), 255–260. doi:10.1080/03637755809375240\

Meier, B. P., Robinson, M. D., Carter, M. S., & Hinsz, V. B. (2010). Are sociable people more beautiful? A zero-acquaintance analysis of agreeableness, extraversion, and attractiveness. Journal of Research in Personality, 44(2), 293–296. doi:10.1016/j.jrp.2010.02.002

Montepare, J. M., & Dobish, H. (2003). The contribution of emotion perceptions and their overgeneralizations to trait impressions. Journal of Nonverbal Behavior, 27(4), 237–254.

Murphy, N. A. (2007). Appearing smart: The impression management of intelligence, person perception accuracy, and behavior in social interaction. Personality and Social Psychology Bulletin, 33(3), 325–339. doi:10.1177/0146167206294871

Murphy, N. A., Hall, J. A., & Colvin, C. R. (2003). Accurate intelligence assessments in social interactions: Mediators and gender effects. Journal of Personality, 71(3), 465–493. doi:10.1111/1467-6494.7103008

Naumann, L. P., Vazire, S., Rentfrow, P. J., & Gosling, S. D. (2009). Personality judgments based on physical appearance. Personality and Social Psychology Bulletin, 35(12), 1661–1671. doi:10.1177/0146167209346309

Nestler, S., Egloff, B., Küfner, A. C. P., & Back, M. D. (2012). An integrative lens model approach to bias and accuracy in human inferences: Hindsight effects and knowledge updating in personality judgments. Journal of Personality and Social Psychology, 103(4), 689–717. doi:10.1037/a0029461

Pedersen, D. M. (1973). Correlates of behavioral personal space. Psychological Reports, 32, 828–830.

Petrican, R., Todorov, A., & Grady, C. (2014). Personality at face value: Facial appearance predicts self and other personality judgments among strangers and spouses. Journal of Nonverbal Behavior, 38(2), 259–277. doi:10.1007/s10919-014-0175-3

Reynolds, D.'A. J., & Gifford, R. (2001). The sounds and sights of intelligence: A lens model channel analysis. Personality and Social Psychology Bulletin, 27(2), 187–200. doi:10.1177/0146167201272005

Riggio, R. E., & Friedman, H. S. (1986). Impression formation: The role of expressive behavior. Journal of Personality and Social Psychology, 50(2), 421–427. doi:10.1037//0022-3514.50.2.421

Riggio, R. E., Lippa, R., & Salinas, C. (1990). The display of personality in expressive movement. Journal of Research in Personality, 24(1), 16–31. doi:10.1016/0092-6566(90)90003-O

Scherer, K. R. (1978). Personality inference from voice quality: The loud voice of extroversion. European Journal of Social Psychology, 8(4), 467–487. doi:10.1002/ejsp.2420080405

Schmid Mast, M., & Hall, J. A. (2004). Who is the boss and who is not? Accuracy of judging status. Journal of Nonverbal Behavior, 28(3), 145–165. doi:10.1023/B:JONB.0000039647.94190.21

Schultheis, O. C., & Brunstein, J. C. (2002). Inhibited power motivation and persuasive communication: A lens model analysis. Journal of Personality, 70(4), 553–582. doi:10.1111/1467-6494.05014

Shrout, P. E., & Fiske, D. W. (1981). Nonverbal behaviors and social evaluation. Journal of Personality, 49(2), 115–128.

Simpson, J. A., Gangestad, S. W., & Biek, M. (1993). Personality and nonverbal social behavior: An ethological perspective of relationship initiation. Journal of Experimental Social Psychology, 29, 434–461.

Stopfer, J. M., Egloff, B., Nestler, S., & Back, M. D. (2014). Personality expression and impression formation in online social networks: An integrative approach to Understanding the processes of accuracy, impression management and meta-accuracy. European Journal of Personality, 28(1), 73–94. doi:10.1002/per.1935

ten Brinke, L., Porter, S., Korva, N., Fowler, K., Lilienfeld, S. O., & Patrick, C. J. (2017). An examination of the communication styles associated with psychopathy and their influence on observer impressions. Journal of Nonverbal Behavior, 41(3), 269–287. doi:10.1007/s10919-017-0252-5

Vazire, S., Naumann, L. P., Rentfrow, P. J., & Gosling, S. D. (2008). Portrait of a narcissist: Manifestations of narcissism in physical appearance. Journal of Research in Personality, 42(6), 1439–1447. doi:10.1016/j.jrp.2008.06.007

Zebrowitz, L. A., Hall, J. A., Murphy, N. A., & Rhodes, G. (2002). Looking smart and looking good: Facial cues to intelligence and their origins. Personality and Social Psychology Bulletin, 28(2), 238–249. doi:10.1177/0146167202282009

Zebrowitz, L. A., & Montepare, J. M. (1992). Impressions of babyfaced individuals across the life span. Developmental Psychology, 28(6), 1143–1152. doi:10.1037//0012-1649.28.6.1143

Zebrowitz, L. A., Voinescu, L., & Collins, M. A. (1996). "Wide-eyed" and "crooked-faced": Determinants of perceived and real honesty across the life span. Personality and Social Psychology Bulletin, 22(12), 1258–1269.

References

Ambady, N., Bernieri, F. J., & Richeson, J. A. (2000). Toward a histology of social behavior-judgmental accuracy from thin slices of the behavioral stream. Advances in Experimental Social Psychology, 32, 201–271.

Ambady, N., & Skowronski, J. J. (Eds.). (2008). First impressions. New York, NY: Guilford Press.

Back, M. D., & Nestler, S. (2016). Accuracy of judging personality. In J. A. Hall, M. S. Mast, & T. V. West (Eds.), The social psychology of perceiving others accurately (98–124). Cambridge, UK: Cambridge University Press.

Back, M. D., Schmukle, S. C., & Egloff, B. (2008). How extraverted is honey.bunny77@hotmail.de? Inferring personality from e-mail addresses. Journal of Research in Personality, 42(4), 1116–1122. doi:10.1016/j.jrp.2008.02.001

Back, M. D., Stopfer, J. M., Vazire, S., Gaddis, S., Schmukle, S. C., Egloff, B., & Gosling, S. D. (2010). Facebook profiles reflect actual personality, not self-idealization. Psychological Science, 21(3), 372–374. doi:10.1177/0956797609360756

Bakemann, R. (2000). Behavioral observation and coding. In H. T. Reis & C. M. Judd (Eds.), Handbook of research methods in social and personality psychology (pp. 138–159). New York, NY: Cambridge University Press.

Bänziger, T., Hosoya, G., & Scherer, K. R. (2015). Path models of vocal emotion communication. PloS One, 10(9), e0136675. doi:10.1371/journal.pone.0136675

Berry, D. S. (1990). Taking people at face value: Evidence for the kernel of truth hypothesis. Social Cognition, 8(4), 343–361.

Blanck, P. D., Rosenthal, R., Snodgrass, S. E., DePaulo, B. M., & Zuckerman, M. (1981). Sex differences in eavesdropping on nonverbal cues: Developmental changes. Journal of Personality and Social Psychology, 41(2), 391–396. doi:10.1037//0022-3514.41.2.391

Borkenau, P., & Liebler, A. (1993). Convergence of stranger ratings of personality and intelligence with self-ratings, partner ratings, and measured intelligence. Journal of Personality and Social Psychology, 65(3), 546–553.

Borkenau, P., & Liebler, A. (1995). Observable attributes as manifestations and cues of personality and intelligence. Journal of Personality, 63(1), 1–25. doi:10.1111/j.1467-6494.1995.tb00799.x

Borkenau, P., Mauer, N., Riemann, R., Spinath, F. M., & Angleitner, A. (2004). Thin slices of behavior as cues of personality and intelligence. Journal of Personality and Social Psychology, 86(4), 599–614. doi:10.1037/0022-3514.86.4.599

Borkenau, P., Mosch, A., Tandler, N., & Wolf, A. (2016). Accuracy of judgments of personality based on textual information on major life domains. Journal of Personality, 84(2), 214–224. doi:10.1111/jopy.12153

Brauner, E., Boos, M., & Kolbe, M. (Eds.). (2018). Cambridge Handbook of Group Interaction Analysis. Cambridge, UK: Cambridge University Press.

Brunswik, E. (1952). The conceptual framework of psychology. International encyclopedia of unified science: v. 1, no. 10. Chicago, IL: University of Chicago Press. Brunswik, E. (1956). Perception and the representative design of psychological experiments (2nd ed.). Berkeley: University of California Press.

Burgoon, J. K., Guerrero, L. K., & Floyd, K. (2010). Nonverbal communication. London: Routledge, Taylor & Francis Group.

Carney, D. R., Hall, J. A., & LeBeau, L. S. (2005). Beliefs about the nonverbal expression of social power. Journal of Nonverbal Behavior, 29(2), 105–123. doi:10.1007/s10919-005-2743-z

Cohen, J. (1992). A power primer. Psychological Bulletin, 112(1), 155–159. doi:10.1037//0033-2909.112.1.155

Colvin, C. R. (1993). "Judgable" people: Personality, behavior, and competing explanations. Journal of Personality and Social Psychology, 64(5), 861–873. doi:10.1037//0022-3514.64.5.861

Connelly, B. S., & Ones, D. S. (2010). An other perspective on personality: Meta-analytic integration of observers' accuracy and predictive validity. Psychological Bulletin, 136(6), 1092–1122. doi:10.1037/a0021212

Connolly, J. J., Kavanagh, E. J., & Viswesvaran, C. (2007). The convergent validity between self and observer ratings of personality: A meta-analytic review. International Journal of Selection and Assessment, 15(1), 110–117. doi:10.1111/j.1468-2389.2007.00371.x

Darwin, C. (1897). The expression of the emotions in man and animals. New York, NY: D. Appleton and Company.

Davis, M. H., & Kraus, L. A. (1997). Personality and empathic accuracy. In W. Ickes (Ed.), Empathic accuracy (pp. 144–168). New York, NY: Guilford.

DeGroot, T., & Gooty, J. (2009). Can nonverbal cues be used to make meaningful personality attributions in employment interviews? Journal of Business and Psychology, 24(2), 179–192. doi:10.1007/s10869-009-9098-0

DePaulo, B. M. (1992). Nonverbal behavior and self-presentation. Psychological Bulletin, 111(2), 203–243. doi:10.1037//0033-2909.111.2.203

Ekman, P. (1994). Strong evidence for universals in facial expressions: A reply to Russell's mistaken critique. *Psychological Bulletin, 115*(2), 268–287.

Ekman, P. (2016). What scientists who study emotion agree about. *Perspectives on Psychological Science, 11*(1), 31–34. doi:10.1177/1745691615596992

Ekman, P., & Friesen, W. V. (1969). Nonverbal leakage and clues to deception. *Psychiatry, 32*(1), 87–106.

Ekman, P., & Friesen, W. V. (1971). Constants across cultures in the face and emotion. *Journal of Personality and Social Psychology, 17*(2), 124–129. doi:10.1037/h0030377

Ekman, P., & Rosenberg, E. L. (Eds.). (1997). *Series in affective science: What the face reveals: Basic and applied studies of spontaneous expression using the facial action coding system (FACS)*. New York, NY: Oxford University Press.

Ekman, P., Sorenson, E. R., & Friesen, W. V. (1969). Pan-cultural elements in facial displays of emotion. *Science, 164*(3875), 86–88. doi:10.1126/science.164.3875.86

Elfenbein, H. A., & Eisenkraft, N. (2010). The relationship between displaying and perceiving nonverbal cues of affect: a meta-analysis to solve an old mystery. *Journal of Personality and Social Psychology, 98*(2), 301–318. doi:10.1037/a0017766

Funder, D. C. (1999). *Personality judgment: A realistic approach to person perception*. San Diego, CA: Academic Press.

Funder, D. C. (2012). Accurate personality judgment. *Current Directions in Psychological Science, 21*(3), 177–182. doi:10.1177/0963721412445309

Gifford, R., Ng, C. F., & Wilkinson, M. (1985). Nonverbal cues in the employment interview: Links between applicant qualities and interviewer judgments. *Journal of Applied Psychology, 70*(4), 729–736. doi:10.1037//0021-9010.70.4.729

Gosling, S. D., Ko, S. J., Mannarelli, T., & Morris, M. E. (2002). A room with a cue: Personality judgments based on offices and bedrooms. *Journal of Personality and Social Psychology, 82*(3), 379–398. doi:10.1037/0022-3514.82.3.379

Grünberg, M., Mattern, J., Geukes, K., Küfner, A. C. P., & Back, M. D. (2018). Assessing group interactions in personality psychology: The Münster Behavior Coding-System (M-BeCoSy). In E. Brauner, M. Boos, & M. Kolbe (Eds.), *Cambridge Handbook of Group Interaction Analysis* (pp. 602–611). Cambridge, UK: Cambridge University Press.

Hall, J. A., & Andrzejewski, S. A. (2008). Who draws accurate first impressions? Personal correlates of sensitivity to nonverbal cues. In N. Ambady & J. J. Skowronski (Eds.), *First impressions* (pp. 87–105). New York, NY: Guilford Press.

Hall, J. A., Andrzejewski, S. A., Murphy, N. A., Mast, M. S., & Feinstein, B. A. (2008). Accuracy of judging others' traits and states: Comparing mean levels across tests. *Journal of Research in Personality, 42*(6), 1476–1489. doi:10.1016/j.jrp.2008.06.013

Hall, J. A., Andrzejewski, S. A., & Yopchick, J. E. (2009). Psychosocial correlates of interpersonal sensitivity: A meta-analysis. *Journal of Nonverbal Behavior, 33*(3), 149–180. doi:10.1007/s10919-009-0070-5

Hall, J. A., & Bernieri, F. J. (2001). *Interpersonal sensitivity: Theory and measurement*. Mahwah, NJ: Erlbaum.

Hall, J. A., Coats, E. J., & LeBeau, L. S. (2005). Nonverbal behavior and the vertical dimension of social relations: A meta-analysis. *Psychological Bulletin, 131*(6), 898–924. doi:10.1037/0033-2909.131.6.898

Hall, J. A., Gunnery, S. D., Letzring, T. D., Carney, D. R., & Colvin, C. R. (2017). Accuracy of judging affect and accuracy

of judging personality: How and when are they related? *Journal of Personality, 85*(5), 583–592. doi:10.1111/jopy.12262

Hall, J. A., Horgan, T. G., & Murphy, N. A. (2018). Nonverbal communication. *Annual Review of Psychology*. Advance online publication. doi:10.1146/annurev-psych-010418-103145

Hall, J. A., Schmidt Mast, M., & West, T. V. (2016). Accurate interpersonal perception: Many traditions, one topic. In J. A. Hall, M. S. Mast, & T. V. West (Eds.), *The social psychology of perceiving others accurately* (pp. 3–22). Cambridge, UK: Cambridge University Press.

Harrigan, J. A., Rosenthal, R., & Scherer, K. R. (Eds.). (2005). *Series in affective science. The new handbook of methods in nonverbal behavior research*. Oxford, UK: Oxford University Press.

Harris, M. J., & Garris, C. P. (2008). You never get a second chance to make a first impression: Behavioral consequences of first impressions. In N. Ambady & J. J. Skowronski (Eds.), *First impressions* (pp. 147–168). New York, NY: Guilford Press.

Hassin, R., & Trope, Y. (2000). Facing faces: Studies on the cognitive aspects of physiognomy. *Journal of Personality and Social Psychology, 78*(5), 837–852. doi:10.1037/0022-3514.78.5.837

Henley, N. (1977). *Body politics: Power, sex, and nonverbal communication*. New York, NY: Simon & Schuster.

Heyman, R. E., Lorber, M. F., Eddy, J. M., & West, T. V. (2014). Behavioral observation and coding. In H. T. Reis & C. M. Judd (Eds.), *Handbook of research methods in social and personality psychology* (2nd ed., pp. 345–372). New York, NY: Cambridge University Press. doi:10.1017/CBO9780511996481.018

Hildebrandt, A., Olderbak, S., & Wilhelm, O. (2015). Facial emotion expression, individual differences in. In James D. Wright, *International Encyclopedia of the Social and Behavioral Sciences* (2nd ed., pp. 667–675). Oxford, UK: Elsevier. doi:10.1016/B978-0-08-097086-8.25008-3

Human, L. J., & Biesanz, J. C. (2011). Target adjustment and self-other agreement: Utilizing trait observability to disentangle judgeability and self-knowledge. *Journal of Personality and Social Psychology, 101*(1), 202–216. doi:10.1037/a0023782

Human, L. J., Biesanz, J. C., Finseth, S. M., Pierce, B., & Le, M. (2014). To thine own self be true: Psychological adjustment promotes judgeability via personality-behavior congruence. *Journal of Personality and Social Psychology, 106*(2), 286–303. doi:10.1037/a0034860

Izard, C. E. (1971). *The face of emotion*. The century psychology series. New York, NY: Appleton-Century-Crofts.

Izard, C. E. (1994). Innate and universal facial expressions: Evidence from developmental and cross-cultural research. *Psychological Bulletin, 115*(2), 288–299. doi:10.1037//0033-2909.115.2.288

Jackson, L. A., Hunter, J. E., & Hodge, C. N. (1995). Physical attractiveness and intellectual competence: A meta-analytic review. *Social Psychology Quarterly, 58*(2), 108–122.

Jussim, L., Cain, T., Crawford, J., Harber, K., & Cohen, F. (2009). The unbearable accuracy of stereotypes. In T. Nelson (Ed.), *Handbook of prejudice, stereotyping, and discrimination* (pp. 199–227). Hillsdale, NJ: Erlbaum.

Kanazawa, S. (2011). Intelligence and physical attractiveness☆. *Intelligence, 39*(1), 7–14. doi:10.1016/j.intell.2010.11.003

Kenny, D. A., Albright, L., Malloy, T. E., & Kashy, D. A. (1994). Consensus in interpersonal perception: Acquaintance and the big five. *Psychological Bulletin, 116*(2), 245–258. doi:10.1037/0033-2909.116.2.245

Knutson, B. (1996). Facial expressions of emotion influence interpersonal trait inferences. *Journal of Nonverbal Behavior, 20*(3), 165–182. doi:10.1007/BF02281954

Kramer, E. (1963). Judgment of personal characteristics and emotions from nonverbal properties of speech. *Psychological Bulletin, 60*(4), 408–420. doi:10.1037/h0044890

Küfner, A. C.P., Back, M. D., Nestler, S., & Egloff, B. (2010). Tell me a story and I will tell you who you are! Lens model analyses of personality and creative writing. *Journal of Research in Personality, 44*(4), 427–435. doi:10.1016/j.jrp.2010.05.003

Langlois, J. H., Kalakanis, L., Rubenstein, A. J., Larson, A., Hallam, M., & Smoot, M. (2000). Maxims or myths of beauty? A meta-analytic and theoretical review. *Psychological Bulletin, 126*(3), 390–423. doi:10.1037//0033-2909.126.3.390

Letzring, T. D. (2008). The good judge of personality: Characteristics, behaviors, and observer accuracy. *Journal of Research in Personality, 42*(4), 914–932. doi:10.1016/j.jrp.2007.12.003

Letzring, T. D., Wells, S. M., & Funder, D. C. (2006). Information quantity and quality affect the realistic accuracy of personality judgment. *Journal of Personality and Social Psychology, 91*(1), 111–123. doi:10.1037/0022-3514.91.1.111

Manusov, V. L. (Ed.). (2004). *The sourcebook of nonverbal measures: Going beyond words* (Digital print). New York, NY: Routledge.

Mitchem, D. G., Zietsch, B. P., Wright, M. J., Martin, N. G., Hewitt, J. K., & Keller, M. C. (2015). No relationship between intelligence and facial attractiveness in a large, genetically informative sample. *Evolution and Human Behavior, 36*(3), 240–247. doi:10.1016/j.evolhumbehav.2014.11.009

Nestler, S., & Back, M. D. (2017). Using cross-classified structural equation models to examine the accuracy of personality judgments. *Psychometrika, 82*(2), 475–497. doi:10.1007/s11336-015-9485-6

Nowicki, S., & Duke, M. P. (1994). Individual differences in the nonverbal communication of affect: The diagnostic analysis of nonverbal accuracy scale. *Journal of Nonverbal Behavior, 18*(1), 9–35. doi:10.1007/BF02169077

Rentfrow, P. J., & Gosling, S. D. (2006). Message in a ballad: The role of music preferences in interpersonal perception. *Psychological Science, 17*(3), 236–242. doi:10.1111/j.1467-9280.2006.01691.x

Scherer, K. R., Scherer, U., Hall, J. A., & Rosenthal, R. (1977). Differential attribution of personality based on multi-channel presentation of verbal and nonverbal cues. *Psychological Research, 39*(3), 221–247. doi:10.1007/BF00309288

Schwarzer, G. (2019). *meta: General package for meta-analysis.* Retrieved from https://cran.r-project.org/web/packages/meta/index.html

Secord, P. (1958). Facial features and inference processes in interpersonal perception. In R. Tagiuri & L. Petrullo (Eds.), *Person perception and interpersonal behavior* (pp. 300–315). Stanford, CA: Stanford University Press.

Smith, E. R., & Zárate, M. A. (1992). Exemplar-based model of social judgment. *Psychological Review, 99*(1), 3–21. doi:10.1037/0033-295X.99.1.3

Taft, R. (1955). The ability to judge people. *Psychological Bulletin, 52*(1), 1–23. doi:10.1037/h0044999

Willis, J., & Todorov, A. (2006). First impressions making up your mind after a 100-ms exposure to a face. *Psychological Science, 17*(7), 592–598.

Youyou, W., Kosinski, M., & Stillwell, D. (2015). Computer-based personality judgments are more accurate than those made by humans. *Proceedings of the National Academy of Sciences of the United States of America, 112*(4), 1036–1040. doi:10.1073/pnas.1418680112

Zebrowitz, L. A. (1997). *Reading faces: Window to the soul?* Boulder, CO: Westview Press.

Zebrowitz, L. A. (2017). First impressions from faces. *Current Directions in Psychological Science, 26*(3), 237–242. doi:10.1177/0963721416683996

Zebrowitz, L. A., & Collins, M. A. (1997). Accurate social perception at zero acquaintance: The affordances of a Gibsonian approach. *Personality and Social Psychology Review, 1*(3), 204–223. doi:10.1207/s15327957pspr0103_2

Zebrowitz, L. A., & Montepare, J. M. (2008). First impressions from facial appearance cues. In N. Ambady & J. J. Skowronski (Eds.), *First impressions* (pp. 171–204). New York, NY: Guilford Press.

Notes

1. With the raw data provided on osf.io/9p64g it is easily possible to compute results for different kinds of allocations (e.g., separate results for dominance and sociability aspects of extraversion; separate results for stylishness related to hairstyles).

2. For more studies and meta-analyses concerning the specific link between attractiveness and intelligence, please refer to Jackson, Hunter, and Hodge (1995), Kanazawa (2011), Langlois et al. (2000), and Mitchem et al. (2015). Mirroring the results we present here, recent research suggests that there is an absent or low correlation between attractiveness and actual intelligence (cf. Mitchem et al., 2015).

3. In this case vector correlations refer to correlations between Fisher z-transformed cue validity/utilization correlations across traits.

Accuracy of Personality Trait Judgments Based on Environmental and Social Media Cues

Helen J. Wall *and* Claire Campbell

Abstract

This chapter provides an overview of the role of physical (e.g., offices, bedrooms) and virtual contexts (e.g., social media such as Facebook and Twitter profiles) on the accuracy of personality judgments. Personality, context, and accuracy are defined, and evidence from studies on trait accuracy are outlined within and across contexts. The availability of cues in online and offline contexts are discussed in terms of Funder's realistic accuracy model (RAM) and Brunswik's lens model. In doing so, the chapter provides some insight into the ways various aspects of a context might affect trait accuracy; specifically, it allows us to consider what aspects of a context affect the cues that are available. The literature described in this chapter sheds light on the importance of the physical and virtual contexts in personality judgments. Context has a differential effect on judgment accuracy in terms of the specific trait, or traits, being judged. The literature presented has also highlighted the need for more research on this topic.

Key Words: personality judgment, judgment accuracy, context, social media, physical context, virtual contexts, realistic accuracy model, lens model

Introduction

Research investigating personality judgments in face-to-face contexts has revealed that people seem to rely on behavioral cues such as tone of voice (McAleer, Todorov, & Belin, 2014), content/fluidity of speech (Isbister & Nass, 2000), use of compliments (Mairesse, Walker, Mehl, & Moore, 2007), attire (Burroughs, Drews, & Hallman, 1991; Gosling & Standen, 1998), and gait (Thoresen, Vuong & Atkinson, 2012), as well as interaction style (e.g., takes charge, smiles, uses hands while talking or moans; Wall, Taylor, Campbell, Heim, & Richardson, 2018) to make judgments about others. In contrast, much can also be learned about individuals from their physical and virtual worlds, as research suggests such contexts are rich with information about their lifestyles, values, and personalities (Gosling, Augustine, Vazire, Holtzman, & Gaddis, 2011; Gosling, Ko, Mannarelli, &

Morris, 2002). Numerous studies have shown that people use the information cues available in everyday physical contexts to form impressions of individuals (Gosling, Gaddis, & Vazire, 2007; Gosling et al., 2002). The utility of exploring cue availability, cue use, and accuracy within physical and virtual contexts is that this work provides us with valuable insight into the ways various aspects of a context might affect trait accuracy. Specifically, it allows us to consider what aspects of a context affect the cues that are available to judges. For example, if people are better at judging personality when interacting over e-mail versus face-to-face, it suggests that language cues alone might be useful cues to another's personality. It also permits an exploration of the types of cues that may be relevant when judging another's personality. We propose that trait accuracy is best understood when judgment accuracy is explored both within and across judgment contexts.

Before outlining the evidence on judgment accuracy within and across contexts, it is imperative to define what is meant by personality, context, and accuracy.

Defining Personality, Context, and Accuracy
Personality

When conceptualizing personality, the five-factor model (FFM; also known as the Big Five) has gained popularity (John & Srivastava, 1999; Pervin, 1994). The Big Five traits—extraversion, agreeableness, conscientiousness, neuroticism, and openness to experience—emerged from decades of research, and the FFM model has been celebrated for its ability to simplify an otherwise overwhelming number of traits (Hofstee, 1994; John, 1990; McCrae & Costa, 1987). Big Five traits have demonstrated good predictive validity in their ability to predict health-relevant and other outcomes (e.g. Emmons, 1995) and show cross-cultural applicability (McCrae & Costa, 1997). In terms of the traits themselves and their meaning, extraversion is associated with sociability, enthusiasm, talkativeness, and assertiveness (McCrae & Costa, 1992). Individuals high in agreeableness tend to be described as interpersonally oriented, warm, trusting, and compliant. Individuals high in conscientiousness tend to be described as planful, responsible, and able to delay gratification. Individuals high in neuroticism[1] are often described as experiencing psychological distress in the form of anger, depression, anxiety and other negative affect (Costa & McCrae, 1990). Finally, individuals who are high in openness to experience tend to be curious, imaginative, unconventional, and to have wide interests. The majority of the studies outlined in this chapter will refer to the Big Five traits as they represent the common framework in the field and have been well researched from an accuracy perspective. Studies investigating judgment accuracy of other traits will also be included to allow for a full review of the field.

Context

Context is often broadly defined as the environmental setting in which a behavior occurs (Bate, 2012; Cappelli & Sherer, 1991). For example, in this chapter we are investigating the personality cues that influence personality judgments and the contexts that we are exploring are the virtual contexts and physical contexts in which the judgments are made. The physical context that provides cues for a personality judgment could be interpreted as relating strictly to the physical objects in very specific personal spaces, for example, the furniture in a bedroom and how it is arranged, the number of books in an office and how they are stacked, and so on. Alternatively, it may be interpreted more broadly to encompass cues outside specific personal spaces an individual occupies such as the geographical location in which the individual resides. For example, research has indicated that geographical personality variations may be linked to factors such as selective migration and social influences (Rentfrow, 2014; Rentfrow, Gosling, & Potter, 2008). Zimmermann and Neyer (2014) have proposed that patterns of geographic personality variations, such as high aggregate levels of openness to experience, may be manifest in the physical environment through accumulated behavioral tendencies associated with this trait. For instance, expressions of this trait may include participation in cultural activities, formal education, and interest in other cultures, which may be evident in the physical environment through the establishment of theaters, universities, and international restaurants. For the purpose of this chapter, we have defined and operationalized the physical context in line with the former, narrower definition as this permits a focus on the specific environmental settings in which a behavior occurs. The majority of research on judgment accuracy also fits within this narrower category.

Virtual contexts are operationalized as online contexts that the individual operates within. As with the physical context, this may also be defined narrowly to include the social networks, blogs, or websites an individual contributes to or on which they have a profile. However, it may also be defined more broadly to include the social networks, blogs, and websites that an individual consumes, or possibly even search engines or operating systems that they use. For example, it is possible that an individual's Internet search history may be just as revealing about personality as the number of Facebook friends they have acquired. Both physical and virtual contexts range from the personal (e.g., bedroom or private e-mail) to the public (e.g., offices or Twitter posts). Again, in the context of the present chapter, we focus on the narrow definition of this context.

The empirical investigation of context has played a key role in the development of all subfields in psychology. For example, within cognitive psychology, context effects are fundamental to our understanding of the encoding and retrieval of information in memory (Tulving & Thomson, 1973). In social psychology, context is central to many of the landmark findings ranging from social influence (Asch, 1951) to social group membership (Tajfel & Turner, 1979). Similarly, in personality psychology context is also central to understanding trait accuracy. Specifically, the information contained within e-mails has been shown to allow comparatively accurate judgments for the trait of openness to experience (Markey & Wells, 2002; Vazire & Gosling, 2004), even though judgments for openness to experience tend to be difficult to make accurately when based on face-to-face interactions (Borkenau & Liebler, 1992). Moreover, extraversion is typically the most accurately judged trait in face-to-face contexts (Funder & Dobroth, 1987; Lippa & Dietz, 2000), whereas examinations of judgments based on physical spaces (Gosling, Ko, Mannarelli, & Morris, 2002), e-mail content (Back, Schmukle, & Egloff, 2008), and stream of consciousness writing (Li & Chignell, 2010; Yee, Harris, Jabon, & Bailenson, 2011) tend to find that judgments of conscientiousness are *more* accurate than judgments of extraversion. Taken together, this differential pattern of trait accuracy highlights the importance of context on accuracy and suggests that much can be learned about the cues used and the types of cognitive processing employed in making personality judgments, and also to consider the implications of each of these for trait accuracy.

Accuracy

The accuracy of personality judgments can be measured in numerous ways. Some studies have used the "realistic accuracy approach," which relies on a reliable and valid measure of a target's personality, which may then be compared to the ratings provided by one or more judges to examine how accurate or correct personality judgments are. Here, researchers tend to define an accurate judgment as a rating made about a target's personality that corresponds with the target's actual personality (Funder, 1987, 1999; Letzring, Wells, & Funder, 2006; Wall, Taylor, & Campbell, 2016; Wall, Taylor, Dixon, Conchie, & Ellis, 2013). The realistic accuracy approach posits that multiple methods of assessment should be used when measuring personality judgments about a person, such as self-reports and informant ratings (Funder, 1999). A common approach to determining judgment accuracy is through self-other agreement. The self-rating is used as the criterion and the judge is said to

be accurate if their rating corresponds with the self-rating. A second approach to measuring the validity of personality judgments is consensus, or the agreement about a target person being judged by two or more judges. This has often been used as a proxy for accuracy, as the benefit of combining several judgments is that errors are likely to cancel each other out (Colvin & Bundick, 2001; Hofstee, 1994). This measure is not without error either, as consensus may not necessarily reflect what the target is actually like, but instead reflect agreement between people about what the target person is like, and people can agree but still be inaccurate. The defining feature of realistic accuracy is the attempt to approach a description of what the target is really like by creating a criterion based on multiple sources of information that includes both self-other agreement, judgment consensus, and ideally behavioral prediction (Webb, Campbell, Schwartz, & Sechrest, 1966). Put another way, if a judge's assessment of a target person's personality matches the realistic criterion (i.e., multiple assessments of personality possibly based on self- and informant ratings and direct behavioral observations), then realistic accuracy is obtained. For the purposes of a comprehensive review, studies employing all of these indices of accuracy are reviewed in this chapter.

How Can a Focus on Context Increase Our Understanding of Judgment Accuracy?

From Instagram sites, websites, and online social networks (OSNs) to offices, bedrooms, and cars—the range of contexts by which to judge another's personality is intriguing. Where should we look when we want to get to know a person? Are some traits judged differently depending on the particular context in which we view, or meet, people? As noted by Gosling et al. (2002), people's judgments are shaped by a number of contextual factors, and he argues it is time to begin finding out exactly how our judgments depend on context.

Judgments across Contexts

A number of studies have compared trait accuracy across contexts and revealed a number of interesting and intriguing findings. For example, a study by Wall et al. (2013) compared trait judgments across three increasingly information-rich interaction contexts (that is, contexts that provide an increasing variety of cues on which to base a personality judgment). These contexts were an e-mail communication, a telephone call, and a face-to-face interaction. While there are many personality cues available in an e-mail context (e.g., message content, emojis, spelling errors), there are arguably more in a telephone call as there are additional paralinguistic cues such as tone and pitch of the speaker. Similarly, in a face-to-face interaction, the judge has access to the message and paralinguistic cues, as well as cues related to appearance and nonverbal cues such as facial expression and gestures. The results of this study indicated that the less interpersonal traits[2] of openness to experience and conscientiousness were rated more accurately in face-to-face interactions than in the information-lean context of an e-mail communication. Such findings indicate that not only are we able to reveal aspects of these traits online, but also that others are able to detect cues relevant to these types of traits and correctly use them. Judgments of extraversion were associated with a linear increase in accuracy as the richness of the context increased; conversely, judgments of conscientiousness increased in accuracy when the context became less rich. These findings suggest that judgment accuracy depends on both the type of trait being judged and the context in which a judgment is made. More specifically, the authors concluded that information-rich contexts are not always preferential when judging personality and that cues relevant to judging traits such as conscientiousness and openness to experience may become less salient in information rich contexts given the breadth of cues that are available (e.g., language cues, tone of voice, nonverbal cues). Put another way, the relevant cues to openness to experience and conscientiousness may be easier to detect via an e-mail relative to face-to-face, as judges are not bombarded by the range of irrelevant cues available in rich contexts (see chapter 8 by Krzyzaniak & Letzring in this handbook for more information on how accuracy differs across traits).

Further support for the differential effect of context on accuracy comes from a study by Holleran and Mehl (2008). Although their focus was to examine accuracy after reading stream of consciousness essays, they summarized findings across a range of studies at a descriptive level. Specifically, they compared studies that had examined accuracy based on a range of contexts (e.g., bedrooms, offices, websites, and stream of consciousness writing). They reported that trait accuracy across different contexts can help to illuminate how personality might be revealed by behavior and judged by others. For example, they theorized that an important dimension by which contexts might vary is in terms of whether they are a public (e.g., face-to-face interactions,

handshakes, personal websites) or a private context (e.g., stream of consciousness essay). This study found that in private contexts, such as a person's stream of consciousness writing, the level of accuracy was substantial and relatively uniform across all Big Five traits. By comparing the findings of this study to other published work investigating public contexts (i.e., Gosling et al., 2002; Mehl, Gosling & Pennebaker, 2006; Vazire & Gosling, 2004), the authors concluded that there were higher levels[3] of accuracy for judgments of agreeableness, conscientiousness, and neuroticism and comparable levels of accuracy for openness to experience in private contexts compared to public contexts. Again, such findings advance our understanding of which traits tend to be the most accurately judged and in which contexts, in addition to developing our understanding about why this might be the case.

Judgments within Contexts

Although it may seem more intuitive to explore how trait accuracy changes across contexts, we argue that it is also fruitful to consider judgment accuracy within contexts, that is, across traits within the same context. Specifically, comparing judgments across traits in one context permits an exploration of the amount and types of context specific cues that may be relevant to certain traits. For example, instead of focusing on whether extraversion is judged more or less accurately via e-mail relative to face-to-face, one can make trait comparisons within a context and consider whether extraversion was judged more accurately than openness to experience. This notion of context influencing the cues to which judges attend has been supported by Ames and Bianchi (2008), who studied personality judgments made by supervisors and supervisees. They found that when participants were able to choose which traits to judge, the traits that they judged appeared to relate to the characteristics that were important for themselves. Specifically, they found that supervisors judged how hardworking their supervisees would be, whereas the student judged how conscientious and reliable the supervisor was, suggesting that perhaps the aspects of personality that are judged are differentially salient depending on the interpersonal needs of each person making the judgment within that specific context. These findings highlight how a focus on trait differences within contexts can increase our understanding of the cues that judges might focus on and the cues that are available within such contexts, and can tell us more about the way in which context is acting on or interacting with the judgment demands.

Understanding How Cues in Physical and Virtual Contexts Affect Accuracy

Theoretical models have been proposed to try to understand how people make judgments. The Brunswikian lens model (1956) is a general model of the judgment process—not just personality judgment—and is a useful tool for determining the relationship between cues that are available, either through behavior or in the environmental context, and judgment accuracy (see Gosling et al, 2002; Naumann, Vazire, Rentfrow, & Gosling, 2009; Vazire & Gosling, 2004; Vazire, Naumann, Rentfrow, & Gosling, 2008; Wall et al., 2018; and chapter 4 by Osterholz, Breil, Nestler, & Back in this handbook). According to Brunswik, environmental cues can serve as a lens through which people indirectly perceive underlying constructs. As noted by Gosling et al. (2002), these cues can be embedded in the environmental context and can be an artifact of the behavior itself. The lens model, as it applies to the process of personality judgment, begins with the occurrence of a behavior that provides cues to personality, and describes cues relevant for making a judgment of each trait as "valid cues." For example, neatness of appearance could be perceived as a lens through which to infer that a person is high in the trait of conscientiousness.

In Brunswik's model, valid cues may be assessed through the coding of each behavior or environmental cue and correlating these aspects with actual personality. As the observer may not necessarily detect (i.e., notice) the relevant cues to each trait, Brunswik's model is also concerned with "cue utility." The cues used are established by correlating the cues in behavior or the environmental context with judgments of the trait of interest. Importantly, the cues used may or may not be valid cues for each trait and the final stage of Brunswik's model addresses the overlap between the valid cues and cues used.

Funder's RAM model (see chapter 2 by Letzring & Funder in this handbook) has applied the lens model to personality judgments (see Funder, 1999). The RAM (Funder, 1995, 1999, 2012) posits that judgment accuracy is a result of a four-stage process whereby cues (i.e., behaviors) need to first be relevant to the trait being judged. Second, the cues to personality need to be available so that the judge can then detect (i.e., notice) and correctly utilize these cues in order to render an accurate judgment. Gosling et al. (2002) note that "overlap" in

Brunswik's model between "cues used" and "valid cues" should lead to accurate personality judgments according to the RAM, as valid cues have been successfully detected and utilized. For example, if a valid cue to extraversion is talkativeness and a judge notices this cue and then correctly infers that this cue is indicative of the trait of extraversion, this overlap between valid cues and cues used should lead to accurate judgment of this trait. In the context of judgment accuracy based on physical and virtual cues, this poses the question of whether there will be relevant cues of the target's personality available in physical and virtual contexts; and, if so, whether judges can detect and correctly utilize these cues to render an accurate judgment.

Personality Cues in Physical and Virtual Contexts

Research to date suggests that as individuals craft and shape their physical personal spaces, they leave traces of their personality, both intentionally and unintentionally. Gosling et al. (2002) applied the lens model and the RAM to judgments of personal spaces and proposed a model of interpersonal perception. Specifically, they proposed mechanisms by which individuals affect their personal environments and leave personality cues in their personal spaces and the processes observers employ to make personality judgments. The two mechanisms outlined by Gosling et al. (2002) by which individuals may affect their personal spaces are through identity claims and behavioral residue.

Identity claims are symbolic statements made by individuals with the aim of shaping how they are perceived by self and others and can be either self-directed or other-directed. *Self-directed identity claims* are directed toward yourself and serve to reinforce or remind one of important aspects of the self. For example, hanging certificates of professional achievement in one's office may communicate pride in the accomplishment or educational and professional values. In the context of virtual spaces such as personal websites and OSNs, this may include posting photos with friends that celebrate valued friendships. *Other-directed identity claims* can be aspirational, strategic, or deceptive attempts to communicate how the individual would like to be perceived by others. For example, an individual may tidy away clutter when expecting visitors in an attempt to appear more conscientious. As Gosling et al. (2002) noted, self-directed and other-directed identity claims may often overlap or be presented in similar ways. For example, if the placement of the books was such so that the individual could look at them and have their view of themselves as an intellectual reinforced, that would be a self-directed identity claim. If the books are placed so that others can also see them in an attempt to create the impression in others that the individual is a professional or an expert, that is an other-directed identity claim.

Behavioral residue differs from identity claims as it refers to personality cues in one's personal space that are the unintentional remnants of an individual's behavior. For example, behavioral residue may include dirty dishes left beside a sink reflecting a low frequency of dishwashing, a juicer on the counter may suggest that the individual is conscientious about healthy eating, while a swimming suit on the clothesline may indicate that the individual is physically active. Behavioral residue can offer an insight into an individual's behaviors conducted within their personal space (*interior behavioral residue*) or activities performed outside that space (*exterior behavioral residue*) (see Gosling et al., 2002, for more detail). Behavioral residue can also be found in OSNs, for example, through their use of social media sites individuals may collect a large number of friends on the site, which has been used as a cue when judging extraversion (Gosling et al., 2011).

In Gosling et al.'s (2002) substantive study, they found that a person's behavioral residue and identity claims affect their physical spaces such as bedrooms and offices; however, subsequent research has also applied this model to more diverse contexts (e.g., Mehl et al., 2006; Rentfrow & Gosling, 2006) including virtual contexts (Vazire & Gosling, 2004). For this reason, we have referred to personal spaces in our description to include both an individual's physical and virtual contexts. Gosling's model of interpersonal perception (Gosling et al., 2002) proposed that physical and virtual cues may affect observer judgments through (1) observer's inferences about the behaviors that may have created the physical evidence, and (2) inferences about the dispositions that may have motivated those behaviors. For example, a long list of Facebook friends may lead an observer to infer that the target is popular online, this in turn may lead the observer to believe that the target is high in extraversion. A study by Back et al. (2010) found that accuracy for extraversion was strongest relative to the remaining Big Five traits. Gosling et al. (2002) also pointed out the possibility that cues in physical and virtual contexts may activate stereotypes, either at the point of making inferences about the behaviors that lead to the presence of these cues, or at the point at which the observers

inferred the motivations for the behaviors. For example, objects or decoration in a room that suggests a female occupant may trigger gendered stereotypes that may influence the observers' trait accuracy. Stereotypes may lead the observers to reach decisions that are not based on evidence in the target's personal space. If observers use invalid stereotypes to guide their decision-making, it may lead them to form inaccurate impressions of the occupant, however, as we know, there is some merit in some stereotypes (Lee, Jussim, & McCauley, 1995; see chapter 16 by Lee, Stevens, & Honeycutt in this handbook), in which case this may lead the observers to make more accurate judgments.

Trait Accuracy in Physical Contexts

As aforementioned, research by Gosling et al. (2002) has applied the lens model and the RAM to judgments of personal spaces and determined which behaviors or aspects of an environmental context were valid cues of each personality trait as outlined in the next section. Their study proposed that personal spaces may contain an abundance of potentially informative cues about an individual and therefore provide rich information to observers for personality judgments. In their paper they explored trait accuracy based solely on examination of an individual's office or bedroom.

Office

In Gosling et al.'s (2002) first study that explored office contexts, judgments of openness to experience showed the strongest consensus, followed by conscientiousness and extraversion. Agreeableness also showed some consensus, while the least consensus was for neuroticism. The pattern of consensus correlations was different from that found in previous zero-acquaintance research,[4] suggesting that the cues available from photographs or short interactions differ from those available from workspaces. Whereas zero-acquaintance research using the Big Five has found the strongest consensus for extraversion and conscientiousness (e.g., Kenny, 1994; Kenny, Horner, Kashy, & Chu, 1992; Park & Judd, 1989), Gosling's study found the strongest consensus for openness to experience, although they still found strong consensus for conscientiousness and extraversion. They found that the level of accuracy also varied across traits. Accuracy was highest for openness to experience, followed by extraversion, conscientiousness, and neuroticism. Judgments of agreeableness were not accurate. Again, the pattern of findings differed from the general pattern of findings in zero-acquaintance research, in which extraversion usually yields the highest accuracy, followed by conscientiousness, with little or no accuracy for neuroticism and openness to experience (Kenny, 1994; Watson, 1989). Consensus and accuracy results were found to have been partially affected by the use of sex stereotypes. The cues that were valid and used to make judgments from offices are discussed later in this section.

Bedroom

In a second study, Gosling et al. (2002) explored the role of cues on accuracy in the context of bedrooms. As in the context of offices, openness to experience showed the strongest consensus, followed by conscientiousness and extraversion, while agreeableness and neuroticism showed the least. In terms of accuracy, openness to experience was also the most accurately judged trait and agreeableness the least accurately judged trait. Consensus and accuracy were found to be only partially mediated by sex and race stereotypes. Observers used similar cues to judge extraversion, agreeableness, and conscientiousness across the office and bedroom contexts. For example, a room being inviting was used as a utilized cue for the trait of agreeableness in both office and bedroom contexts, yet this was not a valid cue for this trait in either context. However, Gosling's findings highlighted that the valid cues to trait accuracy were largely different across contexts and were only similar for the trait of conscientiousness. For example, in comparison to the previous example, many of the cues used to judge the trait of conscientiousness such as a room being in good condition, neat, clean, uncluttered, and organized, were valid cues in both the office and bedroom contexts. This finding highlights the need for research to examine differences across contexts and the ways in which individuals interact with these differences.

In summary, Gosling et al. (2002) employed the Brunswikian lens model to evaluate which cues measured by the researchers were valid cues of each trait and which cues were used by judges when making their personality judgments. This is useful for shedding light on the judgment accuracy for each trait. For example, in the office context valid cues for the trait of openness to experience included how distinctive, stylish, and unconventional the room was. This pattern of accurate detection and utilization of relevant cues has resulted in the comparatively high accuracy for judging this trait in this study. In comparison, in the office context there was only one valid cue measured for the trait of agreeableness, which was whether the office was in a high traffic area. This was not detected by the judges, which can help explain the lack of accurate judgments for this trait. This pattern of the detection and utilization of relevant cues available in the physical context leading to trait accuracy was also found in the bedroom context. For example, while there were only three valid cues for the trait of openness to experience measured in the bedroom context, each of these was utilized by the judges (distinctive room, varied books, varied magazines), which explains the comparatively high level of judgment accuracy for this trait. However, there were no valid cues for neuroticism in the bedroom context and only two for the trait of agreeableness, neither of which were used by judges, which accounts for the poor judgment accuracy for these traits. It is worth noting that a finite number of cues were recorded in this study and it is possible that there were other cues present that were not recorded that informed judges' decisions. This is supported by the judgment accuracy for the trait of extraversion in the bedroom context despite judges failing to use either of the two valid cues for the trait.

Their study also sheds light on the lay theories that the judges employed when making their judgments, for example, this study illustrated that across both contexts there were many more cues employed to inform personality judgments than there were valid cues. All in all, there were less than 20 valid cues measured that were available in each context and yet participants used more than 50 of the cues measured to make their judgments in each context, suggesting that there is a discrepancy between judges' perceptions of relevant cues for a trait and valid cues for a trait. This is illustrated when looking at judgments of the trait of conscientiousness in the office context. When judging this trait judges used a number of valid cues to inform their judgments such as the office being in good condition, and whether offices were clean, organized, neat, uncluttered, and had homogeneous books and CDs. However, judges also employed a number of cues that were not relevant to this trait, for example, whether the office was roomy, empty, expensive, comfortable, inviting, large, distinctive, formal, conventional, a good use of space, had matched contents, organized books, homogeneous stationary, and organized stationery. This suggests that the judges' lay theory of the trait of conscientiousness may be tapping into a broader construct. While the judges were accurate in using cues such as an office being clean, organized, and neat, they seemed to also be associating conscientiousness with something more impressive or possibly luxurious, for example, they employed cues such as an office being expensive, large, roomy, inviting, comfortable, and formal.

It is also interesting that the valid cues to a trait varied across contexts. For example, while being organized, neat, and uncluttered was a valid cue for the trait of conscientiousness in both the office and bedroom contexts, organized books and CDs were valid cues of this trait only in the bedroom context, while homogeneous books and CDs were the valid cues in the office context. Similarly, distinctiveness was a valid cue for the trait of openness to experience across contexts. In the bedroom context this was expressed through cues such varied books and magazines, while in an office context valid cues included the office being perceived as unconventional, stylish, and fresh. While it may be possible to speculate about intuitive explanations about how or why the cues listed here inform judgments of the traits of conscientiousness and openness to experience respectively, it is not wise to do so without first conducting further research. It is unclear why some cues are valid in one context but not another. Again, further research is required to answer this question, particularly as this study is one of a kind.

Trait Accuracy in Virtual Contexts

Although a number of studies have examined first impression accuracy in face-to-face encounters (Bar, Neta, & Linz, 2006; Carney, Colvin, & Hall, 2007; Willis & Todorov, 2006), much less research has examined accuracy in online contexts, which are typically more limited in the number of cues available, particularly regarding nonverbal ones. Knowledge of the specific traits people are more likely to make accurate judgments for and insight into the types of cues that may facilitate or hinder this process is arguably important in a range of contexts such as online dating and job recruitment. When considering the practical means of exploring these issues, the Internet and other virtual settings represents useful contexts in which to explore the expression and perception of personality.

Virtual contexts are an interesting site of research because they offer a context in which to observe an individual engaged in social interactions and also provide an opportunity to access the virtual worlds that they have created for themselves. These virtual spaces are thought to operate in much the same way as physical spaces, displaying the deliberate (e.g., identity claims) and inadvertent (e.g., behavioral

residue) cues to an individual's personality (Vazire & Gosling, 2004).

Language

Numerous aspects of language have been explored in virtual contexts such as the use of text-speak (an informal abbreviated language used in text messaging (Crystal, 2008)), and vocabulary usage, spelling, and pronoun usage (Darbyshire, Kirk, Wall, & Kaye, 2016; Fullwood, Quinn, Chen-Wilson, Chadwick, & Reynolds, 2015; Wall et al., 2013). Writing errors (e.g., grammatical or typography errors) have been found to be related to others' negative judgments of the sender (Boland & Queen, 2016; Queen & Boland, 2015), specifically judging the sender as less conscientious or attentive (Ellison, Heino, & Gibbs, 2006; Vignovic & Thompson, 2010). However, some of these papers have measured perception rather than judgment accuracy. Among those that have measured the latter, language cues seem to influence judgments of the "less interpersonal" traits such as conscientiousness (Darbyshire et al., 2016; Wall et al., 2013). Although the role of language on perceptions, and to a lesser extent judgment accuracy, have been studied, less research has systematically examined how the quantity of language cues shapes trait perception or accuracy. That is, what happens to perceptions of conscientiousness when different types of errors are present, such as typos and/or grammatical errors? This focus on variations in cue type enables quantity and quality of language cues on perceptions to be investigated. In support of the present focus on variations in cue type, a study by Vignovic and Thompson (2010; see also Scott, Sinclair, Short, & Bruce, 2014) found that people tend to be perceived as less conscientious and trustworthy when their e-mails contained many typos (e.g., "abuot" instead of "about"). However, although the existing literature is relatively consistent on the role of language cues on perceptions of conscientiousness, what is less known is the extent to which amount of usage may be relevant here. This is relevant in respect to the RAM, as the quantity of language cues relates to the *availability* stage, and as a result, may foster greater capacity to form accurate judgments.

Research has also examined personality expression in virtual contexts via personal websites (e.g., Vazire & Gosling, 2004), e-mail interaction (e.g., Gill, Oberlander, & Austin, 2006), and usernames in online games (e.g., Graham & Gosling, 2012). For example, Back et al. (2008) examined how strangers judged targets' personality through linguistic features of e-mail addresses, and found that judgments of neuroticism, openness to experience, agreeableness, conscientiousness, and narcissism were reasonably accurate. Neuroticism has been found to be associated with the use of more anxiety words in Facebook profiles (Golbeck, Robles, & Turner, 2011), while agreeable individuals employ more positive emotion words and first-person plural pronouns in blogs (Yarkoni, 2010). People with a higher level of conscientiousness are more likely to discuss others via e-mail communication (Oberlander & Gill, 2006). Taken together, these findings suggest that self-reported personality traits may be differentially associated with specific linguistic patterns in virtual contexts such as microblogs versus nonvirtual contexts such as speech and writing. Importantly, the extent to which judges detect and use these cues is not yet known and is an area for further inquiry.

Emojis

These text-based symbols provide an online alternative to facial expressions in face-to-face interactions, allowing users to communicate their intended emotions (Derks, Bos, & Grumbkow, 2008). Previous work exploring emoji use on Facebook has found that happy emoji use relates to a range of trait perceptions; specifically agreeableness, conscientiousness, and openness to experience (Wall, Kaye, & Malone, 2016). More recently, studies have examined the role of emojis on perceptions of characteristics such as sincerity and friendliness. The use of smiley emojis in a written conversation between two people has been shown to result in perceptions of the person using smiley emojis as friendly and sincere (Wibowo, Ats-Tsiqoh, Sangadah, Komala, & Utomo, 2017). Although this study only examined the role of emojis on perceptions, not accuracy, their findings highlight the importance of context specific cues on shaping personality judgments and further research is needed to explore how cues are differentially related to perception and accuracy.

Twitter

Twitter is a social networking microblog service that permits users to broadcast short posts called *tweets*, which can be up to 140 characters. Members can broadcast tweets and follow other users' tweets and people can search tweets on Twitter whether or not they are a member. Studies exploring the accuracy of personality judgments based on microblogs on Twitter have revealed that unfamiliar raters can accurately judge neuroticism and agreeableness (Qiu

et al., 2012). This is consistent with previous findings that these two dimensions can be judged accurately in self-generated written content (e.g., Holleran & Mehl, 2008).

Webpages

Webpages are usually maintained by one person or organization and devoted to a single topic or several closely related topics on the World Wide Web. A number of studies have examined trait accuracy based on viewing personal webpages and revealed an interesting pattern of findings. A study by Marcus, Machilek, and Schutz (2006) explored the accuracy of personality impressions after viewing a person's personal webpage and found valid judgments for all Big Five traits, in particular for the trait of openness to experience. Interestingly, this study also explored the cues available in webpages that were valid indicators of the website owners' personalities. They found that people high in neuroticism tend to avoid requesting feedback from site visitors, do not reveal their address, and avoid commenting on the external websites linked to their pages. The trait of openness to experience was linked to more use of websites about lyrics and fine arts. Vazire and Gosling (2004) also examined trait accuracy based on personal websites and reported accuracy levels similar to that found in other interpersonal contexts. Specifically, they found that the websites elicited high levels of consensus and accuracy for the two traits of extraversion and agreeableness. They reported accuracy levels higher than those found in zero-acquaintance contexts and suggested that the higher accuracy was due to the identity claims available in this particular context.

Instagram

Instagram is currently the fastest growing photo-sharing social media platform, with more than 400 million active users, nearly 100 million photos shared on the platform daily, and generation of 1.2 billion likes each day (Lay & Ferwerda, 2018). Ferwerda, Schedl, and Tkalcic (2016) found distinct features within Instagram photos, such as their brightness, hues, and saturation,[5] were related to personality traits, indicating that users with different personalities make their pictures look different. For instance, openness to experience was positively associated with cold colors such as green and blue, low brightness, high saturation, cold colors, and few faces; individuals high in conscientiousness tended to post images with more variation in color saturation; agreeable individuals were more likely to post images with few dark and bright areas; neuroticism was related to images with high brightness; extraversion was linked with images of green and blue tones, low brightness, and saturated and unsaturated colors (Ferwerda et al., 2016). This finding that features of Instagram pictures are related to personality judgements expands on previous research that has shown consistent links between openness to experience and aesthetic preferences (Ferwerda et al., 2016). The utility of image characteristics has also been found in research by McManus and Furnham (2006), who found image characteristics to be significantly correlated with openness to experience, followed by agreeableness and conscientiousness.

Selfies

"Selfies" are known as a self-portrait picture taken by oneself, which are then frequently posted on OSN's (Qui, Lu, Yang, Qu, & Zhu, 2015). Selfies are a distinct subgroup of photographs that can be posted in virtual contexts such as Instagram, Facebook, or other websites. From an accuracy perspective, selfies are a very interesting behavior. When taking a selfie, individuals can view what they look like and decide what they want to show. It has been suggested that they are a new medium for self-expression and self-presentation (Qiu et al., 2015). Selfies contain unique cues that are not typically available in other types of photos such as pouting or "duck face," which is a lip pouting expression to give the appearance of fuller lips. Some studies have shown that selfies reveal personality-relevant information (Qiu et al., 2015). Selfies would appear interesting to study from a self-presentation perspective because people *choose* to take selfies. Qiu et al. (2015) were the first researchers to explore how selfies reflect the subject of the photo's personality and the accuracy with which people make personality judgments based on selfies. They found a number of trait-related cues in selfies, for example, selfies taken in a private location were associated with lower levels of conscientiousness, while emotional positivity was found to predict both openness to experience and agreeableness. Interestingly, although there were relevant cues to personality (as measured using a Brunswikian lens model) and judgment consensus among observers for all traits, only openness to experience was judged accurately. This suggests that observers had difficulty detecting and using relevant cues. Another study found that the selfie owners' levels of conscientiousness and openness to experience were the

easiest traits to judge accurately and noted that when judgments were based on selfies, rather than a full-length photograph taken by the researchers, there were greater perceptions of narcissism but lower perceptions of conscientiousness (Kaurin, Heil, Wessa, Egloff, & Hirschmüller, 2018).

Facebook

Facebook is a social networking website that allows registered users to upload photos, keep in touch with friends, send messages, and create profiles. The Big Five traits are considered to be expressed differently across a range of "Facebook behaviors" (Amichai-Hamburger & Vinitzky, 2010). For example, traits are expressed in different ways through a number of online behaviors including number of Facebook friends, disclosure of personal information, uploading and modifying photographs, using different spaces on Facebook for uploading information, and the nature of interactions (Amichai-Hamburger & Vinitzky, 2010; Gosling et al., 2011; Hollenbaugh & Ferris, 2014; Moore & McElroy, 2012; Ross et al., 2009). Patterns of trait accuracy in a Facebook context are consistent with other virtual contexts. A number of studies have shown that extraversion tends to be the most accurately judged personality trait when viewing others' Facebook profiles, and neuroticism the least accurate (Back et al., 2010; Gosling, Gaddis, & Vazire, 2007). This was corroborated in research using personal websites (Vazire & Gosling, 2004) and e-mail correspondence (Gill, Oberlander, & Austin, 2006). Taken together, such trait-specific findings suggest that nuanced context-behavior relations exist.

Interestingly, from a context perspective, these results contrast with those obtained in Qiu, Lin, Ramsay, and Yang (2012) which showed that observers could accurately detect neuroticism and agreeableness from people's Twitter profiles. This suggests that different social media platforms may afford the exhibition of different personality traits. One possible explanation of the observed personality perception results is that microblogging affects the expression of extraversion, openness to experience, and conscientiousness. For example, Twitter encourages people to disclose their inner feelings and share their social activities with others, meaning that all users will appear extraverted to some extent. Similarly, most people tend to tweet about their new experiences or discoveries, giving others the impression that they are open to new experiences.

There are also substantial differences in the cues available through Facebook interactions and those in face-to-face interactions. Crucially, certain behaviors such as a person's facial expressions are not available, or are only available as posed photographs, within online platforms (Amichai-Hamburger & Vinitzky, 2010), however, there are other personality cues that are specific to this context, such as number of online friends and status updates (Gosling, Augustine, Vazire, Holtzman, & Gaddis, 2011; Jarvis, 2010). Given the differences in certain types of behaviors able to be revealed online versus offline and the contextual differences in trait-specific accuracy that have begun to emerge, it is important to continue to examine *how* such judgments are being formed. Although some research has begun to code aspects of behavior in this regard (e.g., Bachrach, Kosinski, Graepel, Kohli, & Stillwell, 2012; Ross et al., 2009), it is also useful to view such coding from the perspective of the target, as Gosling et al. (2011) have done. In this study, Gosling and colleagues found that extraversion was correlated with a large number of self-reported Facebook behaviors, especially those related to maintaining an up-to-date presence and tending to social bonds (e.g., number of Facebook friends and commenting on others' pages). Agreeableness, the other interpersonal Big Five dimension, was also related to OSN usage; those higher in agreeableness viewed all pages (i.e., any, others, and their own pages) more often than those low in agreeableness. Consistent with the idea that OSNs serve as an opportunity for those low in conscientiousness to procrastinate, participants low on conscientiousness spent more time viewing pages and more time on Facebook than did those high in conscientiousness. Finally, openness to experience was related to adding and replacing photographs, which may reflect the fact that individuals high on this trait tend to engage in a wide range of activities. Neuroticism was not related to any of the self-reported Facebook behaviors (Gosling et al., 2011).

Studies adopting a quantitative approach to this issue have tended to correlate behavioral and/or linguistic cues with scores on trait judgments, with the assumption that significant correlations indicate that judges did actually *use* these cues. A complementary qualitative approach can examine the cues that people explicitly report they used when judging others. Darbyshire et al. (2016) have explored individuals' conscious perceptions of the cues used to make personality judgments via the platform of Facebook using thematic analysis of participants' self-reported accounts of how they made their judgments. This study revealed the following cues: vocabulary (an indication for openness to experience) and occupational status (an indication for conscientiousness). Both of these themes contained all language-based predictors for the traits openness to experience and conscientiousness. For example, subthemes of the vocabulary theme included spelling and use of grammar, which are predictors of intelligence, and intelligence is a facet of openness to experience (Costa & McCrae, 1992). It is suggested that an accurate judgment of openness to experience was formed due to the way the judge detected these cues and then used them. It is important that future research replicate this finding to substantiate this claim. Similarly, subthemes of the occupational status theme included organization levels, which was an indicator of conscientiousness (Costa & McCrae, 1992). Recent evidence has shown that Facebook appears to be the least likely place individuals will express neurotic behaviors when comparing Big Five traits (Back et al., 2010). In line with the previous distinction between more and less interpersonal traits, online contexts appear to differentially influence the expression and perception of personality with contexts such as Facebook, and facilitate greater accuracy for less interpersonal traits. Interestingly, the trait of neuroticism has been shown to be poorly judged in many other contexts, including on Facebook (Back et al., 2010; Gosling et al., 2011; Gosling et al., 2007). Such findings attest to the importance of focusing on the role of environmental contexts on personality judgment accuracy, as it can tell us, descriptively, which traits people are more likely to judge accurately, and can begin to illuminate which cues appear to be relevant and even provide a glimpse into how users are interacting with their environmental contexts and the way in which we present ourselves to the world.

Future Directions

The literature described in this chapter has shed light on the importance of physical and virtual contexts in personality judgments. This pioneering research has shown that by exploring the personal space an individual occupies, whether physical or virtual, it is possible to make relatively accurate personality judgments about individuals without ever having met them. To date, this research has fallen within a narrow definition of what a physical or virtual context entails, however, there is scope to explore a broader conceptualization of these contexts. While acknowledging the need to further explore and replicate many of the findings we have discussed in this chapter, we also wish to highlight areas where there is potential to expand the current definitions of physical and virtual contexts.

Replicating and Expanding Current Research

To date there have been a handful of studies that have systematically examined how different contexts contribute to judgment accuracy. There is a need for these studies to be replicated and expanded on. As mentioned previously, there is variation in the cues that are valid indicators of personality traits across contexts. For example, for the trait of conscientiousness, being organized and uncluttered served as valid cues across contexts, while other cues such as a room being clean and in good condition were context specific cues to this trait. It is unclear why this is, and further research on this topic is necessary to develop a better understanding of the expression and perception of personality in and across contexts.

There is also a need to expand the range of physical contexts that have been explored. A possible context for future research includes an individual's vehicle. There is no research to date that has explored the personality cues that an individual's car may provide about the owner's personality, however, Alpers and Gerdes (2006) have demonstrated that judges were able to match cars to their owners with above chance level accuracy. This suggests that cars are providing the judges with some salient cues about their owners. Further research is required in this context to determine whether these cues are salient to trait accuracy. However, this seems to be a promising context for research as it is possible to see how behavioral residue could accumulate in a car and also how a car may be used as a means to convey identity claims.

Another aspect of both physical and virtual contexts that warrants further explorations are cues to social group memberships and other similarities that are shared with the judges. For example, an individual's personal spaces may include many cues to their group memberships such as flags or banners supporting a particular sports team, musical instruments specific to a particular culture, or calligraphy scripts in a specific language. Indeed Gosling et al. (2002) found that cues to age and sex in office and bedroom contexts led to the activation of stereotypes about these groups, which in turn influenced personality judgments. Intragroup and intergroup relationships have also been demonstrated to shape perception in numerous social psychological studies, yet very little research has been conducted to explore how group dynamics influence personality judgments. Letzring (2010) explored the significance of shared gender and ethnicity in trait accu-

racy. The author hypothesized that trait accuracy would be highest when the judge and target were most similar. The results of this study indicated that female judges were more accurate in rating targets that shared their gender and ethnicity than targets that did not. This effect did not hold for men, who were most accurate when judging female targets. A second study in this area has been conducted by Rogers and Biesanz (2014). This study explored the effect of group membership on interpersonal perception, including trait accuracy. They found that perceptions of in-group members showed higher levels of distinctive accuracy than did perceptions of out-group members. Distinctive accuracy is used to refer to the important aspect of accurately judging how a target person is different from the average person. More specifically, it entails understanding how a given target differs from the average person and others on specific traits. However, the results also indicated that judges also rated ingroup members as higher in distinctive assumed similarity (i.e., a tendency for observers to project their own distinctive characteristics onto others). Overall, this study suggests that perceptions of individuals with shared cultural group membership may be more biased as well as more accurate. These studies highlight that intragroup and intergroup dynamics affect personality perceptions, and as group identification is a pervasive aspect of daily life (Tajfel & Turner, 1979), these dynamics should be considered in personality judgments.

Similarly, there is much research on language use in nonvirtual contexts that warrants further investigation in virtual contexts, for example, the connection between self-reported personality and writing style (Pennebaker & King, 1999). A software program called Linguistic Inquiry and Word Count (LIWC) has been widely used to identify linguistic patterns associated with personality traits by calculating word frequencies in psychologically meaningful categories, such as pronouns, social terms, and affect (or emotion) terms (Pennebaker, Booth, & Francis, 2007). Extraverts have been found to produce fewer large words (Mehl et al., 2006), less complex writings, and more social and positive emotional words than introverts (Pennebaker & King, 1999). Küfner, Back, Nestler, and Egloff (2010) found that raters could judge openness to experience and agreeableness via linguistic cues in creative writing samples, while Mehl et al. (2006) found that raters successfully used the presence of swear words and negative emotion words in everyday speech to judge agreeableness. Holleran and

Mehl (2008) found that individuals could accurately judge the Big Five personality traits of unknown others by reading stream of consciousness essays. Future research should explore whether these findings are applicable in a virtual context and whether trait accuracy varies across online platform.

New Avenues for Exploration

As mentioned earlier in this chapter, the definitions of physical and virtual contexts could be broadened to go beyond an individual's own personal space and to include much larger areas that may also provide cues to an individual's personality. In line with research by Rentfrow et al. (2008; see also Zimmermann & Neyer, 2014), which has indicated that there may be personality variation across geographic locations, there is scope for future research to consider how these personality variations shape the local environments, which may in turn influence personality judgments.

Other questions that should be addressed include whether there will be an interaction between the personality cues an individual provides and the cues in the judgment context. That is, will an individual's personality be judged more accurately in contexts where the individual and the context are consistent? For example, it is possible that individuals high in the trait of openness to experience may be judged more accurately in geographic locations that have higher aggregate levels of openness to experience and therefore more infrastructure (e.g., theaters, universities, international restaurants) that would allow the public expression of these traits. Or more importantly, if a person is available to provide personality cues will the judge still attend to environmental cues available in the context? While it may seem intuitive that more cues, whether from an individual or the context, will lead to more accurate judgments, Wall et al. (2013) have illustrated that this is not always the case.

Conclusion

Physical and virtual contexts offer the possibility to explore personality judgments that occur without any direct interaction with the subject of the judgment. This chapter has outlined a range of literature documenting the role of context, including both physical and virtual, on accuracy. We explored the ways that individuals craft and shape their personal spaces and embed personality cues through identity claims and behavioral residue. Research on judgment accuracy in physical and virtual spaces is valuable as it has shown that in many cases trait specific accuracy (e.g., conscientiousness and openness to experience) is greater in these contexts than in face-to-face interactions. The range of contexts that can be examined is broad and ever-growing, and this chapter has made recommendations about areas where the existing research should be replicated and expanded. Overall, this chapter has shown that context has a differential effect on judgment accuracy in terms of the specific trait, or traits, being judged. For the topic of accuracy, a focus on context is key as it concerns understanding more about the way in which humans navigate social situations to make the complex task of judging manageable (Taylor & Fiske, 1978).

References

Alpers, G. W., & Gerdes, A. B. (2006). Another look at "look-alikes": Can judges match belongings with their owners? *Journal of Individual Differences*, *27*(1), 38–41 http://doi.org/10.1027/1614-0001.27.1.38

Ames, D. R., & Bianchi, E. C. (2008). The agreeableness asymmetry in first impressions: Perceivers' impulse to (mis)judge agreeableness and how it is moderated by power. *Personality and Social Psychology Bulletin*, *34*(12), 1719–1736. https://doi.org/10.1177/0146167208323932

Amichai-Hamburger, Y. and Vinitzky, G. (2010) Social network use and personality. *Computers in Human Behavior*, *26*, 1289–1295. http://dx.doi.org/10.1016/j.chb.2010.03.018

Asch, S. E. (1951) Effects of group pressure on the modification and distortion of judgments. In H. Guetzknow (Ed.), *Groups, Leadership and Men* (pp. 177–190). Pittsburgh, PA, Carnegie Press.

Bachrach, Y., Kosinski, M., Graepel, T., Kohli, P., & Stillwell, D. (2012, June). Personality and patterns of Facebook usage. In *Proceedings of the 4th annual ACM web science conference* (pp. 24–32). Association for Computing Machinery. https://doi.org/10.1145/2380718.2380722

Back, M. D., Schmukle, S. C., & Egloff, B. (2008). How extraverted is honey.bunny77@hotmail.de? Inferring personality from e-mail addresses. *Journal of Research in Personality*, *42*(4), 1116–1122. https://doi.org/10.1016/j.jrp.2008.02.001

Back, M. D., Stopfer, J. M., Vazire, S., Gaddis, S., Schmukle, S. C., Egloff, B., & Gosling, S. D. (2010). Facebook profiles reflect actual personality, not self-idealization. *Psychological Science*, *21*(3), 372–374. https://doi.org/10.1177/0956797609360756

Bar, M., Neta, M., & Linz, H. (2006). Very first impressions. *Emotion*, *6*(2), 269–281. https://doi.org/10.1037/1528-3542.6.2.269

Bate, P. (2012). *Context is everything*. London, UK: The Health Foundation, https://www.health.org.uk/sites/default/files/PerspectivesOnContextBateContextIsEverything.pdf

Boland, J. E., & Queen, R. (2016). If you're house is still available, send me an email: Personality influences reactions to written errors in email messages. *PloS One*, *11*(3), e0149885. https://doi.org/10.1371/journal.pone.0149885

Borkenau, P., & Liebler, A. (1992). Trait inferences: Sources of validity at zero acquaintance. *Journal of Personality and Social Psychology*, *62*(4), 645. https://doi.org/10.1037/0022-3514.62.4.645

Brunswik, E. (1956). *Perception and the representative design of psychological experiments*. Berkeley, CA: University of California Press.

Burroughs, J. W., Drews, D. R., & Hallman, W. K. (1991). Predicting personality from personal possessions: A self-presentational analysis. *Journal of Social Behavior and Personality, 6*(6), 147–163.

Cappelli, P., & Sherer, P.D. (1991). The missing role of context in OB: The need for a meso-level approach. *Research in Organisation Behaviour, 13*, 55–110.

Carney, D. R., Colvin, C. R., & Hall, J. A. (2007). A thin slice perspective on the accuracy of first impressions. *Journal of Research in Personality, 41*(5), 1054–1072. https://doi.org/10.1016/j.jrp.2007.01.004

Colvin, C. R., & Bundick, M. S. (2001). In search of the good judge of personality: Some methodological and theoretical concerns. In J. A. Hall & F. J. Bernieri (Eds.), *Interpersonal sensitivity: Theory and measurement*. London, UK: Psychology Press.

Costa, P. T., & McCrae, R. R. (1990). Personality disorders and the five-factor model of personality. *Journal of Personality Disorders, 4*(4), 362–371. https://doi.org/10.1521/pedi.1990.4.4.362

Costa, P. T., & McCrae, R. R. (1992). Normal personality assessment in clinical practice: The NEO Personality Inventory. *Psychological assessment, 4*(1), 5–13. https://psycnet.apa.org/doi/10.1037/1040-3590.4.1.5

Crystal, D. (2008). *Txting: The Gr8 Db8*. Oxford: Oxford University Press. https://doi.org/10.1093/elt/ccm080

Darbyshire, D., Kirk, C., Wall, H. J., & Kaye, L. K. (2016). Don't judge a (face)book by its cover: Exploring judgement accuracy of others' personality on Facebook. *Computers in Human Behavior, 58*, 380–387. https://doi.org/10.1016/j.chb.2016.01.021

Derks, D., Bos, A. E., & Von Grumbkow, J. (2008). Emoticons in computer-mediated communication: Social motives and social context. *CyberPsychology & Behavior, 11*(1), 99–101. doi:10.1089/cpb.2007.9926

DeYoung, C. G., Weisberg, Y. J., Quilty, L. C., & Peterson, J. B. (2013). Unifying the aspects of the Big Five, the interpersonal circumplex, and trait affiliation. *Journal of Personality, 81*(5), 465–475. https//doi.org/10.1111/jopy.12020

Ellison, N., Heino, R., & Gibbs, J. (2006). Managing impressions online: Self-presentation processes in the online dating environment. *Journal of Computer-Mediated Communication, 11*(2), 415–441. https://doi.org/10.1111/j.1083-6101.2006.00020.x

Emmons, R. A. (1995). Levels and domains in personality: An introduction. *Journal of Personality, 63*(3), 341–364. https//doi.org/10.1111/j.1467-6494.1995.tb00499.x

Ferwerda, B., Schedl, M., & Tkalcic, M. (2016). Using Instagram picture features to predict users' personality. In Q. Tian, N. Sebe, G. J. Qi, B. Huet, R. Hong, & X. Liu (Eds.), *MultiMedia Modeling* (pp. 850–861). Lecture Notes in Computer Science, 9516. Cham: Springer International. https://doi.org/10.1007/978-3-319-27671-7_71

Fullwood, C., Quinn, S., Chen-Wilson, J., Chadwick, D., & Reynolds, K. (2015). Put on a smiley face: Textspeak and personality perceptions. *Cyberpsychology, Behavior, and Social Networking, 18*(3), 147–151. https://doi.org/10.1089/cyber.2014.0463

Funder, D. C. (1987). Errors and mistakes: Evaluating the accuracy of social judgment. *Psychological Bulletin, 101*(1), 75–90. https://doi.org/10.1037/0033-2909.101.1.75

Funder, D. C. (1995). On the accuracy of personality judgment: A realistic approach. *Psychological Review, 102*(4), 652–670. https://doi.org/10.1037/0033-295X.102.4.652

Funder, D. C. (1999). *Personality judgment: A realistic approach to person perception*. San Diego, CA: Academic Press.

Funder, D. C. (2012). Accurate personality judgment. *Current Directions in Psychological Science, 21*(3), 177–182. https://doi.org/10.1177/0963721412445309

Funder, D. C., & Dobroth, K. M. (1987). Differences between traits: Properties associated with interjudge agreement. *Journal of Personality and Social Psychology, 52*(2), 409–418. http://dx.doi.org/10.1037/0022-3514.52.2.409

Gill, A. J., Oberlander, J., & Austin, E. (2006). Rating e-mail personality at zero acquaintance. *Personality and Individual Differences, 40*(3), 497–507. https://doi.org/10.1016/j.paid.2005.06.027

Golbeck, J., Robles, C., & Turner, K. (2011, May). Predicting personality with social media. In *CHI '11: Extended abstracts on human factors in computing systems* (pp. 253–262). Vancouver: ACM. https://doi.org/10.1145/1979742.1979614

Gosling, R., & Standen, R. (1998). Doctors' dress. *British Journal of Psychiatry, 172*, 188–189. https://doi.org/10.1192/bjp.172.2.188c

Gosling, S. D., Augustine, A. A., Vazire, S., Holtzman, N., & Gaddis, S. (2011). Manifestations of personality in online social networks: Self-reported Facebook-related behaviors and observable profile information. *Cyberpsychology, Behavior, and Social Networking, 14*(9), 483–488. https://doi.org/10.1089/cyber.2010.0087

Gosling, S. D., Gaddis, S., & Vazire, S. (2007, March). *Personality impressions based on Facebook profiles*. Paper presented at the International Conference on Weblogs and Social Media, Boulder, CO.

Gosling, S. D., Ko, S. J., Mannarelli, T., & Morris, M. E. (2002). A Room with a cue: Personality judgments based on offices and bedrooms. *Journal of Personality and Social Psychology, 82*(3), 379–398. https://doi.org/10.1037/0022-3514.82.3.379

Graham, L. T., & Gosling, S. D. (2012). Impressions of World of Warcraft players' personalities based on their usernames: Interobserver consensus but no accuracy. *Journal of Research in Personality, 46*(5), 599–603. https://doi.org/10.1016/j.jrp.2012.05.002

Hofstee, W. K. B. (1994). Who should own the definition of personality? *European Journal of Personality, 8*(3), 149–162. https://doi.org/10.1002/per.2410080302

Hollenbaugh, E. E., & Ferris, A. L. (2014). Facebook self-disclosure: Examining the role of traits, social cohesion, and motives. *Computers in Human Behavior, 30*, 50–58. https://doi.org/10.1016/j.chb.2013.07.055

Holleran, S. E., & Mehl, M. R. (2008). Let me read your mind: Personality judgments based on a person's natural stream of thought. *Journal of Research in Personality, 42*(3), 747–754. https://doi.org/10.1016/j.jrp.2007.07.011

Isbister, K., & Nass, C. (2000). Consistency of personality in interactive characters: Verbal cues, non-verbal cues, and user characteristics. *International Journal of Human-Computer Studies, 53*(2), 251–267. https://doi.org/10.1006/ijhc.2000.0368

Jarvis, M. M. (2010). *Facebook and personality: What do status updates really communicate?* (Unpublished master's thesis). University of Arizona, Tucson.

John, O. P. (1990). The "Big Five" factor taxonomy: Dimensions of personality in the natural language and in questionnaires.

In L. A. Pervin (Ed.), *Handbook of personality: Theory and research* (pp. 66–100). New York, NY: Guilford Press.

John, O. P., & Srivastava, S. (1999). The Big Five trait taxonomy: History, measurement, and theoretical perspectives. In L. A. Pervin & O. P. John (Eds.), *Handbook of personality: Theory and research* (pp. 102–138). New York, NY: Guilford Press.

Kaurin, A., Heil, L., Wessa, M., Egloff, B., & Hirschmüller, S. (2018). Selfies reflect actual personality—Just like photos or short videos in standardized lab conditions. *Journal of Research in Personality, 76*, 154–164. https://doi.org/10.1016/j.jrp.2018.08.007

Kenny, D. A. (1994). *Interpersonal perception: A social relations analysis.* New York, NY: Guilford Press. https://doi.org/10.1177/026540758800500207

Kenny, D. A., Horner, C., Kashy, D. A., & Chu, L. C. (1992). Consensus at zero acquaintance: Replication, behavioral cues, and stability. *Journal of Personality and Social Psychology, 62*(1), 88. https://doi.org/10.1037/0022-3514.62.1.88

Küfner, A. C., Back, M. D., Nestler, S., & Egloff, B. (2010). Tell me a story and I will tell you who you are! Lens model analyses of personality and creative writing. *Journal of Research in Personality, 44*(4), 427–435. https://doi.org/10.1016/j.jrp.2010.05.003

Lay, A., & Ferwerda, B. (2018). Predicting users' personality based on their "liked" images on Instagram. In *The 23rd International on Intelligent User Interfaces.* Singapore: Association for Computing Machinery. https://doi.org/10.1145/3209219.3209248

Lee, Y. T. E., Jussim, L. J., & McCauley, C. R. (1995). *Stereotype accuracy: Toward appreciating group differences.* Washington, DC: American Psychological Association.

Letzring, T. D. (2010). The effects of judge-target gender and ethnicity similarity on the accuracy of personality judgments. *Social Psychology, 41*(1), 42–51. http://dx.doi.org/10.1027/1864-9335/a000007

Letzring, T. D., Wells, S. M., & Funder, D. (2006). Information quantity and quality affect the realistic accuracy of personality judgment. *Journal of Personality and Social Psychology, 91*(1), 111–123. https://doi.org/10.1037/0022-3514.91.1.111

Li, J., & Chignell, M. (2010). Birds of a feather: How personality influences blog writing and reading. *International Journal of Human-Computer Studies, 68*(9), 589–602. https://doi.org/10.1016/j.ijhcs.2010.04.001

Lippa, R. A., & Dietz, J. K. (2000). The relation of gender, personality, and intelligence to judges' accuracy in judging strangers' personality from brief video segments. *Journal of Nonverbal Behavior, 24*(1), 25–43.

Mairesse, F., Walker, M. A., Mehl, M. R., & Moore, R. K. (2007). Using linguistic cues for the automatic recognition of personality in conversation and text. *Journal of Artificial Intelligence, 30*, 457–500. https://doi.org/10.1613/jair.2349

Marcus, B., Machilek, F., & Schütz, A. (2006). Personality in cyberspace: Personal web sites as media for personality expressions and impressions. *Journal of Personality and Social Psychology, 90*(6), 1014–1031. https://doi.org/10.1037/0022-3514.90.6.1014

Markey, P. M., & Wells, S. M. (2002). Interpersonal perception in internet chat rooms. *Journal of Research in Personality, 36*(2), 134–146. https://doi.org/10.1006/jrpe.2002.2340

McAleer, P., Todorov, A., & Belin, P. (2014). How do you say "Hello"? Personality impressions from brief novel voices. *PLoS One, 9*(3), 1–9. https://doi.org/10.1371/journal.pone.0090779

McCrae, R. R., & Costa, P. T. (1987). Validation of the five-factor model of personality across instruments and observers. *Journal of Personality and Social Psychology, 52*(1), 81. https://doi.org/10.1037/0022-3514.52.1.81

McCrae, R. R., & Costa, P. T., Jr. (1992). Discriminant validity of NEO-PIR facet scales. *Educational and Psychological Measurement, 52*(1), 229–237. https://doi.org/10.1177/001316449205200128

McCrae, R. R., & Costa, P. T., Jr. (1997). Personality trait structure as a human universal. *American Psychologist, 52*(5), 509. http://dx.doi.org/10.1037/0003-066X.52.5.509

McManus, I. C., & Furnham, A. 2006. Aesthetic activities and aesthetic attitudes: Influences of education, background and personality on interest and involvement in the arts. *British Journal of Psychology, 97*(4), 555–587. https://doi.org/10.1348/000712606X101088

Mehl, M. R., Gosling, S. D., & Pennebaker, J. W. (2006). Personality in its natural habitat: Manifestations and implicit folk theories of personality in daily life. *Journal of Personality and Social Psychology, 90*(5), 862–877. https://doi.org/10.1037/0022-3514.90.5.862

Moore, K., & McElroy, J. C. (2012). The influence of personality on Facebook usage, wall postings, and regret. *Computers in Human Behavior, 28*(1), 267–274. https://doi.org/10.1016/j.chb.2011.09.009

Mount, M. K., & Barrick, M. R. (1995). The Big Five personality dimensions: Implications for research and practice in human resources management. *Research in Personnel and Human Resources Management, 13*(3), 153–200. https://doi.org/10.1111/j.1744-6570.1991.tb00688.x

Naumann, L. P., Vazire, S., Rentfrow, P. J., & Gosling, S. D. (2009). Personality judgments based on physical appearance. *Personality and Social Psychology Bulletin, 35*(12), 1661–1671. https://doi.org/10.1177/0146167209346309

Oberlander, J., & Gill, A. J. (2006). Language with character: A stratified corpus comparison of individual differences in e-mail communication. *Discourse Processes, 42*(3), 239–270. https://doi.org/10.1207/s15326950dp4203_1

Park, B., & Judd, C. M. (1989). Agreement on initial impressions: Differences due to perceivers, trait dimensions, and target behaviors. *Journal of Personality and Social Psychology, 56*(4), 493. https://doi.org/10.1037/0022-3514.56.4.493

Pennebaker, J. W., Booth, R. J., & Francis, M. E. (2007). Linguistic inquiry and word count: LIWC2007 [Computer software]. Austin, TX: liwc. net.

Pennebaker, J. W., & King, L. A. (1999). Linguistic styles: Language use as an individual difference. *Journal of Personality and Social Psychology, 77*(6), 1296. http://dx.doi.org/10.1037/0022-3514.77.6.1296

Pervin, L. A. (1994). A critical analysis of current trait theory. *Psychological Inquiry, 5*(2), 103–113. https://doi.org/10.1207/s15327965pli0502_1

Qiu, L., Lin, H., Ramsay, J., & Yang, F. (2012). You are what you tweet: Personality expression and perception on Twitter. *Journal of Research in Personality, 46*(6), 710–718. https://doi.org/10.1016/j.jrp.2012.08.008

Qiu, L., Lu, J., Yang, S., Qu, W., & Zhu, T. (2015). What does your selfie say about you? *Computers in Human Behavior, 52*, 443–449. https://doi.org/10.1016/j.chb.2015.06.032

Queen, R., & Boland, J. E. (2015). I think you're going to like me: Exploring the role of errors in email messages on assessments of potential housemates. *Linguistics Vanguard,* *1*(1), 283–293. https://doi.org/10.1515/lingvan-2015-0011

Rentfrow, P. J. (2014). Geographical differences in personality. In P. J. Rentfrow (Ed.), *Geographical psychology: Exploring the interaction of environment and behavior* (pp. 115–137). Washington, DC: American Psychological Association. https://doi.org/10.1037/14272-007

Rentfrow, P. J., & Gosling, S. D. (2006). Message in a ballad: The role of music preferences in interpersonal perception. *Psychological Science, 17*(3), 236–242. https://doi.org/10.1111/j.1467-9280.2006.01691.x

Rentfrow, P. J., Gosling, S. D., & Potter, J. (2008). A theory of the emergence, persistence, and expression of geographic variation in psychological characteristics. *Perspectives on Psychological Science, 3,* 339–369. https://doi.org/10.1111/j.1745-6924.2008.00084.x

Rogers, K. H., & Biesanz, J. C. (2014). The accuracy and bias of interpersonal perceptions in intergroup interactions. *Social Psychological and Personality Science, 5*(8), 918–926. https://doi.org/10.1177/1948550614537307

Ross, C., Orr, E. S., Sisic, M., Arseneault, J. M., Simmering, M. G., & Orr, R. R. (2009). Personality and motivations associated with Facebook use. *Computers in Human Behavior, 25*(2), 578–586. https://doi.org/10.1016/j.chb.2008.12.024

Scott, G. G., Sinclair, J., Short, E., & Bruce, G. (2014). It's not what you say, it's how you say it: Language use on Facebook impacts employability but not attractiveness. *Cyberpsychology, Behavior, and Social Networking, 17*(8), 562–566. https://doi.org/10.1089/cyber.2013.0584

Tajfel, H., & Turner, J. (1979). An integrative theory of intergroup conflict. In W. Austin & S. Worchel (Eds.), *The social psychology of intergroup relations.* Monterey, CA: Brookes-Cole.

Taylor, S. E., & Fiske, S. T. (1978). Salience, attention, and attribution: Top of the head phenomena. *Advances in Experimental Social Psychology, 11,* 249–288. https://doi.org/10.1016/S0065-2601(08)60009-X

Thoresen, J. C., Vuong, Q. C., & Atkinson, A. P. (2012). First impressions: Gait cues drive reliable trait judgments. *Cognition, 124*(3), 261–271. https://doi.org/10.1016/j.cognition.2012.05.018

Tulving, E., & Thomson, D. M. (1973). Encoding specificity and retrieval processes in episodic memory. *Psychological Review, 80,* 352–373. https://doi.org/10.1037/h0020071

Vazire, S., & Gosling, S. D. (2004). e-perceptions: Personality impressions based on personal websites. *Journal of Personality and Social Psychology, 87*(1), 123–132. https://doi.org/10.1037/0022-3514.87.1.123

Vazire, S., Naumann, L. P., Rentfrow, P. J., & Gosling, S. D. (2008). Portrait of a narcissist: Manifestations of narcissism in physical appearance. *Journal of Research in Personality, 42*(6), 1439–1447. https://doi.org/10.1016/j.jrp.2008.06.007

Vignovic, J. A., & Thompson, L. F. (2010). Computer-mediated cross-cultural collaboration: Attributing communication errors to the person versus the situation. *Journal of Applied Psychology, 95*(2), 265. https://doi.org/10.1037/0022-3514.87.1.123

Wall, H. J., Kaye, L. K., & Malone, S. A. (2016). An exploration of psychological factors on emoticon usage and implications for judgment accuracy. *Computers in Human Behavior, 62,* 70–78. https://doi.org/10.1016/j.chb.2016.03.040

Wall, H. J., Taylor, P. J., & Campbell, C. (2016). Getting the balance right? A mismatch in interaction demands between target and judge impacts on judgment accuracy for some traits but not others. *Personality and Individual Differences, 88,* 66–72. https://doi.org/10.1016/j.paid.2015.08.037

Wall, H. J., Taylor, P. J., Campbell, C., Heim, D., & Richardson, B. (2018). Looking at the same interaction and seeing something different. *Journal of Individual Differences, 39*(3), 123–141. https://doi.org/10.1027/1614-0001/a000257

Wall, H. J., Taylor, P. J., Dixon, J. A., Conchie, S. M., & Ellis, D. A. (2013). Rich contexts do not always enrich the accuracy of personality judgments. *Journal of Experimental Social Psychology, 49*(6), 1190–1195. https://doi.org/10.1016/j.jesp.2013.05.010

Watson, D. (1989). Strangers' ratings of the five robust personality factors: Evidence of a surprising convergence with self-report. *Journal of Personality and Social Psychology, 57*(1), 120. https://doi.org/10.1037/0022-3514.57.1.120

Webb, E. J., Campbell, D. T., Schwartz, R. D., & Sechrest, L. (1966). *Unobtrusive measures: Nonreactive research in the social sciences.* Chicago: Rand McNally.

Wibowo, M. R. F., Ats-Tsiqoh, R., Sangadah, S., Komala, E. S., & Utomo, A. B. (2017). The effect of emoji on person perception. *UI Proceedings on Social Science and Humanities, 1.*

Willis, J., & Todorov, A. (2006). First impressions: Making up your mind after a 100-ms exposure to a face. *Psychological Science, 17*(7), 592–598. https://doi.org/10.1111/j.1467-9280.2006.01750.x

Yarkoni, T. (2010). Personality in 100,000 Words: A large-scale analysis of personality and word use among bloggers. *Journal of Research in Personality, 44*(3), 363–373. https://doi.org/10.1016/j.jrp.2010.04.001

Yee, N., Harris, H., Jabon, M., & Bailenson, J. N. (2011). The expression of personality in virtual worlds. *Social Psychological and Personality Science, 2*(1), 5–12. https://doi.org/10.1177/1948550610379056

Zimmermann, J., & Neyer, F. J. (2014). Places and traces of personality. *Psychologia, 57*(2), 115–132. https://doi.org/10.2117/psysoc.2014.115

Notes

1. The terms neuroticism and emotional stability are used interchangeably in this chapter, as they are labels for the negative and positive poles of the same construct (Mount & Barrick, 1995).

2. Numerous studies refer to the traits of extraversion and agreeableness as "interpersonal traits" (DeYoung, Weisberg, Quilty, & Peterson, 2013).

3. It is worth noting that these conclusions are not based on inferential statistics.

4. Zero acquaintance research explores personality judgments made by pairs of unacquainted participants after a short interaction. Each member of the pair judges their partner's personality and also acts as a target of their partner's personality judgment. Zero-acquaintance research can be conducted with more than just pairs and can be based on observations of pictures or very short videos.

5. Hue refers to the color quality of each pixel and saturation refers to color intensity.

The Role of Normative Information in Judgments of Others

Katherine H. Rogers

Abstract

When forming impressions of an other's personality, people often rely on information not directly related to the individual at hand. One source of information that can influence people's impressions of others is the personality of the average person (i.e., normative profile). This relationship between the normative profile and an impression is called normative accuracy or normativity. In this chapter, you will learn about the average personality, why it is important, the relationship to social desirability and what it means to have a normative impression, as well as correlates and moderators of normativity. More broadly, you will learn about current research and views regarding the normative profile and normative impressions as well as concrete steps for incorporating this approach into your future research on interpersonal perception.

Key Words: normative profile, personality, impression, accuracy, interpersonal perception

It is the first day of class, and two students, Riley and Bruce, are meeting for the first time. They make small talk for a few minutes before the professor indicates that class is beginning. After chatting, Riley reflects on Bruce's personality, as she is hoping to create a study group for the course and wants to determine whether Bruce would be a good addition. Riley perceives Bruce as talkative, hardworking, funny, and assertive. The question then becomes, how did Riley conclude that Bruce is talkative, hardworking, funny, and assertive? For instance, did Riley view Bruce as talkative because Bruce spoke a lot during their interaction, because Riley thinks most people are talkative, or for some other reason? Further, is Riley's impression of Bruce's personality accurate?

It is difficult to imagine that Riley only used cues from Bruce to conclude that he is talkative, hardworking, funny, and assertive, especially given that they chatted for a short period of time. Indeed, there are several sources of information not directly related to their interaction that Riley may have used to fill in any gaps in her understanding of Bruce's

personality. For instance, Riley perhaps perceives Bruce as similar to herself and thus determines that he is also hardworking like she is (a process known as assumed similarity; e.g., Cronbach, 1955). She may have also used social categorical information (Fiske & Neuberg, 1990), such as the fact that Bruce is a political science major, is president of a campus club, and plans to become a lawyer, and this influenced her perception of his assertiveness. Perhaps Bruce had a shirt on that Riley found amusing, thus she determined he was funny or maybe Riley decided she generally liked Bruce, so she just viewed him positively in general. Finally, Riley may have used her knowledge of the average person (which is known as normative knowledge; e.g., Rogers & Biesanz, 2015) to help her understand Bruce, as people tend to be talkative and hardworking.

It may seem strange to think that Riley could have used information not directly related to Bruce to form her first impression, but accurately learning everything about an individual's personality is *hard*[1] and we can only learn so much in a brief encounter. If Riley did use knowledge about the average individual's personality in forming her impression of Bruce, it may have led her slightly astray; perhaps Bruce is not quite as hardworking as Riley thought. As noted by Cronbach (1955), it is possible for individuals to attain some degree of accuracy simply by rating people as average on each trait. For Riley this means that, on average, if she continues to use knowledge about the average personality when forming impressions of new people, she will be more accurate than someone who never uses this information. Moreover, if Riley formed impressions of 100 people and largely relied on the average personality in forming her judgments, she would be fairly accurate, given that, on average, people are similar to the average person. In fact, using data from Rogers and Biesanz (2018), I found that the average correlation between the self-reported personality of two random individuals is $r = 0.23$, and the average correlation between a self-reported personality and the average self-reported personality is $r = 0.50$. In this chapter, I discuss what the average (normative) personality profile is, why it is important to account for the normative profile when assessing agreement or accuracy in impressions across many items or traits at once,[2] what it means to form a normative impression, and how impression normativity varies across individuals and impressions.

What Is the Average Person's Personality?

Before continuing, take a moment and reflect on what you think the average individual's personality is like. Based on your perception of the average individual's personality, indicate the degree to which you *strongly disagree* to *strongly agree* with each of the items below, using Figure 15.1 to sort the following nine personality items from the Big Five Inventory (BFI; John & Srivastava, 1999). Specifically, you will sort one item into each box. For example, if an item was "*is funny*" and I strongly agreed that the average individual *is funny*, I would place that item in the far right box.

Now that you have completed this task, briefly reflect on your experience. Did you find it easy or difficult to complete? Did you want to put many items in the neutral category or in the agree category? One of the reasons to use this modified Q-sort is to force individuals to differentiate between items, otherwise, we might end up without much variance or differences between the items. How confident are you in your responses? Review Figure 15.2 to see how well your responses match up to the average personality profile. What patterns do you notices in how these items were sorted below? Were you sur-

prised to see that "Starts quarrels with others" was not very representative of the average person? Or that "Has a forgiving nature" was fairly representative of the average person?

Given that we frequently must interact with others and have interpersonal relationships, you might be pleased to hear that the average personality is highly socially desirable and positive (Borkenau & Zaltauskas, 2009; Edwards, 1957; Rogers & Biesanz, 2015; Wood, Gosling, & Potter, 2007). This is great since it means we should have to deal with disagreeable, rude, or otherwise unlikable people less often, but it does create some complications when studying impressions and person perception. Indeed, the terms we use to describe personality (e.g., "curious," "moody," "reliable," "quarrelsome") not only communicate descriptive information but also include evaluative information (Peabody, 1967). Being curious and reliable certainly tells us about an individual's personality and can provide insight into their behavior, but these characteristics are also much more positive in nature than being described as moody and quarrelsome. There are also personality descriptors that convey similar information, but do so in very different evaluative manners. For example, "assertive" and "aggressive" provide fairly similar personality information, but "assertive" is perceived to be much more positive than "aggressive." As you might expect, when people are asked to describe their own personality, they tend to ascribe more positive attributes than negative attributes to themselves (Edwards, 1953). This does not seem to be simply a matter of self-report bias, as we see similar positivity when determining the average personality from informant reports, or from people who know an individual well (Leising, Erbs, & Fritz, 2010), and even in first impressions (Rogers & Biesanz, 2015). Of course, individuals who know us, but do not like us, are not as likely to view us as positively (Leising et al., 2010; Wessels, Zimmermann, Biesanz, & Leising, 2018; Zimmermann, Schindler, Klaus, & Leising, 2018). All in all, when self-reports, informant-reports, or first impressions are used to assess personality, the average individual's personality is positive and socially desirable.

Assessing the Average Personality

Now that you understand how the average personality looks, we can discuss the more practical matter of how it is assessed. The average personality profile usually includes item level averages and should include at least eight items with many more being de-

1	2	3	4	5
Strongly Disagree	Disagree	Neutral	Agree	Strongly Agree

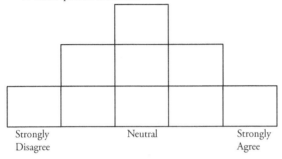

The average individual...

1. Can be moody
2. Has a forgiving nature
3. Is easily distracted
4. Tends to be disorganized
5. Is full of energy
6. Is sophisticated in art, music, or literature
7. Is reserved
8. Remains calm in tense situations
9. Starts quarrels with others

Figure 15.1. Modified Q-sort, similar to the one used in Rogers and Biesanz (2015).

sirable for better profile reliability (Kenny, Kashy, & Cook, 2006; see chapter 5 by Biesanz, in this handbook, for more details). This means you *could* use a brief measure of personality, such as the Ten Item Personality Index (TIPI; Gosling, Rentfrow, & Swann, 2003), but you would be better off using a much longer assessment. For example, if you are using the 44-item measure of the Big Five Inventory (John & Srivastava, 1999), you will determine the average for each of these 44-items to create the normative profile. Notably, you will not reverse code any items.

There are two main methods that researchers use to determine the average person's personality—either by using all the participant self-reports in the dataset they are currently using (e.g., Orehek & Human, 2017; Wood & Furr, 2016) or by using a large set of self-reports from a pool of similar participants (e.g., Human, Biesanz, Finseth, Pierce, & Le, 2014; Letzring, 2015). The normative profile can also be derived from informant reports (e.g., Mosch & Borkenau, 2016) or a combination of informant and self-reports of personality (e.g., Rogers & Biesanz, 2018; Zimmermann et al., 2018). The method to derive the normative profile is typically determined by the criteria used for accuracy, for example, if the accuracy criteria is self-reports, then the normative profile is likely the average self-

reported personality. For example, if you are comparing impressions to self-reports of students at your university, using 400 self-reports of students at your university that you have collected over the last few years would likely capture the average personality for the population well. Additionally, using a sample of 400 may be better than using only the 100 collected in your sample for a given study, as the larger sample should yield more precise estimates and a better representation. You would probably *not* want to use those same 400 self-reports of personality if you were researching older adults in your community, as those are not drawn from similar participant pools (i.e., your 400 undergraduates would not be a random sample of older adults in the community).

Commonly, researchers will generate a separate normative profile for males and for females, and the normative profile is then matched to the gender of the target (the person who is having the impression formed of them; e.g., Human & Biesanz, 2011a), or researchers will generate an overall normative profile (e.g., McDonald & Letzring, 2016). Separating the normative profile based on target gender allows for a cleaner conceptual interpretation, but the results are unlikely to differ dramatically from using a single overall profile as the average personality for males and females typically does not differ drastically. Indeed, using the normative profiles used in

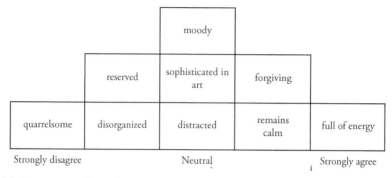

Figure 15.2. Modified Q-sort rating of items based on average individual's profile using data from Rogers and Biesanz (2015).

Rogers and Biesanz (2015), which were derived from 380 self-reports, there is a very strong correlation between the two profiles, $r = 0.94$. It may also be useful to consider the target individual's cultural background, or another important grouping factor such as age, and create separate normative profiles using that information (e.g., Locke et al., 2017; Locke, Zheng, & Smith, 2013; Rogers & Biesanz, 2014a). By matching the normative profile to target characteristics, the discussion of viewing someone as similar to the average person can be more nuanced, that is, a perceiver views a target as similar to an average person appropriate to the target's reference group.

Do People Have Explicit Knowledge of the Average Individual's Personality?

Even though an impression may be highly normative, this does not necessarily mean that the perceiver is *aware* that they are viewing someone as similar to the average person or that they are using average information to fill in any gaps.[3] This leads to the question of whether people have explicit knowledge of the average personality. Based on your previous attempt to rate the average personality, what do you think? Is it reasonable to think that people might know what the average person is like? Yes! Think about the last time you met a new person. Did you enter that interaction wondering if you would be robbed or proposed to? Probably not. We do have some expectations for individuals even when we are first meeting them (Olson, Roese, & Zanna, 1996), likely something along the lines of being pleasant and somewhat talkative. We are not just walking into interactions as blank slates, and there is at least some kernel of truth to general perceptions we hold of others. Indeed, there is some truth to the general perceptions of personality associated with age (Chan et al., 2012; Slotterback & Saarnio, 1996; Wood & Roberts, 2006), music pref-

erence (Rentfrow & Gosling, 2007), facial features (Berry, 1990), and geographic region (Rogers & Wood, 2010). For example, individuals living in New England are perceived as being highly neurotic and these individuals also report being highly neurotic (Rogers & Wood, 2010). Given this evidence, it seems highly plausible that there could also be knowledge about what people generally are like.[4]

Indeed, on average, people do have explicit knowledge of the average individual's personality (Rogers & Biesanz, 2015). We examined whether individuals have explicit knowledge of the average personality profile using a modified Q-sort, similar to the one you completed earlier in this chapter. We used this approach, instead of the more common Likert-style questionnaires, for several reasons. First, we were concerned that if we asked people about the average individual's personality, most people would not differentiate much between some of the items. For example, an individual could simply *agree* that the average individual has a list of fairly positive trait descriptions and *disagree* that the average individual has a list of fairly negative trait descriptions. We also wanted to remove response biases and extreme responses (ways in which an individual responds to a question that are not related to the content of the question), for example, on a 7-point scale, someone might tend to only use 3–5 while another person may tend to use 1–2 and 6–7. Using the modified Q-sort accounted for these issues and meant that the assessment of their explicit knowledge better reflects how they view the average person and not simply how they fill out a questionnaire. This means that participants had to sort each of the personality items into a roughly normally distributed distribution from a scale of 1 (*disagree strongly*) to 7 (*agree strongly*). Since we used 24 items, only 2 items could be placed in the *disagree strongly* category, while 6 could be placed in the *neutral* category. This approach allowed us to see that while, on average, people do have explicit knowledge of the normative profile, there are also wide individual differences in the degree of knowledge, in this case accuracy of the perceptions ranged within $r = -.60$–0.80, with most participants within $r = 0.29$–$.39$. Most people have at least some degree of explicit knowledge regarding the average personality, but there are a few who do not.

Given that people do vary in the degree to which they understand the average person, what characteristics are associated with greater explicit normative knowledge? Additional research has found that agreeableness, neuroticism, and conscientious are associated with greater explicit normative knowledge (Hambleton, Wood-Roberts, Colman, & Letzring, 2016). Beyond the Big Five traits, individuals who engage in more perspective-taking, are more empathetic, have greater life satisfaction, experience less personal distress in interpersonal interactions, and are female have greater explicit knowledge of the average person's personality (Hambleton et al., 2016). Taken together, these traits indicate that individuals who have greater explicit understanding of the average personality are well adjusted, socially skilled, and interested in and concerned about other people.

Why Is It Important to Consider the Average Individual's Personality When Examining Impressions?

When examining accuracy across many traits or items at once, it is necessary to consider the normative profile for several reasons. First, as previously alluded to, an individual could, on average, form fairly accurate impressions simply by rating everyone as average on a trait. While pragmatically this is not the worst way to go about forming impressions, it creates several conceptual issues when studying interpersonal perception. If we are considering raw agreement, we are unable to determine the extent to which this reflects an understanding of the average person (normativity) versus the extent to which this reflects an understanding of how a person is different from others (distinctive accuracy). This makes it difficult to understand the processes behind forming accurate impressions and investigate individual differences in the ability to understand an individual's *unique* characteristics (Cronbach, 1955). Thus, if we only considered raw agreement across traits, the people who appear to be most accurate could just be rating everyone as similar to the average person, which is problematic enough, but additionally, any correlates or moderators of agreement would likely

be dramatically altered. Indeed, distinctive accuracy and normativity have different relationships with a variety of processes and characteristics, such as accuracy motivation (Biesanz & Human, 2010), accuracy awareness (Biesanz et al., 2011), and gender (Chan, Rogers, Parisotto, & Biesanz, 2011). Moreover, there could be interesting and meaningful individual differences in the tendency to view others as similar to the average person and in the tendency to be viewed as similar to the average person.

The second issue has to do with the relationship between the average personality (normative profile) and positivity previously discussed. The relationship between positivity and the average personality makes it difficult to determine the extent to which an impression is due to use of normative information or evaluative bias. Indeed, some researchers have treated normativity as pure bias and have attempted to control for or remove this component of impressions (e.g., Landy, Vance, Barnes-Farrell, & Steele, 1980). However, in doing so, they have ignored important and useful information about the judgment process and potential consequences of these judgments. For example, normative first impressions are associated with liking and desire for future interactions (Human, Sandstrom, Biesanz, & Dunn, 2013; Human, Carlson, Geukes, Nestler, & Back, 2018), and adolescents who view the behavior of their parents more normatively reported lower depression and perceived stress (Human et al., 2016). These findings highlight potential inter- and intrapersonal benefits associated with normative impressions.

Imagine that you compare the impressions formed by 200 perceivers to the personality of 10 targets judged by each perceiver across all 44 items of the Big Five Inventory (John & Srivastava, 1999). If you were to examine raw agreement (i.e., without any adjustments or consideration for the normative profile) between impressions and personality across these items at one time, the overall level of accuracy (i.e., raw agreement) found would reflect a mix of two components—distinctive accuracy and normativity (Furr, 2008; Biesanz, 2010). That is, it would include the perceiver's unique impression of the target and how the target is different from others (distinctive accuracy) as well as the perceiver's tendency to view others as similar to the average person (normativity). As such, we would miss potentially useful information regarding the process and individual differences in forming impressions, and would have inflated perceptions regarding the degree of accuracy. Given that, on average, people are similar to the average person, and the normative profile is highly socially desirable, failing to consider the normative profile when assessing accuracy can substantially alter our understanding of the judgment process, especially when considering correlates and moderators. Fortunately, there are two common approaches that consider the personality of the average person when assessing agreement or accuracy across several attributes at once—profile correlations (Furr, 2008) and multilevel modeling using the social accuracy model (SAM; Biesanz, 2010; see chapter 5 by Biesanz in this handbook). Both approaches provide assessments of accuracy after the average personality has been partialled out (i.e., distinctive accuracy), but only SAM allows for the assessment of individual differences in normativity.

What Does It Mean to View Someone or To Be Viewed as Similar to the Average Person?

Given the strong relationship to social desirability, a highly normative impression is a positive, socially desirable impression. In fact, the relationship between social desirability and normativity is so strong that normativity is sometimes operationalized as an assessment of positivity (e.g., Aiken, Human, Alden, & Biesanz, 2014; Carlson, 2016a). However, despite the strong relationship between the two, it is possible to separate an overly positive impression from an impression relying on the normative profile (Rogers & Biesanz, 2015; Wessels et al., 2018). By including a measure of the normative profile, as well as a measure of social desirability, it is possible to disentangle these two components in impressions, demonstrating that normativity and positivity have unique relationships to other factors. For example, liking a target is associated with forming a more socially desirable impression, while knowing a target is associated with greater normativity (Wessels et al., 2018). Thus, is a normative impression simply a reflection of a positivity bias? In short, no.

What Characteristics and Situations Are Associated with Normative Impressions?

Now that you have a good understanding of the normative profile and normativity, we will discuss individual differences in normativity, both in viewing others and being viewed by others, and when impressions are likely to be normative. Additionally, the discussion for perceivers will highlight the differences between viewing others normatively and viewing others positively. *Perceiver Effects*

Do individuals differ in their tendency to view others normatively and as similar to the average person? There are relatively wide individual differences in the tendency to view others normatively (Biesanz, 2010); that is, some perceivers, on average, tend to view others as very similar to the average while other perceivers tend to see others as not very similar to the average person. Indeed, there several characteristics associated with forming more normative impressions: being well adjusted, emotionally stable, socially connected, positive, agreeable, self-reflective, empathic and tending to engage in perspective-taking, and female (Borkenau, Mosch, Tandler, & Wolf, 2016; Chan et al., 2011; Colman, Letzring, & Biesanz, 2017; Human & Biesanz, 2011b; Letzring, 2015). Additionally, people who have greater explicit knowledge about the average personality and knowledge about nonverbal cues also tend to view others more normatively (Rogers & Biesanz, 2015). On the other hand, individuals who score higher on narcissistic personality disorder, antisocial personality, subclinical sadism, psychopathy, and Machiavellianism form less normative impressions (Rogers, Le, Buckels, Kim, & Biesanz, 2018; Tandler, Mosch, Wolf, & Borkenau, 2016). There is also evidence that individuals with a greater sensitivity to social environment, as assessed by vagal flexibility, tend to form less normative impressions (Human & Mendes, 2018). In sum, it seems that perceivers who tend to form more normative impressions tend to have the following characteristics: being interested in others, positive, well adjusted, and female, and having greater knowledge of the average personality.

However, given the social desirability of the average personality, are these characteristics associated with forming normative impressions or with a positivity bias? While there is less research that has included assessments that capture both normativity and positivity, research has highlighted that these two components of impressions do operate independently and have differential relationships with perceiver characteristics (Rogers & Biesanz, 2015; Wessels et al., 2018; Zimmerman et al., 2018). Indeed, our research demonstrates that females and perceivers who tend to view others positively tend to form more socially desirable impressions, but not more normative impressions. Whereas, perceivers with more accurate explicit perceptions of the average person and greater knowledge of nonverbal cues form more normative impressions, but not more socially desirable impressions. Finally, well-adjusted perceivers form impressions that are both more normative and more socially desirable (Rogers & Biesanz, 2015). By considering normativity and social desirability, we can generate a more nuanced picture of individual differences in impressions.

Beyond the stable individual differences associated with normative impressions, there are circumstances that can result in more or less normative impressions. For example, some researchers have found that when perceivers are motivated to explicitly form more accurate impressions, they tend to form less normative impressions (Biesanz & Human, 2010), but this effect was not replicated in later studies (Colman, 2015). Additionally, idiosyncratic perceptions of attractiveness (i.e., perceiving a target as more attractive than the target tends to be perceived) are associated with more normative impressions (Lorenzo, Biesanz, & Human, 2010). When perceivers like a target or find a target engaging, this is associated with viewing them more normatively, however, when including both social desirability and normativity, liking and engagement are associated with more positive impressions, but not more normative impressions (Rogers & Biesanz, 2015; Wessels et al., 2018). Additionally, when perceivers believe the target does not like them, they form more normative, but less positive, impressions (Zimmermann et al., 2018). The differential relationships between social desirability and normativity again highlight how the two constructs are not identical.

Target Effects

Do individuals differ in their tendency to be viewed by others normatively and as similar to the average person? Compared to differences among perceivers, target individual differences in normativity are often narrower (Biesanz, 2010). That is, there is less variability in the tendency to be viewed normatively than there is in the tendency to view others normatively. Though there is less variability, there are still individual differences in the tendency to be viewed normatively by others. Individuals who are females, well-adjusted, and physically attractive are viewed more normatively (Borkenau et al., 2016; Lorenzo et al., 2010), whereas individuals who score higher on histrionic personality disorder, subclinical sadism, and Machiavellianism are viewed less normatively by others (Rogers et al., 2018; Tandler et al., 2016). As with perceiver effects, there are also circumstances where a target could be viewed more or less normatively than they are on average. For example, targets who self-presented and put their best foot forward were also viewed more normatively (Human, Biesanz, Parisotto, & Dunn, 2012). Thus, while some people tend to be viewed more normatively by others, there are ways in which a person could increase how normatively others view them.

Situational and Contextual Differences in Normativity

Normativity can also vary based on what type of information is used when forming the impression. For example, normativity was lower when a target discussed behaviors, but higher when there was more information about thoughts and feelings (Letzring & Human, 2013). Another approach is to consider the type of interaction that individuals were having when they formed an impression. Forming impressions through more passive approaches, such as viewing videos, reviewing a Facebook profile, or watching an interaction, are associated with less normative impressions compared to impressions formed during a face-to-face interaction (Biesanz, 2015; Biesanz, Rogers, Human, Le, et al., 2014; Biesanz, Rogers, Human, Sandstrom, et al., 2014; Rogers & Biesanz, 2014b). In sum, there is evidence that the type of information provided and the interaction format can influence normativity, but much more research is needed.

Future Directions

There remain many questions about normativity, and there are many options an interested researcher could explore. First, a thorough longitudinal study of how normativity changes over time while also modeling changes in social desirability over time is necessary for understanding how these processes unfold. Previous cross-sectional work found that normativity tended to decrease as relationship length increased from months to years (Biesanz, West, & Millevoi, 2007), while longitudinal work found that normativity tended to increase as relationship length increased over a 3-month period (Human et al., 2018). Thus, research should not only consider how normativity and positivity change in the beginning stages of a relationship but also examine this across a longer time period. Additionally, in line with previous work (Leising et al., 2010; Wessels et al., 2018; Zimmermann et al., 2018) examining this trajectory in people who do not necessarily like each other, but who must interact regularly (e.g., colleagues, classmates) is another important aspect of impression formation that needs to be considered.

Another area to expand on is focusing on perceptions of the average person's personality. One open question is the development of and process through which a person gains accurate knowledge about the average person. Another area to examine is whether people are aware of the degree to which they understand the average person's personality. Finally, disentangling perceptions of the average person with individual assessments of social desirability is necessary so we can understand these effects at the within- and between-person levels.

Conclusion

When examining impressions across several traits at once, it is necessary to consider the personality of the average individual (i.e., the normative profile), as failing to do so can result in erroneous conclusions about the judgment process, as well as causes and consequences of these judgments. Additionally, despite a strong link between social desirability and the normative profile, it is possible to separate these components and doing so can provide a more nuanced understanding of impressions, such as understanding the role of liking. Finally, knowledge of the average individual's personality and normativity are important aspects of impressions to study, not just an artifact that needs to be controlled for, and many questions remain for future research.

References

Aiken, A., Human, L. J., Alden, L. E., & Biesanz, J. C. (2014). Try to find me: Social anxiety and peer first impressions. *Behavior Therapy, 45*, 851–862. doi:10.1016/j.beth.2014.08.001

Back, M. D., & Nestler, S. (2016). Accuracy of judging personality. In J. A. Hall, M. S. Mast, & T. V. West (Eds.), *The social psychology of perceiving others accurately* (pp. 98–124). New York: Cambridge University Press. doi:10.1017/CBO9781316181959.005

Berry, D. S. (1990). Taking people at face value: Evidence for the kernel of truth hypothesis. *Social Cognition, 8*, 343–361. doi:10.1521/soco.1990.8.4.343

Biesanz, J. C. (2010). The social accuracy model of interpersonal perception: Assessing individual differences in perceptive and expressive accuracy. *Multivariate Behavioral Research, 45*, 853–885. doi:10.1080/00273171.2010.519262

Biesanz, J. C. (2015, June). *Towards understanding normative personality assessments*. Presentation at Biannual Conference of the Association for Research in Personality, St. Louis, MO.

Biesanz, J. C., & Human, L. J. (2010). The cost of forming more accurate impressions: Accuracy-motivated perceivers see the personality of others more distinctively but less normatively than perceivers without an explicit goal. *Psychological Science, 21*, 589–594. doi:10.1177/0956797610364121

Biesanz, J. C., Human, L. J., Paquin, A. C., Chan, M., Parisotto, K. L., Sarracino, J., & Gillis, R. L. (2011). Do we know when our impressions of others are valid? Evidence for realistic accuracy awareness in first impressions of personality. *Social Psychological and Personality Science, 2*, 452–459. doi:10.1177/1948550610397211

Biesanz, J. C., Rogers, K. H., Human, L. J., Le, M., Pierce, B., & Oddleifson, L. (2014, July). *The perils of simply observing: Observers' personality impressions are accurate but negatively biased*. Presentation at 16th European Conference on Personality, Lausanne, Switzerland.

Biesanz, J. C., Rogers, K. H., Human, L. J., Sandstrom, G. M., Dunn, E. W., & Le, M. (2014, February). *The consequences and context of accurate first impressions*. Presentation at Annual Conference of the Society for Personality and Social Psychology, Austin, TX.

Biesanz, J. C., West, S. G., & Millevoi, A. (2007). What do you learn about someone over time? The relationship between length of acquaintance and consensus and self-other agreement in judgments of personality. *Journal of Personality and Social Psychology, 92*, 119–135. doi:10.1037/0022-3514.92.1.119

Borkenau, P., Mauer, N., Riemann, R., Spinath, F. M., & Angleitner, A. (2004). Thin slices of behavior as cues of personality and intelligence. *Journal of Personality and Social Psychology, 86*, 599–614. doi:10.1037/0022-3514.86.4.599

Borkenau, P., Mosch, A., Tandler, N., & Wolf, A. (2016). Accuracy of judgments of personality based on textual information on major life domains. *Journal of Personality, 84*, 214–224. doi:10.1111/jopy.12153

Borkenau, P., & Zaltauskas, K. (2009). Effects of self-enhancement on agreement on personality profiles. *European Journal of Personality, 23*, 107–123. doi:10.1002/per.707

Carlson, E. N. (2016a). Do psychologically adjusted individuals know what other people really think about them? The link between psychological adjustment and meta-accuracy. *Social Psychological and Personality Science, 7*, 717–725. doi:10.1177/1948550616646424

Carlson, E. N. (2016b). Meta-accuracy and relationship quality: Weighing the costs and benefits of knowing what people really think about you. *Journal of Personality and Social Psychology, 111*, 250–263. doi:10.1037/pspp0000107

Carney, D. R., Colvin, C. R., & Hall, J. A. (2007). A thin slice perspective on the accuracy of first impressions. *Journal of Research in Personality, 41*, 1054–1072. doi:10.1016/j.jrp.2007.01.004

Chan, M., Rogers, K. H., Parisotto, K. L., & Biesanz, J. C. (2011). Forming first impressions: The role of gender and normative accuracy in personality perception. *Journal of Research in Personality, 45*, 117–120. doi:10.1016/j.jrp.2010.11.001

Chan, W., McCrae, R. R., De Fruyt, F., Jussim, L., Löckenhoff, C. E., De Bolle, M.,...Nakazato, K. (2012). Stereotypes of age differences in personality traits: Universal and accurate? *Journal of Personality and Social Psychology, 103*, 1050–1066. doi:10.1037/a0029712

Colman, D. E. (2015). *Motivated accuracy: Investigating the effect of task goals on normative and distinctive components of accuracy of personality trait judgements* (Unpublished master's thesis). Idaho State University, Pocatello, ID.

Colman, D. E., Letzring, T. D., & Biesanz, J. C. (2017). Seeing and feeling your way to accurate personality judgments: The moderating role of perceiver empathic tendencies. *Social Psychological and Personality Science, 8*, 806–815. doi:10.1177/1948550617691097

Cronbach, L. J. (1955). Processes affecting scores on "understanding of others" and "assumed similarity." *Psychological Bulletin, 52*, 177–193. doi:10.1037/h0044919

Edwards, A. L. (1953). The relationship between the judged desirability of a trait and the probability that the trait will be endorsed. *Journal of Applied Psychology, 37,* 90–93. doi:10.1037/h0058073

Edwards, A. L. (1957). Social desirability and probability of endorsement of items in the interpersonal check list. *Journal of Abnormal and Social Psychology, 55,* 394–396. doi:10.1037/h0048497

Fiske, S. T., & Neuberg, S. L. (1990). A continuum of impression formation, from category-based to individuating processes: Influences of information and motivation on attention and interpretation. In M. P. Zanna (Ed.), *Advances in experimental social psychology* (pp. 1–74). New York: Academic Press.

Funder, D. C., & Colvin, C. R. (1988). Friends and strangers: Acquaintanceship, agreement, and the accuracy of personality judgment. *Journal of Personality and Social Psychology, 55,* 149–158. doi:10.1037/0022-3514.55.1.149

Furr, R. M. (2008). A framework for profile similarity: Integrating similarity, normativeness, and distinctiveness. *Journal of Personality, 76,* 1267–1316. doi:10.1111/j.1467-6494.2008.00521.x

Gosling, S. D., Rentfrow, P. J., & Swann, W. B., Jr. (2003). A very brief measure of the Big-Five personality domains. *Journal of Research in Personality, 37,* 504–528. doi:10.1016/S0092-6566(03)00046-1

Hambleton, J. L., Wood-Roberts, B., Colman, D. E., & Letzring, T. D. (2016, January). *Why you should give people the benefit of the doubt: Positive characteristics associated with explicit normative knowledge.* Poster presentation at Annual Conference of the Society for Personality and Social Psychology, San Diego, CA.

Henrich, J., Heine, S. J., & Norenzayan, A. (2010). The weirdest people in the world? *Behavioral and Brain Sciences, 33*(2–3), 61–83. doi:10.1017/s0140525x0999152x

Human, L. J., & Biesanz, J. C. (2011a). Target adjustment and self-other agreement: Utilizing trait observability to disentangle judgeability and self-knowledge. *Journal of Personality and Social Psychology, 101,* 202–216. doi:10.1037/a0023782

Human, L. J., & Biesanz, J. C. (2011b). Through the looking glass clearly: Accuracy and assumed similarity in well-adjusted individuals' first impressions. *Journal of Personality and Social Psychology, 100,* 349–364. doi:10.1037/a0021850

Human, L. J., Biesanz, J. C., Finseth, S. M., Pierce, B., & Le, M. (2014). To thine own self be true: Psychological adjustment promotes judgeability via personality–behavior congruence. *Journal of Personality and Social Psychology, 106,* 286–303. doi:10.1037/a0034860

Human, L. J., Biesanz, J C., Parisotto, K. L., & Dunn, E. W. (2012). Your best self helps reveal your true self: Trying to make a good impression results in more accurate impressions. *Social Psychological and Personality Science, 3,* 23–30. doi:10.1037/e634112013-507

Human, L. J., Carlson, E. N., Geukes, K., Nestler, S., & Back, M. D. (2018). Do accurate personality impressions benefit early relationship development? The bidirectional associations between accuracy and liking. *Journal of Personality and Social Psychology.* Advance online publication. doi:10.1037/pspp0000214

Human, L. J., Chan, M., Ifthikhar, R., Williams, D., DeLongis, A., & Chen, E. (2016). Accuracy and positivity in adolescent perceptions of parent behavior: Links with adolescent psychological adjustment and proinflammatory profiles. *Social Psychological and Personality Science, 7,* 796–805. doi:10.1177/1948550616660590

Human, L. J., & Mendes, W. B. (2018). Cardiac vagal flexibility and accurate personality impressions: Examining a physiological correlate of the good judge. *Journal of Personality, 86,* 1065–1077. doi:10.1111/jopy.12375

Human, L. J., Sandstrom, G. M., Biesanz, J C., & Dunn, E. W. (2013). Accurate first impressions leave a lasting impression: The long-term effects of accuracy on relationship development. *Social Psychological and Personality Science, 4,* 395–402. doi:10.1177/1948550612463735

John, O. P., & Srivastava, S. (1999). The Big-Five trait taxonomy: History, measurement, and theoretical perspectives. In L. A. Pervin & O. P. John (Eds.), *Handbook of personality: Theory and research* (2nd ed., pp. 102–138). New York: Guilford Press.

Kenny, D. A., Kashy, D. A., & Cook, W. L. (2006). *Dyadic data analysis.* New York: Guilford Press.

Landy, F. J., Vance, R. J., Barnes-Farrell, J. L., & Steele, J. W. (1980). Statistical control of halo error in performance ratings. *Journal of Applied Psychology, 65,* 501–506. doi:10.1037//0021-9010.65.5.501

Leising, D., Erbs, J., & Fritz, U. (2010). The letter of recommendation effect in informant ratings of personality. *Journal of Personality and Social Psychology, 98,* 668–682. doi:10.1037/a0018771

Letzring, T. D. (2015). Observer judgmental accuracy of personality: Benefits related to being a good (normative) judge. *Journal of Research in Personality, 54,* 51–60. doi:10.1016/j.jrp.2014.05.001

Letzring, T. D., & Human, L. J. (2013). An examination of information quality as a moderator of accurate personality judgment. *Journal of Personality, 82,* 440–451. doi:10.1111/jopy.12075

Locke, K. D., Church, A. T., Mastor, K. A., Curtis, G. J., Sadler, P., McDonald, K., … Ortiz, F. A. (2017). Cross-situational self-consistency in nine cultures: The importance of separating influences of social norms and distinctive dispositions. *Personality and Social Psychology Bulletin, 43,* 1033–1049. doi:10.1177/0146167217704192

Locke, K. D., Zheng, D., & Smith, J. (2013). Establishing commonality vs affirming distinctiveness: Patterns of personality judgments in China and the United States. *Social Psychological and Personality Science, 5,* 389–397. doi:10.1177/1948550613506718

Lorenzo, G. L., Biesanz, J. C., & Human, L. J. (2010). What is beautiful is good and more accurately understood: Physical attractiveness and accuracy in first impressions of personality. *Psychological Science, 21,* 1777–1782. doi:10.1177/0956797610388048

McCrae, R. R., Terracciano, A., & 79 members of the Personality Profiles of Cultures Project. (2005). Personality profiles of cultures: Aggregate personality traits. *Journal of Personality and Social Psychology, 89,* 407–425. doi:10.1037/0022-3514.89.3.407

McDonald, J. S., & Letzring, T. D. (2016). Judging personal values and personality traits: Accuracy and its relation to visibility. *Journal of Research in Personality, 65,* 140–151. doi:10.1016/j.jrp.2016.10.009

Mosch, A., & Borkenau, P. (2016). Psychologically adjusted persons are less aware of how they are perceived by others. *Personality and Social Psychology Bulletin, 42,* 910–922. doi:10.1177/0146167216647383

Olson, J. M., Roese, N. J., & Zanna, M. P. (1996). Expectancies. In E. Higgins & A. W. Kruglanski (Eds.), *Social psychology: Handbook of basic principles* (pp. 211–238). New York: Guilford Press.

Orehek, E., & Human, L. J. (2017). Self-expression on social media: Do tweets present accurate and positive portraits of impulsivity, self-esteem, and attachment style? *Personality and Social Psychology Bulletin, 43*, 60–70. doi:10.1177/0146167216675332

Peabody, D. (1967). Trait inferences: Evaluative and descriptive aspects. *Journal of Personality and Social Psychology, 7*(4, Pt. 2), 1–18. doi:10.1037/h0025230

Rauthmann, J. F., & Sherman, R. A. (2017). Normative and distinctive accuracy in situation perceptions: Magnitude and personality correlates. *Social Psychological and Personality Science, 8*, 768–779. doi:10.1177/1948550616687095

Rentfrow, P. J., & Gosling, S. D. (2007). The content and validity of music-genre stereotypes among college students. *Psychology of Music, 35*, 306–326. doi:10.1177/0305735607070382

Rogers, K. H., & Biesanz, J. C. (2014a). The accuracy and bias of interpersonal perceptions in intergroup interactions. *Social Psychological and Personality Science, 5*, 918–926. doi:10.1177/1948550614537307

Rogers, K. H., & Biesanz, J. C. (2014b, February). *Accuracy in first impressions: Perks and perils of simply observing.* Poster Presentation at Annual Conference of the Society for Personality and Social Psychology, Austin, TX.

Rogers, K. H., & Biesanz, J. C. (2015). Knowing versus liking: Separating normative knowledge from social desirability in first impressions of personality. *Journal of Personality and Social Psychology, 109*, 1105–1116. doi:10.1037/a0039587

Rogers, K. H., & Biesanz, J. C. (2018). Reassessing the good judge. *Journal of Personality and Social Psychology.* Advance online publication. doi:10.1037/pspp0000197

Rogers, K. H., Le, M. T., Buckels, E. E., Kim, M., & Biesanz, J. C. (2018). Dispositional malevolence and impression formation: Dark Tetrad associations with accuracy and positivity in first impressions. *Journal of Personality, 86*, 1050–1064. doi:10.1111/jopy.12374

Rogers, K. H., & Wood, D. (2010). Accuracy of United States regional personality stereotypes. *Journal of Research in Personality, 44*, 704–713. doi:10.1016/j.jrp.2010.09.006

Rogers, K. H., Wood, D., & Furr, R. M. (2018). Assessment of similarity and self-other agreement in dyadic relationships: A guide to best practices. *Journal of Social and Personal Relationships, 35*, 112–134. doi:10.1177/0265407517712615

Slotterback, C. S., & Saarnio, D. A. (1996). Attitudes toward older adults reported by young adults: Variation based on attitudinal task and attribute categories. *Psychology and Aging, 11*, 563–571. doi:10.1037/0882-7974.11.4.563

Solomon, B. C., & Vazire, S. (2016). Knowledge of identity and reputation: Do people have knowledge of others' perceptions? *Journal of Personality and Social Psychology, 111*, 341–366. doi:10.1037/pspi0000061

Tandler, N., Mosch, A., Wolf, A., & Borkenau, P. (2016). Effects of personality disorders on self-other agreement and favorableness in personality descriptions. *Journal of Personality Disorders, 30*, 577–594. doi:10.1521/pedi_2015_29_213

Wessels, N. M., Zimmermann, J., Biesanz, J. C., & Leising, D. (2018). Differential associations of knowing and liking with accuracy and positivity bias in person perception. *Journal of Personality and Social Psychology.* Advance online publication. doi:10.1037/pspp0000218

Wood., D., & Furr, R. M. (2016). The correlates of similarity estimates are often misleadingly positive: The nature and scope of the problem and some solutions. *Personality and Social Psychology Review, 20*, 79–99. doi:10.1177/1088868315581119

Wood, D., Gosling, S. D., & Potter, J. (2007). Normality evaluations and their relation to personality traits and well-being. *Journal of Personality and Social Psychology, 93*, 861–879. doi:10.1037/0022-3514.93.5.861

Wood, D., Lowman, G. H., Harms, P. D., & Roberts, B. W. (2018). Exploring the relative importance of normative and distinctive organizational preferences as predictors of work attitudes. *Journal of Applied Psychology.* Advance online publication. doi:10.1037/apl0000356

Wood, D., & Roberts, B. W. (2006). The effect of age and role information on expectations for Big Five personality traits. *Personality and Social Psychology Bulletin, 32*(11), 1482–1496. doi:10.1177/0146167206291008

Zimmermann, J., Schindler, S., Klaus, G., & Leising, D. (2018). The effect of dislike on accuracy and bias in person perception. *Social Psychological and Personality Science, 9*, 80–88. doi:10.1177/1948550617703167

Notes

1. Of course, accuracy in first impressions does exist (see Back & Nestler, 2016, for a review), and certain traits are relatively easy to identify with very little information (e.g., extraversion; Carney, Colvin, & Hall, 2007). However, if you talk to someone for a few minutes you will likely not quite get *all* the unique and interesting components of their personality, even if we limit that to just the Big Five personality traits. After all, you learn more about someone the longer you have known them (e.g., Funder & Colvin, 1988) and the more situations you have seen them in (e.g., Borkenau, Mauer, Riemann, Spinath, & Angleitner, 2004).

2. While this chapter primarily focuses on first impressions, it is also important to consider the normative profile for other measures of correspondence, such as similarity (e.g., Rogers, Wood, & Furr, 2018), meta-perceptions (e.g., Carlson, 2016b) as well as reputation (Solomon & Vazire, 2016) as well as aspects of situations (Rauthmann & Sherman, 2017) and person-environment fit (Wood, Lowman, Harms, & Roberts, 2018).

3. Whether individuals consciously rely on their understanding of the average person when forming impressions remains an open question for researchers to investigate.

4. This is not to say that there is one general "human" personality profile, there are real cultural differences in personality (e.g., Henrich, Heine, & Norenzayan, 2010; McCrae, Terracciano, & 79 members of the Personality Profiles of Cultures Project, 2005) and entering a conversation with individuals from a very different culture with your own cultural expectations can be problematic—it can lead to erroneous judgments, perceptions of disrespect, and worse. There are, of course, hundreds of ways that your expectations can lead you astray, and it is always important to self-correct and be open to feedback.

The Accuracy of Stereotypes About Personality

Lee Jussim, Sean T. Stevens, *and* Nate Honeycutt

Abstract

This chapter first reviews general conceptual and methodological issues in the study of the (in)accuracy of stereotypes. First, the authors define stereotype accuracy. Second, different types of accuracy are discussed and standards for considering a stereotype belief accurate or inaccurate are presented. Finally, the chapter reviews the empirical evidence produced thus far that bears on the (in)accuracy of stereotypes regarding personality. The strongest evidence regarding the (in)accuracy of stereotypes regarding personality have focused on gender, age, and national character stereotypes. Weaker evidence relying primarily on self-reports of individual differences with respect to racial stereotypes and miscellaneous stereotypes (e.g., jazz vs. ballet dancers) is also reviewed. The chapter concludes by developing hypotheses that could help explain the pattern of (in)accuracy in stereotypes regarding personality.

Key Words: stereotype, accuracy, gender, age, national character

Stereotypes are one of the most fundamental social psychological phenomena, because they involve how people perceive other people. As such, they have been studied for nearly one hundred years. For most of that time, scholars defined them as inaccurate or declared that the empirical evidence indicated that they are inaccurate (see Jussim, 2012, for a historical review). Such a conclusion, however, was premature, and not based on much empirical evidence. Rigorous empirical assessments of the accuracy of stereotypes began in the late 1970s, accelerated in the 1990s, and, now, with over 50 empirical studies published, has yielded a surprising conclusion: highly inaccurate stereotypes are the exception; moderate to high accuracy is common. These issues have been amply reviewed elsewhere (e.g., Campbell, 1967; Judd & Park, 1993; Jussim, 2012; Jussim, Cain, Crawford, Harber, & Cohen, 2009; Jussim, Crawford, Anglin, Chambers, Stevens, & Cohen, 2016; Jussim, Crawford, & Rubinstein, 2015; Jussim, Stevens, & Honeycutt, 2018; Lee, Jussim, & McCauley, 1995; Mackie, 1973; Ryan, 2002), and is not a main focus of the present chapter, though we do draw heavily on our prior

work for this review of the evidence regarding the accuracy of stereotypes about personality. Rather than re-list all the reviews just cited each time they are relevant, we hence refer to those reviews with the term "the general stereotype accuracy literature."

The unique contribution of this chapter is that it reviews the evidence specifically regarding the (in)accuracy of stereotypes regarding personality. As such, it is the first review to do so of which we are aware. First, we provide a conceptual overview of what stereotype accuracy is, and then describe how it can be assessed. Second, we identify what types of studies are included and excluded from this review, and explain why. The third section is the core of the chapter—it reviews every study of the (in)accuracy of stereotypes regarding personality that we were able to discover. We end the chapter with some speculative conclusions about what explains patterns of accuracy and inaccuracy in stereotypes regarding personality.

What Is Stereotype Accuracy?

Answering this question requires three steps: (1) defining stereotype, (2) defining accuracy, (3) combining them. Our definition of stereotype is based on that of Ashmore and Del Boca (1981): people's beliefs about groups and their individual members. This leaves the accuracy of stereotypes as an open empirical question.

We use the term "accuracy" to refer to correspondence between a belief and a credible criterion. Stereotype accuracy, therefore, refers to degree of correspondence between a belief about a group and some criterion against which that belief can be evaluated. In the general stereotype accuracy literature, common criteria include Census and government data, meta-analyses of group differences, behavioral observations, and group self-reports. Potential criteria in the general stereotype accuracy literature span a vast variety of characteristics, including academic achievement, beliefs and attitudes, preferences, wealth and income, interpersonal skills, and personality (which is the exclusive focus of the present chapter). The general stereotype accuracy literature has addressed controversies and limitations to various criteria (see Jussim, 2012, for the most extended discussion). In short, self-reports are often considered the weakest of these criteria; however, some self-report criteria have been subject to extensive validation (such as the NEO-PI-R, which is used in many of the studies reviewed herein).

How to Assess the Accuracy of Stereotypes

The general stereotype accuracy literature has long articulated what is necessary to empirically investigate the accuracy of stereotypes: (1) Assess beliefs about one or more groups, (2) Identify criteria for evaluating the validity of those beliefs, and (3) Compare them. To assess the accuracy of a stereotype a *single individual* holds, one needs to: (1) Assess that person's belief about one or more groups, (2) Identify an appropriate criterion for that belief, and (3) Compare them. One can also assess *consensual* accuracy by taking these steps: (1) Assess the average belief held by a group of perceivers about a target group, (2) Identify criteria, and (3) Compare mean perceptions to criteria. Correspondence with criteria is typically assessed with correlations; discrepancies from criteria are typically assessed with difference scores.

Stereotype accuracy is usually assessed with either *discrepancies* or *correlations*. Discrepancies assess how close to criteria people's beliefs come. They can be computed in either of two ways, if the stereotype and criterion are assessed on the same scale. The simplest is direct comparison of stereotype to criteria by subtraction (stereotype minus criteria equals discrepancy). These discrepancy scores can be viewed as assessing: "How close to perfect accuracy are people's stereo-

types?" Sometimes, however, researchers compare standard deviations (SDs); if the SD among stereotype perceptions is larger than that among criteria, it indicates that stereotypes exaggerate real differences; if smaller, it indicates they underestimate real differences. This latter method has the benefit of providing an overall assessment of exaggeration/underestimation across all groups and attributes, and the limitation of not permitting more fine-grained analyses regarding *which* attributes are accurately versus inaccurately perceived. Regardless of the method used, however, smaller discrepancies indicate greater accuracy.

Furthermore, componential approaches can be used to test hypotheses about particular sources of inaccuracy (Judd & Park, 1993; see Jussim, 2012, for a review and critique of several componential approaches). Componential approaches treat discrepancy scores as best understood through analysis of variance. In Judd and Park's (1993) approach, components are divided into effects attributable to perceiver groups (do some groups of perceivers consistently over- or underestimate targets' standing on attributes); target groups (are some groups more likely to be over- or underestimated by perceivers), attributes (are some types of attributes more likely to be over- or underestimated than others), and all possible two-way interactions and the three-way interaction. The meaning and interpretation of the two-way and three-way interactions hinge on the nature of the attributes. If attributes are chosen such that they are stereotypical for one group and counterstereotypical for the other, the three-way interaction has particular significance, because it can reveal in-group bias. If, for example, stereotype exaggeration (overestimation of the difference between stereotypical and counterstereotypical attributes) occurs more when people judge the other group than when they judge their own group (i.e., more when Group A judges Group B and when Group B judges Group A than when Group A judges Group A and Group B judges Group B), one would have evidence of in-group bias.

Correlations assess how well people's beliefs about groups correspond to criteria. Higher correlations indicate greater correspondence—that is, higher accuracy. Correlations assess how sensitive people's stereotypes are to *variability* in the actual differences between criteria.

The different types of information about accuracy provided by discrepancy scores versus correlations can be seen with a simple hypothetical example. A perceiver estimates the average height of Nepalese,

LEE JUSSIM, SEAN T. STEVENS, AND NATE HONEYCUTT

Norwegian, and Nigerian men as 60, 62, and 64 inches. If the real average heights are 72, 74, and 76 inches, the discrepancy is a full foot off—quite inaccurate. And yet the perceiver's estimates correlate 1.0 with the real differences. This occurs because, even though the estimates of average height are far off, they are nonetheless perfectly sensitive to variations in height.

Whether one assesses accuracy via discrepancy scores or correlations, one can assess two types of stereotypes: consensual and personal stereotypes. Consensual (or aggregate) stereotypes are shared by the members of a culture or a particular sample. They have so far always been sample means (e.g., the mean belief about women's height in a sample is the best estimate of the consensual stereotype for women's height for the group sampled; though it is imaginable that other metrics of shared-ness could be justified, such as a sample median). Personal stereotypes are the beliefs about a group held by a single individual, whether or not that belief is shared.

Standards for Considering a Stereotype Accurate or Inaccurate

There is no objective standard for accuracy and there is no established consensus in the literature regarding what constitutes an accurate or inaccurate belief. Indeed, this is both ironic and problematic, given the frequency with which many researchers have declared stereotypes to be "inaccurate." That is, without articulating any standard for (in)accuracy, it is not clear how anyone can justify declaring stereotypes to be either accurate or inaccurate. In order to redress this limitation, we have developed heuristic standards for doing so (see Jussim, 2012; Jussim et al., 2009; Jussim et al., 2016, for extended discussions).

Because there are two broad types of accuracy, discrepancy from perfection and correspondence with real differences, there needs to be two separate standards. For discrepancies, we consider judgments within 10% or 0.25 SDs of the criteria to be accurate, and within 20% and 0.50 SDs to be near misses. We consider judgments that are more than 20% or 0.50 SDs discrepant from criteria to be inaccurate.

For example, McCauley and Stitt (1978) examined the accuracy of racial stereotypes by comparing them to Census data (although they reported results primarily as diagnostic ratios, the original data can be found in McCauley, 1995). At the time, 39% of African Americans had completed high school. Three of five samples estimated that high school completion rate as 40%–48%; by our standard, all three were accurate because 39% +/-10% means anything from 29%–49% would be considered accurate. The other two sample estimates were 50% and 52%, and, by our standards, would be considered near misses (39% +/- 20% means anything outside the 29%–49% range but within 19%–59% would be considered a near miss). If criteria and stereotypes are measured in other sorts of units, SDs could be used in an essentially similar manner. For personality judgments, SDs are more likely to be used than percentages. For example, Rogers and Wood (2010), in a study described later in more detail, examined the accuracy of American regional stereotypes and reported both stereotypes and personality criteria using standardized scores (z scores). Alaskans were seen as quite low on extraversion ($z = -1.88$), which, in fact, they were ($z = -1.63$). Because the stereotype is within 0.25 SDs of the criteria, by our standard, the stereotype of Alaskans' extraversion is accurate.

How much correspondence should be considered "accurate"? Absent reason to do otherwise (and such reasons are usually absent), we use the same standards to which social scientists hold themselves. The standards first articulated by Cohen (1988) are that correlations of 0.4 and higher could be considered accurate because they are "large." Only 24% of social psychological effects exceed 0.3 (Richard et al., 2003). As per Rosenthal's (1991) binomial effect size display, a correlation of 0.4 translates into people being right 70% of the time. This means they are right more than twice as often as they are wrong; $r \geq 0.4$ is a strong standard.

Moderate correspondence reflects a mix of accuracy and inaccuracy. Following the same standards as science (Cohen, 1988; Richard et al., 2003), we characterize correlations between people's beliefs and criteria ranging from 0.25 to 0.4 as moderately accurate. Correlations below 0.25 are considered inaccurate.

These standards for accuracy should not be reified. They have been offered more in a spirit of reasonable heuristic defaults. It is possible that for some purposes different standards could be used and justified. We strongly encourage researchers who wish to make claims about either the accuracy or inaccuracy of stereotypes to articulate standards for doing so. In the absence of such articulation, scientists are in no position to make *any* claims about the (in)accuracy of stereotypes in general, or of particular stereotypes regarding particular groups held by particular people.

What Stereotype Accuracy Is Not

Stereotype accuracy is not the same as group differences or similarities. Stereotypes have sometimes been declared to be "inconsistent with" some stereotype or another, without referring to evidence that actually empirically compares' specific people's measured stereotypes to criteria (e.g., Ellemers, 2018; Hyde, 2014). The only way, however, to know whether group differences (or similarities) confirm or disconfirm people's stereotypes is to assess those stereotypes and compare them to group characteristics. If any piece is lacking—the assessment of the stereotype, the assessment of group characteristics, or the comparison—no conclusions about stereotype (in)accuracy are scientifically justified. Thus, all claims that "stereotypes are inaccurate" that appear in the scientific literature (Ellemers, 2018; Hyde, 2014; see Jussim, 2012; Jussim et al. 2016, for reviews) are themselves not justified because they have never been made on the basis of research that empirically assesses and compares stereotypes to group differences.

When Stereotype Accuracy Cannot Be Assessed

Accuracy of stereotypes cannot always be assessed for both empirical and conceptual reasons. If no empirical criteria for accuracy exist, the validity of the stereotype cannot be evaluated. Conceptually, accuracy can be assessed for descriptive or predictive beliefs, but not for prescriptive or proscriptive beliefs. Descriptive beliefs are supposed to describe reality in some way. "Ohio gets the most rain in April," describes the relative frequency of rain in April (implicitly compared to other months). Similarly, "The Yankees have won more World Series than any other baseball team" described the relative frequency of World Series victories (implicitly compared to other teams). Similarly, the accuracy of predictive beliefs can be evaluated for accuracy. If Jana says, "It will rain here tomorrow," either there will or will not be rain. Similarly, if in 2019 Musa said, "Eighty-five to ninety-five percent of African American voters will vote for the Democratic candidate for President in 2020," this will either turnout true or not.

Prescriptive beliefs describe (one's opinions about) what things or people *should* be like. "Good shoes have arch support" is a prescriptive belief, as is, "children should be seen and not heard." Only descriptive and predictive beliefs, but not prescriptive beliefs, can be evaluated for their accuracy. Whether good shoes always require arch support or children should be quiet is personal preference; and personal preferences cannot be evaluated for their objective accuracy. In contrast, descriptive and predictive beliefs, whether about rain in April or the frequency of World Series victories, can be evaluated for accuracy.

Similarly, personal preferences cannot be evaluated for accuracy regarding the things or people preferred. The accuracy of "I don't like Buddhists" is not a descriptive or predictive belief about Buddhists and therefore, as a statement about Buddhists, cannot be evaluated for accuracy. The accuracy of prescriptive stereotypes, such as "professional football players should be role models," or "girls should wear skirts," cannot be evaluated for accuracy. When stereotypes involve something *other* than descriptive or predictive beliefs, no claims about stereotype (in)accuracy are possible.

What Is Included and Excluded in This Chapter

This chapter focuses exclusively on stereotype accuracy regarding personality. Studies failing to meet the standards described previously, which require assessment of a stereotype, identification of criteria, and a comparison, are excluded. Thus, studies examining only the personality content of some stereotypes are excluded, even if the authors' reached conclusions about accuracy, because, in fact, they have no empirical grounds for doing so. Similarly, studies that merely assess group differences in personality, but not anyone's stereotypes about those groups, are excluded, again, because no empirical assessment of accuracy is possible.

Studies focusing on stereotype accuracy regarding characteristics other than personality are excluded. This includes, but is not restricted to, studies assessing stereotype accuracy regarding demographic characteristics (e.g., wealth, income, likelihood of using social services, likelihood of committing or being victimized by crime, etc.), political attitudes, personal preferences or tastes, academic achievement, and so on. We do include studies of demographic stereotypes *if and only if* those studies assessed stereotypes regarding personality (rather than, e.g., regarding attitudes, wealth, etc.).

One can also think of personality characteristics in terms of stereotypes. Do people have stereotypes of extraverts, introverts, neurotics, and so forth? They probably do, or, at least, could, if they stopped to think about it. However, we know of no research that has assessed the accuracy of such beliefs, so none is reviewed here.

Some prior reviews of stereotype accuracy have also addressed whether perceivers rely primarily on stereotypes or individuating information in person perception, and on whether relying on a stereotype increases or reduces the accuracy of person perception judgments (Jussim, 2012; Jussim et al., 2018). Although these issues are related to issues of stereotype accuracy, they are also quite different. Finding out that, for example, Shakira has an accurate perception regarding Lois's or Mohamed's personality is interesting and important, but it tells us nothing about the overall accuracy of her gender, ethnic, or religious stereotypes. Thus, these issues are not included here (but see chapter by Rogers in this handbook for a discussion of the role of normative information in judgments of others).

The Empirical Evidence

We have discussed much, though not all, of the literature presented in what follows regarding national character, age, and gender stereotypes in our prior reviews of stereotype accuracy (Jussim, 2012; Jussim et al., 2009; Jussim et al., 2016; Jussim et al., 2015). Although more detail can be found in those reviews, our descriptions of the specifics of the studies presented here are often quite similar to that which appeared in one or more prior reviews. Nonetheless, this is the first time any of our reviews have focused specifically on the evidence regarding personality.

The (In)accuracy of National Character Stereotypes

Several studies have examined the accuracy of national or regional personality stereotypes (sometimes referred to as "national character stereotypes") using the NEO-PI-R, which is essentially an updating of what were once called Big Five Personality Inventories. These have been administered to thousands of people worldwide (e.g., Costa & McCrae, 2008; Costa, Terracciano, & McCrae, 2001; McCrae & Allik, 2002, McCrae & Terracciano, 2005), so there is now data on personality characteristics in many different countries. These can be and have been used to assess the accuracy of "national character (i.e., personality) stereotypes."

The first of such studies examined the accuracy of consensual national character *autostereotypes* (stereotypes of their own group—e.g., Italians' beliefs about Italians) in 49 cultures (*N* of almost 4,000) worldwide (Terracciano et al., 2005) which were compared to mean observer ratings of individuals and self-reports on the NEO-PI-R. Correlational accuracy (consensual stereotype accuracy correlations assessed as the intraclass correlation of autostereotypes with observer ratings and self-reports) averaged near zero. Furthermore, consensual stereotypes exaggerated real differences; although they did not directly assess discrepancy scores, they did show that perceived differences between national groups generally exceeded criterion differences. Personal stereotype accuracy was not assessed.

There were, however, several limitations to this research. First, the criterion samples used in this study were haphazard samples of convenience. This meant that low levels of correspondence between stereotype and criteria could have occurred, not because people were inaccurate, but because the criterion sample was not representative of the target population (see Judd & Park, 1993; Jussim et al., 2016 for more on the difficulties that arise when the target sample is mismatched to the stereotype assessed, also referred to as the mismatch limitation).

Heine, Buchtel, and Norenzayan (2008) identified another reason that people's national character stereotypes might have been more accurate than found by Terracciano et al. (2005). They argued that people rely on local cultural norms when arriving at perceptions of themselves (called "the reference group effect") which can distort measurement of cultural differences. To address this issue, they compared stereotypes to behavior, focusing exclusively on conscientiousness; thus their findings do not bear on the other Big Five characteristics (agreeableness, neuroticism, openness to experience, extraversion). Heine et al. (2008) operationalized conscientiousness behaviorally (GDP, longevity, walking speed, clock accuracy, and postal worker speed). The correlations between consensual national autostereotypes and behavior averaged about 0.60, indicating high correspondence accuracy. They assessed neither personal stereotype accuracy nor discrepancy scores.

But the controversy did not end there. A replication (McCrae et al., 2013, *N* > 3,000) of Terracciano et al. (2005) addressed some of the issues raised by Heine et al. (2008), though it still used self-reports on the Big Five as criteria. McCrae et al. (2013) discussed several reasons to be skeptical of low accuracy correlations resulting from the reference group effect. For example, foreigners have shown a pattern similar to that of their national compatriots, strongly suggesting that people are not using local norms as their basis for social judgments. The McCrae et al. (2013) replication, like the original (Terracciano et al., 2005), found almost no evidence of accuracy. These findings are consistent with research showing little accuracy in the personality stereotypes held by over 2000 Austrian, Czech, German, Polish, and Slovak college students regarding each other and their own country (Hrebickova & Graf, 2014). As is typical in this area, the criterion samples were large and international, but not random or representative.

In contrast, another study (Allik, Alyamkina, & Mescheryakov, 2015) of the consensual stereotype accuracy correlations held by two Finno-Urgic ethnic groups (Erzians, Mokshans) and Russians regarding one another's personalities (as measured by the NEO-PI-R), in the Republic of Mordovia (Russian Federation) found: (1) at least moderate accuracy in autostereotypes (correlations of 0.38, 0.51, 0.25, respectively); (2) substantial accuracy in Erzians' stereotypes regarding Mokshans ($r = .39$) and Mokshans' stereotypes of Erzians ($r =. 51$); (3) considerable accuracy in Erzians' ($r = .51$) but not Mokshans' ($r = .07$) stereotypes of Russians; and (4) stereotype accuracy correlations near zero for Russian perceivers regarding Erzians and Mokshans. The accuracy levels obtained in this study may be underestimates, however, because the criterion samples were small (100 for each group) haphazard samples of convenience.

Another study focused on the accuracy of six eastern European ethnic groups' (Finns, Estonians, Latvians, Lithuanians, Poles, and Belarussians) autostereotypes and stereotypes of Russians (Realo et al., 2009). There were 200 or more participants for each perceiver group (most were college students, but there were also subsamples of working adults among the Latvians and Estonians). Convenience samples constituted perceiver and target groups, whose personality and perceptions of national character were assessed on the NEO-PI-R. The evidence of personality stereotype accuracy was mixed. Consensual autostereotype correlations ranged from 0.07 (for Estonian and Latvian students) to 0.52 (for Russians). The only heterostereotype examined was regarding Russians, which was inaccurate (the median of eight consensual stereotype accuracy correlations was near zero).

Overall, then, the pattern of results regarding national character stereotype accuracy is both mixed and limited. We are aware of no studies that have even examined personal stereotype accuracy (either correlational or discrepancies). Nearly all of the remaining work has focused exclusively on correlational accuracy and has found a decidedly mixed pattern. When using the NEO-PI-R (Big Five) to assess traits, which is a self-report measure, albeit a highly validated one, there is much evidence of

inaccuracy (both across traits and across groups), interspersed with some evidence of moderate accuracy. There is only the one study using behavioral criteria (Heine et al., 2008) and it only examined conscientiousness, but it found a high level of consensual stereotype correlational accuracy. What explains these differences in patterns of (in)accuracy is not clear. As such, it would seem to be fertile ground for empirical research that could provide deeper insights into personality, personality measurement, social perception, and stereotypes. We propose some speculative hypotheses about these issues at the end of this chapter.

A Mixed Pattern for American Regional Stereotypes

Rogers and Wood (2010) examined the accuracy of undergraduates' American regional stereotypes of personality (the Big Five). The country was divided into 18 clusters of states, plus Alaska and Hawaii (separately). Results were compared against an Internet sample of over 600,000 people from across the United States who had completed a Big Five Personality inventory.

Although the perceiver sample was small (84), the study is unique in several ways. In addition to being the only study of the accuracy of American regional stereotypes of which we are aware, it is one of few studies to assess consensual discrepancies, consensual accuracy correlations, and personal stereotype accuracy correlations (it did not assess the accuracy of personal discrepancies). There were 100 judgments (the Big Five traits by 20 clusters of states): 21 consensual stereotype discrepancies were accurate; 23 were near misses, and the remaining 56 were inaccurate.

For all regions, consensual stereotype accuracy was high for neuroticism (.59) and openness (.48), but near zero for extraversion, agreeableness, and conscientiousness. However, perceptions regarding Alaska and Hawaii were sufficiently inaccurate to be considered outliers. Without them, the correlation for openness shot up to 0.78; the previously near zero correlation for agreeableness became 0.56; the correlation for neuroticism was largely unchanged at 0.60; the near zero correlation for extraversion stayed near zero; and the previously near zero correlation for conscientiousness became -.55 (i.e., strongly in the wrong direction). Personal stereotype accuracy correlations were moderate for neuroticism and openness (r's = .31 and 0.25, respectively), but near zero for extraversion, agreeableness, and conscientiousness.

The small sample of perceivers means that all of these results should be interpreted as preliminary. Furthermore, although we wish we could tell some compelling narrative about the meaning of these results, there is no obvious explanation (at least to us) for the inconsistent pattern of accuracy. Additionally, because of the small sample, there probably is a great deal of uncertainty (wide confidence intervals) in the results and they probably should not be overinterpreted pending larger-scale assessments of US regional stereotype accuracy regarding personality.

The Accuracy of Age Stereotypes

We know of only one study of the accuracy of age stereotypes of personality. Chan et al. (2012) examined the accuracy of age stereotypes regarding personality in 26 countries among over 3,000 people. Criteria were again self-reports on NEO-PI-R (Big Five). Three patterns emerged. Consensual stereotype accuracy correlations ranged from 0.50 to 0.90. Discrepancy scores, however, showed that people consistently exaggerated real differences among adolescents (14- to 20-year-olds), adults (21–59), and the old (60+). For example, the perceived difference between adolescents and the old were $d = .90$, but the criteria differences were only $d = .54$. A similar pattern was found for extraversion, openness, and conscientiousness (there was a slight tendency to underestimate the real differences on agreeableness).

Last, Chan et al. (2012) assessed personal stereotype accuracy correlations, which averaged 0.34, indicating moderate accuracy. There was a great deal of consistency in these patterns across country, gender, and age of rater. Thus, these patterns may be universal.

Representative samples were available as criteria for some, but not all countries. Analyses showed that levels of accuracy did not vary much based on whether the criterion sample was representative or not. This is the only study we know of to empirically demonstrate that accuracy was essentially the same regardless of whether convenience or representative samples were the basis for criteria. Although representative samples remain the gold standard for criteria, these findings showing similar results regardless of sampling procedure increase the credibility of findings from research on the accuracy of stereotypes regarding personality that has relied exclusively on convenience samples.

The Accuracy of Stereotypes Regarding the Rich

A recent study examined the accuracy of perceptions of personality regarding the rich, who were operationally defined as people with a net worth in excess of one million Euros (the study was conducted in Germany; Leckelt, Richter, Schroder, Kufner, Grabka, & Back, 2019). The personality attributes were the Big Five plus narcissistic admiration and locus of control. They examined (in)accuracy at both consensual and individual levels using both discrepancies and correlations.

This study focused on perceptions of differences. As such, they also obtained personality information from a representative sample of Germans. Perceived differences were then compared to the real differences (as indicated on self-reports on the BFI-S, the short form of the Big Five Inventory). Consensual discrepancies exaggerated real differences on four of the attributes (neuroticism, agreeableness, narcissistic admiration, and locus of control with exaggeration effects $0.23 \leq d < 1.02$). Perceived differences between the very rich and the general population were no more than three-tenths of a scale point (on a scale running from one to seven) for neuroticism, extraversion, openness, and conscientiousness; it was half a scale point for agreeableness. The consensual correlation was quite high ($r = .83$). At the personal (individual perceiver) level, people perceived personality differences between the rich and general population quite accurately, the average correlation between the two was $r = .56$.

Gender

Some of the clearest evidence regarding the accuracy of gender stereotypes regarding personality appeared in a paper strikingly titled, "Gender Stereotypes of Personality: Universal and Accurate?" (Löckenhoff et al., 2014). In this study, over 3,000 participants in 26 countries indicated their perceptions of males and females on the NEO-PI-R (Big Five) personality traits. Women were stereotyped as more agreeable, conscientious, open to experience, and neurotic than men, and as lower than men on extraversion.

These stereotypes were then compared to self-reports on the NEO-PI-R obtained from separate samples in the same countries and to observer reports of sex differences based on prior research. Although these were convenience samples, they totaled over 20,000 people from 26 countries. For all five personality traits, consensual stereotype discrepancies were accurate, ranging from SD differences of 0.01 to 0.22, regardless of whether self-reports or observer reports were used as criteria. There was no tendency to exaggerate differences. Löckenhoff et al. (2014, Table 2) also examined the accuracy of consensual gender stereotype correlations, separately for beliefs about young, adult, or old males and females. In general, these stereotypes met our standards for being considered accurate, ranging from 0.36 to 0.70, with a median of 0.47.

The criterion samples were large, but not representative, so this study suffers from the mismatch limitation. Because mismatch means that the stereotyped target group could differ from convenience criterion samples, the most likely implication is that results reflect a lower bound on accuracy.

Three older studies reported in two papers also assessed gender stereotype accuracy regarding personality. Martin (1987) assessed the accuracy of gender stereotypes in two studies. The first used a version of the Bem Sex Role Inventory (BSRI, Bem, 1981) modified to assess college students' stereotypes about "North American adult males and females" on 30 trait descriptors. The original BSRI was a self-report measure using a 7-point scale; the modification involved asking the college students to identify the percentage of men and women who had each trait. Although not all items were about personality (e.g., "defends beliefs"), many were at least personality-like enough to include in this review (e.g., assertive, dominant, compassionate, affectionate, conscientious, etc.). Unfortunately, the criterion sample was possibly even less representative than a typical convenience sample. It was 94 male and 56 female adult visitors to a campus open house day (who were asked to rate themselves on the BSRI using a true/false format).

Martin (1987) presented the main results as *diagnostic ratios* (DRs, proportion of males/proportion of females, computed separately for the stereotype judgments and criterion self-reports). These tended to exaggerate real differences. For example, 54% of men and 34% of women self-described as dominant, producing a DR of 1.59 for the difference. However, the DR for the perceived difference was 1.98, indicating that people believed there was a greater sex difference in dominance than was reflected in the self-descriptions.

However, DRs have some computational quirks. For example, let's say a perceiver believes 5% of men and 1% of women are assertive, whereas the self-reports are, respectively, 20% and 16%. The perceived difference (4%) exactly equals the real difference. However, the DR will make it appear as if the perceiver exaggerates the real difference, because his DR is 5, whereas the DR for the criterion differences is merely 1.25. One way to view this limitation is that DRs become easily inflated by an overall tendency for people to make low estimates (which is

what Martin, 1987 found), thereby leading to inflated estimates of exaggeration.

However, in the first study, Martin (1987) also presented the raw mean percentage estimates of men and women with each trait. When using these raw percentage estimates (Table 3, p. 493), perceptions of male/female differences were largely accurate using our standards of +/-10%. Specifically, perceptions of differences were accurate 24 times, there were 4 near misses, and 2 judgments were inaccurate. The accuracy could have occurred because: (1) male/female tendencies to self-inflate were comparable; (2) subtracting male minus female self-perceptions implicitly removes that bias; (3) what remains is largely valid; so that (4) perceptions of differences were not very discrepant from the implicitly self-inflation-adjusted real differences. Nonetheless, in absolute terms, 22 judgments were overestimates of differences and 8 were underestimates, indicating that exaggeration occurred more often than underestimation.

Although Martin (1987) did not report consensual stereotype accuracy correlations, they are computable from her data reported in Table 3. Consensual stereotype accuracy correlations were completely inaccurate for male targets ($r = -.10$), but quite accurate for female targets ($r = .72$) and for male/female differences ($r = .80$). Personal stereotype accuracy correlations were not reported.

Study 2 altered the procedure in two major ways. First, self-reports and stereotypes were assessed with a new composite measure, including 32 items from the Extended Personal Attributes Questionnaire (EPAQ; Spence, Helmreich, & Holahan, 1979), and eight from the BSRI. Second, instead of asking about "North American males and females," the stereotype measure asked about the "male and female students at this university" (University of British Columbia). Participants were merely described as 106 female and 33 male undergraduate volunteers. Thus, this is another convenience sample and suffers from a stereotype/criterion sample mismatch problem. Further, the male sample is small.

Martin (1987) did not report the raw percentage values for either the self-reports or stereotype judgments in the second study. The only results reported for the 40 judgments were DRs. Those showed mostly exaggeration of sex differences. However, to assess consensual correlational accuracy, it is easy enough to correlate the 40 DRs on the self-report criteria with the 40 stereotype judgments. That correlation is $r = .53$, indicating considerable accuracy in perceiving gender differences.

Allen (1995) performed a replication and extension of Martin's (1987) second study. One hundred introductory psychology students provided both stereotypes and self-reports on the same 40 items used by Martin (1987, Study 2). Unfortunately, Allen's (1995) method section did not explicitly articulate whom participants were being asked about. However, in Martin's (1987) second study, they were asked about "students at this university." If, as a replication, Allen (1995) did the same, this study suffers from the stereotype/criterion mismatch.

Allen's (1995) main results were reported as DRs. Unfortunately, the raw percentage estimates were not reported. For both stereotype judgments and self-reports, the DRs ranged from 0.16 to 4.22, with one exception: the DR for *unprincipled* was almost 10. This was a bizarre outlier; nearly 10 times as many men as women described themselves as unprincipled. Because this outlier was so extreme, we excluded it from our subsequent summary, which is based on the other 39 attributes. Because Allen (1995) reported DRs rather than raw percentages, we cannot apply any of our standards for evaluating how accurate people were (even using his mismatched criterion sample). As with Martin (1987, both studies), the DR measure indicated exaggeration. Although Allen (1995) did not compute consensual accuracy correlations, they are readily computable from his Table II. That correlation was 0.61 (after excluding the outlier), indicating high accuracy.

Stereotypes of Ballet Versus Modern Dancers

One of the most unique studies of stereotype accuracy was conducted by Clabaugh and Morling (2004), which investigated the accuracy of stereotypes regarding modern dancers and ballet dancers. This study asked perceivers to rate modern dancers and ballet dancers in general, but then used the self-reports of the haphazard samples of dancers (recruited from what they described as seven preprofessional dance camps in Pennsylvania and New York City) in their study as criteria. The study examined stereotypes held by modern ($N = 48$) and ballet ($N = 41$) dancers attending a professional dance camp and by a sample of introductory psychology students ($N = 34$) regarding modern and ballet dancers.

Not all judgments were about personality, but enough were that we have included it in our review. Specifically, they assessed people's beliefs about the self-esteem, body image, physical condition, fear of negative evaluation, need for structure, and need for control regarding the different dancers, and used the dancers' self-reports on these same items as criterion. Unfortunately, the questionnaire assessed beliefs about modern and ballet dancers in general, rather than about those attending the camp, thereby creating mismatch between the stereotype assessed and the criteria.

Clabaugh and Morling (2004) reported the mean differences between groups in self-reports, and the mean perceived differences between the groups. Discrepancy scores showed high accuracy and some systematic error. At the consensual stereotype (aggregate) level, 11 of 18 perceived differences (six traits by three groups of perceivers) were accurate, six were near misses, and one was inaccurate. Of the seven inaccuracies (including the six near misses, four exaggerated the real difference, one underestimated the real difference, and there were two reversals (both groups of dancers believed that modern dancers had higher "body esteem" although ballet dancers reported higher body esteem). They did not report personal discrepancy scores.

Although Clabaugh and Morling (2004) did not report the correlation of perceived with criterion differences, it could be computed from their data. These consensual beliefs about group differences corresponded well with differences in the dancers' self-reports. Consensual stereotypes correlated with the self-reports 0.83, 0.90, and 0.79 for perceivers who were, respectively, ballet dancers, modern dancers, or introductory psychology students.

They also assessed the extent to which personal stereotypes corresponded with the dancers' self-reports. One set of analyses assessed how sensitive people were to different levels of each characteristic within each group (e.g., how sensitive are people to differences in the body image, self-esteem, etc., of ballet dancers). For each perceiver, Clabaugh and Morling (2004) computed the correlation between their perceived level of each characteristic with the self-reported mean level. Among individual psychology students, these correlations indicated only modest sensitivity to variations in the traits of ballet dancers (average correlation between beliefs and criteria was 0.23). Among all other combinations of perceiver group (ballet, modern, intro psych student) and target group (ballet and modern), these correlations were substantial (the average correlations ranging from 0.48 to 0.63). This result is consistent with the *stereotypes as knowledge* hypothesis (Jussim et al., 2016, 2018), because people likely to have far more familiarity with dancers (other dancers) were more accurate than were those less likely to be familiar with dancers (introductory psychology students).

They also assessed people's sensitivity to differences between ballet and modern dancers (how well do perceived differences correspond to the self-reported differences?). Again, these were personal stereotypes, because they computed these correlations for each perceiver. These average correlations were strikingly·high: 0.67 for ballet perceivers, 0.71 for modern dance perceivers, and 0.62 for the introductory psychology students.

Summary of the Literature

Given how long social scientists have been studying stereotypes and, especially, making claims about their inaccuracy (Lippmann, 1991[1922]), there has been a surprising paucity of empirical research on stereotype accuracy until fairly recently (see reviews by Jussim, 2012; Jussim et al., 2018), and only a fraction of that literature has assessed the accuracy of stereotypes regarding personality.

Even when there is a substantial literature, as is the case with national character stereotypes, it has so many limitations and/or contradictory findings that it is not possible at this time to tell a simple compelling narrative about the data. National character stereotypes, when measured by Big Five and related instruments, have usually been found to be highly inaccurate, though there is some evidence of moderate accuracy in some studies. Moreover, the one study that used behavioral rather than self-report measures as criteria (Heine et al., 2008) found high consensual correlational accuracy for conscientiousness but did not assess any other trait or type of accuracy. Because there is ample evidence for the validity of the NEO-PI-R (McCrae & Terracciano, 2005), our view is that a breezy dismissal of the difference cannot be easily attributed to "it's just self-report." It is self-report, but when self-report scales have been highly validated, breezy dismissals are not justified. American regional stereotypes are probably conceptually similar to national character, and also showed evidence of moderate accuracy, though these have been the subject of only a single, small-scale study (Rogers & Wood, 2010). On the other hand, there were considerably higher levels of accuracy in stereotypes of personality regarding age, gender, and wealthy people.

To their credit, most of the national character studies have had very large samples and have examined stereotype accuracy cross-culturally. On the other hand, most used convenience criterion samples, which risks underestimating accuracy because of mismatch between stereotype and criterion, although the

one study (Chan et al., 2012) that included both haphazard and representative samples had similar patterns of accuracy. Furthermore, far more work has examined consensual than personal stereotypes.

Although the *exaggeration* hypothesis has long and venerable roots in social psychology (e.g., Allport, 1954; Campbell, 1967), the general stereotype accuracy literature provides little systematic support for it, except in the case of political stereotypes (Jussim et al., 2016). The research on stereotypes about personality provides weak and inconsistent support for exaggeration. One national character study found exaggeration (Terracciano et al., 2005; others did not assess it); the one study of age stereotypes of personality also found exaggeration (Chan et al., 2012). Studies of gender stereotypes of personality (with larger and more diverse samples, and better match of stereotype to criteria) have tended not to find exaggeration (Löckenhoff et al., 2014; Swim, 1994), though an early study using mismatched samples did find exaggeration (Martin, 1987). There was also a modest tendency toward exaggeration in the study of stereotypes of ballet versus modern dancers (Clabaugh & Morling, 2004).

Some Speculative Hypotheses

In this section, we offer three speculative hypotheses regarding stereotypes about personality that are inspired by the existing pattern of findings. We say "inspired by" rather than "empirically demonstrated" because, though there are data consistent with these hypotheses, our view is that the state of the data is currently too thin and uncertain to declare these hypotheses confirmed. As such, testing these hypotheses in future studies would be valuable. We refer to these as "wisdom of crowds," "stereotypes as knowledge," and the "more accuracy for stereotypes of differences" hypotheses, and discuss each next.

WISDOM OF CROWDS

When both consensual and personal stereotypes are assessed, both in the literature reviewed here and in the general stereotype accuracy literature, consensual stereotype accuracy is usually higher. This is almost certainly a wisdom of crowds effect, whereby combining independent judgments or predictions is well-established at producing higher accuracy than nearly all of the individual judgments (e.g., Surowiecki, 2004; see Jussim, 2012, for an extended application to stereotype accuracy). Evidence of accuracy strongly suggests that a major source of at least some stereotypes is *social reality*—people's beliefs about groups are often strongly linked to what those groups are actually like. The simplest explanation for this is that sometimes people learn quite a lot about what many groups are like.

STEREOTYPES AS KNOWLEDGE HYPOTHESIS

Wisdom of crowds effects are also consistent with a *stereotypes as knowledge* hypothesis. Wisdom of crowds effects can only occur if there is some element of validity in most people's judgments. If stereotypes are (at least in part) a form of everyday knowledge, then more informed people should hold more accurate stereotypes. Consistent with this, stereotypes held by multicultural migrants (ethnic Finns who had lived in Russia but who had migrated back to Finland; Russian emigrants to Finland) were considerably more accurate than many other national stereotypes (Lönnqvist et al., 2012). This increased accuracy might have occurred because the migrants had more direct experience with—and therefore, increased knowledge of—both cultures. Outside of personality, other research has found increased racial stereotype accuracy among the highly educated (Kaplowitz et al., 2003) and among those encouraged to recognize, as opposed to ignore, group differences (Wolsko et al., 2000).

The flip side of *stereotypes as knowledge* is that, absent knowledge, stereotypes are likely to be inaccurate. This may explain the pervasive inaccuracy of national character stereotypes of personality (as measured by the Big Five), inasmuch as most people have little direct contact with many individuals from lots of other nations. In contrast, most people do have extensive experience with men and women, and with the young and old—which may help explain the accuracy found by so many studies of gender stereotypes (Hall & Carter, 1999; Löckenhoff et al., 2014; McCauley et al., 1988), and age stereotypes (Chan et al., 2012).

MORE ACCURACY FOR STEREOTYPES OF DIFFERENCES

Most evidence for inaccuracy comes from the work on national character stereotypes, and much (though not all) of that is derived from work on autostereotypes when compared against self-report criteria such as the NEO-PI-R/Big Five. The reference group effect and lack of knowledge about people in distant cultures may therefore at least partially account for low levels of accuracy in such autostereotypes. In contrast, heterostereotypes (those of other groups) of personality, especially perceptions of *differences*, often moderately to strongly correlated with real differences (age: Chan et al., 2012; the rich: Leckelt et al., 2019; gender: Allen, 1995, Löckenhoff et al., 2014, Martin, 1987; ballet dancers: Clabaugh & Morling, 2004). It is distinctly possible that people are better at detecting *differences between groups* than they are at detecting the *absolute levels of traits* within groups. We know of no obvious theoretical basis for predicting this pattern. Thus, it would be useful for future research to develop or identify relevant theories making alternative predictions, and then tested as an a priori (and preferably preregistered) hypothesis.

Conclusion

Our review indicates that stereotypes of personality are a mixed bag. Most, but not all, of the evidence regarding national character stereotypes shows low accuracy. Much, but not all, of the rest of the evidence regarding gender, age, and other stereotypes, shows high correlational accuracy and more mixed results regarding discrepancies. Although these mixed results provide no basis for supporting the blanket emphasis on inaccuracy and exaggeration that once was common in the stereotype literature (see Jussim, 2012, for a review), they do provide a strong justification for the need for additional research. Stereotype (in)accuracy goes to the heart of several long-standing major issues in psychology: the (ir)rationality of judgment; the extent to which social beliefs and attitudes create versus reflect social realities; and the role of cognition in discrimination. Research on stereotype accuracy regarding personality has already contributed to these areas by its very mixed nature, thereby providing no easy support for absolutist views of social judgment either as fundamentally flawed or as fundamentally sound. For decades, the error and bias paradigm was dominant in social cognition (e.g., Fiske & Taylor, 1991; Ross, Lepper, & Ward, 2010). Testaments to the power of error and bias are legion (see Gigerenzer, 2018; Jussim, 2012, for reviews). Nonetheless, there has been a slow-moving revolution in both cognitive (Gigerenzer, 2018) and social psychology (Jussim, 2012), the latter driven in part by research repeatedly showing some, and sometimes a great deal, of accuracy in stereotypes (the present review; see also reviews by Hall & Goh, 2017; Jussim et al., 2016; Jussim et al., 2015). Some of the strongest evidence for accuracy occurred for demographic stereotypes, such as age and sex (and, outside of personality, also for race and ethnicity, see Jussim et al., 2016). This strongly suggests that, despite whatever truth there is to the claim that stereotypes are cognitive sources of prejudice and discrimination (Fiske & Neuberg, 1990), a simplistic storyline of bad and irrational stereotypes producing nothing but bias is no longer justified. It remains possible, that, in the fullness of time, as the results of many more studies of stereotype accuracy of personality and other attributes come in, they will more clearly support one view or the other. For now, however, such strong conclusions would be premature.

References

Allen, B. P. (1995). Gender stereotypes are not accurate: A replication of Martin (1987) using diagnostic vs. self-report and behavioral criteria. *Sex Roles, 32*, 583–600. http://dx.doi.org/10.1007/BF01544213

Allik, J., Alyamkina, E., & Meshcheryakov, B. (2015). The personality stereotypes of three cohabiting ethnic groups: Erzians, Mokshans, and Russians. *Cross-Cultural Research, 49*(2), 111–134. https://doi.org/10.1177/1069397114540861

Allport, G. W. (1954/1979). *The nature of prejudice.* Reading, MA: Addison-Wesley.

Ashmore, R. D., & Del Boca, F. K. (1981). Conceptual approaches to stereotypes and stereotyping. In D. L. Hamilton (Ed.), *Cognitive processes in stereotyping and intergroup behavior* (pp. 1–35). Hillsdale, NJ: Erlbaum.

Bem, S. L. (1981). *The Bem Sex-Role Inventory: A professional manual.* Palo Alto, CA: Consulting Psychologists Press.

Campbell, D. T. (1967). Stereotypes and the perception of group differences. *American Psychologist, 22*, 817–829. http://dx.doi.org/10.1037/h0025079

Chan, W., McCrae, R. R., De Fruyt, F., Jussim, L., Löckenhoff, C., De Bolle, M., & Terracciano, A. (2012). Stereotypes of age differences in personality traits: Universal and accurate? *Journal of Personality and Social Psychology, 103*, 1050–1066. https://doi.org/10.1037/a0029712

Clabaugh, A., & Morling, B. (2004). Stereotype accuracy of ballet and modern dancers. *Journal of Social Psychology, 144*, 31–48. https://doi.org/10.3200/SOCP.144.1.31-48

Cohen, J. (1988). *Statistical power analysis for the behavioral sciences.* New York, NY: Academic Press.

Costa, P. T., Jr., & McCrae, R. R. (2008). The revised NEO Personality Inventory (NEO-PI-R). In G. J. Boyle, G. Matthews, & D. H. Salclofske (Eds.), *The Sage handbook of personality theory, and assessment: Personality measurement and testing* (Vol. 2, pp. 179–198). London: Sage Publications. http://dx.doi.org/10.4135/9781849200479.n9

Costa, P. T., Jr., Terracciano, A., & McCrae, R. R. (2001). Gender differences in personality traits across cultures: Robust and surprising findings. *Journal of Personality and Social Psychology, 81*, 322–331. http://dx.doi.org/10.1037/0022-3514.81.2.322

Ellemers, N. (2018). Gender stereotypes. *Annual Review of Psychology, 69*(1), 275–298. https://doi.org/10.1146/annurev-psych-122216-011719

Fiske, S. T., & Neuberg, S. L. (1990). A continuum of impression formation, from category-based to individuating processes: Influences of information and motivation on attention and interpretation. In M. P. Zanna (Ed.), *Advances in experimental social psychology*, (Vol. 23, pp. 1–74). New York: Academic Press.

Fiske, S. T., & Taylor, S. E. (1991). *Social cognition* (second edition). New York: McGraw-Hill.

Gigerenzer, G. (2018). The bias bias in behavioral economics. *Review of Behavioral Economics, 5*, 303–336. http://dx.doi.org/10.1561/105.00000092

Hall, J. A., & Carter, J. D. (1999). Gender-stereotype accuracy as an individual difference. *Journal of Personality and Social Psychology, 77*, 350–359. http://dx.doi.org/10.1037/0022-3514.77.2.350

Hall, J. A., & Goh, J. X. (2017). Studying stereotype accuracy from an integrative social-personality perspective. *Social and Personality Psychology Compass, 11*(11), e12357. https://doi.org/10.1111/spc3.12357

Heine, S. J., Buchtel, E. E., & Norenzayan, A. (2008). What do cross-nation comparisons of personality traits tell us? The case of conscientiousness. *Psychological Science, 19*, 309–313. https://doi.org/10.1111/j.1467-9280.2008.02085.x

Hrebickova, M., & Graf, S. (2014). Accuracy of national character stereotypes in central Europe: Outgroups are not better than ingroup in considering personality traits of real people. *European Journal of Personality, 28*, 60–72. https://doi.org/10.1002/per.1904

Hyde, J. S. (2014). Gender similarities and differences. *Annual Review of Psychology, 65*, 373–398. https://doi.org/10.1146/annurev-psych-010213-115057

Judd, C. M., & Park, B. (1993). Definition and assessment of accuracy in social stereotypes. *Psychological Review, 100*, 109–128. http://dx.doi.org/10.1037/0033-295X.100.1.109

Jussim, L. (2012). *Social perception and social reality: Why accuracy dominates bias and self-fulfilling prophecy.* New York, NY: Oxford University Press.

Jussim, L., Cain, T., Crawford, J., Harber, K., & Cohen, F. (2009). The unbearable accuracy of stereotypes. In T. Nelson (Ed.), *Handbook of prejudice, stereotyping, and discrimination* (pp. 199–227). Hillsdale, NJ: Erlbaum.

Jussim, L., Crawford, J. T., Anglin, S. M., Chambers, J. R., Stevens, S. T., & Cohen, F. (2016). Stereotype accuracy: One of the largest and most replicable effects in all of social psychology. In T. Nelson (Ed.), *Handbook of prejudice, stereotyping, and discrimination*, (2nd ed., pp. 31–63). New York, NY: Psychology Press.

Jussim, L., Crawford, J. T., & Rubinstein, R. S. (2015). Stereotype (in)accuracy in perceptions of groups and individuals. *Current Directions in Psychological Science, 24*, 490–497. https://doi.org/10.1177/0963721415605257

Jussim, L., Stevens, S. T., & Honeycutt, N. (2018). Unasked questions about stereotype accuracy. *Archives of Scientific Psychology, 6*, 214–229. http://dx.doi.org/10.1037/arc0000055

Kaplowitz, S. A., Fisher, B. J., & Broman, C. I. (2003). How accurate are perceptions of social statistics about blacks and whites? *Public Opinion Quarterly, 67*, 237–243. https://doi.org/10.1086/374400

Leckelt, M., Richter, D., Schroder, C., Kufner, A. C. P., Grabka, M. M., & Back, M. D. (2019). The rich are different: Unraveling the perceived and self-reported personality profiles of high net-worth individuals. *British Journal of Psychology, 110*(4), 669–689. https://doi.org/10.1111/bjop.12360

Lee, Y. T., Jussim, L., & McCauley, C. R. (Eds.). (1995). *Stereotype accuracy: Toward appreciating group differences.* Washington, DC: American Psychological Association.

Lippmann, W. (1991). *Public opinion.* Piscataway, NJ: Transaction Publishers. First published 1922.

Löckenhoff, C. E., Chan, W., McCrae, R. R., De Fruyt, F., Jussim, L., De Bolle, M.,...Terracciano, A. (2014). Gender stereotypes of personality: Universal and accurate? *Journal of Cross-Cultural Psychology,* *45,* 675–694. https://doi.org/10.1177/0022022113520075

Lönnqvist, J.-E, Yijälä, A., Jasinskaja-Lahti, I., & Verkasalo, M, (2012). Accuracy and contrast in national value stereotypes—A case study using Ingrian-Finns as bi-cultural experts. *International Journal of Intercultural Relations, 36,* 271–278. https://doi.org/10.1016/j.ijintrel.2011.08.002

Mackie, M. (1973). Arriving at "truth" by definition: The case of stereotype inaccuracy. *Social Problems, 20,* 431–447. https://doi.org/10.2307/799706

Martin, C. L. (1987). A ratio measure of sex stereotyping. *Journal of Personality and Social Psychology, 52,* 489–499. http://dx.doi.org/10.1037/0022-3514.52.3.489

McCauley, C. R. (1995). Are stereotypes exaggerated? A sampling of racial, gender, academic, occupational, and political stereotypes. In Y. T. Lee, L. Jussim, & C. R. McCauley (Eds.), *Stereotype accuracy: Toward appreciating group differences* (pp. 215–243). Washington, DC: American Psychological Association. http://dx.doi.org/10.1037/10495-009

McCauley, C., & Stitt, C. L. (1978). An individual and quantitative measure of stereotypes. *Journal of Personality and Social Psychology, 36*(9), 929–940. https://doi.org/10.1037/0022-3514.36.9.929

McCauley, C., Thangavelu, K., & Rozin, P. (1988). Sex stereotyping of occupations in relation to television representations and census facts. *Basic and Applied Social Psychology, 9,* 197–212. https://doi.org/10.1207/s15324834basp0903_3

McCrae, R. R., & Allik, J. (Eds.). (2002). *The five-factor model of personality across cultures.* New York, NY: Kluwer Academic/Plenum Publishers. https://doi.org/10.1007/978-1-4615-0763-5_2

McCrae, R. R., Chan, W., Jussim, L., De Fruyt, F., Löckenhoff, C. E., De Bolle, M., & Avdeyeva, T. V. (2013). The inaccuracy of national character stereotypes. *Journal of Research in Personality, 47,* 831–842. https://doi.org/10.1016/j.jrp.2013.08.006

McCrae, R. R., & Terracciano, A. (2005). Universal features of personality traits from the observer's perspective: Data from 50 cultures. *Journal of Personality and Social Psychology, 88,* 547–561. https://doi.org/10.1037/0022-3514.88.3.547

Realo, A., Allik, J., Lonnqvist, J., Verkasalo, M., Kwiatkowska, A., Koots, L., & Renge, V. (2009). Mechanisms of the national character stereotype: How people in six neighboring countries of Russia describe themselves and the typical Russian. *European Journal of Personality, 23,* 229–249. http://dx.doi.org/10.1002/per.719

Richard, F. D., Bond, C. F., Jr., & Stokes-Zoota, J. J. (2003). One hundred years of social psychology quantitatively described. *Review of General Psychology, 7,* 331–363. http://dx.doi.org/10.1037/1089-2680.7.4.331

Rogers, K. H., & Wood, D. (2010). Accuracy of United States regional personality stereotypes. *Journal of Research in Personality, 44,* 704–713. https://doi.org/10.1016/j.jrp.2010.09.006

Rosenthal, R. (1991). Effect sizes: Pearson's correlation, its display via the BESD, and alternative indices. *American Psychologist, 46,* 1086–1087. http://dx.doi.org/10.1037/0003-066X.46.10.1086

Ross, L. D., Lepper, M., & Ward, A. (2010) History of social psychology: Insights, challenges, and contributions to theory and application. In S. T. Fiske, D. T. Gilbert, & G. Lindzey (Eds.), *Handbook of social psychology* (5th ed., Vol. 1, pp. 3–50). Hoboken, NJ: Wiley. https://doi.org/10.1002/9780470561119.socpsy001001

Ryan, C. S. (2002) Stereotype accuracy. *European Review of Social Psychology, 13,* 75–109. https://doi.org/10.1080/10463280240000037

Spence, J. X., Helmreich, R. L., & Holahan, C. K. (1979). Negative and positive components of psychological masculinity and femininity and their relationships to self-reports of neurotic and acting out behaviors. *Journal of Personality and Social Psychology, 37,* 1673–1682. http://dx.doi.org/10.1037/0022-3514.37.10.1673

Surowiecki, J. (2004). *The wisdom of crowds: Why the many are smarter than the few and how collective wisdom shapes business, economies, societies, and nations.* New York, NY: Doubleday.

Swim, J. K. (1994). Perceived versus meta-analytic effect sizes: An assessment of the accuracy of gender stereotypes. *Journal of Personality and Social Psychology, 66,* 21–36. http://dx.doi.org/10.1037/0022-3514.66.1.21

Terracciano, A., Abdel-Khalek, A. M., Adam, N., Adamova, L., Ahn, C., Ahn, H. N., & Meshcheriakov, B. (2005). National character does not reflect mean personality trait levels in 49 cultures. *Science, 310,* 96–100. https://dx.doi.org/10.1126%2Fscience.1117199

Wolsko, C., Park, B., Judd, C. M., & Wittenbrink, B. (2000). Framing interethnic ideology: Effects of multicultural and color-blind perspectives on judgments of groups and individuals. *Journal of Personality and Social Psychology, 78,* 635–654. http://dx.doi.org/10.1037/0022-3514.78.4.635

Implications and Applications of Trait Accuracy Research

Accuracy and Bias of Trait Judgments in Romantic Relationships

Shanhong Luo *and* David Watson

Abstract

This chapter provides a review of recent theoretical developments and empirical evidence regarding accuracy and biases of trait judgments in romantic relationships. Consistent with prior theorizing, personality judgments may be conceptualized to consist of *accurate perceptions*, *systematic biases*, and *random errors*. Two common biases in romantic relationships—*positivity bias* and *similarity bias*—are the focus of the chapter. The two major approaches to conceptualizing and assessing accuracy and biases—the *variable-centered approach* and the *person-centered approach*—are discussed. A review of the literature on partner personality judgments in both approaches suggests that individuals tend to perceive their partners with both substantial accuracy and a considerable amount of bias. Judges' personal characteristics, trait properties, and relationship factors may moderate the extent to which the judgments are accurate and biased. Finally, accuracy, positivity bias, and similarity bias all have important positive implications for romantic relationship functioning.

Key Words: accuracy, positivity bias, similarity bias, partner personality judgment, variable-centered approach, person-centered approach, relationship functioning

Classical theory and research on personality judgment tend to have two foci. First, they focus on the accuracy, validity, or consensus of personality judgment. Second, they primarily take an informational approach to studying the accuracy of personality judgment; that is, how perceivers gather and use information to form their judgments of a target's personality. By comparison, there is far less theorizing and empirical research on biases. For example, Funder's (1995, 2012) widely known Realistic Accuracy Model (RAM) proposes accurate personality judgment relies on four factors: good judge, good target, good traits, and good information. The RAM emphasizes opportunities to observe behavioral manifestations of a target's traits and how such information is used in personality judgment. Although briefly mentioned as a possible factor in partner judgments (e.g., in influencing whether or not someone is a good judge), judges' motivations—particularly those for developing systematic biases—are not extensively discussed.

The context of romantic relationships provides a unique setting to study personality judgment because both informational and motivational factors are most likely to play a critical role in shaping one's perceptions of one's partner. Compared to other personality judgment contexts ranging from zero-acquaintance to friendship, romantic relationships arguably are the setting wherein partners have the most opportunities to learn about each other's personality; they therefore would be expected to have the most abundant information to form accurate judgments, which allows for a solid information base for accuracy. Moreover, from the perspective of error management theory (Haselton & Buss, 2000), partners also have strong motivations to be accurate in their understanding of each other's personality because serious erroneous partner judgments may lead to poor relationship decision-making and can be highly consequential in a negative way.

At the same time, there are both significant motivational and cognitive factors that may cause partner judgments to be systematically biased. On one hand, individuals may be motivated to see their partners in an overly positive light (e.g., Fletcher, Simpson, & Thomas, 2000) or as overly similar to themselves (Murray, Holmes, Bellavia, Griffin, & Dolderman, 2002). On the other hand, biases may occur due to cognitive mechanisms. For example, assumed similarity has been suggested as a cognitive heuristic used in forming judgments when information is unavailable, for example, when judging strangers or assessing less visible traits (e.g., Watson, Hubbard, & Wiese, 2000). Kruger (1999) provided a cognitive account for a positivity bias in self-perceptions, arguing that individuals may hold a self-serving bias simply because of the anchoring heuristic—self-information is more accessible and thus overly represented in our self-judgments compared to information about others. Although it has not been empirically tested, it is possible that people's judgments about their partner's personality are also overly anchored in partner information simply due to its better accessibility.

Given these strong, somewhat unique cognitive and motivational factors involved in personality judgment in the context of romantic relationships, it is particularly important to examine both accuracy and biases in partner judgments. In this chapter we conduct a thorough analysis of individuals' judgments of their partner's personality and the implications of such judgments for romantic functioning. We first discuss different approaches to conceptualizing and assessing accuracy and biases in partner personality judgments. Second, we review the empirical evidence regarding the degree of accuracy and biases in partner trait judgments. Third, we discuss several moderators that influence the level of accuracy and biases of partner trait judgments. Finally, we review the role of accuracy and biases of trait judgments in romantic relationship functioning. Note that the term "trait judgment" is commonly used in personality research, whereas the same process is often referred to as "personality perception" in close relationship research. In this chapter these two terms are used interchangeably.

Conceptualization and Assessment of Accuracy and Biases in Personality Judgments in Romantic Relationships

Whereas there is only one type of accurate judgment, systematic biases can take different forms. In the romantic relationship context, the two most commonly discussed biases are *positivity bias*—holding overly positive perceptions of one's partner, and *similarity bias*—seeing the partner as more similar to the self than is actually the case (e.g., Luo & Snider, 2009). Positivity bias also has been referred to as "positive illusions" (Murray, Holmes, & Griffin, 1996a, 1996b), "enhancement bias" (Taylor & Brown, 1988), and "directional bias" (Fletcher & Kerr, 2010; West & Kenny, 2011). Positivity bias may further display different, albeit related, subtypes, including seeing one's partner in a socially desirable manner (Luo & Snider, 2009), projecting one's own ideal self-images onto one's perceptions of the partner (e.g., Klohnen & Luo, 2003), and projecting one's own ideal partner images into partner perceptions (e.g., Fletcher et al., 2000). It is one of the most pervasive biases in romantic relationships (e.g., Murray et al., 1996a, 1996b; Rusbult, Van Lange, Wildschut, Yovetich, & Verette, 2000). Similarity bias has been labeled "projection bias" (Ruvolo & Fabin, 1999; West & Kenny, 2011), "egocentrism" (Murray et al., 2002), "assumed similarity" (Thielmann, Hilbig, & Zettler, 2018; Watson et al., 2000), and the "self-based heuristic" (Ready, Clark, Watson, & Westerhouse, 2000).

To date, two major approaches have been used to study accuracy and bias. One is the *logical impossibility approach*. This approach nicely demonstrates the existence of biases through logical inferences (for reviews, see Kruger, 1999; Taylor & Brown, 1988); however, it bypasses the tricky task of defining accuracy and bias. The other is the *accuracy benchmark approach*. Researchers following this approach explicitly define accuracy and biases, which allows them to examine accurate perceptions and biases at both the individual and sample level (e.g., Murray et al., 1996a, 1996b).

The Logical Impossibility Approach

This approach is popular among social psychologists interested in social comparison processes. In a typical example of this approach, participants are asked to compare themselves relative to average others. Results show the majority of people rate desirable attributes as more descriptive of themselves than of average others. For example, 89 percent of respondents rated their ability to get along with others as better than average; 70 percent rated their leadership as better than average (College Board Survey cited by Kruger, 1999). This "better than average effect" generalizes from skills and abilities to positive traits such as rating oneself as interesting, organized, attractive, and so forth (see Brown, 1986;

Kruger, 1999). Because most personal attributes conform to a quasi-normal distribution, it is logically impossible for the large majority to be truly better than the average; that is, some people must be exaggerating. This self-serving tendency is considered to be a bias (see Taylor & Brown, 1988).

As the old saying "beauty is in the eye of the beholder" illustrates, the "better than average effect" not only is seen in self-perceptions but also extends to perceptions of one's close others, including romantic partners (e.g., Murray & Holmes, 1997), friends (e.g., Brown, 1986; Suls, Lemos, & Stewart, 2002), and family members (e.g., Endo, Heine, & Lehman, 2000). Among dating and married individuals, the majority of them believe their own partners are more virtuous than average or typical partners (e.g., Endo et al., 2000; Murray & Holmes, 1997) and are better than their friends' partners (e.g., Murray, Holmes, Dolderman, & Griffin, 2000).

Although the logical impossibility approach clearly shows that some people must be biased, it does not allow researchers to distinguish those who are truly better than average others from those whose perceptions are positively biased. Furthermore, it provides little insight as to how people construct such biases. In contrast, the *accuracy benchmark approach* clearly defines the "benchmark" for accurate judgments, thereby allowing researchers to examine the degree to which individuals' perceptions of their partners are accurate, how their perceptions systematically deviate from the benchmark, and which judges are more accurate.

The Accuracy Benchmark Approach

The first key task that researchers must undertake in this approach is to define an accuracy benchmark (or accuracy criterion), against which individuals' perceptions can be evaluated. The similarity between individuals' perceptions and the accuracy benchmark represents accuracy; any systematic differences between the two are considered to represent a bias, whereas nonsystematic differences are viewed as random errors. This approach is popular among psychologists who study self-perceptions and personality judgments of others. It is important to note that unlike object perceptions (e.g., shape, size), for which there are more objective criteria to judge whether or not the perceptions are accurate, there is no perfect "objective truth" or accuracy benchmark in person perceptions. Thus, any accuracy benchmark is only relative and more than one accuracy benchmark may be justifiable depending on particular research purposes.

Two frequently used benchmarks for evaluating the accuracy of partner personality judgment are: self-ratings provided by the partners themselves (e.g., Kenny & Acitelli, 2001; Klohnen & Mendelsohn, 1998; Luo & Snider, 2009; Murray et al., 1996a, 1996b; Watson et al., 2000), and ratings provided by an outside observer of the couple, for example, a common friend to both partners (e.g., John & Robins, 1994; Murray et al., 2000). Since far more research has used partners' self-ratings as the benchmark, this is the focus of our review.

Following the establishment of the accuracy benchmark, the second major task is to evaluate the degree to which one's judgments of partner personality are accurate or biased. Two major approaches have been used to conceptualize and assess accuracy and biases: the *variable-centered approach* (VCA) and the *person-centered approach* (PCA) (see Kenny, Kashy, & Cook, 2006; Luo & Klohnen, 2005).

VARIABLE-CENTERED APPROACH

The VCA concerns the agreement (or the lack thereof—discrepancy) between (1) the personality judgment about one's partner and (2) the accuracy benchmark on distinct individual traits (e.g., on extraversion). To quantify accuracy, researchers typically compute a correlation between judges' partner perceptions and partners' own self-ratings on a given trait using the entire sample. This correlation is the traditional self-other agreement correlation in personality research. Fletcher and Kerr (2010) referred to this sample-level VCA agreement correlation as "tracking accuracy."

To index similarity bias, researchers simply correlate judges' partner perceptions with the judges' own self-perceptions on a particular trait (e.g., extraversion), which is called "assumed similarity" (Thielmann et al., 2018; Watson et al., 2000) or "projection" (West & Kenny, 2011). Assumed similarity can sometimes be accurate if the judge and the target are truly similar to each other. To address this, the targets' self-ratings can be partialled out from this correlation. The resulting partial correlation is considered a more pure form of "similarity bias" because any accurate similarity perceptions would have been removed from this partial correlation (Luo & Snider, 2009).

To index positivity bias, researchers typically compute a difference score by subtracting the partners' self-ratings from the judges' partner perceptions on a given trait (e.g., extraversion). Fletcher and Kerr (2010) referred to this as "mean-level bias." Although technically a difference score can be either positive or negative, in the area of partner personality perceptions in romantic relationships, the difference scores computed this way tend to be consistently positive on desirable traits (e.g., extraversion) and negative on undesirable traits (e.g., neuroticism), both of which indicate a positivity bias—that is, seeing the partner in a more positive light than the partner sees him/herself. In fact, Fletcher and Kerr (2010) concluded that "almost all research findings and related theories are conceptualized in terms of positivity bias" (p. 630). Our review therefore follows this tradition. West and Kenny's (2011) truth-bias model outlined a creative regression approach that provides simultaneous estimates for VCA-based accuracy, positivity bias, and similarity bias (details provided in the next section).

PERSON-CENTERED APPROACH

The PCA, on the other hand, focuses on the congruence between the overall profiles of (1) each judge's partner personality judgments and (2) the accuracy benchmark across a number of related or unrelated characteristics (e.g., ratings across all five items in conscientiousness or across all 44 items of the Big Five Inventory). To indicate this profile congruence (i.e., perception accuracy), researchers compute a profile correlation[1] by correlating the judge's partner ratings and the target's self-ratings (i.e., the benchmark) across all items in a given personality inventory. This profile correlation is computed for every judge in the sample. In a hypothetical example of a married couple John and Mary, we compute an index of Mary's accuracy in her judgment of John's conscientiousness by correlating Mary's perceptions of John on the five items in conscientiousness (i.e., 3, 2, 4, 4, 2) with John's self-ratings on these five items (i.e., 4, 3, 5, 4, 2). In this hypothetical case, their profile correlation is 0.88, which indicates that the correspondence between Mary's perceptions and John's self-ratings is high; that is, Mary is quite accurate in her perceptions of the way John's conscientiousness is manifested in the five individual items. For instance, Mary agrees with John that he is more "efficient" and "thorough" than "neat" and "punctual." To evaluate the sample's overall accuracy, all judges' profile accuracy correlations are averaged across the entire sample. Note that even when a sample shows PCA accuracy in partner trait judgments, it may or may not display VCA accuracy. These two approaches capture different types of accuracy in judgments and are independent of each other.

The PCA also allows researchers to easily assess distinct types of systematic biases in addition to examining the accuracy of partner personality judgments. For example, Luo and Snider (2009) created a PCA-based index for positivity bias by correlating each judge's partner perceptions with a preestablished positivity prototype profile across all items for a personality inventory (e.g., Big Five Inventory) while controlling for the target's self-perceptions. Likewise, they constructed a similarity bias index by correlating each judge's partner perceptions with the judge's own self-perceptions while controlling for the target's self-perceptions. Similar to the accuracy index, the PCA positivity bias and similarity bias also are individual-based—each judge receives his or her bias "scores." To evaluate at the sample level, all judges' bias scores (i.e., the aforementioned partial correlations) are averaged across the entire sample.

Researchers often need to examine how partner judgment accuracy is associated with other variables, such as relationship outcomes or moderators of judgment accuracy. This becomes a major challenge in VCA because VCA produces one accuracy correlation and one similarity bias correlation per sample. Thus, to test how accuracy and similarity bias are associated with other variables in VCA, more complicated statistical approaches must be used such as interactions either in ANOVA or regression (see Griffin, Murray, & Gonzalez, 1999). For the VCA positivity bias, the difference score can be computed at the individual level; that is, each judge can have a difference score as an index of his or her positivity bias, which then can be used to correlate with other variables.

An advantage of PCA over VCA is that in PCA, because each judge receives profile correlation-based indices of accuracy, positivity bias, and similarity bias, it is very easy to associate these judgment properties with other variables either by correlations or regressions. Although the use of difference scores and profile correlations as an indicator of similarity or accuracy has been questioned, most researchers agree that both can be used when certain assumptions are met and careful measures are taken (for discussions surrounding the statistical issues of using difference scores, interactions, and profile similarity, see Edwards, 2001; Griffin et al., 1999; Kenny et al., 2006; Rogers, Wood, & Furr, 2018).

Because accuracy and biases are conceptualized and measured in distinctly different ways in VCA and PCA, it is important to note that the VCA-based accuracy and PCA-based accuracy may very well be independent of each other. Likewise, the biases derived from the two approaches can be quite distinct as well. We believe that VCA and PCA nicely complement each other and together they provide a more complete understanding of partner personality judgment. In the rest of the chapter, we review research from both approaches.

How Accurate and Biased Are Judgments of Partner Traits?

The meta-analysis by Fletcher and Kerr (2010) did an excellent job of evaluating the degree to which intimates are accurate in their judgments of each other's personality (as well as judgments of five nonpersonality domains), using studies conducted primarily from the VCA perspective. Their meta-analysis, however, did not examine similarity bias. Moreover, it did not cover accuracy and bias research from the PCA perspective. Our review provides a summary of the findings from Fletcher and Kerr's (2010) meta-analysis, an update of evidence since their publication, and additional coverage for similarity bias, as well as a review of PCA-based research.

VCA-Based Accuracy and Biases

For VCA accuracy (in the form of correlations or regressions), Fletcher and Kerr (2010) collected a total of 28 studies that reported such a correlation or regression in partner personality judgments. According to their analyses, the effect size for accuracy was 0.43, suggesting that on average the correlation between individuals' partner personality judgments and their partners' self-ratings was 0.43, which was quite substantial in size by Cohen's (1988) criteria. In another series of meta-analyses that evaluated the accuracy of observers' personality judgments, Connelly and Ones (2010) reported that spouses and dating partners showed the highest accuracy in judging their partner's traits, compared to other types of judges, including parents, friends, coworkers, and roommates.

In terms of VCA positivity bias based on difference scores, Fletcher and Kerr (2010) identified a total of 16 studies that reported such positivity bias in partner personality judgments. Their meta-analysis showed an effect size of 0.15 for mean-level bias, which indicates that in general, individuals' partner personality judgments were elevated from targets' self-ratings. However, the degree of this positivity bias was considered small according to Cohen's (1988) effect size criteria. In other words, people are only slightly positively biased in their judgments of partners' personality.

With regard to similarity bias, past research also has provided consistent evidence that people in dating and married relationships perceive their partner to resemble themselves on a variety of personality traits (e.g., Ready et al., 2000; Ruvolo & Fabin, 1999; Watson et al., 2000), whereas in reality there is little actual personality similarity in romantic couples (e.g., Botwin, Buss, & Shackelford, 1997; Luo, 2009; Watson et al., 2004).

Following West and Kenny's (2011) truth-bias model, Wood, Oldham, Reifman, and Niehuis (2017) took a regression approach to estimate accuracy, positivity bias, and similarity bias simultaneously in a sample of newlywed couples. They regressed partner personality judgments on perceivers' own self-ratings and the targets' self-ratings. The regression coefficient for the target's self-ratings was considered an indicator of accuracy, while the regression coefficient for the perceiver's self-ratings was considered an indicator of similarity bias. The intercept was considered an indicator of positivity bias. Their findings showed that spouses displayed highly consistent, substantial accuracy in their partner personality judgments. The two biases showed less consistency and strength, although wives showed greater biases than husbands. One important aspect of this study was that their sample consisted of 154 newlywed couples with a greater representation of Hispanic couples than usual (>50%). Currently it is unclear whether such perception patterns depend on ethnicity/race or culture.

PCA-Based Accuracy and Biases

By comparison, there is far less PCA partner judgment research. However, the amount of PCA research is on the rise in the early 21st century (e.g., Decuyper, De Bolle, & De Fruyt, 2012; Human, Sandstrom, Biesanz, & Dunn, 2012; Letzring & Noftle, 2010; Luo & Snider, 2009; Murray et al., 2002, 2011; Neff & Karney, 2005). Almost all PCA partner judgment studies examined accuracy, albeit their specific approach to constructing the PCA accuracy index has varied. Despite the differences in the way the accuracy index is constructed, the evidence for accuracy is strong and consistent: Although there is substantial variability in the degree of accuracy from person to person, overall, individuals' judgments of their partners' personality profiles are quite accurate; that is, these judgments strongly align with the targets' self-perceptions (Decuyper et al., 2012; Letzring & Noftle, 2010; Luo & Snider, 2009; Murray et al, 1996a, 1996b; Neff & Karney, 2005).

With regard to PCA evidence for positivity bias, Murray and colleagues conducted a series of studies on the role of positivity bias in the framework of enhancing partner perceptions according to the perceivers' ideal partner images (Murray et al., 1996a, 1996b, 2011). The researchers tended to use both VCA and PCA in order to test the robustness of the findings. The PCA findings have shown that intimates hold substantial positivity bias through the process of idealizing the partner, which echoes the VCA evidence for mean-level bias in the same study. Other researchers operationalized the PCA positivity bias in other formats. For instance, Luo and Snider (2009) defined positivity bias as the degree to which partner perceptions match a positivity prototype that was based on a separate group of judges' ratings of trait social desirability. Human et al. (2012) indexed positivity bias by the degree to which partner perceptions matched a normative profile, which was the average self-ratings from the entire sample and tended to be very positive. Regardless of the exact operationalization of positivity bias, these studies yielded consistent evidence that intimates hold positive illusions for each other (Luo & Snider, 2009; Murray et al., 1996a, 1996b, 2011).

Similarity bias is the least studied among the three PCA-based judgments. So far only three studies have examined PCA similarity bias. Although specific estimates vary, overall, there is evidence that individuals tend to project their own images in the judgments of their partner (Decuyper et al., 2012; Luo & Snider, 2009; Murray et al., 2002). This is true even after the effect of partners' self-ratings has been statistically removed from the partner judgments, indicating that assumed similarity tends to be exaggerated and, in fact, represents a systematic judgment bias.

Taken together, both VCA- and PCA-based research have provided converging evidence that partners judge each other's personality with substantial accuracy, while also showing evidence of systematic biases such as positivity bias and similarity bias. Furthermore, there is strong evidence indicating that being accurate appears to be independent from holding biases at several different levels. For example, Fletcher and Kerr (2010) concluded from their meta-analysis that mean-level positivity bias is conceptually and empirically independent from correlation-based accuracy. Neff and Karney (2005) found that newlywed couples tended to universally hold positive partner biases on global characteristics, while varying considerably in their perceptual accuracy of specific attributes. Luo and Snider (2009) further demonstrated that accuracy and

biases were both evident in the same set of perceptions of partner personality traits.

These findings are consistent with the fundamental shift in theoretical models of accuracy and bias in person perceptions from the simplified "either accurate or biased" fashion to a more integrative, dialectical approach. Specifically, accuracy and bias in partner perceptions no longer are conceptualized to be mutually exclusive; rather, it increasingly is recognized that they can coexist (e.g., Gagne & Lydon, 2004; Kenny & Acitelli, 2001; Luo & Snider, 2009; West & Kenny, 2011). In light of these developments, we agree with some prior models that posit partner perceptions are best conceptualized to consist of three distinct components: *accurate perceptions*, *systematic biases*, and *random errors* (e.g., Murray et al., 1996a; West & Kenny, 2011). According to this conceptualization, it is possible that when one of the three components changes, it does not necessarily translate into direct, one-to-one changes in the others. An important next task then is to identify the factors that influence accuracy and biases.

When Are Partners More Accurate or Biased?

One clear finding evident from both PCA and VCA research is that there are significant individual differences in the degree of accuracy and biases in partner personality judgments, which suggests the existence of important moderators that influence them. Given the unique context of romantic relationships, we consider the following key moderators in this review: personal characteristics of the judge (e.g., judge's gender, personality), trait properties (e.g., trait visibility), and relationship factors (e.g., relationship length). Due to a lack of published PCA-based research examining potential moderators of accuracy and biases, the following review is primarily based on VCA research.

Personal Characteristics of the Judge

Gender likely is the most studied personal characteristic in intimate relationships. Although women tend to be better lay psychologists than men when it comes to personality judgment (see Fletcher, 2002), Fletcher and Kerr's (2010) meta-analysis concluded that overall, gender failed to exert a significant moderating influence on either tracking accuracy or directional positivity bias; however, women did show significantly higher levels of absolute (i.e., nondirectional) bias than men. In contrast, Wood et al.'s (2017) regression-based results indicated a clear gender difference with women being more biased, particularly in similarity bias. The limited PCA research echoed this gender difference: Luo and Snider (2009) found that wives tended to be more accurate, but also showed greater positivity bias and similarity bias in their partner personality judgments. Taken together, women appear to be more biased than men, although this gender difference is likely to be small in magnitude.

In addition to gender, it is conceivable that individuals' levels of judgment accuracy and bias may be a function of the perceiver's personality characteristics (see chapter 6 by Colman in this handbook for more discussions of the "Good Judge"). For example, individuals with more positive self-views tend to be more generous in idealizing their partner perceptions (e.g., Murray et al., 1996a, 1996b), whereas lower perceiver self-esteem is associated with less positivity bias (Murray, Holmes, & Griffin, 2000) and reduced accuracy (Wood et al., 2017). However, Neff and Karney (2005) reported that personality variables (measured by the Eysenck Personality Questionnaire) and depression did not moderate PCA-based accuracy in either of their two newlywed samples.

It is important to note that research in this area to date has focused on perceiver personality characteristics of direct impact on relationships, such as self-esteem and depression. Personal characteristics that are not central to relationship functioning also may play a role in moderating accuracy and biases. For example, individuals higher on need for cognition (Cacioppo & Petty, 1982) or need for closure (Webster & Kruglanski, 1994) are expected to pursue higher accuracy in their perceptions (see Gagne & Lydon, 2004) simply for cognitive reasons. However, this hypothesis has not been empirically tested.

Trait Properties
Fletcher and colleagues suggested that traits vary in their relevance to romantic relationships and trait relevance should moderate the extent to which people are accurate and biased in judging their partners (Fletcher & Kerr, 2010; Fletcher, Simpson, & Boyes, 2006). Two studies have shown that both mean-level positivity bias and tracking accuracy were higher on dimensions more critical to relationships, such as warmth, attractiveness, and status; in contrast, both positivity bias and tracking accuracy were reduced on traits that were less central to mate selection or the success of romantic relationships, such as sensation-seeking and artistic ability (Boyes & Fletcher, 2007; Gill & Swann, 2004). These findings

have been interpreted from a motivational perspective: for relationship-relevant traits, intimates may be motivated to strive for greater accuracy to ensure a solid understanding of each other; at the same time, they may be motivated to pursue stronger positivity bias to make their feelings of love seem worthy.

From the cognitive perspective, it has been argued that trait "visibility" is likely to be another moderator of accuracy and bias (see also Funder, 1995, and chapter 8 by Krzyaniak & Letzring in this handbook). Specifically, more readily observable traits (e.g., extraversion) should display greater judgment accuracy, whereas more nuanced internal traits (e.g., neuroticism) may be prone to biases and errors (e.g., Connelly & Ones, 2010; Funder, 1995). In support of that, Watson et al. (2000) found that on less visible traits, accuracy was lower whereas assumed similarity was higher, suggesting that projecting one's self-images onto one's partner judgments likely is a cognitive heuristic used to make up the gap when information is insufficient. Connelly and Ones's (2010) meta-analyses provided further evidence showing that the accuracy of spouse ratings was highest on extraversion and lowest on neuroticism and openness to experience. In a recent article, Thielmann et al. (2018) identified an additional trait property that plays a role in the assumed similarity effect—namely, trait relevance to the judge's personal values; specifically, the more important a trait is to the judge's own values (e.g., honesty/humility, openness), the more assumed similarity is observed.

In addition to trait visibility, trait evaluativeness may also have significant implications for judgment accuracy (Funder, 1995). Trait evaluativeness refers to the extent to which possessing a specific characteristic is associated with being socially valuable or desirable. Among the Big Five traits, agreeableness is considered the most evaluative trait whereas extraversion is least evaluative in North American cultures (John & Robins, 1993). The meta-analyses by Connelly and Ones (2010) indicated that partner judgments of highly evaluative traits such as agreeableness tend to be less accurate in comparison to less evaluative traits; more importantly, this reduced accuracy is more likely to be due to greater idiosyncrasies in the judges' perceptions of their partner's trait rather than to the targets' self-presentation efforts.

Taking a slightly different perspective, Neff and Karney (2005) suggested that whether a judgment occurs at a global or specific level may also moderate the degree of accuracy and bias in partner judgments. Further, they argued that intimates' love may be conceptualized as "a hierarchically organized collection of beliefs, feelings, and perceptions of the partner" (p. 481). There are both motivational and cognitive reasons that romantic partners, particularly newlyweds, would show universal "global adoration" at the most general, abstract level but would vary in "specific accuracy" at the more concrete perceptions of individual attributes. The results from two newlywed couple samples provided replicable evidence that while most newlyweds held positivity biases for their partners in terms of global evaluations (e.g., "I feel positively about my partner"), they showed ample variability in the accuracy of judging partners' specific attributes (e.g., "my partner is tidy"). Moreover, judges' neuroticism and depression, the length of time spouses had known one another, whether the couple had lived together prior to marriage, and whether the couple received premarital counseling did not moderate spouses' accuracy of their partner judgments.

Relationship Factors

Relationship satisfaction undoubtedly can be theorized as a powerful moderator because it provides strong motives for both accuracy and bias. In this review, we reserve the discussion of the associations between perceptual properties and relationship outcomes for the next section on implications for romantic relationships. It is important to note that the exact role of relationship satisfaction in perceivers' partner judgments is debatable, depending on whether it is theorized to be a cause, a moderator, or an outcome of such judgments.

Other than relationship quality, relationship length is a commonly studied moderator of judgment accuracy (see chapter 9 by Beer in this handbook for a discussion on information quantity and quality). Counter to what one might expect— namely, that as partners spend more time together, their accuracy should increase—previous studies have provided quite consistent evidence that acquaintanceship or relationship length does not play a significant role in moderating the accuracy or bias of intimates' perceptions of each other, regardless of whether accuracy and biases are measured by VCA (Fletcher & Kerr, 2010; Wood et al., 2017) or by PCA (Letzring & Noftle, 2010; Neff & Karney, 2005). Additionally, Watson et al. (2000) reported that not only acquaintanceship length but relationship closeness and number of shared activities also did not moderate accuracy of partner trait judgments in all three samples: married couples, dating couples, and friend dyads. However, accuracy tended to be substantially higher in the married

couples than in the dating couples and friend dyads. Connelly and Ones's (2010) meta-analyses yielded an interesting interaction between trait visibility and relationship intimacy: although more visible traits tend to receive higher judgment accuracy in general, the impact of trait visibility on partner judgment accuracy is attenuated as relationship intimacy (rather than frequency of interactions) increases. These findings suggest that something unique about the intimacy dynamics in romantic relationships, particularly in married couples, rather than acquaintanceship alone, may play a significant role in moderating intimates' judgments.

Fletcher and Kerr's meta-analyses (2010) examined relationship length as a moderator of the link between trait judgments and relationship quality. Their analyses showed that as relationship length increases, the link between positive mean-level bias and relationship quality decreases in size, whereas the link between accuracy and relationship quality increases. Taking these findings together, it appears that accuracy and biases in partner judgments are established fairly early on in the relationship; however, their roles in relationship functioning may change over time, which is discussed in greater detail in the next section.

Implications of Accuracy and Bias for Relationship Outcomes

Perhaps the most important question—and a unique question to address in research on accuracy and bias of personality judgment in the context of romantic relationships—is the "so what" question; that is, how are accuracy and bias related to relationship functioning? Are they beneficial or detrimental? There has been a long debate regarding whether accuracy or positive bias is more adaptive. Some researchers argue that positivity or enhancement bias is more adaptive (e.g., Endo et al., 2000; Martz et al., 1998; Murray et al., 1996a, 1996b; Murray & Holmes, 1997; Taylor & Brown, 1988), whereas others argue that accurate perceptions are most beneficial (e.g., Colvin, Block, & Funder, 1995; De La Ronde & Swann, 1998; Kobak & Hazan, 1991; Swann, De La Ronde, & Hixon, 1994). As the area starts to shift the conceptualization of accuracy and biases from a mutually exclusive perspective to a coexisting one (e.g., Gagne & Lydon, 2004; Luo & Snider, 2009), it increasingly seems plausible that accuracy and biases both can be adaptive.

Thus far, VCA research consistently has shown that partners holding stronger positivity bias report higher relationship satisfaction and better quality (e.g., Fletcher et al., 2000; Fowers, Lyons, & Montel, 1996; Martz et al., 1998; Murray et al., 1996a, 1996b; Murray & Holmes, 1997). Longitudinal research also has found that relationships are more likely to persist when intimates idealize their partners and relationships (Fletcher et al., 2000; Helgeson, 1994; Murray et al., 1996b; Murray & Holmes, 1997; Rusbult et al., 2000). It is important to note that the relation between positivity bias and relationship satisfaction may not be strictly linear. Katz and her colleagues found this association to be curvilinear, indicating that although people tend to idealize their partners, their perceptions are also constrained by reality; perceptions that are too positive with little basis in reality may backfire and have negative impacts on relationships (Katz, Anderson, & Beach, 1997; Katz & Joiner, 2002).

There is far less VCA research relating accuracy to relationship outcomes and virtually none on similarity bias and relationship outcomes. Available evidence suggests that accuracy in partner personality perceptions, in general, is associated with positive relationship outcomes (e.g., De La Ronde & Swann, 1998; Kobak & Hazan, 1991; Murray et al., 1996a, 1996b; see Fletcher & Boyes, 2008, for a review) with some exceptions (e.g., Murray et al., 2002). Finally, Fletcher and Kerr's (2010) meta-analyses confirmed that positivity bias in partner judgments was strongly associated with better relationship quality; however, tracking accuracy surprisingly was unrelated with relationship outcomes. However, this was a collective finding based on a host of relationship-related perceptions that went beyond personality judgments.

With regard to PCA research, there have been quite a few studies that related PCA-based accuracy to relationship outcomes, such as satisfaction, closeness, intimacy, and stability. The evidence is mixed, although it tends to support the adaptive value of accuracy: Whereas a number of studies reported that accuracy was related to better relationship functioning (Decuyper et al., 2012; Letzring & Noftle, 2010, Study 1; Luo & Snider, 2009; Murray et al., 1996b; Neff & Karney, 2005) as well as greater relationship stability (Neff & Karney, 2005), two other studies failed to find any significant association (Letzring & Noftle, 2010, Study 2; Murray et al., 1996a, 2002).

The link between PCA positivity bias and relationship outcomes, however, has proven to be highly robust: available studies consistently found positivity bias to be a significant associate of relationship quality (e.g., Luo & Snider, 2009; Murray

et al., 1996a, 1996b, 2011). Further, newlyweds holding positively biased partner perceptions are more able to battle the decline in relationship satisfaction as part of the "honeymoon" effect (e.g., Murray et al., 2011); young dating couples are less likely to break up when they idealize the partner perceptions (Fletcher et al., 2000; Murray et al., 1996b). In terms of the PCA similarity bias, it has been shown to be associated with higher relationship satisfaction (Decuyper et al., 2012; Luo & Snider, 2009; Murray et al., 2002).

Taking both VCA and PCA findings together, it is evident that accuracy, positivity bias, and similarity bias all tend to be associated with positive relationship outcomes. Given the newer conceptualization of the independent coexisting relationship between accuracy and biases, it is important to test how these three perceptual properties operate together in relationship functioning. To date, two studies have examined all three of them in the same setting and both studies followed the PCA. Luo and Snider (2009) simultaneously modeled the effects of accuracy, positivity bias, and similarity bias in predicting newlywed satisfaction. Findings across several personality domains showed that all three perceptual indices made strong, independent contributions to the prediction of the perceiver's satisfaction, suggesting that accuracy, similarity bias, and positivity bias all serve important but different functions in maintaining a satisfying relationship. Although not particularly focusing on romantic couples, Human et al. (2012) examined accuracy, positivity bias, and assumed similarity in a one-semester longitudinal study of newly met college students. Their results suggested that more accurate personality impressions of new classmates, as well as positively biased first impressions, were strong predictors of initial and subsequent relationship development, whereas assumed similarity only showed significant associations with initial liking and interest in future interactions.

In light of the findings indicating a possible adaptive role for both accuracy and biases, Lackenbauer, Campbell, Rubin, Fletcher, and Troister (2010) took a step further and experimentally examined the effects of accuracy and positivity bias of partner trait judgment on the target's relationship well-being. Specifically, participants were led to believe that their partner's judgments of them were either high or low in profile accuracy and mean-level positivity bias. The results suggested that artificially induced accuracy and positivity bias in partner judgments had independent and additive beneficial effects on targets' relationship experiences—they rated their relationship most favorably and reported highest intimacy when the feedback from their partner was both accurate and positively biased.

Overall, these exciting new findings support the notion that accuracy and biases not only coexist but also play different beneficial roles in a happy, satisfying relationship. Although their exact functions remain to be discovered, let us use a hypothetical example to illustrate how the three perceptions may work independently to enhance relationship satisfaction. Recall John and Mary, the newlywed couple we mentioned before. Recently John lost his job due to an economic recession. It is likely that Mary's accurate perceptions of John would be beneficial to his job search because such perceptions may help John to evaluate himself more correctly and assess the situation more clearly. Additionally, her positivity bias for John would enable her to continue or even strengthen her faith in their love in spite of the temporary difficulties he is facing. Finally, believing that they are similar to each other may allow Mary to better appreciate John's frustrations and offer more useful support to him. Although this example is fictitious, it demonstrates that accuracy, positivity bias, and similarity bias all can play a unique constructive role in relationship maintenance. It is conceivable that some optimal combination of moderate accuracy and biases may be most adaptive for relationship functioning; that is, accuracy without bias, or bias without accuracy, or simply too much bias all can have detrimental effects on relationships (see also Gagne & Lydon, 2004; Neff & Karney, 2005).

Conclusions and Further Considerations

The aim of this chapter was to review theories and research relevant to accuracy and biases of partner personality judgment in romantic relationships. Consistent with prior theorizing (Murray et al., 1996a; West & Kenny, 2011), we suggested that personality judgments may be conceptualized to consist of three components: *accurate perceptions*, *systematic biases*, and *random errors*. We focused on two common biases in romantic relationships—positivity bias and similarity bias. We discussed the two major approaches to conceptualizing and assessing accuracy and biases—VCA and PCA. A review of the literature on partner personality judgment in both approaches suggests that, overall, individuals in romantic relationships tend to perceive their partners with substantial accuracy but also with a considerable amount of bias. However, there are abundant individual differences in the degree of

accuracy and bias. Moderator analyses suggest that judges' personal characteristics, trait properties, and relationship factors can have a significant moderating effect on the degree to which one is accurate and biased. Finally, accuracy, positivity bias, and similarity bias in partner trait judgments all have important positive implications for romantic relationship functioning.

As we were analyzing the relevant theories and findings, we identified several important, broad questions about accuracy and bias in partner judgments that have not yet been adequately addressed. For example, what are the processes underlying partner judgments? How stable are partner personality judgments? Do partner personality judgments contain both implicit and explicit components?

What Are the Processes Underlying Partner Judgments?

It appears that there might be several processes underlying the development of partner personality judgments. Striving for an accurate understanding of their partners certainly would be one of the most important processes (e.g., Gagne & Lydon, 2004). At the same time, multiple motivational processes may contribute to systematic biases: for example, people may be motivated to see their partners as similar to their own actual self (e.g., Murray et al., 2002), their own ideal self (e.g., Klohnen & Luo, 2003), or their own ideal partner (e.g., Fletcher et al., 2000; Murray et al., 1996a, 1996b), and to perceive partners simply in a socially desirable way (e.g., Luo & Snider, 2009). Additionally, cognitive processes such as the assumed similarity heuristic (e.g., Watson et al., 2000) and the anchoring heuristic (Kruger, 1999) may also lead to systematic judgment biases. It is possible that some of these processes may be overlapping, or that some of them may subsume some of the others. So far no study has investigated all of these processes together.

Furthermore, there has been evidence for a "self-fulfilling prophecy" in partner perceptions—that is, targets gradually incorporate perceivers' images and feedback of the targets into their self-perceptions over time. In a longitudinal study of 121 dating couples, Murray and colleagues (1996b) reported that the targets' self-perceptions became more aligned with the perceivers' idealized perceptions of them a year ago. Additional diary studies by Murray, Griffin, Rose, and Bellavia (2003, 2006) further corroborated this finding, showing that chronic perceptions of the partner's regard about themselves predicted people's day-to-day state self-esteem, particularly in response to their perception of the partner's acceptance the day before. These findings suggested that individuals internalize both their partner's chronic and immediate judgments of them to become part of their own self-concepts. One implication of this process for partner trait judgment is that accuracy of partner judgment likely will increase as a result of the "self-fulfilling prophecy" effect.

Our review indicated that both accurate and biased partner judgments are strongly associated with relationship outcomes. It is often theorized that accuracy, positivity bias, and similarity bias lead to better relationship well-being. For example, an accurate assessment of partner attributes may foster a sense of predictability and security on the part of the perceivers (e.g., Kenny & Acitelli, 2001; Swann et al., 1994), while they provide the targets a feeling of validation (Reis & Shaver, 1988). Positivity bias may enable perceivers to justify their relationship and to counteract the attractiveness of potential alternative partners (e.g., Murray et al., 1996a), as well as make targets feel valued (e.g., Rusbult et al., 2000). Similarity bias may benefit perceivers by strengthening feelings of closeness (Aron, Aron, Tudor, & Nelson, 1991) and bring a sense of connection for the targets (e.g., Murray et al., 2002). On the other hand, it is also conceivable that better relationship functioning leads to greater accuracy and stronger biases. For instance, there has been some evidence suggesting that experimentally elicited attraction leads to greater positivity bias and similarity bias (Luo, 2007). Further, more recent experimental findings suggested that initial liking, induced from positive self-presentation, can also increase accuracy, possibly because self-presenters may release more information and perceivers may pay more attention to the target (Human, Biesanz, Parisotto, & Dunn, 2012). It is highly likely that the associations between partner trait judgments and relationship outcomes are bidirectional in nature.

Stability and Change in Partner Personality Judgments

Relationship representations, including partner perceptions, are often theorized to be stable over time (e.g., Bowlby, 1969; Shaver, Hazan, & Bradshaw, 1988); yet it is likely they are also open to change. Pietromonaco, Laurenceau, and Barrett (2002) discussed two possible mechanisms through which one's relationship representations can be modified: reframing existing knowledge and incorporating new knowledge. Individuals' partner trait judgments may also change through these processes. For example, integra-

tive couple therapy has two related goals: increasing emotional acceptance of the differences between two partners and promoting positive changes to better accommodate the needs of the other (Jacobson & Christensen, 1998). Acceptance does not entail adding new information, but rather reevaluating the existing knowledge, which leads to a new, positive judgment of the partner and the relationship. Accommodation, on the other hand, involves making active changes in judgments, decision-making, and actions.

Very few empirical studies have explicitly tested how partner judgments change over time. One challenge in examining this issue is that the target's self-perceptions may also change. When the perceiver's judgments of the target change, it remains to be determined whether the perceiver accurately reflects the changes that the target him/herself has experienced, or whether the perceiver simply has changed the judgments unilaterally. Watson and Humrichouse (2006) followed 291 newlywed couples over the course of 2 years to examine personality changes during this critical period. One interesting finding was that little convergence existed between participants' self-rated personality changes and the corresponding spouse-rated changes; in other words, partners did not see eye to eye in terms of each other's personality changes, at least in the first few years of their marriage. Assuming the self-rated changes are "real," this result can be explained in several possible ways, including (1) the perceiver fails to update his/her judgments of the target, whose self-perceptions have changed, or (2) the perceiver has made some invalid unilateral updates in the partner trait judgments. It is important for future research to examine the stability of partner trait judgments and delineate the underlying processes.

It is important to recognize that intimates' self-perceptions and partner perceptions are interactive in nature. For example, intimates tend to adopt partners' perceptions of them into their self-perceptions over time (e.g., Murray et al., 1996b). Moreover, they also tend to gradually incorporate perceptions of the partner into their ideal partner standards (Fletcher et al., 2000; Murray et al., 1996b). So far, the majority of research relevant to partner trait judgments has focused on individuals currently in stable relationships. Only a few studies examined partner perceptions at the early stages of relationship development (e.g., Aron et al., 1991; Fletcher et al., 2000; Klohnen & Luo, 2003). Virtually no research has been conducted on how individuals judge their ex-partners after the relationship has dissolved (see "fatal attraction" research [Felmlee, 1995] for an exception). We believe it is very important to follow individuals throughout the entire course of their relationship and compare their partner judgments at different times, particularly in the initial crush or attraction stage and in the post-breakup stage. Despite the difficulty of conducting this type of longitudinal research, it is extremely valuable in that it not only informs us regarding both stability and change in partner judgments but also helps to disentangle the complex links between judgments and relationship development.

Do Partner Personality Judgments Contain Both Implicit and Explicit Components?

Research on personality judgment so far primarily has relied on perceivers' responses obtained from self-report measures, which are considered as tapping conscious or explicit perceptions, given that participants are well aware of these perceptions. However, the bulk of the social psychology literature on social cognition, judgments, attitudes, and stereotypes suggests that these perceptual processes contain both implicit and explicit components (for a review, see Greenwald & Banaji, 1995; also see chapter 4 by Osterholz, Breil, Nestler, & Back in this handbook, on lens and dual lens models). To what extent do partner perceptions also contain explicit and implicit components? Attachment theorists suggest that internal working models contain both explicit and implicit components. For example, Bowlby (1980) proposed that while the more conscious aspects of working models serve self-defensive functions, working models may well operate without conscious awareness. Bartholomew (1997) further elaborated on this issue: although it has been commonly observed that dismissing individuals show positive self-models and preoccupied individuals hold positive other models when assessed with explicit measures, at some unconscious level dismissing individuals actually feel negatively about themselves, yet they manage to maintain a positive self-image as a way to avoid depending on their partners. Similarly, preoccupied individuals may hold implicit negative models of others, while their conscious positive other models are a defense against the fact that their significant others are unable to meet their emotional needs.

Given that working models of attachment are a specific part of personality, it is likely that partner judgments on personality traits also contain both implicit and explicit components. We believe that research on partner judgments would benefit from the use of more implicit measures (e.g., the Implicit Association Test) and the examination of judgments that are less masked by self-defense or self-presentation motives. Future research may investigate (1) whether there are systematic discrepancies between responses obtained from explicit measures and from implicit measures of partner trait judgments, (2) what individual difference dimensions may be related to these discrepancies, (3) how explicit and implicit judgments influence the processing of incoming information and instant decision-making in the relationship context, and (4) whether explicit and implicit judgments are differentially associated with personal and relationship well-being.

We believe that the topic of personality judgments in romantic relationships is highly intriguing and exciting in that the study of personality judgments integrates social cognition, personality judgments, and close relationships. It has important implications for many areas of psychological science, including social, personality, developmental, and clinical psychology. This challenging work will also require creative, sophisticated methodologies that combine techniques typically employed by social psychologists (e.g., priming, response latencies), paradigms typically used by personality psychologists (e.g., self- and other-ratings, longitudinal designs), and research designs typically used by relationship researchers (e.g., dyadic or multilevel designs). We hope this chapter provides a useful beginning of a more comprehensive framework that will stimulate another new wave of high-quality research on partner personality judgments.[1]

References

Aron, A., Aron, E. N., Tudor, M., & Nelson, G. (1991). Close relationships as including other in the self. *Journal of Personality and Social Psychology, 60*, 241–253. doi:10.1037/0022-3514.60.2.241

Bartholomew, K. (1997). Adult attachment processes: Individual and couple perspectives. *British Journal of Medical Psychology, 70*, 249–263. doi:10.1111/j.2044-8341.1997.tb01903.x

Botwin, M. D., Buss, D. M., & Shackelford, T. K. (1997). Personality and mate preferences: Five factors in mate selection and marital satisfaction. *Journal of Personality, 65*, 107–136. doi:10.1111/j.1467-6494.1997.tb00531.x

Bowlby, J. (1969). *Attachment and loss: Vol. 1. Attachment.* New York: Basic.

Bowlby, J. (1980). *Attachment and loss: Vol. 3. Loss: Sadness and depression.* New York: Basic.

Boyes, A. D., & Fletcher, G. J. O. (2007). Metaperceptions of bias in intimate relationships. *Journal of Personality and Social Psychology, 92*, 286–306. doi:10.1037/0022-3514.92.2.286

Brown, J. D. (1986). Evaluations of self and others: Self-enhancement biases in social judgments. *Social Cognition, 4*, 353–376. doi:10.1521/soco.1986.4.4.353

Cacioppo, J. T., & Petty, R. E. (1982). The need for cognition. *Journal of Personality and Social Psychology, 42*, 116–131. doi:10.1037/0022-3514.42.1.116

Cohen, J. (1988). *Statistical power analysis for the behavioral sciences* (2nd ed.). Hillsdale, NJ: Erlbaum.

Colvin, C. R., Block, J., & Funder, D. C. (1995). Overly positive self-evaluations and personality: Negative implications for mental health. *Journal of Personality and Social Psychology, 68,* 1152–1162. doi:10.1037/0022-3514.68.6.1152

Connelly, B. S., & Ones, D. S. (2010). An other perspective on personality: Meta-analytic integration of observers' accuracy and predictive validity. *Psychological Bulletin, 136,* 1092–1122. doi:10.1037/a0021212

De La Ronde, C., & Swann, W. B. (1998). Partner verification: Restoring shattered images of our intimates. *Journal of Personality and Social Psychology, 75,* 374–382. doi:10.1037/0022-3514.75.2.374

Decuyper, M., De Bolle, M., & De Fruyt, F. (2012). Personality similarity, perceptual accuracy, and relationship satisfaction in dating and married couples. *Personal Relationships, 19,* 128–145. doi:10.1111/j.1475-6811.2010.01344.x

Edwards, J. R. (2001). Ten difference score myths. *Organizational Research Methods, 4,* 265–287. doi:10.1177/109442810143005

Endo, Y., Heine, S. J., & Lehman, D. R. (2000). Culture and positive illusions in close relationships: How my relationships are better than yours. *Personality and Social Psychology Bulletin, 26,* 1571–1586. doi:10.1177/01461672002612011

Felmlee, D. H. (1995). Fatal attractions: Affection and disaffection in intimate relationships. *Journal of Social and Personal Relationships, 12,* 295–311. doi:10.1177/0265407595122009

Fletcher, G. J. O. (2002). *The new science of intimate relationships.* Malden, MA: Blackwell.

Fletcher, G. J. O., & Boyes, A. D. (2008). Is love blind? Reality and illusion in intimate relationships. In J. P. Forgas & J. Fitness (Eds.), *Social relationships: Cognitive, affective, and motivational processes* (pp. 101–114). Hove, UK: Psychology Press.

Fletcher, G. J. O., & Kerr, P. S. G. (2010). Through the eyes of love: Reality and illusion in intimate relationships. *Psychological Bulletin, 136,* 627–658. doi:10.1037/a0019792

Fletcher, G. J. O., Simpson, J. A., & Boyes, A. D. (2006) Accuracy and bias in romantic relationships: An evolutionary and social psychological analysis. In M. Schaller, J. A. Simpson, & D. T. Kenrick (Eds.), *Evolution and social psychology.* New York: Psychology Press.

Fletcher, G. J. O., Simpson, J. A., & Thomas, G. (2000). Ideals, perceptions, and evaluations in early relationship development. *Journal of Personality and Social Psychology, 79,* 933–940. doi:10.1037/0022-3514.79.6.933

Fowers, B. J., Lyons, E. M., & Montel, K. H. (1996). Positive marital illusions: Self-enhancement or relationship enhancement? *Journal of Family Psychology, 10,* 192–208. doi:10.1037/0893-3200.10.2.192

Funder, D. C. (1995). On the accuracy of personality judgment: A realistic approach. *Psychological Review, 102,* 652–670. doi:10.1037/0033-295X.102.4.652

Funder, D. C. (2012). Accurate personality judgment. *Current Directions in Psychological Science, 21,* 177–182. doi:10.1177/0963721412445309

Gagne, F. M., & Lydon, J. E. (2004). Bias and accuracy in close relationships: An integrative review. *Personality and Social Psychology Review, 8,* 322–338. doi:10.1207/s15327957pspr0804_1

Gill, M. J., & Swann, W. B., Jr. (2004). On what it means to know someone: A matter of pragmatics. *Journal of Personality and Social Psychology, 86,* 405–418. doi:10.1037/0022-3514.86.3.405

Greenwald, A. G., & Banaji, M. R. (1995). Implicit social cognition: Attitudes, self-esteem, and stereotypes. *Psychological Review, 102,* 4–27. doi:10.1037/0033-295X.102.1.4

Griffin, D., Murray, S., & Gonzalez, R. (1999). Difference score correlations in relationship research: A conceptual primer. *Personal Relationships, 6,* 505–518. doi:10.1111/j.1475-6811.1999.tb00206.x

Haselton, M. G., & Buss, D. M. (2000). Error management theory: A new perspective on biases in cross-sex mind reading. *Journal of Personality and Social Psychology, 78,* 81–91. doi:10.1037/0022-3514.78.1.81

Helgeson, V. S. (1994). The effects of self-beliefs and relationship beliefs on adjustment to a relationship stressor. *Personal Relationships, 1,* 241–258. doi:10.1111/j.1475-6811.1994.tb00064.x

Human, L. J., Biesanz, J. C., Parisotto, K. L., & Dunn, E. W. (2012). Your best self helps reveal your true self: Positive self-presentation leads to more accurate personality impressions. *Social Psychological and Personality Science, 3,* 23–30. doi:10.1177/1948550611407689

Human, L. J., Sandstrom, G. M., Biesanz, J. C., & Dunn, E. W. (2012). Accurate first impressions leave a lasting impression: The long-term effects of accuracy on relationship development. *Social Psychological and Personality Science, 4,* 395–402. doi:10.1177/1948550612463735

Jacobson, N. S., & Christensen, A. (1998). *Acceptance and change in couple therapy: A therapist's guide to transforming relationships.* New York: W. W. Norton.

John, O. P., & Robins, R. W. (1993). Determinants of interjudge agreement on personality traits: The Big Five domains, observability, evaluativeness, and the unique perspective of the self. *Journal of Personality, 61,* 521–551. doi:10.1111/j.1467-6494.1993.tb00781.x

John, O. P., & Robins, R. W. (1994). Accuracy and bias in self-perception: Individual differences in self-enhancement and the role of narcissism. *Journal of Personality and Social Psychology, 66,* 206–219. doi:10.1037/0022-3514.66.1.206

Katz, J., Anderson, P., & Beach, S. R. H. (1997). Dating relationship quality: Effects of global self-verification and self-enhancement. *Journal of Social and Personal Relationships, 14,* 829–842. doi:10.1177/0265407597146007

Katz, J., & Joiner, T. E. J. (2002). Being known, intimate, and valued: Global self-verification and dyadic adjustment in couples and roommates. *Journal of Personality, 70,* 33–58. doi:10.1111/1467-6494.00177

Kenny, D. A., & Acitelli, L. K. (2001). Accuracy and bias in the perception of the partner in a close relationship. *Journal of Personality and Social Psychology, 80,* 439–448. doi:10.1037/0022-3514.80.3.439

Kenny, D. A., Kashy, D. A., & Cook, W. L. (2006). *Dyadic data analysis.* New York: Guilford.

Klohnen, E. C., & Luo, S. (2003). Interpersonal attraction and personality: What is attractive—Self similarity, ideal similarity, complementarity, or attachment security? *Journal of Personality and Social Psychology, 85,* 709–722. doi:10.1037/0022-3514.85.4.709

Klohnen, E. C., & Mendelsohn, G. A. (1998). Partner selection for personality characteristics: A couple-centered approach. *Personality and Social Psychology Bulletin, 24,* 268–278. doi:10.1177/0146167298243004

Kobak, R., & Hazan, C. (1991). Attachment in marriage: Effects of security and accuracy of working models. *Journal of Personality and Social Psychology, 60*, 861–869. doi:10.1037/0022-3514.60.6.861

Kruger, J. (1999). Lake Wobegon be gone! The "below-average effect" and the egocentric nature of comparative ability judgments. *Journal of Personality and Social Psychology, 77*, 221–232. doi:10.1037/0022-3514.77.2.221

Lackenbauer, S. D., Campbell, L., Rubin, H., Fletcher, G. J. O., & Troister, T. (2010). The unique and combined benefits of accuracy and positive bias in relationships. *Personal Relationships,17*,475–493.doi:10.1111/j.1475-6811.2010.01282.x

Letzring, T. D., & Noftle, E. E. (2010). Predicting relationship quality from self-verification of broad personality traits among romantic couples. *Journal of Research in Personality, 44*, 353–362. doi:10.1016/j.jrp.2010.03.008

Luo, S. (2007). *Does love make us blind? Effects of attraction on self and partner perceptions*. Riga, Latvia: VDM Verlag.

Luo, S. (2009). Partner selection and relationship satisfaction in early dating couples: The role of couple similarity. *Personality and Individual Differences, 47*, 133–138. doi:10.1016/j.paid.2009.02.012

Luo, S., & Klohnen, E. C. (2005). Assortative mating and marital quality in newlyweds: A couple-centered approach. *Journal of Personality and Social Psychology, 88*, 304–326. doi:10.1037/0022-3514.88.2.304

Luo, S., & Snider, A. G. (2009). Accuracy and biases in newlyweds' perceptions of each other: Not mutually exclusive but mutually beneficial. *Psychological Science, 20*, 1332–1339. doi:10.1111/j.1467-9280.2009.02449.x

Martz, J. M., Verette, J., Arriaga, X. B., Slovik, L. F., Cox, C. L., & Rusbult, C. E. (1998). Positive illusion in close relationships. *Personal Relationships, 5*,159–181. doi:10.1111/j.1475-6811.1998.tb00165.x

Murray, S. L., Griffin, D. W., Derrick, J. L., Harris, B., Aloni, M., & Leder, S. (2011). Tempting fate or inviting happiness? Unrealistic idealization prevents the decline of marital satisfaction. *Psychological Science, 22*, 619–626. doi:10.1177/0956797611403155

Murray, S. L., Griffin, D. W., Rose, P., & Bellavia, G. M. (2003). Calibrating the sociometer: The relational contingencies of self-esteem. *Journal of Personality and Social Psychology, 85*, 63–84. doi:10.1037/0022-3514.85.1.63

Murray, S. L., Griffin, D. W., Rose, P., & Bellavia, G. M. (2006). For better or worse? Self-esteem and the contingencies of acceptance in marriage. *Personality and Social Psychology Bulletin, 32*, 866–880. doi:10.1177/0146167206286756

Murray, S. L., & Holmes, J. G. (1997). A leap of faith? Positive illusions in romantic relationships. *Personality and Social Psychology Bulletin, 23*, 586–604. doi:10.1177/0146167297236003

Murray, S. L., Holmes, J. G., Bellavia, G., Griffin, D. W., & Dolderman, D. (2002). Kindred spirits? The benefits of egocentrism in close relationships. *Journal of Personality and Social Psychology, 82*, 563–581. doi:10.1037/0022-3514.82.4.563

Murray, S. L., Holmes, J. G., Dolderman, D., & Griffin, D. W. (2000). What the motivated mind sees: Comparing friends' perspectives to married partners' views of each other. *Journal of Experimental Social Psychology, 36*, 600–620. doi:10.1006/jesp.1999.1417

Murray, S. L., Holmes, J. G., & Griffin, D. W. (1996a). The benefits of positive illusions: Idealization and the construction of satisfaction in close relationships. *Journal of Personality and Social Psychology, 70*, 79–98. doi:10.1037/0022-3514.70.1.79

Murray, S. L., Holmes, J. G., & Griffin, D. W. (1996b). The self-fulfilling nature of positive illusions in romantic relationships: Love is not blind, but prescient. *Journal of Personality and Social Psychology, 71*, 1155–1180. doi:10.1037/0022-3514.71.6.1155

Murray, S. L., Holmes, J. G., & Griffin, D. W. (2000). Self-esteem and the quest for felt security: How perceived regard regulates attachment processes. *Journal of Personality and Social Psychology, 78*, 478–498. doi:10.1037/0022-3514.78.3.478

Neff, L. A., & Karney, B. R. (2005). To know you is to love you: The implications of global adoration and specific accuracy for marital relationships. *Journal of Personality and Social Psychology, 88*, 480–497. doi:10.1037/0022-3514.88.3.480

Pietromonaco, P. R., Laurenceau, J. P., & Barrett, L. F. (2002). Change in relational knowledge structures. In H. Reis, M. A. Fitzpatrick, & A. Vangelisti (Eds.), *Stability and change in relationship behavior. Advances in personal relationships* (pp. 5–34). Cambridge, UK: Cambridge University Press.

Ready, R. E., Clark, L. A., Watson, D., & Westerhouse, K. (2000). Self- and peer-related personality: Agreement, trait ratability, and the "self-based heuristic." *Journal of Research in Personality, 34*, 208–224. doi:10.1006/jrpe.1999.2280

Reis, H. T., & Shaver, P. (1988). Intimacy as an interpersonal process. In S. W. Duck (Ed.), *Handbook of personal relationships* (pp. 367–389). New York: Wiley.

Rogers, K. H., Wood, D., & Furr, R. M. (2018). Assessment of similarity and self-other agreement in dyadic relationships: A guide to best practices. *Journal of Social and Personal Relationships, 35*, 112–134. doi:10.1177/0265407517712615

Rusbult, C. E., Van Lange, P. A. M., Wildschut, T., Yovetich, N. A., & Verette, J. (2000). Perceived superiority in close relationships: Why it exists and persists. *Journal of Personality and Social Psychology, 79*, 521–545. doi:10.1037/0022-3514.79.4.521

Ruvolo, A. P., & Fabin, L. A. (1999). Two of a kind: Perceptions of own and partner's attachment characteristics. *Personal Relationships, 6*, 57–79. doi:10.1111/j.1475-6811.1999.tb00211.x

Shaver, P. R., Hazan, C., & Bradshaw, D. (1988). Love as attachment: The integration of three behavioral systems. In R. J. Sternberg & M. Barnes (Eds.), *The psychology of love* (pp. 68–99). New Haven, CT: Yale University Press.

Suls, J., Lemos, K., & Stewart, H. L. (2002). Self-esteem, construal, and comparisons with the self, friends, and peers. *Journal of Personality and Social Psychology, 82*, 252–261. doi:10.1037/0022-3514.82.2.252

Swann, W. B., De La Ronde, C., & Hixon, J. G. (1994). Authenticity and positivity strivings in marriage and courtship. *Journal of Personality and Social Psychology, 66*, 857–869. doi:10.1037/0022-3514.66.5.857

Taylor, S. E., & Brown, J. D. (1988). Illusion and well-being: A social psychological perspective on mental health. *Psychological Bulletin, 103*, 193–210. doi:10.1037/0033-2909.103.2.193

Thielmann, I., Hilbig, B. E., & Zettler, I. (2018, October 15). Seeing me, seeing you: Testing competing accounts of assumed similarity in personality judgments. *Journal of Personality and Social Psychology*. Advance online publication. doi:10.1037/pspp0000222

Watson, D., Hubbard, B., & Wiese, D. (2000). Self-other agreement in personality and affectivity: The role of acquaintanceship, trait visibility, and assumed similarity. *Journal of Personality and Social Psychology, 78,* 546–558. doi:10.1037/0022-3514.78.3.546

Watson, D., & Humrichouse, J. (2006). Personality development in emerging adulthood: Integrating evidence from self-ratings and spouse ratings. *Journal of Personality and Social Psychology, 91,* 959–974. doi:10.1037/0022-3514.91.5.959

Watson, D., Klohnen, E. C., Casillas, A., Simms, E. N., Haig, J., & Berry, D. S. (2004). Match makers and deal breakers: Analyses of assortative mating in newlywed couples. *Journal of Personality, 72,* 1029–1068. doi:10.1111/j.0022-3506.2004 .00289.x

Webster, D. M., & Kruglanski, A. W. (1994). Individual differences in need for cognitive closure. *Journal of Personality and Social Psychology, 67,* 1049–1062. doi:10.1037/0022-3514.67.6.1049

West, T. V., & Kenny, D. A. (2011). The truth and bias model of judgment. *Psychological Review, 118,* 357–378. doi:10.1037/ a0022936

Wood, W. I., Oldham, C. R., Reifman, A., & Niehuis, S. (2017). Accuracy and bias in newlywed spouses' perceptions of each other's personalities. *Personal Relationships, 24,* 886–901. doi:10.1111/pere.12219

Note

1. There are multiple options to compute this profile correlation, including Pearson correlation (e.g., Luo & Snider, 2009), intraclass correlation (e.g., Murray et al., 2002), I_{pa} index (Decuyper et al., 2012), regression coefficient (Neff & Karney, 2005), and so forth.

Self–Other Agreement on Ratings of Personality Disorder Symptoms and Traits

Three Meta-Analyses

Joshua R. Oltmanns *and* Thomas F. Oltmanns

Abstract

The present chapter considers the factors important to self–other agreement on personality disorder, reviews the literature on this topic, and presents three meta-analyses with a total of fifty-three studies of self–other agreement on personality disorder (total N = 11,812). Meta-analyses were completed on (1) overall self–other agreement on personality disorder symptoms and traits, (2) self–other agreement on DSM personality disorders, and (3) self–other agreement on maladaptive personality traits measured dimensionally by the Personality Inventory for DSM-5 (PID-5). Overall median self-other agreement was r = 0.37. Self–other agreement on DSM PDs ranged from r = . 32 (dependent PD) to r = 0.51 (antisocial PD). Median self–other agreement was somewhat higher on the PID-5 maladaptive trait domains (r = 0.45), which is in line with prior estimates of the magnitude of self–other agreement on "normal" FFM trait domains.

Key Words: self–other agreement, personality disorder, five-factor model, personality assessment, Personality Inventory for DSM-5, informant-report, meta-analysis

The five-factor model (FFM) of personality is a dimensional model of mostly adaptive levels of personality traits (Goldberg, 1993; John, Naumann, & Soto, 2008). It was originally developed through the study of the English language (Allport, 1937) and consists of five broad personality trait "domains" (neuroticism, extraversion, openness, agreeableness, and conscientiousness) that each contain more specific "facets" of personality. Personality *disorder* is defined as an "enduring pattern of inner experience and behavior" (American Psychiatric Association [APA], 2013, p. 645) that is inconsistent with an individual's culture, is rigid and stable, begins in adolescence, and is associated with distress (APA, 2013). Personality disorders, as defined by the *Diagnostic and Statistical Manual of Mental Disorders 5th Edition* (DSM-5; APA, 2013), can be thought of as "maladaptive variants" of FFM personality traits (Widiger, Gore, Crego, Rojas, & Oltmanns, 2017). For example, high levels of FFM conscientiousness are associated with adaptive characteristics such as

being punctual and hard-working. The maladaptive variant of the FFM conscientiousness domain is compulsivity,[1] including the traits of rigidity, perfectionism, and workaholism—characteristic of the DSM obsessive-compulsive personality disorder category—which are maladaptive because they cause impairment in life (Boudreaux, 2016; Livesley, 2007; Samuel, Riddell, Lynam, Miller, & Widiger, 2012). The research supporting the FFM conceptualization of personality disorder is extensive and is described later in this chapter. The differences between personality "symptoms" and "traits" can be complicated. However, because research indicates that symptoms converge with FFM traits—and symptoms that compose the personality disorders in the DSM personality disorder categories are defined as being "enduring" and "stable" (APA, 2013, p. 645)—we use the words "trait" and "symptom" interchangeably in this chapter.

Self–other agreement on personality traits has been of interest to psychological researchers for many years, largely because self–other agreement on personality traits provides convergent validation evidence for their existence (Campbell & Fiske, 1959; Costa & McCrae, 1988; Norman, 1963). This line of research simultaneously tests the validity of personality traits and the uniqueness of personality data reported by the self and by others. The magnitude of self–other agreement on personality traits such as those in the more adaptive ranges of the FFM is moderate (e.g., Connelly & Ones, 2010). In contrast, self–other agreement has been shown to be relatively lower on the maladaptive personality traits that constitute personality disorders (e.g., Klonsky, Oltmanns, & Turkheimer, 2006). Findings in this area are nuanced, however, and they rely on numerous factors. Because—to our knowledge—there have not been follow-up reviews or a meta-analysis of this literature, no further conclusions have been drawn since publication of a systematic review on self–other agreement on personality disorder by Klonsky et al. (2002).

Further, a paradigm shift is underway in personality disorder classification (Clark, 2007; Krueger, Derringer, Markon, Watson, & Skodol, 2012; Widiger & Trull, 2007). Dimensional measures and models of personality disorder traits are now being used more often to investigate self–other agreement, which may influence conclusions about self–other agreement on personality disorder. Dimensional measures and models of personality disorder view personality disorders as collections of maladaptive personality traits that are measured on scales from low to high, rather than criteria (i.e., symptoms or traits) that are categorically rated as being present or absent.

In this chapter, we discuss factors related to self–other agreement on personality disorder traits, review research findings, and provide three meta-analyses on this topic in hopes of better understanding the extent of self–other agreement on personality disorder. We provide meta-analyses for (1) overall median self–other agreement correlations on personality disorder traits across multiple conceptualizations of personality disorder, (2) self–other agreement correlations on traits from specific DSM personality disorder categories (i.e., the more traditional way of classifying personality disorder), and (3) self–other agreement correlations on maladaptive personality trait domains from the dimensional Criterion B of the DSM-5 Section-III alternative model of personality disorders (AMPD; APA, 2013)—that can be understood as maladaptive extensions of the FFM trait domains.

Self–other agreement on personality disorder traits has implications for personality assessment and for the construct validity of personality disorder. Self–other agreement is usually measured in two ways: (1) Rank-order stability agreement, which is the correlation between self- and informant reports of the same trait and indicates an individual's rank on a personality disorder trait compared to other people in the sample, and (2) Mean-level agreement, which is the correspondence of mean-levels of the same personality disorder trait and indicates how the mean-level of a personality disorder trait self-reported by a sample of targets compares to the mean-level reported for those targets by informants. Agreement indicates convergent validity; that is, when both perspectives provide similar information about the same trait, we develop support for the existence of personality disorder traits. Disagreement on both forms (i.e., rank-order agreement and mean-level agreement) indicates that different information about personality disorder traits is being provided by targets compared to informants. It may raise questions about the validity of inferences regarding the presence of personality pathology. Substantial disagreement leads to important questions: (1) are the reports valid? and (2) which source is more accurate in their description of targets' levels of the respective trait? Importantly, levels of self–other agreement on personality disorder traits are not necessarily proxy measures of accuracy. For example, it is possible that one source may be more accurate than the other, which would decrease self–other agreement, but not the accuracy of the more accurate source (it is also possible that both reports are inaccurate—and either agree or disagree with each other).

Self–other agreement on personality disorder traits may depend on any of several important factors such as type of informant (e.g., spouses, close others, clinicians, or classmates), length and quality of the relationship, target age, target gender, sample type, assessment method, specific instrument, reliability of ratings from each source, and differential item functioning on measurement instruments across perspectives (see Section II on moderators of accuracy in this handbook). Theories on the judgment of more adaptive personality traits have posited that the type of relationship between a target and an informant can affect the shared observable information that there is available to agree on (Funder, 1995). For example, spouses and clinicians may have more information about less observable characteristics such as the target's tendency to experience negative emotion, while classmates and friends may have more accessible information about more observable characteristics such as talkativeness and gregariousness (Funder, 1995; Vazire, 2010). Spouses may also be less apprehensive than friends, classmates, or other family members to report on evaluative traits such as conscientiousness and agreeableness because of their closeness to the target. Target age may influence self–other agreement as a result of personality maturation; that is, as personality matures—and becomes more stable—self–other agreement may increase (Rohrer, Egloff, Kosinski, Stillwell, & Schmukle, 2018).

Adaptive dimensional models of personality, such as the FFM, have been shown to capture personality disorder traits (e.g., Samuel & Widiger, 2008). Haigler and Widiger (2001) showed that simply by altering the NEO-Personality Inventory-Revised (Costa & McCrae, 1992) items, correlations between the NEO-PI-R openness, agreeableness, and conscientiousness scales and personality disorder increased. For example, the correlations between the NEO-PI-R conscientiousness domain and three measures of obsessive-compulsive personality disorder were small, but the correlations between NEO-PI-R conscientiousness items that were experimentally altered to include maladaptivity (e.g., changing the item "I keep my belongings neat and clean" to "I keep my belongings excessively neat and clean") and three measures of obsessive-compulsive personality disorder were large (Haigler & Widiger, 2001). Miller (2012) has demonstrated that simply adding together the facets of the NEO-PI-R deemed characteristic of certain personality disorders—by expert researchers and clinicians (Lynam & Widiger, 2001; Samuel & Widiger, 2004)—creates personality disorder scores that correlate as highly with personality disorder measures as personality disorder measures correlate with each other (Trull, Widiger, Lynam, & Costa, 2003). Indeed, FFM personality disorder (FFMPD) measures have been developed for most of the DSM personality disorders (e.g., Widiger et al., 2017; Widiger, Lynam, Miller, & Oltmanns, 2012). It should be noted, however, that FFMPD scales can and should be used in any combination across FFMPD measures (e.g., for clinical assessment or research on maladaptive low agreeableness, maladaptive low agreeableness scales from FFMPD borderline, narcissistic, and/or antisocial personality disorders can be used in combination).

It is likely that theories of accuracy from adaptive personality models would extend to the judgment of maladaptive personality traits. Agreement studies on maladaptive traits often find that disinhibition (i.e.,

maladaptive low conscientiousness), detachment (i.e., maladaptive low extraversion), and exhibitionism (e.g., maladaptive high extraversion traits) have the highest self–other agreement (Jopp & South, 2015; Keulen et al., 2011; Markon et al., 2013; Oltmanns, Crego, & Widiger, 2018; Ready & Clark, 2002; Samuel, Suzuki, Bucher, & Griffin, 2018). This finding is consistent with studies on adaptive trait models showing higher self–other agreement on conscientiousness and extraversion (Connelly & Ones, 2010). There are exceptions, however, in which relatively higher agreement has been found on antagonistic traits (i.e., maladaptive low agreeableness), compared to other maladaptive trait domains—a pattern that would not be expected based on accuracy theories of normal range traits (Kelley et al., 2018; Sleep, Lamkin, Lynam, Campbell, & Miller, 2019). These mixed findings indicate that a meta-analysis of the growing literature would be useful.

Self–other agreement is undoubtedly affected by measurement considerations. For example, (1) The assessment method (e.g., interview or questionnaire) should be considered in self–other agreement on personality disorder traits. Clinical interviews are often used to collect information on personality disorder traits from patients and informants (Klonsky et al., 2002). Method effects unique to certain instruments may influence self–other agreement. Further, different specific instruments using the same method may even have different levels of agreement (e.g., one self-report questionnaire may demonstrate higher self–other agreement than another self-report questionnaire). (2) Reliability can also affect self–other agreement. For example, low internal consistency of the items on a test scale limits the maximum correlation that would be possible between two scores (i.e., attenuation; Furr & Bacharach, 2008). Interestingly, informant-ratings often demonstrate higher internal consistency than self-ratings (Balsis, Cooper, & Oltmanns, 2015). (3) Differential item functioning across perspectives in the assessment of personality disorder traits may also be important (Balsis, Loehle-Conger, Busch, Ungredda, & Oltmanns, 2017; Cooper, Balsis, & Oltmanns, 2012). Informant-reports of personality disorder traits have demonstrated differential item functioning, in that informants may indicate the presence of pathological traits at lower levels than self-reports (i.e., to "agree" on a maladaptive personality trait question might reflect the presence of more significant pathology in a target when it is reported by an informant than when it is reported by the target; Balsis et al., 2017). If this finding is replicated, it could have ramifications for understanding mean-level self–other agreement on personality disorder traits—because mean-levels on the same scales would have different meanings between self- and informant-reports.

A practical implication of low self–other agreement is that one source may be more valid for the prediction of important criteria. Self-reports of personality disorder traits have been shown to predict behavior and consequential life outcomes (Dixon-Gordon, Whalen, Layden, & Chapman, 2015; Powers & Oltmanns, 2012). Likewise, informant-reports of personality disorder traits have been shown to predict behavior and important outcomes (Kaurin et al., 2018; Klein, 2003; Fiedler, Oltmanns, & Turkheimer, 2004). Neither source is necessarily more valid than the other. Incremental validity analyses have even demonstrated that—for some purposes and under certain conditions—informant-reports of personality disorder traits predict behavior and consequential outcomes over and above self-reports (Cruitt & Oltmanns, 2018; Galione & Oltmanns, 2013; Ready, Watson, & Clark, 2002). For example, informant-reports of personality disorder traits are predictive of targets' dismissal from the military (Fiedler et al., 2004), neutral-observer behavioral ratings (Kaurin et al., 2018), and social adjustment (Klein, 2003) over and above self-reports. These findings are important because they may have implications for clinical assessment, treatment, and the ultimate prevention of health problems. For example, if a clinician is interested in the risk of a certain life outcome given a certain personality trait, the clinician may defer to an informant-report of that trait rather than a self-report.

Self–other agreement on personality disorder also depends on the way that personality disorder is classified. Personality disorders are currently defined in the DSM-5 Section II as categorical types. Many people in the lay public have heard of borderline, paranoid, and narcissistic personality disorders. This traditional conceptualization, however, is plagued with problems—the largest being that personalities do not fall into personality types (or categories). Personality disorders can be understood similarly to normal personality—as dimensions, or constellations of traits.

21st-Century Shift in the Conceptualization and Classification of Personality Disorder

The release of explicit criteria sets for categorical personality disorders in the DSM-III (APA, 1980) was a significant development in the clinical and empirical classification of personality disorders. For example, instead of short descriptions for different types of personality disorder, personality disorders now contained detailed lists of specific criteria, or symptom sets. If a person were to present with a certain number of the criteria (e.g., at least five of nine symptoms listed for borderline personality disorder), they could be diagnosed with the personality disorder. This system represented a huge improvement because clinicians across the United States could now refer to the same criteria while diagnosing personality disorders. Unfortunately, the criteria for each personality disorder were still largely developed on the basis of clinical experience and anecdotal evidence (Widiger & Clark, 2000). This unscientific method that was used for the development of the criteria sets has proven problematic because of (1) the arbitrary cutoff thresholds (e.g., people with four symptoms likely have impairment levels similar to those with five symptoms, but may not meet the threshold for a personality disorder diagnosis), (2) high rates of co-occurrence across the categorical personality disorder types (e.g., borderline and dependent, and many other combinations are often present within the same person), and (3) heterogeneity within disorders (e.g., people with the same personality disorder diagnosis may have almost entirely different symptoms; Clark, 2007; Widiger & Trull, 2007).

Research over the past few decades has demonstrated that the facets and domains of the FFM can be extended to capture DSM personality disorders (Lynam & Widiger, 2001; Samuel & Widiger, 2008). Further, new measures that assess maladaptive variants of the FFM facets can be used to better capture personality disorder traits (Widiger et al., 2017). This evidence suggests that personality disorders can be conceptualized as "constellations" of maladaptive variants of personality traits from the FFM (Lynam & Widiger, 2001). Subsequent research has demonstrated that the FFM can address problems related to the traditional DSM categorical approach to the diagnosis of personality disorders. For example, there are no arbitrary diagnostic cutoffs, no "types" of personality disorder, and fewer co-occurrences and heterogeneity within types. There are only constellations of maladaptive traits. The FFM was developed based on the "lexical hypothesis," which postulates that the importance of personality trait terms is based on their level of representation in the language: More important traits presumably have more synonym terms (Allport, 1937; Goldberg, 1993). Thus, the FFM not only helps resolve problems of heterogeneity and unreliable categories/types—it rests on a firm scientific base.[2]

Section-III of the DSM-5 includes an alternative dimensional model of personality disorder (the AMPD). It was designed to be a replacement for the traditional DSM categorical model, and it resembles closely many of the features of an FFM approach to personality disorder. The AMPD model includes Criterion A, which describes problematic self and interpersonal functioning, and Criterion B, which includes a five-domain maladaptive trait model. The AMPD states, "these five broad domains are maladaptive variants of the five domains of the extensively validated and replicated personality model known as the 'Big Five' or Five Factor Model of personality (FFM)" (APA, 2013, p. 773). Underneath the five broad domains are listed 25 more specific facets of maladaptive personality that can be understood as maladaptive variants of FFM traits (see Krueger et al., 2012, for a review; and Crego, Oltmanns, & Widiger, 2018). This model is a promising leap for personality disorder classification, but its official adoption was rejected by the APA Board of Trustees (Widiger, 2013). Although it currently appears in the DSM-5 Section III entitled "Emerging Measures and Models," it is generating considerable interest among researchers and clinicians (Al-Dajani, Gralnick, & Bagby, 2016). The upcoming release of the World Health Organization's (WHO) *International Classification of Diseases, 11th edition* (ICD-11; WHO, 2018) has proposed a similar dimensional trait model of personality disorder—including (1) a general level of personality disorder severity and (2) five maladaptive trait domains (Tyrer, Mulder, Kim, & Crawford, 2019). The DSM-5 AMPD was an important step toward the official adoption of a dimensional model of personality disorder. The adoption of an official dimensional personality disorder trait model in the ICD-11 is an even more important step, because the ICD is the authoritative mental disorder diagnostic system for 194 WHO member countries around the world (Oltmanns & Widiger, 2018)—the DSM is the system for mental disorder diagnosis only in the United States. The adoption of a dimensional personality disorder model in ICD-11 would indicate that, moving forward, personality disorder will be classified dimensionally using maladaptive trait domains in the DSM and in the ICD.

Self–Other Agreement on Personality Disorder: A Brief Literature Review

More than 50 studies have been published regarding self–other agreement on the presence of person-

ality disorder traits and symptoms. There are important distinctions in methodology among these studies, and their results vary in important ways (as discussed previously). We review influential findings in the following sections.

Rank-Order Agreement

Our compilation of over 50 studies of self–other agreement on personality disorder reported a range of rank-order correlation sizes from $r = 0.12$ to $r = 0.90$, with a median of $r = 0.35$ (see Table 18.1). There are college, clinical, and community samples presenting a range of effect sizes from small (e.g., Tackett et al., 2013; Yalch & Hopwood, 2017 Zimmerman et al., 1988) to large (e.g., Coolidge et al., 1995; Few et al., 2013; Kelley et al., 2018; Miller et al., 2011). Likewise, there are studies with clinicians, classmates, partners, close others, and parents serving as informants that present both small (Ferro & Klein, 1997; Hill et al., 2000; McKeeman & Erickson, 1997; Samuel et al., 2014; Tackett et al., 2013) and large effect sizes (Coolidge et al., 1995; Few et al., 2013; Kelley et al., 2018; Peselow, Sanfilipo, Fieve, & Gulbenkian, 1994; Tromp & Koot, 2010). A similar pattern is found when considering differences in effect sizes for studies with similar target age and gender, length of acquaintance, method of assessment, and assessment instrument. Sample size does not appear to influence the magnitude of the correlation. The variability in these findings and in the methodologies used might reflect the lack of controlled systematic research on this topic. The findings indicate the need for more careful studies controlling for several of these variables while examining the effects more specifically. The only firm conclusion that can be drawn to date is that, based on a number of factors, agreement appears variable. Interestingly, the presence of personality disorder in target persons has been shown to reduce agreement on FFM personality traits (Furr, Dougherty, Marsh, & Mathias, 2007).

Mean-Level Agreement

Mean-level agreement is also important in the consideration of self–other agreement, but it has been studied less frequently than rank-order agreement. Studies that have compared mean self-reported levels of personality disorder traits to mean informant-reported levels of personality disorder traits have produced inconsistent findings. In terms of the DSM personality disorders, many studies with clinical samples have reported similar diagnostic rates between self and informant-reports—indicating self–other agreement on diagnosis (Bernstein

Table 18.1 Studies Included in Meta-Analysis

Author(s)	Year	Median r	N	Sample Type	Target Age (M)	Target% Female	Informant Type	Assessment Method
Bernstein et al.	1997	0.47	62	clinical	40.6	10	close others	interview
Bottesi et al.	2018	0.40	80	community	31.5	80	close others	questionnaire
Bradley et al.	2007	0.33	54	clinical	30.0	57	clinician	questionnaire
Caspi et al.	2001	0.49	67	community	33.0	0	partners	interview
Clifton et al.	2004	0.15	2013	military	20.0	38	training groups	questionnaire
Coolidge et al. 1	1995	0.51	52	college	35.9	50	spouses	questionnaire
Coolidge et al. 2	1995	0.36	52	college	35.9	50	friends	questionnaire
Decuyper et al. 1	2014	0.36	197	community	18.2	72	mothers	questionnaire
Decuyper et al. 2	2014	0.35	197	community	18.2	72	mothers	questionnaire
Dowson	1992	0.38	60	clinical	34.1	77	close others	questionnaire
Dreessen et al.	1998	0.31	42	clinical	33.4	46	close others	interview
Ferro & Klein	1997	0.18	224	mixed	32.2	74	close others	interview
Few et al.	2013	0.63	109	clinical	35.9	71	clinicians	questionnaire
Fowler & Lilienfeld	2007	0.32	60	college	18.9	75	close others	questionnaire
Hill et al.	2000	0.18	56	clinical	41.0	52	couples	interview
Jopp & South	2015	0.34	48	couples	25.7	100	couples	questionnaire
Jopp & South	2015	0.45	48	couples	26.6	0	couples	questionnaire
Kaurin et al. 1	2018	0.43	256	college	19.8	51	close others	questionnaire
Kaurin et al. 2	2018	0.23	256	college	19.8	51	close others	questionnaire
Kelley et al.	2018	0.52	87	college	18.9	64	roommates	questionnaire
Keulen et al. 1	2011	0.27	24	forensic	37.6	0	clinicians	questionnaire
Keulen et al. 2	2011	0.20	24	forensic	37.6	0	clinicians	questionnaire
Lawton et al.	2011	0.46	760	community	59.5	55	close others	questionnaire
Lukowitsky & Pincus	2013	0.15	437	college	21.2	41	classmates	questionnaire
Markon et al. 1	2013	0.48	40	community	N/A	48	close others	questionnaire
Markon et al. 2	2013	0.30	221	community	41.7	45	close others	questionnaire
McKeeman & Erickson	1997	0.27	75	college	21.2	100	roommates	questionnaire
Miller et al. 1	2004	0.47	69	clinical	36.1	58	close others	questionnaire
Miller et al. 2	2005	0.51	69	clinical	36.1	58	close others	interview
Miller et al. 3	2011	0.67	32	community	38.8	53	close others	questionnaire
Oltmanns & Turkheimer	2006	0.23	1686	college	18.5	67	hallmates	questionnaire
Oltmanns et al. 1	2014	0.23	1437	community	59.6	55	close others	questionnaire
Oltmanns et al. 2	2018	0.35	137	college	19.0	65	close others	questionnaire
Ouimette et al.	1995	0.35	63	college	19.4	60	close others	questionnaire

Author(s)	Year	Median r	N	Sample Type	Target Age (M)	Target% Female	Informant Type	Assessment Method
Peselow et al. 1	1994	0.90	58	clinical	42.4	52	close others	interview
Peselow et al. 2	1994	0.73	58	clinical	42.4	52	close others	interview
Ready & Clark	2002	0.37	90	clinical	35.0	81	close others	questionnaire
Ready et al.	2000	0.44	189	college	19.7	64	friends	questionnaire
Riso et al.	1994	0.36	105	clinical	31.9	74	close others	interview
Samuel et al. 1	2013	0.35	320	clinical	32.9	62	clinicians	mixed
Samuel et al. 2	2013	0.22	320	clinical	32.9	62	clinicians	questionnaire
Samuel et al. 3	2014	0.12	130	clinical	37.4	31	clinicians	questionnaire
Samuel et al. 4	2014	0.15	130	clinical	37.4	31	clinicians	mixed
Samuel et al. 5	2018	0.41	54	clinical	39.8	52	clinicians	questionnaire
Schuppert et al.	2012	0.35	122	clinical	15.9	95	parents	questionnaire
Sleep et al.	2019	0.37	197	community	26.9	60	close others	questionnaire
South et al.	2011	0.36	82	community	32.0	100	partners	questionnaire
South et al.	2011	0.39	82	community	34.0	0	partners	questionnaire
Tackett et al.	2013	0.25	489	community	14.3	54	parents	questionnaire
Tromp & Koot	2010	0.47	110	clinical	15.6	65	parents	questionnaire
Tyrer et al.	1979	0.12	15	clinical	N/A	N/A	clinicians	interview
Yalch & Hopwood	2017	0.22	101	college	20.0	76	close others	questionnaire
Zimmerman et al.	1988	0.28	66	clinical	37.0	65	close others	interview

Note. Numbered studies have more than one effect size based on different sample or informant types.

JOSHUA R. OLTMANNS AND THOMAS F. OLTMANNS

et al., 1997; Case et al., 2007; Dreessen et al., 1998; Walters, Moran, Choudhury, Lee, & Mann, 2004). However, several studies have found significant mean-level differences where informants report significantly more narcissistic and borderline personality pathology than is found in the self-reports (Keulen et al., 2011; Miller et al., 2005; Modestin & Puhan, 2000; Riso et al., 1994; Schuppert et al., 2012). Several studies have found mean-level self-reports of avoidant and obsessive-compulsive personality pathology to be significantly higher than informant-reports (Clifton, Turkheimer, & Oltmanns, 2005; Miller et al., 2005; Modestin & Puhan, 2000; South, Oltmanns, Johnson, & Turkheimer, 2011).

Regarding maladaptive traits, Samuel et al. (2018) found that clients generally rated themselves higher on maladaptive personality traits than their therapists rated them, particularly with regard to traits in the domain of psychoticism, which largely composes traits of schizotypal personality disorder. The effect was so large that it might reflect a misunderstanding of the psychoticism items on the part of the clients. Indeed, the PID-5 psychoticism items include delusions that are characteristic of schizophrenia—not schizotypal personality traits (see Crego & Widiger, 2017, for an in-depth discussion of this issue). Other studies have failed to find mean-level differences between self- and informant-reported levels of maladaptive personality traits (Fowler & Lilienfeld, 2007). South and colleagues (Jopp & South, 2015; South et al., 2011) have found that, within romantic couples, partners tend to attribute more pathological traits to themselves than to their partners. Overall, studies using dimensional maladaptive trait perspectives have found that self-reports show higher mean-levels than informant-reports, with discrepancies between studies. Several single studies have found higher mean-levels of maladaptive traits from the informant-perspective, but, to our knowledge, these specific findings have not yet been replicated: In single studies, informant-reports have been significantly higher on negative temperament and disinhibition (Keulen et al., 2011), psychopathy (on one out of three measures; Miller et al., 2011), and rejection (Tromp & Koot, 2010).

Future research studies should include mean-level comparisons, which can be useful for identifying which source reports more personality pathology and for identifying the variables that may be responsible for mean-level differences. However, as mentioned previously, mean self- and informant-report ratings on maladaptive traits may not be equivalent. For example, on a scale from 1 to 5 (with "5" being the most maladaptive response), a "3" rating from the informant-report might be just as maladaptive as a "4" rating from the self-report. This would be evidence that informants report maladaptive personality at lower levels (Balsis and colleagues have demonstrated this; Balsis et al., 2017). This may directly reduce mean-level agreement between self- and informant-reports. In this case, mean-level comparisons between self- and informant-reports may not be particularly useful—because the self and informants complete items differently. Alternative methods may have to be used in order to meaningfully compare mean-level self–other agreement.

Meta-Analyses

The surge of studies on self–other agreement for personality disorder traits and the inconsistencies in the literature indicate that new meta-analyses would be useful. Klonsky et al. (2002) reviewed 17 studies and concluded that agreement was "modest at best" (p. 300). Klonsky and colleagues examined agreement on categorical personality disorder diagnoses using the kappa statistic and found unequivocally low self–other agreement. The low kappa statistics might reflect problems associated with the categorical personality disorder classification (i.e., it is harder for self and informant to agree when an arbitrary threshold must be met to contribute to the agreement statistic). In the present analyses, we focused on rank-order correlations between continuous measures of either DSM-type personality disorder symptoms or maladaptive personality traits, which are probably more accurate measures of self–other agreement because they are not categorical. Since Klonsky's systematic review, more than 30 studies have been conducted on self–other agreement for personality disorders. Studies were selected for the present meta-analysis if they presented original empirical data in which self–other agreement was quantified by comparing scores on self- and informant-report personality disorder instruments using correlations of ordinal test scores. An additional literature search on PsychINFO was conducted using all combinations of the search terms from each of the three following groups with all terms from the other groups: (1) "personality disorder," "maladaptive personality," and "personality pathology"; (2) "agreement," "correspondence," "convergence," and "correlation"; and (3) "informant," "observer," "other," and "spouse." The search was conducted on studies published through August 2018.

Meta-analyses were conducted on 53 studies of self–other agreement on personality disorder symptoms and traits (including several qualifying studies that were included in the Klonsky review; see Table 1). We present three meta-analyses: (1) a meta-analysis of overall self–other agreement on personality disorder as measured by DSM symptoms and dimensional maladaptive traits, (2) a meta-analysis of self–other agreement on traditional DSM personality disorder symptoms, and 3) a meta-analysis of self–other agreement on maladaptive personality disorder traits from the perspective of emerging dimensional models of personality disorder (i.e., the PID-5). The analyses were conducted in R statistical software (R Core Team, 2013) using the robumeta (Fisher & Tipton, 2015) and metafor (Viechtbauer, 2010) packages. Random-effects models were fit using a restricted maximum-likelihood estimator. The data file compiled from the studies and R syntax are available online at: https://osf.io/gd6tc/.

Overall Meta-Analysis of Self–Other Agreement on Personality Disorder

All 53 studies were used in the first meta-analysis examining the overall median correlation of self–other agreement on personality disorder features (symptoms/traits). The degree of heterogeneity was significant (τ^2 = 0.0320, SE = 0.0084, 95% CI [.0202, 0.0605]), indicating that there were significant differences in the study effect sizes. I^2 was 86.87% (95% CI [80.64, 92.58]), indicating that 86.87% of the variation in effect sizes was reflective of actual differences in the population mean. The Q statistic (Q = 298.3725) had 52 degrees of freedom and was statistically significant ($p < 0.0001$), indicating that the studies did not share a common effect size. The estimated model coefficient (i.e., summary effect size) was r = 0.37, 95% CI [.32, 0.42]). A forest plot of all studies is presented in Figure 18.1.

A set of diagnostic tests derived from standard regression that is used to identify outliers (studies with large effects on overall study heterogeneity) is included in the metafor package (Viechtbauer & Cheung, 2010). One study (Peselow et al., 1994; pretreatment group, median r = 0.90) fulfilled criteria as an influential study (Q = 221.6024; see Figure 18.2). These tests indicate that Peselow et al.'s study showed a significantly higher level of self–other agreement than the other studies. A funnel plot was created (see Figure 18.3) and Egger's regression and rank correlation tests were completed to check for publication bias (Quintana, 2015). The regression test for funnel plot asymmetry was statis-

tically significant at z = 2.4491, p = 0.0143, but the rank correlation test was not significant (Kendall's τ = 0.144, p = 0.1286), suggesting some presence of publication bias. However, heterogeneity can occur for several reasons, including heterogeneity in the methodology of the studies included in the meta-analysis (Sterne et al., 2011), which was indeed present in this case. Further, studies on self–other agreement on personality disorder traits often include tests of many traits at the same time, some of which may be significant and others not. As a result, the evidence for publication bias is unclear.

Moderator analyses were completed to check for the influence of several variables that were presented in all studies on the heterogeneity of findings across studies. Target age and target gender did not moderate the overall effect size ($QM[1]$ = 2.52, p = 0.1123 and $QM[1]$ = 0.00, p = 0.9706, respectively), nor did dummy-coded sample type variables (community ($QM[1]$ = 0.12, p = 0.7289), clinical ($QM[1]$ = 2.14, p = 0.1433), college ($QM[1]$ = 0.72, p = 0.3961), or informant relationship variables (parent ($QM[1]$ = 0.05, p = 0.8262), partner ($QM[1]$ = 0.11, p = 0.7342), or clinician ($QM[1]$ = 1.45, p = 0.2283)). There is some evidence that use of assessment interviews ($QM[1]$ = 4.04, p = 0.0445) moderated the relationship—the use of questionnaires did not ($QM[1]$ = 1.81, p = 0.1787).

Meta-Analysis of Self–Other Agreement on Symptoms from Specific DSM Personality Disorder Types

The number of studies used in meta-analyses for median self–other correlations on each of the ten specific DSM personality disorders ranged from 20 (schizoid) to 27 (borderline), with a median of 23.5. The degrees of heterogeneity were significant, ranging from τ^2 = 0.0569 (SE = 0.0216; schizoid) to τ^2 = 0.136 (SE = 0.0466; narcissistic), with a median of τ^2 = 0.0817. I^2 ranged from 94.14% (borderline) to 97.72% (narcissistic), with a median of 96.10%, indicating the percentages of variation in effect sizes was reflective of actual differences in the population means. The Q statistic ranged from Q = 223.1648 (schizotypal) to Q = 332.5484 (obsessive-compulsive), with a median of Q = 267.7654. The Q statistics were all significant ($p < 0.0001$), indicating that the studies displayed a significant amount of heterogeneity (i.e., did not share a common effect size).

To account for multiple effect sizes that were compiled from individual studies using the same sample (i.e., dependency in the data), robust variance estimation (RVE; Hedges, Tipton, & Johnson, 2010)

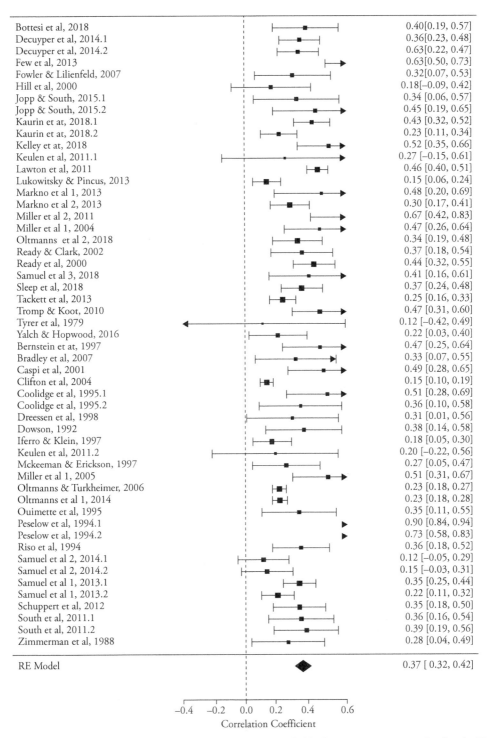

Bottesi et al, 2018		0.40 [0.19, 0.57]
Decuyper et al, 2014.1		0.36 [0.23, 0.48]
Decuyper et al, 2014.2		0.63 [0.22, 0.47]
Few et al, 2013		0.63 [0.50, 0.73]
Fowler & Lilienfeld, 2007		0.32 [0.07, 0.53]
Hill et al, 2000		0.18 [−0.09, 0.42]
Jopp & South, 2015.1		0.34 [0.06, 0.57]
Jopp & South, 2015.2		0.45 [0.19, 0.65]
Kaurin et at, 2018.1		0.43 [0.32, 0.52]
Kaurin et at, 2018.2		0.23 [0.11, 0.34]
Kelley et at, 2018		0.52 [0.35, 0.66]
Keulen et al, 2011.1		0.27 [−0.15, 0.61]
Lawton et al, 2011		0.46 [0.40, 0.51]
Lukowitsky & Pincus, 2013		0.15 [0.06, 0.24]
Markno et al 1, 2013		0.48 [0.20, 0.69]
Markno et al 2, 2013		0.30 [0.17, 0.41]
Miller et al 2, 2011		0.67 [0.42, 0.83]
Miller et al 1, 2004		0.47 [0.26, 0.64]
Oltmanns et al 2, 2018		0.34 [0.19, 0.48]
Ready & Clark, 2002		0.37 [0.18, 0.54]
Ready et al, 2000		0.44 [0.32, 0.55]
Samuel et al 3, 2018		0.41 [0.16, 0.61]
Sleep et al, 2018		0.37 [0.24, 0.48]
Tackett et al, 2013		0.25 [0.16, 0.33]
Tromp & Koot, 2010		0.47 [0.31, 0.60]
Tyrer et al, 1979		0.12 [−0.42, 0.49]
Yalch & Hopwood, 2016		0.22 [0.03, 0.40]
Bernstein et at, 1997		0.47 [0.25, 0.64]
Bradley et al, 2007		0.33 [0.07, 0.55]
Caspi et al, 2001		0.49 [0.28, 0.65]
Clifton et al, 2004		0.15 [0.10, 0.19]
Coolidge et al, 1995.1		0.51 [0.28, 0.69]
Coolidge et al, 1995.2		0.36 [0.10, 0.58]
Dreessen et al, 1998		0.31 [0.01, 0.56]
Dowson, 1992		0.38 [0.14, 0.58]
Iferro & Klein, 1997		0.18 [0.05, 0.30]
Keulen et al, 2011.2		0.20 [−0.22, 0.56]
Mckeeman & Erickson, 1997		0.27 [0.05, 0.47]
Miller et al 1, 2005		0.51 [0.31, 0.67]
Oltmanns & Turkheimer, 2006		0.23 [0.18, 0.27]
Oltmanns et al 1, 2014		0.23 [0.18, 0.28]
Ouimette et al, 1995		0.35 [0.11, 0.55]
Peselow et al, 1994.1		0.90 [0.84, 0.94]
Peselow et al, 1994.2		0.73 [0.58, 0.83]
Riso et al, 1994		0.36 [0.18, 0.52]
Samuel et al 2, 2014.1		0.12 [−0.05, 0.29]
Samuel et al 2, 2014.2		0.15 [−0.03, 0.31]
Samuel et al 1, 2013.1		0.35 [0.25, 0.44]
Samuel et al 1, 2013.2		0.22 [0.11, 0.32]
Schuppert et al, 2012		0.35 [0.18, 0.50]
South et al, 2011.1		0.36 [0.16, 0.54]
South et al, 2011.2		0.39 [0.19, 0.56]
Zimmerman et al, 1988		0.28 [0.04, 0.49]
RE Model		0.37 [0.32, 0.42]

Figure 18.1. Forest plot of overall median effect size correlations for studies of self–other agreement on personality disorder. Triangles indicate ranges less than −.40 or greater than .60. Numbers following study years denote different samples.

was used to calculate meta-analytic summary effect size coefficients. Meta-analytic summary effect size estimates are presented in Table 18.2. They ranged from 0.32 (dependent) to 0.51 (antisocial), with a median of 0.38, indicating that the average effect size

of self–other agreement on personality disorders measured continuously was moderate.

Funnel plots, Egger's regression test, and rank correlation tests were completed for each of the 10 DSM personality disorders to check for publication bias

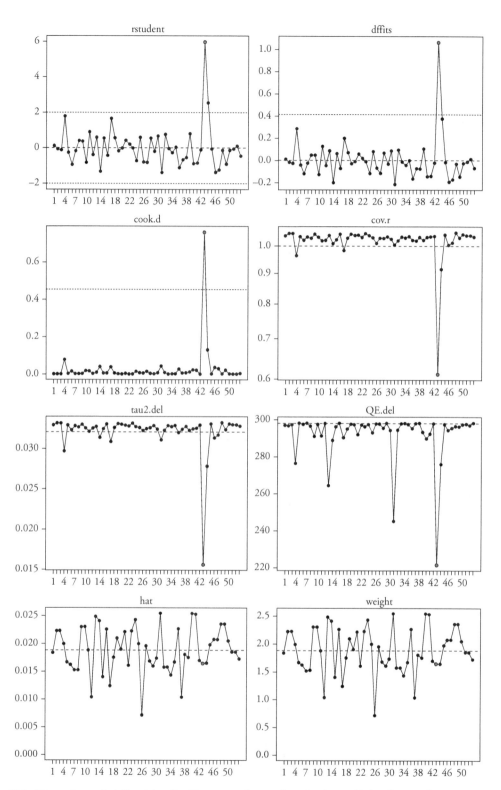

Figure 18.2. Diagnostic tests for influential studies. The one significant outlier is Peselow et al.'s (1994) reported pretreatment median rank-order agreement coefficient.

Table 18.2 Meta-Analytic Self–Other Agreement Correlation Effect Sizes

	R	SE	t	df	p	95% CI	RVE τ	k
DSM PDs								
Paranoid	0.38	0.08	4.53	17	<.001	.20, 0.56	.0389	23
Schizoid	0.42	0.07	6.20	14	<.001	.27, 0.56	.0358	20
Schizotypal	0.37	0.06	6.01	19	<.001	.24, 0.50	.0274	26
Antisocial	0.51	0.07	7.19	18	<.001	.36, 0.66	.0411	25
Borderline	0.44	0.06	7.11	20	<.001	.31, 0.56	.0300	27
Histrionic	0.43	0.10	4.48	15	<.001	.22, 0.63	.0357	21
Narcissistic	0.37	0.10	3.52	15	0.003	.15, 0.59	.0444	21
Avoidant	0.38	0.07	5.38	17	<.001	.23, 0.53	.0432	24
Dependent	0.32	0.08	4.02	15	0.001	.15, 0.49	.0390	21
Obsessive	0.37	0.08	4.80	18	<.001	.21, 0.54	.0426	26
PID-5 Domains							RVE ω	
Negative Affect	0.45	0.06	6.98	5.57	<.001	.29, 0.62	.0832	8
Detachment	0.50	0.06	8.08	5.56	<.001	.35, 0.66	.0910	8
Psychoticism	0.33	0.05	6.85	5.61	<.001	.21, 0.45	.0487	8
Antagonism	0.43	0.04	11.4	5.62	<.001	.34, 0.53	.0241	8
Disinhibition	0.53	0.06	9.06	5.61	<.001	.38, 0.67	.0214	8

Note. RVE = robust variance estimation, DSM PDs = personality disorders from the *Diagnostic and Statistical Manual of Mental Disorders*, PID = Personality Inventory for DSM-5, k = number of outcomes.

(Quintana, 2015). The regression and rank correlation tests for funnel plot asymmetry were statistically significant for borderline, histrionic, dependent, and obsessive-compulsive personality disorders. For schizotypal, the rank correlation test was significant but not the regression test, and the opposite was true for avoidant. These results similarly indicated publication bias in the literature. Similar to the overall funnel plot (Figure 18.3), the results for specific DSM personality disorder studies showed imbalance where studies appeared to be missing from the right side of the plot. This would indicate that the effect size estimates for four of the personality disorders (borderline, histrionic, dependent, obsessive-compulsive) and possibly two more (schizotypal and avoidant), are perhaps larger than the coefficients that are presented here. However, again the heterogeneity may be due to other methodological reasons besides publication bias (Sterne et al., 2011).

Meta-Analysis of Self–Other Agreement on DSM-5 Maladaptive Trait Domains (from the AMPD)

Eight studies were used in meta-analyses for median self–other correlations on each of the five the DSM-5 maladaptive trait domains. The degrees of heterogeneity were significant, ranging

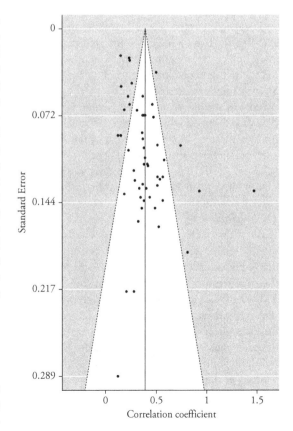

Figure 18.3. Funnel plot of all studies.

from τ^2 = 0.0027 (SE = 0.0070; antagonism) to τ^2 = 0.0254 (SE = 0.0207; detachment), with a median of τ^2 = 0.0134. I^2 statistics were 19.56% (antagonism), 47.12% (psychoticism), 54.61% (disinhibition), 67.89% (negative affect), and 69.56% (detachment), indicating the percentages of variation in effect sizes were reflective of actual differences in the population means for the domains besides antagonism. The Q statistic ranged from Q = 7.6585 (antagonism) to Q = 25.3377 (detachment), with a median of Q = 14.9629. The Q statistics were significant for negative affectivity (p = 0.0016), detachment (p = 0.0007), and disinhibition (p = 0.0365), indicating that these domains displayed a significant amount of heterogeneity (i.e., did not share a common effect size).

To account for multiple effect sizes as well as small sample sizes, robust variance estimation (RVE) was again used to calculate meta-analytic summary effect size coefficients adjusted for small samples (Tipton, 2015). Meta-analytic summary effect size estimates are presented in Table 2. They ranged from 0.33 (psychoticism) to 0.50 (detachment), with a median of 0.45, indicating that the average effect size of self–other agreement on maladaptive personality traits was moderate.

Diagnostic tests indicated that one study (Few et al., 2013; median r = 0.63, N = 109) fulfilled criteria as an influential study in the meta-analyses in each PID-5 trait domain, and that Markon et al. (2013) Study 2 fulfilled criteria as an influential study specifically in the antagonism meta-analysis (r = 0.31, N = 221). Egger's regression test and rank correlation tests were completed for each of the five maladaptive trait domains to check for publication bias (Quintana, 2015). None of the tests were significant, indicating no publication bias in the literature.

Discussion

Results from the present meta-analysis indicate that, overall, self–other agreement on personality disorder symptoms and traits is r = 0.37. Agreement on the maladaptive trait domains of the DSM-5 AMPD displayed relatively better agreement than the symptoms of the DSM-5 Section II personality disorder categories. The assessment of personality disorder traits on continua as opposed to dichotomous categories appears to improve agreement. The Klonsky et al. (2002) review's conclusions were perhaps influenced by the consistently very low kappa statistics that measure diagnostic agreement on dichotomous personality disorder categories. Only 13 studies of self–other agreement on personality dis-

order were reviewed at that point, and only 11 included correlation coefficients. In contrast, the present meta-analysis used 53 studies meeting our criteria for inclusion. Further, in the years since the Klonsky et al. review was published, dimensional models and measures have been further developed and validated that may contribute to enhanced self–other agreement on personality disorder traits.

Moderation analyses suggested that neither target age nor gender, sample type, nor target/informant relationship type moderated levels of self–other agreement. There was slight evidence that agreement was better when both target and informant were assessed by interview. The lack of significant moderator findings in general may have to do with imbalance of study methodologies—because there is such variety, for each potential moderating variable only a small number of studies have been reported. Sufficient evidence is not yet available to conclude that these variables truly do not moderate self–other agreement. We suggest that more research is needed considering each of these potential moderating variables. Self–other agreement may also depend on the number of items used to assess a specific construct. Agreement has been lower in DSM-related studies, which often rely only on one item per DSM criterion, whereas agreement on maladaptive traits from a dimensional perspective is typically based on several items per facet scale. Yalch and Hopwood (2017) found lower agreement on dimensional maladaptive traits when they were measured from both self- and informant-perspectives using only one item per trait. This is yet another area that would benefit from further research.

Agreement was higher for the antisocial, histrionic, and borderline personality disorders compared to the other DSM personality disorders. These personality disorders have historically been part of the "Cluster B" group of personality disorders that is characterized by outgoing and externalizing symptoms. According to adaptive personality models of self–other agreement, outgoing and externalizing features may be more observable to the self and others, more noticeable, and therefore more easily reportable (Funder, 1995; Vazire, 2010; see also chapter 8 by Krzyzaniak & Letzring in this handbook). Narcissistic personality disorder is also traditionally part of Cluster B, but it has displayed relatively lower agreement across a variety of relationship types (Klonsky et al., 2002; Lukowitsky & Pincus, 2013; Oltmanns, Crego, & Widiger, 2018). This could be the result of vulnerable features characterizing narcissism—such as shame, anger, and insecurity (Miller et al., 2018)—that are associated with lower self–other agreement (Oltmanns et al., 2018). On the other hand, borderline personality disorder also has internalizing features with relatively higher agreement. Perhaps the different distinctive features of borderline personality disorder, such as recklessness and rashness, are more observable and easier to rate for both the self and others compared to the vulnerable and internalizing presentation that can accompany narcissism (Pincus & Lukowitsky, 2010). The remaining DSM personality disorders displayed relatively lower agreement, with the exception of schizoid. The relatively higher agreement on schizoid features may result from the core of detachment (low extraversion) that is characteristic of schizoid personality disorder (Krueger et al., 2012; Samuel & Widiger, 2008). Maladaptive low-extraversion behavior might be more noticeable to the self and others.

In the meta-analysis of maladaptive traits, agreement was highest for detachment and disinhibition—the maladaptive low poles of extraversion and conscientiousness, respectively. This finding supports the hypothesis that agreement should be higher on traits related to extraversion and conscientiousness because they are more observable and therefore more reportable by informants (c.f. Vazire, 2010). Agreement was relatively lower on negative affectivity (the high pole of neuroticism) and antagonism (the low pole of agreeableness). This finding also aligns with the hypothesis that neuroticism and agreeableness traits are more internal, less observable, more evaluative, and therefore less agreed on by the self and others. These meta-analytic findings indicate that studies demonstrating relatively higher self–other agreement on antagonistic or negative affective traits may be the exception, rather than the rule. Psychoticism displayed the lowest self–other agreement. Samuel and colleagues (2018) have noted conspicuously lower agreement on psychoticism traits between patients and their therapists, and the results of our meta-analysis corroborate this finding.

Conclusions and Future Directions

The current meta-analysis indicates that the average level of self–other agreement on personality disorder traits is $r = 0.37$ and may be described as moderate (Cohen, 1992). Dimensional trait models of personality disorder appear to have better self–other agreement, perhaps in part because they typically include more assessment items per trait domain. There is significant variability across studies, and more careful research is obviously needed. In particular, more research is needed to identify moderators that explain the variability. Valuable information could be gained by more systematic studies including multiple age groups and multiple assessments (in addition to sources of information)—perhaps in the same studies—to examine potential moderating variables. We recommend that researchers always report, at least, the following self and informant characteristics: age, sex/gender identity, race/ethnicity, the number of informants per target, relationship type, length of acquaintance, closeness, a rating of liking, and several methodological variables: measurement type (i.e., interview, questionnaire), the specific assessment instrument (for both the target and informant), reliability information, and target and informant variable means with tests for significant mean-level differences and effect sizes. It must be noted that small changes in study design might lead to dramatic changes in self–other agreement. For example, the relationship type between the target and the informant or the specific instrument used to measure personality disorder traits might significantly influence the level of agreement. Additional research on mean-level differences in self–other agreement on personality disorder traits is also warranted. Further, research considering sensitivity (i.e., from an item response theory perspective; c.f. Balsis et al., 2017) of self- versus informant-measures of personality disorder traits would be particularly important for understanding these differences. This work will continue to shed light on factors that influence levels of self–other agreement on personality disorder traits. The results could have important implications for assessment, diagnosis, treatment, and prediction.

References

Al-Dajani, N., Gralnick, T. M., & Bagby, R. M. (2016). A psychometric review of the Personality Inventory for DSM–5 (PID–5): Current status and future directions. *Journal of Personality Assessment, 98*, 62–81. doi: 10.1080/00223891.2015.1107572

Allport, G. W. (1937). *Personality: A psychological interpretation.* New York: Holt, Rinehart & Winston.

American Psychiatric Association. (1980). *Diagnostic and statistical manual of mental disorders* (3rd ed.). Washington, DC: Author.

American Psychiatric Association. (2013). *Diagnostic and statistical manual of mental disorders* (5th ed.). Washington, DC: Author.

Balsis, S., Cooper, L. D., & Oltmanns, T. F. (2015). Are informant reports of personality more internally consistent than self reports of personality? *Assessment, 22*, 399–404. doi: 10.1177/1073191114556100

Balsis, S., Loehle-Conger, E., Busch, A. J., Ungredda, T., & Oltmanns, T. F. (2017). Self and informant report across the borderline personality disorder spectrum. *Personality Disorders: Theory, Research, and Treatment, 9*, 429–436. doi: 10.1037/per0000259

Bernstein, D. P., Kasapis, C., Bergman, A., Weld, E., Mitropoulou, V., Horvath, T., ... Siever, L. J. (1997). Assessing Axis II disorders by informant interview. *Journal of Personality Disorders, 11*, 158–167. doi: 10.1521/pedi.1997.11.2.158

Boudreaux, M. J. (2016). Personality-related problems and the five-factor model of personality. *Personality Disorders: Theory, Research, and Treatment, 7*, 372–383. doi: 10.1037/t62931-000

Bradley, R., Hilsenroth, M., Guarnaccia, C., & Westen, D. (2007). Relationship between clinician assessment and self-assessment of personality disorders using the SWAP-200 and PAI. *Psychological Assessment, 19*, 225–229. doi: 10.1037/1040-3590.19.2.225

Campbell, D. T., & Fiske, D. W. (1959). Convergent and discriminant validation by the multitrait-multimethod matrix. *Psychological Bulletin, 56*, 81–105. doi: 10.1037/h0046016

Case, B. G., Biel, M. G., Peselow, E. D., & Guardino, M. (2007). Reliability of personality disorder diagnosis during depression: The contribution of collateral informant reports. *Acta Psychiatrica Scandinavica, 115*, 487–491. doi: 10.1111/j.1600-0447.2007.00995.x.

Caspi, A., Taylor, A., Smart, M., Jackson, J., Tagami, S., & Moffitt, T. E. (2001). Can women provide reliable information about their children's fathers? Cross-informant agreement about men's lifetime antisocial behaviour. *Journal of Child Psychology and Psychiatry and Allied Disciplines, 42*, 915–920. doi: 10.1017/S0021963001007636.

Clark, L. A. (2007). Assessment and diagnosis of personality disorder: Perennial issues and an emerging reconceptualization. *Annual Review of Psychology, 58*, 227–257. doi: 10.1146/annurev.psych.57.102904.190200

Clifton, A., Turkheimer, E., & Oltmanns, T. F. (2005). Self-and peer perspectives on pathological personality traits and interpersonal problems. *Psychological Assessment, 17*, 123–131. doi: 10.1037/1040-3590.17.2.123.

Clifton, A., Turkheimer, E., & Oltmanns, T. F. (2004). Contrasting perspectives on personality problems: Descriptions from the self and others. *Personality and Individual Differences, 36*, 1499–1514. doi: 10.1016/j.paid.2003.06.002.

Cohen, J. (1992). A power primer. *Psychological Bulletin, 112*, 155–159. https://psycnet.apa.org/doi/10.1037/0033-2909.112.1.155.

Connelly, B. S., & Ones, D. S. (2010). An other perspective on personality: Meta-analytic integration of observers' accuracy and predictive validity. *Psychological Bulletin, 136*, 1092–1122. doi: 10.1037/a0021212.

Coolidge, F. L., Burns, E. M., & Mooney, J. A. (1995). Reliability of observer ratings in the assessment of personality disorders: A preliminary study. *Journal of Clinical Psychology, 51*, 22–28. doi: 10.1002/1097-4679(199501)51:1<22::AID-JCLP2270510105>3.0.CO;2-9.

Cooper, L. D., Balsis, S., & Oltmanns, T. F. (2012). Self-and informant-reported perspectives on symptoms of narcissistic personality disorder. *Personality Disorders: Theory, Research, and Treatment, 3*, 140–154. doi: 10.1037/a0026576.

Costa, P. T., & McCrae, R. R. (1992). *Revised NEO Personality Inventory (NEO PI-R) and NEO Five-Factor Inventory (NEO-FFI) professional manual*. Odessa, FL: Psychological Assessment Resources.

Costa, P. T., & McCrae, R. R. (1988). Personality in adulthood: A six-year longitudinal study of self-reports and spouse ratings on the NEO Personality Inventory. *Journal of Personality and Social Psychology, 54*, 853–863. doi: 10.1037/0022-3514.54.5.853.

Crego, C., Oltmanns, J. R., & Widiger, T. A. (2018). FFMPD scales: Comparisons with the FFM, PID-5, and CAT-PD-SF. *Psychological Assessment, 30*, 62–73. doi: 10.1037/pas0000495.

Crego, C., & Widiger, T. A. (2017). The conceptualization and assessment of schizotypal traits: A comparison of the FFSI and PID-5. *Journal of Personality Disorders, 31*, 606–623. doi: 10.1521/pedi_2016_30_270.

Cruitt, P. J., & Oltmanns, T. F. (2018). Incremental validity of self- and informant-report of personality disorders in later life. *Assessment, 25*, 324–335. doi: 10.1177/1073191117706020.

Decuyper, M., De Caluwé, E., De Clercq, B., & De Fruyt, F. (2014). Callous-unemotional traits in youth from a DSM-5 trait perspective. *Journal of Personality Disorders, 28*, 334–357. doi: 10.1521/pedi_2013_27_120.

Dixon-Gordon, K. L., Whalen, D. J., Layden, B. K., & Chapman, A. L. (2015). A systematic review of personality disorders and health outcomes. *Canadian Psychology/Psychologie Canadienne, 56*, 168–190. doi: 10.1037/cap0000024.

Dowson, J. H. (1992). Assessment of DSM–III–R personality disorders by self-report questionnaire: The role of informants and a screening test for co-morbid personality disorders (STCPD). *British Journal of Psychiatry, 161*, 344–352. doi: 10.1192/bjp.161.3.344.

Dreessen, L., Hildebrand, M., & Arntz, A. (1998). Patient-informant concordance on the Structured Clinical Interview for DSM-III-R personality disorders (SCID-II). *Journal of Personality Disorders, 12*, 149–161. doi: 10.1521/pedi.1998.12.2.149.

Ferro, T., & Klein, D. N. (1997). Family history assessment of personality disorders: I. Concordance with direct interview and between pairs of informants. *Journal of Personality Disorders, 11*, 123–136. doi: 10.1521/pedi.1997.11.2.123.

Few, L. R., Miller, J. D., Rothbaum, A. O., Meller, S., Maples, J., Terry, D. P., ... MacKillop, J. (2013). Examination of the Section III DSM-5 diagnostic system for personality disorders in an outpatient clinical sample. *Journal of Abnormal Psychology, 122*, 1057–1069. doi: 10.1037/a0034878.

Fiedler, E. R., Oltmanns, T. F., & Turkheimer, E. (2004). Traits associated with personality disorders and adjustment to military life: Predictive validity of self and peer reports. *Military Medicine, 169*, 207–211. doi: 10.7205/MILMED.169.3.207.

Fisher, Z., & Tipton, E. (2015). *Robumeta: Robust Variance Meta-regression. R Package Version 1.6*. Available at: http://CRAN.R-project.org/package=robumeta.

Fowler, K. A., & Lilienfeld, S. O. (2007). The Psychopathy Q-Sort: Construct validity evidence in a nonclinical sample. *Assessment, 14*, 75–79. doi: 10.1177/1073191106290792.

Funder, D. C. (1995). On the accuracy of personality judgment: A realistic approach. *Psychological Review, 102*, 652–670. http://dx.doi.org.libpublic3.library.isu.edu/10.1037/0033-295X.102.4.652.

Furr, R. M., & Bacharach, V. R. (2008). *Psychometrics: An introduction*. Thousand Oaks, CA: Sage Publications.

Furr, R. M., Dougherty, D. M., Marsh, D. M., & Mathias, C. W. (2007). Personality judgment and personality pathology: Self–other agreement in adolescents with conduct disorder. *Journal of Personality, 75*, 629–662. doi: 10.1111/j.1467-6494.2007.00451.x.

Galione, J. N., & Oltmanns, T. F. (2013). Identifying personality pathology associated with major depressive episodes: Incremental validity of informant reports. *Journal of Personality Assessment, 95*, 625–632. doi: 10.1080/00223891.2013.825624.

Goldberg, L. R. (1993). The structure of phenotypic personality traits. *American Psychologist, 48*, 26–34. doi: 10.1037/0003-066X.48.1.26.

Haigler, E. D., & Widiger, T. A. (2001). Experimental manipulation of NEO-PI-R items. *Journal of Personality Assessment, 77*, 339–358. doi: 10.1207/S15327752JPA7702_14.

Hedges, L. V., Tipton, E., & Johnson, M. C. (2010). Robust variance estimation in meta-regression with dependent effect size estimates. *Research Synthesis Methods, 1*, 39–65. doi: 10.1002/jrsm.5.

Hill, J., Fudge, H., Harrington, R., Pickles, A., & Rutter, M. (2000). Complementary approaches to the assessment of personality disorder: The Personality Assessment Schedule and Adult Personality Functioning Assessment compared. *British Journal of Psychiatry, 176*, 434–439. doi: 10.1192/bjp.176.5.434.

John, O. P., Naumann, L. P., & Soto, C. J. (2008). Paradigm shift to the integrative Big Five trait taxonomy: History: Measurement, and conceptual issue. In O. P. John, R. W. Robins, & L. A. Pervin (Eds.), Handbook of personality: Theory and research (pp. 114–158). New York: Guilford Press.

Jopp, A. M., & South, S. C. (2015). Investigating the Personality Inventory for DSM-5 using self and spouse reports. *Journal of Personality Disorders, 29*, 193–214. doi: 10.1521/pedi_2014_28_153.

Kaurin, A., Sauerberger, K. S., & Funder, D. C. (2018). Associations between informant ratings of personality disorder traits, self-reports of personality, and directly observed behavior. *Journal of Personality, 86*, 1078–1101. doi: 10.1111/jopy.12376.

Kelley, S. E., Edens, J. F., Donnellan, M. B., Mowle, E. N., & Sörman, K. (2018). Self-and informant perceptions of psychopathic traits in relation to the triarchic model. *Journal of Personality, 86*, 738–751. doi: 10.1111/jopy.12354.

Keulen-de-Vos, M., Bernstein, D. P., Clark, L. A., Arntz, A., Lucker, T. P., & de Spa, E. (2011). Patient versus informant reports of personality disorders in forensic patients. *Journal of Forensic Psychiatry and Psychology, 22*, 52–71. doi: 10.1080/14789949.2010.511242.

Klein, D. N. (2003). Patients' versus informants' reports of personality disorders in predicting 7 1/2-year outcome in outpatients with depressive disorders. *Psychological Assessment, 15*, 216–222. doi: 10.1037/1040-3590.15.2.216.

Klonsky, E. D., Oltmanns, T. F., & Turkheimer, E. (2002). Informant-reports of personality disorder: Relation to self-reports and future research directions. *Clinical Psychology: Science and Practice, 9*, 300–311. doi: 10.1093/clipsy .9.3.300.

Krueger, R. F., Derringer, J., Markon, K. E., Watson, D., & Skodol, A. E. (2012). Initial construction of a maladaptive personality trait model and inventory for DSM-5. *Psychological Medicine, 42*, 1879–1890. doi: 10.1017/S0033291711002674.

Lawton, E. M., Shields, A. J., & Oltmanns, T. F. (2011). Five-factor model personality disorder prototypes in a community sample: Self-and informant-reports predicting interview-based DSM diagnoses. *Personality Disorders: Theory, Research, and Treatment, 2*, 279–292. doi: 10.1037/a0022617.

Livesley, W. J. (2007). A framework for integrating dimensional and categorical classifications of personality disorder. *Journal of Personality Disorders, 21*, 199–224. doi: 10.1521/pedi.2007.21.2.199.

Lukowitsky, M. R., & Pincus, A. L. (2013). Interpersonal perception of pathological narcissism: A social relations analysis. *Journal of Personality Assessment, 95*, 261–273. doi: 10.1080/00223891.2013.765881.

Lynam, D. R., & Widiger, T. A. (2001). Using the five-factor model to represent the DSM-IV personality disorders: An expert consensus approach. *Journal of Abnormal Psychology, 110*, 401. doi: 10.1037/0021-843X.110.3.401.

Markon, K. E., Quilty, L. C., Bagby, R. M., & Krueger, R. F. (2013). The development and psychometric properties of an informant-report form of the Personality Inventory for DSM-5 (PID-5). *Assessment, 20*, 370–383. doi: 10.1177/1073191113486513.

McKeeman, J. L., & Erickson, M. T. (1997). Self and informant ratings of SCID-II personality disorder items for nonreferred college women: Effects of item and participant characteristics. *Journal of Clinical Psychology, 53*, 523–533. http://dx.doi.org. libpublic3.library.isu.edu/10.1002/(SICI)1097-4679(199710)53:6%3C523::AID-JCLP1%3E3.0.CO;2-L.

Miller, J. D. (2012). Five-factor model personality disorder prototypes: A review of their development, validity, and comparison to alternative approaches. *Journal of Personality, 80*, 1565–1591. doi: 10.1111/j.1467-6494.2012.00773.x.

Miller, J. D., Jones, S. E., & Lynam, D. R. (2011). Psychopathic traits from the perspective of self and informant reports: Is there evidence for a lack of insight? *Journal of Abnormal Psychology, 120*, 758–764. doi: 10.1037/a0022477.

Miller, J. D., Lynam, D. R., Vize, C., Crowe, M., Sleep, C., Maples-Keller, J. L.,...& Campbell, W. K. (2018). Vulnerable narcissism is (mostly) a disorder of neuroticism. *Journal of Personality, 86*, 186–199. doi: 10.1111/jopy.12303.

Miller, J. D., Pilkonis, P. A., & Clifton, A. (2005). Self-and other-reports of traits from the five-factor model: Relations to personality disorder. *Journal of Personality Disorders, 19*, 400–419. doi: 10.1521/pedi.2005.19.4.400.

Miller, J. D., Pilkonis, P. A., & Morse, J. Q. (2004). Five-factor model prototypes for personality disorders: The utility of self-reports and observer ratings. *Assessment, 11*, 127–138. doi: 10.1177/1073191104264962.

Modestin, J., & Puhan, A. (2000). Comparison of assessment of personality disorder by patients and informants. *Psychopathology, 33*, 265–270. doi: 10.1159/000029156.

Norman, W. T. (1963). Toward an adequate taxonomy of personality attributes: Replicated factor structure in peer nomination personality ratings. *Journal of Abnormal and Social Psychology, 66*, 574–583. doi: 10.1037/h0040291.

Oltmanns, J. R., Crego, C., & Widiger, T. A. (2018). Informant assessment: The Informant Five-Factor Narcissism Inventory. *Psychological Assessment, 30*, 31–42. doi: 10.1037/pas0000487.

Oltmanns, J. R., & Widiger, T. A. (2018). A self-report measure for the ICD-11 dimensional trait model proposal: The Personality Inventory for ICD-11. *Psychological Assessment, 30*, 154. doi: 10.1037/pas0000459.

Oltmanns, T. F., Rodrigues, M. M., Weinstein, Y., & Gleason, M. E. (2014). Prevalence of personality disorders at midlife in a community sample: Disorders and symptoms reflected in interview, self, and informant reports. *Journal of Psychopathology and Behavioral Assessment, 36*, 177–188. doi: 10.1007/s10862-013-9389-7.

Oltmanns, T. F., & Turkheimer, E. (2006). Perceptions of self and others regarding pathological personality traits. In R. F. Krueger & J. L. Tackett (Eds.), *Personality and psychopathology* (71–111). New York: Guilford Press.

Ouimette, P. C., & Klein, D. N. (1995). Test-retest stability, mood-state dependence, and informant-subject concordance of the SCID-Axis II Questionnaire in a nonclinical sample. *Journal of Personality Disorders, 9*, 105–111. doi: 10.1521/pedi.1995.9.2.105.

Peselow, E. D., Sanfilipo, M. P., Fieve, R. R., & Gulbenkian, G. (1994). Personality traits during depression and after clinical recovery. *British Journal of Psychiatry, 164*, 349–354. doi: 10.1192/bjp.164.3.349.

Pincus, A. L., & Lukowitsky, M. R. (2010). Pathological narcissism and narcissistic personality disorder. *Annual Review of Clinical Psychology, 6*, 421–446. doi: 10.1146/annurev.clinpsy.121208.131215.

Powers, A. D., & Oltmanns, T. F. (2012). Personality disorders and physical health: A longitudinal examination of physical functioning, healthcare utilization, and health-related behaviors in middle-aged adults. *Journal of Personality Disorders, 26*, 524–538. doi: 10.1521/pedi.2012.26.4.524.

Quintana, D. S. (2015). From pre-registration to publication: A non-technical primer for conducting a meta-analysis to synthesize correlational data. *Frontiers in Psychology, 6*, 1–9. doi: 10.3389/fpsyg.2015.01549.

R Core Team (2013). R: A language and environment for statistical computing. Vienna, Austria: R Foundation for Statistical Computing. <http://www.R-project.org/>.

Ready, R. E., & Clark, L. A. (2002). Correspondence of psychiatric patient and informant ratings of personality traits, temperament, and interpersonal problems. *Psychological Assessment, 14*, 39–49. doi: 10.1037//1040-3590.14.1.39.

Ready, R. E., Clark, L. A., Watson, D., & Westerhouse, K. (2000). Self-and peer-reported personality: Agreement, trait ratability, and the "self-based heuristic." *Journal of Research in Personality, 34*, 208–224. doi: 10.1006/jrpe.1999.2280.

Ready, R. E., Watson, D., & Clark, L. A. (2002). Psychiatric patient- and informant-reported personality: Predicting concurrent and future behavior. *Assessment, 9*, 361–372. doi: 10.1177/1073191102238157.

Riso, L. P., Klein, D. N., Anderson, R. L., Ouimette, P. C., & Lizardi, H. (1994). Concordance between patients and informants on the personality disorder examination. *American Journal of Psychiatry, 151*, 568–573. doi: 10.1176/ajp.151.4.568.

Rohrer, J. M., Egloff, B., Kosinski, M., Stillwell, D., & Schmukle, S. C. (2018). In your eyes only? Discrepancies and agreement between self- and other-reports of personality from age 14 to 29. *Journal of Personality and Social Psychology, 115*, 304–320. doi: 10.1037/pspp0000142.

Samuel, D. B., Añez, L. M., Paris, M., & Grilo, C. M. (2014). The convergence of personality disorder diagnoses across different methods among monolingual (Spanish-speaking only) Hispanic patients in substance use treatment. *Personality Disorders: Theory, Research, and Treatment, 5*, 172–177. doi: 10.1037/per0000033.

Samuel, D. B., Riddell, A. D., Lynam, D. R., Miller, J. D., & Widiger, T. A. (2012). A five-factor measure of obsessive-compulsive personality traits. *Journal of Personality Assessment, 94*, 456–465. doi: 10.1080/00223891.2012.677885.

Samuel, D. B., Sanislow, C. A., Hopwood, C. J., Shea, M. T., Skodol, A. E., Morey, L. C.,…Grilo, C. M. (2013).

Convergent and incremental predictive validity of clinician, self-report, and structured interview diagnoses for personality disorders over 5 years. *Journal of Consulting and Clinical Psychology, 81*, 650–659. doi: 10.1037/a0032813.

Samuel, D. B., Suzuki, T., Bucher, M. A., & Griffin, S. A. (2018). The agreement between clients' and their therapists' ratings of personality disorder traits. *Journal of Consulting and Clinical Psychology, 86*, 546–555. doi: 10.1037/ccp0000304.

Samuel, D. B., & Widiger, T. A. (2004). Clinicians' personality descriptions of prototypic personality disorders. *Journal of Personality Disorders, 18*, 286–308. doi: 10.1521/pedi.18.3.286.35446.

Samuel, D. B., & Widiger, T. A. (2008). A meta-analytic review of the relationships between the five-factor model and DSM-IV-TR personality disorders: A facet level analysis. *Clinical Psychology Review, 28*, 1326–1342. doi: 10.1016/j.cpr.2008.07.002.

Schuppert, H. M., Bloo, J., Minderaa, R. B., Emmelkamp, P. M., & Nauta, M. H. (2012). Psychometric evaluation of the Borderline Personality Disorder Severity Index—IV—adolescent version and parent version. *Journal of Personality Disorders, 26*, 628–640. doi: 10.1521/pedi.2012.26.4.628.

Sleep, C. E., Lamkin, J., Lynam, D. R., Campbell, W. K., & Miller, J. D. (2019). Personality disorder traits: Testing insight regarding presence of traits, impairment, and desire for change. *Personality Disorders: Theory, Research, and Treatment, 10*, 123–131. doi: 10.1037/per0000305.

South, S. C., Oltmanns, T. F., Johnson, J., & Turkheimer, E. (2011). Level of agreement between self and spouse in the assessment of personality pathology. *Assessment, 18*, 217–226. doi: 10.1177/1073191110394772.

Sterne, J. A., Sutton, A. J., Ioannidis, J. P., Terrin, N., Jones, D. R., Lau, J.…Tetzlaff, J. (2011). Recommendations for examining and interpreting funnel plot asymmetry in meta-analyses of randomised controlled trials. *BMJ, 343*, d4002.

Tackett, J. L., Herzhoff, K., Reardon, K. W., Smack, A. J., & Kushner, S. C. (2013). The relevance of informant discrepancies for the assessment of adolescent personality pathology. *Clinical Psychology: Science and Practice, 20*, 378–392. doi: https://doi.org/10.1111/cpsp.12048.

Tipton, E. (2015). Small sample adjustments for robust variance estimation with meta-regression. *Psychological Methods, 20*, 375–393. doi: 10.1037/met0000011.

Tromp, N. B., & Koot, H. M. (2010). Self-and parent report of adolescent personality pathology: Informant agreement and relations to dysfunction. *Journal of Personality Disorders, 24*, 151–170. doi: 10.1521/pedi.2010.24.2.151.

Trull, T. J., Widiger, T. A., Lynam, D. R., & Costa, P. T., Jr. (2003). Borderline personality disorder from the perspective of general personality functioning. *Journal of Abnormal Psychology, 112*, 193–202. doi: 10.1037/0021-843X.112.2.193.

Tyrer, P., Alexander, M. S., Cicchetti, D., Cohen, M. S., & Remington, M. (1979). Reliability of a schedule for rating personality disorders. *British Journal of Psychiatry, 135*, 168–174. doi: 10.1192/bjp.135.2.168.

Tyrer, P., Mulder, R., Kim, Y., & Crawford, M. J. (2019). The development of the ICD-11 classification of personality disorders: An amalgam of science, pragmatism and politics. *Annual Review of Clinical Psychology, 15*, 481–502. doi: 10.1146/annurev-clinpsy-050718-095736.

Vazire, S. (2010). Who knows what about a person? The self–other knowledge asymmetry (SOKA) model. *Journal of*

Personality and Social Psychology, 98, 281–300. http://dx.doi.org.libpublic3.library.isu.edu/10.1037/a0017908.

Viechtbauer, W. (2010). Conducting meta-analyses in R with the metaphor package. *Journal of Statistics Software, 36*, 1–43.

Viechtbauer, W., & Cheung, M. W. L. (2010). Outlier and influence diagnostics for meta-analysis. *Research Synthesis Methods, 1*, 112–125. doi: 10.1002/jrsm.11.

Walters, P., Moran, P., Choudhury, P., Lee, T., & Mann, A. (2004). Screening for personality disorder: A comparison of personality disorder assessment by patients and informants. *International Journal of Methods in Psychiatric Research, 13*, 34–39. doi: 10.1002/mpr.162.

Widiger, T. A. (2013). A postmortem and future look at the personality disorders in DSM-5. *Personality Disorders: Theory, Research, and Treatment, 4*, 382–387. doi: 10.1037/per0000030.

Widiger, T. A., & Clark, L. A. (2000). Toward DSM-V and the classification of psychopathology. *Psychological Bulletin, 126*, 946–963. doi: 10.1037/0033-2909.126.6.946.

Widiger, T. A., Gore, W. L., Crego, C., Rojas, S. L., & Oltmanns, J. R. (2017). Five factor model and personality disorder. In T. A. Widiger (Ed.), *The Oxford handbook of the five factor model* (pp. 449–478). New York: Oxford University Press.

Widiger, T. A., Lynam, D. R., Miller, J. D., & Oltmanns, T. F. (2012). Measures to assess maladaptive variants of the five-factor model. *Journal of Personality Assessment, 94*, 450–455. doi: 10.1080/00223891.2012.677887.

Widiger, T. A., & Trull, T. J. (2007). Plate tectonics in the classification of personality disorder: Shifting to a dimensional model. *American Psychologist, 62*, 71–83. doi: 10.1037/0003-066X.62.2.71.

World Health Organization. (2018). ICD-11 beta draft. Retrieved from: http://www.who.int/classifications/icd/revision/en/.

Yalch, M. M., & Hopwood, C. J. (2017). Target-, informant-, and meta-perceptual ratings of maladaptive traits. *Psychological Assessment, 29*, 1142–1156. doi: 10.1037/pas0000417.

Zimmerman, M., Pfohl, B., Coryell, W., Stangl, D., & Corenthal, C. (1988). Diagnosing personality disorder in depressed patients: A comparison of patient and informant interviews. *Archives of General Psychiatry, 45*, 733–737. doi: 10.1001/archpsyc.1988.01800320045005.

Notes

1. Compulsivity is analogous to "Anankastia" in the International Classification of Diseases-11 (World Health Organization, 2018).

2. Assessment of maladaptive personality traits at the facet level will be important for future classification, as assessment of only broad maladaptive trait domains may lead to similar heterogeneity problems as in broad DSM personality disorder types.

Trait Accuracy in the Workplace

Melinda Blackman

Abstract

The importance of accurate trait judgments about employees within organizational contexts is highlighted. More specifically, how the employees' traits affect both positive and negative work outcomes is illustrated. Next, a description of how personality judgments are used to predict these outcomes both during the hiring process and throughout an employee's tenure (e.g., performance evaluation, decisions about advancement, and formation of workgroups) is given. The remainder of the chapter focuses on the accurate assessment of the job candidate's personality during the employment interview, with several points of discussion revolving around methods to improve trait judgments about prospective hires.

Key Words: accurate trait judgment, organizational context, personality judgment, employment interview, job candidate, personality

Record-setting sales, heightened corporate creativity, and low turnover are every employer's dream come true. Positive outcomes such as these can be achieved when organizations implement methods to accurately assess their employees' personality traits (Barrick & Mount, 1991; van Aarde, Meiring, & Wiernik, 2017). Employers who invest a substantial amount of time in accurately assessing their employees' personalities can be assured of a lucrative return on their investment. On the flip side, consider embezzlement, fist-fights with coworkers, narcissistic tantrums, sexual misconduct, on-the-job drug use, and employee theft. These are just some of the detrimental outcomes that can occur if a company does not carefully vet the personality traits of its employees (DePaulo et al., 2003; Ozer & Benet-Martinez, 2006; Townsend, Bacigalupi, & Blackman, 2007). The accurate assessment of an employee's personality traits is more important than it has ever been in our world's economic history as the stakes are high for letting even one unsuitably matched employee into an organization (Pinkovitz, Moskal, & Green, 1997). Moreover, these positive and negative outcomes make a compelling case for

employers to adopt the practice of accurately screening employees' personalities.

Back in 1997 when I submitted my first manuscript with regard to accurately assessing an employee's personality, I received a short, succinct rejection letter from the journal editor. The statement read something to this effect, "We do not see the relevance of accurately assessing an employee's personality. We feel that what should be focused upon is accurately determining the employee's skill set." What the editor did not realize is that personality characteristics, whether they are assessed during the hiring process, performance evaluation process, or promotion process, are job-relevant criteria and do indeed predict job performance (Barrick & Mount, 1991; Hogan et al., 1996). Since that time, notable and newsworthy incidences of workplace violence, interview/resume fraud, sexual misconduct, and employee counterproductive behavior have been highly publicized and even caused the demise of major corporations (Blackman, 2012). Interestingly, many of these incidents of workplace deviance could have been predicted if the employers had just taken the additional step of assessing the employee's job-relevant personality traits (Ones, Viswesvaran, & Schmidt, 1993; Townsend et al., 2007).

An employee's personality traits affect many important work outcomes and behaviors, so accurately assessing them is very important. One of the most obvious goals of accurate personality assessment is to determine *person-job fit*. In other words, does the job candidate possess the traits that lead to successful performance in a particular position (Kristof, 2000)? For instance, for a sales position, a job applicant who is extraverted and persuasive would likely have a high level of person-job fit. Or for high-stress jobs such as law enforcement and mental health care, it would be of the utmost importance to assess the applicant's level of resilience (e.g., his/her capacity to recover from difficulties) to determine person-job fit. Individuals with this key trait are less likely to experience job burnout and to contribute to organizational turnover (Stoddart & Clance, 2017). We should also be mindful to accurately assess the candidate's potential to engage in counterproductive behavior on the job such as bullying, employee theft, and dishonesty. Accurate personality assessment is important beyond just hiring decisions and should be focused on when considering candidates for promotions or for putting together compatible work groups. Ensuring that an employee has potential leadership abilities would be crucial if they are to be promoted into a managerial position. Similarly, employees who will be working in groups should be vetted for traits that facilitate group productivity and harmony.

But how can we accurately assess the traits that matter in the workplace? Some organizations give job candidates a battery of standardized personality tests during the screening and selection process. Numerous studies have found that such assessments, while often expensive, can be useful (Barrick & Mount, 1991; Blackman, 2002a; Hogan et al., 1996; Ones et al., 1993). More often, however, the assessment of a job candidate's traits is made, either formally or informally, by human judges during the hiring interview. But are these judgments accurate? Can interviewers accurately assess job-relevant traits? What are the factors that make such judgments more or less likely to be accurate? How can we improve our hiring processes so that we hire the best employees?

In this chapter, I first discuss the importance of accurate trait judgments in organizations by highlighting how employees' traits affect both positive and negative work outcomes. Next, I describe how

personality judgments are used to predict these outcomes both during hiring and throughout an employee's tenure, explaining their current use in screening and selection, performance evaluation, decisions about advancement, and formation of workgroups. I then briefly review research on the accuracy of trait judgments when used for these purposes. In order to fully explain how organizations might improve the accuracy of judgments about work-relevant traits, I describe how to improve trait judgments about prospective hires. Because many work-relevant personality traits are first assessed by human judges during the interview process, the remainder of the chapter focuses on the accurate assessment of the job candidate's personality during the employment interview. The employment interview is the organization's first of many encounters with an employee that may lead to tenure and lasting ties with an organization.

Before I go in-depth with regard to accurately assessing an employee's personality traits during the employment interview, I want to focus briefly on three organizational aspects where personality assessment is also very relevant: performance evaluations, promotions, and the formation of workgroups. When an organization hires an employee, they are hopeful that the employee will stay with the organization for a substantial period of time and have strong yearly performance evaluations. Wouldn't it be ideal if an organization could predict that employee's yearly performance evaluations? Well they can, by implementing personality assessment. Time and time again, the employee's personality has been found to be a strong predictor of his/her performance evaluations in a wide array of occupations (Barrick & Mount, 1991; Detrick & Chibnall, 2002; Hogan et al., 1996; Wang & Cui, 2008). For example, in a study conducted by Detrick and Chibnall (2002), police officers upon being hired were given the Inwald Personality Inventory (IPI), which is used to predict traits related to failure in high-risk jobs. A year later, the police officers' IPI results were found to predict their one-year performance evaluations given by their supervisors.

The predictive validity of personality assessments for performance evaluations is also strong across cultures. Out of the many personality traits, conscientiousness (e.g., being organized, reliable, and careful) has been found to be a robust predictor of performance in Western cultures. Jiang, Wang, and Zhou (2009) wanted to determine if this finding was generalizable to the Chinese culture. The participants were local Chinese government executives who were participating in a one-month public administration training program. The researchers found that indeed conscientiousness was a strong predictor of the task performance and contextual performance (activities that support the social, psychological, and general environment of the organization) of these executives. While meta-analyses have shown that the Big Five personality factors[1] are consistent predictors of workplace performance in Western culture, van Aarde and colleagues (2017) set out to examine the generalizability of the findings to South Africa. After conducting a meta-analysis of 33 South African studies, the researchers found that the strongest predictor of performance out of the Big Five traits was conscientiousness, and the other four factors showed strong predictive validity for specific performance criteria and subsamples (van Aarde, Meiring, & Wiernik, 2017).

In addition to predicting performance evaluations, personality assessment is a valid predictor of an employee's promotion potential. Upon hiring an employee, future-oriented supervisors are hopeful that the employee will be capable of taking on additional responsibilities and roles. Accurate personality assessments of the employees can predict the likelihood of being promoted. In New Zealand, 309 high school seniors were given the Sixteen Personality Factor Questionnaire (16PF), which measures normal personality, and were then retested 5 years later (Barton & Cattell, 1972). It was found that those participants who were high in warmheartedness and shrewdness were promoted significantly more than their counterparts with lower levels of these traits. Longenecker and Fink's (2008) study supports this finding as well. They sent out 311 surveys to US service and manufacturing managers in 100 cities throughout the country asking them for 5 specific criteria that lead an employee to promotion. From there, the researchers created 10 factors. Six of the 10 factors were indeed personality-related traits (e.g., integrity, trustworthiness). These results support the utility of personality assessment in yet another work-related realm.

Sometimes tasks in various organizations are best completed by multimember workgroups. Supervisors are then faced with deciding which employees to put together in these groups. Factors such as an employee's compatibility, past productivity level, and knowledge base should be considered when selecting employees to work together. Again, an employee's personality characteristics have been shown to strongly predict the effective functioning of a work team (Driskell, Hogan, & Salas, 1987). More specifically, extraversion and self-efficacy were found to be important personality characteristics that contribute to effective management teams (de Jong, Bouhuys, & Barnhoorn, 1999). Kline (1999) subsequently developed a Team Player Inventory (TPI) that measures the degree to which individuals' personalities are positively predisposed toward being successful in teamwork environments. As one can see, there are many facets within organizations that can use the strong predictive validity of personality assessments that are beyond the initial hiring and screening process. Though these aspects are important, the remaining portion of the chapter focuses on the assessment of personality traits within the interview process, as this is the first point of contact that organizations have with their future employees.

The Importance of Accurately Assessing a Job Candidate's Traits

Consider this, once a job candidate is hired for a position, he or she will be representing the organization in various ways. This person will be interacting with customers and colleagues, perhaps handling money or even operating expensive equipment. In addition, the employee could have a tenure with the organization for several decades. For these reasons and several more that will be discussed, it is optimal to accurately assess a job candidate's personality traits at this juncture to determine if he or she is a good fit for the position and the organization as a whole.

Person-Job Fit

Accurately determining the job candidate's person-job fit is of the utmost importance during the interview process (Kristof, 2000). More specifically, organizations need to ask themselves, does the candidate's personality fit the type of position that he or she will be doing on a daily basis? Research indicates that job-relevant personality traits increase employee performance (Frieder, Wang, & Oh, 2018). The most obvious example of this relationship would be hiring an individual for a sales position. During the interview process, one would want to ensure that the job candidate is extraverted and conscientious, as research indicates that individuals with these traits perform well in sales positions (Stewart, 1996). Interestingly, these two traits also accurately predict the performance of food servers (Zeigler-Hill, Besser, Vrabel, & Noser, 2015). For positions that have yet to be researched for their job-relevant personality traits, interviewers would want to cull traits that they feel are desirable in a candidate or perhaps are indicative of the successful incumbent. The interviewers could look to the job description and its stated duties as a guide for identifying these traits. Once these traits are agreed on, the interviewers should focus on accurately judging these characteristics. For instance, for a kindergarten teacher, an interview committee might decide that they are looking for a job candidate who is empathetic, caring, and creative. During the interview process, these job-relevant traits can be targeted for assessment. Employers who do not invest an effort in accurately assessing person-job fit may find themselves with underperforming employees who have low job satisfaction. Ultimately, this lack of fit of personality-relevant traits frequently leads to increased organizational turnover (Tett, Jackson, & Rothstein, 1991).

Organizational Culture

Another factor to consider with regard to accurate personality judgment is fit with the culture of the organization. Each organization has a culture or vibe that employees create or adhere to. A culture may, for instance, have a supportive norm that is necessary for employees who work in a stressful environment like an emergency call center. In this environment, supportive traits like compassion, agreeableness, and the ability to work well with others are helpful for reducing tensions among co-workers, thus facilitating culture-fit (García-Herrero, Mariscal, Gutiérrez, & Ritzel, 2013). Another example of workplace culture would be an environment where "everyone is out for themselves" such as the environment you might find in a commission-based business where the stakes and earning potential are high and the competition is fierce. Hence in this environment, an employee with personality traits such as "goal oriented and tenacious" might have a high likelihood of fitting into this culture. The culture could also be one that requires creativity, like that encouraged at computer gaming companies or organizations like Google. Traits such as "open-minded" and "autonomous" might work well in this environment. So, if you are not judged to be an individual who appreciates a worksite where radical candor is encouraged, like that at Google, you would be screened out in the first round of interviews if the interview team is astute in determining person-culture fit (Chatman, 1991; Rynes & Gerhart, 1990). Achieving workplace-culture fit is imperative, as a misfit in the culture can disrupt the equilibrium

and cause other norm-abiding employees to feel discomfort that could affect their productivity. Ideally, interview teams should have a clear understanding of their organization's culture and screen for candidates who would easily assimilate into the organization.

Organizational Citizenship

Organizational citizenship behavior (OCB) is another important set of traits and behavior patterns to screen for during the interview process (Ocampo et al., 2018). Employees who possess a high level of OCB are employees who are willing to cooperate with others in the organization for the common good of the organization and who possess prosocial traits such as being considerate, thoughtful, and communally oriented (Neuman & Kickul, 1998; Penner, Midili, & Kegelmeyer, 1997). These employees are willing to stay late to work on projects, cover other employees' work if they have a medical appointment, volunteer for projects that no one else is willing to tackle, and generally cooperate on superordinate goals within the organization. Organizational citizenship behavior is not about self-promotion (though a promotion may be in order down the line for this type of individual), but about selfless devotion to the organization because one believes in its mission. If one breaks OCB down into some of its component traits (e.g., is agreeable, works well with others, considerate) one can accurately judge the extent to which a job candidate possesses each specific quality.

Counterproductive Behavior

Assessing an employee's potential to engage in counterproductive behavior (e.g., dishonesty, lack of integrity, bullying, employee theft, procrastination) is a common hiring practice (Ones et al., 1993). It is essentially the first hoop that many candidates are forced to jump through on their job-hunting journey. These days one cannot apply for a minimum-wage-earning position at a major organization without being asked to take a test that measures counterproductive behaviors such as lack of integrity and dishonesty (Ones et al., 1993; Townsend et al., 2007).

Emotional Intelligence

Another personality characteristic that interviewers should aim to judge accurately is the applicant's level of emotional intelligence. Emotional intelligence, commonly referred to as EI, involves the ability of the individual to accurately read one's own emotions and that of others, and manage these emotions appropriately (Caruso, Bienn, & Kornacki, 2006). This personality characteristic is important in managerial, human services positions, and many others that lead to higher levels of employee and customer satisfaction (Zeidner, Matthews, & Roberts, 2004).

Maladaptive Traits

One last category of characteristics that employers are advised to accurately detect in the job candidate are maladaptive traits that could lead to interpersonal problems in the workplace (e.g., narcissism, Machiavellianism). Though the job candidate may be able to do the job effectively with this cluster of traits, employers need to ask themselves, "Will this personality trait or pattern of related behaviors disrupt the culture of the workplace?" "Will coworkers feel uncomfortable around this individual?" "Will turnover or loss of productivity occur due to this person's uniqueness?" "Is the organization putting itself at risk with the hiring of this individual?" For instance, an individual with a known antisocial behavioral disorder may be charming to customers and increase sales dramatically, but his lack of ethics may lead to embezzlement of the company's funds. These are some important trade-offs for the interview committee to consider. These individuals can be quite charming at first and are practiced social chameleons, but once hired show their true colors through arrogance and self-absorption (DuBrin, 2012). These individuals can be so convincing in their arguments that they will have a coworker believing that black is white and red is blue and that the other coworker is the one who is self-absorbed.

Eliciting Good Information from the Job Applicant

But how does one accurately judge each of these characteristics during the hiring process? To gain theoretical knowledge in how accurate personality judgments are achieved, employers and their team of interviewers should turn to the realistic accuracy model (RAM; Funder, 1995; see also chapter 2 by Letzring & Funder in this handbook). The RAM is instrumental in laying the foundation for how employers should tackle accurately assessing an employee's personality traits. The RAM states that accurate personality judgments can be achieved when relevant behavioral information or cues are available to the judge of personality and the judge detects and correctly utilizes the cues. The RAM has four moderator variables of accurate personality judgment: good information, the good trait, the good judge, and the good target (see Section II of this hand-

book). These four moderators help facilitate accurate personality judgments. First, the good information moderator consists both of the quality and quantity of information available to the judge of personality. The better the quality and increased quantity of information that the judge is able to garner, the higher the likelihood of an accurate personality judgment being made. Next, the good trait moderator reflects that some traits have more visible cues than others, making them easier and more accurate to judge. With regard to the good judge, RAM purports that some individuals are better judges of personality than others, thus producing more accurate personality judgments. Finally, the good target moderator reflects that some targets are easier to judge than others, as their behavior is more consistent.

Ideally, when an organization is developing their interview process format, they should first focus on the good information moderator variable (Blackman 2017; Letzring, Wells, & Funder, 2006; see chapter 9 by Beer in this handbook) because the quality and quantity of information that is available to the judge of personality is of the utmost importance when hiring personnel. But what is the best way to obtain good information? Employers should pay particular attention to interview formats that will enhance both the quantity and quality of information that is available to the interviewer with regard to the job candidate's personality in order to enhance trait judgment accuracy.

When setting up the mechanics of hiring personnel, employers have historically turned to the structured interview format as their go-to process to vet relevant information from job candidates (Campion, Palmer, & Campion 1997; Ulrich & Trumbo, 1965). Most of us are familiar with the structured interview format and have probably participated in this tried and true method. The format entails job applicants being interviewed in a formal setting in which they are asked preset, structured questions that do not deviate from candidate to candidate. Very little small talk is encouraged during this interview format and rarely are follow-up questions asked by the interviewers. Typically the list of interview questions is developed from a job analysis, which is a procedure that is conducted to reveal relevant skills and duties of the position. Interviewers usually have a structured rating form that they use to rate the candidate's responses to the questions and for overall fit to the position.

The structured interview format has a strong level of predictive validity with regard to the job candidate's skill set and potential performance on the job (Campion, Pursell, & Brown, 1988; Levashina,

Hartwell, Morgeson, & Campion, 2014). However, this interview format does not successfully predict the job applicant's relevant personality characteristics that are imperative to carry out the job (Blackman 2002a; Townsend et al., 2007). The structured interview format elicits significantly shorter and more succinct responses from the job candidate in comparison to the unstructured interview with its free flowing format. The nonverbal behavior displayed by the job candidates during a structured interview is also very minimal (Blackman 2002a). Ultimately, in terms of RAM, the structured interview format provides a limited quantity and quality of information about personality traits to the interviewer (Blackman, 2002a; Townsend et al., 2007).

To peel back the layers of the job candidate's persona during the interview process and see to the heart of his/her real personality traits (i.e., obtain good information), one should use another type of interview format—the unstructured format. The *unstructured interview format* differs from the structured format in that there is not a list of preset questions that are asked of the interviewee. The setting in which the job candidate is interviewed in tends to be informal, such as over a cup of coffee or a meal. Sometimes the interview is so informal that the applicant is unaware that he or she is being interviewed. Due to the informal format, the applicant may see the interviewer as a friend or even a confidant. Typically with this format, applicants loosen up and their true personality characteristics start to appear. Reasons for leaving their last position may suddenly be brought up by the applicant, true feelings about their last employers might be shared, and many pieces to an accurate portrait of the applicant's personality can be gleaned by the interviewer. Funder (1995) makes the point that weaker situations like an unstructured interview, which inherently don't have strong scripts, are situations in which an individual's personality becomes more apparent than in strong situations that naturally elicit scripted behavior. The unstructured interview by nature does not have a clear script that candidates can anticipate and practice ahead of time. The structured format, on the other hand, is considered a strong situation in which a predictable line of behavior is expected by the candidate and can be rehearsed prior to the interview to strengthen the quality of the candidate's responses.

Research has shown that unstructured interview formats produce significantly more accurate personality judgments of the job candidates when self-judge agreement and peer-judge agreement are used as the criteria (Blackman, 2002a; Townsend et al., 2007). In an experimental design, job applicants were randomly assigned to either a structured or unstructured interview for a student clerk position (Blackman, 2002a). Interviewers in the structured interview condition were given a list of preset interview questions to ask that were derived from a job analysis. The interviewers were then told to ask the same exact questions to the applicant without follow-up questions. On the other hand, interviewers in the unstructured condition were not given any interview questions (just a copy of the job description) and were told to ask whatever questions came to mind. Coders, who were blind to the hypothesis, sat in on each interview to record the length of the interview and code the extent of nonverbal behavior given off by the job candidate. Nonverbal behaviors such as gesturing, fidgeting, and smiling were coded. After the interview, the interviewers completed the California Q-set rating inventory with regard to the applicant's personality traits. The California Q-set consists of 100 mid-level traits in which the judge of personality rates the target person on a Likert scale from 1 "least characteristic" to 5 "highly characteristic" of the target person (Bem & Funder, 1978; Block, 1978; Furr & Funder, 1999). Prior to their interviews, the job applicants were asked to complete the California Q-set to describe their own personality traits. To gather another point of view about the job applicant's personality, the job applicants were given an additional California Q-set form to have a well-acquainted peer or friend describe the interviewee's personality characteristics. Average agreement correlations between the job applicant and the judge of personality were then derived, as well as correlations between the acquaintance and judge, for the structured interview condition and for the unstructured interview condition. Self-interviewer agreement correlations and peer-interviewer agreement correlations were significantly higher for the unstructured interview condition in comparison to the structured condition. A variety of factors were analyzed to determine why these correlations differed. Based on the coded results, the unstructured interviews were on average significantly longer than the structured interviews, as the job applicants spent longer periods of time talking. It would follow that longer interviews would provide a greater quantity of information to the judge of personality (the interviewer) to use in the judgment process. It can also be surmised that the increased quantity of information from the candidates might be due to the fact they felt more comfortable and thus revealed more about themselves and elaborated more on their answers.

More specifically, candidates tended to use more positive nonverbal behavior and facial animation during the unstructured interview format, indicating their higher comfort level. These cues also helped to supply the judge with additional relevant cues of that individual's personality. So, ultimately, the quantity and quality of information that was produced about the job applicant were significantly more when an interviewer used an unstructured format, even though there was not a significant difference in the number of questions asked between the two interview formats. The unstructured format encouraged the interviewer to ask follow-up questions so that they could gain clarity on any responses that might have been vague. The structured interview format, in its truest sense, does not allow for follow-up or probing questions. Again, the structured format by nature reduces the quantity and quality of information available for judging personality.

Though the unstructured interview method yields better information for personality assessment, it is not to say that the structured interview is of little value during the interview process, but quite the contrary. The structured interview format does a wonderful job, as mentioned previously, of vetting the job candidate's relevant job related skills while ensuring that the same information is elicited from each candidate. Ideally, an interviewer would want to use the structured format first in the hiring process to narrow down the list of candidates to those who would be able to successfully perform the job skills if hired. Once this list has been narrowed down, interviewers should then implement the unstructured interview to elicit a better quality and increased quantity of information about the job candidate's personality.

To capitalize even more on the RAM's good (quantity) information moderator variable, longer and variable interviews should be conducted. With multiple follow-up interviews, more information will be collected about the job candidate, thus giving the interviewers more information on which to base their judgment. Interviewers should also focus on the other component of the good information moderator variable, which is the quality of information received about the job candidate. By varying the interview venues, the quality of the information obtained from the job candidate should be richer. For instance, the candidates can be given a pseudo-tour of the organization while, unbeknownst to him/her, they are being interviewed. Most job candidates prepare for the structured job interview format, but rarely prepare for an unstructured format. Due to this lack of preparation for this format, many job candidates do not know how to conduct themselves because there is no scripted behavior to rely on or practice ahead of time. This is when nonverbal behavior that is indicative of lying or lack of integrity has the highest likelihood of appearing (Townsend et al., 2007). When a job applicant tries to lie they usually focus on preparing their upper body to mask what they believe are their facial clues to deceit (Ekman, 2009). But as Paul Ekman points out, many of the telltale clues of deceit can be seen below the target person's waist in what is termed "leakage." Target persons unconsciously use hand gestures below the waist called "emblems" that indicate their true feelings at the moment that may sharply contradict their facial and verbal messages. Interestingly, most interviews take place in an office in which the interviewer is positioned behind a desk, thus blocking their view of the job candidate's entire body. By using an unstructured interview that does not involve a desk and has the job candidate move freely around, such as on a tour of the organization, many of these clues to deceit can be easily seen (Blackman & Funder, 2002).

It is most advantageous to the interviewer to gather a high quality of information about the job candidate from various venues to make an accurate personality judgment about them. Other venues to consider that offer high quality information are restaurants, coffee houses, golf courses, or even a baseball stadium. Many employers might balk at the time and cost of conducting multiple interviews in several different venues. It is important for these individuals to look farther down the path than the immediate future of filling a job opening as quickly as possible. With multiple interviews and different venues, an employer can feel confident after the process is over that they have done all that is possible to gather the highest quality and quantity of information about the job candidates, which can then be used to make more accurate judgments of personality (Funder, 1995).

Other Interview Formats and Good Information

We have only talked about two interview formats—structured and unstructured—with regard to their accuracy to predict a job candidate's personality traits. Many variations of these two interview formats exist, with several variables to consider as well. First, there is the type of format to consider: structured versus unstructured versus semistructured. Within these formats, they can be conducted face-to-face or via a conference/video call. The number of applicants present during the interview can also vary, such as a single versus multiple applicant/group interview. Likewise, the number of interviewers present can also vary (Blacksmith, Willford, & Behrend, 2016; Dixon, Wang, Calvin, Dineen, & Tomlinson, 2002; Tran & Blackman, 2006).

The group interview has become extremely popular as a prescreening interview for organizations that need to hire many employees in a short amount of time (e.g., seasonal help, the opening of a casino). While these interviews can to some degree narrow down the group of candidates to those who possess relevant job skills, these formats produce a low level of accuracy with regard to the job candidate's personality (Townsend et al., 2007). When using a group interview or a structured format, research indicates that applicants' responses to interview questions are significantly shorter than in the unstructured one-on-one interview (providing a poor quality and quantity of information to the judge of personality) and applicants' display of nonverbal behavior is minimal. This could be due to both the presence of many applicants and the structured nature of the format. Also, because interviewers have to multitask by focusing on six to eight persons at a time, interviewers are also significantly less observant at noticing and processing the cues that the job candidates are displaying.

The one-on-one conference call interview, without the video portion, has a similar accuracy rate to that of the group interview (Blackman, 2002b). Again, with both of these interview formats, we see that the job applicant's interview responses are significantly shorter and less complex than in the unstructured interview, while having less animation and inflection in their vocal tones. These interview formats provide the interviewer with a paucity of information with regard to the candidate's personality, yet they should not be dismissed. They are definitely efficient for narrowing down a large group of job applicants with a relevant skill set to a smaller pool of qualified candidates who will proceed to the next round of interviewing.

Judging "Good Traits" during the Interview Process

As the interviewer prepares to conduct an interview, he/she needs to have a clear idea of the traits that he/she will be able to most accurately assess. Traits that have numerous highly visible behavioral cues tend to be easy to judge (Funder, 1995; see also chapter 8 by Krzyzaniak & Letzring in this handbook), so interviewers need to be aware of the job-relevant traits that will produce the most visible cues for the interviewers to process (Funder, 2012). Interviewers will thus be more accurate in judging these particular traits. Before beginning the hiring process, the interviewer should become familiar with the job-relevant traits that are the easiest to judge. The interviewer can also develop behavioral interview questions or work task samples that will bring out the cues to those visible traits even more readily, thus ensuring accurate judgment.

It is advisable for interviewers to become familiar with the visible behavioral cues related to traits that they are judging. For instance, interviewers who are interviewing applicants for an accounting position might want to assess the job candidate on the traits of meticulousness, reliability, and dependability to evaluate the person-job fit. During an interview, the interviewer should focus on finding visual cues of meticulousness (attention to detail) that the applicant exudes. For example, visible cues with regard to this trait might be whether the candidate is taking notes during the interview, how clearly and thoroughly he or she answers each interview question, and perhaps even the attention to detail that the applicant has put into their appearance. These cues are very visible, thus increasing the likelihood that the judge of personality will accurately detect and perceive the relevant cues.

Some job-relevant traits may not be highly visible. If an organization were to interview applicants for the position of a nurse, for example, one might like to detect this individual's level of compassion. This is a personality trait that does not have several visible cues that naturally appear during an interview. In such a case, it may be necessary to use other methods to obtain visible trait-relevant information. In this case, the interviewer could ask the applicant to perform a job sample to obtain better information about this particular trait. A job sample consists of the job candidate actually performing the job or task while the interviewer or committee evaluates him or her. If the job candidate were to perform a procedure on a patient as a job sample, the likelihood of relevant and visible cues relating to his or her compassion for the patient would increase dramatically. The interviewer would then be able to detect them and then accurately judge the applicant's level of compassion. Ultimately, interviewers need to ensure that the interview venue best elicits the most relevant and visible cues to the important traits that the job position requires.

Another option for gathering a substantial number of cues relevant to less visible traits might involve putting the job candidate into various settings during the interview process in which he or she will interact with potential colleagues or customers. If this is not feasible in the interview process, then an interviewer would want to ask several behavioral interview questions. Behavioral interview questions consist of hypothetical work scenarios (e.g., what would you do if a customer...?) in which the applicant must give a spontaneous response (Huffcutt, Weekley, Wiesner, DeGroot, & Jones, 2001; Motowidlo, 1999). These interview questions can also draw on the applicant's past work experience by asking a question such as, "Tell us about a time when you had a disagreement with your boss. What was the disagreement about and how did you resolve it?" These behavioral questions will at least give insight into the implicit (thinking) processes of the applicant and reveal a healthy supply of explicit relevant cues toward their level of compassion.

Finding the Optimal Interviewer/Judge

The "good judge" of personality is also a key moderator in accurately judging the target's personality (Funder, 1995; Letzring, 2008; see also chapter 6 by Colman in this handbook). If possible, the organization should use an interviewer who is known for their competent social skills, agreeableness, and mental stability (Letzring, 2008). These individuals usually have much practice and experience working with others and are adept at creating situations with their personalities and behaviors that draw out relevant cues from the target person. In other words, the targets feel comfortable with the judge of personality and thus reveal more relevant cues for the judge to utilize. Christiansen et al.'s (2005) research focused on another aspect of the good judge—his/her intelligence level. The researchers found that the good judge has a solid understanding of personality and how it relates to behavior (termed dispositional intelligence). In addition, these "good judges" had high general mental ability/intelligence and possessed a high level of openness to new experiences.

Findings with regard to the gender of the "good judge" have been mixed. Kolar (1995) found higher levels of self-other agreement among male judges who rated themselves as "not anxious" and "not concerned with what others think" and were "interpersonally experienced." In addition, he found high self-other agreement among female judges who rated themselves high on intelligence and openness

to experience. Chan, Rogers, Parisotto, and Biesanz (2011) also examined this gender issue. They found that female judges of personality were significantly more accurate than their male counterparts with regard to normative accuracy (perceiving what others are like in general) versus distinctive accuracy (perceiving how others are different from the average person). Interestingly, there has been no *one* strong consistent finding with regard to the personality characteristics and gender of the good judge. Letzring (2008) believes that this may in part be due to the different criteria for accuracy that the researchers have used. So whom should an employer choose to judge the personality of the job candidate? If an employer can find a judge of personality who is the epitome of the majority of the previously mentioned traits, then there is a high likelihood that he or she will be a good judge of personality.

Good Targets

The fourth moderator variable of the RAM is "the good target." The RAM states that some target individuals are simply easier to judge than others (Colvin, 1993; Funder, 1995; Human & Biesanz, 2013; see also chapter 7 by Mignault & Human in this handbook). Some job candidates, therefore, will be easier to judge than others. Some applicants are like an open book and they are not afraid to share a lot of information with the interviewer. The good target's behavior is also very consistent across several situations and contexts. More specifically, interviewers, regardless of the format that they used, should find themselves in agreement about the good target's behavior gleaned from the various interview formats. On the flip side, we must acknowledge that some targets are very hard to judge. These hard-to-judge individuals may be people you have known your entire life, yet you feel that you really don't know them at all. This type of job candidate may be very difficult to assess accurately. They may be very close-mouthed and reluctant to share information about themselves. The hard-to-judge target's behavior can be very inconsistent across situations, sometimes pointing to mental health issues. For instance, they may be very outgoing in one interview context and then become very withdrawn in a follow-up interview or vice-versa. To be on the safe side, hard-to-judge targets with inconsistent behavior should be red-flagged or dropped from the applicant pool. However, if their skill set is extremely promising, they could be brought back for several follow-up interviews until an accurate assessment can be made.

Final Thoughts

Next to accurately assessing the job candidate's relevant job skills, it is of the utmost importance that the job candidate's job-relevant personality traits be judged accurately. As discussed earlier in the chapter, one bad hire can scar the organization through lawsuits and financial woes (Brown, Jones, Terris, & Steffy, 1987). Organizations should not look on the hiring and interview process lightly or as a one-step process. The vetting of the job candidate's personality traits is definitely a multiple-step process that involves utilizing the RAM's moderators of personality judgment to put the judge of personality (interviewer) at the greatest advantage during the hiring process. It is recommended that organizations research the desired personality qualities that they are looking for in their new hire, keeping in mind concepts such as person-job fit, organizational citizenship behavior, integrity, and emotional intelligence, while screening out maladaptive traits. Using the successful incumbent's personality traits is usually a good template to start with. Once the desired traits are agreed on, organizations are advised to develop a structured interview format (with standardized preset questions). This format most accurately predicts the job applicant's skill set and future job-related performance (van Iddekinge, Raymark, Eidson, & Attenweiler, 2004). Optimally, employers should narrow down the applicant pool based on resume content. Next, the organization should call the promising candidates in for a structured interview format to assess their job-relevant skills. At this point, employers could turn the interview into an unstructured interview to assess job-relevant personality traits, as the unstructured interview is the optimal format to accurately assess traits (Blackman, 2002a; Townsend et al., 2007). The unstructured interview should be conducted in a very informal setting (e.g., over coffee, while playing golf, at a park) that allows the candidate to relax and reveal their true personality characteristics. This informal venue will allow the judge of personality to glean a high quality of information about the job candidate's personality, thus utilizing RAM's good information moderator of personality judgment.

Also, to tap into RAM's "good judge" moderator variable, the organization should use the successful incumbent(s) as one of the interviewers. The incumbent would be very familiar with the job duties and could add insight into the person-job fit more so than an interviewer who does not perform the duties on a daily basis. And last, the hiring team should be aware of the "good trait" moderator variable and

know which of the desired personality attributes have the most visible cues. Those traits with the most visible cues will likely be judged most accurately. It is important to keep in mind that some traits that are screened for, such as neuroticism and resilience, are less visible and more difficult to judge. However, these very relevant traits can be judged accurately if the job candidate is put into a situation that actually elicits trait relevant cues (Hirschmüller, Egloff, Schmukle, Nestler, & Back, 2015). For instance, the interview team could manipulate the interview settings to make the trait of "resilience" more visible by placing the job candidate in a timed job sample that involves stress and a lot of interruptions, thus bringing any cues relevant to this trait to the forefront. As one can see, if an interview team diligently sets up their interview process to tap into the good information, good judge, and good trait moderator variables of the RAM, they can be assured of achieving a high level of accuracy concerning the job candidate's personality portrait.

Other Sources for Personality-Relevant Information

In addition to accurately judging the job candidate's personality during the interview process, what else can an organization do to ensure that the candidate is a good personality fit with the organization? I recommend looking into that individual's social media accounts as indicators of that individual's personality characteristics (Back et al., 2010; Gosling, Augustine, Vazire, Holtzman, & Gaddis, 2011). Research indicates that online social media such as Facebook accurately portrays individuals' personality characteristics (Azucar, Marengo, & Settanni, 2018). Another suggestion, if feasible, is to have a 60- to 90-day probationary period for the newly hired employee. During this period, supervisors, coworkers, and customers can evaluate the employee actually executing his/her position while interacting with relevant personnel. Any red flags with regard to questionable behavior can be addressed with the employee at this time. During or after the probationary period, the organization can make a truly informed decision about the tenure of the employee after seeing his/her on-the-job behavior for a significant period of time, as the quantity and quality of information that they will have gathered will have increased significantly, making their judgment more accurate. If organizations could also keep a record of their success rate in hiring, that would in turn help them shed light on the effectiveness of their hiring and personality vetting practices. In other words, if they recorded how many of the probationary hires were kept on to full-time and achieve some type of tenure within the organization, this would be meaningful data about their hiring practices. If the organization finds that their success rate was extremely low, they would then want to perhaps lengthen their probationary period or revise their screening process. Also, tracking their turnover rate would give additional insight into the success of an organization's personality judgments. Specifically, if turnover decreased significantly upon instituting a careful personality vetting process, then the organization could be confident that its screening process was effective. Organizations would be more apt to use a multistep, multi-interviewer process, while incorporating the moderators of the RAM, if they could see the benefits of it on paper. Many researchers implement into their research designs a pretest (or baseline dimension) as well as a post-test to measure the effectiveness of the intervention that they used. Organizations that have preexisting data (a baseline) with regard to their turnover rate and success of new hires could compare this data to the data after they have implemented a multistep interview process (the intervention) to effectively determine the success of their interview and personality judgment process. Then changes to the existing process could be made based on the data.

Another suggestion to gather additional trait information on one's employees, new or existing for potential promotions, is for the supervisors to practice MBWA (Management by Walking Around) (Luria & Morag, 2012). Many employers are rarely seen by their employees and have their office door closed to focus on their daily routine. This is dangerous, as they are not in touch with their employees and seeing their interactions on a daily basis. Managers who keep an open door and frequently walk around the business premise talking to the employees and customers have a higher likelihood of witnessing or hearing about any red flag behavior committed by their new or existing hires. Vigilance is the key to keeping a healthy organization that exudes organizational citizenship from each of its employees. Also it reveals to the employees that they are cared about and that their work is valued.

I am optimistic that the importance of accurately assessing employees' personality characteristics will soon be recognized by employers and human resource managers alike. Hopefully, organizations will then integrate smart interview, promotion, and performance evaluation practices that incorporate the assessment of the employee's personality into the process so it will become a mainstay in organizational practices. This practice will undoubtedly lead to a win-win situation for employers and employees alike.

References

Azucar, D., Marengo, D., & Settanni, M. (2018). Predicting the Big 5 personality traits from digital footprints on social media: A meta-analysis. *Personality and Individual Differences, 124*, 150–159. https://doi.org/10.1177/0963721419827849

Back, M. D., Stopfer, J. M., Vazire, S., Gaddis, S., Schmukle, S. C., Egloff, B., & Gosling, S. D. (2010). Facebook profiles reflect actual personality, not self-idealization. *Psychological Science, 21*, 372–374. doi: 10.1177/0956797609360756

Barrick, M. R., & Mount, M. K. (1991). The Big Five personality dimensions and job performance: A meta-analysis. *Personnel Psychology, 44*(1), 1–26. https://doi.org/10.1111/j.1744-6570.1991.tb00688.x

Barton, K., & Cattell, R. B. (1972). Personality factors related to job promotion and turnover. *Journal of Counseling Psychology, 19*(5), 430–435.

Bem, D. J., & Funder, D. C. (1978). Predicting more of the people more of the time: Assessing the personality of the situation. *Psychological Review, 85*, 485–501.

Blackman, M. C. (2002a). Personality judgment and the utility of the unstructured employment interview. *Basic and Applied Social Psychology, 24*(3), 240–249. https://doi.org/10.1207/S15324834BASP2403_6

Blackman, M. C. (2002b). The employment interview via the telephone: Are we sacrificing accurate personality judgments for cost efficiency? *Journal of Research in Personality, 36*(3), 208–223. doi:10.1006/jrpe.2001.2347

Blackman, M. C. (2012, May 12). *What Yahoo CEO's false bio tells us about resume fraud.* Retrieved from https://www.cnn.com/2012/05/12/opinion/blackman-resume-fraud/index.html

Blackman, M. C. (2017). *Using interviewing in personnel selection.* In H. W. Goldstein, E. D. Pulakos, J. Passamore, & C. Semedo (Eds.), *Handbook of the psychology of recruitment, selection, and retention* (pp. 182–201). West Sussex, UK: Wiley Blackwell.

Blackman, M. C., & Funder, D. C. (2002). Effective interview practices for accurately assessing counterproductive traits. *International Journal of Selection and Assessment, 10*(1/2), 109–116. https://doi.org/10.1111/1468-2389.00197

Blacksmith, N., Willford, J. C., & Behrend, T. S. (2016). Technology in the employment interview: A meta-analysis and future research agenda. *Personnel Assessment and Decisions, 2*, 12–20. doi:10.25035/pad.2016.002

Block, J. (1978). *The Q-sort method in personality assessment and psychiatric research.* Palo Alto, CA: Consulting Psychologists Press.

Brown, T. S., Jones, J. W., Terris, W., & Steffy, B. D. (1987). The impact of pre-employment integrity testing on employee turnover and inventory shrinkage losses. *Journal of Business and Psychology, 2*, 136–149. https://link.springer.com/article/10.1007/BF01014208

Campion, M. A., Palmer, D. K., & Campion, J. E. (1997). A review of structure in the selection interview. *Personnel Psychology, 50*(3), 655–702. https://doi.org/10.1111/j.1744-6570.1997.tb00709.x

Campion, M. A., Pursell, E., & Brown, B. (1988). Structured interviewing: Raising the psychometric properties of the employment interview. *Personnel Psychology, 41*, 25–42. https://doi.org/10.1111/j.1744-6570.1988.tb00630.x

Caruso, D. R., Bienn, B., & Kornacki, S. A. (2006). Emotional intelligence in the workplace. In J. Ciarrochi, J. R. Forgas, J. D. Mayer, J. Ciarrochi, J. R. Forgas, J. D. Mayer (Eds.), *Emotional intelligence in everyday life*(pp. 187–205). Hove, UK: Psychology Press/Erlbaum (UK) Taylor & Francis.

Chan, M., Rogers, K. H., Parisotto, K. L., & Biesanz, J. C. (2011). Forming first impressions: The role of gender and normative accuracy in personality perception. *Journal of Research in Personality, 45*, 117–120. https://doi.org/10.1016/j.jrp.2010.11.001

Chatman, J. A. (1991). Matching people and organizations: Selection and socialization in public accounting firms. *Administrative Science Quarterly, 36*, 459–484. doi:10.2307/2393204

Christiansen, N. D., Wolcott-Burnam, S., Janovics, J. E., Burns, G. N., & Quirk, S. W. (2005). The good judge revisited: Individual differences in the accuracy of personality judgments. *Human Performance, 18*, 123–149. http://dx.doi.org/10.1207/s15327043hup1802_2

Colvin, C. R. (1993). Judgable people: Personality, behavior, and competing explanations. *Journal of Personality and Social Psychology, 64*, 861–873. http://dx.doi.org/10.1037/0022-3514.64.5.861

de Jong, R. D., Bouhuys, S. A., & Barnhoorn, J. C. (1999). Personality, self-efficacy and functioning in management teams: A contribution to validation. *International Journal of Selection and Assessment, 7*(1), 46–49. https://doi.org/10.1111/1468-2389.00103

DePaulo, B. M., Lindsay, J. L., Malone, B. E., Muhlenbruck, L., Charlton, K., & Cooper, H. (2003). Cues to deception. *Psychological Bulletin, 129*, 74–118. doi:10.1037/0033-2909.129.1.74

Detrick, P., & Chibnall, J. T. (2002). Prediction of police officer performance with the Inwald Personality Inventory. *Journal of Police and Criminal Psychology, 17*(2), 9–17. http://dx.doi.org/10.1007/BF02807111

Dixon, M., Wang, S., Calvin, J., Dineen, B., & Tomlinson, E. (2002). The panel interview: A review of empirical research and guidelines for practice. *Public Personnel Management, 31*(3), 397–428. https://doi.org/10.1177/009102600203100310

Driskell, J. E., Hogan, R., & Salas, E. (1987). Personality and group performance. In C. Hendrick (Ed.), *Group processes and intergroup relations* (pp. 91–112). Thousand Oaks, CA: Sage Publications.

DuBrin, A. J. (2012). *Narcissism in the workplace: Research, opinion and practice.* Northampton, MA: Edward Elgar.

Ekman, P. (2009). *Telling lies: Clues to deceit in the marketplace, politics, and marriage.* New York, NY: W. W. Norton.

Frieder, R. E., Wang, G., & Oh, I.-S. (2018). Linking job-relevant personality traits, transformational leadership, and job performance via perceived meaningfulness at work: A moderated mediation model. *Journal of Applied Psychology, 103*(3), 324–333. doi: 10.1037/apl0000274

Funder, D. C. (1995). On the accuracy of personality judgment: A realistic approach. *Psychological Review, 102*, 652–670.

Funder, D. C. (2012). Accurate personality judgment. *Current Directions in Psychological Science, 21*, 177–182. https://doi.org/10.1177/0963721412445309

Furr, R. M., & Funder, D. C. (April, 1999). *A comparison of Q-sort and Likert rating methods.* Poster presented at the Western Psychological Association Conference, Irvine, CA.

García-Herrero, S., Mariscal, M. A., Gutiérrez, J. M., & Ritzel, D. O. (2013). Using Bayesian networks to analyze occupational stress caused by work demands: Preventing stress through social support. *Accident Analysis and Prevention, 57*, 114–123. doi: 10.1016/j.aap.2013.04.009

Gosling, S. D., Augstine, A. A., Vazire, S., Holtzman, N., & Gaddis, S. (2011). Manifestations of personality in online social networks: Self-reported Facebook-related behaviors and observable profile information. *Cyberpsychology, Behavior, and Social Networking, 14*, 483–488. doi:10.1089/cyber.2010.0087

Hirschmüller, S., Egloff, B., Schmukle, S. C., Nestler, S., & Back, M. D. (2015). Accurate judgments of neuroticism at zero acquaintance: A question of relevance. *Journal of Personality, 83*(2), 221–228. doi:10.1111/jopy.12097

Hogan, R., Hogan, J., & Roberts, B. W. (1996). Personality measurement and employment decisions: Questions and answers. *American Psychologist, 51*(5), 469–477. http://dx.doi.org/10.1037/0003-066X.51.5.469

Human, L., & Biesanz, J. (2013). Targeting the good target: An integrative review of the characteristics and consequences of being accurately perceived. *Personality and Social Psychology Review, 17*, 248–272. doi:10.1177/1088868313495593

Huffcutt, A. I., Weekley, J., Wiesner, W. H., DeGroot, T., & Jones, C. (2001). Comparison of situational and behavior description interview questions for higher-level positions. *Personnel Psychology, 54*, 619–644. http://dx.doi.org/10.1111/j.1744-6570.2001.tb00225.x

Jiang, C., Wang, D., & Zhou, F. (2009). Personality traits and job performance in local government organizations in China. *Social Behavior and Personality: An International Journal, 37(4)*, 451–458. https://doi.org/10.2224/sbp.2009.37.4.451

Kline, T. J. (1999). The team player inventory: Reliability and validity of a measure of predisposition toward organizational team-working environments. *Journal for Specialists in Group Work, 24*(1), 102–112. http://dx.doi.org/10.1080/01933929908411422

Kolar D. W. (1995). *Individual differences in the ability to accurately judge the personality characteristics of others* (Unpublished doctoral dissertation). University of California, Riverside.

Kristof, A. L. (2000). Perceived applicant fit: Distinguishing between recruiters' perceptions of person-job and person-organization fit. *Personnel Psychology, 53*, 643–671. http://dx.doi.org/10.1111/j.1744-6570.2000.tb00217.x

Letzring, T. D. (2008). The good judge of personality: Characteristics, behaviors, and observer accuracy. *Journal of Research in Personality, 42*, 914–932. doi:10.1016/j.jrp.2007.12.003

Letzring, T. D., Wells, S., & Funder, D. C. (2006). Quantity and quality of available information affect the realistic accuracy of personality judgment. *Journal of Personality and Social Psychology, 91*, 111–123. doi:10.1037/0022-3514.91.1.111

Levashina, J., Hartwell, C. J., Morgeson, F. P., & Campion, M. A. (2014). The structured employment interview: Narrative and quantitative review of the research literature. *Personnel Psychology, 67*, 241–293. https://doi.org/10.1111/peps.12052

Longenecker, C. O., & Fink, L. S. (2008). Key criteria in twenty-first century management promotional decisions. *Career Development International, 13*(3), 241–251. https://doi.org/10.1108/13620430810870494

Luria, G., & Morag, I. (2012). Safety management by walking around (SMBWA): A safety intervention program based on both peer and manager participation. *Accident Analysis and Prevention, 45,* 248–257. doi: 10.1016/j.aap.2011.07.010

Motowidlo, S. J. (1999). Asking about past behavior versus hypothetical behavior. In R. W. Eder & M. M. Harris (Eds.), *The employment interview handbook* (pp. 179–190). Thousand Oaks, CA: Sage.

Neuman, G. A., & Kickul, J. R. (1998). Organizational citizenship behaviors: Achievement orientation and personality. *Journal of Business and Psychology, 13*(2), 263–279. https://www.jstor.org/stable/25092637

Ocampo, L., Acedillo, V., Bacunador, A. M., Balo, C. C., Lagdameo, Y. J., & Tupa, N. S. (2018). A historical review of the development of organizational citizenship behavior (OCB) and its implications for the twenty-first century. *Personnel Review, 47*(4), 821–862. http://dx.doi.org/10.1108/PR-04-2017-0136

Ones, D. S., Viswesvaran, C., & Schmidt, F. L. (1993). Comprehensive meta-analysis of integrity test validities: Findings and implications for personnel selection and theories of job performance [Monograph]. *Journal of Applied Psychology, 78,* 679–703. http://dx.doi.org/10.1037/0021-9010.78.4.679

Ozer, D. J., & Benet-Martínez, V. (2006). Personality and the prediction of consequential outcomes. *Annual Review of Psychology, 57,* 401–421. doi: 10.1146/annurev.psych.57.102904.190127

Penner, L. A., Midili, A. R., & Kegelmeyer, J. (1997). Beyond job attitudes: A personality and social psychology perspective on the causes of organizational citizenship behavior. *Human Performance, 10*(2), 111–131. https://doi.org/10.1207/s15327043hup1002_4

Pinkovitz, W. H., Moskal, J., & Green, G. (1997). *How much does your employee turnover cost?* Madison: University of Wisconsin, Extended Education, Center for Community Economic Development.

Rynes, S., & Gerhart, B. (1990). Interviewer assessments of applicant "fit": An exploratory investigation. *Personnel Psychology, 43,* 13–35. https://doi.org/10.1111/j.1744-6570.1990.tb02004.x

Stewart, G. L. (1996). Reward structure as a moderator of the relationship between extraversion and sales performance. *Journal of Applied Psychology, 81,* 619–627. doi:10.1037/0021-9010.81.6.619

Stoddart, P. E., & Clance, P. R. (2017). Identifying and managing personality styles that impair resilience in the workplace. In M. F. Crane (Ed.), *Managing for resilience: A practical guide for employee wellbeing and organizational performance* (pp. 32–52). New York, NY: Routledge/Taylor & Francis Group.

Tett, R. P., Jackson, D. N., & Rothstein, M. (1991). Personality measures as predictors of job performances: A meta-analytic review. *Personnel Psychology, 44,* 703–741. doi:10.1111/j.1744-6570.1991.tb00696.x

Townsend, R. J., Bacigalupi, S. C., & Blackman, M. C. (2007). The accuracy of lay integrity assessments in simulated employment interviews. *Journal of Research in Personality, 41,* 540–557. https://doi.org/10.1016/j.jrp.2006.06.010

Tran, T., & Blackman, M. C. (2006). The dynamics and validity of the group selection interview. *Journal of Social Psychology, 146*(2), 183–201. doi:10.3200/SOCP.146.2.183-201

Ulrich, L., & Trumbo, D. (1965). The selection interview since 1949. *Psychological Bulletin, 63,* 100–116. http://dx.doi.org/10.1037/h0021696

van Aarde, N., Meiring, D., & Wiernik, B. M. (2017). The validity of the Big Five personality traits for job performance: Meta-analyses of South African studies. *International Journal of Selection and Assessment, 25*(3), 223–239. https://doi.org/10.1111/ijsa.12175

van Iddekinge, C. H., Raymark, P. H., Eidson, C. E., Jr., & Attenweiler, W. (2004). What do structured interviews really measure? The construct validity of behavior description interviews. *Human Performance, 17,* 71–93. http://dx.doi.org/10.1207/S15327043HUP1701_4

Wang, D. F., & Cui, H. (2008). Predicting job performance of Chinese local government executives with QZPS and NEO PI-R. *Acta Psychologica Sinica, 40*(7), 828–838. doi:10.3724/SP.J.1041.2008.00828

Zeidner, M., Matthews, G., & Roberts, R. D. (2004). Emotional intelligence in the workplace: A critical review. *Applied Psychology: An International Review, 53*(3), 371–399. https://doi.org/10.1111/j.1464-0597.2004.00176.x

Zeigler-Hill, V., Besser, A., Vrabel, J., & Noser, A. E. (2015). Would you like fries with that? The roles of servers' personality traits and job performance in the tipping behavior of customers. *Journal of Research in Personality, 57,* 110–118. https://doi.org/10.1016/j.jrp.2015.05.001

Note

1. The Big Five traits or factors are openness to experience, conscientiousness, extraversion, agreeableness, and neuroticism.

Training and Improving Accuracy of Personality Trait Judgments

Danielle Blanch-Hartigan *and* Krista Hill Cummings

Abstract

Given that accurate trait judgments are related to myriad positive characteristics and outcomes, this chapter focuses on approaches for improving trait judgment accuracy. The chapter outlines potential trait judgment training approaches aligned with the realistic accuracy model (RAM) and presents available evidence from previous training research in other domains of person perception and basic personality research. In addition, the chapter examines how characteristics of the trait, target, and judge can potentially impact training effectiveness. More research is needed to develop effective, generalizable, and impactful training interventions for personality and trait judgment accuracy.

Key Words: training, intervention, feedback, accuracy, trait judgment, personality

As seen throughout the chapters in this handbook, making accurate judgments of others' traits and personalities is associated with a whole host of characteristics and positive interpersonal outcomes in a variety of applied contexts. With many well-documented positive associations, the next logical step might be to think about ways to *improve* the ability to make personality trait judgments through training programs or interventions. More accurate trait judgments as the result of training could be associated with better interpersonal and applied outcomes. For example, if customer service professionals could quickly judge the personality or other key traits of customers, they could more effectively tailor communication or marketing to improve satisfaction or increase sales. Training accurate trait judgment in human resource professionals could mean better screening of potential candidates for desired characteristics. In clinical encounters, healthcare providers could better assess characteristics of their patients that are stable over time, such as their tendency to catastrophize pain or be conscientious about adhering to medication regimens. In interpersonal interactions, training people to better detect and identify personality or trait characteris-

tics could help them identify potential friends or relationship partners and avoid individuals with traits that might yield unhealthy relationships.

Training in All Domains of Person Perception

Researchers have been studying training to improve accuracy in person perception for a century (Blanch-Hartigan, Andrzejewski, & Hill, 2016). Interventions to improve our ability to make judgments of others have used a variety of approaches, including motivating individuals to be more accurate, providing instruction or discussion of key indicators of accuracy, and allowing for practice with or without feedback about performance. Meta-analyses have attempted to determine the most effective training approaches for improving various aspects of person perception accuracy (Blanch-Hartigan, Andrzejewski, & Hill, 2012; Driskell, 2012; Hall et al., 2009; Hauch, Sporer, Michael, & Meissner, 2016; Sprung, Münch, Harris, Ebesutani, & Hofmann, 2015). A 2012 meta-analysis of 30 experimental studies that tested different training approaches demonstrated that practice with feedback about performance was the most effective way to improve person perception accuracy

(Blanch-Hartigan et al., 2012). Simply instructing people about what cues to look for on its own did not seem to be an effective approach, a result consistent with a meta-analysis focused just on training in the domain of deception detection (Driskell, 2012). However, multiple training approaches used in combination with practice with feedback was more effective than a single approach (Blanch-Hartigan, 2012; Driskell, 2012; Ruben, Hall, Curtin, Blanch-Hartigan, & Ship, 2015). Training length did not seem to matter, as shorter trainings were just as effective as longer trainings (Blanch-Hartigan et al., 2012; Sprung et al., 2015). A 2009 meta-analysis of motivational interventions for improving person perception demonstrated that motivation was overall not an effective intervention to improve accuracy, especially for judgments that relied on nonverbal cues (Hall et al., 2009). Imploring someone to do better, paying or rewarding them, or appealing to their ego did not improve performance on various person perception tasks.

These meta-analyses, and the studies included within them, give us some indication of what might work, and what might not work, when trying to improve the accuracy of judging others. However, the previous findings need to be qualified when applied to the domain of personality and trait judgment. Unfortunately, despite a century of research in this area, the majority of studies of training person perception have been in domains outside of personality. In fact, in the 2012 meta-analysis of training approach effectiveness described previously (Blanch-Hartigan et al., 2012), only two experimental studies attempted to improve judgments of traits (Crow, 1957; Heneman, 1988).

The 1957 study by Crow asked 72 medical students to estimate target patients' self-reported personality and scores on the Minnesota Multiphasic Personality Inventory (MMPI) scales based on videos of their inpatient interactions with a physician (Crow, 1957). Half the medical students were randomly assigned to a clinic that instructed them on patient–provider communication and allowed them to have increased contact with their patients. The results went in the opposite direction hypothesized and showed that the increased interpersonal-focused training group was actually less accurate at judging personality than the control group. The intervention did lead to increased variability in estimates of targets' personality for those medical students in the experimental condition, but this did not result in increased accuracy. The findings support Cronbach's hypothesis that just increasing the ability to differentiate one target from another will not necessarily lead to greater accuracy (Cronbach, 1955). Although the Crow study did not demonstrate increased accuracy, it may be a function of the training approach. The interpersonal exposure and communication instruction did not specifically focus on personality judgments. In addition, the MMPI is primarily a measure of psychopathology and not normal range personality traits (Butcher, 2015; Hathaway & McKinley, 1951). It is unclear whether a different, more targeted, approach to training or a different personality assessment might have increased the effectiveness of the intervention.

What is known about training effectiveness for improving accuracy of trait judgments is largely driven by the literature on person perception. However, to the extent that judgments of personality are different from judgments made in other domains of person perception, more research is needed to understand the training approaches that might work best in the personality domain. In addition, improving the ability to detect and identify interpersonal cues to personality is just one aspect of increasing accurate judgments of personality. There are other components of personality judgments that may be amenable to training.

Training at Each Step of the Realistic Accuracy Model

As discussed in the chapter 2 by Letzring and Funder in this handbook, Funder's realistic accuracy model (RAM) outlines the steps that must occur in order for one to make an accurate judgment of another's personality (Funder, 1995). These steps include (1) Relevance: a cue must exist that is relevant to or diagnostic of the personality attribute of interest, (2) Availability: the cue must be visible to the judge, (3) Detection: the judge must detect the cue, and (4) Utilization: the judge must utilize or interpret the cue correctly as to its meaning for personality. If any of the four steps are not accomplished, accurate judgment will not occur. Thus, it is important for training to improve all four steps of accurate personality judgment. The next section describes each step, the obstacles a judge may face at each step, and how training may improve the judge's ability to accomplish the step. Table 20.1 provides a brief outline of this discussion. Examples are provided of what a training may look like using the context of an employment interview.

Table 20.1. Training Approaches at Each Step of the Realistic Accuracy Model

Stages of the Realistic Accuracy Model (RAM)	Definition	What might be included in a training approach focused on this step	Examples of training approaches from an interview context
Relevance	Cues exist that are informative and can be used to make trait judgments.	Learn what types of questions or situations will result in personality-relevant cues. Discuss the types of situations that will distinguish among those high and low on a trait. Identify ways to create a comfortable and relaxing environment.	Have candidates work for a day in the office rather than complete a task with specific instructions. Expose interviewers to exemplars of a particular trait.
Availability	The cue emitted by the target is one that is visible to or detectable by the judge.	Emphasize the importance of knowing a target across diverse situations over time. Train judges to identify how situations differ and how certain situations may allow for more visible behavior emissions.	Ask candidates to engage in a variety of tasks and activities throughout a day-long interview.
Detection	The available, relevant information from the targets is perceived by the judge.	Teach judges emotional regulation exercises. Provide information on what cues a judge may wish to focus on by discussing literature that has looked at visible behavioral indicators of personality.	Engage interviewers in emotion regulation activities to optimize their own mental and physical state. Instruct interviewers to look for and even write down known behavioral indicators of a particular trait, like conscientiousness.
Utilization	The judge interprets the detected information to make a judgment about the target's personality.	Provide information on associations between traits and cues. Discuss common biases, heuristics, and errors people make during the judgment process. Allow for practice and feedback on whether cues have been utilized correctly to make accurate judgments.	Conduct mock interviews where interviewers practice making judgments of candidates' personalities and then receive feedback based on candidate ratings.

Step 1—Training Relevance

The first step, relevance, requires the existence of cues that are relevant to the trait being judged, that is, the cue is potentially informative about a target's personality. For example, speaking in a loud voice can be a valid and informative indicator of extraversion (Scherer, 1978). One of the factors that stands in the way of step 1 occurring is situational constraint. Some situations are stronger than others (Ickes, Snyder, & Garcia, 1997). If a situation is strong, most individuals in the situation will behave similarly; therefore, the situation itself will not encourage individual differences in behavior and may limit our ability to distinguish relevant personality cues. Weak situations may not dictate as much in terms of prescribed behavior to the individuals in the situation. When a situation is weak, individuals are freer to express themselves and may display more relevant and more variable personality cues.

Knowing about situational constraint can help improve personality judgment accuracy.

It is important for judges to know how to create situations that distinguish among those at various levels of a given personality trait. Judges of personality can be encouraged or even trained to create weak situations where targets can emit relevant cues that are informative of their personalities. Relevant situations may be particularly important for traits demonstrated to be more difficult to judge, such as neuroticism (Funder, 2012; Vazire, 2010). Hirschmüller and colleagues examined judges' neuroticism judgment accuracy in four situations (Hirschmüller, Egloff, Schmukle, Nestler, & Back, 2015). Judges were more accurate in judging targets' neuroticism in the trait-relevant self-introduction scenario than in three other scenarios. Judgments were more accurate because more cues to neuroticism were present and utilized by the judges in this situation.

In an interview context, a judge can be trained to create weak and trait-relevant situations, including questions or activities that are more open-ended and will allow for more freedom of expression. For example, asking all candidates to complete a task in a computer program with specific instructions may not be as informative of conscientiousness as having them work for a day in the office and observing their behaviors. If the goal is to encourage targets to freely express themselves to encourage the emission of relevant personality cues, judges may want to create comfortable and welcoming environments in which targets feel relaxed and open to expressing themselves. It is also important to consider who the target is when designing relevant situations. For example, accuracy of trait judgments of children may vary less across situations than accuracy of trait judgments of adults. Children may be less constrained by situational features, allowing for their true personality to emerge more so than for adults (Tackett, Herzhoff, Kushner, & Rule 2016).

Step 2—Training Availability

The second step in training to improve trait judgments focuses on the availability of the cues. Although relevant cues to a target's personality may exist (see step 1), cues may not be available for use by a judge in making the trait judgment. Some behaviors are imperceptible or inaccessible to the judge. For example, traits that are considered mostly internal or cognitive such as neuroticism may be associated with relevant cues that are also largely internal to the target such as experiencing anxious thoughts or feelings. Although these anxious thoughts and feelings are relevant cues to neuroticism, the target may not display these cues to the judge. The second step (availability) is also situationally dependent. There may be situations that do or do not elicit relevant cues as seen in step 1, but also situations in which cues may be more or less available to a judge.

In terms of improving trait judgment, the best way to improve availability of trait-relevant cues may be through increasing the quantity of information a judge can receive. If in every situation, only a fraction of the behaviors a target emits are available, then the hope is that by increasing the number of situations (and the diversity of the situations), enough information will become available for a judge to use. In terms of training, it is important for judges to first recognize the importance of information quantity and quality and when it may be rare to see a trait-relevant behavior. For example, judges can accurately perceive extraversion in a 50 ms look at a target's photo (Borkenau, Brecke, Möttig, & Paelecke, 2009) because behavioral cues to extraversion may be more readily available (Beer & Watson, 2008a, 2008b). But other traits, like neuroticism, are harder to detect because behavioral cues might be less available to the judges (e.g., Borkenau, et al., 2009; Hall, Andrzejewski, Murphy, Mast, & Feinstein, 2008; Hirschmüller, Egloff, Schmukle, Nestler, & Back, 2015; Vazire & Gosling, 2004; Vazire, Naumann, Rentfrow, & Gosling, 2008). Judges can be trained on which traits are likely to manifest in overt behavior and which are less likely to have visible cues. Judges can be trained to provide several diverse situations in which to observe a target to allow for the diverse expression of the targets' traits. For example, interviewers who are interested in assessing how a specific candidate's traits are different from other candidates' traits, known as distinctive accuracy (Biesanz and Human, 2010), should discuss with the candidate how they think, feel, and behave in different scenarios (Letzring & Human, 2013).

Although this chapter focuses on training the judge to improve the judges' trait judgment accuracy, it is worth noting that there are a number of training approaches that could focus on training the target, especially at step 1 and step 2 of the RAM. Targets could be taught how to more explicitly, deliberately, or consciously display cues to construct a specific impression of their personality (Leary & Kowalski, 1990). However, training targets to portray a specific personality may not necessarily lead to being judged more accurately. Training targets could perhaps reduce accuracy if the way the target wants to be perceived is discrepant from their actual self.

Step 3—Training Detection

If target behavior is both relevant to the trait judgment and available to the judge, the next step is for the judge to detect the cues. A variety of factors can interfere with judges' ability to detect the relevant and available information. Judges may be inattentive, distracted, or unperceptive. Certain cues may be harder to detect because they are less dramatic or less obvious or because they take more effort by the judge to perceive. Either way, accurate trait judgment would likely be hampered by judges' inability to detect relevant and available cues.

In terms of training detection, the focus can be on increasing a judge's attentional accuracy, meaning teaching them to pay attention to the target and important cues being emitted. For example, it is unlikely a physician would pick up on a relevant, available behavioral cue to pain catastrophizing, such as increased facial muscle movement in response to pain (Ruben & Hall, 2016), if they are looking at the electronic medical records and not the patient.

Given that there is a lot of potential information to detect, judges can learn and practice attending to what is most important in a situation. For example, are nonverbal or verbal behaviors more predictive of the trait of interest? Unfortunately, the literature on visible cues of personality is still not fully developed, but the work that is out there could be shared with judges (Borkenau & Liebler, 1992; Liebler & Borkenau, 1995). Lens models can examine which cues judges use when making judgments of a particular trait and compare that to which cues actually produce more accurate judgments (Back & Nestler, 2016; Nestler & Back, 2013; see also chapter 4 by Osterholz et al. in this handbook). Training judges to direct their attention to more accurate cues and away from less accurate cues to a given trait may increase their ability to detect these cues. For example, in deception detection, judges across the world universally report targets' gaze aversion as a signal to deception (Global Deception Research Team, 2006). Lens models suggest that people's stated beliefs about deception cues and actual cues that indicate deception are not necessarily aligned (Hartwig & Bond, 2011). For example, despite judges' beliefs, gaze aversion is not typically a valid cue to deception. Meta-analyses on training deception detection demonstrate that increased accuracy can result from training participants to focus on specific cues (Hauch et al., 2016), such as verbal content indicators of truthfulness, which include that the statement is detailed and logically structured (Vrij, 2005).

Judges can also be trained to reduce internal and external distractions that might interfere with their ability to detect cues. For example, a judge who is making judgments of seven traits at once may be less able to detect cues than a judge focusing on only one trait. A judge making a trait judgment while completing other cognitive tasks may be less accurate. In person perception for state judgments, accuracy can decrease when judges are experiencing cognitive load (Phillips, Channon, Tunstall, Hedenstrom, & Lyons, 2008; Phillips, Tunstall, & Channon, 2007). Judges could be trained to create judgment-situations that do not include other cognitive tasks. For optimal detection, judges might also want to be in a certain emotional state. Although work in this area is still relatively nascent, there is some indication that person perception accuracy decreases when judges are experiencing the state emotion of sadness (Ambady & Gray, 2002). Teaching judges how to regulate their own emotions as well as reduce their cognitive load before going into the judgment situation might improve accuracy. However, there is a lot more work to be done in this area, as it is not fully known which trait judgments might improve with deliberate processing and which might not.

Step 4—Training Utilization

The final step of the RAM model involves interpreting the information gathered during the first three steps. The relevant, available information emitted by a target and detected by the judge is used by the judge to interpret and draw conclusions about a target's traits. Accuracy here means drawing accurate conclusions about the traits. Is the person high or low in neuroticism? Is this cue a signal of the target's extraversion?

In many ways, this is most akin to other person perception judgment tasks, like emotion recognition or deception detection, where a judge is presented with a cue and asked to say whether the person is happy or sad, lying or telling the truth. Therefore, although there has not been a meta-analysis focused on training approaches for personality or trait judgments, here is where previous work in person perception training might be most applicable. Training judges using multiple approaches, and including practice with feedback about accuracy, may be the most effective approach (Blanch-Hartigan et al., 2012). Judges may get little feedback in everyday interactions about the accuracy of their personality judgments; moreover, the criterion for the "truth" in trait judgments is more difficult to assess, particularly in real-world interactions (Funder, 2012). Accuracy for personality judgments might increase if given more feedback about accuracy because it will allow judges to ascertain how a given set of cues might be related to different traits.

There is still a lot more research that needs to be done to understand whether exposing errors or biases through feedback is an effective approach for improving personality judgments. Making automatic, unconscious processing of trait judgments more deliberate and conscious might actually hinder trait judgment accuracy. For example, having more time to judge dominance from facial features does not necessarily improve accuracy (Rule, Adams, Ambady, & Freeman, 2012). The effectiveness of practice and feedback, especially compared to instruction alone, in general person perception research suggests that improving accuracy may mean internalizing feedback to make accurate judgments more automatic, but this needs to be further explored.

Previous Training Studies

To date, the majority of studies that have looked at the effectiveness of training have included trainings that focus on the last two steps of the RAM (detection and utilization). For example, Powell and Goffin (2009) created a training program to enhance raters' knowledge of personality cues in an employment interview context (Powell & Goffin 2009). The training group began by watching a video of a mock interview. Participants were asked to rate the interviewee on three personality traits they were told were important for the job (vulnerability, self-discipline, and assertiveness). Next, participants began the training by receiving a brief lecture on the three personality traits and the behavioral cues associated with them. Participants then wrote the verbal and nonverbal cues that they based their ratings on and then shared with the rest of the members in the group their personality ratings of the interviewee in the video. In the final stage of the training, participants were informed of the ratings experts had given the target in the video and provided with an explanation for why those ratings were made. After the training, participants watched three additional interviews and rated the candidates on the same personality traits as well as additional traits (cheerfulness, order, and self-consciousness) to examine whether the training had broader utility in terms of judging personality in general. The training group scored higher than the control group on stereotype accuracy. Stereotype accuracy is "accuracy of the relative distinctions made among the average trait levels, averaged across the group of targets…how accurate a rater is in indicating that the group of targets tends to be higher on some traits than others" (p. 457). Furthermore, the training group scored higher than the control group on differential accuracy. Differential accuracy is "accuracy that reflects the rater's sensitivity to target differences in patterns of traits…a measure of the accuracy with which a rater evaluates the pattern of interviewee levels across traits" (p. 457). Looking at the individual traits using difference scores and expert ratings as the criterion, training was effective for improving judgment accuracy on two of the three personality traits on which the training focused (assertiveness and self-discipline) and two additional traits (cheerfulness and order). Thus, providing support that the training was not only able to improve judgments of the trained traits, but also had broader utility in terms of judging personality in general. The researchers suggested this generalized improvement may be the result of participants learning to utilize new categories of personality cues such as voice qualities, physical characteristics, and mannerisms.

Powell and Bourdage (2016) conducted a similar study to train people to be more accurate judges of personality from videotaped employment interviews (Powell & Bourdage 2016). Informed by the last two steps of the RAM, the study tested different training approaches to improve the detection and utilization processes involved in accurate trait judgment. Participants watched six videos, 5–6 minutes in length. The first video and ratings were before the training, the remaining five were after the training. The study included 144 undergraduate participants randomly assigned to four small group training conditions: (1) Detection: feedback on detecting and recalling cues to personality (participants wrote down which cues they remembered after listening to the interview, experimenters suggested additional cues to look for, the group discussed cues they detected and were instructed to attend to these cues in the next interviews); (2) Utilization: feedback on utilizing cues to make inferences about personality (participants shared their personality ratings for each trait, then the experimenter provided expert ratings and cues that led experts to those ratings and the group discussed); (3) A combined condition of the two previous trainings with feedback on detecting *and* utilizing personality cues; and (4) A control group that rated the first video but did not receive feedback or discuss their ratings. All participants in the study also had a motivation manipulation; the top 10 percent of raters received $20. Accuracy on the five videos rated post-training was measured by a profile correlation with expert ratings. Results showed that accuracy was significantly better for the utilization and combined conditions than for the detection and control conditions, although the utilization and combined conditions did not significantly differ from each other. Training individuals to detect cues alone did not improve personality judgment accuracy in this study. Feedback on how to apply cues to trait judgments was key.

Also in an employment context, Heneman (1988) conducted an experiment in 87 supervisors at a utility company using a three-hour accuracy training that focused on the process of making judgments instead of the content of particular scenarios that might yield accurate trait judgments (Heneman, 1988). They compared a control group, which did not receive any training, to a Rater Error Training group that focused on eliminating heuristic biases like the halo and leniency effect, and a Rater Accuracy Training group that focused on how to identify job-related and performance behaviors instead of more general trait behaviors. Those assigned to the Rater Error and Rater Accuracy Trainings practiced making trait ratings, received feedback, and discussed the process and accuracy of their judgments. Neither training significantly improved participants' ability to accurately judge 187 job-related traits like "has common sense," "seldom sticks to business," and "is self-controlled."

Lievens (2001) conducted a training experiment with industrial-organizational psychology students (N = 221) and managers enrolled in an MBA program (N = 161) to examine the impact of different training approaches on the accuracy of judging work-related constructs from videotaped sales presentations (Lievens, 2001). Four scripted portrayals of a job candidate for a district sales manager position were developed to vary behavioral indicators of three traits: problem analysis and solving, interpersonal sensitivity, and planning and organization. Lievens experimentally compared the effectiveness of two types of training approaches: a data-driven assessor training that focused on systematically observing and documenting key behaviors before making evaluations, and a schema-driven assessor training that focused on using frames of reference of good, average, and poor performance to make overall evaluative judgments without distinguishing specific behaviors. Both of these training approaches included practice making ratings, discussing ratings given, and receiving feedback on accuracy of these ratings. A control group practiced making ratings, but did not receive either of these trainings, or feedback or discussion about their ratings. While both of these training approaches yielded higher accuracy than controls, the schema-driven approach was most effective. This study, conducted in the context of performance evaluations, suggests that training

programs may be more effective if they begin with a set of parameters for the characteristics and norms that form the basis of good performance or if participants have high, average, and low exemplars for a particular trait. In terms of the RAM steps, Lievens's work suggests that accurately detecting specific behaviors may be less important than effectively utilizing those behaviors based on a given frame. Relevance may also be important; something the previous studies had not included. This study suggests training is most effective when the person making the judgment is instructed on a set schema or frame-of-reference, which can be highly specific to the context, and even the organization.

Gaps and Unknowns

There are many gaps in our existing knowledge on training accuracy of personality trait judgments. More research is needed that systematically explores not only the approaches to training, but also looks across outcomes and domains of person perception, verbal and nonverbal cue channels, and potential moderating factors to understand the complex picture of effectively improving personality judgment accuracy.

For this chapter, accuracy in judging the personality of a target has been the primary outcome of training. However, some studies have examined the effect of training on dispositional reasoning or dispositional intelligence (Hall, 2015; Powell & Bourdage, 2016). Dispositional reasoning and intelligence are not the actual accuracy of the judgments themselves, but instead reflect an individual's general knowledge of personality cues and how behaviors are related to personality. Dispositional intelligence is related to accurate personality judgments (Christiansen, Wolcott-Burnam, Janovics, Burns, & Quirk, 2005), much as nonverbal cue knowledge is correlated to person perception accuracy (Rosip & Hall, 2004). Improving the dispositional reasoning and intelligence of the judge may actually serve as a training approach for improving judgment accuracy. Powell and Bourdage (2016) also found a correlation between judges' accuracy and their dispositional intelligence (as measured by Christiansen et al.'s 2005 scale); however, they did not report whether dispositional intelligence moderated the effectiveness of training condition on accuracy. Future research should assess how individual differences, such as knowledge of the role of behaviors in personality, could impact the effectiveness of training. Perhaps certain training approaches are more effective for those who are less skilled and less knowledgeable to begin with.

Professional experience matters in trait judgment accuracy; however, its impact on training effectiveness has not been explored. Professional recruiters are somewhat more accurate judges of personality than college students without human resource experience (Schmid Mast, Bangerter, Bulliard, & Aerni, 2011). Clinicians with more experience are slightly more accurate at clinical judgments that include personality dimensions compared to clinicians with less experience (Spengler et al., 2009). The effectiveness of training should be compared in more and less experienced populations.

Because interjudge agreement in personality increases with acquaintanceship (Satchell 2019; see chapter 9 by Beer in this handbook), research on improving trait judgments should also examine the length of the relationship between targets and judges as a moderator of training effectiveness. Satchell (2019) found that trait judgments of neuroticism, extraversion, and psychopathic boldness became more accurate after just a 5-minute unstructured interaction with a stranger as compared to ratings made after viewing a facial photograph of that person (Satchell, 2019). An interesting follow-up to this study could randomly assign participants to a brief training either before or after their unstructured interaction and determine effects on accuracy. Researchers might also want to know if certain training approaches improve personality judgment accuracy for zero-acquaintance/first impression contexts (i.e., a first date, a job interview) but not in more established relationships. Perhaps different steps in the RAM process are more effective training approaches when two people know each other well compared to making trait judgments of strangers.

There is also a dearth of research on how trainings in one domain of person perception impact other domains of person perception. For example, does training focused on improving the ability to recognize emotional states lead to an increased ability to accurately judge personality? Although person perception accuracy may be more strongly related within domains (i.e., the ability to judge anger is more closely related to the ability to judge other emotions than it is to the ability to judge deception), there is evidence for individual differences in the general ability to perceive others accurately across multiple domains (Schlegel, Boone, & Hall, 2017). It is likely that training person perception would operate similarly. For example, a training program designed to improve judgment accuracy of the Big 5 personality

traits (openness to experience, conscientiousness, extraversion-introversion, agreeableness, and neuroticism; McCrae & Costa, 1987) may be effective at improving judgments of other personality dimensions (i.e., the Dark Triad of narcissism, Machiavellianism, and psychopathy; Paulhus & Williams, 2002). However, it may also improve accuracy in other domains of person perception, such as emotion recognition. Moreover, the order of judgment might be important. It is hypothesized, given evidence about the relationship between state and trait judgments, that state judgments come before trait judgments and that these judgments of traits may actually be informed by the previous state judgments in situations where there is no prior information available (Hall, Gunnery, Letzring, Carney, & Colvin, 2017). This theoretical temporal relationship between state and trait judgments is described in the state and trait accuracy model (STAM; Hall et al., 2017; see also chapter 2 by Letzring & Funder in this handbook). For this reason, training approaches designed to improve state judgment accuracy may improve trait judgment accuracy.

In addition, training approaches for both verbal and nonverbal cue channels should be developed and tested. Much of the work in training in person perception in general has looked at how to improve the ability to detect and interpret nonverbal cues (Blanch-Hartigan et al., 2012). However, motivational approaches, such as offering financial incentives for accurate judgments, ego-motivations, and framing the skill as highly desirable, or even begging participants to try hard, are more effective for judgments based on verbal cues than nonverbal cues (Hall et al., 2009). Personality traits can also be accurately judged through purely verbal channels, including curricula vitae (Cole, Feild, & Giles, 2003) and short text excerpts (Hall, Goh, Mast, & Hagedorn, 2016). Traits that can be accurately judged from verbal cues may be more amenable to training, particularly certain training approaches, like motivation, that may not work as well for judgments based on nonverbal cues.

Another largely unexplored research area is the potential impact of a judge's own personality characteristics on the effectiveness of training. For example, would certain training approaches be more effective if tailored for individuals with certain personality traits? In laying out a research agenda for using virtual reality to train interpersonal accuracy and other social skills, Schmid Mast and colleagues postulate that the personality dimension of extraversion would moderate training effectiveness (Schmid Mast, Kleinlogel, Tur, & Bachmann, 2018). Specifically, they hypothesized that because extraverts are more likely to feel immersed in a virtual world (Laarni, Ravaja, Saari, & Hartmann, 2004), training may be more effective for extraverts. However, other research shows that introverts feel more immersed than extraverts in high-stress virtual scenarios (Alsina-Jurnet & Gutiérrez-Maldonado, 2010), so high-stress training environments might be more effective for introverts. These types of questions have not previously been explored. If the goal is to create the most effective training program for trait judgment accuracy, how judges' personality characteristics impact training should also be considered.

To determine the impact of training approaches to improve trait judgment accuracy, accuracy must be systematically assessed multiple times. To determine effectiveness of different training approaches, accuracy across studies should be comparable. The lack of a comprehensive, standardized measure to assess trait judgment accuracy is problematic for moving this field forward. Because no standard, validated, and widely used set of targets exists for personality and trait accuracy research, each research group or study may end up using different assessment approaches with different targets to measure the effectiveness of their training approach. In addition, the way accuracy is calculated across these studies may matter. Judging across different targets for a given trait (trait accuracy) and judging within one target across multiple traits (profile accuracy) may represent different judgment processes—even though they are both aspects of accurately judging personality (Hall et al., 2018; see also the chapter by 5 Biesanz in this handbook). Researchers creating multiple tests of personality judgment accuracy or calculating accuracy in different ways not only limits the ability to infer across studies, across labs, and across domains, but is also time-consuming and tedious, slowing the pace of research in this field. The field could be advanced by a validated and widely used test of personality and trait judgment accuracy to systematically assess training effectiveness.

Conclusion

Given a limited amount of experimental studies and significant research gaps in our knowledge on training personality and trait judgment accuracy, one might jump to the conclusion that training this skill is not effective or useful. However, available evidence from the relatively few studies within the domain of trait judgments, together with meta-analyses across other domains of person perception accuracy, suggest that training may be effective and useful for improving our ability to accurately judge the personality and traits of others. The evidence suggests that training should include the ability to practice and receive feedback on the accuracy of trait judgments. Training may be more effective by including practice and feedback on cue utilization and not just detection or noticing cues. However, these recommendations should be viewed somewhat hesitantly given the unknowns. Even the extent to which our knowledge about effective training in other domains of person perception translates to trait judgments is uncertain.

The effectiveness of training to improve trait judgment accuracy is an area ripe for future research. The RAM supports developing further research in this area by systematically testing training approaches that focus on each step of accurate judgment. In addition, an increased systematic focus on potential training approaches, outcomes, and moderating factors is also essential to move this field forward and determine effective ways to improve our ability to accurately judge the traits of others.

References

Alsina-Jurnet, I., & Gutiérrez-Maldonado, J. (2010). Influence of personality and individual abilities on the sense of presence experienced in anxiety triggering virtual environments. *International Journal of Human Computer Studies, 68*(10), 788–801. doi:10.1016/j.ijhcs.2010.07.001

Ambady, N., & Gray, H. M. (2002). On being sad and mistaken: Mood effects on the accuracy of thin-slice judgments. *Journal of Personality and Social Psychology, 83*(4), 947–961. doi:10.1037//0022-3514.83.4.947

Back, M. D., & Nestler, S. (2016). Accuracy of judging personality. In J. A. Hall, M. S. Mast, & T. V. West (Eds.), *The social psychology of perceiving others accurately* (pp. 98–124). Cambridge, UK: Cambridge University Press. doi:10.1017/cbo9781316181959.005

Beer, A., & Watson, D. (2008a). Personality judgment at zero acquaintance: Agreement, assumed similarity, and implicit simplicity. *Journal of Personality Assessment, 90*(3), 250–260. doi:10.1080/00223890701884970

Beer, A., & Watson, D. (2008b). Asymmetry in judgments of personality: Others are less differentiated than the self. *Journal of Personality, 76*(3), 535–560. doi:10.1111/j.1467-6494.2008.00495.x

Biesanz, J. C., & Human, L. J. (2010). The cost of forming more accurate impressions: Accuracy-motivated perceivers see the personality of others more distinctively but less normatively than perceivers without an explicit goal. *Psychological Science, 21*(4), 589–594. doi:10.1177/0956797610364121

Blanch-Hartigan, D. (2012). An effective training to increase accurate recognition of patient emotion cues. *Patient Education and Counseling, 89*(2), 274–280. doi:10.1016/j.pec.2012.08.002

Blanch-Hartigan, D., Andrzejewski, S. A., & Hill, K. M. (2012). The effectiveness of training to improve person perception accuracy: A meta-analysis. *Basic and Applied Social Psychology, 34*(6), 483–498. doi:10.1080/01973533.2012.728122

Blanch-Hartigan, D., Andrzejewski, S. A., & Hill, K. M. (2016). Training people to be interpersonally accurate. In J. A. Hall, M. S. Mast, & T. V. West (Eds.), *The social psychology of perceiving others accurately* (pp. 253–269). Cambridge, UK: Cambridge University Press. doi:10.1017/cbo97813161819 59.012

Borkenau, P., Brecke, S., Möttig, C., & Paelecke, M. (2009). Extraversion is accurately perceived after a 50-ms exposure to a face. *Journal of Research in Personality, 43*(4), 703–706. doi:10.1016/j.jrp.2009.03.007

Borkenau, P., & Liebler, A. (1992). Trait inferences: Sources of validity at zero acquaintance. *Journal of Personality and Social Psychology, 62* (4), 645. doi:10.1037/0022-3514.62.4.645

Butcher, J. N. (2015). Minnesota multiphasic personality inventory. In J. Wright (Ed.), *International encyclopedia of the social and behavioral sciences* (2nd ed.). Elsevier. doi:10.1016/B978-0-08-097086-8.25019-8

Christiansen, N. D., Wolcott-Burnam, S., Janovics, J. E., Burns, G. N., & Quirk, S. W. (2005). The good judge revisited: Individual differences in the accuracy of personality judgments. *Human Performance, 18*(2), 123–149. doi:10.1207/s15327043hup1802_2

Cole, M. S., Feild, H. S., & Giles, W. F. (2003). What can we uncover about applicants based on their resumes? A field study. *Applied Human Resource Management Research, 8*(2), 51–62. http://applyhrm.asp.radford.edu/2003/MS%208_2_%20 Cole.pdf

Cronbach, L. (1955). Processes affecting scores on "understanding of others" and "assumed similarity." *Psychological Bulletin, 52*(3), 177–193. doi:10.1037/h0044919

Crow, W. J. (1957). The effect of training upon accuracy and variability in interpersonal perception. *Journal of Abnormal Psychology, 55*(3), 355–359. https://psycnet.apa.org/record/1959-00281-001

Driskell, J. E. (2012). Effectiveness of deception detection training: A meta-analysis. *Psychology, Crime and Law, 18*(8), 713–731. doi:10.1080/1068316X.2010.535820

Funder, D. C. (1995). On the accuracy of personality judgment: A realistic approach. *Psychological Review, 102*(4), 652–670. https://psycnet.apa.org/buy/1996-11222-001

Funder, D. C. (2012). Accurate personality judgment. *Current Directions in Psychological Science, 21*(3), 177–182. doi:10.1177/0963721412445309

Global Deception Research Team. (2006). A world of lies. *Journal of Cross-Cultural Psychology, 37*(1), 60–74. doi:10.1177/0022022105282295

Hall, J. (2015). *The effect of schema-based training on dispositional reasoning components: comparing frame-of-reference training and schema-feedback training* (Unpublished doctoral dissertation). University of Cape Town, Cape Town, South Africa.

Hall, J. A., Andrzejewski, S. A., Murphy, N. A., Mast, M. S., & Feinstein, B. A. (2008). Accuracy of judging others' traits and states: Comparing mean levels across tests. *Journal of Research in Personality, 42*(6), 1476–1489. doi:10.1016/j.jrp.2008.06.013

Hall, J. A., Back, M. D., Nestler, S., Frauendorfer, D., Schmid Mast, M., & Ruben, M. A. (2018). How do different ways of measuring individual differences in zero-acquaintance personality judgment accuracy correlate with each other? *Journal of Personality, 86*(2), 220–232. doi:10.1111/jopy.12307

Hall, J. A., Blanch, D. C., Horgan, T. G., Murphy, N. A., Rosip, J. C., & Schmid Mast, M. (2009). Motivation and interpersonal sensitivity: Does it matter how hard you try? *Motivation and Emotion, 33*, 291–302. doi:10.1007/s11031-009-9128-2

Hall, J. A., Goh, J. X., Mast, M. S., & Hagedorn, C. (2016). Individual differences in accurately judging personality from text. *Journal of Personality, 84*(4), 433–445. doi:10.1111/jopy.12170

Hall, J. A., Gunnery, S. D., Letzring, T. D., Carney, D. R., & Colvin, C. R. (2017). Accuracy of judging affect and accuracy of judging personality: How and when are they related? *Journal of Personality, 85*(5), 583–592. doi:10.1111/jopy.12262

Hartwig, M., & Bond, C. F. (2011). Why do lie-catchers fail? A lens model meta-analysis of human lie judgments. *Psychological Bulletin, 137*(4), 643. doi:10.1037/a0023589

Hathaway, S. R., & McKinley, J. C. (1951). *Minnesota multiphasic personality inventory: Manual, revised*. Psychological Corp.

Hauch, V., Sporer, S. L., Michael, S. W., & Meissner, C. A. (2016). Does training improve the detection of deception? A meta-analysis. *Communication Research, 43*(3), 283–343. doi:10.1177/0093650214534974

Heneman, R. L. (1988). Traits, behaviors, and rater training: Some unexpected results. *Human Performance, 1*(2), 85–98. doi:10.1207/s15327043hup0102_1

Hirschmüller, S., Egloff, B., Schmukle, S. C., Nestler, S., & Back, M. D. (2015). Accurate judgments of neuroticism at zero acquaintance: A question of relevance. *Journal of Personality, 83*(2), 221–228. doi:10.1111/jopy.12316

Ickes, W., Snyder, M., & Garcia, S. (1997). Personality influences on the choice of situations. In R. Hogan, J. Johnson, & S. Briggs (Eds.), *Handbook of personality psychology* (pp. 165–195). Cambridge, MA, USA: Academic Press. doi:10.1016/b978-012134645-4/50008-1

Laarni, J., Ravaja, N., Saari, T., & Hartmann, T. (2004). Personality-related differences in subjective presence. In *Proceedings of the Seventh Annual International Workshop Presence* (pp. 88–95).

Leary, M. R., & Kowalski, R. M. (1990). Impression management: A literature review and two-component model. *Psychological Bulletin, 107*(1), 34–47. doi:10.1037//0033-2909.107.1.34

Letzring, T. D., & Human, L. J. (2013). An examination of information quality as a moderator of accurate personality judgment: Information about thoughts and feelings and behaviors increases distinctive accuracy. *Journal of Personality, 82*, 440–451. doi:10.1111/jopy.12075

Liebler, A., & Borkenau, P. (1995). Observable attributes as manifestations and cues of personality and intelligence. *Journal of Personality, 63*(1), 1–25. doi:10.1111/j.1467-6494.1995.tb00799.x

Lievens, F. (2001). Assessor training strategies and their effects on accuracy, interrater reliability, and discriminant validity. *Journal of Applied Psychology, 86*(2), 255–264. doi:10.1037/0021-9010.86.2.255

McCrae, R. R., & Costa, P. T. (1987). Validation of the five-factor model of personality across instruments and observers. *Journal of Personality and Social Psychology, 52*(1), 81–90. doi:10.1037/0022-3514.52.1.81

Nestler, S., & Back, M. D. (2013). Applications and extensions of the lens model to understand interpersonal judgments at zero acquaintance. *Current Directions in Psychological Science, 22*(5), 374–379. doi:10.1177/0963721413486148

Paulhus, D. L., & Williams, K. M. (2002). The dark triad of personality: Narcissism, Machiavellianism, and psychopathy. *Journal of Research in Personality, 36*(6), 556–563. doi:10.1016/S0092-6566(02)00505-6

Phillips, L. H., Channon, S., Tunstall, M., Hedenstrom, A., & Lyons, K. (2008). The role of working memory in decoding emotions. *Emotion, 8*(2), 184–191. doi:10.1037/1528-3542.8.2.184

Phillips, L. H., Tunstall, M., & Channon, S. (2007). Exploring the role of working memory in dynamic social cue decoding using dual task methodology. *Journal of Nonverbal Behavior, 31*(2), 137–152. doi:10.1007/s10919-007-0026-6

Powell, D. M., & Bourdage, J. S. (2016). The detection of personality traits in employment interviews: Can "good judges" be trained? *Personality and Individual Differences, 94,* 194–199. doi:10.1016/j.paid.2016.01.009

Powell, D. M., & Goffin, R. D. (2009). Assessing personality in the employment interview: The impact of training on rater accuracy. *Human Performance, 22*(5), 450–465. doi:10.1080/08959280903248450

Rosip, J. C., & Hall, J. A. (2004). Knowledge of nonverbal cues, gender, and nonverbal decoding accuracy. *Journal of Nonverbal Behavior, 28*(4), 267–286. doi:10.1007/s10919-004-4159-6

Ruben, M. A., & Hall, J. A. (2016). A lens model approach to the communication of pain. *Health Communication, 31*(8), 934–945. doi:10.1080/10410236.2015.1020261

Ruben, M. A., Hall, J. A., Curtin, E. M., Blanch-Hartigan, D., & Ship, A. N. (2015). Discussion increases efficacy when training accurate perception of patients' affect. *Journal of Applied Social Psychology, 45*(6), 355–362. doi:10.1111/jasp.12301

Rule, N. O., Adams, R. B., Jr., Ambady, N., & Freeman, J. B. (2012). Perceptions of dominance following glimpses of faces and bodies. *Perception, 41*(6), 687–706. doi:10.1068/p7023

Satchell, L. P. (2019). From photograph to face-to-face: Brief interactions change person and personality judgments. *Journal of Experimental Social Psychology, 82,* 266–276. doi:10.1016/j.jesp.2019.02.010

Scherer, K. R. (1978). Personality inference from voice quality: The loud voice of extroversion. *European Journal of Social Psychology, 8*(4), 467–487, doi:10.1002/ejsp.2420080405

Schlegel, K., Boone, R. T., & Hall, J. A. (2017). Individual differences in interpersonal accuracy: A multi-level meta-analysis to assess whether judging other people is one skill or many. *Journal of Nonverbal Behavior, 41*(2), 103–137. doi:10.1007/s10919-017-0249-0

Schmid Mast, M., Bangerter, A., Bulliard, C., & Aerni, G. (2011). How accurate are recruiters' first impressions of applicants in employment interviews? *International Journal of Selection and Assessment, 19*(2), 198–208. doi:10.1111/j.1468-2389.2011.00547.x

Schmid Mast, M., Kleinlogel, E. P., Tur, B., & Bachmann, M. (2018). The future of interpersonal skills development: Immersive virtual reality training with virtual humans. *Human Resource Development Quarterly, 29*(2), 125–141. doi:10.1002/hrdq.21307

Spengler, P. M., White, M. J., Ægisdóttir, S., Maugherman, A. S., Anderson, L. A., Cook, R. S., & Rush, J. D. (2009). The meta-analysis of clinical judgment project: Effects of experience on judgment accuracy. *The Counseling Psychologist, 37*(3), 350–399. doi:10.1177/0011000006295149

Sprung, M., Münch, H. M., Harris, P. L., Ebesutani, C., & Hofmann, S. G. (2015). Children's emotion understanding: A meta-analysis of training studies. *Developmental Review, 37,* 41–65. doi:10.1016/j.dr.2015.05.001

Tackett, J. L., Herzhoff, K., Kushner, S. C., & Rule, N. (2016). Thin slices of child personality: Perceptual, situational, and behavioral contributions. *Journal of Personality and Social Psychology, 110*(1), 150–166. doi:10.1037/pspp0000044

Vazire, S. (2010). Who knows what about a person? The self–other knowledge asymmetry (SOKA) model. *Journal of Personality and Social Psychology, 98*(2), 281–300. doi:10.1037/a0017908.

Vazire, S., & Gosling, S. D. (2004). E-perceptions: Personality impressions based on personal websites. *Journal of Personality and Social Psychology, 87*(1), 123–132. doi:10.1037/0022-3514.87.1.123

Vazire, S., Naumann, L. P., Rentfrow, P. J., & Gosling, S. D. (2008). Portrait of a narcissist: Manifestations of narcissism in physical appearance. *Journal of Research in Personality, 42*(6), 1439–1447. doi:10.1016/j.jrp.2008.06.007

Vrij, A. (2005). Criteria-based content analysis: A qualitative review of the first 37 studies. *Psychology, Public Policy, and Law, 11*(1), 3–41. doi:10.1037/1076-8971.11.1.3

PART 6

Conclusions and Future Directions for the Study of Accurate Personality Judgment

Conclusions and Future Directions for the Study of Accurate Personality Judgment

Tera D. Letzring

Abstract

This chapter identifies several well-established findings and overarching themes within personality trait accuracy research, and highlights especially promising directions for future research. Topics include (1) theoretical frameworks for accuracy, (2) moderators of accuracy and the context or situation in which judgments are made, (3) the important consequences of accuracy, (4) interventions and training programs to increase judgmental ability and judgability, (5) the generalizability of previous findings, and (6) standardized tests of the accuracy of judging personality traits. The chapter ends by stating that it is an exciting time to be a researcher studying the accuracy of personality trait judgments.

Key Words: trait, judgment, accuracy, personality, moderator, context, situation, consequence, intervention, training program

The goal of this chapter is to offer concluding remarks based on the other chapters in the *Oxford Handbook on Accurate Personality Judgment*. In general, people can be accurate when making judgments of the personality traits of others and of themselves, and this is not the first time this overall conclusion has been made (see Murphy, 2016). Additionally, people vary in how accurately they judge others and are judged by others, and understanding this variability is useful for many reasons. This chapter identifies several major themes and well-established findings within personality accuracy research, and highlights especially promising directions for future research.

Theoretical Frameworks for Accuracy

One major theme of this book is the importance of theoretical models or frameworks that can be used to understand the underlying process of making accurate judgments. It is highly useful to understand the factors that are related to this process and how they affect levels of accuracy. One influential theoretical framework that has contributed significantly to our understanding of accurate personality

judgment is provided by the realistic accuracy model (RAM). The RAM, which was proposed by Funder (1995), was largely based on the ecological approach of Brunswik (1955) as described in his lens model (Funder & Sneed, 1993). Ecological approaches to accurate trait judgment attempt to identify the factors that impact how judges detect and utilize relevant cues to a target's personality, and ultimately how these factors affect the accuracy of personality judgments. The RAM and the lens model have guided a large portion of the research on personality judgment accuracy, and are discussed and applied in many chapters in this handbook. These chapters review previous work that has tested various aspects of the RAM and used the lens model framework, and also provide a roadmap for how future work could be inspired by these models.

Another important model for personality judgment is the social relations model (SRM), which was proposed by Kenny and LaVoie (1985), and later reconceptualized as the PERSON model (Kenny, 2004). The SRM and PERSON models focus on specification of how various sources of information contribute to consensus, or agreement among judges, about what targets are like. These models also have relevance for the study of the accuracy of personality judgments, as is evident in the models proposed by Malloy in chapter 3 of this handbook that are based on the SRM and PERSON models.

In addition to these more theoretical models, an analytical model was proposed by Biesanz (2010) to facilitate analyzing data that are gathered to test predictions about accuracy of personality judgments (see chapter 5 by Biesanz in this handbook). An important aspect of this model is the simultaneous estimation of distinctive accuracy and normative accuracy or normativity. Distinctive accuracy reflects the degree to which judgments are consistent with how targets are distinctive or different from the average person, while normativity reflects the degree to which judgments of targets are consistent with what the normative or average person is like. Much research evidence supports the importance of considering the components of distinctive accuracy and normativity separately, as results often differ depending of the type of accuracy that is assessed (Human, Sandstrom, Biesanz, & Dunn, 2013; Krzyzaniak, Colman, Letzring, McDonald, & Biesanz, 2019; Letzring & Human, 2014).

Research has also supported the validity of the process of accurate judgment and the importance of the moderators of accuracy as described in the RAM, and the importance of the components or sources of information that contribute to judgments of others identified in the SRM and PERSON. It is important that researchers remain grounded in theory to facilitate the cumulative nature of knowledge in this area, to think about which model or models apply best to their research questions, and to propose expansions or modifications of models to fit new processes (such as meta-accuracy) or contexts (such as judgments based on social media).

Moderators of Accuracy and the Impact of Contexts and Situations

A second major theme in this handbook is the importance of moderators and the context or situation in which judgments are made. The four chapters in Section II are each devoted to one of the moderators originally identified in the RAM, which are the good judge, good target, good trait, and good information. Additionally, the level of accuracy that can be expected in a research study or real-world situation is influenced by many factors that often interact with each other. For example, research has demonstrated the importance of the situation for judgment

accuracy, largely because cues relevant to different traits are likely to be available in different situations. It is also possible that targets might be more willing to make relevant cues available in some situations (e.g., Hirschmüller, Egloff, Schmukle, Nestler, & Back, 2015; see also chapter 8 by Krzyaniak & Letzring and chapter 14 by Wall & Campbell in this handbook), such as when meeting with a new medical professional or counselor for whom accurate personality judgments might lead to more appropriate treatment recommendations. To add to the complexity, targets with certain characteristics might strive to make relevant cues available in certain situations, while targets with other characteristics might attempt to be deceptive. For example, an athlete trying out for a team who has high levels of determination and passion would likely want the coaches to judge these traits accurately and would strive to make relevant cues available, whereas an athlete with low levels of determination and passion would not want the coaches to be accurate and would strive to be deceptive. A more systematic evaluation of interactions between moderators, and between moderators and context, would likely deepen our understanding of what is needed for highly accurate judgments to be possible and illuminate possible ways to increase accuracy of judgments.

Finally, additional research on the generalizability of previous findings to newer contexts, such as social media, will allow for important refinements of theory and models of accuracy. Most simply, accuracy should be examined in additional physical and psychological contexts. For example, Wall and Campbell (see chapter 14 in this handbook) suggested examining how accurately people could be judged based on their cars, where there are likely to be many cues to personality. As the Internet continues to grow and expand, accuracy researchers should also consider new ways that personality could be expressed in online contexts and examine the accuracy of judgments based on exposure to these contexts. Examining these additional contexts addresses questions about the generalizability of previous findings and may reveal important nuances and insights about the process of accuracy or the availability, validity, and use of cues in various situations.

Relatedly, there has been a renewed interest in the context or situation in personality psychology in general, as evidenced by a new taxonomy of situations (Rauthmann et al., 2014), the International Situations Project (Sherman, Nave, & Funder, 2010, 2012, 2013), and whole trait theory and the density distribution approach to understanding the variability of state-manifestations of personality traits (Fleeson, 2001; Fleeson & Jayawickreme, 2015; Jones, Brown, Serfass, & Sherman, 2017). Taking the situation into account when deciding what kinds of stimulus materials to use or interactions to create between participants will be important in order to more fully understand how situations influence judgment accuracy. Additionally, types of relationships could be thought of as different situations, and therefore examining accuracy in different types of relationships and being clear about the nature of relationships between judges and targets is important (see chapter 17 by Luo & Watson in this handbook for a discussion of accuracy in romantic relationships). Furthermore, different information is likely to be available in different types of relationships, and this may also have important effects on accuracy of judgments.

Accuracy of Contextualized Personality

Another way to think about context is in terms of different levels of personality. For example, McAdams (1995) proposed three levels of personality in which the second level is personal concerns that are contextualized in time, place, and role of the individual. This includes constructs such as motivations, intentions, and coping strategies. This differs from the first level, which consists of broad and decontextualized personality traits that are relatively consistent across time and situations. Most personality accuracy research focuses on this broad level. Future research that examines personal concerns would be informative about the process and accuracy of judgments for aspects of personality that are not expected to be highly consistent and stable across time and situations.

Important Consequences of Accuracy

A third major theme is that accuracy has many important consequences for life outcomes and behaviors, romantic relationships (see chapter 17 by Luo & Watson in this handbook), clinical assessment, diagnosis, treatment, and prediction (see chapter 18 by Oltmanns & Oltmanns in this handbook), and successful employee hiring and other workplace issues (see chapter 19 by Blackman in this handbook). This theme highlights that research on trait accuracy seeks to answer consequential questions that matter to everyone and will promote the basic goals of increasing relationship satisfaction, job productivity and satisfaction, and overall well-being and quality of life. Researchers should continue to examine how trait accuracy predicts important outcomes so we have a more complete understanding

of the implications of this skill and the consequences of high and low levels of accuracy.

Interventions and Training Programs to Increase Accuracy

Many chapters include suggestions for how to use empirical findings to design interventions to increase judgmental ability and judgability, for both accuracy and meta-accuracy. The chapters in Section II describe many factors that are related to accuracy in terms of the four moderators that were originally proposed with the RAM, and much is known about how accuracy relates to the characteristics of judges, targets, traits, and information. Other chapters also point out ways to increase accuracy, such as using self-observations of behavior, providing feedback to increase meta-accuracy (see chapter 12 by Carlson & Elsaadawy in this handbook), being aware of how traits are related to cues in different contexts (see chapter 14 by Wall & Campbell in this handbook), and increasing how much information is available when decisions are made about whom to hire for a job (see chapter 19 by Blackman in this handbook). Chapter 20 by Blanch-Hartigan and Cummings is specifically focused on training and improving accuracy of trait judgments. This information could be used to design more effective training programs by increasing people's awareness of what is needed to make more accurate judgments and the situations in which the attainment of accuracy tends to be especially easy or challenging. Research in this area has primarily focused on how to make judges more accurate, but it would also be useful to know what targets can do to increase how accurately they are judged by others. Future research should continue to explore how to most effectively increase accuracy for judges and targets in multiple situations (including casual and professional settings) and for multiple purposes (making decisions about potential new friends or romantic partners and work-related decisions).

Application of Findings to Other Cultures and Age Groups

Much of accuracy research has been conducted in Western countries such as the United States, Canada, Australia, and several European countries. These have been referred to as WEIRD (Western, educated, industrialized, rich, and democratic) countries, and the acronym fits because most of the world's population is not WEIRD (Henrich, Heine, & Norenzayan, 2010). Little is known about whether the findings from accuracy research generalize to other, non-WEIRD countries that are likely to differ in many ways, including how the self and the stability of traits are conceptualized, the level of importance placed on the individual versus the group, cultural complexity, flexibility, emotional experience and expression, and styles of communication (Benet-Martínez & Oishi, 2008; Triandis, 1989; Triandis & Suh, 2002). These and other culture-level variables could have important implications for typical levels of accuracy and how accuracy is achieved. Additionally, there is little research on the accuracy of cross-cultural judgments of traits. Accuracy of judging emotions across cultures has been examined extensively (Ekman et al., 1987; Elfenbein & Ambady, 2002; Laukka et al., 2016), and similar research that examines accuracy of trait judgments would reveal the similarities and differences of judging traits of people within and between cultural groups.

Furthermore, most accuracy research has been conducted with college students, young adults, and middle adults, so little is known about whether findings generalize to both judges and targets of younger and older age groups, or how accuracy develops over the lifespan. Learning about the development of the ability to make accurate judgments may also shed new light on the process of accuracy and reveal additional moderators or important outcomes of accuracy.

Standardized Tests of Personality Judgment Accuracy

A final important future direction is based on the fact that there is not a standard way to assess personality accuracy, in terms of how to expose people to personality cues, which cues to include, which situations to sample from, or how to compute accuracy scores, among other issues. Standardized tests exist for assessing accuracy of judgments of other domains, most notably emotions (Blanch-Hartigan, 2011; Buck, 1976; Nowicki & Duke, 1994; Rosenthal et al., 1979), but there is not a standardized test for accuracy of judgments of personality. As a start to more systematic and similar stimuli, researchers could share their stimulus materials with others by posting them in online repositories, such as on the Open Science Framework website (https://osf.io) or the Inter-University Consortium for Political and Social Research (ICPSR, https://www.icpsr.umich.edu/icpsrweb/content/about/), so that others could use the same materials in their own studies. Researchers would also need to post the accuracy criteria along with

the stimulus materials so that other researchers have this information to use when computing accuracy scores. This would help with replicability, reproducibility, and transparency (Asendorpf et al., 2013; Finkel, Eastwick, & Reis, 2017), but it is not the same as creating a standardized test. To create a standardized test, a high-quality set of videos would need to be identified or created, valid accuracy criteria would need to be collected, and the accuracy of judgments that are made based on observations of those videos would need to be evaluated for reliability and validity. Such a test would allow research on trait judgment accuracy to progress at a faster pace because researchers would not have to create their own stimulus materials, and would allow for much easier comparisons of findings across studies and research labs.

References

Asendorpf, J. B., Conner, M., De Fruyt, F., De Houwer, J., Denissen, J. J. A., Fiedler, K.,...Wicherts, J. M. (2013). Recommendations for increasing replicability in psychology: Recommendations for increasing replicability. *European Journal of Personality, 27*, 108–119. doi:10.1002/per.1919

Benet-Martínez, V., & Oishi, S. (2008). Culture and personality. In O. P. John, R. W. Robins, & L. A. Pervin (Eds.), *Handbook of personality: Theory and research* (3rd ed., pp. 542–567). New York, NY: Guilford Press.

Biesanz, J. C. (2010). The social accuracy model of interpersonal perception: Assessing individual differences in perceptive and expressive accuracy. *Multivariate Behavioral Research, 45*, 853–885. doi:10.1080/00273171.2010.519262

Blanch-Hartigan, D. (2011). Measuring providers' verbal and nonverbal emotion recognition ability: Reliability and validity of the Patient Emotion Cue Test (PECT). *Patient Education and Counseling, 82*, 370–376. doi:10.1016/j.pec.2010.11.017

Brunswik, E. (1955). Representative design and probabilistic theory in a functional psychology. *Psychological Review, 62*, 193–217. doi:10.1037/h0047470

Buck, R. (1976). A test of nonverbal receiving ability: Preliminary studies. *Human Communication Research, 2*, 162–171. https://academic.oup.com/hcr/article/2/2/162-171/4637518

Ekman, P., Friesen, W. V., O'Sullivan, M., Chan, A., Diacoyanni-Tarlatzis, I., Heider, K.,...Tzavaras, A. (1987). Universals and cultural differences in the judgments of facial expressions of emotion. *Journal of Personality and Social Psychology, 53*, 712–717. doi:10.1037/0022-3514.53.4.712

Elfenbein, H. A., & Ambady, N. (2002). On the universality and cultural specificity of emotion recognition: A meta-analysis. *Psychological Bulletin, 128*, 203–235. doi:10.1037/0033-2909.128.2.203

Finkel, E. J., Eastwick, P. W., & Reis, H. T. (2017). Replicability and other features of a high-quality science: Toward a balanced and empirical approach. *Journal of Personality and Social Psychology, 113*, 244–253. doi:10.1037/pspi0000075

Fleeson, W. (2001). Toward a structure- and process-integrated view of personality: Traits as density distributions of states. *Journal of Personality and Social Psychology, 80*, 1011–1027. doi:10.1037/0022-3514.80.6.1011

Fleeson, W., & Jayawickreme, E. (2015). Whole trait theory. *Journal of Research in Personality, 56*, 82–92. doi:10.1016/j.jrp.2014.10.009

Funder, D. C. (1995). On the accuracy of personality judgment: A realistic approach. *Psychological Review, 102*, 652–670.

Funder, D. C., & Sneed, C. D. (1993). Behavioral manifestations of personality: An ecological approach to judgmental accuracy. *Journal of Personality and Social Psychology, 64*, 479–490.

Henrich, J., Heine, S. J., & Norenzayan, A. (2010). The weirdest people in the world? *Behavioral and Brain Sciences, 33*(2–3), 61–83. doi:10.1017/S0140525X0999152X

Hirschmüller, S., Egloff, B., Schmukle, S. C., Nestler, S., & Back, M. D. (2015). Accurate judgments of neuroticism at zero acquaintance: A question of relevance. *Journal of Personality, 83*, 221–228. doi:10.1111/jopy.12097

Human, L. J., Sandstrom, G. M., Biesanz, J. C., & Dunn, E. W. (2013). Accurate first impressions leave a lasting impression: The long-term effects of distinctive self-other agreement on relationship development. *Social Psychological and Personality Science, 4*(4), 395–402. doi:10.1177/1948550612463735

Jones, A. B., Brown, N. A., Serfass, D. G., & Sherman, R. A. (2017). Personality and density distributions of behavior, emotions, and situations. *Journal of Research in Personality, 69*, 225–236. doi:10.1016/j.jrp.2016.10.006

Kenny, D. A. (2004). PERSON: A general model of interpersonal perception. *Personality and Social Psychology Review, 8*, 265–280. doi:10.1207/s15327957pspr0803_3

Kenny, D. A., & La Voie, L. (1985). Separating individual and group effects. *Journal of Personality and Social Psychology, 48*, 339–348 doi:10.1037/0022-3514.48.2.339

Krzyzaniak, S. L., Colman, D. E., Letzring, T. D., McDonald, J. S., & Biesanz, J. C. (2019). The effect of information quantity on distinctive accuracy and normativity of personality trait judgments. *European Journal of Personality, 33*(2), 197–213. doi:10.1002/per.2196

Laukka, P., Elfenbein, H. A., Thingujam, N. S., Rockstuhl, T., Iraki, F. K., Chui, W., & Althoff, J. (2016). The expression and recognition of emotions in the voice across five nations: A lens model analysis based on acoustic features. *Journal of Personality and Social Psychology, 111*, 686–705. doi:10.1037/pspi0000066

Letzring, T. D., & Human, L. J. (2014). An examination of information quality as a moderator of accurate personality judgment. *Journal of Personality, 82*(5), 440–451. doi:10.1111/jopy.12075

McAdams, D. P. (1995). What do we know when we know a person? *Journal of Personality, 63*, 365–396. doi:10.1111/j.1467-6494.1995.tb00500.x

Murphy, N. A. (2016). What we know and the future of interpersonal accuracy research. In J. A. Hall, M. Schmid-Mast, & T. V. West (Eds.), *The social psychology of perceiving others accurately* (pp. 404–424). Cambridge, United Kingdom: Cambridge University Press. doi:10.1017/CBO9781316181959.019

Nowicki, S., & Duke, M. P. (1994). Individual differences in the nonverbal communication of affect: The diagnostic analysis of nonverbal accuracy scale. *Journal of Nonverbal Behavior, 18*, 9-35. doi:10.1007/BF02169077

Rauthmann, J. F., Gallardo-Pujol, D., Guillaume, E. M., Todd, E., Nave, C. S., Sherman, R. A., ...Funder, D. C. (2014). The situational eight DIAMONDS: A taxonomy of major dimensions of situation characteristics. *Journal of Personality and Social Psychology, 107*, 677–718. doi:10.1037/a0037250

Rosenthal, R., Hall, J. A., DiMatteo, M. R., Rogers, P. L., & Archer, D. (1979). *Sensitivity to nonverbal communication: The PONS Test.* Baltimore: The Johns Hopkins University Press.

Sherman, R. A., Nave, C. S., & Funder, D. C. (2010). Situational similarity and personality predict behavioral consistency. *Journal of Personality and Social Psychology, 99*, 330–343. doi:10.1037/a0019796

Sherman, R. A., Nave, C. S., & Funder, D. C. (2012). Properties of persons and situations related to overall and distinctive personality-behavior congruence. *Journal of Research in Personality, 46*, 87–101. doi:10.1016/j.jrp.2011.12.006

Sherman, R. A., Nave, C. S., & Funder, D. C. (2013). Situational construal is related to personality and gender. *Journal of Research in Personality, 47*, 1–14. doi:10.1016/j.jrp.2012.10.008

Triandis, H. C. (1989). The self and social behavior in differing cultural contexts. *Psychological Review, 96*, 506–520. doi:10.1037/0033-295X.96.3.506

Triandis, H. C., & Suh, E. M. (2002). Cultural influences on personality. *Annual Review of Psychology, 53*, 133–160. doi:10.1146/annurev.psych.53.100901.135200

NAMES INDEX

Note: Tables and figures are indicated by an italic "*t*" and "*f*", respectively, following the page number.

For the benefit of digital users, indexed terms that span two pages (e.g., 52–53) may, on occasion, appear on only one of those pages.

Erber, R. 107–8
Erbs, J. 141, 153, 180–1, 236, 241
Erickson, E. A. 109–10
Erickson, M. T. 280
Erickson, T. M. 102
Estes, S. G. 87–9, 133
Evans, J. St. B. 10
Evans, J. St. B. T. 53
Everett, J. J. 111
Eyde, L. D. 147

F

Fabin, L. A. 262, 265
Fabrigar, L. R. 107, 136–8, 142, 143*f*
Fagan, P. J. 135
Fareri, D. S. 136
Fast, L. A. 23–4
Feeney, M. G. 63–4
Feild, H. S. 314
Feinstein, B. 50–2
Feinstein, B. A. 94, 105, 207, 310
Felmlee, D. H. 271–2
Fenigstein, A. 103
Ferguson, L. W. 133
Fernandez, G. 89
Ferris, A. L. 228
Ferro, T. 281*t*
Ferwerda, B. 227–8
Few, L. R. 280, 281*t*
Fiedler, E. R. 169, 279
Fiedler, K. 324
Fieve, R. R. 280, 281*t*, 284, 286*f*
Fink, L. S. 296
Finkel, E. J. 110, 324
Finn, S. E. 147
Finseth, S. M. 12, 102, 213, 237
Fisher, B. J. 255
Fisher, Z. 284
Fiske, D. W. 163, 213, 276–7
Fiske, S. T. 24–5, 91, 93, 107–8, 181,
    185–6, 231, 235, 255–6
Fivush, R. 18
Fleeson, W. 122, 124, 127–9,
    167–8, 182, 322–3
Fleming, J. J. 139–40
Fletcher, G. J. O. 89, 110, 262–72
Floyd, K. 196
Foo, M. D. 17
Forest, A. L. 102, 110–11
Forest, C. 26, 30, 32, 35*f*, 36–40, 178
Förster, J. 155
Fowers, B. J. 153, 268–9
Fowler, K. A. 281*t*, 283
Francis, M. E. 230–1
Frauendorfer, D. 46, 56, 75, 105, 315
Freeman, J. B. 311–12
Frieder, R. E. 296–7
Friedman, H. S. 104–7, 213
Friedman, R. S. 155
Friesen, C. A. 141
Friesen, W. V. 53, 106, 196, 323–4
Fritz, U. 141, 153, 180–1, 236, 241
Frost, J. H. 110

Fudge, H. 281*t*
Fuhrman, R. W. 107
Fukuno, M. 185
Fullwood, C. 226
Funder, D. C. 5, 9–12, 14–17, 23–4,
    26, 28, 36, 46, 50–2, 62–4,
    85–8, 93–5, 100–1, 105, 107,
    119–20, 122–3, 126, 128,
    132–4, 137, 139–40, 143–4, 151–2,
    157–8, 163–4, 167, 169, 175–6,
    176*f*, 178, 181–2, 184, 195, 212,
    220–1, 223, 244, 261, 267–8, 277–9,
    281*t*, 288–9, 298–302, 308–11,
    321–3
Furnham, A. 227–8
Furr, R. M. 63–4, 67, 86, 122, 124,
    127–8, 164, 173–5, 178, 180–2,
    185–6, 237, 239–40, 244, 264, 280,
    299–300

G

Gaddis, S. 14–15, 147, 196, 219–20,
    224, 228–9, 303–4
Gaertner, L. 152–3
Gage, N. L. 25, 96
Gagne, F. M. 266–8, 270
Galfano, G. 183, 185–6
Galinsky, A. D. 104, 108, 111
Galione, J. N. 279
Gallardo-Pujol, D. 169, 322–3
Gallrein, A. M. B. 158, 178
Gangestad, S. W. 46, 213
Garcia, S. 309
García-Herrero, S. 297
Gardner, W. L. 108–9
Garris, C. P. 45, 195
Gaucher, D. 102
Gawronski, B. 52–3
Ge, F. 147
Gebauer, J. E. 158
Gerdes, A. B. 230
Gerhart, B. 297
Gesn, P. R. 92
Geukes, K. 100, 102, 107, 110, 158,
    198, 241
Gibbs, J. 226
Gibson, J. 23–4, 28–9
Gifford, R. 46, 49–51, 196, 212–13
Gigerenzer, G. 255–6
Gilbert, D. T. 101, 179–80
Giles, W. F. 314
Gill, A. J. 226–8
Gill, M. J. 109, 267
Gillath, O. 147
Gillis, R. L. 72–3, 239
Gilovich, T. 177–80
Gilpin, A. T. 18–19
Gino, F. 111
Giovannini, S. 109–10
Glassman, N. S. 165
Gleason, M. E. J. 174–5, 178, 281*t*
Glinski, A. J. 136
Goffin, R. D. 312

Goffman, E. 104
Goh, J. X. 55, 90, 92, 255–6, 314
Golbeck, J. 226–7
Gold, D. A. 165
Goldberg, L. R. 22, 93, 102–3, 121, 123,
    133–4, 136, 138, 168, 276, 279–80
Gonzalez, R. 264
Goodwin, S. A. 108, 185–6
Gooty, J. 196
Gore, W. L. 276, 278–80
Gosling, R. 219–20
Gosling, S. D. 13–15, 46, 49–50, 55,
    64, 125, 138–9, 147, 151–2, 163–4,
    168, 178–9, 196–8, 219–31, 236–8,
    303–4, 310
Gottfredson, L. S. 87
Gough, H. G. 93, 123
Grabka, M. M. 251, 255
Graepel, T. 228–9
Graf, S. 249–50
Graham, L. T. 226–7
Graham, T. 92
Gralnick, T. M. 280
Gray, H. M. 139, 311
Graziano, W. G. 62, 102–3
Green, G. 294
Greenberg, A. 108–9
Greenwald, A. G. 52–3, 272
Gregg, A. P. 111, 152
Grich, J. 19
Griffin, D. 264
Griffin, D. W. 153, 262–3, 265–72
Griffin, S. A. 278, 281*t*, 283, 289
Griffiths, T. L. 30
Grilo, C. M. 104, 281*t*
Gromet, D. M. 110–11
Gros, D. F. 136
Gross, J. J. 106, 109–10
Gruenfeld, D. H. 104, 108
Grünberg, M. 198
Gschwendner, T. 52–3
Guardino, M. 280–3
Guarnaccia, C. 281*t*
Gubin, A. 108, 185–6
Guenther, C. I. 165
Guerrero, L. 53
Guerrero, L. K. 196
Guillaume, E. 23–4, 169
Guillaume, E. M. 169, 322–3
Guinote, A. 108
Gulbenkian, G. 280, 281*t*, 284, 286*f*
Gunderson, J. G. 104
Gunnery, S. D. 17, 56, 92, 196,
    201*t*, 314
Guterman, H. A. 51
Gutiérrez, J. M. 297
Gutiérrez-Maldonado, J. 314–15
Gyurak, A. 109–11

H

Hagedorn, C. 90, 92, 314
Hagemeyer, B. 53
Haig, J. 265

Morgeson, F. P. 298–9
Moritz, D. 184
Morling, B. 122, 253–5
Morris, C. N. 77–8
Morris, M. E. 50, 125, 147, 196, 219–25, 230
Morse, J. Q. 281*t*
Mosch, A. 196, 237, 240–1
Moskal, J. 294
Moskowitz, D. S. 63–4, 104
Motowidlo, S. J. 52, 302
Möttig, C. 125, 138–9, 310
Mount, M. K. 184, 234, 294–5
Mowle, E. N. 278, 280, 281*t*
Mroczek, D. K. 168
Mücke, D. 52–3
Muhlenbruck, L. 294
Mulder, R. 280
Münch, H. M. 307–8
Murphy, N. A. 46, 49–52, 91–2, 94, 104–5, 107–8, 139, 178, 196–7, 207, 212–13, 307–8, 310, 314, 321
Murray, S. 264
Murray, S. L. 153, 262–3, 265–72

N

Nakazato, K. 238
Nardone, N. 103–4
Nash, D. L. 151–2
Nass, C. 219–20
Naumann, L. P. 13, 22, 46, 49–50, 55, 89, 93, 121, 125, 138–9, 196–8, 223, 276, 310
Nauta, M. H. 281*t*
Nauta, M. M. 136
Navarro, D. 62
Nave, C. S. 63–4, 169, 322–3
Neff, L. A. 110, 153, 265–70
Neisser, U. 10–11
Nelson, G. 107, 271–2
Nelson, M. 122
Nestler, S. 13, 45–8, 47*f*, 50–6, 75, 100, 102, 104, 107, 110, 120, 125, 127–8, 138–40, 178, 196, 212–13, 230–1, 241, 244, 303, 309–11, 315, 322
Neta, M. 226
Neuberg, S. L. 88, 91, 93, 104, 107–9, 181, 235, 255–6
Neuman, G. A. 297
New, J. 101
New, M. 41
Newcomb, T. M. 33–4
Newman, D. A. 104
Newman, M. G. 102
Neyer, F. J. 220, 231
Ng, C. F. 196
Nguyen, L. 105
Niehuis, S. 265–8
Nisbett, R. E. 5, 10, 143, 154
Niznikiewicz, M. A. 136
Noftle, E. E. 167–8, 265, 268–9
Norenzayan, A. 142–3, 244, 249–50, 254, 323–4

Norman, W. T. 133–4, 136, 138, 276–7
Norton, M. I. 110
Norton, P. J. 185
Noser, A. E. 296–7
Nowicki, S., Jr. 94, 196, 324

O

Oberlander, J. 226–8
Ocampo, L. 297
Ochsner, K. 26, 100–1
Oddleifson, L. 241
Oh, I.-S. 296–7
Ohtsubo, Y. 185
Oishi, S. 323–4
Olderbak, S. 196
Oldham, C. R. 265–8
Oliver, P. V. 174–5
Olsen, J. A. 35, 35*f*, 38–9, 42
Olson, J. M. 238
Oltmanns, J. R. 276, 278–80, 281*t*, 288–9
Oltmanns, T. F. 169, 174–5, 177–8, 180–6, 276–83, 281*t*, 288–9
Omoto, A. M. 135
Ones, D. S. 12–13, 15–16, 49–51, 63–4, 87, 105, 122, 125, 127–8, 137–8, 137*f*, 142–4, 143*f*, 147, 153, 158, 163–4, 166, 177–8, 207, 265, 267–8, 276–8, 294–5, 297
Orehek, E. 53, 237
Oriña, M. M. 19
Orr, E. S. 228–9
Orr, R. R. 228–9
Ortiz, F. A. 237–8
Osborne, R. E. 179–80
Ouimette, P. C. 281*t*
Overbeck, J. R. 108
Ozer, D. J. 89, 168, 294

P

Pacini, R. 53–4
Packer, D. J. 111
Paelecke, M. 125, 138–9, 310
Palmer, D. K. 298
Paquin, A. C. 72–3, 239
Paris, J. 104
Paris, M. 281*t*
Parisotto, K. L. 15, 51, 72–3, 92, 104, 106–8, 111, 239–41, 271, 302
Park, B. 108, 134–5, 224–5, 245–6, 249, 255
Park, G. 14–15
Parke, R. D. 106
Parks, L. 184
Patton, G. K. 87
Paula, A. D. 102
Paulhus, D. L. 105–6, 120, 134–5, 138, 153, 162–3, 165, 178–9, 185, 314
Paunonen, S. V. 12, 102–3, 121–4, 128, 133–4
Pavan, G. 183, 185–6
Peabody, D. 236
Pelham, B. W. 101, 109

Pennebaker, J. W. 168, 222, 224, 230–1
Penner, L. A. 297
Pennington, N. 14–15
Pervin, L. A. 220
Peselow, E. D. 280–4, 281*t*, 286*f*
Peters, S. 34
Peterson, D. 89
Peterson, J. B. 234
Petrican, R. 135
Petty, R. E. 267
Pfohl, B. 280, 281*t*
Phillips, L. H. 311
Phillipson, H. 26
Pickett, C. L. 108–9
Pickles, A. 281*t*
Pierce, B. 12, 102, 213, 237, 241
Pierucci, J. M. 18–19
Pietromonaco, P. R. 109, 271
Pilkonis, P. A. 280–3, 281*t*
Pincus, A. L. 102, 281*t*, 288–9
Pinkovitz, W. H. 294
Pirke, K. M. 155
Poehlman, T. A. 52–3
Pontari, B. A. 51, 107
Potter, J. 220, 231, 236
Powell, D. M. 56, 312–14
Powers, A. D. 279
Premack, D. R. 88
Price, J. H. 168
Prince, L. M. 104, 107
Pronin, E. 110–11, 139–40, 151–2, 154, 165
Puhan, A. 280–3
Pursell, E. 298–9

Q

Qiu, L. 14–15, 227–8
Qu, W. 228
Queen, R. 226
Quilty, L. C. 234, 278, 281*t*, 288
Quinn, S. 226
Quintana, D. S. 284–8
Quirk, S. W. 12, 14–15, 51–2, 87–9, 92, 96, 184, 302, 313–14

R

Rafaeli, E. 19
Ramsay, J. 14–15, 227–8
Rasinski, K. A. 28
Ratcliff, N. J. 15, 108, 183, 185–6
Rauthmann, J. F. 16, 95, 169, 244, 322–3
Ravaja, N. 314–15
Rawsthorne, L. J. 102
Raymark, P. H. 303
R Core Team 284
Read, S. J. 152–3
Ready, R. E. 123–4, 128, 262, 265, 278–9, 281*t*
Realo, A. 14, 63, 70–1, 75, 87, 122–4, 128, 134–5, 140–1, 143–4, 250
Reardon, K. W. 280, 281*t*
Reber, R. 110

Shields, A. J. 281*t*
Shiner, R. 168
Ship, A. N. 307–8
Shoda, Y. 39–40, 102, 141
Short, E. 226
Shriver, E. R. 15, 108, 183, 185–6
Shrout, P. E. 213
Shuttleworth, F. K. 23–4, 26
Siever, L. J. 280–3, 281*t*
Simmering, M. G. 228–9
Simms, E. N. 265
Simms, L. J. 136
Simpson, J. A. 19, 46, 213, 262, 267–72
Sinclair, D. 179–80
Sinclair, J. 226
Sisic, M. 228–9
Skodol, A. E. 277, 280, 281*t*, 288–9
Skowronski, J. J. 4, 151–2, 178–9, 195
Sleep, C. 288–9
Sleep, C. E. 278, 281*t*
Slotterback, C. S. 238
Slovic, P. 5
Slovik, L. F. 268–9
Smack, A. J. 280, 281*t*
Smart, M. 281*t*
Smith, D. M. 88, 104
Smith, E. R. 88, 198–9
Smith, J. 237–8
Smith, N. C. 109–10
Smith, R. E. 111
Smoll, F. L. 111
Smoot, M. 15, 104–5, 108–9, 183, 218
Sneed, C. D. 10–11, 50–1, 178, 321
Snider, A. G. 110, 143, 262–70
Snodgrass, S. E. 196
Snyder, M. 104, 108–9, 135, 309
Solomon, B. C. 153, 244
Sorenson, E. R. 196
Sörman, K. 278, 280, 281*t*
Sorokowska, A. 147
Sorokowski, P. 147
Soto, C. J. 22, 64, 89, 93, 121, 129, 276
South, S. C. 278, 280–3, 281*t*
Spain, J. S. 126, 157–8, 166–8
Sparling, S. 136
Spence, J. X. 252
Spengler, P. M. 314
Spiegel, N. H. 106
Spies, K. 111
Spinath, F. M. 36–7, 40, 63–4, 105, 139, 197, 212, 240–1, 244
Sporberg, D. 178–9
Sporer, S. L. 307–8, 311
Sprung, M. 307–8
Spry, W. L. 166
Srivastava, S. 62–4, 72, 151–2, 158, 180–2, 220, 236–7, 239–40
Stahl, G. 111
Standen, R. 219–20
Stangl, D. 280, 281*t*
Starzyk, K. B. 136–8, 142, 143*f*
Stauner, N. 169
Steele, J. W. 239

Steffel, M. 139–40
Steffy, B. D. 303
Stein, M. B. 184
Stein-Seroussi, A. 179–80
Sterne, J. A. 284–7
Stevens, S. T. 245, 247–9, 253–6
Stewart, D. W. 108–9
Stewart, G. L. 296–7
Stewart, H. L. 263
Stewart, J. 69, 75
Stewart, J. E. 108–9
Stewart, T. R. 50, 55
Stillwell, D. 214, 228–9, 277–8
Stillwell, D. J. 14–15
Stinson, D. A. 102
Stitt, C. L. 247
Stoddart, P. E. 295
Stokes-Zoota, J. J. 247
Stone, J. I. 17
Stone, S. V. 135
Stopfer, J. M. 50, 55, 147, 178, 196, 224, 228–9, 303–4
Storms, M. D. 154
Stringfield, D. O. 102–3
Strube, M. J. 152–3
Sugarman, D. B. 29, 40
Suh, E. M. 323–4
Sullivan, H. S. 24–5, 31, 35–6
Sullivan, M. 53, 323–4
Suls, J. 162–3, 165, 167, 263
Suls, J. M. 141, 158
Surowiecki, J. 254–5
Susa, K. J. 54
Sutton, A. J. 284–7
Suzuki, T. 278, 281*t*, 283, 289
Svenson, O. 152
Swaim, G. W. 104, 107
Swann, W. B., Jr. 24–5, 28, 39–40, 64, 104, 108–11, 152–3, 178–80, 236–7, 267–9, 271
Swim, J. K. 254
Syed, M. 18
Szmajke, A. 147

T

Tabor, L. E. 151–2
Tackett, J. L. 280, 281*t*, 310
Taft, R. 51–2, 89–90, 133, 196
Tagami, S. 281*t*
Tagiuri, R. 25, 33–4
Tajfel, H. 220–1, 230
Takezawa, M. 185
Tamir, D. I. 109
Tandler, N. 196, 240–1
Tangney, J. P. 102
Tanke, E. D. 108–9
Tarlatzis, I. 323–4
Taylor, A. 281*t*
Taylor, P. J. 139–40, 219–21, 223, 226, 231
Taylor, S. E. 154, 231, 255–6, 262–3, 268

Tenenbaum, J. B. 30
Tennen, H. 167
Tenney, E. R. 158
Terracciano, A. 244, 249–52, 254–5
Terrin, N. 284–7
Terris, W. 303
Terry, D. P. 280, 281*t*
Tett, R. P. 51, 296–7
Tetzlaff, J. 284–7
Thangavelu, K. 255
Thibodeau, R. B. 18–19
Thielmann, I. 157–8, 262–3, 267
Thingujam, N. S. 323–4
Thomas, G. 262, 268–72
Thompson, L. F. 226
Thomson, D. M. 220–1
Thoresen, J. C. 219–20
Throckmorton, B. 93
Tice, D. M. 102, 104
Tipton, E. 284–5, 288
Tkalcic, M. 227–8
Tobey, E. L. 104
Todd, E. 23–4, 169, 322–3
Todd, F. J. 50
Todorov, A. 173, 195, 219–20, 226
Tofighi, D. 73
Toguchi, Y. 152–3
Tomlinson, E. 300–1
Toner, K. 169–70
Tooby, J. 101
Tost, L. P. 111
Townsend, R. J. 294, 297–301, 303
Tracy, J. L. 153
Tran, T. 300–1
Trapnell, P. D. 103
Triandis, H. C. 323–4
Troister, T. 110, 269–70
Tromp, N. B. 280, 281*t*, 283
Trope, Y. 10, 197–8
Trull, T. J. 277–9
Trumbo, D. 298
Tskhay, K. O. 147
Tucker, J. 90
Tudor, M. 107, 271–2
Tulving, E. 220–1
Tunnel, G. 104
Tunstall, M. 311
Tupa, N. S. 297
Tur, B. 314–15
Turiano, N. A. 168
Turkheimer, E. 169, 174–5, 177–8, 276–83, 281*t*, 288–9
Turner, J. 220–1, 230
Turner, K. 226–7
Turner, R. G. 103
Turnley, W. H. 184
Tversky, A. 5, 10, 23–5, 30
Tyrer, P. 280, 281*t*
Tzavaras, A. 323–4

U

Uhlmann, E. L. 52–3
Ulrich, L. 298

SUBJECT INDEX

Note: Tables and figures are indicated by an italic "*t*" and "*f*", respectively, following the page number.

For the benefit of digital users, indexed terms that span two pages (e.g., 52–53) may, on occasion, appear on only one of those pages.

perceiver effects 240
positivity and 236, 239
social desirability of 240–1
target effects of 241

B

base rate 30
base rate meta-accuracy 31
bedrooms, trait accuracy in context
of 225–6
behavior
counterproductive 297
everyday, naturalistically observed 156
Facebook and 228
interpersonal theories of dyadic 24–5
of judges 92–3
moral 157
organizational citizenship 297
personality judgment and 178
predicting 164, 168
prosocial 157
self-observations of 178–9
behavioral cues 219–20
behavioral measures 164
behavioral residue 224
being liked 111
beliefs
descriptive 248
predictive 248
prescriptive 248
self-beliefs 4
Bem Sex Role Inventory (BSRI) 252
BESD. See binomial effect size display
better than average effect 262–3
BFI. See Big Five Inventory
bias
in close others' perceptions 153–4
egoistic 165
moralistic 165
of partner trait judgments 265–6
PCA and 265–6
positivity 126, 262, 265, 270
research on 5
self-judges and 165–6
self-perceptions and 152–3
in self-report measures 165
similarity 262
systematic 266, 270
VCA and 265
Big Five Inventory (BFI) 64, 93
average personality and 236–7,
239–40
Big Five Personality Inventories 249
Big Five traits 46, 220. See also five factor
model
evaluativeness and 124
hindsight effects and 55
judge's personality and 89
lens model and 49
meta-accuracy indexing and 174–5
national character stereotypes and 249
self-other agreement and 166
self-rating 168

binomial effect size display (BESD) 40
bivariate approach 31
blind spots 165
blogs 220
body language 196–7
extraversion and 203*t*
neuroticism and 202*t*
openness and 205*t*
borderline personality disorder 104,
288–9
BRICK test 155
Brunswick lens model. See lens model
BSRI. See Bem Sex Role Inventory

C

California Adult Q-Set (CAQ) 122–3,
166, 168, 299–300
cars 230
children, peer judgments of 29
close others
biases in perceptions of 153–4
information access by 154
cognitive ability, paralanguage and 197
cognitive functioning, of judges 87–9
communication skills 107
compliments 219–20
componential approach to accuracy
25–6, 30–1
interpersonal meta-accuracy and 31–3
conference/video call interviews 300–1
conscientiousness 121–2, 201*t*
judgment accuracy and 90
maladaptive variant of 276
nonverbal cues and 207, 209*t*
self-ratings of 168–9
consensual autostereotype accuracy
correlations 250
for American regional stereotypes 250
consensus 5, 27–8, 133
constructivist approaches, to person
perception 4–5
construct validity approaches 164
context 322–3. See also physical contexts;
virtual contexts
accurate judgments and 14–15
cues and 223
defining 220–1
face-to-face 219–20
judgment accuracy and 221–3
judgments across 221–2
judgments within 222–3
meta-perceptions and 178
normativity and 241
private differences from public 222
relationships and 125–6
richness of 139–40
shared 14–15
social 178
contexts, virtual 220
correlations 62–3
consensual autostereotype
accuracy 250
profile 120–1

rank-order 152
stereotype accuracy assessment and 246
counterproductive behavior 297
criterion problem 26, 163–5
Cronbach critiques 24
SRM and 40–1
cue detection, power and 108
cue relevance 101
extraversion and 105
personality coherence and 102
physical attractiveness and 104
power and 104, 111
psychological adjustment and 102
self-knowledge and 103
social skills and 104
cues 101, 147n.6, 235. See also nonverbal
cues
behavioral 219–20
context and 223
feedback and hearsay as 179–80
information 219–20
meta-accuracy and 177–81
observable 47, 53, 55–6
self-observations of behavior as
178–9
self-perceptions and 177–8
spontaneous 53
vocal 197
cue utilization 54
agreeableness 208*t*
conscientiousness 209*t*
extraversion and 203*t*
intelligence 210*t*
neuroticism 202*t*
nonverbal cues and 198–9
openness and 205*t*
power and 108
cue-utilization processes 54
cue validity 54
agreeableness 208*t*
conscientiousness 209*t*
extraversion and 203*t*
intelligence 210*t*
neuroticism 202*t*
nonverbal cues 199, 208*t*
openness and 205*t*

D

daily life experience
predicting activities 168
predicting emotional 167
self-judgment accuracy and 166–8
deceit 300
decoders 46
defining traits 185
deliberate judgments 53
Delphi 162
density distribution 128–9
depression 184
descriptive beliefs 248
detection stage 15, 50
good targets and 107–9
training for 310–11

Heisenberg uncertainty principle 27–8
HEXACO 93, 124
HEXACO-PI-R 122
hindsight effects 55
hiring 295
histrionic personality disorders 288–9
honesty 157
Honesty-Humility 122

I

IAT. *See* Implicit Association Test
ICD-11. See *International Classification of Diseases, 11th edition*
identity claims 223–4
idiographic approaches 26
Implicit Association Test (IAT) 52–3
implicit personality self-concept 52–3
impression evaluation, average personality and 239–40
impression formation 47, 52
    meta-stereotypes and 181–4
    normative profile in 239
impression management 55
impressions 61
indistiguishable dyad members
    APM and 38, 39*f*
    ARRMA and 35
individual level APM 36–8, 36*f*
individual level ARRMA model 33–4, 33*f*
informant judgment 4
informant reports
    average personality assessment with 237
    self-other agreement in personality disorders and 278–9
information
    accuracy and 6, 51, 139
    close others and 154
    cues 219–20
    differences in 134
    effect sizes of 140–1
    emotion expression and 106
    evaluation of, as moderator 140–2
    future research directions for, as moderator 142–3
    joint evaluations of quantity and quality 139
    judges and 185
    meta-accuracy and 182
    nonverbal cues and 212–13
    in personality judgment 7, 133
    quality 12, 182
    quantity 12, 182
    in SAM 86
    scarcity of studies on, as moderator 141–2
    self-other agreement and 141
    self-perception and 154
    self-relevant 152–3
    stereotype accuracy assessment and 246–7

studies of pure quality of 139–40, 142
studies of pure quantity of 139, 141–2
zero 138
ingroup members 230
Instagram 14–15, 221
    as virtual context 227–8
intelligence
    dispositional 88, 313–14
    of judges 87
    nonverbal cues and 207, 210*t*
    personality judgment and 87
    RAM and 87–8
    self-knowledge of 152
    verbal 88
interaction style 219–20
interior behavioral residue 224
International Classification of Diseases, 11th edition (ICD-11) 280
International Personality Item Pool (IPIP) 123
interpersonal accuracy. *See also* accuracy; judgment accuracy; judgmental ability; meta-accuracy; trait accuracy
    APM and 36–7
    componential approach to 30–1
    research methods for 24
    SRM and 40–1
interpersonal behavior, theories of 24–5
interpersonal effectiveness 85
interpersonal meta-accuracy, componential approach to 31–3
interpersonal perception. *See also* person perception
    accuracy of 23–4
    Cronbach critiques of 24
interpersonal relationships, good targets and 110
interpersonal sensitivity 90
interpersonal theories of dyadic behavior 24–5
interpersonal trait judgments, social relations component of 26–30
intimacy level 125, 127, 136
introversion 201*t*
intuitive judgments 53
Inwald Personality Inventory (IPI) 295
IPIP. *See* International Personality Item Pool
IQ tests 152, 155

J

job candidates
    assessment of 295
    eliciting good information from 298–301
    importance of accurately assessing traits of 296–8
job-relevant traits 301–2
judge moderators 6
judges 46. *See also* perceivers
    accuracy and 51–2
    accurate self- 166–9
    applied opportunities for good 95
    attention and 88, 91

behavior of 92–3
biased 165–6
characteristics of good 87–93
cognitive functioning of 87–9
defining 119–20
distracted 88
empathic response of 90
feedback and training 311
future research directions on 94–6
gender of 92
information and 185
intelligence of 87
memory of 89
meta-accuracy and 183–4
meta-perception and 176–7, 183–4
motivation of 91–2
partner trait judgments and 266–7
personality of 89–91
psychological adjustment of 90
RAM stages and 175–6
in SAM 86
self-fulfilling prophecy and 91
theoretical and methodological considerations for 93–4
training and development of good 95–6, 310
traits and 185
judgment accuracy. *See also* accuracy; interpersonal accuracy; judgmental ability; meta-accuracy; trait accuracy
    consequences of 19
    across contexts 221–2
    within contexts 222–3
    contexts and understanding 221–3
    empathic response and 90
    future research directions for traits and 128–9
    modeling occurrence of 86
judgmental ability. *See also* accuracy; interpersonal accuracy; judgment accuracy; meta-accuracy; trait accuracy
    assessing developmental trajectory of 95
    contextual specificity of 95
    development of 18–19
    standardizing assessment of 94–5
judgments. *See also* personality judgment; trait judgments
    deliberate 53
    intuitive 53

K

knowledge. *See also* self-knowledge; self-other knowledge asymmetry model
    of average personality 238–9
    of goals of others 136
    limits of 23–4
    measures of extent of 135
    normative 180–1
    self 7, 103, 111, 152–3
    stereotypes as, hypothesis of 253–5